WHITAKER'S WORLD OF FACTS

RUSSELL ASH

WHITAKER'S WORLD OF FACTS

A & C Black • London

This edition published 2010
First published in 2005 by
A&C Black Publishers Ltd
36 Soho Square
London W1D 3QY
www.acblack.com

www.whitakersworld.com

Produced for A&C Black by
White-Thomson Publishing Ltd
0843 208 7460
www.wtpub.co.uk

Illustrators Alan Baker (Illustration), Julian Baker, KJA-artists

Religions consultant Martin Palmer, ICOREC

Sports consultant Ian Morrison

A CIP catalogue record for this book is available from the British Library.

ISBN 978-1-4081-3007-0

Printed and bound in China by Toppan

This book is produced using paper that is made from wood grown in managed, sustainable forests. It is natural, renewable and recyclable. The logging and manufacturing processes conform to the environmental regulations of the country of origin.

WORLD HISTORY

COUNTRIES OF THE WORLD

PEOPLE

BELIEFS AND IDEAS

CONFLICT AND CRIME

WORK AND HOME

BUILDINGS AND STRUCTURES

TRANSPORT AND TRAVEL

LANGUAGE AND LITERATURE

EDUCATION AND THE ARTS

MUSIC AND PERFORMANCE

FILM, TV AND RADIO

SPORTS

LAST LISTS

Welcome to the sixth annual edition of *Whitaker's World of Facts*. It has been updated with many new and astonishing facts and hundreds of exciting pictures to help you to keep track of recent world record-breakers, find out about the latest scientific discoveries and medical marvels, new technology and gadgets and anniversaries coming in 2011.

Facts, figures and freaky stuff

Whitaker's World of Facts is divided into 20 sections – Film, TV and Radio, People, World History and The Human Body, to name but a few. **Detailed lists and charts** show global comparisons, while **special features, factfiles** and **FactDisks** provide fast information on a huge range of subjects, with data from authoritative sources and specialists on every subject imaginable - the environment, the people and the crucial events that shape our marvellous world. The countless new entries include London's most haunted theatre and the youngest person to sail round the world; facts about animals with the biggest brains to giant squid and the life raft sunk by an elephant; the bestselling albums, the richest actors and the highest-earning films; the most expensive work of art ever sold, the most valuable comics, the largest drum, the smallest gun, the biggest Ferris wheel and the fastest roller coaster; the world's most-watched sporting leagues, the top Olympic medal-winners – and the heaviest heavyweight boxer.

A section on **countries** gives up-to-date and crucial information, including population, capital city and currency for every country in the world, as well as the flag of each one. **Timelines** on subjects such as communications, astronomy, wars and inventions give a see-at-a-glance overview and pinpoint important milestones up to the present day.

Useful maps, tables and formulae include conversions, mathematical symbols and scales, from Beaufort (weather) to Richter (earthquakes).

Other features

Web link boxes suggest useful websites to help you explore subjects further. **See also** boxes guide you to information on a particular subject elsewhere in the book. There is an extensive **index** at the back of the book, as well as a **list of sources**.

Whitaker's World Website

You can write to me with comments, suggestions and corrections at the publisher's address on page four or via the *Whitaker's World of Facts* website www.whitakersworld.com

Russell Ash

About this book

216 AIR TRANSPORT

Aviation firsts

First flight
Orville Wright (USA, 1871–1948) made the first ever flight, a distance of approximately 37 m (121 ft) at Kitty Hawk, North Carolina, USA, on 17 December 1903.

First Channel crossing
On 25 July 1909 Louis Blériot (France, 1872–1936) became the first person to fly across the English Channel, in a time of 37 minutes.

First flight in the UK
American-born showman and aviator Samuel Franklin Cody made the first flight in Britain, a distance of 424 m (1,360 ft), at Farnborough, Hampshire, on 16 October 1908. He was killed in a plane crash in 1913.

First non-stop Transatlantic flight
On 14–15 June 1919 John Alcock (UK, 1892–1919) and Arthur Whitten Brown (1886–1948) completed the first ever non-stop flight across the Atlantic, from Newfoundland to Ireland.

First solo Transatlantic flight
In his aircraft, *The Spirit of St Louis*, Charles Lindbergh (USA, 1902–74) became the first pilot to fly solo across the Atlantic, from New York to Paris, on 20–21 May 1927.

First non-stop US coast-to-coast flight
US pilots Oakley G. Kelly and John A. Macready flew a Fokker T-2 monoplane from New York to California, landing on 3 May 1923 after a 4,034-km (2,521-mile) flight lasting 26 hours 50 minutes.

First to fly over Mount Everest
In an expedition led by Douglas Douglas-Hamilton (then Lord Clydesdale, UK, 1903–73), two open-cockpit Westland biplanes flew over Everest on 3 April 1933.

First non-stop round-the-world
Dick Rutan (USA, 1938–) and Jeana Yeager (USA, 1952–) flew the *Voyager* aircraft round the world, a distance of 40,211 km (24,986 miles), on 14–23 December 1986.

Concorde

Concorde fact file

Concorde, the only passenger aircraft ever to fly faster than the speed of sound, was first named in a speech by General de Gaulle on 13 January 1963. The Anglo-French project began the following year.

- The first prototype Concorde was shown at the Toulouse Air Show on 11 December 1967.
- The first French flight took place on 2 March 1969.
- The first British flight took place on 9 April 1969.
- The first landing at London Heathrow was on 13 September 1970.
- The first Concorde landing in the USA was at Dallas-Fort Worth on 20 September 1973.
- The only Concorde crash was near Paris, 25 July 2000, when 109 passengers and crew and four people on the ground died.
- Concorde's last flight took place on 24 October 2004. All surviving BA and Air France Concordes are on public display in museums and airports in the USA, UK, France, Germany and Barbados.

Rocket man
On 26 September 2008 Swiss pilot and inventor Yves Rossy, nicknamed FusionMan, became the first ever to fly a jet-powered wing across the English Channel. He took off from an aircraft above Calais, France, and landed in Dover, UK, a distance of 35 km (miles), 13 minutes later, reaching a top speed of 299 km/h (186 mph) and landing by parachute.

Rocket man, Yves Rossy, crossing the English Channel

See also
Steve Fossett: page 153

217 TRANSPORT AND TRAVEL

Breaking the sound barrier

Charles "Chuck" Yeager became the first person to break the sound barrier on 14 October 1947. His Bell X-1 rocket plane was dropped from a carrier aircraft above Muroc Dry Lake, California. At 12,800 m (42,000 ft) he reached a speed of 1,078 km/h (670 mph). He did not break the air speed record because only aircraft that take off and land under their own power are eligible. The speed of sound is not fixed and varies according to height and air conditions. In dry air at sea level the speed of sound is 1,229 km/h (763.67 mph), but at high altitudes, where air density is less, it is lower.

High-level railway
The Qingzang railway from Beijing, China, to Lhasa, once the world's highest capital city, climbs to 5,072 m (16,640 ft) across the Tanggula Pass where the altitude is so thin that passengers are supplied with oxygen. The Fenghuoshan tunnel on this line is the world's highest at 4,905 m (16,093 ft) above sea level, which is higher than Mont Blanc, Europe's tallest mountain.

www.flyingmachines.org search

First manned balloon flights

The first balloons worked on the principle that when air is heated, it rises. They were filled with hot air by burning things under them, such as paper, straw and wool – and even old shoes and rotten meat!

The balloons often caught fire and once the air cooled, they quickly came down. Soon after the first hot-air flights, people realized that the gas hydrogen could be used instead. Hydrogen is the lightest of all elements – almost 15 times lighter than air. Gas balloons can also be filled with helium, which is not as light as hydrogen but does not catch fire so easily. Most balloons today use hot air made by burning propane gas.

The first hot-air balloon flight
The Montgolfier brothers, Joseph and Etienne, tested their first unmanned hot-air balloon on 5 June 1783. On 21 November 1783, François Laurent, Marquis d'Arlandes and Jean-François Pilâtre de Rozier took off from the Bois de Boulogne, Paris, in a Montgolfier hot-air balloon. They travelled about 9 km (5.6 miles) in 23 minutes.

First hydrogen balloon flight
On 1 December 1783, Jacques Alexandre César Charles and Nicholas-Louis Robert made the first flight in a hydrogen balloon. They took off from the Tuileries, Paris, watched by a crowd of 400,000, and travelled 43 km (27 miles) north to Nesle in about two hours. Charles then took off again alone, so was the first ever solo pilot.

First British flight
On 27 August 1784 James Tytler, a doctor and newspaper editor, took off in a home-made balloon from Comely Gardens, Edinburgh. He reached an altitude of 107 m (350 ft) in a 0.8 km (0.5 miles) hop.

First Channel crossing
On 7 January 1785 Jean-Pierre Blanchard made the first Channel crossing in a balloon with Dr John Jeffries (the first American to fly). They also carried the first airmail letter. As they lost height, they had to reduce weight, so they threw almost everything overboard – including their clothes!

First flight in the USA
On 9 January 1793 in Philadelphia, Blanchard made the first balloon flight in America. He took a small black dog with him as a passenger.

First hot-air balloon flight

The flight was watched by George Washington, who gave Blanchard a passport permitting his flight, which was the first pilot's licence and America's first airmail document.

First non-stop solo flight
US adventurer Steve Fossett made the first non-stop solo and fastest round-the-world balloon flight, 19 June to 3 July 2002.

Coloured bars identify each section of the book

Follow these web links for more information

FactDisks identify unique facts

Find cross-references throughout the book in these boxes

86 COMPUTERS AND THE INTERNET

Computer use worldwide

In 2010 it was estimated that there are 1.35 billion personal computers in use, one for every five people on the planet. Some 311 million of them, one for nearly every person, are in North America (the USA and Canada), with almost as many (302.6 million) in Western Europe. China has seen a huge increase since 2000, when there were just 20.6 million computers in the entire country.

The computer mouse
The first computer mouse – so called because its size, shape and tail-like cable resemble a mouse – was patented by Douglas Engelbart (USA) as early as 1968. Mice were not widely used until they were supplied with Apple Macintosh computers from 1984 onwards. Since then most desktop computers have used them. Leading manufacturer Logitech announced in 2008 that it had made its billionth mouse.

Computer countries
These are the countries with the most computers.

Country	Computers in use 2010 estimate
USA	273,094,500
China	111,540,800
Japan	68,457,600
Germany	66,513,900
UK	57,841,000
Brazil	54,902,800
France	54,880,700
India	53,195,000
Canada	38,131,200
South Korea	31,432,500

Laptops
Although there were some early attempts at making laptops, the first successful model with a screen that folds inside the case was the British-designed Grid Compass 1110, launched in 1982 and used by astronauts on the Space Shuttle. Improvements in displays and battery life, Wi-Fi and the use of lightweight components have led to such advanced models as Apple's MacBook Air. In 2005 the OLPC – One Laptop Per Child – charity was set up to provide inexpensive laptops for people in developing countries. By 2009 over 1 million had been distributed, including the XO-1, specially designed for use by children.

Apple's MacBook Air, 2008

Laptops being used in a school in Africa

Most offices worldwide now rely on computers to transact business

87 SCIENCE AND TECHNOLOGY

Most popular social networking sites

	Network	Registered users
1	MySpace	471,152,724
2	Facebook	350,000,000
3	Qzone	200,000,000
4	Windows Live Spaces	120,000,000
5	Habbo	117,000,000
6	Friendster	90,000,000
7	hi5	80,000,000
8	Tagged	70,000,000
9	Orkut	67,000,000
10	Flixter	63,000,000

Internet milestones

In little over 10 years, the Internet has become a global phenomenon. In 1995 it was used by about 45 million people around the world. By 2008 the figure had more than doubled to 1,463,632,361. By the time you read this, the figures will have increased again.

1960s
During the 1960s scientists in the USA began trying to work out how organizations could keep in touch with one another after a nuclear attack. In 1965 ARPA (Advanced Research Projects Agency) suggested linking computers. In 1969 computers at four US universities were connected and could "talk" to each other for the first time.

1970s
The network was extended. At the same time, electronic mail (e-mail) was being used more and more to send messages between computers. In 1979 the first Usenet newsgroups (online discussion groups) began.

1980s
By 1981 the ARPA network had 213 hosts (sites to which users could connect). In 1982 a language called TCP/IP was invented which allowed all Internet computers to communicate with each other and the network was first called an Internet. The Internet began to be used commercially and by governments and universities.

1990s
In 1991 the World Wide Web (www) was created. By 1994 about 40 million people were connected to the Internet. They could exchange information, sell goods and work from any computer with a phone line. By 1996 users in almost 150 countries around the world were connected to the Internet.

2000s
High-speed broadband and Wi-Fi access is now widespread and many businesses offer goods and services on the Internet. The number of people using the Internet increased almost three times from 2000 to 2009, with the number of users in China and India growing by more than 1,000%. Almost 1.5 billion people use the Internet worldwide.

Most-visited websites

	Website	Launched*
1	Google.com	15 Sep 1997
2	Facebook.com	26 Sep 2006
3	Youtube.com	23 Apr 2005
4	Yahoo.com	18 Jan 1995
5	Windows Live	28 Dec 1994
6	Wikipedia.org	15 Jan 2001
7	Blogger.com	31 Jul 2000
8	Baidu.com	11 Oct 1999
9	Msn.com	24 Aug 1995
10	qq.com	4 May 1995

*In some instances test versions started earlier

Computer timeline

1600s
1642 Blaise Pascal, France, makes a numerical wheel calculator, an early mechanical adding machine
1694 Gottfried von Leibniz, Germany, makes a machine that can multiply numbers
1820 Charles Xavier de Colmar, France, makes an "Arithometer" that can add, subtract, multiply and divide
1822 Charles Babbage, England, devises his Difference Engine
1829 Wheatstone uses punched paper tape to store data
1834 Babbage conceives the Analytical Engine
1889 Hollerith's punch card machine used in US Census
1928 IBM adopts 80-column punched card
1944 Harvard's Mark I, first digital computer
1952 Univac computer accurately predicts the US presidential election winner
1953 First IBM electronic digital computer (IBM 701)
1956 First hard disk drive (IBM). Term "artificial intelligence" devised
1958 First chess game between computer and human
1960 USA has 6,000 computers
1963 ASCII (American Standard Code for Information Interchange) introduced
1967 IBM releases floppy disk
1970 Douglas Engelbart patents first computer mouse
1971 Intel builds the micro-processor, "computer on a chip". Wang 1200, first word processor
1972 E-mail invented by Ray Tomlinson. First electronic video game, PONG
1975 Microsoft founded by William Gates, later to become the world's richest person
1976 First Apple computer, Cray-1, first supercomputer
1979 Compuserve launches first commercial Bulletin Board (BBN) service
1980 USA has more than one million computers. First laptop computers
1981 First Nintendo home video game. Commercial introduction of the computer mouse. Microsoft introduces software for IBM personal computers.
1982 Worldwide, 200 computers connected to the Internet
1984 Apple Macintosh computers launched
1985 Microsoft ships Windows 1.0
1986 USA has more than 30 million computers
1988 4.7 million microcomputers, 120,000 minicomputers and 11,500 mainframe computers sold in USA
1989 100,000 hosts on the net
1990 World Wide Web described by Tim Berners-Lee. First palmtop computers
1991 First use of the phrase "surfing the net", by Jean Armour Polly
2000s
1993 Mosaic, the first graphical Internet browser, launched
1994 135 million PCs worldwide. First ads on the World Wide Web (ad for Wired magazine claimed as first)
1995 Amazon.com Internet bookseller founded. Microsoft's Internet Explorer browser launched
2002 iPod digital music players launched
2008 Over 1.5 billion Internet users, 100 million websites and 1 trillion URLs worldwide.
2009 India launched the Sakshat, claimed to be the world's cheapest computer
2010 Apple's iPad released

www.computer.howstuffworks.com search

FactDisks highlight key facts

Timelines give you all the key milestones up to the present day

Lists give you the latest facts and figures, dates and rankings for all kinds of subjects

WHITAKER'S WORLD OF FACTS

Time

Counting down

In 2010, the Doomsday Clock, a symbolic clock maintained since 1947 by the Bulletin of the Atomic Scientists, was put back one minute. The clock is advanced or rewound based on how close the world is estimated to be to global nuclear disaster (midnight). The closest it has come is 11.59 pm in 1953, during Soviet and United States thermonuclear tests such as this explosion over Bikini Atoll in 1954. The clock currently stands at 11.54 pm, due to increased worldwide cooperation to reduce nuclear arsenals.

The Universe in a year!

The American astronomer Carl Sagan (1934–96) first suggested a "cosmic calendar" as a way of helping people understand the history of the Universe. He put everything into the scale of a calendar year: the galaxies are formed over nine months and the Earth appears in September.

Human history is crowded into the last five minutes of the year. Recent time is divided into seconds and fractions of a second. So everything that happened in the last 475 years takes place in less than the last second of the last minute of the year.

Earth's life in a year

1 Jan (midnight) Big Bang – Universe forms
15 Mar First stars and galaxies form
1 May Milky Way galaxy forms
8 Sep Sun forms
9 Sep Solar system forms
12 Sep Earth forms
13 Sep Moon forms
20 Sep Earth's atmosphere forms
1 Oct Earliest known life on Earth
7 Oct Earliest known fossils
18 Dec First many-celled life forms
19 Dec First fish
21 Dec First land plants; first insects
23 Dec First reptiles
24 Dec First dinosaurs
26 Dec First mammals
27 Dec First birds
28 Dec First flowering plants
28 Dec Dinosaurs extinct
31 Dec (11:55 pm) *Homo sapiens* (modern humans)

The last day

11:59.50.487 pm Great Pyramid is built (2520 BC)
11:59.55.333 pm Great Wall of China built (215 BC)
11:59.56.785 pm Roman Empire falls (AD 476)
11:59.58.026 pm Battle of Hastings (1066)
11:59.58.921 pm Columbus lands in America (1492)
11.59.59.pm Shakespeare writes his first plays (1588–90)
11:59.59.865 pm World War II ends (1945)
11:59.59.882 pm Mount Everest is climbed (1953)
11:59.59.916 pm Man lands on the Moon (1969)
11:59.59.998 pm President Barack Obama is elected (2008)
Midnight Today

Royal Observatory, Greenwich; the "time ball" on the roof falls daily at 1.00 pm

The Earth in a day

The Earth rotates once in a day, and also orbits the Sun at 107,218 km/h (66,622 mph) or 29.78 km (18.50 miles) every second, so in a day everyone on Earth will travel 2,573,232 km (1,598,932 miles) in space.

Timetellers 1500BC

The following are some landmarks in the history of telling the time.

1500–1300 BC Sundials are used in Egypt: as the Earth rotates, the gnomon – the upright part of the sundial – casts a shadow which moves to indicate the time

c. 400 BC Water clocks are used in Greece: as water drains from a container, each level it reaches represents a period of time

c. 890 In England people use candles marked with time intervals

12th century The hourglass, familiar to us as an eggtimer, is used by monks to show times of prayer

1325 The first clock with a dial is installed in Norwich Cathedral, England

1335 The first clock to strike the hours is made in Milan, Italy

1350 The oldest known surviving alarm clock is made in Würzburg, Germany

1364 Clocks are first used in people's homes

1386 The clock is installed in Salisbury Cathedral, England. This is the world's oldest clock in working order.

1462 The earliest description of a watch is written in Italy

1641 The pendulum clock is proposed by Vincenzio Galilei, son of the astronomer Galileo

1657 The first pendulum clocks are made in Holland

Time zones

The Earth is constantly turning on its axis. If people everywhere set their clocks to the same time, midnight would be in the middle of the night on one side of the globe, but the middle of the day on the opposite side. To avoid this problem the Earth is divided into artificial time zones. These generally follow lines of longitude – imaginary lines running from the North to the South Pole. Some large countries, such as the USA, cover several time zones. Mainland USA is divided into Atlantic, Eastern, Central, Mountain, Pacific and Alaska zones, with Hawaii and other islands falling into further zones.

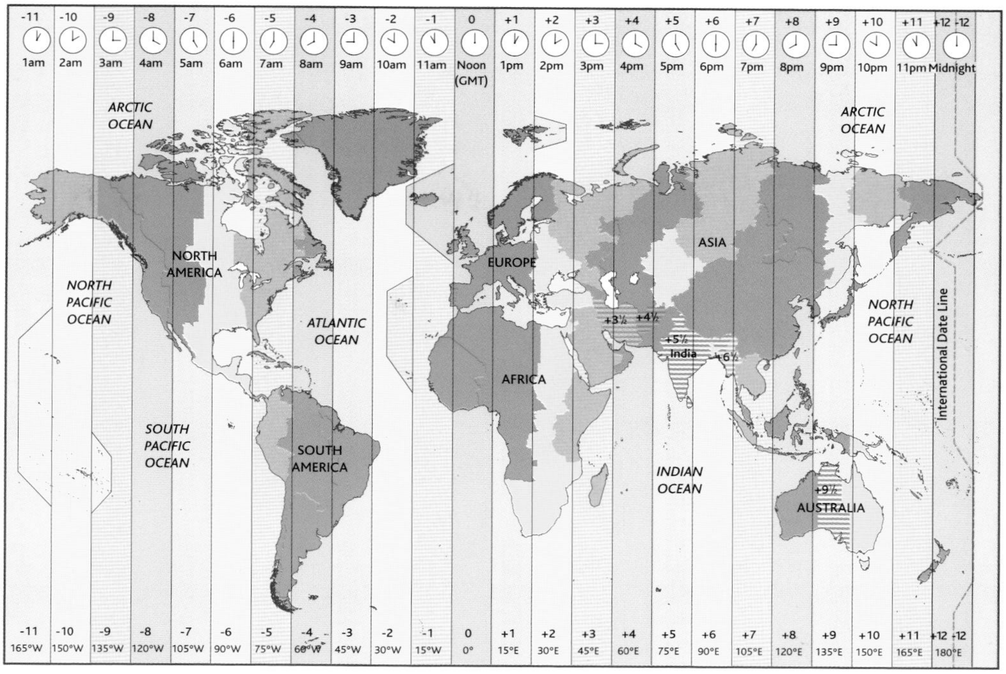

World time zones and the International Date Line

Since the Greenwich Prime Meridian (0°) was established in 1884, there have been 24 time zones, each of 15° longitude and an hour apart. Those to the east are ahead of Greenwich by one hour per zone.

Those to the west are behind by one hour each. Some countries, such as India, have chosen zones halfway between those on either side, so that the whole country can use the same time.

Two sides of the Earth

The International Date Line

The Earth makes one complete turn in every 24 hours. In that time, each of the 360 degrees of longitude passes the Sun. This means that time progresses eastwards by four minutes for every degree of longitude.

The International Date Line is an imaginary line between the North and South Poles. It marks the end of one day and the start of another. Countries to the east of the Date Line are always a day ahead of those to the west. Travellers who cross the line gain or lose a day, depending on which direction they are going.

Most of the Date Line follows the 180° Meridian (on the opposite side of the globe from 0°, the Greenwich Meridian). The line generally passes through sea, but where it would pass through or near certain land areas, it is adjusted. It zigzags around islands, putting them either into the west or the east, and avoids dividing Siberia in north-east Asia into two time zones.

See also
Galileo Galilei: page 26

2010

c. 1665 The first watches with minute and second hands are made

1759 John Harrison's marine chronometer is made. Accurate timekeeping at sea is important for calculating position, but previously the rolling of a ship had made it impossible.

1880 Greenwich Mean Time becomes the standard from which time around the world is set

1880 The first practical wristwatches are made for the German navy

1928 The first quartz crystal clock is made in the USA

1949 The first atomic clock is built in the USA

1957 The first battery watches are marketed in the USA

1969 Quartz wristwatches are first sold in Japan

1970 Digital watches and displays become widely used worldwide and can be made and sold cheaply

2011 ACES (Atomic Clock Ensemble in Space), an atomic clock on the International Space Station, will provide the most accurate time measurements ever

www.rog.nmm.ac.uk search

Thor was the Scandinavian god of thunder and war. He is often shown brandishing a hammer. Thursday, or Thor's day, is named after him.

Names of months

The names of the months in English (as well as in many other languages) come from Latin words.

January
Januarius – this month was dedicated to Janus, the Roman god of doors. Janus had two faces, one looking back at the old year and the other looking forward to the new year.

February
Februarius – Februa was the Roman purification festival, which took place at this time of year.

March
Martius – from Mars, the Roman god of war.

April
Aprilis – from *aperire*, Latin for open, because plants begin to open during this month.

May
Maius – probably comes from Maia, the Roman goddess of growth and increase.

June
Junius – either from a Roman family name Junius, which means young, or perhaps after the goddess Juno.

July
Julius – after Julius Caesar. This month was named in Caesar's honour by Mark Antony in 44 BC. Previously this month was called Quintilis from the word *quintus*, five, as it was the fifth month in the Roman calendar.

August
Augustus – named in 8 BC in honour of Emperor Augustus.

September
September – from *septem*, seven, because it was the seventh month in the Roman calendar.

October
October – from *octo*, eight (as in octopus, which has eight legs), the eighth month in the Roman calendar.

November
November – from *novem*, nine, the ninth month in the Roman calendar.

December
December – from *decem*, ten, the tenth month in the Roman calendar.

Revolutionary calendar

In 1793, after the French Revolution, France adopted a new calendar with 10 days in each week and 12 months of 30 days each, with names relating to the seasons, such as *Nivôse* ('snowy') and *Thermidor* ('summer heat'). It was unpopular and was abandoned in 1805.

Naming the days of the week

The ancient Babylonians, then the Romans, named the days of the week after planets and other bodies they saw in the sky. Some names we know today come from the names of Scandinavian gods.

Monday
Moon's day

Tuesday
Tiu's day: Mars, the Roman god of war, was adopted in Scandinavian mythology as the warrior Tiu or Tiw.

Wednesday
Woden's day: the Roman god Mercury became the Scandinavian god Woden.

Thursday
Thor's day: like the Roman god Jupiter, Thor was a thunder god.

Friday
Freyja's day: like Venus, Freyja or Frigg was the goddess of love.

Saturday
Saturn's day

Sunday
Sun's day

How long does it take?

One beat of a fly's wing (1/1,000 second) 0.001 seconds
Flash of lightning (1/1,000 second) 0.001 seconds
One beat of a hummingbird's wing (80 times a second) 0.0125 seconds
Mouse heartbeat (10.8 times a second) 0.09 seconds
Blink of a human eye 0.33 seconds
Human heartbeat 1.0 seconds
Land speed record: car *ThrustSSC* travelling 1 km (0.62 miles) 2.9 seconds
Record-breaking Jamaican athlete Asafa Powell to run 100 m (328 ft) 9.77 seconds
Bullet train to travel 1 km (0.62 miles) 13.75 seconds
Space Shuttle to travel 100 km (62 miles) 15 seconds
Light reaching Earth from the Sun 497 seconds

Watches at sea

At sea, the 24-hour day is traditionally divided into seven watches, during which some of a ship's crew are on duty.

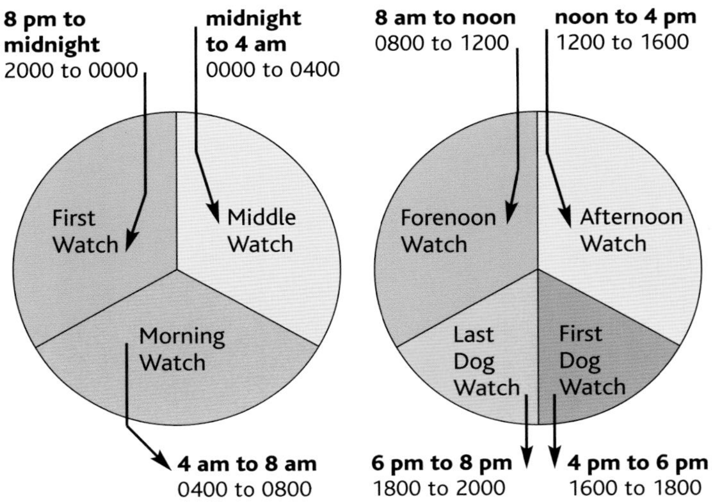

www.physics.nist.gov/Genint/Time search

Just a second

It will take you almost five seconds to read this sentence. During an average-length film more than 5,000 seconds will pass. In a lifetime of 80 years, there are more than 2.5 billion seconds – but you will spend more than 800 million of them asleep!

1 minute 60 seconds
1 hour 3,600 seconds
1 day 86,400 seconds
1 week 604,800 seconds
1 year 31,536,000 seconds

ThrustSCC set the first supersonic land-speed record, at 1,227.986 km/h (763.035 mph).

Time words

Here are some of the words used for units of time.

chronon
One-billionth of a trillionth of a second (the time a photon would take to cross the width of one electron at the speed of light)

femtosecond
0.000000000000001 of a second

picosecond
0.000000000001 (one-trillionth) of a second

nanosecond
0.000000001 (one-billionth) of a second

microsecond
0.000001 (one-millionth) of a second

millisecond
0.001 (one-thousandth) of a second; the blink of an eye takes 50–80 milliseconds

centisecond
0.01 (one-hundredth) of a second

second
1/60 of a minute

minute
60 seconds

hour
60 minutes

day
Sunrise to sunrise, or sunset to sunset, or midnight to midnight; 24 hours

week
Seven days; in Shakespeare's time, it was also called a sennight, or seven nights

fortnight
Two weeks (from the Old English for 14 nights)

month
Full Moon to full Moon; 1/12 of a year; 4 weeks, or 28, 29, 30 or 31 days, depending on month

bimester
Two months

trimester
A period of three months

year
365¼ days, 52 weeks, or 12 months

solar day
The time it takes for a place on the Earth directly facing the Sun to make one revolution and return to the same position (about 23 hours 56 minutes)

solar year
The time it takes for the Earth to make a complete revolution around the Sun, equal to 365.24219 solar days or 365 days, 5 hours 48 minutes, 45.51 seconds; also called a tropical year or astronomical year

leap year
366 days

decade
10 years; also called a decennium

century
100 years

millennium
1,000 years; also called a chiliad

bimillennium
2,000 years

era
A period of time measured from some important event

aeon or eon
A long period of time, usually thousands of years; in geology and astronomy it is one billion years

epoch
A geological era or very long period of time

See also
Geological time chart: page 34

Gregorian calendar

The Gregorian calendar is the one most used nowadays. It is named after Pope Gregory XIII who introduced it in 1582. There is a leap year every four years (or more precisely, 97 leap years every 400 years). This means that the year corresponds closely with the astronomical year (365.24219 days) so that it gets just one day out of sync in every 3,300 years.

Calendar problems

Some non-Catholic countries such as Britain refused to adopt the Gregorian calendar at first. The Julian calendar previously used in Britain was based on a solar year, the time taken for the Earth to rotate around the Sun. This is 365.25 days, which is fractionally too long (it is actually 365.24219 days), so the calendar steadily fell out of line with the seasons. In 1752 Britain decided to correct this by abandoning the Julian calendar in favour of the Gregorian. By doing so, 3 September instantly became 14 September – and, as a result, nothing whatsoever happened in British history between 3 and 13 September 1752. Many people believed their lives would be shortened. They protested in the streets, demanding, "Give us back our 11 days!"

1 January 31 days
2 February 28 days*
3 March 31 days
4 April 30 days
5 May 31 days
6 June 30 days
7 July 31 days
8 August 31 days
9 September 30 days
10 October 31 days
11 November 30 days
12 December 31 days

* In a leap year, February has 29 days.

Mayan calendar

The Mayan people lived in the Yucatan area of present-day Mexico and the neighbouring region. They built many amazing pyramids and temples, and had an astonishing knowledge of astronomy.

Mayan culture had declined by the time Spanish invaders occupied their territory in the 16th century, but we know something about it from the remains found. The Haab or civil calendar of the Maya had 18 months made up of 20 days each. Five extra days were added at the year's end, known as Uayeb, giving a year of 365 days.

Mayan calendar

The year round

The Mayans had one calendar to record a single year and another for the 'Long Count' – a period of thousands of years. The next 'Long Count' ends in December 2012, when some people believe catastrophic events will occur.

Calendar timeline

Most of the world's countries and cultures use the Gregorian calendar, but some base their calendars on more ancient systems. Other countries have adopted an alternative calendar at some point in their history.

3761 BC Jewish calendar starts
2637 BC Original Chinese calendar starts
45 BC Julian calendar adopted by Roman Empire
AD 1 Christian calendar starts
79 Hindu calendar starts
597 Julian calendar adopted in Britain
622 Islamic calendar starts
1582 Gregorian calendar introduced in Catholic countries
1752 Julian calendar abandoned, Gregorian calendar adopted in Britain and its colonies, including America
1873 Japan adopts the Gregorian calendar
1949 China adopts the Gregorian calendar

Mayan months

1 Pop
2 Uo
3 Zip
4 Zotz
5 Tzec
6 Xul
7 Yaxkin
8 Mol
9 Chen
10 Yax
11 Zac
12 Ceh
13 Mac
14 Kankin
15 Muan
16 Pax
17 Kayab
18 Cumku

Chinese calendar

Present-day China uses the Gregorian calendar for most purposes, but traditional festivals, such as Chinese New Year, take place according to the ancient Chinese calendar. Legend has it that this was started during the reign of Emperor Huangdi in 2637 BC, and relates to the positions of the Moon and Sun.

The ancient Chinese calendar follows a 60-year cycle which combines a heavenly stem and earthly branch, represented by a zodiac animal. The first year of the cycle is jia-zi, the second yi-chou, and so on; the 11th year is jia-xu, 12th yi-hai and 13th bing-zi. This continues until the 60th year (gui-hai) and then starts again. Each earthly branch is believed to be linked with certain qualities.

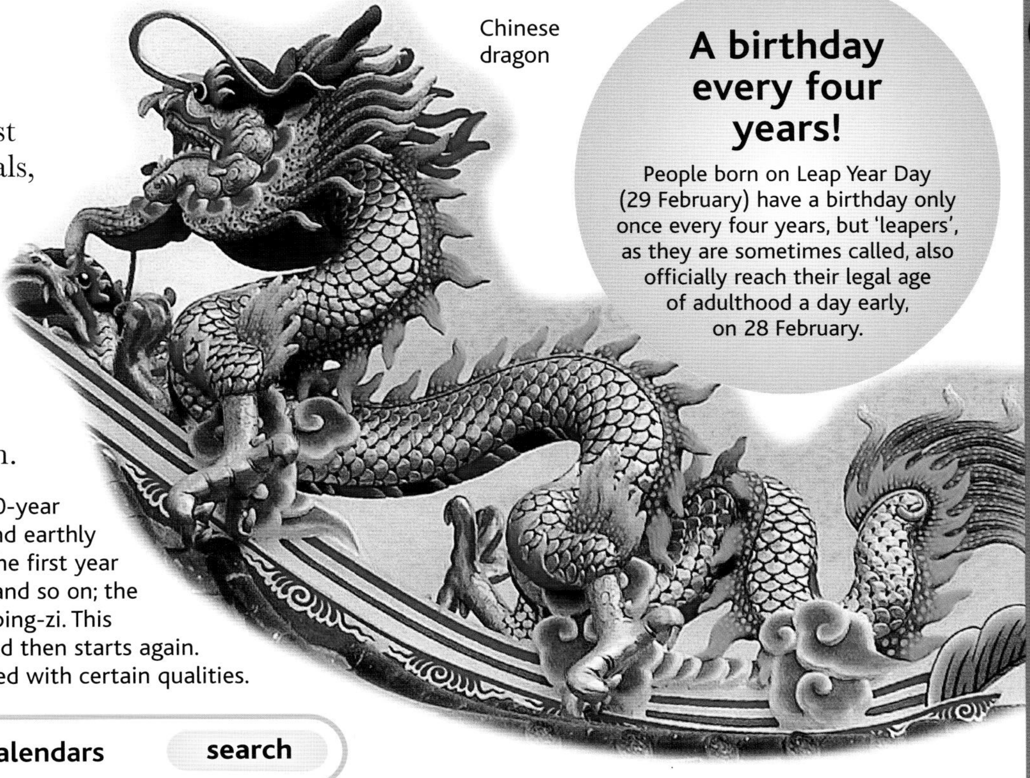
Chinese dragon

A birthday every four years!

People born on Leap Year Day (29 February) have a birthday only once every four years, but 'leapers', as they are sometimes called, also officially reach their legal age of adulthood a day early, on 28 February.

http://webexhibits.org/calendars search

Hebrew and Islamic calendars

The Hebrew (Jewish) and Islamic (Muslim) calendars are based on the lunar (Moon) cycle. Every month starts approximately on the day of a new Moon, or when a crescent moon is first seen.

The visibility of the Moon varies according to the weather so the start date cannot be determined in advance. Printed calendars may vary by a few days. Tishri/Muharram corresponds approximately with September/October in the Gregorian calendar, Heshvan/Safar with October/November, and so on.

Hebrew	Islamic	Hebrew	Islamic
1 Tishri	Muharram* (30 days)	**7 Nisan**	Rajab* (30 days)
2 Heshvan	Safar (29 days)	**8 Iyar**	Sha'ban (29 days)
3 Kislev	Rabi'a I (30 days)	**9 Sivan**	Ramadan † (30 days)
4 Tevet	Rabi'a II (29 days)	**10 Tammuz**	Shawwal (29 days)
5 Shevat	Jumada I (30 days)	**11 Av**	Dhu al-Q'adah* (30 days)
6 Adar	Jumada II (29 days)	**12 Elu**	Dhu al-Hijjah (29 days)

* Holy months † Month of fasting

Indian calendar

The Indian calendar is based on the motions of the Sun and Moon and is dated from the so-called Saka Era, equivalent to AD 79. It is used for dating religious and other festivals, but the Gregorian calendar is used for official dates.

Month	Length	Gregorian calendar
1 Caitra	30 days*	22 March
2 Vaisakha	31 days	21 April
3 Jyaistha	31 days	22 May
4 Asadha	31 days	22 June
5 Sravana	31 days	23 July
6 Bhadra	31 days	23 August
7 Asvina	30 days	23 September
8 Kartika	30 days	23 October
9 Agrahayana	30 days	22 November
10 Pausa	30 days	22 December
11 Magha	30 days	21 January
12 Phalguna	30 days	20 February

* In a leap year, Caitra has 31 days and 1 Caitra = 21 March

Chinese calendar and Gregorian equivalents

HEAVENLY STEMS	EARTHLY BRANCHES	
1 jia	1 zi (rat)	11 xu (dog)
2 yi	2 chou (ox)	12 hai (pig or boar)
3 bing	3 yin (tiger)	
4 ding	4 mao (hare or rabbit)	
5 wu	5 chen (dragon)	
6 ji	6 si (snake)	
7 geng	7 wu (horse)	
8 zxin	8 wei (sheep or ram)	
9 ren	9 shen (monkey)	
10 gui	10 you (rooster)	

Zodiac animal	Gregorian calendar year beginning	Zodiac animal	Gregorian calendar year beginning
Hare	16 Feb 1999	Dog	29 Jan 2006
Dragon	5 Feb 2000	Pig	18 Feb 2007
Snake	24 Jan 2001	Rat	7 Feb 2008
Horse	12 Feb 2002	Ox	26 Jan 2009
Sheep	1 Feb 2003	Tiger	14 Feb 2010
Monkey	22 Jan 2004	Rabbit	3 Feb 2011
Rooster	9 Feb 2005	Dragon	23 Jan 2012

WHITAKER'S WORLD OF FACTS

Space

Virgin Galactic *SpaceShipTwo*

Designed to carry six space tourists and two crewmembers to the edge of space, Virgin's spaceships are in development with a planned launch date of 2011. The first, called *VSS Enterprise* after the spaceship in *Star Trek*, was named by California Governor Arnold Schwarzenegger in 2010. The first stage *WhiteKnightTwo* carrier aircraft transports *SpaceShipTwo* to a height of 18.3 km (11 miles), after which the rocket-powered spacecraft detaches and travels at 4,200 km/h (2,600 mph) to 110 km (68 miles) above the Earth's surface. The craft will be launched from the first-ever space airport, Spaceport America, in New Mexico, USA. The cost of a ticket is $200,000.

Twinkle twinkle little star...

Stars appear to twinkle because we see them through the layers of the Earth's atmosphere. Light is distorted as it passes through these layers, so that the amount we see changes constantly. Stars nearest the horizon seem to twinkle the most because the light is passing through a greater depth of atmosphere. Stars do not twinkle when viewed from space, so telescopes in space, such as the Hubble, give the best possible view of distant stars and galaxies.

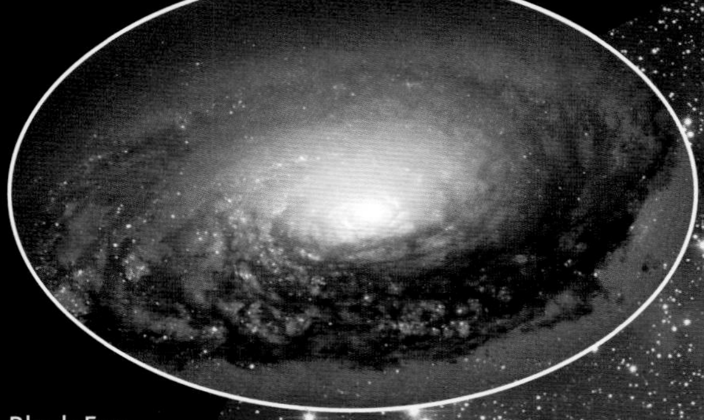
Black Eye Galaxy

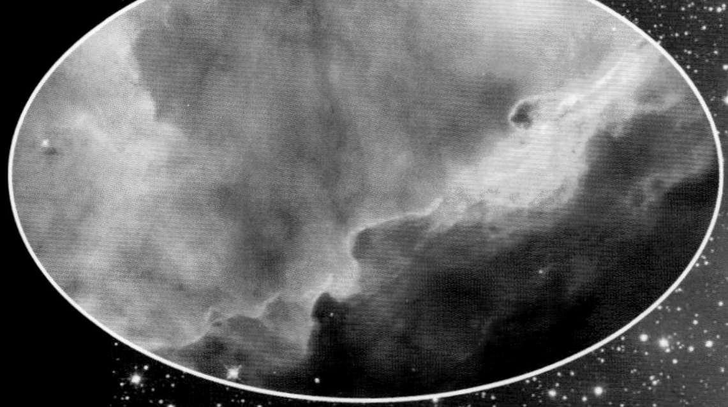
Swan Nebula

Star facts

A star is a luminous body of gas, mostly hydrogen and helium. Stars generate light, which makes it possible for us to see them with a telescope or the naked eye.

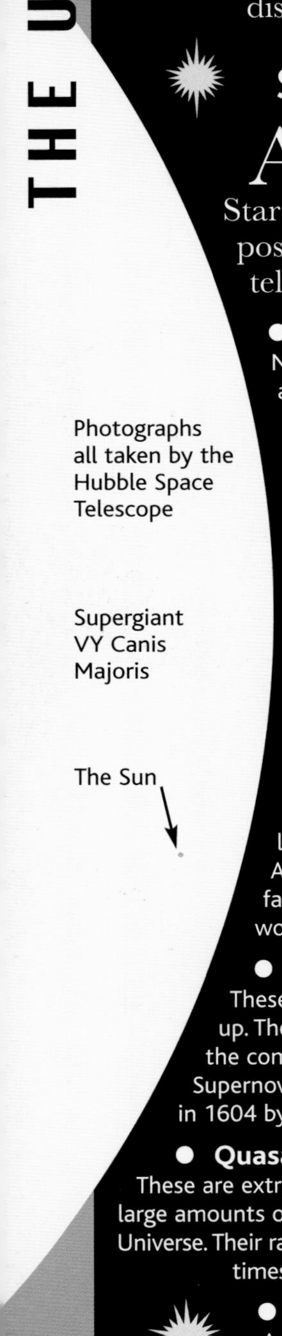

Photographs all taken by the Hubble Space Telescope

- **Brightest**
Not counting the Sun, the brightest star as seen from Earth is Sirius, known as the dog star, in the constellation of Canis Major. It has a diameter of 149,598,020 km and is more than 24 times brighter than the Sun. The star LBV 1806–20 in the constellation of Sagittarius may be 40 million times as bright as our Sun, but dust clouds make it almost invisible from Earth.

- **Largest**
The largest star is VY Canis Majoris, which has an estimated diameter of about 1,950 times greater than the Sun. For comparison, if it were a football, the Sun would be no bigger than a pinhead.

- **Nearest**
Proxima Centauri, discovered in 1915, is 4.22 light years (39,953,525,879,212 km) from Earth. A spaceship moving at 40,000 km/h – which is faster than any human has yet travelled in space – would take more than 114,000 years to reach it.

- **Supernovae**
These are vast explosions in which a whole star blows up. They are extremely bright, rivalling for a few days the combined light output of all the stars in the galaxy. Supernovae are rare – the last one in our galaxy was seen in 1604 by the German astronomer Johannes Kepler.

- **Quasars**
These are extremely distant radio galaxies – galaxies giving out large amounts of radio energy – and the brightest objects in the Universe. Their radio emission is typically 1,000,000 to 100,000,000 times greater than that of a normal galaxy.

- **Black holes**
A black hole is a star that has collapsed into itself. It has a surface gravity so powerful that nothing can escape from within it.

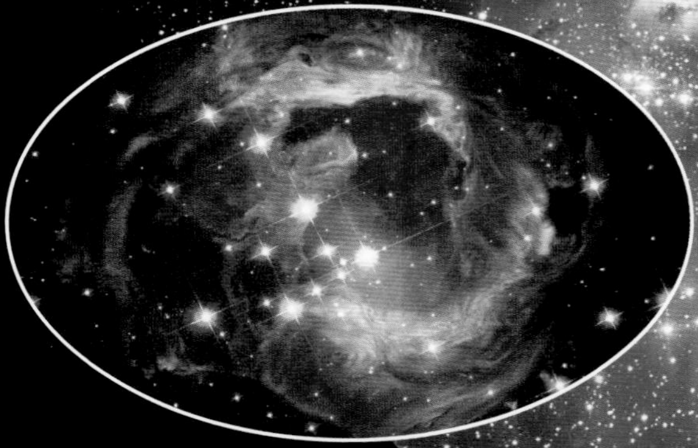
Monocerotis V838 (a red supergiant star surrounded by dust)

Travelling at the speed of light

In space, light travels at a speed of 299,792.46 km a second, or 1,079,252,956 km an hour. When we look at even the nearest star, we see light that left it more than four years ago. Here are the times it takes light to reach Earth from various bodies in space.

- **Light years**
A light year measures distance, not time. Distances in space are often described as light years, the distance light travels in a year.

Galaxy facts

Galaxies are groups of billions of stars held together by the force of gravity. Most are either spiral or elliptical, but some are irregular in shape.

● **The Milky Way**
This is the best-known galaxy. The word galaxy comes from the Greek for milk. Before telescopes were powerful enough to prove that they were made up of individual stars, galaxies looked like milky or cloudy areas in the sky. Our Solar System is only one of 100–200 billion stars in the Milky Way, which is 100,000 light years in diameter. The Sun and all the planets take about 200,000,000 years to complete one orbit around its centre.

● **Brightest**
The Large Magellanic Cloud, which is visible only in the southern hemisphere, is 170,000 light years from Earth and 39,000 light years in diameter.

● **Largest**
The central galaxy of the Abell 2029 galaxy cluster was discovered in 1990. It is 1,070 million light years distant and has a diameter of 5.6 million light years, 80 times the diameter of our own galaxy. It has a total light output equivalent to 2 trillion times that of the Sun.

● **Nearest**
Discovered in 1993, the Canis Major Dwarf galaxy is approximately 25,000 light years from the Solar System.

Small Magellanic Cloud

Constellations

Groups of stars form patterns in the night sky, which are called constellations. There are 88 known constellations. The Sumerians, a Middle Eastern civilization, probably named them, about 5,000 years ago.

The largest is Hydra, the sea serpent, and the smallest is Crux Australis, the Southern Cross. Centaurus, the Centaur, has the most stars that can be seen with the naked eye (94). Others include Aquila, the Eagle; Canis Major, the Great Dog; and Orion, the Hunter.

Crux Australis – the Southern Cross

Canis Major – the Great Dog

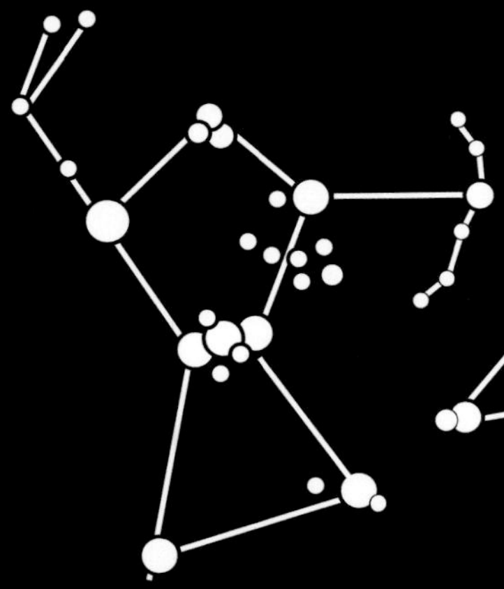

Orion – the Hunter

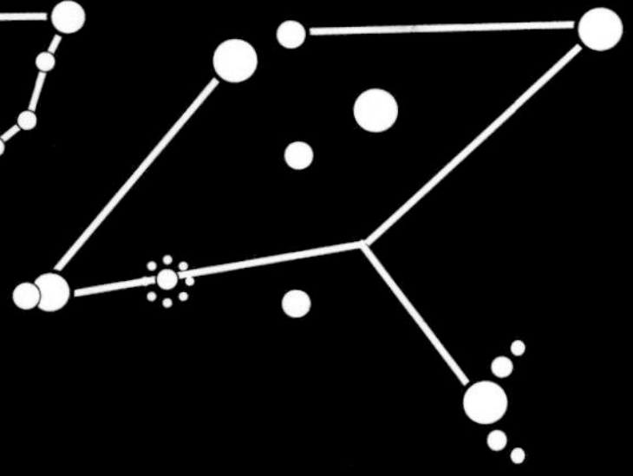

Aquila – the Eagle

Moon 1.26 seconds
Sun 8 minutes 17 seconds
Furthest planet (Neptune) 4 hrs 21 mins when the planet is at its maximum distance from Earth
Nearest star 4.22 years
Distance at which the Sun would no longer be visible to the naked eye 60 years
Most distant star in our galaxy 62,700 years
outside our galaxy 174,000 years
Furthest visible star 2,309,000 years
Most distant known quasar 14,000,000,000 years

www.astronautix.com search

T… was formed about 4,560 million years ago. It is made up of the eight planets – Mercury, Venus, Earth, Mars, Jupiter, Saturn, Uranus and Neptune – as well as their moons, comets and other bodies. These all orbit our Sun, to which they are attracted by gravity.

Mercury

Mercury was named after the speedy messenger of the gods because it seemed to move more quickly than the other known planets. In 2004 NASA launched its MESSENGER probe, which is due to reach Mercury in 2011.

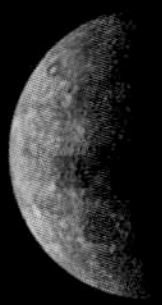

Diameter: 4,880 km
Mass: 3,302,000,000,000 tonnes
Average distance from Sun: 57,909,175 km
Rotation: 58.6462 days
Orbit: 87.969 days
Average temperature: +166.86°C
Moons: 0

Venus

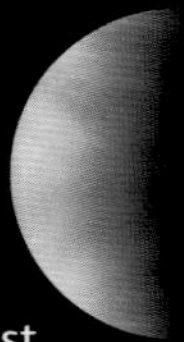

In size, mass, density and volume Venus is the planet most similar to Earth. Venus rotates backwards, from east to west, so the Sun would appear to rise in the east and set in the west. In April 2006 the European Space Agency's *Venus Express* spacecraft reached Venus. Japan's Venus Climate Orbiter *PLANET-C* will be launched in 2010.

Diameter: 12,103.6 km
Mass: 48,690,000,000,000 tonnes
Average distance from Sun: 108,208,930 km
Rotation: 243.0187 days
Orbit: 224.701 days
Average temperature: +456.85°C
Moons: 0

See also
Planets visited by spacecraft: page 29

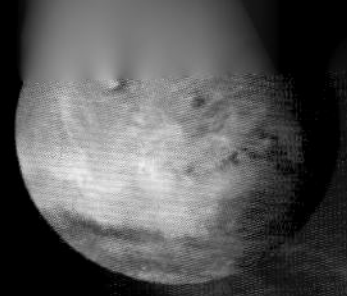

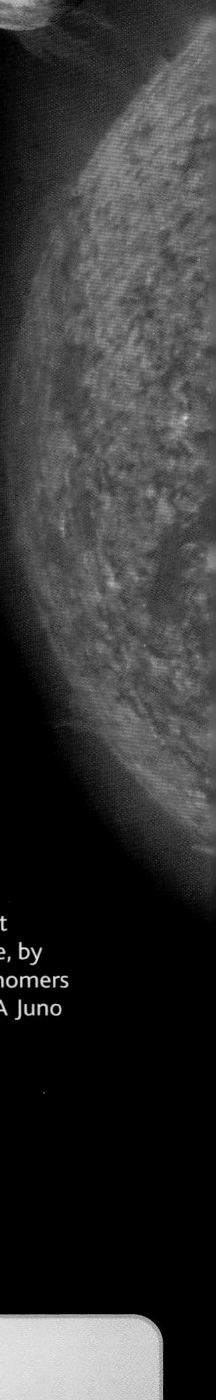

…pace probes have flown past or landed on Mars, providing information on its atmosphere and features, such as the volcano Olympus Mons. This stands 27 km high – more than three times the height of Mount Everest. The latest craft to visit the red planet are NASA's *Mars Reconnaissance Orbiter*, which began its four-year orbit in 2006, and the *Phoenix Mars* lander, which descended to the surface on 25 May 2008.

Diameter: 6,794 km
Mass: 6,421,900,000,000 tonnes
Average distance from Sun: 227,940,000 km
Rotation: 1.025957 days
Orbit: 686.98 days
Average temperature: -63°C
Moons: 2

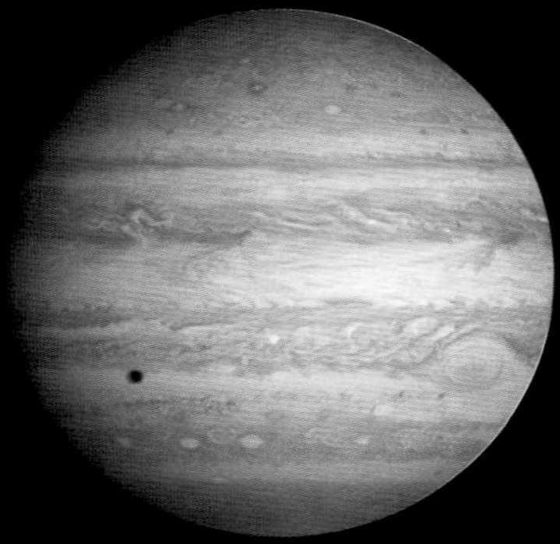

Jupiter

Jupiter is the largest planet in the Solar System and is big enough to contain more than a thousand Earths. Four of its many moons were among the first ever astronomical discoveries made with a telescope, by Galileo in 1610. More were identified by later astronomers and in 1979 by the space probe *Voyager 2*. The NASA Juno mission to Jupiter is planned for launch in 2011.

Diameter: 142,984 km
Mass: 18,986,000,000,000,000 tonnes
Average distance from Sun: 778,412,010 km
Rotation: 9 hours 50 minutes
Orbit: 11 years 314 days
Average temperature: -150° C
Moons: 63

Earth

Earth is a watery planet – 70 per cent of its surface appears blue – and the only one that can support life. From space, astronauts have observed cities, forest fires, roads, airports, dams and other large structures, such as the Great Pyramid and the Great Wall of China.

Diameter: 12,756.3 km
Mass: 59,720,000,000,000 tonnes
Average distance from Sun: 149,600,000 km
Rotation: 0.99727 days
Orbit: 365.256 days
Average temperature: +15°C
Moons: 1

www.nineplanets.org search

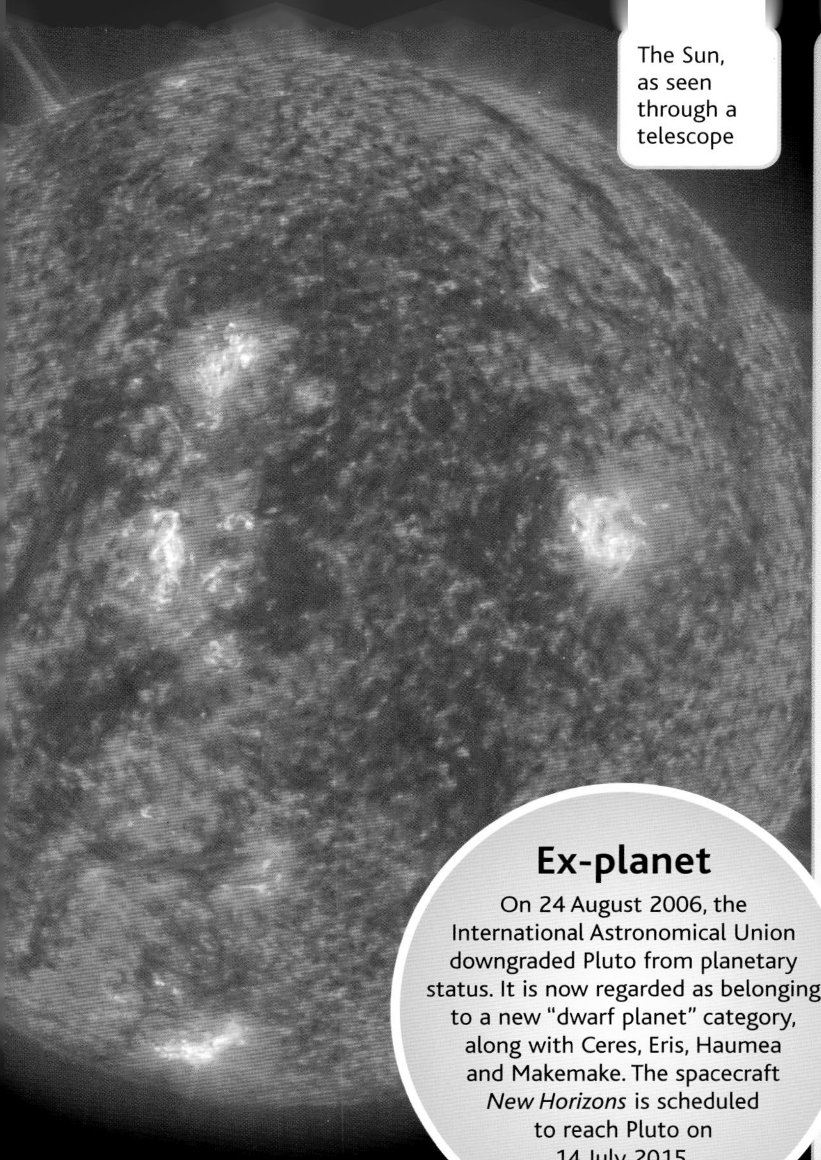

The Sun, as seen through a telescope

Sun facts

The Sun is 149,597,893 km from Earth and has a diameter of 1,391,940 km. This is more than 100 times larger than Earth. Its mass is equivalent to 99.98 per cent of the mass of the entire Solar System.

Elements

The Sun is mostly made up of two light gases, 75 per cent hydrogen and 23 per cent helium, with relatively small quantities of other elements – including metals such as gold. Helium was discovered in the Sun before it was detected on Earth. Its name comes from *helios*, the Greek word for sun.

Temperature

The Sun has a surface temperature of 5,880 K but it can be 56,000,000 K at its core. (K represents Kelvin, which is an astronomical temperature; it can be converted to Celsius by subtracting 273.16.) At the Sun's centre, nuclear fusion constantly changes hydrogen into helium, and the energy and heat released from this process rise to the surface. The yellow surface we see is called the photosphere.

The corona

The outermost layer of the Sun extends millions of kilometres into space but is visible only during eclipses. At a height of 75,000 km in the corona, the temperature may reach 2,000,000 K.

Rotation

The Sun rotates once every 25.4 days, but because it is not solid, the poles spin at a different rate, taking as much as 36 days to complete a single revolution.

Solar eclipses

When the Moon is between Earth and the Sun, it blocks out the light causing a partial or total eclipse. At this time, astronomers are able to observe the corona in detail.

Ex-planet

On 24 August 2006, the International Astronomical Union downgraded Pluto from planetary status. It is now regarded as belonging to a new "dwarf planet" category, along with Ceres, Eris, Haumea and Makemake. The spacecraft *New Horizons* is scheduled to reach Pluto on 14 July 2015.

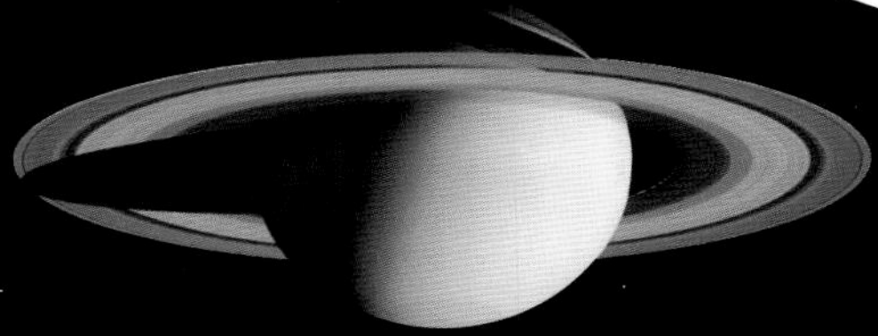

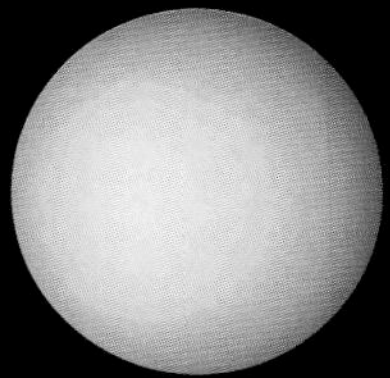

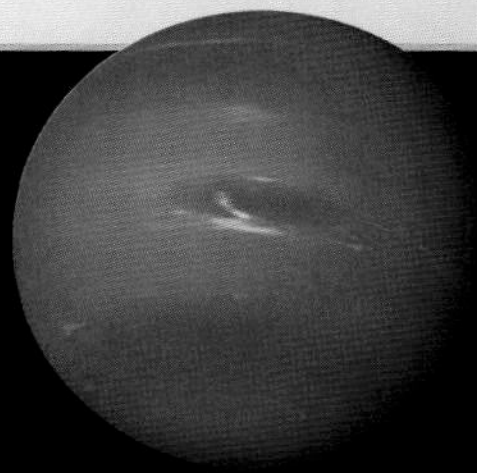

Saturn

Saturn and its rings are being examined by NASA/European Space Agency's *Cassini* probe, which reached it in 2004. It released the *Huygens* probe to orbit Titan in 2005 and began flybys of Saturn's moons Iapetus in 2007 and Enceladus, Titan and others in 2008–10.

Diameter: 120,536 km
Mass: 5,684,600,000,000,000 tonnes
Average distance from Sun: 1,426,725,400 km
Rotation: 10 hours 34 minutes
Orbit: 29 years 168 days
Average temperature: -139.5°C

Uranus

All the satellites of Uranus are called after characters from either William Shakespeare's plays or Alexander Pope's poem *The Rape of the Lock*. Uranus has rings like those of Saturn, but they are visible only with a powerful telescope.

Diameter: 51,118 km
Mass: 868,320,000,000,000 tonnes
Average distance from Sun: 2,870,972,200 km
Rotation: 17 hours 17 minutes
Orbit: 84 years 4 days
Average temperature: -197.15°C

Neptune

Neptune is the furthest body from the Sun. Surface winds are the strongest of any planet at up to 2,000 km/h. Neptune's year is so long that it has not completed an orbit round the Sun since its discovery and will not do so until 12 July 2011.

Diameter: 49,522 km
Mass: 1,024,700,000,000,000 tonnes
Average distance from Sun: 4,498,252,900 km
Rotation: 16 hours 7 minutes
Orbit: 164 years 298 days
Average temperature: -200.15°C

Buzz Aldrin, walking on the Moon

The Moon's near side

Our Moon's far side
The far side of our Moon always faces away from Earth, so it was unknown until October 1959, when the Soviet *Luna 3* probe sent pictures of it back to Earth.

Asteroid facts

Asteroids are often called minor planets. They are lumps of rock orbiting the Sun, mostly in the asteroid belt between the orbits of Mars and Jupiter.

- Ceres was once considered the largest asteroid but it has been recently reclassified as a dwarf planet. It is 936 km in diameter and was found on New Year's Day, 1801. Since then thousands of asteroids have been found. Twelve of them are more than 250 km wide and 26 are larger than 200 km in diameter. As telescopes have improved, more small asteroids have been detected. Up to 2009, over 200,000 asteroids had been identified. It has been estimated that there are more than one million asteroids larger than 1 km in diameter.
- Vesta, the fourth asteroid to be found (in 1807), is the only one bright enough to be seen without a telescope.

Moon facts

Earth's Moon is the most familiar and also the largest satellite in relation to its planet in the Solar System. It is the first body in the Solar System on which vehicles from Earth landed, and the only one to be explored by humans.

Diameter: 3,475.6 km
Distance from Earth: 406,711 km (furthest, 1912) to 356,375 km (closest, 1984), 384,403 km (average)
Mass: 734,556,000,000 tonnes; a person weighing 65 kg on Earth would weigh 10.79 kg on the Moon
Rotation: 27 days 7 hours 43 minutes 11.5 seconds
Surface temperature: -163°C to +117°C
Largest crater: South Pole Aitken (far side) 2,100 km diameter, 12 km deep (largest in the Solar System)

Part of the Bayeux Tapestry, showing Halley's comet top left

Halley's comet

240BC **1450s**

British astronomer Edmond Halley (1656–1742) was the first to prove that comets travel in orbits, making it possible to calculate when they will next be seen from Earth. He predicted that the comet he saw in 1682 would return in 1759. It did and was named in his honour. The regular orbit of Halley's comet means that we can find historical accounts of its appearances going back more than 2,000 years. They were often believed to foretell great events.

25 May 240 BC Seen in China
10 October 12 BC Believed to mark the death of Roman general Agrippa
28 June AD 451 Believed to mark the defeat of Attila the Hun
20 March 1066 William (later William the Conqueror) believed the comet foretold victory over King Harold at the Battle of Hastings. The comet and battle are later depicted in the Bayeux Tapestry.
9 June 1456 The defeat of the Turkish army by Papal forces was thought to be linked to the comet.

- Astronomers believe that, on average, one asteroid larger than 0.4 km strikes Earth every 50,000 years. Some 65 million years ago a 10 km diameter asteroid crashing to Earth may have been responsible for wiping out the dinosaurs. It would have caused a catastrophic explosion, affecting the climate and chemical composition of the atmosphere and destroying the plants and animals on which the dinosaurs fed. As recently as 1991 a small asteroid came within 170,600 km of Earth, the closest recorded near miss. On 30 Jan 2052 an asteroid is predicted to pass as close as 119,678 km.

- Toutatis (asteroid 4,179) was discovered in 1989. It is named after the Celtic god Toutatis, whose name is used as an oath by the comic strip character Astérix the Gaul. Toutatis measures 4.6 by 2.4 by 1.9 km. It passes Earth every four years and is one of the largest space objects to come so close to us. On 29 September 2004 Toutatis came within 1,555,818 km of Earth. Its next visit will be on 9 November 2008, when it will come within 7,524,773 km.

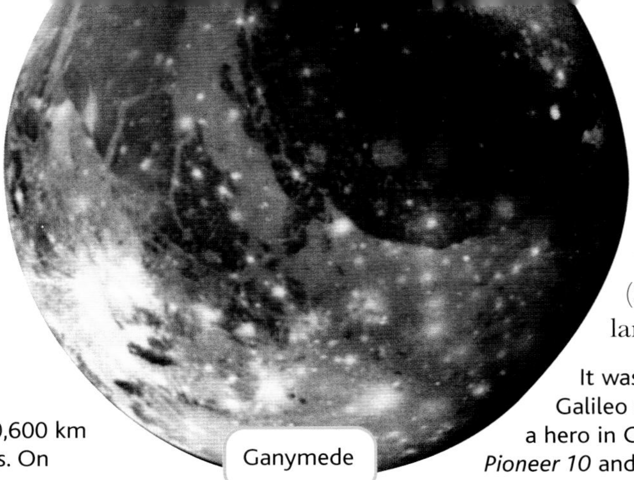

Ganymede

Biggest moon

Ganymede, one of the 63 moons of the planet Jupiter, is the largest moon in the Solar System. At 5,262.4 km (3,269.9 miles) in diameter it is larger than the planet Mercury.

It was discovered by Italian astronomer Galileo on 11 January 1610 and named after a hero in Greek mythology. It was visited by the *Pioneer 10* and *Pioneer 11* space probes in the early 1970s and in 1979 by *Voyager 1* and *2*, which sent back detailed images. Launched in 1989, NASA's *Galileo* probe reached Ganymede in June 1996 and data sent back indicated an ocean beneath its icy surface, while the Hubble space telescope later detected a small amount of oxygen in the atmosphere. In 2007 the probe *New Horizons* made further discoveries.

Old names for new discoveries

Recently discovered features on Ganymede, such as craters and ridges, have been given the names of ancient Greek, Egyptian and other gods, places in Egypt and ancient Babylon, with larger regions named after important astronomers.

Longest tail

In 1996 amateur Japanese astronomer Yuji Hyakutake discovered a comet that was named after him. Its tail is 550 million km (342 million miles) long, more than twice as long as the tail of any comet previously seen.

Hyakutake's comet

2000s

15 September 1682 Observed by Edmond Halley, who predicted its return

13 March 1759 The comet's first return, as predicted by Halley, proving his calculations correct

16 November 1835 The American author Mark Twain is born. He always believed that his fate was linked to that of the comet, and soon after it reappeared in 1910, he died.

10 April 1910 There was panic as many believed the world would come to an end

9 February 1986 The Japanese *Suisei* probe, Soviet *Vega 1* and *Vega 2* and the European Space Agency's *Giotto* passed close to Halley's comet. Astronomers concluded that the comet is made of dust held together by water and carbon dioxide ice.

28 July 2061 Next due to appear. The orbit of Halley's comet is not exactly 76 years. Astronomers have to take into account the gravitational pull from planets when calculating its return.

www.spacetoday.org search

Famous astronomers

John Couch Adams (Britain, 1819–92) studied the Leonid meteor shower and predicted the existence of Neptune, which was discovered in 1846.

Edward Emerson Barnard (USA, 1857–1923) discovered Barnard's Star and Amalthea, a moon of Jupiter.

Nicolaus Copernicus (Poland, 1473–1543) showed that the Sun was at the centre of the Solar System.

Galileo Galilei (Italy, 1564–1642) made important discoveries concerning gravity and motion. He built some of the first telescopes used in astronomy and used them to discover many previously unknown space objects.

George Ellery Hale (USA, 1868–1938) pioneered the astronomical study of the Sun and founded observatories, one with a major telescope named after him.

Edmond Halley (Britain, 1656–1742) predicted the orbits of comets, including the one that bears his name.

William Herschel (Germany/Britain, 1738–1822) built huge telescopes, compiled catalogues of stars and discovered moons of Saturn and Uranus.

Edwin Hubble (USA, 1889–1953) made important discoveries about galaxies. The Hubble Space Telescope was named in his honour.

Christiaan Huygens (Holland, 1629–95) discovered Saturn's rings and devised the wave theory of light.

Percival Lowell (USA, 1855–1916) was founder of the Lowell Observatory, Arizona. He predicted that a planet would be found in the region where Pluto was later discovered.

Charles Messier (France, 1730–1817) studied comets and eclipses, but he is best known for his catalogue of stars first published in 1774.

Yerkes Observatory, Wisconsin, USA

Isaac Newton (Britain, 1643–1727) is considered one of the greatest of all astronomers. His theories of gravity and the motions of planets revolutionized the subject.

Telescopes and observatories

The following are some of the world's most famous telescopes and observatories.

Royal Observatory, Greenwich, London
Founded by King Charles II in 1675, but atmospheric and light pollution in London reduced its efficiency. In 1884 the Prime or Greenwich Meridian, 0°, which passes through the Observatory, was adopted as the basis for all mapping and measurements. Longitude measurements refer to west or east of the meridian.

Herschel's "Forty-foot" reflector, Slough
A giant telescope built in 1788 with a 1.2 m (3.9 ft) mirror.

Birr Castle, Co. Offaly, Ireland
The Earl of Rosse's 1.8 m (5.9 ft) reflecting telescope, built in 1845, was used to discover the spiral form of galaxies. It was the world's largest until the opening of Mount Wilson.

Yerkes Observatory, Williams Bay, Wisconsin, USA
This 1 m (3.25 ft) telescope is the biggest refracting instrument made up to this time. It was completed in 1897.

Mount Wilson Observatory, California, USA
The telescope was installed in 1917 with a mirror size of 2.5 m (8.2 ft). It was the world's largest until the Hale.

Hale Telescope, Palomar Observatory, California, USA
The Hale's 5 m (16.4 ft) telescope was first used in 1949.

Jodrell Bank, Cheshire
Britain's first, and once the world's largest radio telescope, with a 76 m (249.3 ft) dish, began operating in 1957.

Arecibo Observatory, Puerto Rico
Completed in 1963, this is the world's most powerful radio telescope. Its uses include searching for pulsars and quasars and the search for alien life forms under the SETI (Search for Extra-Terrestrial Intelligence) programme. Its giant 305 m (1,000.65 ft) dish features in the final scenes of the James Bond film *Golden Eye* (1995).

Astronomy milestones

Astronomy is the scientific study of the Universe and the bodies it contains (excluding Earth). Astronomers are the scientists who study astronomy.

585 BC First prediction of eclipse of the Sun

130 BC Hipparchus calculates distance and size of Moon

AD 1543 Copernicus shows that the Sun is at the centre of the Solar System

1609 Johannes Kepler describes laws of planetary motion

1610 Galileo Galilei discovers moons of Jupiter

1655 Christiaan Huygens discovers Titan, moon of Saturn

1600s

1668 Isaac Newton builds first reflecting telescope

1687 Isaac Newton publishes theories of motions of planets, etc

1705 Edmond Halley predicts return of comet

1671–84 Giovanni Cassini discovers four moons of Saturn

1774 Charles Messier compiles star catalogue

1781 William Herschel discovers 7th planet, Uranus

1800s

1801 First asteroid, Ceres, discovered by Giuseppe Piazzi

1846 Johann Galle and Urbain Le Verrier discover 8th planet Neptune

1787–89 Herschel finds two moons of Uranus and two of Saturn

1839–40 First photographs of the Moon

1894 Flagstaff Observatory, Arizona, founded

1905 Einstein's Special Theory of Relativity first proposed

Hubble Space Telescope
The HST was launched in 1990 and orbits 600 km (372.8 miles) above Earth's atmosphere. It can photograph distant objects with ten times the detail possible with ground-based telescopes.

Keck I & II Telescopes, Mauna Kea Observatory, Hawaii, USA
The two Keck telescopes were opened in 1992–96. They are situated 4,000 m (13,123 ft) up a Hawaiian mountain, so above 40 per cent of the Earth's atmosphere. They are the world's most powerful ground-based instruments, with a 10.82 m (35.5 ft) total aperture made up of 36 hexagonal mirrors.

Hobby-Eberly Telescope, McDonald Observatory, Texas, USA
This telescope is designed to collect light for spectrum analysis rather than for visual exploration. It has been in operation since 1999, and has an overall diameter of 11 m (36.1 ft), making it one of the largest ever optical telescopes.

Large Binocular Telescope, Arizona, USA
The Large Binocular Telescope, completed in 2007, is the largest and most advanced optical telescope ever built. Sited at the Mount Graham International Observatory, it has two 8.4 m (27.5 ft) mirrors, giving a total area equal to one giant 11.4 m (37.4 ft) diameter mirror. It is expected to produce images as much as 10 times the resolution of those produced by the much smaller Hubble Space Telescope.

Kepler telescope
Launched in 2009, NASA's Kepler Mission uses a powerful telescope to discover Earth-like planets, known as extrasolar planets, in orbit around distant stars.

NASA technicians work on the Kepler telescope at its base in Florida, USA

1900s

1930 Pluto discovered by Clyde Tombaugh
1959 First photographs of the far side of the Moon by Soviet satellite *Luna 3*
1961 First quasars discovered
1967 First pulsars identified
1971 Black hole first detected
1973 *Skylab* space laboratory launched
1976 Rings of Uranus are discovered
1977 *Voyager* deep space probes are launched
1971 *Mariner 9* spacecraft maps Mars
1980 *Voyager 1* explores Saturn
1978 Space probes *Pioneer 1* and *2* reach Venus
1985–89 *Voyager 2* discovers moons of Uranus and Neptune
1994 Comet Shoemaker-Levy observed crashing into Jupiter
1995 *Galileo* probe reaches Jupiter
1997 *Mars Pathfinder* lands
1997 *Cassini* probe launched to Saturn
1998 *International Space Station* construction starts

2000s

2003 *Galileo* probe deliberately crash-landed on Jupiter
2006 *New Horizons* space probe launched to Pluto
2008 *Phoenix* mission to Mars landed on the planet
2009 International Year of Astronomy celebrates 400th anniversary of Galileo's first telescope observations
2010–11 Tiangong 1, Chinese unmanned space station launched.

www.absoluteastronomy.com search

Animal space pioneers

Before humans went into space animals were used to test equipment. The first animal to be sent up in a rocket – but not into space – was Albert 1, a male rhesus monkey, in 1948. He and his successor, Albert 2, died during the tests.

However, on 20 September 1951, a monkey and 11 mice were recovered after a launch in a US *Aerobee* rocket. Many further animal experiments were carried out before the first manned space flight.

Space teddies

In 2008 a helium balloon carried four teddy bears to the edge of space, a height of 30 km (18.6 miles). An experiment by schoolchildren in Cambridge, UK, it was designed to test which spacesuit best protected the teddies at temperatures of –53°C.

Space dogs, and a cat

Laika, a female Samoyed husky, became the first animal in orbit after being launched by the USSR in *Sputnik 2* in November 1957. There was no way to bring her down and she died after ten days in space. Two female huskies, Belka and Strelka, orbited successfully in August 1960. Strelka later gave birth to puppies, one of which was given to US President John F. Kennedy. In October 1963, a French *Veronique AGI* rocket put a cat called Félix into space and returned him safely to Earth by parachute.

Monkey business

Able, a female rhesus monkey, and Baker, a female squirrel monkey, were launched by the USA in May 1959. They did not orbit and successfully returned to Earth. In November 1961 Enos, a male chimpanzee, completed two orbits and survived. The USSR's first space primates were monkeys Abrek and Bion, who orbited in December 1983 in one of a series of Bion satellite experiments.

Flying frogs

In November 1970, the USA's Orbiting Frog Otolith satellite (OFO-A) launched two bullfrogs into orbit for a week. In December 1990, Toyohiro Akiyama, a Japanese journalist, took six green tree frogs to the Soviet *Mir* space station to conduct weightlessness experiments.

Worldwide web

Arabella, a garden spider, went to the US *Skylab-3* in July 1973. She spent almost 60 days in orbit in an experiment to test the effect of weightlessness on her web-weaving skills.

A space menagerie

The *STS-90* mission of space shuttle *Columbia* (April/May 1998) contained the *Neurolab* – a space menagerie with 170 baby rats, 18 mice, 229 swordtail fish, 135 snails, four oyster toad fish and 1,514 cricket eggs and larvae.

Space butterflies and worms

In 2009 Space shuttle *Atlantis* carried larvae of Painted lady and Monarch butterflies as part of a US school experiment and *Caenorhabditis elegans* roundworms for a University of Nottingham experiment into how these creatures behave in weightless conditions.

The *Ares V* launch vehicle is designed to carry heavy equipment into space after the retirement of the Space Shuttle in 2010. It will be able to carry seven times the weight of a Space Shuttle into orbit.

http://kids.msfc.nasa.gov search

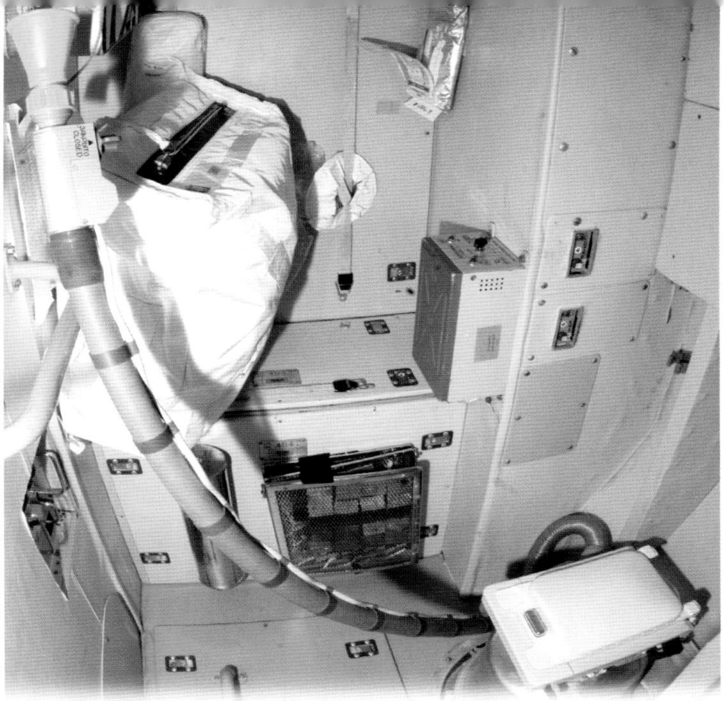

The toilet on the International Space Station was specially designed to operate in zero gravity

Space toilets

Because the first space flights were short, no one had thought about what would happen if an astronaut needed to use a toilet, so on 5 May 1961, when Alan Shepard was kept waiting on the launchpad for four hours, he was given permission to relieve himself in his spacesuit.

- **Nappies**

As missions grew longer, the problem of zero gravity, where liquids and solids float around the cabin, had to be overcome. At first, astronauts used nappies and, on the Apollo Moon missions, plastic bags known as 'Apollo bags' that were held on with sticky tape.

- **Waste Collection System**

Space toilets were first installed on the roomier space shuttle, with the Waste Collection System first used on shuttle mission STS-54 (1993) and an improved version on the International Space Station. This resembles an ordinary toilet, but with foot restraints, Velcro straps and handholds to prevent astronauts from floating around while they are using it. It features a fan-driven suction system and anti-bacteria filters to prevent odours. Solid waste is collected in removable plastic bags that are stored and returned to Earth, while liquids are either stored, recycled or vented into space in a 'water dump': in the intense cold, they instantly form a cloud of ice crystals that reflect light and can be seen from Earth.

Artificial satellites

The USSR's *Sputnik 1* was the first artificial satellite to enter Earth's orbit. This 83.6 kg (184 lb) metal sphere transmitted signals back to Earth for three weeks before its batteries failed.

In 1958 the USA began to launch its own satellites. Five went into orbit. All of the earliest satellites have since crashed back to Earth, except *Vanguard 1* (USA, 1958) which is still in space – and likely to remain so for another 200 years.

Over the past 50 years, many more artificial satellites have been launched, with a greater range of uses.

Astronomy

The Hubble Space Telescope has been taking photographs of distant galaxies since 1990. In 2008 the Herschel Space Observatory is scheduled for launch. This new telescope will have the biggest mirror ever in space (3.5 m across).

Communications

Over 5,000 satellites have been launched to transmit telephone, radio and television signals around the world. Fewer than half are still orbiting, and many have stopped working.

Earth observation satellites

These transmit images of the weather and the Earth's environment. They helped to show the depletion of the ozone layer.

Military satellites

Governments use these "spies in the sky" for surveillance but their precise functions are secret.

Global Positioning System

This is a system of 24 linked satellites that allows people to pinpoint their exact position anywhere on Earth. The system is operated by the US Department of Defense and is used by aircraft and ships. GPS systems are now common in cars, too.

Return to the Moon?

No human has set foot on the Moon since 1972. NASA planned a return to the Moon in 2020 with the *Constellation* programme, but in 2010 it was cancelled as part of the US Government's cost-savings. Russia, Japan, India and the European Space Agency have all put forward plans to set up Moon bases, but none has been confirmed.

Planets visited by spacecraft

No human has yet set foot on any space body other than Earth and the Moon. But unmanned spacecraft have taken photographs, made scientific readings and gathered data from all the planets in the Solar System, either by flying past or landing.

Venus *Mariner 2* (USA) flyby 1962; *Venera 4* (USSR) landed 1967; *Venus Express* (European Space Agency), in orbit 2005; *MESSENGER* (USA) flybys 2006, 2007; *PLANET–C* (Japan), planned for 2010

Mars *Mariner 4* (USA) flyby 1965; *Mars Pathfinder* (USA) landed 1997; *MER-A* and *MER-B* landed 2004; *Mars Reconnaissance Orbiter* (USA) in orbit 2006– ; *Phoenix Mars* (USA) landed in 2008; *Dawn* (USA) flyby 2009

Jupiter *Pioneer 10* (USA) flyby 1973; *Galileo* (USA) landed* 2003; *New Horizons* (USA) flyby 2007

Mercury *Mariner 10* (USA) flyby 1974; *MESSENGER* (USA) flybys 2008, 2009; orbiter 2011–12

Saturn *Pioneer 11* (USA) flyby 1979; *Cassini/Huygens* (USA/ESA) orbiter/lander 2004/2005

Uranus *Voyager 2* (USA) flyby 1986

Neptune *Voyager 2* (USA) flyby 1989

* Deliberately destroyed entering Jupiter's atmosphere, rather than risk contaminating moon Europa with bacteria from Earth.

Manned space missions

During the 1950s, there was a "space race" between the USA and USSR to be the first country to send a human into space. NASA's *Mercury* missions were originally unmanned, or carried only animals. The USSR launched the first man into orbit in 1961.

Each country's subsequent space missions had different aims. The USA focused on Moon landings with their *Apollo* programme and later the re-usable space shuttle. The Soviets and later Russia concentrated on long-duration missions, with the *Mir* space station. The latest manned mission is the *International Space Station*, which is four times larger than *Mir*.

Mission	Country	Years
Mercury	USA	1959–63
Vostok	USSR	1961–63
Voskhod	USSR	1964–65
Gemini	USA	1965–66
Apollo	USA	1967–72
Soyuz	USSR	1967–76
Salyut	USSR	1971–82
Skylab	USA	1973
Apollo Soyuz	USA/USSR	1975
Space shuttle	USA	1981
Mir space station	USSR/Russia	1986–2001
International Space Station	USA, Canada, Japan, European Space Agency, Russia, Brazil	1998–
Shenzhou	China	2003–

International Space Station

Astronauts and cosmonauts

The word "astronaut" was first used in 1880 by the British writer Percy Greg. It was the name he gave to a spaceship in his novel *Across the Zodiac*. By the 1950s it was the word used for a space voyager. The Russian word is cosmonaut.

12 April 1961 First person in space Soviet cosmonaut Yuri Gagarin made a single orbit of Earth in *Vostok 1*, a flight that lasted 1 hour 48 minutes.

5 May 1961 First US astronaut America's first astronaut Alan B. Shepard Jr, entered space aboard *Mercury 3* but did not orbit during his 15 minute 22 second mission.

6 August 1961 First flight of over 24 hours Gherman S. Titov (USSR) in *Vostok 2* made the first flight of more than 24 hours. He was also the youngest ever astronaut at 25 years 10 months 25 days.

20 February 1962 First US orbit John H. Glenn Jr in the *Friendship 7* capsule made the first US orbit, completing three orbits in 4 hours 55 mins.

16 June 1963 First woman in space Valentina V. Tereshkova (USSR) in *Vostok 6* was the first woman in space. She spent 2 days 22 hours 50 minutes 8 seconds in space. She remains the youngest (26 years 3 months 10 days) woman in space.

18 March 1965 First space walk Aleskei Leonov (USSR) made the first space walk, from *Voskhod 2*. It took 24 minutes and it almost ended in disaster when his spacesuit ballooned. He was unable to return through the airlock until he reduced the pressure in his suit to a dangerously low level.

23 March 1965 First two-man US mission John Young and Virgil "Gus" Grissom made the first two-man US mission in *Gemini 3*.

3 June 1965 First US spacewalk Edward H. White II made a 36 minute spacewalk from *Gemini 4*.

24 April 1967 First space death After 18 orbits in *Soyuz 1*, Vladimir M. Komarov (USSR) died when his parachute got tangled and his capsule crash-landed.

24 December 1968 First manned spacecraft to orbit the Moon *Apollo 8* (followed in 1969 by *Apollo* missions 9 and 10) orbited the Moon but did not land.

All the men on the Moon

The human exploration of the Moon lasted just over three years and involved a total of six missions. In each, a pair of US astronauts went down to the surface in a LEM (lunar excursion module) while a third orbited in a CSM (command service module). The missions provided scientists with a huge amount of information about the Moon.

Astronaut	Spacecraft	Total EVA* hr:min	Mission dates
1 Neil A. Armstrong	*Apollo 11*	2:32	16–24 Jul 1969
2 Edwin E. "Buzz" Aldrin	*Apollo 11*	2:15	16–24 Jul 1969
3 Charles Conrad Jr	*Apollo 12*	7:45	14–24 Nov 1969
4 Alan L. Bean	*Apollo 12*	7:45	14–24 Nov 1969
5 Alan B. Shepard	*Apollo 14*	9:23	31 Jan–9 Feb 1971
6 Edgar D. Mitchell	*Apollo 14*	9:23	31 Jan–9 Feb 1971
7 David R. Scott	*Apollo 15*	19:08	26 Jul–7 Aug 1971
8 James B. Irwin	*Apollo 15*	18:35	26 Jul–7 Aug 1971
9 John W. Young	*Apollo 16*	20:14	16–27 Apr 1972
10 Charles M. Duke Jr	*Apollo 16*	20:14	16–27 Apr 1972
11 Eugene A. Cernan	*Apollo 17*	22:04	7–19 Dec 1972
12 Harrison H. Schmitt	*Apollo 17*	22:04	7–19 Dec 1972

* Extra vehicular activity: time spent out of the lunar module on the Moon. The six US *Apollo* missions above resulted in successful Moon landings. *Apollo 13*, 11–17 April 1970, was aborted and returned to Earth after an oxygen tank exploded.

Astronaut Christer Fuglesang resumes construction work on the *International Space Station*, December 2006

Most in space

The first time the most astronauts were in space together was in March 1995, but the 13 of them were in separate spacecraft. The first occasion 13 were together occurred on 17 July 2009, when representatives of the USA, Russia, Canada, Belgium and Japan assembled in the International Space Station.

STS-116 Patch design shows the names of the astronauts who went in *Discovery* to continue construction of the *International Space Station* in December 2006

International Space Station

Work began on constructing the International Space Station (ISS) in 1998. It has been manned permanently since 2000 and is scheduled for completion in 2011. The project is a cooperative venture between a number of countries led by the USA, Russia, Japan, Canada and the European Space Agency.

For research

It is used for research in physics, astronomy and meteorology and the study of the effects on the human of long-duration stays in space. An understanding of these effects will be important as manned flights to planets are planned in the future.

Getting bigger

As each new mission arrives, further components are added, so the Space Station has steadily increased in size – it will weigh some 450 tonnes when complete and measures 93 x 73 m (306 x 240 ft). It orbits Earth over 15 times a day at a height of 350 km (217 miles). It is solar powered and has systems for generating oxygen and processing water, but relies on supply ships from Earth for food for the crew.

Most visited

Members of the crew are replaced, with previous personnel returning to Earth: it is the most-visited spacecraft ever, with over 160 people travelling to it since its launch.

20 July 1969 First Moon landing Neil Armstrong and Edwin E. "Buzz" Aldrin became the first men on the Moon.

18 June 1983 First US woman in space Sally Ride was launched in the space shuttle *Challenger STS-7*, which was the first reusable space vehicle.

18 May 1991 First British astronaut Helen Sharman travelled to the *Mir* space station and spent a week in space.

29 June 1995 First space shuttle/space station docking Space shuttle *Atlantis STS-71* docked with the Soviet space station *Mir*.

26 September 1996 US endurance record On her 5th mission, US astronaut Shannon Lucid completed 188 days aboard the Russian *Mir* station, setting a world record for women. Lucid was born in China. She flew more missions than any woman and at 53 was the oldest woman in space.

4 December 1998 International Space Station First stage of the *International Space Station* was established.

2 November 2000 First crew on ISS An American and Russian crew began living aboard the *International Space Station*.

28 April–6 May 2001 First space tourist US millionaire Dennis Tito became the first space tourist, paying $20 million for his Russian *Soyuz TM-32* flight to the *International Space Station*.

15–16 October 2003 First astronaut launched by China Chinese astronaut Lang Liwei made eight orbits of Earth in a *Shenzhou 5* spacecraft.

2010 Virgin Galactic plans space tourism flights to over 100 km (62 miles) in *SpaceShipOne*, which carries six passengers at a cost of $200,000 per person.

2010 Last space shuttle retires STS–133 *Endeavour* – probable last space shuttle flight, due to launch September 16. The shuttle has been in use since 1981. It will be replaced by Orion spacecraft, planned for launch in 2014.

2011 DragonLab reusable spacecraft developed by SpaceX company takes over from Shuttle.

http://amazingspace.stsci.edu search

Planet Earth

Haitian earthquake

On 12 January 2010 an earthquake measuring 7.0 on the Richter Scale devastated parts of Haiti. About 280,000 buildings, including the Presidential Palace and the Port-au-Prince cathedral, were destroyed or seriously damaged and 230,000 people killed and 92,000 injured. Haiti is one of the world's poorest countries and many people lost their homes and livelihoods, while schools and businesses were destroyed. International organizations have provided funds and sent practical assistance, including medical aid, shelter, food and other supplies.

Layers of the Earth

The Earth is made up of a number of layers. At the top is the crust – the thinnest layer. Next is the mantle, then the outer and inner cores. The outer core is probably liquid and the inner core solid.

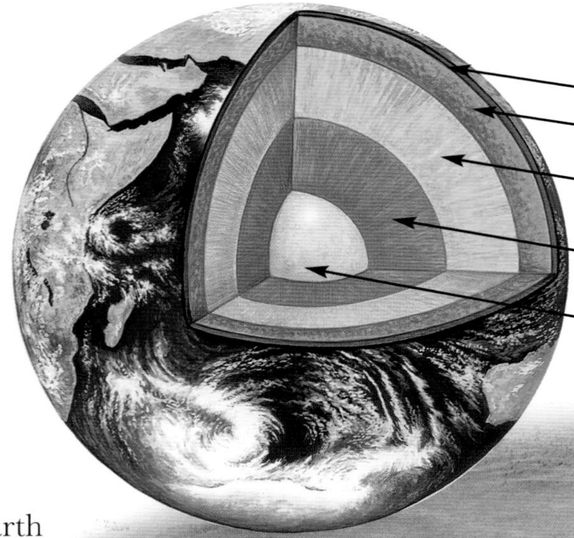

Inside the Earth showing the average depth of its layers

The largest meteorite craters

About 500 meteorites reach Earth every year. Many collision sites have been altered by weather over millions of years, and scientists are unsure whether some craters are actually the craters of extinct volcanoes. Those below are all agreed to be meteorite craters.

1 Vredefort, South Africa 300 km (186 miles) in diameter
2 Sudbury, Ontario, Canada 250 km (155 miles) in diameter
3 Chicxulub, Yucatan, Mexico 170 km (106 miles) in diameter
4 Manicougan, Canada 100 km (62 miles) in diameter
5 Popigai, Russia 100 km (62 miles) in diameter

Meteor Crater, Arizona

The 10 degrees of hardness

The Mohs scale, named after German mineralogist Friedrich Mohs (1773–1839), is used for comparing the relative hardness of minerals. Each mineral on the scale can be scratched by the harder ones below it.

Metals most mined

Mineral	Production 2008 (million tonnes)
Iron	2,318.00
Aluminium	39.00
Chromium	21.50
Magnesium	18.30
Manganese	12.80
Zinc	10.90
Lead	8.28
Titanium	2.26
Zirconium	1.36
Nickel	1.34

Geological time 2011

CENOZOIC ERA
Quaternary period
Recent/Holocene epoch: 11,000 years ago (y.a.) to present day – modern humans
Pleistocene epoch: 1,800,000 to 11,000 y.a. – humans

Tertiary period
Pliocene epoch: 5,000,000 to 1,800,000 y.a. – ape-like human ancestors
Miocene epoch: 23,000,000 to 5,000,000 y.a. – apes and whales
Oligocene epoch: 38,000,000 to 23,000,000 y.a. – cats and dogs
Eocene epoch: 54,000,000 to 37,000,000 y.a. – grasslands
Palaeocene epoch: 65,000,000 to 54,000,000 y.a. – large mammals

MESOZOIC ERA
Cretaceous period: 146,000,000 to 65,000,000 y.a. – flowering plants; dinosaurs became extinct
Jurassic period: 208,000,000 to 146,000,000 y.a. – birds and mammals
Triassic period: 245,000,000 to 208,000,000 y.a. – dinosaurs and flying reptiles

Uluru

The rock formerly known as Ayers Rock in Northern Territory, Australia, is believed to be the world's largest free-standing rock. It is made of sandstone and is 335 m (1,100 ft) high, 3.6 km (2.2 miles) long and 2 km (1.5 miles) wide. It was originally called after South Australian premier Sir Henry Ayers, but it is now known by the name given to it by local Aborigines, to whom it is sacred.

Iron from space!

Inuit people of Greenland did not have the technology to produce iron, but more than 1,000 years ago they were known to have iron tools such as knives and harpoons, which they sometimes traded with other Arctic inhabitants. The mystery was solved when it was discovered that they had hacked iron fragments from the 58.2-tonne Cape York meteorite, which landed on Earth some 10,000 years ago and is now in the American Museum of Natural History, New York, USA.

Rocks

There are three categories of rock – igneous, sedimentary and metamorphic.

- Igneous rocks originate deep in the Earth. They erupt from volcanoes as magma and cool or solidify as they rise to the upper layers. Basalt is an igneous rock and so is granite, a very hard rock often used in building. Pumice stone is a soft igneous rock that is ejected from volcanoes. As it cools, it often fills with so many air bubbles that it floats in water.
- Sedimentary rocks can be formed by deposits in water and occasionally by wind. Sandstone is a common example. Organic sedimentary rocks are formed by living plants and animals – coal comes from plant matter and limestone from the calcium from billions of plants and animals. Chemical sedimentary rocks occur when chemical processes take place and minerals are deposited.
- Metamorphic rocks are igneous or sedimentary rocks that have changed as a result of high temperatures or pressures. Slate used on roofs is a familiar example.

www.webmineral.com search

Minerals

Minerals are naturally occurring substances with a definite chemical composition. Most mineral names end in "ite". Many have a practical use or contain a chemical compound or element that can be extracted and used commercially. Bauxite, for instance, is the main source of aluminium. Gems are minerals that are highly prized for their rarity or appearance, eg diamonds, sapphires, emeralds and rubies.

4,500,000,000 years ago

PALAEOZOIC ERA

Permian period: 286,000,000 to 245,000,000 y.a. – deciduous plants

Carboniferous Pennsylvanian period: 325,000,000 to 286,000,000 y.a. – reptiles

Carboniferous Mississippian period: 360,000,000 to 325,000,000 y.a. – winged insects

Devonian period: 410,000,000 to 360,000,000 y.a. – amphibians

Silurian period: 440,000,000 to 410,000,000 y.a. – land plants and insects

Ordovician period: 500,000,000 to 440,000,000 y.a. – corals and molluscs

Cambrian period: 544,000,000 to 500,000,000 y.a. – fish and shelled creatures

PRECAMBRIAN ERA

Proterozoic period: 2,500,000,000 to 544,000,000 y.a. – earliest fossils; jellyfish

Archaic period: 3,800,000,000 to 2,500,000,000 y.a. – living cells

Hadean period: 4,500,000,000 to 3,800,000,000 y.a. – environment unable to support life; from 4,500,000,000 or earlier – the Earth was formed

Largest deserts

Deserts cover about a third of the world's land area. They range from extremely arid and barren sandy deserts (about four per cent of the total land surface of the globe), through arid (15 per cent) to semi-arid (just under 15 per cent).

Most deserts have features of all these, with one zone merging into the next, so the start and finish of any desert is not exact. Many of the world's largest deserts are broken down by geographers into smaller desert regions – the Australian Desert includes the Gibson, Great Sandy, Great Victoria and Simpson, for example.

1 Sahara, Northern Africa – 9,100,000 sq km (3,514,000 sq miles)
2 Australian, Australia (Includes Gibson, Great Sandy, Great Victoria and Simpson) – 3,400,000 sq km (1,313,000 sq miles)
3 Arabian Peninsula, Southwest Asia (Includes an-Nafud and Rub al Khali) – 2,600,000 sq km (1,004,000 sq miles)
4 Turkestan, Central Asia (Includes Kara-Kum and Kyzylkum) – 1,900,000 sq km (734,000 sq miles)
5 Gobi, Central Asia – 1,300,000 sq km (502,000 sq miles)
6 North American Desert, US/Mexico (Includes Great Basin, Mojave, Sonorah and Chihuahuan) – 1,300,000 sq km (502,000 sq miles)

The Devil's Marbles in the Australian desert

Mount Everest, the world's highest mountain

The highest mountain?

The height of mountains is usually measured from sea level. Mauna Kea in Hawaii is only 4,245 m (13,957 ft) above sea level, but it rises a total of 10,203 m (33,474 ft) from the floor of the Pacific Ocean, making its real height 1,353 m (4,439 ft) greater than Mount Everest!

Highest mountains

People used to think that Kangchenjunga in Nepal/India was the highest mountain. Then the Great Trigonometrical Survey of India measured all the country's land features. The survey was completed in 1852 and showed that Everest (then called Peak XV) was the world's highest mountain.

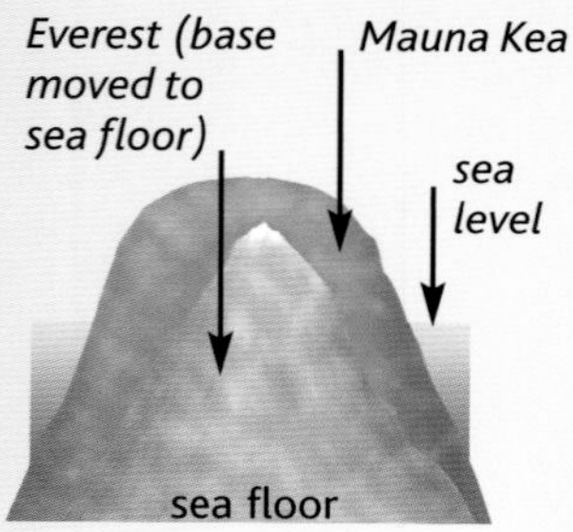

Everest's height was then reckoned to be 8,840 m (29,002 ft). This has since been adjusted as improved measuring methods have been used. The mountain's name was suggested in 1865 as a tribute to Sir George Everest, the Surveyor General of India, who had led the survey.

Highest mountains

1 Everest, Nepal/China – 8,850 m (29,035 ft)
2 K2 (Chogori), Pakistan/China – 8,607m (28,238 ft)
3 Kangchenjunga, Nepal/India – 8,598 m (28,208 ft)
4 Lhotse, Nepal/China – 8,511 m (27,923 ft)
5 Makalu I, Nepal/China – 8,481 m (27,824 ft)

Largest island

An island is a piece of land surrounded by water. Australia is so large it is a continent, not an island; otherwise it would rank first. The smallest island with country status is Pitcairn, at 4.53 sq km (1.75 sq miles).

1 Greenland (Kalaatdlit Nunaat) – 2,175,600 sq km (840,070 sq miles)
2 New Guinea – 789,900 sq km (312,190 sq miles)
3 Borneo – 751,000 sq km (289,961 sq miles)
4 Madagascar (Malagasy Republic) – 587,041 sq km (226,674 sq miles)
5 Baffin Island, Canada – 507,451 sq km (195,926 sq miles)
6 Sumatra, Indonesia – 422,200 sq km (163,011 sq miles)
7 Honshu, Japan – 230,092 sq km (88,839 sq miles)
8 Great Britain – 218,041 sq km (84,185 sq miles)
9 Victoria Island, Canada – 217,290 sq km (83,896 sq miles)
10 Ellesmere Island, Canada –196,236 sq km (75,767 sq miles)
11 Celebes, Indonesia – 179,000 sq km (69,100 sq miles)
12 South Island, New Zealand – 151,971 sq km (58,676 sq miles)
13 Java, Indonesia – 126,900 sq km (49,000 sq miles)
14 North Island, New Zealand – 114,489 sq km (44,204 sq miles)
15 Newfoundland, Canada – 108,860 sq km (42,031 sq miles)
16 Cuba – 104,945 sq km (40,519 sq miles)
17 Luzon, Philippines – 104,688 sq km (40,420 sq miles)
18 Iceland – 102,819 sq km (39,699 sq miles)
19 Mindanao, Philippines – 94,630 sq km (36,537 sq miles)
20 Ireland 84,406 sq km (32,589 sq miles)
(Area excludes offshore islands)

Lowest places on land

Sea level is the average height of the sea at a point midway between high and low tides. The shore of the Dead Sea is the lowest exposed ground below sea level. Some land in Antarctica is 2,538 m (8,327 ft) below sea level, but is covered by a 2,100 m (6,890 ft)-deep ice cap.

1 Dead Sea, Israel/Jordan – 400 m (1,312 ft) below sea level
2 Lake Assa, Djibouti – 156 m (511 ft) below sea level
3 Turfan Depression, China – 154 m (505 ft) below sea level
4 Qattâra Depression, Egypt – 133 m (436 ft) below sea level
5 Mangyshlak Peninsula, Kazakhstan – 132 m (433 ft) below sea level

Floating in the Dead Sea

Dead Sea

The shores of the Dead Sea are the lowest point below sea level on Earth. The salt and other chemicals in the water are concentrated by evaporation in the region's high temperatures, which makes it almost impossible to sink.

The seven continents

The Americas are named after the explorer Amerigo Vespucci (1451–1512). Africa was perhaps originally a Berber tribal name. This was adopted by the Romans as the name of their province and later spread to the whole continent.

The name of Europe may simply mean mainland. Asia is probably from the Assyrian, *asu*, meaning sunrise or east. Australis is Latin for southern; Australia, with New Zealand and other islands, is also considered as part of Oceania, a name invented by the geographer Conrad Malte-Brun (1775–1826). Antarctica is Greek for opposite the Arctic. Arctic comes from the Greek for bear, because the region lies under the stars of the Great Bear constellation.

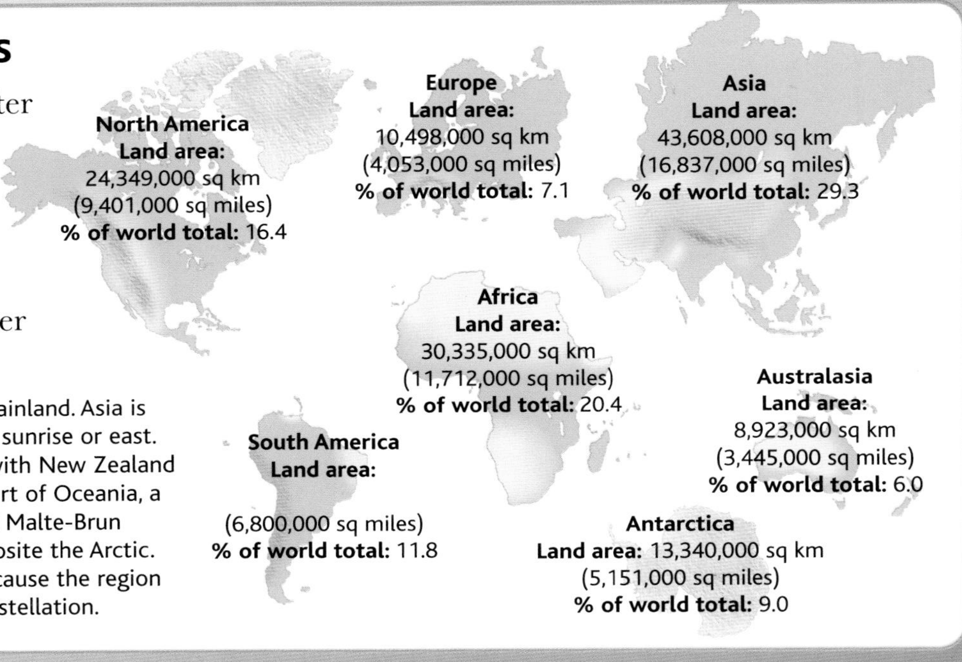

Niagara Falls

Longest river

The source of the Nile was discovered by Europeans in 1858 when British explorer John Hanning Speke reached Lake Victoria Nyanza, in what is now Burundi. About one hundred years later, in 1953, the source of the Amazon was identified as a stream called Huarco flowing from the Misuie glacier in the Peruvian Andes mountains.

By following the Amazon from its source and up the Rio Pará, it is possible to sail for 6,750 km (4,195 miles), which is slightly more than the length of the Nile. But geographers do not consider the entire route to be part of the Amazon basin, so the Nile is considered the world's longest river.

1 Nile* flows through Burundi, Dem. Rep. of Congo, Egypt, Eritrea, Ethiopia, Kenya, Rwanda, Sudan, Tanzania, Uganda – 6,695 km (4,158 miles)
2 Amazon flows through Peru and Brazil – 6,448 km (4,007 miles)
3 Chang Jiang (Yangtze) flows through China – 6,378 km (3,964 miles)
4 Huang He (Yellow) flows through China – 5,464 km (3,395 miles)
5 Amur flows through China and Russia – 4,415 km (2,744 miles)
* In 2006 the British and New Zealand Ascend the Nile team sailed from the mouth to the source of the river. Using Global Positioning, they measured their journey and came up with a total length 107 km (66.5 miles) longer than the official figure.

Greatest waterfalls

The flow of many waterfalls varies according to the season, and some have been reduced by building dams to harness their power for hydro-electric plants.

The flow of the Boyoma waterfall is equivalent to 17m. litres (36m. gall) a second – enough to fill more than 140,000 baths per second, or enough for every person on Earth to have two baths a day!

1 Boyoma (Stanley), Democratic Republic of Congo – 17,000 m^3/sec (22,235 yd^3/sec)
2 Khône, Laos † – 11,330 m^3/sec (14,819 yd^3/sec)
3 Niagara (Horseshoe), Canada – 5,830 m^3/sec (7,625 yd^3/sec)
4 Grande, Uruguay – 4,500 m^3/sec (5,886 yd^3/sec)
5 Paulo Afonso, Brazil – 2,800 m^3/sec (3,662 yd^3/sec)
(Based on volume of water)
† Also the widest waterfall at 10.8 km (6.7 miles)

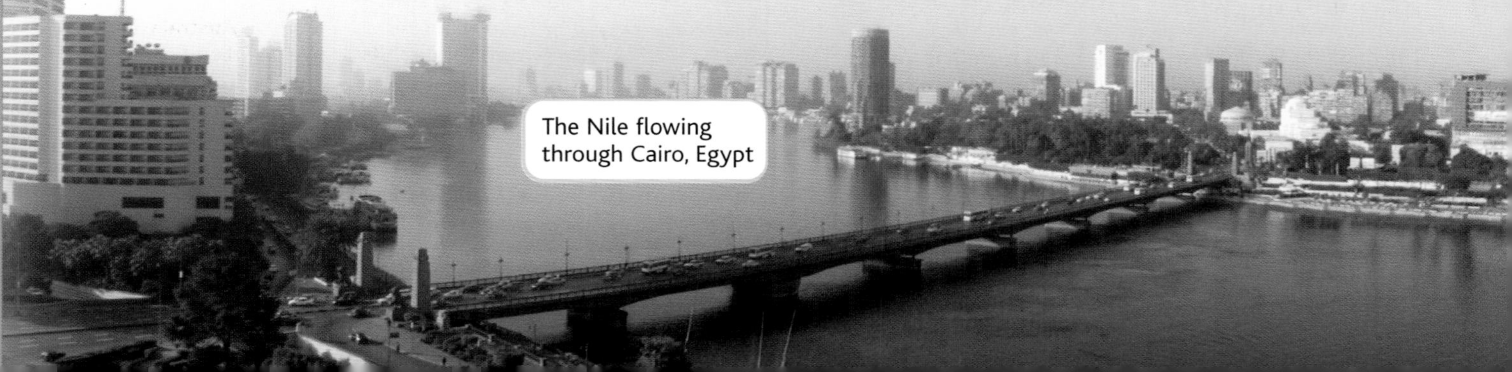
The Nile flowing through Cairo, Egypt

Highest waterfalls

Waterfalls form when a river or stream goes over a drop, often where softer rocks are eroded faster than harder ones. The drop is the distance from top to bottom of the waterfall.

1 Angel Falls, Carrao river, Venezuela – 979 m (3,212 ft)*
2 Tugela Falls, Tugela river, South Africa – 948 m (3,110 ft)
3 Ramnefjellsfossen, Jostedal Glacier, Nesdale, Norway – 800 m (2,625 ft)
4 Mongefossen Falls, Monge river, Mongebekk, Norway – 774 m (2,540 ft)
5 Gocta Falls, Cocahuayco river, Peru – 771 m (2,531 ft)
6 Mutarazi Falls, Mutarazi river, Zimbabwe – 762 m (2,499 ft)
7 Yosemite Falls, Yosemite Creek, California, USA – 739 m (2,425 ft)
8 Østre Mardøla Foss, Mardals river, Eikisdal, Norway – 656 m (2,152 ft)
9 Tyssestrengane Falls, Tysso river, Hardanger, Norway – 646 m (2,120 ft)
10 Cuquenán Falls, Arabopo river, Venezuela – 610 m (2,000 ft)
* Longest single drop 807 m (2,648 ft)

The Great Lakes

The Great Lakes are a group of five freshwater lakes in North America on the border between the USA and Canada. Superior is so called because it is higher upstream that the others. Huron takes its name from the name French settlers gave to a local Indian tribe (from *hure*, a boar's head). No one knows where the name Michigan comes from, but Erie and Ontario are both from the Iroquois language. Erie means cat, the animal the tribe used as its symbol. Ontario simply means beautiful lake.

1 Superior, Canada/USA – 82,414 sq km (31,820 sq miles)
2 Huron, Canada/USA – 59,596 sq km (23,010 sq miles)
3 Michigan, USA – 58,016 sq km (22,400 sq miles)
4 Erie, Canada/USA – 25,719 sq km (9,930 sq miles)
5 Ontario, Canada/USA – 19,477 sq km (7,520 sq miles)

Longest glaciers

During the last Ice Age, more than 30 per cent of the Earth's surface was covered by glaciers – frozen rivers of ice that move very slowly. Today, almost 10 per cent is covered with glaciers.

The Lambert-Fisher Glacier is the longest in the world and was discovered (from the air) in 1956. The longest glacier in North America is the Hubbard Glacier, Alaska, which measures 146 km (91 miles). The longest in Europe is the Aletsch Glacier, Switzerland, at 35 km (22 miles).

1 Lambert-Fisher, Antarctica – 515 km (320 miles)
2 Novaya Zemlya, Russia – 418 km (260 miles)
3 Arctic Institute, Antarctica – 362 km (225 miles)
4 Nimrod-Lennox-King, Antarctica – 290 km (180 miles)
5 Denman, Antarctica – 241 km (150 miles)

Glaciers

Glaciers hold about 75 per cent of the world's fresh water. If all the glaciers melted, the world's sea level would rise about 70 m (230 ft).

Greatest rivers

The volume of water flowing from the mouth of a river varies according to the season. The figures given are highest averages. The outflow of the Amazon would fill almost two million baths every second.

1 Amazon flows into the South Atlantic, Brazil at 219,000 m^3/sec (286,441 yd^3/sec)
2 Ganges flows into the Bay of Bengal, Bangladesh at 43,900 m^3/sec (57,419 yd^3/sec)
3 Zaïre (Congo) flows into the South Atlantic, Angola/Congo at 41,800 m^3/sec (54,672 yd^3/sec)
4 Chang Jiang flows into the Yellow Sea, China at 31,900 m^3/sec (41,724 yd^3/sec)
5 Orinoco flows into the South Atlantic, Venezuela at 31,900 m^3/sec (41,724 yd^3/sec)
6 Plata-Paraná-Grande flows into the South Atlantic, Uruguay at 25,700 m^3/sec (33,614 yd^3/sec)
(Based on rate of discharge at mouth)

Lake fact file

● Largest lake by volume and area

The Caspian Sea (Russia, Kazakhstan, Turkmenistan, Azerbaijan and Iran) has a volume of 78,200 cubic km (18,760 cubic miles) and an area of 374,000 sq km (144,402 sq miles), making it the world's largest body of inland water. It would take 400 years for the entire contents of the Caspian to flow over Niagara Falls!

● Largest freshwater lake by area

Some geographers think that Lake Michigan and Lake Huron are one lake. They have a combined area of 117,612 sq km (45,410 sq miles) and have a larger area than half the world's countries.

● Largest freshwater lake by volume and deepest lake

Lake Baikal, Russia, contains 22,995 cubic km (5,517 cubic miles) of water. It has an average depth of 730 m (2,395 ft) and is 1,741m (5,712 ft) at its deepest point – deep enough to cover more than four Empire State Buildings piled on top of one another.

● Fastest-shrinking lake

In 1960, The Aral Sea (Kazakhstan and Uzbekistan) was 64,501 sq km (24,904 sq miles). Since then, feeder rivers have been diverted for irrigation and the lake has shrunk to about 28,000 sq km (10,811 sq miles). It is now in danger of disappearing.

www.geography.learnontheinternet.co.uk search

Wave height scale

The wave height scale describes the sort of waves that sailors might meet at sea. Wave height varies according to wind speed. High waves can be very dangerous, especially to small boats which can be turned over and even smashed.

0 **Glassy** – 0.0 m (0.0 ft)
1 **Calm** – 0.0–0.30 m (0.0–1.0 ft)
2 **Rippled** – 0.30–0.60 m (1.0–2.0 ft)
3 **Choppy** – 0.60–1.2 m (2.0–4.0 ft)
4 **Very choppy** – 1.2–2.4 m (4.0–7.9 ft)
5 **Rough** – 2.4–4.0 m (8.0–13.0 ft)
6 **Very rough** – 4.0–6.0 m (13.0–20.0 ft)
7 **High** – 6–9 m (20.0–30.0 ft)
8 **Very high** – 9.0–14 m (30.0–45.0 ft)
9 **Ultra high** –14.0 m+ (45.0 ft+)

Huge waves breaking over a lighthouse in Havana, Cuba during a hurricane

Tsunami

The word tsunami comes from the Japanese *tsu* (meaning port) and *nami* (meaning wave). A tsunami is not a tidal wave, but a powerful surge of moving water caused by an earthquake or volcanic eruption beneath the sea bed.

There may be advance warning signs, such as bubbling water, a roaring noise and a sudden rise in water temperature. Tsunamis are rarely as high as tidal waves. However, powerful ones can cross huge distances, raising the sea level and destroying entire islands and coastal areas in their path. Lisbon, the capital of Portugal, was almost completely destroyed in 1755 by the combined effects of an earthquake, tsunami and fire. The worst recorded tsunami occurred in 2004 in South East Asia.

Animal survivors

Amazingly, few animals died in the tsunami that hit Sri Lanka and other areas in 2004. Elephants, buffalo and tigers, as well as smaller animals, moved to high ground in time. Scientists think that they sensed soundwaves and changes in air pressure in advance of the wave and this gave them time to escape.

Iceberg fact file

An iceberg is a large piece of ice that has broken away from a glacier or ice shelf. In the North Atlantic most came from Greenland glaciers, and in the South Atlantic from Antarctica.

- The word iceberg probably comes from the Dutch *ijsberg*, or ice hill.
- Icebergs float because they are made of fresh water, which is less dense than sea water.
- Seven-eighths of an iceberg is below the surface of the sea, hence the expression "the tip of the iceberg", which means that more is hidden than can be seen.
- The tallest iceberg measured was 168 m (551 ft) high. It was seen in 1958 off Greenland and was as tall as a 50-storey skyscraper.
- Icebergs less than 1 m (3.25 ft) high and 5 m (16.25 ft) wide are known as growlers because of the noise they make.
- Icebergs larger than growlers are called bergy bits; then they are graded small, medium, large or very large. Very large icebergs are those measuring more than 75 m (246 ft) high and 213 m (699 ft) wide.
- One of the biggest icebergs of recent times, known as B-15, broke away from the Ross Ice Shelf, Antarctica, in March 2000. It had an average length of 295 km (183 miles) and width of 37 km (23 miles), making it about the size of Jamaica!
- About 10,000 to 15,000 new icebergs are formed every year. The process is called "calving".
- The air trapped in icebergs is "harvested" and sold for use in drinks. It may be 3,000 years old.
- At least 500 incidents have been recorded of ships striking icebergs. The worst disaster involving an iceberg happened when the *Titanic* struck one on 14 April 1912 and 1,503 people died.

Longest coastlines

The coastline of Canada, including all its islands, is more than six times as long as the distance round the Earth at the Equator (40,076 km [24,902 miles]). Greenland (Kalaalit Nunaat) is not in this list as it is part of Denmark, not a separate country, but its coastline is 44,087 km (27,394 miles) long.

1 Canada – 265,523 km (164,988 miles)
2 USA – 133,312 km (82,836 miles)
3 Russia – 110,310 km (68,543 miles)
4 Indonesia – 95,181 km (59,143 miles)
5 Chile – 78,563 km (48,817 miles)
6 Australia – 66,530 km (41,340miles)
7 Norway – 53,199 km (33,056 miles)
8 Philippines – 33,900 km (21,064 miles)
9 Brazil – 33,379 km (20,741 miles)
10 Finland – 31,119 km (19,336 miles)
11 China 30,017 km (18,652 miles)
12 Japan 29,020 km (18,032 miles)

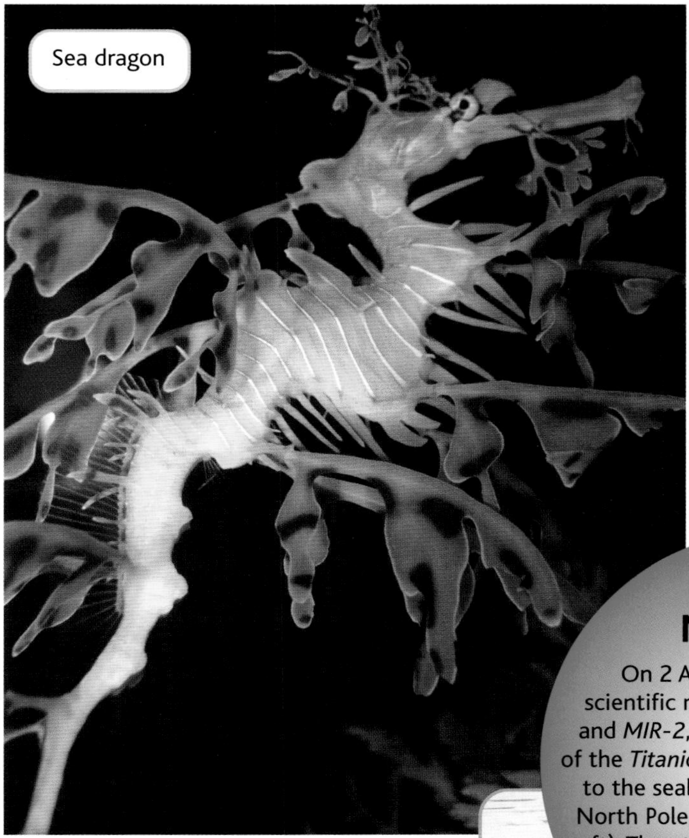
Sea dragon

Deepest oceans and seas

The Pacific Ocean is the deepest ocean. Its greatest depth is 10,924 m (35,837 ft) with an average depth of 4,028 m (13,215 ft). The Indian Ocean is 7,455 m (24,460 ft) at its deepest point and has an average depth of 3,963 m (13,002 ft). The Atlantic Ocean comes next with a greatest depth of 9,219 m (30,246 ft) and an average depth of 3,926 m (12,880 ft).

Under the North Pole

On 2 August 2007 two Russian scientific research submersibles *MIR-1* and *MIR-2*, which had filmed the wreck of the *Titanic* for the 1997 film, descended to the seabed beneath the Geographic North Pole, a depth of 4,261 m (13,980 ft). They took soil and water samples and *MIR-1* planted a titanium alloy Russian flag and a time capsule on the ocean floor.

Oceans and seas

Ocean is the term used for the world's sea water, except for landlocked seas such as the Caspian.

More than 70 per cent of the planet's surface is occupied by oceans – the Pacific Ocean alone is more than 25 per cent larger than the planet's entire land area. Smaller divisions of some oceans are separately named as seas.

Pacific Ocean – 166,240,000 sq km (64,185,629 sq miles)
Atlantic Ocean – 86,560,000 sq km (33,421,006 sq miles)
Indian Ocean – 73,430,000 sq km (28,351,484 sq miles)
Arctic Ocean – 13,230,000 sq km (5,108,132 sq miles)
South China Sea – 2,974,600 sq km (1,148,499 sq miles)
Caribbean Sea – 2,753,000 sq km (1,062,939 sq miles)
Mediterranean Sea – 2,510,000 sq km (969,116 sq miles)
Bering Sea – 2,261,000 sq km (872,977 sq miles)
Gulf of Mexico – 1,542,985 sq km (595,749 sq miles)
Sea of Okhotsk – 1,527,570 sq km (589,798 sq miles)
East China Sea – 1,249,150 sq km (482,299 sq miles)
Sea of Japan – 1,012,945 sq km (391,100 sq miles)
Andaman Sea – 797,700 sq km (307,993 sq miles)
Hudson Bay – 730,380 sq km (282,001 sq miles)

- During World War II, Lord Mountbatten led a programme to build artificial icebergs to use as aircraft carriers, but the project, codenamed Habbakuk, was abandoned.
- Cruise ship *MS Explorer* struck an iceberg in the Antarctic and sank on 23 November 2007. All 154 passengers and crew were rescued.

Russian *MIR* submersibles are used for deep-sea exploration

See also
Worst natural disasters: page 47

www.oceansatlas.org search

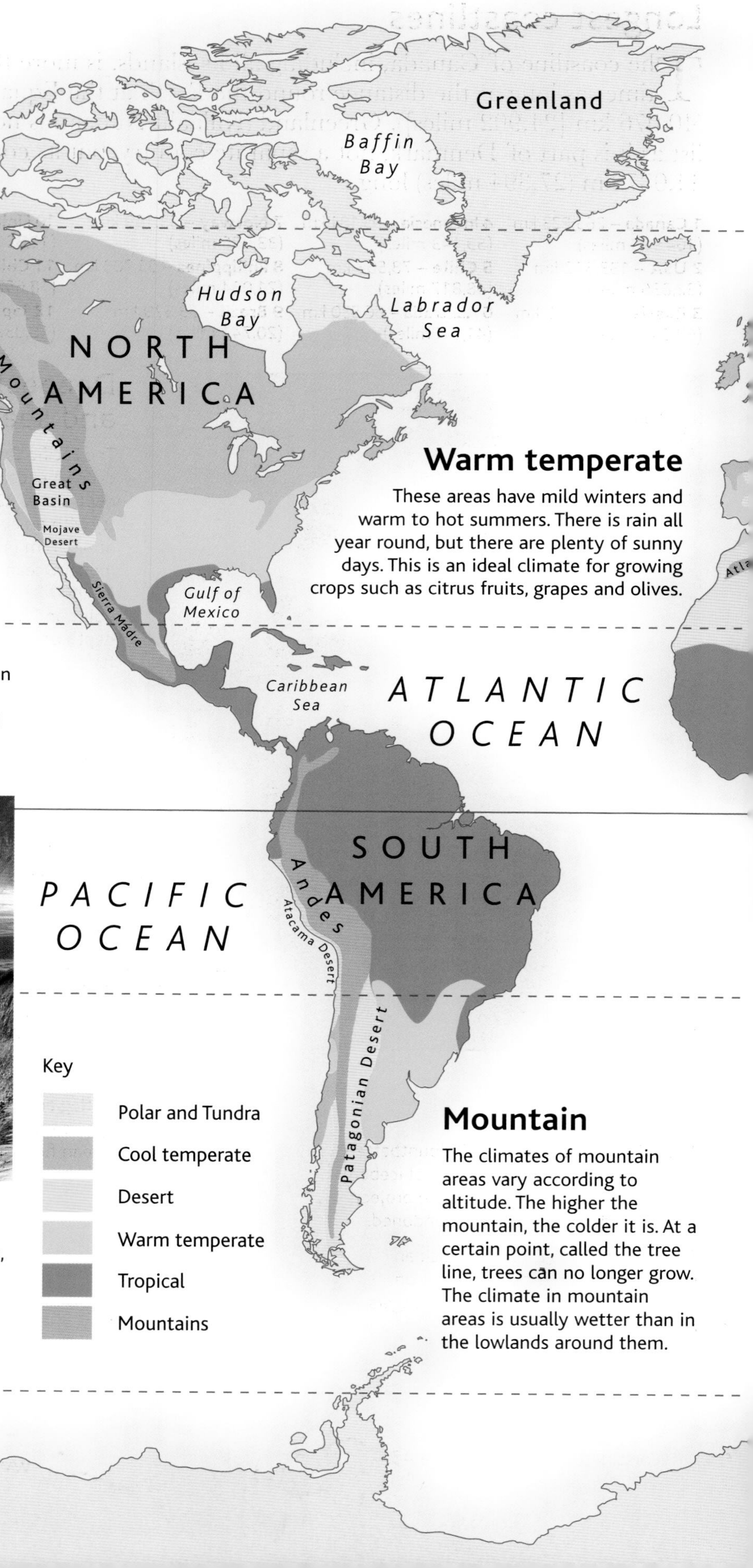

Climate

Weather and climate are not the same. Weather is how hot, cold or wet a place is at a particular time. Climate is the average weather of an area over time.

Several things decide the climate of an area, including how far it is from the Equator, how far from the sea, its height above sea level and its wind systems. The position of a place on an area of land and the size of that land area also affects the climate. Scientists divide the world into different climate regions: polar and tundra, temperate, tropical, desert and mountain.

Warm temperate

These areas have mild winters and warm to hot summers. There is rain all year round, but there are plenty of sunny days. This is an ideal climate for growing crops such as citrus fruits, grapes and olives.

The sea affects the climate of coastal regions, keeping them warmer than inland areas in winter and cooler in summer.

Climate change

Climates have changed naturally throughout history. But scientists think that human activities, such as burning fossil fuels, are producing greenhouse gases such as carbon dioxide, and these are causing global warming. The effects include ocean currents altering, ice sheets melting, sea levels rising and severe weather, such as cyclones and floods, becoming more common.

Mountain

The climates of mountain areas vary according to altitude. The higher the mountain, the colder it is. At a certain point, called the tree line, trees can no longer grow. The climate in mountain areas is usually wetter than in the lowlands around them.

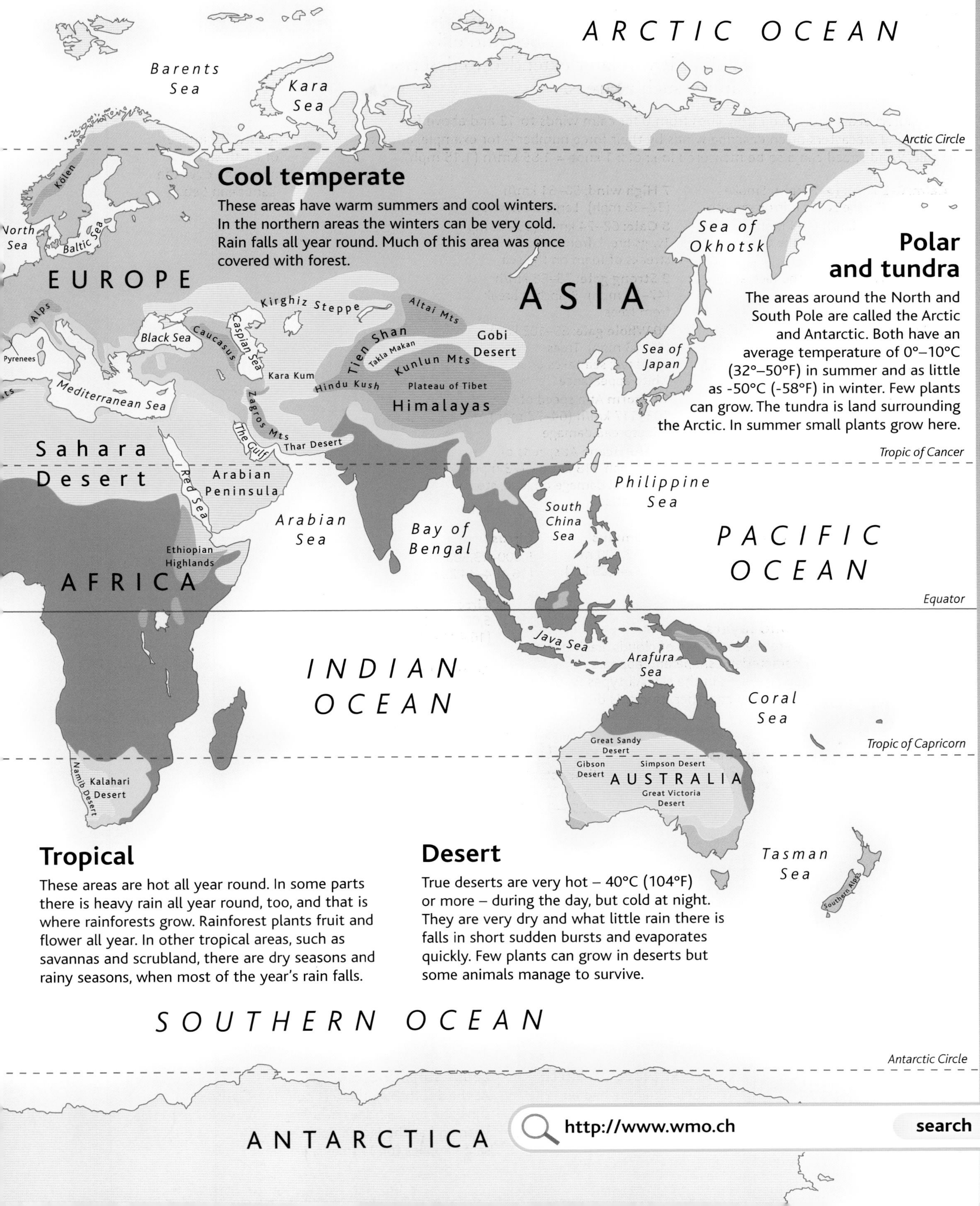

Cool temperate

These areas have warm summers and cool winters. In the northern areas the winters can be very cold. Rain falls all year round. Much of this area was once covered with forest.

Polar and tundra

The areas around the North and South Pole are called the Arctic and Antarctic. Both have an average temperature of 0°–10°C (32°–50°F) in summer and as little as -50°C (-58°F) in winter. Few plants can grow. The tundra is land surrounding the Arctic. In summer small plants grow here.

Tropical

These areas are hot all year round. In some parts there is heavy rain all year round, too, and that is where rainforests grow. Rainforest plants fruit and flower all year. In other tropical areas, such as savannas and scrubland, there are dry seasons and rainy seasons, when most of the year's rain falls.

Desert

True deserts are very hot – 40°C (104°F) or more – during the day, but cold at night. They are very dry and what little rain there is falls in short sudden bursts and evaporates quickly. Few plants can grow in deserts but some animals manage to survive.

http://www.wmo.ch search

The Beaufort scale

The Beaufort scale was introduced in 1806 by British Admiral Sir Francis Beaufort (1774–1857) to describe wind effects on a fully rigged man-of-war ship. It was later extended to describe how winds affect land features such as trees.

The Beaufort scale is divided into values from 0 for calm winds to 12 and above for hurricanes. Forecasters often describe winds by their force number – for example, a force 10 gale. Wind speed can also be measured in knots: 1 knot = 1.85 km/h (1.15 mph).

0 Calm: 0–2 km/h (> 1 mph) Smoke rises vertically; the sea is mirror smooth
1 Light air: 3–6 km/h (1–3 mph) Smoke indicates the direction of the wind
2 Slight breeze: 7–11 km/h (4–7 mph) Wind felt on the face and leaves rustle in trees
3 Gentle breeze: 12–19 km/h (8–12 mph) Wind extends a light flag
4 Moderate breeze: 20–28 km/h (13–18 mph) Loose paper blows around; frequent whitecaps at sea
5 Fresh breeze: 29–38 km/h (19–24 mph) Small trees sway
6 Strong breeze: 39–49 km/h (25–31 mph) Wind whistles in telephone wires; some spray on the sea's surface
7 High wind: 50–61 km/h (32–38 mph) Large trees sway
8 Gale: 62–74 km/h (39–46 mph) Twigs break from trees; long streaks of foam on the sea
9 Strong gale: 75–88 km/h (47–54 mph) Branches break from trees
10 Whole gale: 89–102 km/h (55–63 mph) Trees uprooted; sea takes on a white appearance
11 Storm At a speed of 103–117 km/h (64–72 mph) Widespread damage
12 Hurricane At speeds of more than 118 km/h+ (73 mph+) Structural damage on land; storm waves at sea

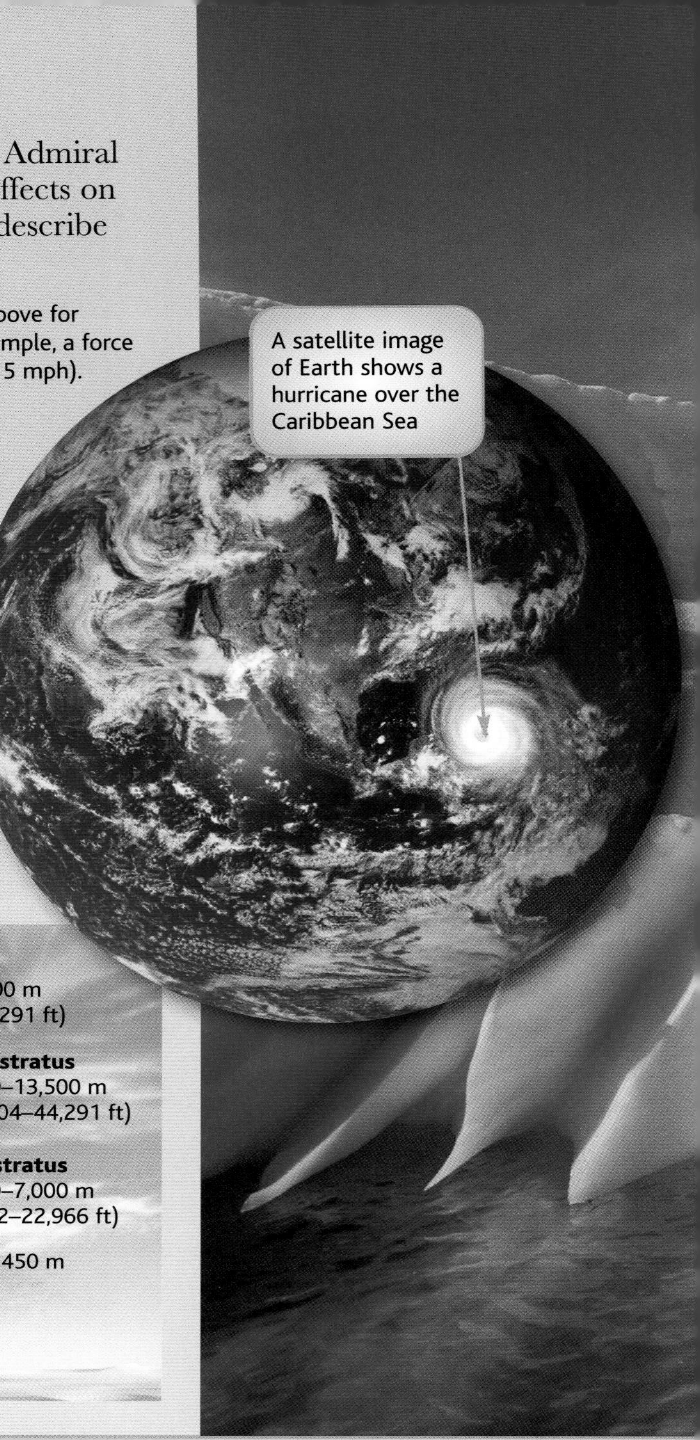

A satellite image of Earth shows a hurricane over the Caribbean Sea

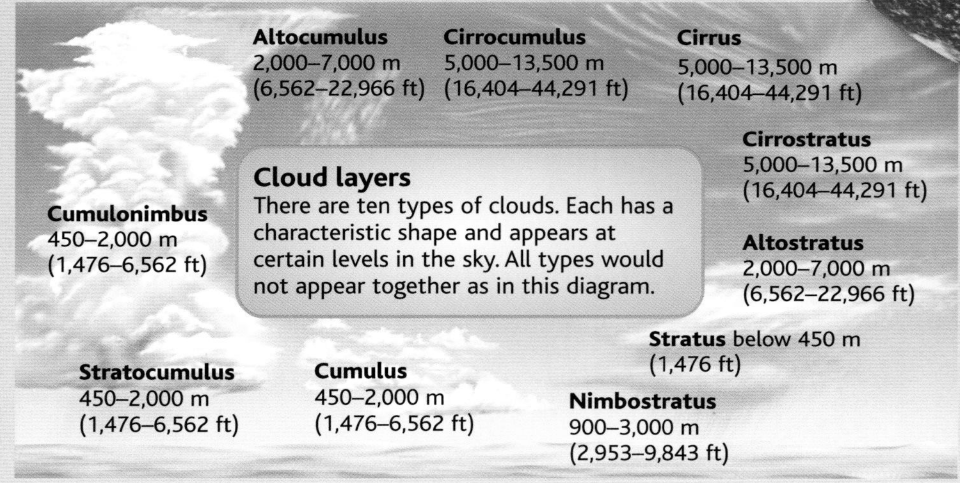

Cloud layers

There are ten types of clouds. Each has a characteristic shape and appears at certain levels in the sky. All types would not appear together as in this diagram.

World extremes

Windiest place on Earth
Commonwealth Bay, Antarctica, has some consistently high wind speeds, occasionally reaching 320 km/h (200 mph). The highest individual gust of wind measured was 371 km/h (231 mph) at Mt Washington, USA, on 12 April 1934.

Tornado wind speed
Fastest 450 km/h (280 mph) at Wichita Falls, Texas, USA, on 2 April 1958.

Hurricane wind speed
The fastest sustained winds in a hurricane in the USA measured 322 km/h (200 mph), with 338 km/h (210 mph) gusts, on 17–18 August 1969, when Hurricane Camille hit the Mississippi/Alabama coast.

Hottest place on Earth
Dallol in Ethiopia had an average temperature of 34.4°C (94°F) during 1960–66.

Highest shade temperature recorded
Al'Aziziyah, Libyan desert, 57.8°C (136°F) on 13 September 1922. A temperature of 56.6°C (134°F) was recorded at Death Valley, California, USA, on 10 July 1913.

Least sunshine
At the South Pole there is no sunshine for 182 days every year, and at the North Pole the same applies for 176 days.

Driest place
Atacama Desert, Chile, where average annual rainfall is officially nil (also longest drought – 400 years up to 1971). The average rainfall on the Pacific coast of Chile between Arica and Antofagasta is less than 1 mm (0.04 in).

Coldest place
Vostok, Antarctica, -89.2°C (-129°F) on 21 July 1983.

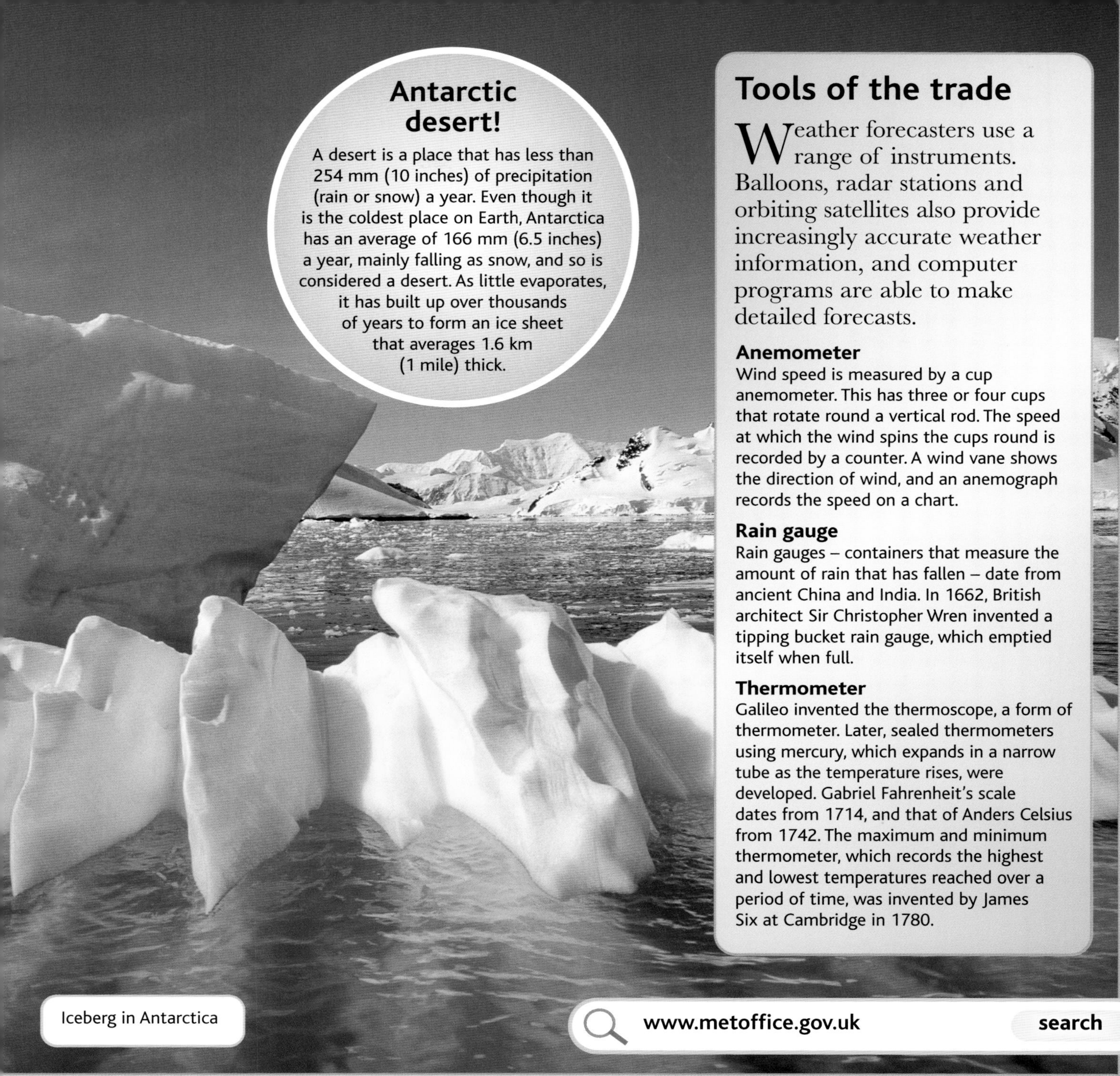

Antarctic desert!

A desert is a place that has less than 254 mm (10 inches) of precipitation (rain or snow) a year. Even though it is the coldest place on Earth, Antarctica has an average of 166 mm (6.5 inches) a year, mainly falling as snow, and so is considered a desert. As little evaporates, it has built up over thousands of years to form an ice sheet that averages 1.6 km (1 mile) thick.

Tools of the trade

Weather forecasters use a range of instruments. Balloons, radar stations and orbiting satellites also provide increasingly accurate weather information, and computer programs are able to make detailed forecasts.

Anemometer

Wind speed is measured by a cup anemometer. This has three or four cups that rotate round a vertical rod. The speed at which the wind spins the cups round is recorded by a counter. A wind vane shows the direction of wind, and an anemograph records the speed on a chart.

Rain gauge

Rain gauges – containers that measure the amount of rain that has fallen – date from ancient China and India. In 1662, British architect Sir Christopher Wren invented a tipping bucket rain gauge, which emptied itself when full.

Thermometer

Galileo invented the thermoscope, a form of thermometer. Later, sealed thermometers using mercury, which expands in a narrow tube as the temperature rises, were developed. Gabriel Fahrenheit's scale dates from 1714, and that of Anders Celsius from 1742. The maximum and minimum thermometer, which records the highest and lowest temperatures reached over a period of time, was invented by James Six at Cambridge in 1780.

Iceberg in Antarctica

www.metoffice.gov.uk search

Greatest snowfall in 12 months

31,102 mm (1,224 in) at Mt Rainier, Washington, USA, from 19 February 1971 to 18 February 1972. This is an incredible 31 m (102 ft), equivalent to 17 people standing on each other's heads!

Greatest depth of snow

11.46 m (38 ft) at Tamarac, California, USA, in March 1911.

Freak snow storm

In the Sahara Desert, Algeria, 18 February 1979.

Heaviest hailstones

Coffeyville, Kansas, USA, 0.75 kg (1.65 lb), 3 September 1970. The largest hailstone – 17.8 cm (7 in) diameter – fell in Aurora, Nebraska on 22 June 2003.

Most rainfall in 24 hours

Cilaos, La Réunion, 1,870 mm (74 in), 15–16 March, 1952.

Greatest annual rainfall (extreme example)

Cherrapunji, Assam, India, 26,461 mm (1,042 in) between 1 August 1860 and 31 July 1861 – which is close to the length of a tennis court! Also, at the same place, the greatest in one calendar month – 9,300 mm (366 in) – fell in July 1861. That's about the same as five people standing on each other's heads.

Greatest annual rainfall (annual average)

Mawsynram, India, with 11,870 mm (467 in) a year; and Tutunendo, Colombia, 11,770 mm (463 in).

Most rainy days in a year

Mt Waialeale, Kauai, Hawaii, USA, up to 350 days a year. The total rainfall is about 11,684 mm (460 in), which approaches the annual record.

Volcanic eruptions

Santorini
The eruption of the Greek island of Santorini in c1450 BC is believed to have been one of the most powerful ever.

Vesuvius, Italy
On 24 August AD 79 Vesuvius erupted with little warning, engulfing the Roman city of Herculaneum in a mud flow. Nearby Pompeii was buried under a vast layer of pumice and volcanic ash. This preserved the city, including the bodies of many of its inhabitants, until it was excavated by archaeologists in the 19th and 20th centuries. As many as 20,000 people died. Vesuvius erupted again in 1631, killing up to 18,000 people.

Laki, Iceland
Iceland is one of the most volcanically active places on Earth, but the population is small so eruptions seldom cause many deaths. On 11 June 1783 the largest lava flow ever recorded engulfed many villages in a river of lava up to 80 km (50 miles) long and 30 m (98 ft) deep. It released poisonous gases that killed those who managed to escape the lava flow – up to 20,000 people.

Unsen, Japan
On 1 April 1793 the volcanic island of Unsen, or Unzen, completely disappeared, killing all 53,000 inhabitants.

Tambora, Indonesia
On the island of Sumbawa the eruption of Tambora between 5 and 12 April 1815 killed about 10,000 islanders immediately. A further 82,000 died later from disease and famine. This made it the worst-ever eruption for loss of human life.

Krakatoa, Sumatra/Java
The uninhabited island of Krakatoa exploded on 27 August 1883 with what may have been the biggest bang ever heard by humans. People heard it up to 4,800 km (2,980 miles) away!

Mont Pelée, Martinique
Mont Pelée began to erupt in April 1902, after lying dormant for centuries. The 30,000 residents of the main city, St Pierre, were told that they were not in danger, so stayed in their homes. They were there on 8 May when the volcano burst apart and showered the port with molten lava, ash and gas, destroying all buildings and killing as many as 40,000 people.

Nevado del Ruiz, Colombia
In 1985 this Andean volcano gave warning signs that it was about to erupt, but the local people were not evacuated soon enough. On 13 November the hot steam, rocks and ash ejected from Nevado del Ruiz melted its icecap, causing a mudslide. This completely engulfed the town of Armero, killing 22,940 people.

Earthquake detector
Chinese astronomer Chan Heng (AD 78–139) invented an earthquake detector made of a vase adorned with dragons' heads and surrounded by metal frogs. In each of the dragons' jaws was a carefully balanced ball. When the first tremors of an earthquake made the device vibrate, the balls fell into the frogs' mouths, making a noise to warn of the coming danger.

Evacuation!
The 2009 eruption of Mayon, a volcano on Luzon island, Philippines, led to the evacuation of 44,394 people from within 8 km (5 mile) of its base.

A volcano erupts on Réunion Island in the Indian Ocean. (Inset) Lava pouring from an erupting volcano

The Richter scale

Seismic waves are vibrations from earthquakes that travel through the Earth. Sensitive instruments called seismographs can record the waves, even at great distances, and calculate their strength and location.

The Richter scale indicates the magnitude or strength of an earthquake based on the size of the seismic waves (the distance the ground moves). The biggest earthquake (9 on the Richter scale) is a billion times greater than the smallest.

0 Detected by sensitive seismographs (some can detect magnitudes of less than zero!)
1 Detected by instruments
2 Lowest felt by humans
3 Slight vibration; more than 100,000 a year around the world
4 Up to 15,000 a year; at 4.5, would be detected by seismographs worldwide, but cause little damage
5 3,000 a year; the 1960 earthquake in Agadir, Morocco was 5.6
6 100 a year worldwide
7 20 a year; the 1995 earthquake in Kobe, Japan was 7.2
8 Major destructive earthquakes; average two a year; the 1904 San Francisco earthquake was probably 8.25
9 No quake higher than 8.9 has been recorded, but 9.0 or even higher is theoretically possible

Earthquake

Earthquakes are movements of the Earth's surface, often as a result of a fault, or fracture, in the crust. They happen more often in some parts of the world than others. In heavily populated areas, they cause great damage to buildings and loss of life.

Worst ever
An earthquake affecting the Middle East and North Africa on 20 May 1202 may have been the worst in human history. Up to 1,000,000 people were killed, 110,000 in Cairo, Egypt alone.

Longest-lasting
Most earthquakes last only a minute or two, but the Alaska earthquake of 27 March 1964 continued for at least five minutes and registered 8.6 on the Richter scale. It killed only 131 people but caused more than $450 million (£162 million) worth of damage.

Most powerful
The worst earthquake affecting an inhabited area was in Assam, India on 12 June 1897. It is reckoned to have reached 8.7, killing about 1,500. The Colombia/Ecuador earthquake of 31 January 1906 was 8.9 on the Richter scale. Fortunately, it was 300 km (200 miles) off the coast, and so resulted in fewer than 1,000 deaths on land.

Worst modern earthquakes
A devastating earthquake in Haiti on 12 January 2010 killed at least 200,000 people and injured about 300,000.

Worst natural disasters

Drought
Severe droughts kill people and livestock and destroy crops, and property. A total of 173 died and 414 were injured in Australia's 'Black Saturday' bushfires on 7 February 2009, with thousands of sheep, cattle and houses destroyed.

Flood
Floods caused by China's Huang He, or Yellow River, were first recorded in 2297 BC. The river has flooded at least 1,500 times since. In 1887 floods killed between 1.5 and 7 million people, making it the worst flood ever.

Tsunami
On 26 December 2004 a tsunami created by an undersea earthquake caused catastrophic floods in Indonesia, Sri Lanka, Myanmar, the Maldives, Malaysia, India and parts of Africa. More than 283,100 people died.

Cyclone
The worst cyclone of the 21st century has been Cyclone Nargis (2008) which killed an estimated 140,000 in Myanmar (Burma), with more than 2.5 million more gravely affected.

WHITAKER'S WORLD OF FACTS

Life Sciences

Saving the tiger

In 2010 the Indian Government announced that it was intending to ban tourists from visiting the country's 37 tiger reserves. The total number of tigers in the wild in India is uncertain, ranging from 800–1,400 but it is known to be dwindling. Although they attract many tourists, fear of extinction in some reserves caused by poaching and the stress resulting from the presence of tourist vehicles and luxury resorts in the tigers' territory has made this policy necessary.

Top food plants

Every year the people of the world eat more than 2.3 billion tonnes of cereals, 893 million tonnes of vegetables and 500 million tonnes of fruit. These figures come from the Food and Agriculture Organization of the United Nations, or FAO, which is based in Rome. The aim of the FAO is to help people around the world grow more food and eat a better diet.

Sugar cane 1,557,664,978 tonnes per annum
Maize 784,786,580 tonnes p.a.
Rice 651,742,616 tonnes p.a.
Wheat 607,045,683 tonnes p.a.
Potatoes 321,736,483 tonnes p.a.
Sugar beet 247,878,893 tonnes p.a.
Cassava 228,138,068 tonnes p.a.
Soybeans 216,144,262 tonnes p.a.
Barley 136,209,179 tonnes p.a.
Sweet potatoes 126,299,661 tonnes p.a.
Tomatoes 126,246,708 tonnes p.a.
Watermelons 93,173,368 tonnes p.a.
Bananas 81,263,358 tonnes p.a.
Cabbages 69,214,270 tonnes p.a.
Grapes 66,271,676 tonnes p.a.
Sorghum 64,589,459 tonnes p.a.
Onions 64,475,126 tonnes p.a.
Apples 64,255,520 tonnes p.a.
Oranges 63,906,064 tonnes p.a.
Coconuts 54,716,444 tonnes p.a.

Bananas grow well in tropical climates.

Banana facts

- Although bananas grow on trees, botanically the banana is a herb.
- Bananas grow upwards, not down.
- A cluster of bananas is called a hand and consists of 10 to 20 bananas, which are known as fingers – the word *banan* is Arabic for finger.
- The first bananas grown in the Americas were planted in 1516 on the island of Hispañiola by Spanish missionary Tomás de Berlanga.
- India grows more bananas than any other country in the world, nearly 22 million tonnes a year, more than a quarter of the total world crop.
- Worldwide, more than 80 million tonnes of bananas are eaten every year.

Important crops

These are the most important crops grown for uses other than food.

Cotton (clothing, household items) 72,504,406 tonnes per annum
Rubber (tyres, shoes, balls, erasers) 10,035,915 tonnes p.a.
Tobacco (cigarettes, cigars) 6,326,252 tonnes p.a.
Jute (sacks, rope) 3,225,551 tonnes p.a.

Going Bananas

- The phrase 'going bananas' was first recorded in the 1930s, perhaps because of their connection with the wild behaviour of monkeys.
- In 1987 Peter Dowdeswell (UK) set a record for eating 17 bananas in 1 minute 47 seconds.
- In an average year there are more than 300 banana-related accidents in Britain, most involving people slipping on skins.
- Billy Jones's recording of the song *Yes! We Have No Bananas* was US No.1 for five weeks in 1923.

The dense undergrowth of a tropical rainforest.

World forests

Forests cover 29.6 per cent of Earth's land and almost a quarter of these are in Russia. There are three main types of forest which grow in particular climates in different parts of the world.

- Tropical forests or rainforests grow near the Equator where it is always hot and wet. Here, temperatures are about 20–25˚C (68–77°F) and there is more than 200 cm (79 in) of rain a year.
- Temperate forests grow in places that have hot summers and cold winters. The summers can be as hot as 30˚C (86°F) and winters as cold as -30˚C (-22°F). Average rainfall is about 75–150 cm (30–59 in) a year. Many trees are deciduous (drop their leaves in autumn).
- Boreal or taiga forests grow in Russia, Canada and elsewhere in the far north. Winters are long and very cold. There is rainfall of 40–100 cm (16–39 in) a year, but most falls as snow. Most trees are evergreen conifers (cone-producing trees with needle-like leaves).

Dangerous plants

- Potatoes are safe to eat when cooked, but the stems and leaves of the plants contain a poison called solanine. If potatoes turn green, they may also contain solanine.
- Ricin is extracted from the seeds of the castor oil plant and is more poisonous than cyanide or snake venom. Even minute doses of ricin can be fatal.
- Opium is extracted from the juice of a poppy and contains morphine. Small quantities of both are used legally as painkillers and illegally as drugs. Both can easily cause death.
- The death cap is a highly poisonous mushroom. It is responsible for almost 90 per cent of deaths from eating fungi. The poison causes severe diarrhoea and vomiting.
- Curare is extracted from the bark of certain trees and is used by South American Indian tribes to tip their poison arrows when they go hunting.
- Deadly nightshade is also known as belladonna. It contains a poison called atropine. Less than 10 milligrams (0.0004 oz) could kill a child.
- Nicotine is a yellow oily liquid found in tobacco. About 50 milligrams (0.002 oz) of nicotine would kill an adult within minutes.
- The leaves of the purple foxglove contain digitalis and eating just a few can be fatal. Digitalis is used in tiny doses to treat people suffering from heart disease.

Purple foxglove

Record-breaking plants

- **Tallest tree**
The world's tallest tree is called the Stratosphere Giant. It grows in the Rockefeller Forest, Humboldt Redwoods State Park, California. At 112.32 m (369 ft), this redwood is almost three times the height of the Statue of Liberty in New York.

- **Biggest living thing**
The General Sherman giant sequoia in Sequoia National Park, California, USA, is the world's largest living thing. It is 83.8 m (275 ft) tall and measures 2.53 m (8.3 ft) round its mighty trunk. Including its huge root system, the tree weighs about 2,000 tonnes.

- **Smallest flowering plant**
Wolffia, a kind of duckweed, is just 0.6 mm (0.024 in) long and weighs about as much as two grains of salt. Its seeds are also the tiniest known – they weigh only 70 micrograms (0.0000025 oz), as much as a single grain of salt.

Bristlecone pine tree

Oldest trees

The bristlecone pines in California and Nevada, USA, are almost 5,000 years old and were long believed to be the oldest trees. Latest research suggests that creosote bushes in the USA's Mojave Desert may be even older – some of these plants began life nearly 12,000 years ago.

www.fao.org search

Grouping living things

Living things are organized by scientists into five groups called kingdoms. These are: Animals (Animalia); Algae and protozoans (Protoctista); Bacteria (Prokaryotae); Mushrooms, moulds and lichens (Fungi); Plants (Plantae).

The animal kingdom alone has thousands of different species. A species is a type of animal, and animals of the same species can breed successfully with each other. Similar species are grouped in a genus. Genera are grouped into families, families into orders, right up to the level of phylum. The phylum chordata contains all vertebrate animals – animals with a backbone. Here's how a human and a giant panda are classified.

	Human	**Giant panda**
Phylum	Chordata	Chordata
Class	Mammalia	Mammalia
Order	Primates	Carnivores
Family	Hominidae	Ursidae
Genus	*Homo*	*Ailuropoda*
Species	*sapiens*	*melanoleuca*

Animal species

Below is a list of the animals we know about. No one knows exactly how many species there may be altogether, but one recent estimate puts the total at 1,105,589. New species are often being found and there may be millions not yet discovered.

Some experts think there may be millions of species of insects and at least a million species of deep-sea fish that no one has ever seen. About half of all known creatures and plants live in tropical rainforests. In a study of just 19 trees in a tropical rainforest, 1,200 beetle species were found. About 80 per cent of these had not been seen before.

- **Arachnids** 98,000 (spiders, scorpions, etc)
- **Molluscs** 81,000 (snails, clams, etc)
- **Nematodes** 80,000 (unsegmented worms)
- **Crustaceans** 40,000 (shrimps, crabs, etc)
- **Fish** 30,700
- **Flatworms** 25,000
- **Segmented worms** 15,000
- **Sponges** 10,000
- **Birds** 9,990
- **Jellyfish, coral, etc** 9,000
- **Reptiles** 8,734
- **Starfish** 7,000
- **Amphibians** 6,347
- **Mammals** 5,488

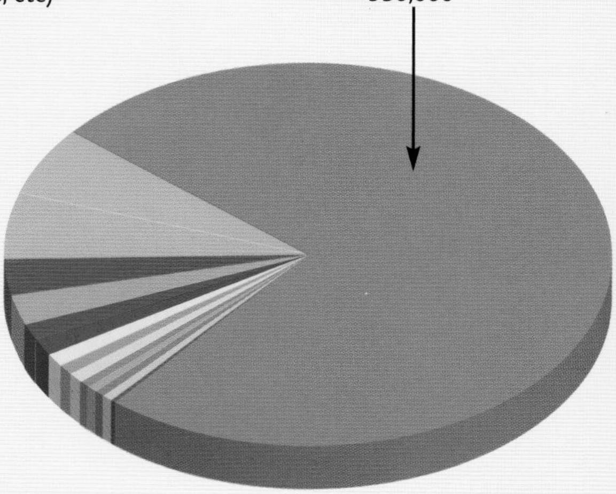

The first zoos

Panda in captivity

- As long ago as 2000 BC, the rulers of ancient Mesopotamia, Egypt and China had collections of animals. In medieval England King Henry I kept animals including a lion, leopard and camels at his palace at Woodstock, Oxford.
- Aztec ruler Montezuma II's animal collection in Tenochtitlán (modern Mexico City) contained many exotic creatures, such as jaguars, ocelots, snakes, monkeys and even human freaks.
- The imperial menagerie of Tiergarten Schönbrunn, Vienna, Austria, was built by Emperor Francis in 1752, and opened to the public in 1779. Its present-day inhabitants include giant pandas.
- London Zoo in Regent's Park was originally established in 1828 for the scientific study of animals, but was opened to the public in 1847. Officially called the Zoological Gardens, its name was shortened to 'zoo', which became used worldwide.
- Melbourne Zoo, opened in 1862, was Australia's first.
- Travelling menageries toured the USA in the early 19th century. The first permanent zoo was established in Philadelphia in 1859, but the Civil War delayed its opening until 1874. Meanwhile, Central Park Zoo, New York, opened in 1864 and Lincoln Park, Chicago, in 1868.

Life on Earth — 3,900 million years ago

The first simple life forms began to appear on Earth almost four billion years ago. More familiar animals appeared about 500 million years ago, and humans only within the past two million. We know a little about extinct creatures and early humans from fossil remains found in rocks from each period.

3,900–2,500 million years ago
Archaean period – the earliest marine life form (blue-green algae)

2,500–540 million years ago
Proterozoic period – the first many-celled organisms evolve

540–490 million years ago
Cambrian period – the first fossils of animals with shells and skeletons

490–443 million years ago
Ordovician period – molluscs, some corals and fishlike vertebrates

443–417 million years ago
Silurian period – fish develop jaws; first sharks

417–354 million years ago
Devonian period – fish dominant; amphibians (the first land animals) evolve

354–290 million years ago
Carboniferous period – insects; first reptiles

290–248 million years ago
Permian period – insects evolve into modern types; reptiles evolve

248–206 million years ago
Triassic period – early dinosaurs; marine reptiles

How fast?

Most of the creatures in this list can keep up these speeds for only a short time – less than an hour. The peregrine falcon achieves its speed as it dives through the air to catch prey, not in level flight.

Peregrine falcon (diving speed) 298 km/h (185 mph)
Spine-tailed swift 171 km/h (106 mph)
Eider duck 113 km/h (70 mph)
Sailfish (fastest fish) 110 km/h (68 mph)
Cheetah (fastest on land) 105 km/h (65 mph)
Pronghorn antelope 89 km/h (55 mph)
Racing pigeon 80 km/h (50 mph)
Lion (charging) 80 km/h (50 mph)
Brown hare 72 km/h (45 mph)
Ostrich (fastest flightless bird) 72 km/h (45 mph)
Blue shark 69 km/h (43 mph)
Horse 69 km/h (43 mph)
Greyhound 68 km/h (42 mph)
Killer whale 56 km/h (35 mph)
Death's head hawkmoth (fastest-flying insect) 53 km/h (33 mph)
Guano bat (fastest-flying mammal) 51 km/h (32 mph)
Skipper butterfly 48 km/h (30 mph)
California sea lion 40 km/h (25 mph)
Dolphin 40 km/h (25 mph)
Fastest man over 100 m (328 ft) 37km/h (23 mph)

Peregrine falcon

Heartbeats in a lifetime

Small animals such as hamsters have heartbeats of 450 or more per minute, compared with humans, whose hearts beat at an average 70 (that's 36.8 million a year, 2.94 billion in an 80–year lifetime). This explains why small pets often die young, having 'used up' their heartbeats, while elephants and large mammals have relatively long lifespans.

How long do they live?

Who would have thought that a sea anemone could live for 80 years? All these figures are the longest ever recorded. Most of these animals have much shorter lives.

Marine clam 200
Giant tortoise 150
Human 122
Killer whale 90
Sea anemone 80
Asiatic elephant 78
American alligator 66
Blue macaw 64
Horse 62
Chimpanzee 56
Hippopotamus 54
Slow-worm 54
Beaver 50
Bactrian camel 50
Grizzly bear 50
Blue whale 45
Boa constrictor 40
Domestic cat 34
Lion 30
Pig 27
Common rabbit 18
Queen ant 18
Giant centipede 10
Millipede 7
House mouse 6
Bedbug 6 months
Common housefly (male) 2 weeks

Giant tortoise

2000s

206–144 million years ago
Jurassic period – reptiles dominate land, sea and air; *Archaeopteryx* (first bird) appears; first mammals

144–65 million years ago
Cretaceous period – dinosaurs become extinct; snakes and lizards appear

65–55 million years ago
Palaeocene period – first large land mammals

55–34 million years ago
Eocene period – modern land mammals and whales appear

34–24 million years ago
Oligocene period – modern mammals dominant

24–5 million years ago
Miocene period – modern mammals eg primates; birds

5–1.8 million years ago
Pliocene period – human-like apes appear

1.8–10,000 million years ago
Pleistocene period – humans appear

10,000 million years ago to present
Holocene period – human civilization

http://animaldiversity.ummz.umich.edu search

Types of mammal

A mammal is a warm-blooded vertebrate (animal with a backbone) with some hair on its body. Female mammals feed their young on milk from their mammary glands. Most mammals give birth to live young which develop inside the mother's body, but echidnas and the platypus lay eggs.

Marsupial mammals such as kangaroos give birth to live young, but they are very small and weak. They finish their development in a pouch on the mother's body. There are 21 main groups, or orders, of mammals. Listed below are the names of the main mammal groups, examples of the animals and the approximate number of known species. Common names are given where possible.

Rodents Beavers, squirrels, mice, rats, porcupines, voles, guinea pigs, chinchillas 2,052
Chiroptera Bats 977
Insectivores Shrews, moles, hedgehogs, tenrecs 440
Marsupials Opossums, koalas, bandicoots, kangaroos, wallabies, numbat 292
Primates Lemurs, lorises, tarsiers, marmosets, monkeys, gibbons, apes, humans 270
Carnivores Dogs, foxes, wolves, cats, bears, hyenas, raccoons, civets, mongooses, weasels, pandas 249
Even-toed ungulates Pigs, peccaries, giraffe, okapi, hippopotamuses, deer, camels, llamas, antelopes, cattle 225
Cetacea Whales, dolphins, porpoises 83
Lagomorphia Rabbits, hares, pikas 80
Pinnipedia Seals, sea-lions, walruses 34
Edentates Anteaters, sloths, armadillos 29
Odd-toed ungulates Horses, asses, zebras, rhinos, tapirs 19
Scandentia Tree shrews 19
Macroscelidea Elephant-shrews 15
Monotremes Duck-billed platypus, echidnas 5
Hyracoidea Hyraxes 8
Pholidota Pangolins 7
Sirenia Manatees, dugong 4
Proboscidea Elephants 3
Dermoptera Flying lemurs 2
Tubulidentata Aardvark 1

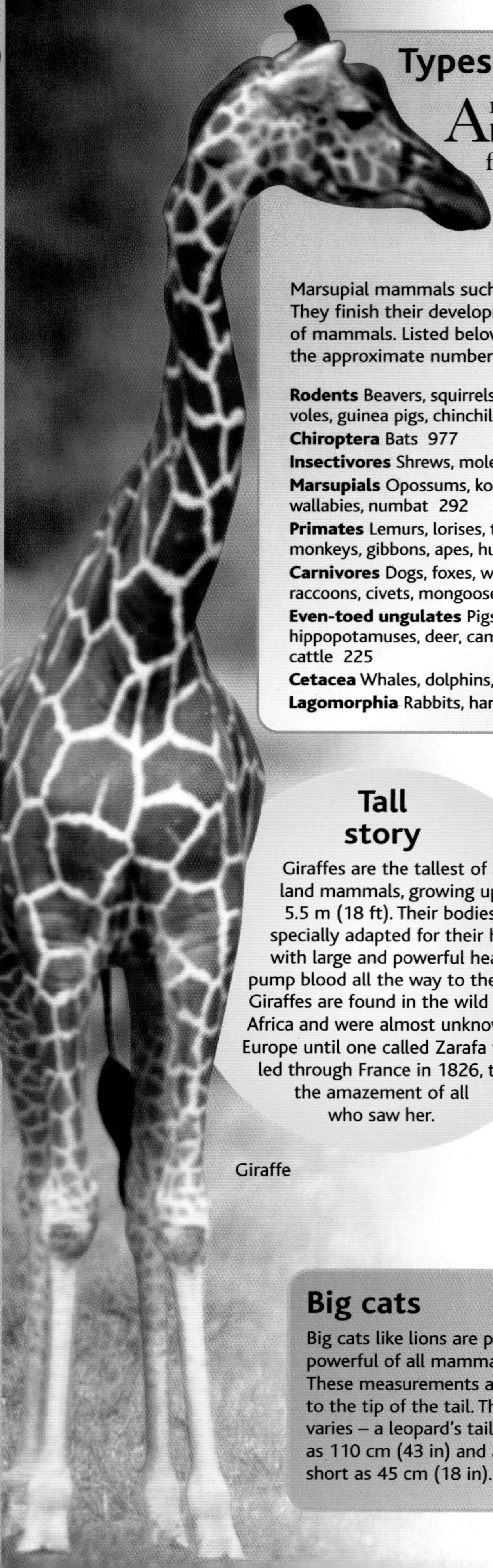

Giraffe

Tall story

Giraffes are the tallest of all land mammals, growing up to 5.5 m (18 ft). Their bodies are specially adapted for their height, with large and powerful hearts to pump blood all the way to their brain. Giraffes are found in the wild only in Africa and were almost unknown in Europe until one called Zarafa was led through France in 1826, to the amazement of all who saw her.

Biggest and smallest

The following are the biggest land mammals according to weight:

African elephant 7,000 kg (14,432 lb)
White rhinoceros 3,600 kg (7,937 lb)
Hippopotamus 2,500 kg (5,512 lb)
Giraffe 1,600 kg (3,527 lb)
American bison 1,000 kg (2,205 lb)
Arabian camel (dromedary) 690 kg (1,521 lb)
Polar bear 600 kg (1,521 lb)

The following are the smallest land mammals, according to length:

Kitti's hog-nosed bat 2.9 cm (1.1 in)
Pygmy shrew 3.6 cm (1.4 in)
Pipistrelle bat 4.0 cm (1.6 in)
Little brown bat 4.0 cm (1.6 in)
Masked shrew 4.5 cm (1.8 in)
Southern blossom bat 5.0 cm (2.0 in)
Harvest mouse 5.8 cm (2.3 in)

Big cats

Big cats like lions are perhaps the most powerful of all mammal predators. These measurements are from the nose to the tip of the tail. The length of tail varies – a leopard's tail can be as long as 110 cm (43 in) and a jaguar's tail as short as 45 cm (18 in).

Tiger (Asia) 330 cm (130 in)
Leopard (Asia, Africa) 320 cm (126 in)
Lion (Africa, Asia) 280 cm (110 in)
Jaguar (North, Central and South America) 271 cm (107 in)
Mountain lion (North, Central and South America) 245 cm (96 in)
Snow leopard (Asia) 240 cm (94 in)
Cheetah (Africa, Asia) 220 cm (87 in)
Clouded leopard (Asia) 197 cm (75 in)

Bears of the world

Scientists have long argued about whether the giant panda should be grouped with the raccoon family or the bears. DNA tests have now proved that it belongs with the bears. The koala, often called koala bear, is actually a marsupial not a bear.

Polar bear (Arctic) Length up to 257cm (101 in); weight 200–800 kg (440–1,760 lb)
Brown (grizzly) bear (North America, Europe, Asia) Length up to 290 cm (114 in); weight 136–390 kg (300–860 lb)
American black bear (North America) Length 127–191 cm (50–75 in); weight 60–300 kg (130–660 lb)
Asiatic black bear (Southern Asia) Length 127–188 cm (50–74 in); weight 100–200 kg (220–440 lb)
Sloth bear (Asia) Length 152–191 cm (60–75 in); weight 80–140 kg (175–310 lb)
Giant panda (China) Length 122–152 cm (48–60 in); weight up to 125 kg (275 lb)
Spectacled bear (South America) Length 152–183 cm (60–72 in); weight 70–113 kg (150–250 lb)
Sun bear (Asia) Length 122–152 cm (48–60 in); weight 27–65 kg (60–145 lb)

Cheetah running at full speed

Fastest mammal

Its long limbs and claws that help it grip enable the cheetah to accelerate as fast as a Formula One racing car, reaching a top speed of 96 km/h (60 mph). However, it is unable to maintain this speed further than 500 m (1,640 ft), so could be outrun by an antelope that can maintain a high speed for a long distance.

Champion divers

Lots of mammals can dive underwater, including humans, but whales are the champions. All have to hold their breath. These are average dives.

Northern bottlenose whale 120 mins
Sperm whale 112 mins
Greenland whale 60 mins
Seal 22 mins
Beaver 20 mins
Dugong 16 mins
Hippopotamus 15 mins
Porpoise 15 mins
Muskrat 12 mins
Duck-billed platypus 10 mins
Sea otter 5 mins
Human pearl diver 2.5 mins
Human 1 min

Monkeys and apes

Monkeys and apes (and humans) belong to the group of mammals called primates. There are 256 known species of primate. The smallest is the pygmy mouse lemur, which weighs only 30 g (1 oz). The largest is the gorilla, which weighs 220 kg (485 lb). The human comes next at 77 kg (170 lb).

Western lowland gorilla

Siberian tiger cubs in the snow

Marine mammals

The biggest creatures in the sea are whales, which are mammals not fish. The blue whale is the largest creature that has ever lived. Whales spend all their lives in the sea, but there are other mammals that spend most of their time in water and some time on land. These include seals, sea lions and otters.

Dolphins

- Dolphins are found worldwide. There are 33 species of marine dolphin and four river dolphins. The orca, or killer whale, is the largest dolphin. It can be as big as 9.8 m (32 ft) long and weigh 10 tonnes – as much as a double-decker bus.
- Dolphins are believed to be highly intelligent, and can be trained by navies to locate underwater mines and lost divers.
- The first dolphinarium, where dolphins perform for the public, was opened in St Augustine, Florida, USA, in 1938.
- Bottlenose dolphins can leap 7 m (23 ft) out of the water and turn a somersault in mid-air.

Biggest marine mammals

- The blue whale is 33.5 m (110 ft) long and weighs 130.0 tonnes
- The fin whale is 25.0 m (82 ft) long and weighs 45.0 tonnes
- The right whale is 17.5 m (57.4 ft) long and weighs 40.0 tonnes
- The sperm whale is 18.0 m (59 ft) long and weighs 36.0 tonnes

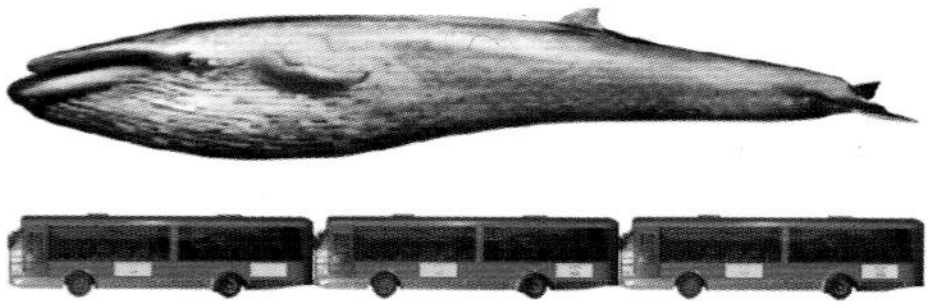

Blue whales can be as long as three buses

Top food fish

Fish and shellfish are popular foods worldwide. Although most are caught by traditional capture techniques, using lines and nets, increasing quantities are raised in special fish farms by modern aquaculture methods.

Type of fish	Total catch in 2007 (tonnes)
Herrings, sardines, anchovies	19,739,459
Carps, barbels, cyprinid	19,720,495
Cod, hake, haddock	8,327,605
Shrimps, prawns	6,529,041
Tunas, bonitos, billfish	6,326,329
Clams, cockles, arkshell	5,001,706
Oysters	4,549,819
Squids, cuttlefish, octopus	4,375,475
Salmon, trout, smelts	3,403,685
Tilapias, cichlids	3,275,401
Top 10 total	*81,249,015*
Aquaculture	*50,329,007*
Capture	*90,063,851*
World total caught for food	*140,392,858*

Danger in the water

Most creatures living in the world's oceans and rivers are harmless to people, but there are a few that can be very dangerous if you encounter or provoke them.

- The tiny candiru fish lives in South American rivers. It can enter your body and kill you unless it is surgically removed.
- Cone-shells, found in the South Pacific and Indian Oceans, have poisonous barbs that cause paralysis and occasionally death if you touch them. The geographer cone is probably the most dangerous of all.
- Freshwater electric eels live in South America and are the most powerful of all the electric eels. They can release up to 650 volts, which is nough to kill a person. Fortunately, this rarely happens.
- Certain parts of the Japanese puffer fish, also known as the maki-maki or deadly death puffer fish, contain a powerful nerve poison that can kill you if you eat it. There is no known antidote. Despite the danger, puffer fish are eaten in Japan, where they are a very expensive delicacy. People are specially trained to prepare them because eating the wrong part causes death in about 60 per cent of cases. About 50 people a year in Japan die after eating incorrectly prepared puffers.
- Several species of octopus are dangerous. The sting of the blue-ringed octopus, which

Big fish

Whale sharks are probably the biggest fish in the world. They are usually up to 12 m (39 ft) long – though one caught off Thailand in 1919 was reckoned to be 18 m (59 ft) long.

Whale sharks eat only plankton – tiny plants and animals that float in water. Basking sharks also eat plankton, but most other big fish hunt.

Whale shark 22 tonnes (4,850 lb)
Basking shark 16 tonnes (3,527 lb)
Giant manta 3 tonnes (661 lb)
Beluga 2 tonnes (441 lb)
Great white shark 2 tonnes (441 lb)
Sharptail mola 2 tonnes (441 lb)
Greenland shark 1 tonne (220 lb)
Ocean sunfish 1 tonne (220 lb)

Giant squid

Although the giant squid is the biggest of all molluscs, tales told by sailors and in Jules Verne's novel *Twenty Thousand Leagues Under the Sea* started a belief that some were so huge that they could drag large ships to the bottom of the sea.

Whale sharks with divers

Deep sea divers

- Emperor penguins sometimes dive to depths of 265 m (870 ft).
- In 1987 a leatherback turtle fitted with a depth-gauge reached a depth of 1,200 m (3,937 ft).
- Sperm whales regularly dive to 1,200 m (3,937 ft) and experts think they may sometimes go down to twice this depth.
- Fish called brotulids are the deepest-living vertebrate animals. They have been found in deep-sea trenches at 8,300 m (27,230 ft) – that is almost as deep as Mount Everest is high.

Amazing sea creatures

Most eggs
The black marlin fish lays as many as 226 million eggs.

Largest crustacean
The giant spider crab's body measures up to 30.5–35.6 cm (12–14 in) across and it has a claw span of 2.4–2.7 m (7.8–8.8 ft).

Smallest crustacean
Pea crabs measure only about 64 mm (2.5 in) across the shell.

Heaviest crustacean
An Atlantic lobster weighing 19.25 kg (42.44 lb) was caught off Virginia, USA in 1934. It was nicknamed Mike.

Heaviest mollusc
A giant squid caught in 1878 had tentacles 10.7 m (35 ft) long and weighed about 1,814 kg (4,000 lb).

Largest clam
A clam known as *Tridacna derasa* measures up to 124 cm (49 in) across and weighs 263 kg (580 lb).

Largest gastropod
The gastropod group includes snails. The largest gastropod is the trumpet or baler conch. It lives off Australian coasts and weighs up to 18 kg (40 lb). Its shell measures 77 cm (30 in) long and 101 cm (40 in) round.

Largest jellyfish
The lion's mane jellyfish (*Cyanea arctica*) is up to 2.3 m (7.5 ft) long, with tentacles that add an extra 37 m (121 ft).

Largest sponge
The barrel sponge of the Caribbean is up to 1.8–2.4 m (6–8 ft) tall.

lives in the Australian seas, can cause paralysis and even death.

- Piranha are small but incredibly ferocious fish which live in rivers in parts of South America. They hunt in groups, attacking any creatures in the water – including humans unlucky enough to encounter them. They strip their prey to the bone in minutes.
- Sea wasps, also known as box jellyfish, live off the coast of Australia. They have tentacles up to 9 m (29 ft) long and venom as powerful as that of a cobra. Australian lifeguards often wear nylon tights to protect them against stings, which can cause death within three minutes.
- Most sharks are harmless but a few species have been known to attack people. The great white, tiger and bull shark are the most dangerous. Of 2,199 attacks on humans recorded from 1580 to 2007, 471 were fatal.
- Stonefish lie on the seabed where they resemble rocks encrusted with seaweed. Unsuspecting swimmers who tread on the fish receive a very painful sting from their spines. In severe cases, victims may die.

www.fishbase.org search

Bird fact file

Birds are vertebrate animals with two legs and front limbs that have become adapted to form wings. All birds have feathers and most, but not all, can fly. Birds reproduce by laying eggs from which their young hatch.

Smallest bird

The smallest bird is the bee hummingbird, which is 5.7 cm (2.2 in) long and weighs 1.6 g (0.056 oz).

Longest beak

The bird with the longest beak in relation to its body is the sword-billed hummingbird – its beak is 10.5 cm (4.1 in) long and its body is 13.5 cm (5.3 in) long. The bird with the longest beak of all is the Australian pelican. Its beak is 47 cm (18.5 in) long.

Highest flyer

Ruppell's griffon is the highest-flying bird. In 1973 one was recorded at 11,278 m (37,000 ft) above sea level – 2,427 m (7,963 ft) higher than Mt Everest – after colliding with an airliner.

Longest migration

The Arctic tern migrates further than any other bird. Every year it flies from the Arctic to Antarctica and back again – a round trip of at least 40,000 km (25,000 miles).

Hummingbird

One and only

The kakapo of New Zealand is an endangered bird that is vulnerable to predators because it is the only parrot that is unable to fly. The heaviest of all parrots, the kakapo can run quickly and climb trees. It is also unusual as it is nocturnal – hence its alternative nameof 'owl parrot'.

All about feathers

The body of a feather is called its vane, the shaft is known as the rachis and the individual tufts are known as barbs. The barbs have hooks called barbules that cling to the others like Velcro to make a smooth surface.

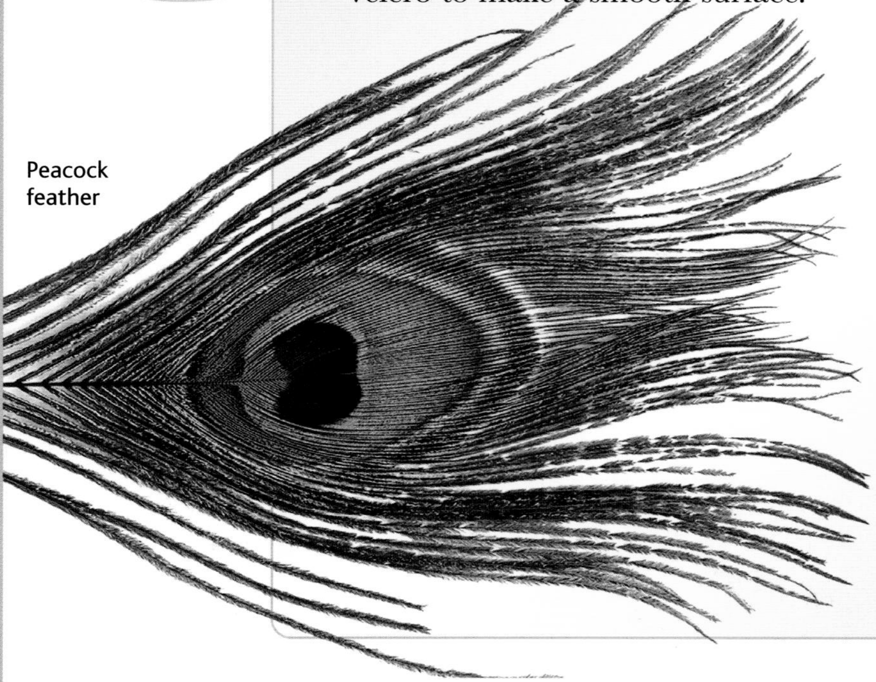

Peacock feather

- Feathers are made of keratin, the same material as our hair and nails.
- Birds shed their feathers at intervals and grow new ones. This process is called moulting. Feathers fall in a set pattern and in pairs, one from each side, so that the bird's flight is not unbalanced. Birds that do not fly, such as penguins, moult all over.
- A songbird such as a sparrow has about 3,000 feathers in the summer but as many as 3,500 in the winter to keep it warm. A swan may have 25,216 or more – up to 20,000 of them on its head and neck. The bird with the fewest feathers is the ruby-throated hummingbird with only 940.
- Pens for writing were once made from the quills, or feathers, of geese, turkeys and other birds. The word pen comes from the Latin *penna*, a feather.
- Grebes eat their own feathers. They are thought to form pellets that help the birds regurgitate (bring up) the bones and scales of the fish they eat.
- The Japanese phoenix fowl is a domestic bird. It has tail feathers measuring up to 10.6 m (34.8 ft), the longest of any bird. Various types of pheasant have tail feathers of 2 m (6.6 ft) long or more and a peacock's tail feathers can be 1.5 m (5 ft) long.
- Each feather weighs very little, but together they make up a large part of the weight of a bird, especially as flying birds have very light skeletons. The skeleton of the frigate bird, a large bird with a 2.1 m (6.9 ft) wingspan, weighs just 113 g (4 oz), less than the weight of all its feathers.

Largest flightless birds

- **Ostrich**: height 2.74 m (9 ft); weight 156.5 kg (345 lb)
- **Emu**: height 1.52 m (5 ft); weight 40.0 kg (88.2 lb)
- **Cassowary**: height 1.52 m (5 ft); weight 33.5 kg (73.9 lb)
- **Rhea**: height 1.37 m (4.5 ft); weight 25.0 kg (55.1 lb)
- **Emperor penguin**: 1.30 m (4.3 ft); weight 29.4 kg (64.8 lb)

Largest flying birds

- **Great bustard**: wingspan 2.7 m (9 ft); weight 20.9 kg (46 lb)
- **Trumpeter swan**: wingspan 3.4 m (11 ft); weight 16.8 kg (37 lb)
- **Mute swan**: wingspan 3.1 m (10 ft); weight 16.3 kg (36 lb)
- **Albatross**: wingspan 3.7 m (12 ft); weight 15.8 kg (34.8 lb)
- **Whooper swan**: wingspan 3.1 m (10 ft); weight 15.8 kg (34.8 lb)

Birds' eggs

The biggest ostrich eggs weigh up to 2.35 kg (5.18 lb), but they are not the largest eggs of all time. The extinct elephant bird (*Aepyornis maximus*) of Madagascar laid eggs that were up to 33 cm (13 in) long.

This is larger than the eggs of any dinosaur, seven times bigger than an ostrich egg, 180 times bigger than a chicken egg and over 20,000 times the size of a hummingbird's egg!

Ostrich 1,600 g (56.44 oz)
Albatross 595 g (20.99 oz)
Kiwi 450 g (15.87 oz)
Emperor penguin 450 g (15.87 oz)
Mute swan 340 g (11.99 oz)
Eagle 145 g (5.11 oz)
Snowy owl 83 g (2.93 oz)
Domestic hen 65 g (2.29 oz)
Mallard 54 g (1.90 oz)
Peregrine falcon 52 g (1.83 oz)
Sparrow 3.0 g (0.106 oz)
Vervain hummingbird 0.375 g (0.013 oz)

Emperor penguins

The Emperor penguin is the largest penguin. It lives in Antarctica, where there are about 200,000 breeding pairs. The female lays one egg, then goes off to feed for about two months. The male keeps the egg warm on his feet, beneath his body. Chicks stay with their mothers for about seven weeks, then gather together in a group to keep warm.

Flying mammals

Bats are the only mammals capable of true flight. They belong to the order Chiroptera, which means hand-wing. Instead of front legs, bats have wings made of skin which are supported by the bones of the arms and hands.

- There are about 977 species of bat. Flying foxes are among the largest. These bats are 45 cm (17.7 in) long, have wings that span 1.7 m (5.6 ft) and weigh up to 1.6 kg (3.5 lb). The Kitti's hog-nosed bat, which lives in Thailand, is the smallest. It weighs 2 g (0.07 oz), which is less than a table tennis ball. It is only 2.9 cm (1.1 in) long, making it the smallest of all mammals.
- Bats sleep during the day and wake up at night, when they go in search of food. Most bats are insect-eaters – a little brown bat can catch 1,200 insects in an hour – but others eat fruit or nectar from plants. Some larger species catch frogs, birds and fish.
- Many bats live in large groups called colonies. Bracken Cave in Texas, USA contains the world's largest bat colony, with about 20 million animals. This is one of the densest populations of any mammal and there can be as many as 5,000 newborn babies per square metre (11 square feet). These bats eat 1,000 tonnes of insects every night.

Emperor penguins and their young

www.bsc-eoc.org/avibase/avibase.jsp search

Tarantula

Fastest runner
Australian tiger beetles can run at 2.5 m a second (5.6 mph). If their relative sizes are taken into account, scaling this speed up, a human could run at about 720 mph, almost breaking the sound barrier!

Loudest insect
The African cicada makes a sound measured at 106.7 decibels at a distance of 50 cm (19.7 ins) – as loud as a car horn on the far side of a road.

Largest swarm
In 1954 a swarm of desert locusts in Kenya was estimated to cover 200 sq km (77 sq ml) and contain 10 billion locusts.

Spiders

Spiders are not insects. They belong to a separate group called arachnids, which also includes scorpions. A spider's body is divided into two parts linked by a narrow waist. It has four pairs of legs tipped with claws, but no wings. All spiders can make silk but not all spin webs.

There are at least 35,000 species of spider. Most are harmless but a few can be deadly. The banana spider of Central and South America produces enough venom to kill six adults. Other deadly spiders are the funnel-web, which lives in Australia, and the wolf spider of Central and South America. The black widow and various tarantulas are also dangerous and can kill.

Biggest spider
The goliath bird-eating spider, which lives in South American rainforests, has legs up to 25 cm (9.8 in) long.

Smallest spider
A species called *Patu marplesi* from Western Samoa is the smallest known spider. It is only 0.46 mm (0.018 in) long.

Amazing insects

Most abundant
Insects called springtails live in topsoil all over the world. There are probably as many as 600 million per hectare (1.5 billion per acre). Together, they weigh more than the entire human race.

Longest
Stick insects have the longest bodies. Some measure up to 51 cm (20.07 in) long, including their legs.

Heaviest
Goliath beetles can be 11 cm (4.33 in) long and weigh 100 g (3.5 oz).

Largest wingspan
The wings of the female Queen Alexandra birdwing butterfly of Papua New Guinea measure 28 cm (11 in) across.

Smallest
The wings of a battledore wing fairy fly, which is a kind of parasitic wasp, measure only 0.21 mm (0.008 in).

Longest-lived
Jewel beetle larvae, or young, may live inside timber for up to 30 years or more before emerging and turning into adult insects.

Types of insect

The body of most insects has three parts – head, thorax and abdomen. Insects have three pairs of legs and many have two pairs of wings. Listed here are the main groups, or orders, of insects. Numbers are just the species that we know about and have been named. There may be thousands more still to be discovered. Total numbers are huge. Together, all the insects in the world would weigh at least 12 times as much as all the people in the world.

Coleoptera meaning "hard wings": 370,000 species, eg beetles

Hymenoptera "membrane wings": 198,000 species, eg ants, bees, wasps

Lepidoptera "scaly wings": 165,000 species, eg butterflies and moths

Diptera "two-wings": 122,000 species, eg midges, mosquitoes, true flies

Hemiptera "half wings": 82,000 species, eg aphids and cicadas

Orthoptera "straight wings": 20,000 species, eg crickets and locusts

Trichoptera "hairy wings": 8,000 species, eg caddisflies

Collembola "sticky peg": 6,500 species, eg springtails

Phthiraptera "louse wings": 6,000 species, eg biting and sucking lice

Odonata "toothed flies": 5,500 species, eg dragonflies

Bee facts

There are about 20,000 types of bee. The best known is probably the honeybee, but not all bees live in colonies like the honeybee. Many live alone and build their own nests.

- Honeybees are the only insects that make food which humans eat. Bees make honey to feed the inhabitants of their hives during winter. The honey they do not eat is harvested by beekeepers. Bees also make beeswax which is used for making candles and furniture polish.
- Wallace's giant bees are the world's largest at up to 4 cm (1.6 in) long. They were first found in Indonesia in 1858 but were then thought to have become extinct. In 1981 the bees were rediscovered.

www.insectguide.net search

Honey bee on a flower

Colony Collapse Disorder

Colony Collapse Disorder is the name given to a recent phenomenon where entire colonies of honey bees suddenly die. It may result from pollution, a virus or some other unknown cause. It is of worldwide concern because bees are vital for pollinating many important food crops.

Some stick insects can be as long as a person's arm

- Honeybees visit up to five million flowers to make 1 kg (2.2 lb) of honey. In doing so, they fly a total distance equal to flying four times round the Earth.
- The smallest bee is the Brazilian *Trigona duckei* at 2–5 mm (0.08–0.20 in) long.
- One beehive may contain 50,000 worker bees – these are the bees which collect nectar from flowers to make honey.
- Honeybees' wings beat 11,400 times a minute. These wing movements make the bees' familiar buzz.
- 1.3 million tonnes of honey are produced worldwide every year. China is the main producer with 276,000 tonnes, followed by the USA with 82,000.
- Some people are allergic to bee stings, which can even be fatal. In 1962 in Rhodesia, Johanne Relleke was stung 2,243 times by wild bees, but survived!
- Queen bees can lay two or three thousand eggs a day – as many as 200,000 eggs a year. They may live as long as five years, so can produce a million eggs.

Thysanoptera "fringed wings": 5,000 species, eg thrips

Neuroptera "net-veined wings": 4,000 species, eg lace-wings

Blattodea "insect avoiding light": 4,000 species, eg cockroaches

Pscoptera "milled wings": 3,500 species, eg hook lice

Isoptera "equal wings": 2,750 species, eg termites

Ephemeroptera "living for a day": 2,500 species, eg mayflies

Phasmatodea "like a ghost": 2,500 species, eg leaf insects

Mantodea "like a prophet": 2,000 species, eg mantids

Plecoptera "Wickerwork wing": 2,000 species, eg stoneflies

Siphonaptera "tube without wings": 2,000 species, eg fleas

Dermaptera "leathery wings": 1,900 species, eg earwigs

Mecoptera "long wings": 550 species, eg hanging flies

Thysanura "fringed tail": 370 species, eg silverfish

Archaeognatha "ancient jaw": 350 species, eg bristletails

Embioptera "lively wings": 300 species, eg web-spinners

Megaloptera "large wings": 250 species, eg alderflies

Raphidioptera "embroidered wings": 150 species, eg snakeflies

Zoraptera "pure + wingless": 30 species, eg angel insects

Grylloblattodea "cricket cockroach": 25 species, eg rock crawlers

Reptiles

A reptile is a vertebrate animal with a body covered in tough scales. Most reptiles live on land, but turtles and some kinds of snake live in water.

Crocodiles and their relatives spend time on land and in water. There are more than 8,000 species of reptiles, which are divided into the following groups.

Lizards 4,765 species
Snakes 2,978 species
Turtles and tortoises 307 species
Amphisbaenians (worm lizards) 165 species
Crocodiles, alligators, caimans 23 species
Tuataras 2 species

Alligators and crocodiles

The crocodile family contains 23 species, including alligators, caimans and gavials. All are large reptiles with long bodies and short legs. Most crocodiles have narrow V-shaped snouts, but alligators and caimans have wider, U-shaped snouts. The gavial has long slender jaws – just right for catching fish.

In alligators and caimans the teeth of the lower jaw fit into pits in the upper jaw and cannot be seen when the mouth is closed. In crocodiles the fourth tooth on each side of the lower jaw fits into a notch on the upper jaw, so they are always visible. Crocodiles are generally bigger and more aggressive than alligators.

Alligators

American alligator (southern USA) 4–4.5 m (13.1–14.8 ft)
Chinese alligator (China) 2 m (6.6 ft)
Spectacled caiman (South America) 2–2.5 m (6.6–8.2 ft)
Broad-snouted caiman (South America) 2 m (6.6 ft)
Yacaré caiman (South America) 2.5–3 m (8.2–9.8 ft)
Black caiman (South America) 4–6 m (13.1–19.7 ft)
Cuvier's dwarf caiman (South America) 1.5–1.6 m (4.9–5.2 ft)
Schneider's or Smooth-fronted caiman (South America) 1.7–2.3 m (5.6–7.5 ft)

Crocodiles

American crocodile (southern USA, Mexico, Central and South America) 5 m (16.4 ft)
Slender-snouted crocodile (West Africa) 2.5 m (8.2 ft)
Orinoco crocodile (northern South America) 6 m (19.7 ft)
Australian freshwater crocodile (Australia) 2.5–3 m (8.2–9.8 ft)
Philippine crocodile (Philippines) 3 m (9.8 ft)
Morelet's crocodile (Central America) 3 m (9.8 ft)
Nile crocodile (Africa) 5 m (16.4 ft)
New Guinea crocodile (New Guinea) 3.5 m (11.5 ft)
Mugger or marsh crocodile (India, Sri Lanka) 4–5 m (13.1–16.4 ft)
Estuarine or saltwater crocodile (Southeast Asia, Australia) 6–7 m (19.7–23 ft)
Cuban crocodile (Cuba) 3.5 m (11.5 ft)
Siamese crocodile (Southeast Asia, very rare) 3–4 m (9.8–13.1 ft)
African dwarf crocodile (Central and West Africa) 1.9 m (6.2 ft)
False gharial or gavial (Southeast Asia) 5 m (16.4 ft)

Gavials

Indian gavial or gharial (India, Pakistan, Bangladesh, Nepal) 5–6 m (16.4–19.7 ft)

Man-eaters?

As snakes have no limbs, they are unable to hold their prey and rip it apart, but they have powerful jaw and throat muscles, no breastbone or shoulder muscles, and a very elastic skin. These enable them to eat whole animals much larger than themselves – there are even reports of African rock pythons swallowing humans!

Amphibians

An amphibian is a vertebrate animal that spends at least some of its life in water. Its skin is not scaly. There are about 5,578 species of amphibian, divided into:

Frogs and toads 4,896 species
Newts and salamanders 517 species
Caecilians (legless amphibians) 165 species

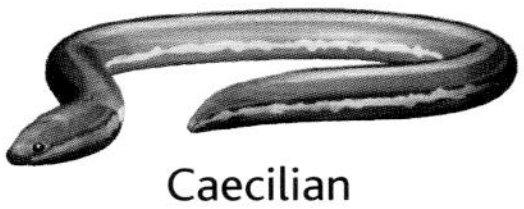
Caecilian

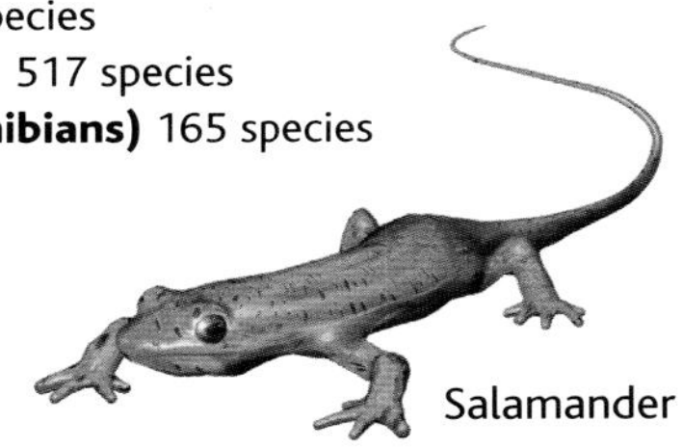
Salamander

Snake facts

Largest snakes

Many people believe that the South American anaconda is the longest snake. There are reports of anacondas up to 36.5 m (120 ft) long, but this has never been proved. The reticulated or royal python is probably the longest snake at up to 10.7 m (35 ft), but the anaconda may be the heaviest at up to 230 kg (500 lb).

Smallest snake

Discovered in 2008, the Barbados threadsnake *Leptotyphlops carlae* grows to just 10 cm (4 in).

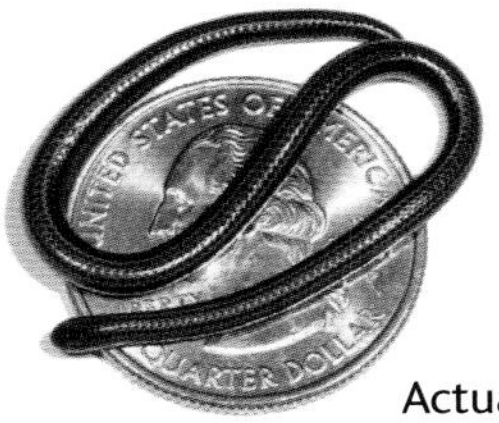
Actual size

Turtles and tortoises

These reptiles all have a hard shell that protects the body. There are about 250 species, some of which live in the sea, others in fresh water and the rest on land.

Biggest

- Fossils of the extinct turtle *Stupendemys geographicus* have been found with shells up to 3 m (10 ft) long. They would have weighed more than 2,040 kg (4,497 lb).
- The largest living turtle is the leatherback. A male washed up on the coast of Wales in 1988 holds the record – he was 291 cm (113.5 in) long and weighed 916 kg (2,019 lb).
- The Aldabra giant tortoise, which lives on an island in the Seychelles, weighs up to 304 kg (670 lb) and is the largest land-living tortoise. It is also one of the slowest tortoises. It moves at an average speed of 0.27 km/h (0.17 mph).

Aldabra tortoises

Smallest

The smallest turtle or tortoise is the common musk turtle which is 7.62 cm (3 in) long and weighs 227 g (8 oz).

Blue poison dart frog

Fantastic frogs and toads

Largest frogs and toads

- The world's largest known frog is the goliath frog, which lives in central Africa. It measures up to 87.63 cm (34.5 in) long and weighs as much as 3.66 kg (8.1 lb).
- The largest tree frog is *Hyla vasta*, which lives only on the island of Hispaniola. It is more than 12 cm (4.7 in) long and has huge round finger and toe disks which grip like superglue.
- The world's largest toad is the South American marine toad. It can have a body length of over 23 cm (9.1 in) and weigh up to 1.2 kg (2.6 lb).

Smallest frog

The smallest frog and the world's smallest amphibian is the *Eleutherodactylus limbatus* frog, which measures only 8.5–12 mm (0.3–0.5 in).

Newest frogs

In 2006, 20 previously unknown frog species were discovered in an expedition to Indonesia (see page 69) including a tiny microhylid frog that measures less than 14 mm (0.6 in).

Egg laying

The marine toad lays 35,000 eggs a year, but the Cuban arrow-poison frog lays only one egg.

Highest and lowest homes

The green toad has been seen at 8,000 m (26,247 ft) in the Himalayas and toads have been discovered more than 3,048 m (10,000 ft) down a coal mine.

Most poisonous

The poison-arrow frogs of Central and South America are the most deadly. The world's most poisonous amphibian is the golden poison-arrow frog of western Colombia. One adult contains enough highly toxic poison in its skin to kill 1,000 people.

Smelliest

The smelliest frog is the Venezuela skunk frog, which was discovered in 1991. It warns off its enemies by releasing a bad-smelling chemical identical to the one produced by skunks.

Longest jumps

- On 21 May 1977, a female sharp-nosed frog leaped 10.2 m (33.5 ft) in three consecutive jumps at a frog derby at Larula Natal Spa, Paulpietersburg in South Africa.
- The cricket frog is only 3.5 cm (1.4 in) and can jump 36 times its own length. If an adult human jumped 36 times his own length, the long-jump record could stand at 65.8 m (216 ft)!

Life on man

As many as 100 trillion viruses and bacteria live on each of us. However much we wash, there are always ten million or so bacteria on every square centimetre of our skin. There are also many tiny creatures called parasites, which can live inside or on the human body, feeding on our blood.

- Parasites such as roundworms, hookworms, flukes and tapeworms – which can grow as long as 9.75 m (32 ft) – can live inside our bodies. They may cause such diseases as elephantiasis, in which the patient's limbs swell to gigantic sizes. Head lice live on human heads and feed on blood. The lice lay little white eggs, called nits, which cling to individual hairs.
- Follicle mites are in everyone's hair, even among our eyelashes. They were first described by 19th-century scientist Richard Owen (the man who first named dinosaurs), but are so tiny that few people have ever seen them or are even aware that they are there.
- Some of the tiny creatures that feed on us may also transmit diseases. Tsetse flies carry African sleeping sickness. Mosquitoes can infect humans with diseases such as malaria, dengue fever and yellow fever when they bite. Malaria has killed more people in human history than any other disease.
- Ticks can carry diseases such as encephalitis and Lyme disease. Mites and chiggers (baby mites) cause skin diseases and may transmit typhus.

See also
Black Death: page 104

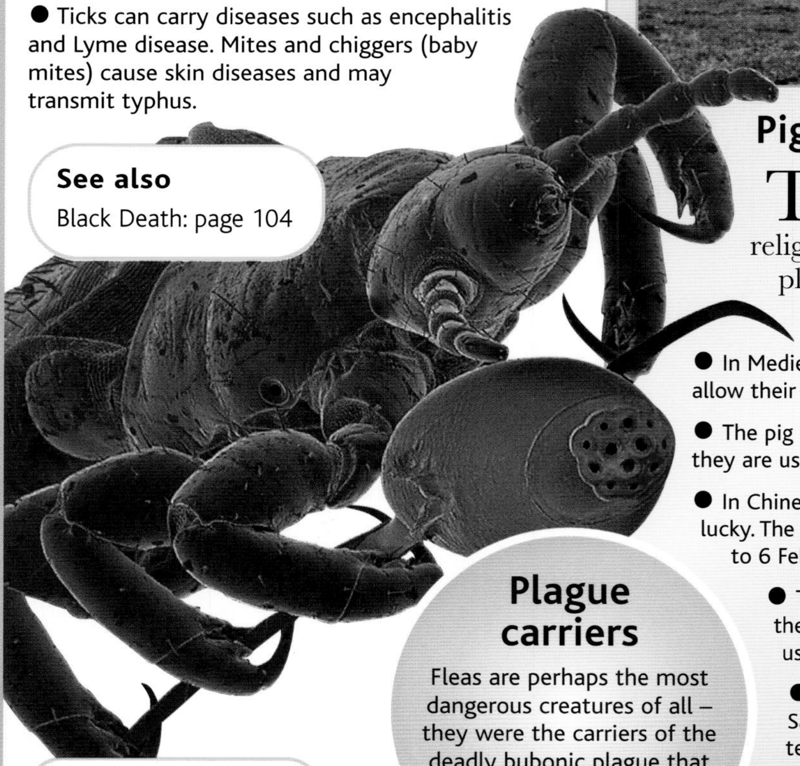

Head louse with egg

Plague carriers

Fleas are perhaps the most dangerous creatures of all – they were the carriers of the deadly bubonic plague that killed millions of people in medieval times.

Animal heroes

St Bernard

St Bernard dogs have traditionally been used to aid mountain rescue crews. One of the most famous was Barry (1800–14), who lived at the monastery at the St Bernard Pass, on the border of Switzerland and Italy, and rescued many travellers trapped in the snow. His body is preserved in the Natural History Museum, Berne, Switzerland.

Animal war heroes

In 2004, a statue was unveiled in Park Lane, London, with the inscription 'Animals In War. This monument is dedicated to all the animals that served and died alongside British and allied forces in wars and campaigns throughout time.' Since 1943, animal war heroes have been awarded the Dickin Medal, often described as the animals' Victoria Cross.

Gorilla

On 16 August 1996 a three-year-old boy fell into the gorilla enclosure at Brookfield Zoo, Chicago, USA, and was knocked unconscious. Binti Jua, a female gorilla, protected the boy from another gorilla until he was rescued.

Pig tales

There are over 900 million pigs in the world. Although considered 'unclean' in some religions, including Judaism and Islam, the pig has played an important part in human culture since it was first domesticated thousands of years ago.

- In Medieval times, 'pannage' was the legal right of pig owners to allow their animals to graze in forests on acorns and beech nuts.
- The pig has a highly developed sense of smell: in France, they are used to hunt for truffles, a valuable edible fungus.
- In Chinese culture, being born in the Year of the Pig is considered lucky. The latest year spanned the period from 18 February 2007 to 6 February 2008.
- The bodies of pigs are similar to those of humans: pigs coat themselves with mud to avoid sunburn and their hearts are used to make replacement valves for human hearts.
- Exhibited in London in the early 19th century, 'Toby, the Sapient [wise] Pig' was said to be able to read, count and tell the time.
- At Aquarena Springs in Texas, USA, the 'Swine Dive' featured Ralph, a performing pig, diving into a swimming pool.

Humans and animals

Since ancient times humans have used many types of animals for a vast range of different purposes.

Meat, milk and honey

Humans have always hunted and eaten wild animals. Milk from such animals as cows, goats, sheep, camels, buffalo, reindeer, llamas and yaks is drunk, used in cooking and made into butter and cheese. The eggs from birds such as hens, ducks, geese and quail are another important food. Honey has long been taken from the hives of wild bees, and now from domesticated bees kept in artificial hives.

Wool, fur and skin

Wool is shorn from live sheep, which then regrow their coats. The fur and leather of many other animals can be taken only after the animal has been killed. Cattle, goats, rabbits, mink, seals, wolves, foxes, kangaroos, big cats such as leopards, and alligators and snakes are among the many animals that have been used in this way. There are some very special uses for animal skin: for example, medieval manuscripts were written on vellum, made from calfskin.

Silk

Silk comes from the silkworm, the caterpillar of the silkmoth. Silkworms eat a tonne of mulberry leaves to make 5 kg (11 lb) of silk.

Beasts of burden and transport

Strong animals such as horses, donkeys, camels, reindeer and buffalo are used to pull agricultural equipment and carts, and to carry people. Elephants drag heavy logs, pit ponies once drew trucks in coal mines, and dogs – usually huskies – pull sledges.

Security

Guard dogs (and even guard geese), police dogs and sniffer dogs (to detect drugs) are widely used.

Helpers

Sheepdogs, hunting hounds, retrievers and guide dogs for the blind are among the best known, but other animals, such as monkeys, can be trained to aid the disabled. Search and rescue dogs help to find missing people, lost walkers and climbers, and earthquake victims. Less well-known human helpers include pigs used to find truffles (edible fungi) and cats kept by the British Post Office to prevent mice from eating the mail! Animals kept as pets also provide millions of people with companionship.

Military

The warhorse is one of the most familiar of all military animals, but elephants have also been successfully used in battles. Many military organizations use dogs, goats and other animals as regimental mascots. Message-carrying dogs and carrier pigeons have been used by armies. During the Iraq war in 2004, dolphins were trained to find mines.

Swine flu

An outbreak of H1N1 influenza virus that began in Mexico in March 2009 was called 'swine flu' because it is found in pigs, although it is actually transmitted from human to human and can not be caught from eating pork products. Despite this, pigs were slaughtered in some countries and exports of meat banned. Most people who caught it suffered only mild symptoms, but a number died, leading to fears of a global pandemic like that of 1918–19, when millions died. Countries across the world introduced emergency measures, including travel restrictions, issuing of facemasks and a programme of vaccination. By early 2010, it seemed that the threat had been much less serious than expected, with fewer than 15,000 confirmed deaths worldwide, rather than the many millions that had been predicted.

Sporting animals

Animals that are raced by humans range from camels and dogs to ostriches, mice and even snails. Horses are perhaps the best known racing animals, and are also used to play polo – as are elephants.

A galloping horse

Countries with most pets

These totals include cats, dogs, birds, fish, small mammals (hamsters, guinea pigs, etc) and reptiles.

USA 371,262,000
China 276,685,000
Brazil 80,412,500
Germany 77,925,000
Turkey 72,033,000
France 68,420,000
Japan 68,346,000
Italy 60,475,000
Russia 59,985,000
UK 50,390,000
Philippines 37,442,100
Netherlands 30,795,300
Mexico 27,841,000
Canada 26,409,600
Ukraine 24,257,000
Spain 24,099,800
Argentina 23,904,700
Australia 22,215,000
Poland 21,060,000
South Africa 16,002,000

Top UK pets

Some 43% (11,200,000 households) in the UK own at least one pet, ranging from dogs, cats and rabbits to more exotic creatures such as snakes and spiders.

Dog 23% = 6,000,000 households (hh)
Cat 20% = 5,200,000 hh
Indoor fish 10% = 2,600,000 hh
Outdoor fish 8% = 2,100,000 hh
Rabbit 2.8% = 700,000 hh
Indoor birds 1.8% = 500,000 hh
Guinea pigs 1.3% = 300,000 hh
Hamster 1.3% = 300,000 hh
Domestic fowl 0.8% = 280,000 hh
Gerbils 0.5% = 130,000 hh
Snakes 0.4% = 104,000 hh
Lizards 0.4% = 104,000 hh
Horses/ponies 0.3% = 78,000 hh
Tortoises/turtles 0.3% = 78,000 hh
Rats 0.3% = 78,000 hh

Long-haired cat

The first cat show

The first cat show was held at Crystal Palace, London, on 13 July 1871. It was organised by writer, animal artist and cat-lover Harrison Weir. The first in the USA took place in New York on 8–11 May 1895.

Cat-alogue

Heaviest
Himmy, owned by Thomas Vyse of Queensland, Australia, weighed 21.3 kg (47 lb). He had a 38.1 cm (15 in) neck and an 84 cm (33 in) waist – similar to that of an adult human! He died in 1986 at the age of ten.

Smallest
Tinker Toy, a male Blue Point Himalayan owned by Katrina and Scott Forbes of Illinois, USA, is 7 cm (2.8 in) tall, 19cm long and weighs 625 g (1.4 lb).

Biggest breed
Maine Coons are a North American breed of muscular, big-boned cats. Males often reach 6–8 kg (13–17.5 lb) in weight.

Oldest
There are several contenders for this title. The most reliable record is that of the French-born cat Grandpa Rex's Allen. This was a Sphynx cat owned by Jake Perry of Austin, Texas, USA. The cat died in 1998 at the age of 34.

Largest litter
In 1970 Tarawood Antigone, a female Burmese owned by Valerie Gane of Kingham, Oxfordshire, gave birth to 19 kittens. Fifteen of the litter survived.

Racing greyhounds

The fastest dogs
Greyhound 67.14 km/h (41.72 mph)
Saluki 64+ km/h (40+ mph)
Ibizan hound 60.8–64 km/h (38–40 mph)
Whippet 54.42 km/h (36.52 mph)
Sloughi 57.6 km/h (36 mph)

Weird pets

Bear
Hercules, a grizzly bear owned by Scottish wrestler Andy Robin, appeared in TV adverts and in films including the James Bond film *Octopussy* (1983).

Dormouse
Xarifa, a dormouse owned by illustrator Beatrix Potter as a child, appears in her book *The Fairy Caravan* (1929).

Hippo
In 1927 Billy, a pygmy hippo, was given to US President Calvin Coolidge, who also owned a wallaby, lion cubs and other animals. He gave it to a zoo rather than keep it at the White House.

Kinkajou
Paris Hilton kept a kinkajou or honey bear, called Baby Luv, until it bit her.

Pot-bellied pig
US actor George Clooney owned a 136-kg (300-lb) pig called Max who died in 2006.

Tigers
American boxer Mike Tyson once kept four white Bengal tigers at his Texas home.

Wombats
At his London house Victorian painter and poet Dante Gabriel Rossetti kept two wombats as well as owls, kangaroos, wallabies, armadillos, parakeets, peacocks, a racoon, a Canadian marmot, a Japanese salamander, two laughing jackasses and a zebu.

Zebra
Lord Rothschild (1868–1937) was a famous zoologist – 239 animals were named after him. Among other animals he kept six zebra that he used to pull his carriage.

Sloth bear in captivity

Intelligent dogs

American psychology professor and pet trainer Stanley Coren ranked 133 breeds of dogs for intelligence. He studied their responses to a range of IQ tests, as well as the opinions of dog obedience judges. The five top breeds were the border collie, poodle, German shepherd, golden retriever and Doberman pinscher.

Dog-alogue

Largest dog
In 1989 Aicama Zorba of La-Susa, an Old English mastiff owned by Chris Eraclides of London, weighed 155.58 kg (343 lb) and measured 2.5 m (8.25 ft) from nose to tail.

Smallest dog
A Yorkshire terrier owned by Arthur Marples of Blackburn in the 1940s was just 6.3 cm (2.5 in) tall and weighed 113 g (4 oz).

Oldest dog
Bluey, an Australian cattle-dog owned by Les Hall of Victoria, Australia, died in 1938 at the age of 29 years 5 months.

Largest litter
In 1944, Lena, an American foxhound, produced 23 puppies, all of which survived. Other dogs have equalled this record, but not all the pups have survived.

Longest jumper
Bang, a greyhound, jumped 9.14 m (30 ft) while chasing a hare at Brecon Lodge in Gloucestershire.

Greatest climber
Tschingel, a beagle, climbed more than 50 peaks in the Alps, including the 4,165 m (13,664 ft) Jungfrau and the 3,974 m (13,038 ft) Eiger.

Famous dog-lovers

Francis Barraud and Nipper
British artist Francis Barraud sold a painting called *His Master's Voice* to the Gramophone Company. It showed his dog Nipper listening to a gramophone. The company adopted it as its trademark and later changed its company name to His Master's Voice or HMV.

J.M. Barrie and Luath
Luath, a Newfoundland dog, was the model for Nana in Barrie's book *Peter Pan*.

George Bush and Millie
Millie, the springer spaniel belonging to US President George Bush (Snr) had a bestselling "autobiography" *Millie's Book*, written by First Lady Barbara Bush.

Elizabeth Barrett Browning and Flush
The English poet's cocker spaniel became famous from Virginia Woolf's book *Flush: A Biography* (1933), which looks at the world from the dog's point of view.

John Gray and Greyfriars Bobby
Bobby was a Skye terrier who faithfully guarded his master's grave at Greyfriars, Edinburgh, for 14 years from 1858. The true story of the devoted dog has been the subject of books and films.

Charles Schulz and Spike
American cartoonist Charles Schulz based his comic character Snoopy on his family's Basset hound Spike. In later strips a dog called Spike appears as Snoopy's brother.

Tyrannosaurus rex skull and reconstruction (below)

Dinosaurs

Dinosaurs first appeared about 230 million years ago. These amazing reptiles then dominated life on Earth until they became extinct 65 million years ago. The first dinosaurs to be described were *Megalosaurus* (great lizard) by William Buckland in 1824 and *Iguanodon* (iguana tooth) by Gideon Mantell in 1825.

They were named before the word "dinosaur" had been invented. The name *dinosauria* (terrible lizards) was suggested by British scientist Richard Owen in July 1841. Since then 700 species have been identified. Not all dinosaurs were enormous – some measured less than 60 cm (24 in) long, about the size of a chicken. Sizes of dinosaurs are mostly estimates worked out from the size of bones. The largest known complete skeleton is of a *Brachiosaurus* and is 22.3 m (73.2 ft) long. The skeleton is in the Humboldt Museum, Berlin, Germany.

Biggest dinosaurs

Amphicoelias weight 122.4 tonnes; length 40–60 m (131–198 ft)
Supersaurus weight 35–40 tonnes; length 33–34 m (108–112 ft)
Bruhathkayosaurus weight 139 tonnes; length 28–34 m (92–111 ft)
Futalognkosaurus weight 73–88 tonnes; length 32–34 m (105–111 ft)
Diplodocus weight 38 tonnes; length 33.5 m (110 ft)
Argentinasaurus weight 73–88 tonnes; length 30 m (98 ft)

Dinosaur facts

- The biggest dinosaurs were all herbivores. *Tyrannosaurus rex*, one of the largest carnivorous dinosaurs, measured up to 15 m (49.2 ft) long and weighed 60,000 kg (132,277 lb) or more. Its huge jaws were packed with 60 teeth, the biggest of which were 23 cm (9 in) long!
- A new type of tyrannosaur called *Guanlong wucaii* has recently been discovered in China. It lived 160 million years ago, measured about 3 m (10 ft) long, and looked like a miniature version of *Tyrannosaurus rex*.
- The largest flying prehistoric creatures were pterosaurs. The wings of the biggest pterosaur, *Quetzalcoatlus*, measured 10.96 m (36 ft) from tip to tip.
- The largest known dinosaur egg belonged to *Hypselosaurus*. The 100 million-year-old egg measures 30 by 25.5 cm (12 by 10 in), about three times the volume of an ostrich egg.
- The fastest dinosaur, *Ornithomimus*, could probably run at a speed of up to 70 km/h (43.5 mph). The ostrich runs at a similar speed today.
- Dinosaurs have been in space! Fragments of bone and an eggshell of *Maiasaura peeblesorum* were taken into space by astronaut Loren Acton in 1985. A *Coelophysis* skull was taken into space by astronaut Bonnie Dunbar in 1998.

Giant pliosaur

In 2009 the discovery in Dorset, UK, of a 2.4 m (7 ft 10 in) skull of a pliosaur from the Jurassic era (about 150 million years ago) was announced and is being studied by scientists before being put on display. It may have been up to 16 m (52 ft) long and weighed as much as 12 tonnes, making it the largest marine 'dinosaur' ever found – twice the size of a killer whale. Pliosaurs were a type of huge sea reptile that belonged to a group known as plesiosaurs. Their heads were like those of crocodiles, with powerful jaws and sharp teeth, but were so big that it has been claimed one could have eaten a Tyrannosaurus rex whole.

Animals in danger

In the past 500 years, hundreds of species of animals have become extinct – they have disappeared from Earth for ever. In many cases this is because of human actions. The animals have been hunted, or the areas where they lived have been destroyed.

Some creatures become extinct in the wild but have survived in artificial settings, such as zoos. If they can be successfully bred, they may be taken back to the wild. Przewalski's horse, for example, became extinct in the wild but has since been bred in captivity. Now there are herds of these wild horses in their old home around the Gobi Desert. Other species are defined as "threatened", or in danger of becoming extinct. According to the degree of threat they may be considered "critically endangered", "endangered" or "vulnerable".

Amphibians 6,347 known species; 1,895 threatened
Fishes 30,700 known species; 1,414 threatened
Birds 9,990 known species; 1,223 threatened
Mammals 5,488 known species; 1,142 threatened
Molluscs 81,000 known species; 1,036 threatened
Insects 950,000 known species; 711 threatened
Crustaceans 40,000 known species; 606 threatened
Reptiles 8,734 known species; 469 threatened
Corals 2,175 known species; 235 threatened

Dodo

Last seen alive

Sabre-toothed tiger 12,000 years ago
Woolly mammoth 10,000 years ago
Moa 1,000 years ago
Aurochs (giant wild ox) 1627
Aepyornis (elephant bird) 1649
Dodo 1681
Steller's sea cow 1768
Great auk 1844
Tarpan (wild horse) 1851
Labrador duck 1875
Quagga (zebra-like creature) 1883
Pilori muskrat 1902
Badlands bighorn sheep 1905
Japanese grey wolf 1905
Passenger pigeon 1914
Carolina parakeet 1918
California grizzly bear 1922
Schomburgk's deer 1938
Arabian ostrich 1941
Euler's flycatcher 1955
Eskimo curlew 1963
Guam flying fox 1968
Pyrenean ibex 2000
Yangtze River dolphin 2006
Western black rhinoceros 2006
Madeiran large white butterfly 2007

www.bbc.co.uk/dinosaurs search

Lost and found

Although many animals have been declared extinct, some have been rediscovered. The Yunnan box turtle was believed to have died out, but one was sold in a market in China in 2004, since when other specimens have been found. The Cyprus spiny mouse was thought to have vanished in 1980, but four animals were identified in 2007. The Tasman booby is a large seabird that was apparently hunted to extinction by hungry sailors in the late 18th century, but in 2009 DNA testing proved that another species, the Masked booby, was identical to the 'lost' one.

Saving the turtle

Despite being on Earth for over 100 million years, marine turtles have become endangered in recent times as a result of human activity. This includes hunting them for their meat and shells and for use in traditional medicine, stealing their eggs, destroying and polluting their habitats and nesting beaches and killing them by accidentally catching them in fishing nets.

There are seven main turtle species that are endangered:

- Green turtle • Loggerhead • Flatback • Hawksbill
- Leatherback • Olive ridley • Kemp's ridley

Green turtles, which can weigh up to 270 kg (600 lb), were the main ingredient of turtle soup, once considered a great delicacy in the UK and USA. As they became scarce and expensive and catching them was banned, imitation or 'mock' turtle soup, which uses other meats, was served instead. The Mock Turtle in Alice in Wonderland was based on the joke that it was made from a creature called a Mock Turtle.

The beaches where turtles lay 100–150 eggs at a time are protected in many countries. Some have established conservation projects, including Turtle Islands National Park, Malaysia, where the first hatchery (a safe place for turtle eggs to hatch so that they are not taken by predators or poachers) was set up 1966, and the Tortuguero National Park, Costa Rica, the main nesting site for the Leatherback turtle, in 1976. Similar programmes are in operation in the USA, Brazil, Gabon, Thailand, India, Bali, Australia and other countries.

Marine turtle

Pollution fact file

Pollution happens when unwanted gases and other materials escape into the environment. It causes waste, financial losses and damage to human, animal and plant health. Huge growth in industry and in the world's population in the last 100 years have led to more and more industrial processes and pollution. Deliberate dumping and accidents such as oil spillages have seriously affected the Earth's air, land and water.

Loggers cutting down rainforest in Borneo

Air pollution

Most air pollution comes from burning fossil fuels (coal, oil and gas) and solid waste, or from gases released into the air. Carbon monoxide from vehicle exhausts is poisonous because it prevents the absorption of oxygen. Nitrogen oxide reacts with sunlight to produce smog (a combination of smoke and fog).

Acid rain

Acid rain is caused when nitrogen oxide, sulphur dioxide and other chemicals from volcanic eruptions and human sources combine with rain and fall as acid. It can damage buildings, kill fish and harm trees and other plants.

Land pollution

Soil can be damaged by the dumping of chemicals, toxic (poisonous), radioactive and other waste as well as the overuse of pesticides and fertilizers. Polluted land is unsafe for anything to live on.

Global warming

Greenhouse gases in Earth's atmosphere, such as carbon dioxide, nitrous oxide, water vapour and methane, help to trap heat and stop too much of it escaping into space. Without these gases, the Earth would not be warm enough for us to live on. But more and more greenhouse gases are being released into the atmosphere from human activities, and too much heat is being trapped. The Earth became 0.5°C (0.9°F) warmer during the 20th century and a further rise of even a couple of degrees will damage its natural balance.

10:10

Founded in the UK in 2009, 10:10 is a campaign that aims to cut carbon emissions by 10 per cent by 2010. It has the support of the British Government and major political parties, celebrities and private individuals, schools and colleges, newspapers and businesses.

Destroying forests

About 90,000 sq km (34,749 sq miles) of forest are cut down every year worldwide to obtain timber or to clear land so it can be used for farming. This is about the same area as Portugal.

Cutting down forests increases the amount of carbon dioxide in the atmosphere, which can affect climate and destroy the homes of many animals and plants.

Country	Average annual forest loss 2000–2005
Brazil	34,660 sq km (13,382 sq miles)
Indonesia	14,448 sq km (5,578 sq miles)
Sudan	11,780 sq km (4,548 sq miles)
Zambia	5,322 sq km (2,055 sq miles)
Mexico	3,950 sq km (1,525 sq miles)

City skyline in smog

How much water?

People worldwide use 3,802,300,000,000,000 litres (8,035,600,000,000,000 pt) of water every year. On average everybody in the world uses 633,000 litres (1,337,767 pt) a year, or 1,734 litres (3,665 pt) a day. Of this, 9 per cent (156 litres [330 pt]) a day is used in homes, 20 per cent (347 litres [733 pt]) by industry and 71 per cent (1,231 litres [2,602 pt]) by agriculture.

In the UK we use 163,000 litres (344,480 pt) per head a year – 9,500,000,000,000 litres (20,100,000,000,000 pt) in total.

Household water usage

Brushing teeth (tap off) 2.5 litres (5.3 pt)
Brushing teeth (tap on) 5 litres (10.6 pt)
Toilet flush 5–20 litres (10.6–42.3 pt)
Shower (per minute) 22 litres (46.5 pt)
Washing machine 120 litres (253.6 pt)
Bath (full) 170 litres (359.3 pt)
Washing car 200 litres (422.7 pt)
Watering garden (1 hour) 600–1,500 litres (1,268–3,170 pt)

Worst polluters

Carbon dioxide (CO_2) pollution enters the atmosphere from three main sources – burning fossil fuel (coal and oil), cement manufacturing and gas burning.

These figures show the total amounts produced by some of the leading industrial countries in 2008 measured in tonnes of carbon, one of the components of carbon dioxide, rather than the weight of CO_2. CO_2 is produced naturally by animals, forest fires and other sources. But natural production has been overtaken by the amount produced by human activities. More carbon dioxide in the atmosphere increases the amount of heat absorbed, and this leads to global warming (see Pollution fact file).

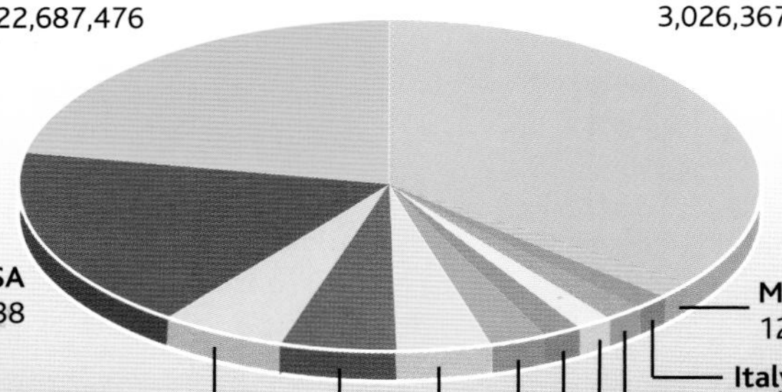

Worst oil tanker spills

About two million tonnes of oil are spilled into the sea every year from oil tankers, mostly during collisions or other accidents. Most spills are small (7 tonnes or less), but some are much more serious. When huge quantities of oil are discharged into the sea and washed up on shorelines they harm many birds and other creatures.

The 1989 grounding of the *Exxon Valdez* in Prince William Sound, Alaska, caused the USA's worst oil spill. The quantity spilled was smaller than the spills listed (35,000 tonnes), but thousands of birds, fish, otters, seals and whales were killed.

Atlantic Empress and ***Aegean Captain***, off Tobago, 1979, 287,000 tonnes
ABT Summer, off Angola, 1991, 260,000 tonnes
Castillio de Bellver, off Saldanha Bay, South Africa, 1983, 252,000 tonnes
Olympic Bravery, off Ushant, France, 1976, 250,000 tonnes
Amoco Cadiz, off Finistère, France, 1978, 223,000 tonnes

Smog

Smog – a word that combines 'smoke' and 'fog' – resulting from smoke from coal fires during cold weather – was once the UK's worst type of air pollution. The 'Great Smog' of 1952 killed as many as 12,000 people in London.

www.environment-agency.gov.uk search

A brief history of rubbish

The ancient world

In ancient times, nomadic peoples simply left their rubbish and moved on. Once people settled in villages, they were faced with the problem of having to dispose of rubbish where they lived. Often they just covered it with earth. The first anti-dumping law was issued in Athens, Greece in 320 BC, when citizens were compelled to bury their rubbish or put it in pits outside the city.

The Middle Ages

In medieval cities, people often threw their rubbish into the street, causing the spread of rats, mice – and disease. In London, kites and ravens scavenged among the rubbish tips. The birds were so important that killing one was punishable by death.

The 19th century

Rag-and-bone men were a common sight in 19th-century streets. They went from house to house with a horse and cart, gathering anything that could be re-sold. Dustmen collected cinders from home fires to be used in brickmaking; human waste and horse manure were taken to farms for fertilizer; and dog droppings were used in the leather tanning trade. The first rubbish-burning incinerator, called The Destructor, was built in Nottingham in 1874. The first dustbin appeared in Paris, France in 1883.

The 20th century

During the 20th century, thousands of new, disposable goods were invented and fewer people had open fires so more rubbish was thrown away. Disused electronic equipment including TVs, computers, mobile phones and fax machines began to join the growing rubbish dumps.

The 21st century

Since the start of the new millennium, the use of plastic bags and amount of food packaging have been reduced. Taxes on landfill and legislation have encouraged more recycling: over 85% of the materials used in motor vehicles must be recycled when they are scrapped, and many products, from printer cartridges to batteries, can now be returned to their manufacturers and reused rather than being disposed of.

Household waste

per person per year (OECD countries only)

Ireland
800 kg (1,764 lb)
Norway
800 kg (1,764 lb)
USA
760 kg (1,676 lb)
Denmark
740 kg (1,631 lb)
Switzerland
700 kg (1,543 lb)
Australia
689 kg (1,518 lb)
Luxembourg
680 kg (1,499 lb)
The Netherlands
625 kg (1,379 lb)
Spain
600 kg (1,323 lb)
Austria
585 kg (1,290 lb)
UK
585 kg (1,290 lb)

How much rubbish is that?

Every person in the UK produces more than half a tonne of household rubbish every year, which means that the UK as a whole produces 30 million tonnes. That's enough to fill dustbins stretching from the Earth to the Moon.

A further 312.4 million tonnes – over five tonnes per person – comes from demolition and construction – bricks, soil, etc (109 million), mining and quarrying (105 million tonnes), industrial waste (45 million), commercial waste (35 million), dredged spoils from rivers and harbours (17 million), sewage (1 million) and agriculture (400,000).

How long to rot

Cotton rags 1–5 months
Paper 2–5 months
Orange peel up to 6 months
Wool socks 1–5 years
Cigarette ends 1–12 years
Plastic-coated drink cartons 5 years
Plastic bags 10–20 years
Photo film 20–30 years
Leather shoes 25–50 years
Artificial fibre clothes (nylon, etc) 30–40 years
Tin cans 50–100 years

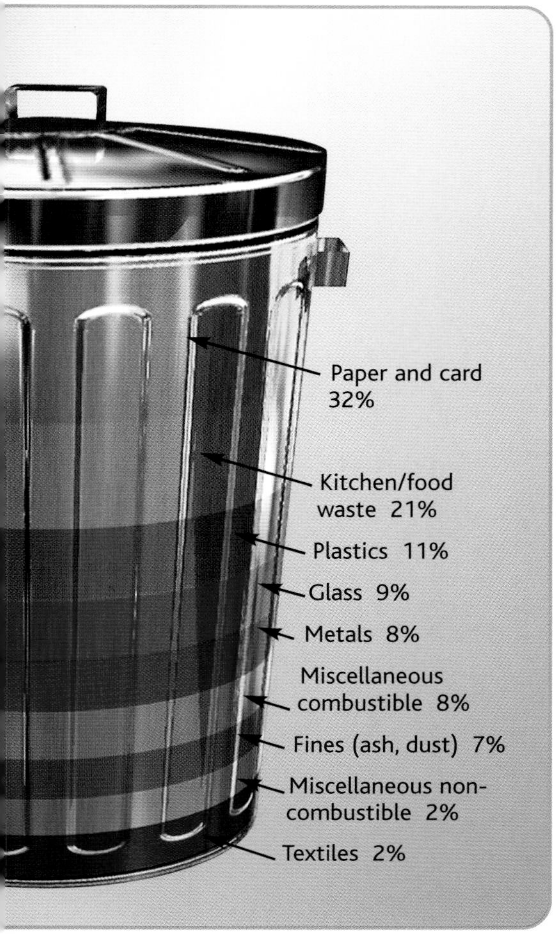

Where does it go?

Landfills

Most waste ends up underground – in giant municipal pits, or landfill sites, where it can rot out of sight. These are usually lined to prevent dangerous chemicals seeping into the ground. However, many discarded objects take decades, even centuries to break down, and we are running out of suitable places to bury waste.

Incineration

Burning rubbish is another solution. Burning gets rid of most kinds of waste and the heat can be converted into energy for other uses. The problem is that incineration releases harmful gases, some of which may contribute to global warming.

www.wasteonline.org.uk search

Compost is recycled organic waste

Recycling

Recycling uses old waste to make new products. It cuts down the amount of rubbish and saves natural resources by reducing the need for new raw materials. Items most suitable for recycling are organic matter (plant and animal) which can be composted and used as fertilizer, metals (such as aluminium cans), glass and paper.

Reduce and reuse

The most sustainable solution is to reduce the amount of waste we create. Compared with 50 years ago, food cans are 50 per cent lighter, yoghurt pots are 60 per cent lighter, glass bottles are 50 per cent lighter and plastic carrier bags are half as thick. Shoppers can help by choosing not to buy goods with lots of packaging or disposable containers, as these make up 10–20 per cent of all domestic rubbish.

Ways to reduce waste

1 Use a shopping bag and refuse unnecessary carrier bags
2 Buy refills
3 Buy fruits and vegetables loose, not pre-packed
4 Buy recycled goods
5 Buy reusable nappies
6 Buy soft drinks in large bottles and pour into smaller bottles for daily use
7 Reuse wrapping paper, packing materials and envelopes
8 Pack your lunch in a reusable box rather than foil or clingfilm
9 Choose durable products over disposable ones, eg rechargeable batteries
10 Donate unwanted clothes to charity shops or jumble sales
11 Donate unwanted furniture to a furniture recycling project
12 Buy drinks in glass bottles – they can be reused 20 times
13 If it's broken, mend it – don't throw it away!
14 Return clothes hangers to dry cleaners
15 Take glass, cans, paper and cardboard to recycling banks
16 Compost leftover food, garden waste, paper (in small amounts) and vacuum cleaner dust

The WEEE Man

Designed by Paul Bonomini and displayed at the Eden Project in Cornwall, UK, the WEEE (Waste Electrical and Electronic Equipment) Man stands 7 metres (23 ft) tall. He represents the amount of these goods the average British person throws away in a lifetime, a total of more than 3 tonnes, including fridges, computers, microwaves, TVs, mobile phones and computers.

4

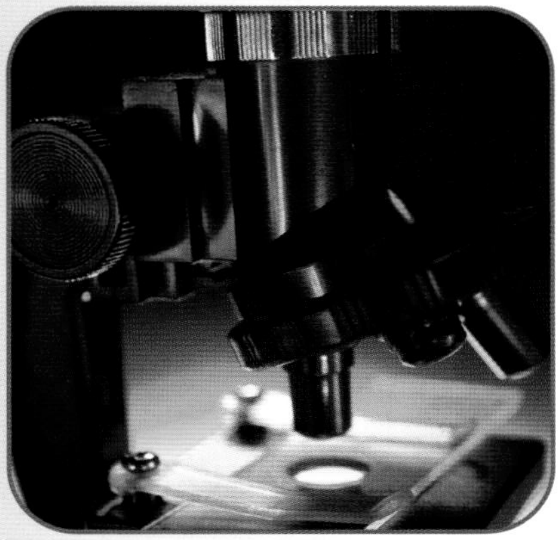

Science & Technology

AquaPenguin

German design and technology company Festo's Bionic Learning Network has created a robot penguin that can perform in water just like a real penguin using flippers and tail at speeds of up to 5 km/h (3 mph) – it is even able to swim backwards! It has a flexible 77-cm (30-in) plastic body and weighs 9.6 kg (21 lb). It is powered by electric motors and uses 3-D sonar to detect obstacles in the water and navigate round them. Its practical applications include designing equipment that performs as efficiently as the creatures they copy while using little energy.

How dense?

A cubic metre (m^3) (35.31 ft^3) of pure water weighs 1,000 kg (2,204.62 lb) or one tonne. Materials that have a density greater than water sink, and those that are less dense float.

Lightweight metals such as aluminium and titanium are important to engineers – for example, for building aircraft that need to be strong but light enough to fly. These are the average densities of some of the substances around us.

	kg/m^3	(lb/ft^3)
Air at 0°C	1.29	(0.08)
Styrofoam	100	(6.24)
Balsa wood	150	(9.36)
Cork	240	(14.98)
Steam	600	(37.46)
Petrol	730	(45.57)
Oak	750	(46.82)
Butter	900	(56.19)
Paper	900	(56.19)
Ice	920	(57.43)
Olive oil	920	(57.43)
Rubber	940	(58.68)
Wax	950	(59.31)
Pure water at 0°C	1,000	(62.43)
Milk	1,030	(64.30)
Sea water	1,030	(64.30)
Ebony	1,200	(74.91)
Spider silk	1,260	(78.66)
Coal	1,400	(87.40)
Bone	1,800	(112.37)
Brick	2,100	(131.10)
Salt	2,165	(135.16)
Carbon	2,267	(141.52)
Chalk	2,300	(143.58)
China	2,300	(143.58)
Concrete	2,300	(143.58)
Sand	2,500	(156.07)
Glass	2,600	(162.31)
Aluminium	2,700	(168.56)
Marble	2,700	(168.56)
Human tooth enamel	2,900	(181.04)
Diamonds	3,500	(218.50)
Titanium	4,507	(281.36)
The Earth (average for whole planet)	5,520	(344.60)
Iron	7,874	(491.56)
Copper	8,920	(556.86)
Silver	10,490	(654.86)
Lead	11,340	(707.93)
Mercury	13,570	(847.15)
Tungsten	19,250	(1,201.74)
Gold	19,300	(1,204.86)
Platinum	21,090	(1,316.61)
Osmium	22,610	(1,411.5)

Strange studies

Angelology Angels
Aphnology Wealth
Biometrology The effect of weather on people
Cereology Crop circles
Cryology Snow, ice and frozen ground
Cryptology Codes and ciphers
Diabology Devils
Draconology Dragons
Enigmatology Puzzles
Eremology Deserts
Fromology Cheese
Garbology Rubbish
Gelotology Laughter
Googlology The Google search engine
Googology Large numbers
Hypnology Sleep
Ichnology Fossilized footprints
Kalology Beauty
Limacology Slugs
Loimology Plagues
Momilogy Mummies
Nanotechnology Very small objects
Nephology Clouds
Osmology Smells
Pharology Lighthouses
Polemology Wars
Pomology Fruit-growing
Rhinology Noses
Siphonapterology Fleas
Teratology Monsters
Toxicology Poisons
Tsiology Tea
Ufology Unidentified flying objects
Vermeology Worms
Xylology Wood

Cork is harvested from cork trees. Its buoyancy makes it useful for such products as fishing floats. Lifejackets used by sailors and fishermen were once made of blocks of cork.

See also
Conversions: page 84

www.exploratorium.edu search

Acids and alkalis

The pH (potential Hydrogen) system was invented in 1909 by Danish chemist Søren Sørensen (1868–1939). In this, pH is a measure of the concentration of hydrogen ions, which shows whether something is acid or base (also known as alkali).

Pure water has a pH of 7.0. Substances that have a pH of less are acid. Substances with a pH of more than 7.0 are base (alkali). Acids make lemon juice and vinegar taste sharp, and acid rain harms trees and other plants. The traditional way of testing pH is by using litmus paper – acidic substances turn blue litmus red, while alkalis turn red litmus blue.

Substance	pH	Substance	pH
Hydrochloric acid	0	Orange juice	3.7
Car battery acid	1.0	Wine/beer	4.0
Gastric (digestive) juices	1–3	Tomato juice	4.3
Lime juice	2.3	Normal rainfall	5.6
Lemon juice	2.4	Saliva	6.4–6.9
Acid rain	2.4–3.6	Milk	6.6
Apple	3.0	Pure water	7.0
Vinegar	3.0	Human blood	7.4
Grapefruit	3.2	Sea water	7.8–8.3

A rainbow is created when sunlight passes through water droplets.

Spectrum colours

The electromagnetic spectrum includes all forms of light, from radio waves and microwaves at one end of the scale to X-rays and gamma rays at the other. In between is visible or white light, which is made up of a range of colours.

We can see the individual colours when they are split up by water droplets and form a rainbow, or by passing white light through a prism. The colours of the spectrum are red, orange, yellow, green, blue, indigo and violet.

Sound levels

The decibel (dB) is a way of measuring sound. Sounds of 80–90 dB or more can damage hearing and it is dangerous for people to work in sound levels of more than 90 dB.

Sounds above 130 dB become painful, and people should wear hearing protectors with sounds of more than 140 dB. A decibel level of more than 150 dB can cause permanent deafness.

Silence	0 dB
Rustle of leaves	10 dB
Quiet whisper at 5 m (16.25 ft); library	20–30 dB
Normal conversation; soft music	30 dB
Sailing boat	35 dB
Quiet countryside; ticking watch	40 dB
Inside average home	45–50 dB
Restaurant; office; loud conversation	50–60 dB
Background music; motorboat	60 dB
Hairdryer	60–80 dB
Workshop	65 dB
Radio; telephone ring; busy traffic; orchestra; loud TV	70 dB
Inside car; underground train	80 dB
Pneumatic drill at 15 m (48.75 ft); Niagara Falls; top level of comfort	85 dB
Very loud snore	88 dB
Heavy traffic at 15 m (48.75 ft); roaring lion	90 dB
Loud shout at 15 m (48.75 ft); lawnmower; chainsaw; blender	100 dB
Heavy truck 1 m (3.25 ft) away; orchestra playing Beethoven's Ninth Symphony	105 dB
Circular saw at 1 m (3.25 ft); car horn at 5 m (16.25 ft)	110 dB
Shouting in someone's ear	114 dB
Personal stereo	115 dB
Loud scream; thunder; explosion; submarine engine room	120 dB
Loud rock music	120–130 dB
Racing car	125 dB
Motorbike (without silencer)	130 dB
Banger; jumbo jet takeoff at 30 m (98.4 ft)	140 dB
Rock music (peak at 5 m [16.25 ft] from speaker)	150 dB
Level at ear of person firing powerful rifle	160 dB
Launch of *Saturn V* space rocket	172 dB
Blue whale call	188 dB
Volcanic eruption	272 dB

Brightness scale

A candela is a unit of light intensity. It was originally equivalent to the amount given out by a candle, but is now more precise.

Candelas per m^2 (ft^2)	
Overcast sky	2,000 (186)
Moon	2,500 (232)
Clear sky (average)	8,000 (743)
Candle (brightest spot)	10,000 (929)
Domestic light bulb	100,000 (9,290)
Sun at Equator	1,600,000 (148,645)
Flash of lightning	80,000,000 (7,432,243)
Atom bomb	2,000,000,000 (185,806,087)

A flash of lightning gives out 80,000,000 candelas

What is an element?

The elements are sometimes called the building blocks of the Universe because everything in the Universe – including ourselves – is made of them. The nucleus of each element consists of atoms with the same number of protons. Each element is unique, although elements can exist in different forms – for example, carbon may be soft graphite or hard diamond. Elements cannot usually be broken down into any other substance.

There are about 118 elements altogether, and 91 occur naturally on Earth. Others can be created in laboratories, but in minute quantities and they have very short lifespans of only thousandths of a second. Each element is also known by a one- or two-letter symbol as well as its name; for example, Fe is iron.

A chemical compound is a combination of two or more elements linked together, which can be broken down again into their constituent parts but no further. Water, for example, is made up of two hydrogen atoms linked to one oxygen atom. Salt, or sodium chloride, is a compound of sodium and chlorine.

Krypton and kryptonite

In 1904 William Ramsay, a British scientist, received the Nobel Prize for Chemistry for his discovery of gaseous elements including the gas krypton (named after the Greek word for 'hidden'), which he had found in 1898. Forty years later, 'Krypton' was the name given to the planet from which comic book superhero Superman came, with the imaginary element 'kryptonite' claimed to be the only thing that could take away his power. The real krypton is a rare element, one of six known as 'noble gases', so called because, like 'noble metals' such as gold, they react very little with other chemicals such as acids. It is used in special lasers and photographic and other light bulbs.

Swedish scientist

Jöns Jakob Berzelius (1779–1848) discovered four elements, silicon, selenium, thorium and cerium. He also invented the chemical symbols for elements, scientific terms such as catalyst and protein, and laboratory equipment including filter papers and rubber tubing.

See also
Air transport: pages 216–17

Various weights of gold in a gold refinery

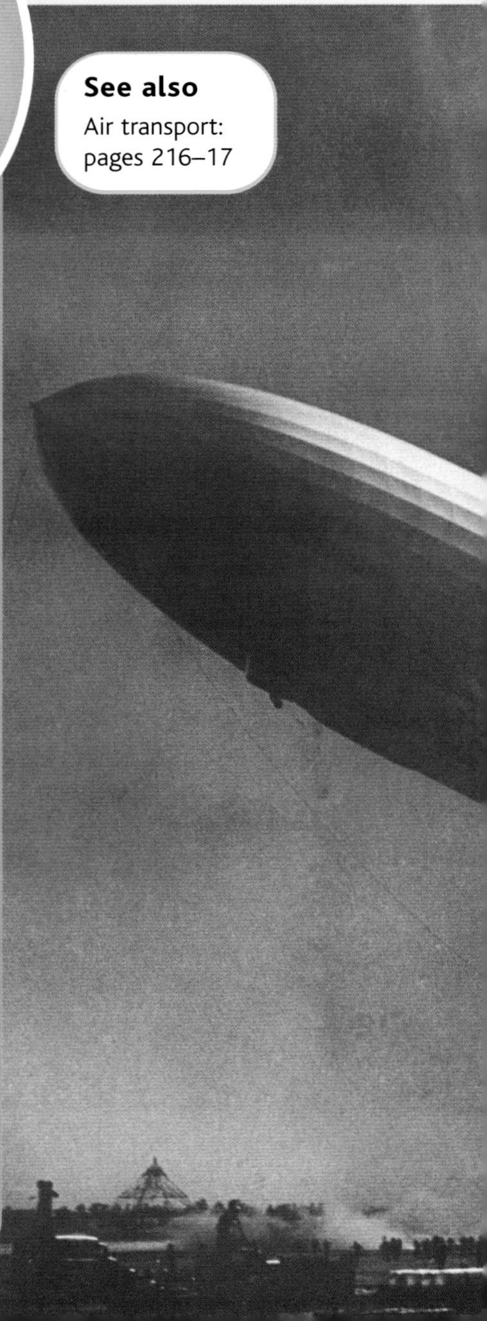

The heaviest elements

● Osmium
Osmium is the heaviest element (22.61 g/cm^3 [13.07 oz/in^3]). It was discovered in 1803. It was named after the Greek word for smell because it smelt bad. Osmium is very hard, and is used to make hard-wearing points, such as the nibs of fountain pens.

● Platinum
Platinum was used before anyone realized that it was an element. It weighs almost as much as osmium (21.45 g/cm^3 [12.39 oz/in^3]) and is used to make jewellery. It is also used in catalytic converters in cars to reduce the pollution from exhaust gases.

● Plutonium
Plutonium was discovered in 1941 and is a heavy and highly radioactive metal. It is used as a nuclear fuel and in nuclear weapons – a kilogram of plutonium produces an explosion equivalent to 20,000 tonnes of TNT.

● Gold
Gold is the best-known of all heavy metals – though at 19.29 g/cm^3 (11.15 oz/in^3) it is less heavy than the others here. Gold has been prized since ancient times and has many uses beyond coins and jewellery.

The lightest elements

● Hydrogen

Hydrogen is the simplest and lightest element, and the most common – 93 per cent of all atoms in the universe are hydrogen atoms. On Earth, it is relatively rare in the atmosphere – only 5 of every 100 million litres (8.8 of 176 million pints) of air are hydrogen, but hydrogen combined with oxygen forms all the water in the world. Hydrogen is very light. This is why it was used in balloons carrying human passengers: the second-ever flight, in Paris on 1 December 1783, was in a hydrogen balloon. Hydrogen was also used in giant airships until 6 May 1937, when the giant German airship *Hindenburg* exploded, killing 36 people, at Lakehurst, New Jersey, USA. Today, hydrogen fuel cells are used to power clean-energy cars.

● Helium

Helium is twice as heavy as hydrogen, but it is still only one-seventh the weight of air. Unlike hydrogen, helium does not burn, so it is used in modern airships.

● Lithium

Lithium was discovered in 1817 and takes its name from the Latin word for rock, although it is actually a metal. Lithium is so light and so soft that it can be easily cut with a knife. It floats because it is half as heavy as water and lighter than some types of wood. It is used to make lithium batteries.

● Potassium and sodium

Both were discovered in 1807. Both are metals that are lighter than water. In a laboratory, potassium and sodium are usually kept in paraffin because if they come into contact with water they will catch fire. Potassium is vital for plant growth and human well-being – our bodies contain about 140 g (5 oz) of it. Sodium is relatively common as part of a compound: in combination with chlorine it is ordinary table salt.

Female element discoverers

Marie Curie was the first woman to discover an element, radium, for which she received a Nobel prize in 1911 (her daughter Irène was the second woman to get a Nobel prize for her work on elements). Her experiments with radium gave Marie leukaemia, from which she died.

Lise Meitner (Austria), co-discoverer of protactinium, was the second female to discover an element – meitnerium was later named after her. Ida Eva Noddack (Germany), was the third female discoverer (rhenium), jointly with her husband Walter Noddack, and Marguerite Perey (France) the fourth (francium).

The *Hindenburg*, a giant airship filled with hydrogen, bursts into flames

Elements on Earth

There is calcium in the Earth and sea in the form of calcium carbonate. Sodium exists in the form of sodium chloride, the salt in the sea and on our tables.

The quantities of both calcium and sodium are so vast that these elements are considered unlimited.

There are quite small amounts of some precious metals on Earth, which is why they are so valuable. For example, there are about one million tonnes of silver and 15,000 tonnes of gold. Elements are constantly being taken from Earth, but new discoveries are being made.

www.webelements.com search

Leonardo da Vinci

Italian Leonardo da Vinci (1452–1519) is best known as a painter, anatomist, sculptor and architect. *The Last Supper* and *Mona Lisa* are among the most famous paintings of all time.

But he is also hailed as one of the greatest inventors. Among his notebooks he left plans for countless advanced machines, often with descriptions written in secret mirror writing. Many of them were never built, but they anticipated modern inventions, often by hundreds of years. They include the following:

- Air conditioner
- Alarm clock
- Crane
- Diving suit and diving bell
- Double-hull ship
- Flying machine
- Gas mask
- Gears
- Giant catapults and crossbows
- Helicopter
- Lifebelt
- Magnetic compass
- Mileometer
- Multi-barrelled machine gun
- Parachute
- Revolving stage
- Shrapnel bomb
- Spectacles
- Steam engine
- Tank-like armoured vehicle
- Telescope
- Water turbine

Crazy inventions

Safety coffin

Frank Vester received a patent for this device in 1868, one of many similar inventions of the period – which allows anyone accidentally buried alive to summon help by means of a bell, or even to escape from his early grave via a ladder.

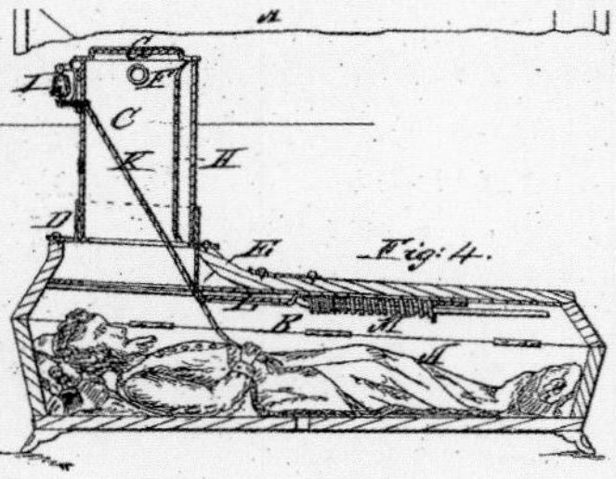

Dog scuba-diving apparatus

This 2001 invention by Dwane L. Folsom was designed for a performing dog called Shadow, but could be adapted for use by any animal.

What is a patent?

A patent is granted by a government to an inventor. It gives him or her the right for a limited period – usually 20 years – to stop others from making, using or selling the invention without the inventor's permission. The patent is territorial and protected only in the country in which it is patented. The first patent was granted to Filippo Brunelleschi in Florence in 1421, for a barge crane to transport marble.

Automatic haircutter

Patented by John J. Boax in 1951, it was designed to make hair stand on end by means of a vacuum attachment. It would then be trimmed off by mechanical cutters.

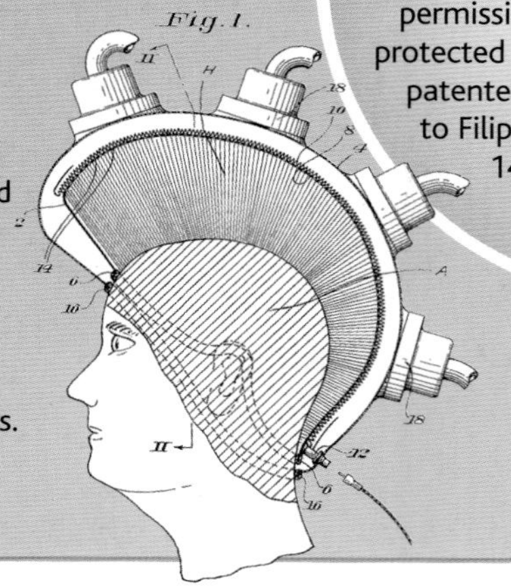

Scream muffler

Moira J. and Frank M. Figone patented this foam-insulated muffler in 1989. Users can shout and scream without disturbing their neighbours.

Thumb wrestling ring

Devised by Richard B. Hartman in 1991, players poke their thumbs into a miniature wrestling ring and fight with each other.

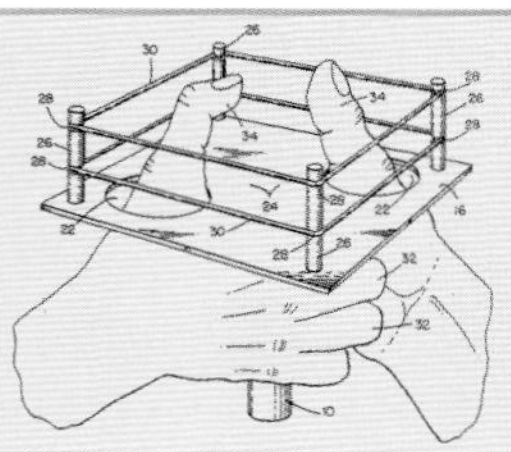

100+ years of everyday inventions 1900s

1903 the safety razor was invented by King Camp Gillette

1904 the ice cream cone was invented by Italo Marcioni

1906 the electric washing machine was invented by Alva J. Fisher

1907 vacuum cleaners with bags were invented by J. Murray Spangler

1913 the crossword puzzle was invented by Arthur Wynne

1913 the zip fastener was invented by Gideon Sundback

1920 the tea bag was invented by Joseph Krieger

1924 frozen food was invented by Clarence Birdseye

1926 the aerosol spray was invented by Erik Rotheim

1927 the pop-up toaster was invented by Charles Strite

1928 elastoplast was invented by Horatio Nelson Smith

1928 sliced bread was invented by Otto Rohwedder

1931 the electric razor was invented by Col. Jacob Schick

1934 the trampoline was invented by George Nissen and Larry Griswold

1938 the ballpoint pen was invented by László Biro

1938 instant coffee was invented by the Nestlé company

1945 the microwave oven was invented by Percy LeBaron Spencer

1945 Tupperware (food containers) was invented by Earl W. Tupper

1947 the long-playing record was invented by Goldmark

1950 the credit card was invented by Frank X. McNamara

The modern trampoline was invented by George Nissen when he was a student

Brainchildren: young inventors

Horatio Adams
Adams was only 16 when he assisted his father, Thomas, in his experiments with chicle, the dried sap of a Mexican jungle tree. This led to the invention of chewing gum.

Charles Babbage
Babbage was 19 when he first thought of the idea of the mechanical computer.

Louis Braille
He invented Braille, the raised-dot writing used by blind people, at the age of 15. Louis himself was blind.

Peter Chilvers
Chilvers was 12 when he invented boardsailing (windsurfing) in 1958 off Hayling Island, UK.

Frank Epperson
The Popsicle or ice lolly was invented by 11-year-old Frank Epperson of San Francisco, California, in 1905. He had the idea when he left a fruit drink out during a freezing winter night and originally called it the Epsicle. He did not apply for a patent until 1923, by which time his son had renamed it Popsicle.

Chester Greenwood
Greenwood of Farmington, Maine, USA, was aged 15 in 1873 when he invented earmuffs. He started Greenwood's Ear Protector Factory and made a fortune by supplying his product to US soldiers in World War I.

Sam Houghton
At the age of three Sam Houghton of Buxton, UK, invented the double-headed broom. It was patented in 2007 (GB Patent No. 2,438,091) when he was aged five, making him the youngest-ever British patentee.

Walter Lines
British schoolboy Lines invented the scooter at the age of 15. He later founded Triang Toys, once Britain's leading toy manufacturer.

George Nissen
George Nissen (1914-2010), an American gymnast, came up with the idea of the trampoline when he was still at school. He built his first prototype in 1934 and started a company to manufacture them. Trampolining became so popular that in 2000 it was introduced as an Olympic sport.

Austin Meggitt
American schoolboy Meggitt was nine when he invented a device for carrying a baseball bat, ball and glove safely on the handlebars of a bicycle. In 2000 he received US Patent No. 6,029,874.

John J. Stone-Parker
In 1989, when he was only four years old, John and his sister, Elaine W. Stone-Parker, invented a star-shaped gadget to prevent ice from slipping out of a drinking-glass. He is the youngest holder of a patent in the United States.

See also
Computer timeline: page 86

2000s

- **1955** Lego was invented by Gotfried Kirk Christiansen
- **1956** Velcro was invented by Georges de Mestral
- **1958** videotape was invented by A.M. Poniatoff
- **1963** the ring-pull can was invented by Alcoa
- **1971** the digital watch was invented by George Theiss and Willy Crabtree
- **1971** E-mail was invented by Ray Tomlinson
- **1971** the pocket calculator was invented by the Sharp company
- **1974** the personal computer was invented by MITS
- **1975** the digital camera was invented by Steven Sasson and Kodak
- **1979** Post-it notes were invented by Spencer Silver and 3M
- **1979** the mobile phone was invented by NTT
- **1979** the Walkman was invented by Akio Morita
- **1981** the compact disc was invented by Philips
- **1982** the camcorder was invented by Sony
- **1989** the World Wide Web was invented by Tim Berners-Lee
- **1994** the GPS (completed) was invented by I. Getting and B. Parkinson
- **2000** the iPod digital music player was invented by Apple Computer, Inc
- **2001** Self-cleaning glass was invented by Kevin Sanderson
- **2008** MyVu launches personal media viewer (video glasses)

Roman numerals

Roman numerals use seven letters (I, V, X, L, C, M and D). A small numeral in front of a larger one is subtracted from it, so 90 is written as X (10) subtracted from C (100) – XC. A small number after a larger one is usually added to it – for example, XI (11).

Roman numerals are still in use today. You can find them in the introduction pages of books (i, ii, iii, iv, etc), on traditional clock and watch faces, in film and TV credits (2007 will appear as MMVII), in serial film titles (such as *Star Wars: Episode III – Revenge of the Sith*). They are also used in the names of sporting events – the Beijing 2008 Olympics will be the XXIX (29th) Games.

Roman	Arabic	Roman	Arabic	Roman	Arabic
I	1	XX	20	CCC	300
II	2	XXX	30	CCCC	400
III	3	XL	40	D	500
IV	4	L	50	DC	600
V	5	LX	60	DCC	700
VI	6	LXX	70	DCCC	800
VII	7	LXXX	80	CM	900
VIII	8	XC	90	M	1,000
IX	9	C	100	MM	2,000
X	10	CC	200		

Mega multiples

Certain prefixes are used in the metric system. The prefixes are the same whether describing weight, such as a kilogram, distance, such as a kilometre, or other measurements.

Prefix	Name	Value
exa-	quintillion	1,000,000,000,000,000,000
peta-	quadrillion	1,000,000,000,000,000
tera-	trillion	1,000,000,000,000
giga-	billion	1,000,000,000
mega-	million	1,000,000
kilo-	thousand	1,000
hecto-	hundred	100
deca-	ten	10
	one	1
deci-	tenth	0.1
centi-	hundredth	0.01
milli-	thousandth	0.001
micro-	millionth	0.000,001
nano-	billionth	0.000,000,001
pico-	trillionth	0.000,000,000,001
femto-	quadrillionth	0.000,000,000,000,001
atto-	quintillionth	0.000,000,000,000,000,001

Useful mathematical formulae

Area of a rectangle	length x height
Area of a triangle	½ length x height
Area of a circle	π x radius^2
Diameter of a circle	radius x 2
Circumference of a circle	π x diameter
Volume of a sphere	$\frac{4}{3}\pi$ x radius^3
Surface of a sphere	$4 \times \pi^2$
Volume of a cylinder	π x radius^2 x height
Curved area of cylinder	2 x π x radius x height
Area of a cone	π x radius x length
Volume of a cone	$\frac{1}{3}\pi$ x radius^2 x height

π = pi, pi = 3.14159265

Mathematical symbols

Symbol	Meaning	Symbol	Meaning
+	Plus or positive	%	Per cent
–	Minus or negative	>	Greater than
±	Plus or minus, positive or negative	<	Less than
x	Multiplied by	√	Square root
÷ or /	Divided by	Σ	Sum of
=	Equal to	π	Pi
≠	Not equal to	°	Degree
~	Of the order of, similar to	∞	Infinity

"Big Ben", London, uses Roman numerals.

Big numbers

The terms used for big numbers differ between the UK and the USA and other parts of the world. A billion used to be a million million in the UK, but a thousand million elsewhere. The UK has changed this definition to match the rest of the world, but other numbers are still different.

Number	Equivalent to	Zeros US	Zeros UK
Trillion	1,000 billion	12	18
Quadrillion	1,000 trillion	15	24
Quintillion	1,000 quadrillion	18	30
Sextillion	1,000 quintillion	21	36
Septillion	1,000 sextillion	24	42
Octillion	1,000 septillion	27	48
Nonillion	1,000 octillion	30	54
Decillion	1,000 nonillion	33	60
Undecillion	1,000 decillion	36	66
Duodecillion	1,000 undecillion	39	72
Tredecillion	1,000 duodecillion	42	78
Quattuordecillion	1,000 tredecillion	45	84
Quindecillion	1,000 quattuordecillion	48	90
Sexdecillion	1,000 quindecillion	51	96

- There are names for even bigger numbers, including a centillion (303 zeros in the USA and 600 zeros in the UK), a trigent-billillion (60,000,003 zeros) and sextent-billillion (1,800,000,003 zeros).
- In 1938, nine-year-old Milton Sirotta came up with the word googol, which means a one followed by 100 zeros. Milton was the nine-year-old nephew of an American mathematician called Edward Kasner (1878–1955).
- A googolplex is an even bigger number – a one with a googol of zeros, or 10 to the googol power. This number is so vast that, as Kasner explained, "... there would not be enough room to write it, if one went to the furthest stars, touring all the nebulae in the Universe and putting down zeros every inch of the way."
- There is no such number as a zillion – the word just means a really huge amount.

www.factmonster.com/mathmoney.html search

Prime numbers

A prime number is a whole number that can be divided only by one and itself, and not by any other number. Examples include 2, 3, 5, 7, 11 and 13. All prime numbers, except for 2, are also odd numbers. There are 168 prime numbers under 1,000.

Regular polygons

A polygon is a shape enclosed by straight lines. Regular polygons have sides of equal length and the angles inside are all the same. A regular polygon fits inside a circle with all its points touching the circumference. An irregular polygon does not.

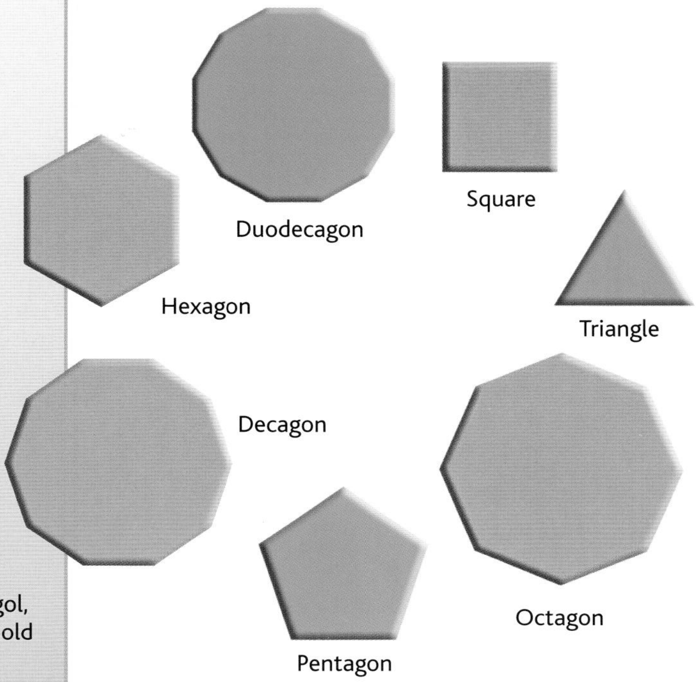

Polygon	Number of sides	Each internal angle	Sum of internal angles
Triangle	3	60°	180°
Square (or quadrilateral)	4	90°	360°
Pentagon	5	108°	540°
Hexagon	6	120°	720°
Heptagon	7	128.57°	900°
Octagon	8	135°	1,080°
Nonagon	9	140°	1,260°
Decagon	10	144°	1,440°
Undecagon	11	147.27°	1,620°
Duodecagon (or dodecagon)	12	150°	1,800°
Quindecagon	15	156°	2,340°
Icosagon	20	162°	3,240°

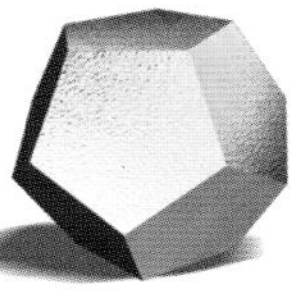
Dodecahedron (12 sides)

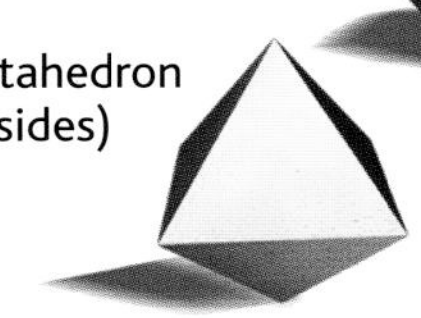
Octahedron (8 sides)

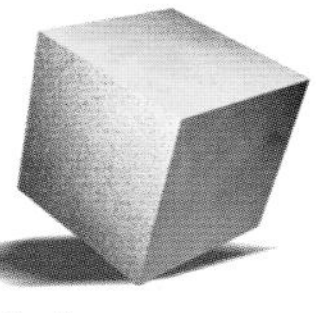
Cube (6 sides)

Tetrahedron (4 sides)

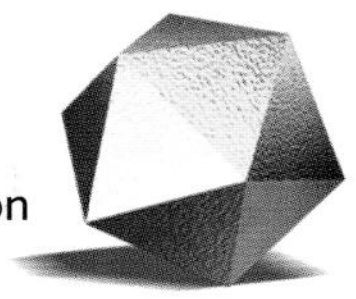
Isosahedron (20 sides)

Regular solids

There are five types of regular solid. All faces on a regular solid are exactly the same shape. If you put a regular solid inside a sphere, all its points will touch the surface of the sphere.

Conversions

There are two systems of measuring length, area, weight, volume and so on – metric and imperial. Here's how to convert between the two different systems.

From	To	Multiply by
Area		
Square centimetres (cm^2)	Square inches (in^2)	0.1550
Square inches (in^2)	Square centimetres (cm^2)	6.4516
Square metres (m^2)	Square feet (ft^2)	10.7639
Square feet (ft^2)	Square metres (m^2)	0.0929
Square metres (m^2)	Square yards (yd^2)	1.1960
Square yards (yd^2)	Square metres (m^2)	0.8361
Square kilometres (km^2)	Square miles (ml^2)	0.3861
Square miles (ml^2)	Square kilometres (km^2)	2.5900
Hectares (ha)	Acres	2.4711
Acres	Hectares (ha)	0.4047
Speed		
Metres per second (m/s)	Feet per second (ft/s)	3.2808
Feet per second (ft/s)	Metres per second (m/s)	0.3048
Kilometres per hour (km/h)	Miles per hour (mph)	0.6214
Miles per hour (mph)	Kilometres per hour (km/h)	1.6093

From	To	Multiply by
Weight		
Grams (g)	Ounces (oz)	0.0353
Ounces (oz)	Grams (g)	28.3495
Kilograms (kg)	Pounds (lb)	2.2046
Pounds (lb)	Kilograms (kg)	0.4536
Stones	Kilograms (kg)	6.3503
Kilograms (kg)	Stones	0.1575
Hundredweight (cwt)	Kilograms (kg)	50.8024
Kilograms (kg)	Hundredweight (cwt)	0.0197
Tonnes	Tons (long)	0.9842
Tons (long)	Tonnes	1.0160
Tonnes	US short tons	1.1023
US short tons	Tonnes	0.9072
Length		
Centimetres (cm)	Inches (in)	0.3937
Inches (in)	Centimetres (cm)	2.5400
Metres (m)	Feet (ft)	3.2808
Feet (ft)	Metres (m)	0.3048
Metres (m)	Yards (yd)	1.0936
Yards (yd)	Metres (m)	0.9144
Kilometres (km)	Miles (ml)	0.6214
Miles (ml)	Kilometres (km)	1.6093

Namesakes

These measurements were named after the people who discovered them.

Ampere is a measure of electrical current. It was named after André-Marie Ampère (French, 1775–1836).

Beaufort scale measures wind speed and was named after Sir Francis Beaufort (British, 1774–1857).

Marie Curie in her laboratory

Bel/decibel is a measure of sound named after Alexander Graham Bell (Scots/USA, 1847–1922).

Celsius is a temperature measure. It was named for Anders Celsius (Swedish, 1701–44).

Curie is a measure of radiation named after Marie Curie (Polish/French, 1867–1934).

Fahrenheit is a measure of temperature named after Gabriel Fahrenheit (German, 1686–1736).

Joule is a measure of energy named after James Prescott Joule (British, 1818–89).

Kelvin is a temperature measure. It was named after William Thomson, Lord Kelvin (British, 1824–1907).

Mercalli scale measures earthquakes. It was named after Giuseppe Mercalli (Italian, 1850–1914).

Mohs' scale measures hardness and was named after Friedrich Mohs (German, 1773–1839).

Ohm/Mho measures electrical resistance. It was named after Georg Simon Ohm (German, 1787–1854).

Richter scale measures earthquakes and was named after Charles Richter (USA, 1900–85).

Volt is a measure of electromagnetic force. It was named after Alessandro Volta (Italian, 1745–1827).

Watt is a measure of power and was named after James Watt (British, 1736–1819).

Volume conversions

From	To	Multiply by
Cubic centimetres (cc)	Cubic inches (in^3)	0.0610
Cubic inches (in^3)	Cubic centimetres (cc)	16.3871
Cubic feet (ft^3)	Cubic metres (m^3)	0.0283
Cubic metres (m^3)	Cubic feet (ft^3)	35.3147
Cubic yards (yd^3)	Cubic metres (m^3)	1.3080
Cubic metres (m^3)	Cubic yards (yd^3)	0.7646
Cubic kilometres (km^3)	Cubic miles (ml^3)	0.2399
Cubic miles (ml^3)	Cubic kilometres (km^3)	4.1682
Litres (l)	Pints	1.7598
Pints	Litres (l)	0.5683
Litres (l)	UK gallons (gal)	0.2200
UK gallons (gal)	Litres (l)	4.5461
Litres (l)	US gallons (gal)	0.2642
US gallons (gal)	Litres (l)	3.78532

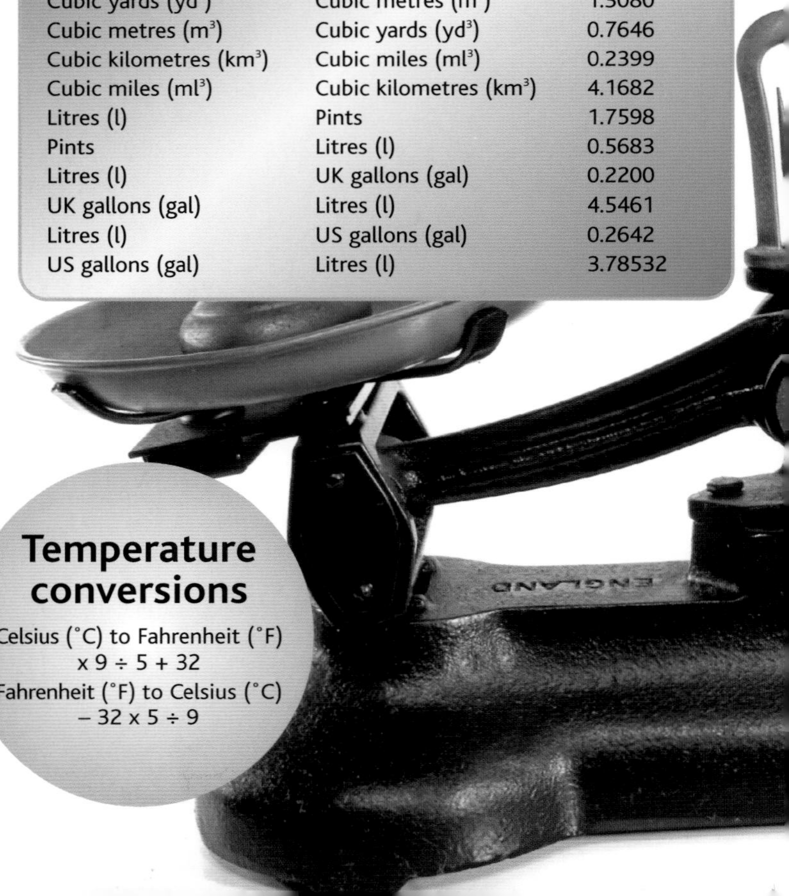

Temperature conversions

Celsius (°C) to Fahrenheit (°F)
x 9 ÷ 5 + 32

Fahrenheit (°F) to Celsius (°C)
– 32 x 5 ÷ 9

The world's smallest

Aircraft The *Bumble Bee II* built by Robert H. Starr (USA) in 1988 measured only 2.7 m (8 ft 10 in) long with a wingspan of 1.68 m (5 ft 6 in). It was destroyed in a crash.

Gun SwissMiniGun 5.5 cm long and weighs 19.8 gm, but is capable of killing a person.

Mobile phone Introduced in 2008, the Modu mobile phone is smaller than a credit card, measuring 72 x 37 x 8 mm (2.8 x 1.5 x 0.3 in) and weighing 40 gm (1.4 oz). It is designed to be slotted into other electronic devices and even incorporated into clothing.

Mini mobile

Weighty words

Acre
An acre describes an area of land and comes from the Old English word *aecer*, meaning a ploughed field. It was the area a team of oxen could plough in one day. In the UK in 1824, an acre was set as 4,840 square yards.

Celsius
A temperature scale invented in 1742 by Swedish astronomer Anders Celsius. A Celsius degree is 1/100th of the difference between the freezing and boiling points of water (0° and 100°).

Fahrenheit
This temperature scale was devised by German physicist Gabriel Fahrenheit. On this scale the freezing point of water is 32°.

Foot
Foot originally meant the average length of an adult foot, and has been used since ancient times. Before France invented the metric system, the French foot was based on the length of the Emperor Charlemagne's foot.

Metre
The metre was introduced in France in June 1799. It was first set as one ten-millionth of a quarter of the circumference of the Earth. It was later set as the distance between two lines on a metal bar which was kept in Sèvres, France. The distance is now more precise. It is the distance light travels in a vacuum in 1/299792458th of a second. A centimetre is 1/100th of a metre. A millimetre is 1/1,000th of a metre and a kilometre is 1,000 metres.

Gram/kilogram
Gram comes from the same ancient Greek word that gave us grammar, and means a marked-off division. A kilogram is 1,000 grams. Kilo comes from the Greek chilioi, meaning one thousand.

Hectare
This is used for measuring land areas and comes from the ancient Greek hekaton, meaning one hundred. One hectare is equivalent to 10,000 square metres or 2.4711 acres.

Hundredweight/ton
A hundredweight is 1/20th of a ton. A British or long hundredweight is 112 pounds, and a long ton is 2,240 pounds. An American or short hundredweight is 100 pounds. A short ton is 2,000 pounds.

Special measurements

Carat
The weight of diamonds and other valuable gems is measured in carats. The word comes from the carob bean, which has a consistent weight of 0.2 of a gram (0.007 oz).

Hand
The height of horses is measured in hands. The measurement is taken from the ground to the highest point on the animal's shoulder. One hand is 10.16 cm (4 in).

Knot
Speed at sea is measured in knots, which is the time it took a ship to travel the length of a knotted rope. A knot is now the same as a nautical mile, which is 1,852 m (6,076 ft).

Point
This is used by typographers and printers and refers to the size of a letter such as an x. One point is equal to 0.3528 mm (0.0139 in), so 6-point type is 2.116 mm (0.083 in) high.

Troy ounce
This name comes from the city of Troyes, France, where dealers in precious stones and metals gathered in medieval times. Gold and other rare metals are still measured in troy ounces (31.1035 g/1.1677 oz).

Computer use worldwide

In 2010 it was estimated that there are 1.35 billion personal computers in use, one for every five people on the planet. Some 311 million of them, one for nearly every person, are in North America (the USA and Canada), with almost as many (302.6 million) in Western Europe. China has seen a huge increase since 2000, when there were just 20.6 million computers in the entire country.

The computer mouse

The first computer mouse – so called because its size, shape and tail-like cable resemble a mouse – was patented by Douglas Engebart (USA) as early as 1968. Mice were not widely used until they were supplied with Apple Macintosh computers from 1984 onwards. Since then most desktop computers have used them. Leading manufacturer Logitech announced in 2008 that it had made its billionth mouse.

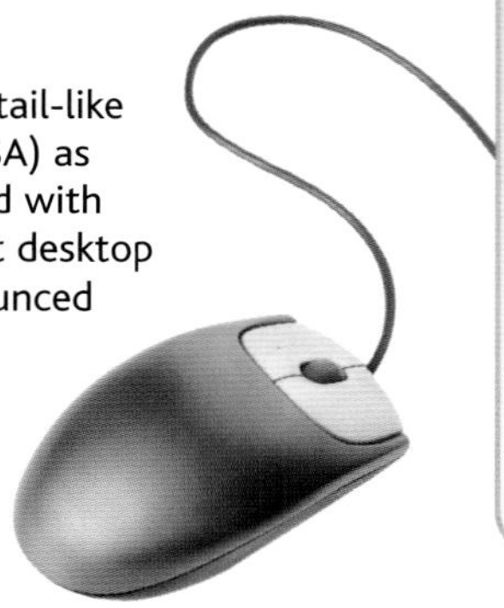

Computer countries

These are the countries with the most computers.

Country	Computers in use 2010 estimate
USA	273,094,500
China	111,540,800
Japan	68,457,600
Germany	66,513,900
UK	57,841,000
Brazil	54,902,800
France	54,880,700
India	53,195,000
Canada	38,131,200
South Korea	31,432,500

Laptops

Although there were some early attempts at making laptops, the first successful model with a screen that folds inside the case was the British-designed Grid Compass 1110, launched in 1982 and used by astronauts on the Space Shuttle. Improvements in displays and battery life, Wi-Fi and the use of lightweight components have led to such advanced models as Apple's MacBook Air. In 2005 the OLPC – One Laptop Per Child – charity was set up to provide inexpensive laptops for people in developing countries. By 2009 over 1 million had been distributed, including the XO-1, specially designed for use by children.

Apple's MacBook Air, 2008

Laptops being used in a school in Africa

Computer timeline

1600s

1642 Blaise Pascal, France, makes a numerical wheel calculator, an early mechanical adding machine

1694 Gottfried von Leibniz, Germany, makes a machine that can multiply numbers

1820 Charles Xavier de Colmar, France, makes an "Arithometer" that can add, subtract, multiply and divide

1822 Charles Babbage, England, devises his Difference Engine

1829 Wheatstone uses punched paper tape to store data

1834 Babbage conceives the Analytical Engine

1889 Hollerith's punch card machine used in US Census

1928 IBM adopts 80-column punched card

1944 Harvard's Mark I, first digital computer

1952 Univac computer accurately predicts the US presidential election winner

1953 First IBM electronic digital computer (IBM 701)

1956 First hard disk drive (IBM). Term "artificial intelligence" devised

1958 First chess game between computer and human

1960 USA has 6,000 computers

1963 ASCII (American Standard Code for Information Interchange) introduced

1967 IBM releases floppy disk

1970 Douglas Engelbart patents first computer mouse

1971 Intel builds the micro-processor, "computer on a chip". Wang 1200, first word processor

1972 E-mail invented by Ray Tomlinson. First electronic video game, *PONG*

1975 Microsoft founded by William Gates, later to become the world's richest person

1976 First Apple computer. Cray-1, first supercomputer

1979 Compuserve launches first commercial Bulletin Board (BBN) service

Most offices worldwide now rely on computers to transact business

Most popular social networking sites

	Network	Registered users
1	MySpace	471,152,724
2	Facebook	350,000,000
3	Qzone	200,000,000
4	Windows Live Spaces	120,000,000
5	Habbo	117,000,000
6	Friendster	90,000,000
7	hi5	80,000,000
8	Tagged	70,000,000
9	Orkut	67,000,000
10	Flixter	63,000,000

Internet milestones

In little over 10 years, the Internet has become a global phenomenon. In 1995 it was used by about 45 million people around the world. By 2008 the figure had more than doubled to 1,463,632,361. By the time you read this, the figures will have increased again.

1960s

During the 1960s scientists in the USA began trying to work out how organizations could keep in touch with one another after a nuclear attack. In 1965 ARPA (Advanced Research Projects Agency) suggested linking computers. In 1969 computers at four US universities were connected and could "talk" to each other for the first time.

1970s

The network was extended. At the same time, electronic mail (e-mail) was being used more and more to send messages between computers. In 1979 the first Usenet newsgroups (online discussion groups) began.

1980s

By 1981 the ARPA network had 213 hosts (sites to which users could connect). In 1982 a language called TCP/IP was invented which allowed all Internet computers to communicate with each other and the network was first called an Internet. The Internet began to be used commercially and by governments and universities.

1990s

In 1991 the World Wide Web (www) was created. By 1994 about 40 million people were connected to the Internet. They could exchange information, sell goods and work from any computer with a phone line. By 1996 users in almost 150 countries around the world were connected to the Internet.

2000s

High-speed broadband and Wi-Fi access is now widespread and many businesses offers goods and services on the Internet. The number of people using the Internet increased almost three times from 2000 to 2009, with the number of users in China and India growing by more than 1,000%. Almost 1.5 billion people use the Internet worldwide.

Most-visited websites

	Website	Launched*
1	Google.com	15 Sep 1997
2	Facebook.com	26 Sep 2006
3	Youtube.com	23 Apr 2005
4	Yahoo.com	18 Jan 1995
5	Windows Live	28 Dec 1994
6	Wikipedia.org	15 Jan 2001
7	Blogger.com	31 Jul 2000
8	Baidu.com	11 Oct 1999
9	Msn.com	24 Aug 1995
10	qq.com	4 May 1995

*In some instances test versions started earlier

2000s

1980 USA has more than one million computers. First laptop computers

1981 First Nintendo home video game. Commercial introduction of the computer mouse. Microsoft introduces software for IBM personal computers.

1982 Worldwide, 200 computers connected to the Internet

1984 Apple Macintosh computers launched

1985 Microsoft ships Windows 1.0

1986 USA has more than 30 million computers

1988 4.7 million microcomputers, 120,000 minicomputers and 11,500 mainframe computers sold in USA

1989 100,000 hosts on the net

1990 World Wide Web described by Tim Berners-Lee. First palmtop computers

1991 First use of the phrase "surfing the net", by Jean Armour Polly

1993 Mosaic, the first graphical Internet browser, launched

1994 135 million PCs worldwide. First ads on the World Wide Web (ad for *Wired* magazine claimed as first)

1995 Amazon.com Internet bookseller founded. Microsoft's Internet Explorer browser launched

2002 iPod digital music players launched

2008 Over 1.5 billion Internet users, 100 million websites and 1 trillion URLs worldwide.

2009 India launched the Sakshat, claimed to be the world's cheapest computer

2010 Apple's iPad released

www.computer.howstuffworks.com search

The first telegraph message was sent by Morse code using a hand-operated key.

From fixed cables to satellites

In the early years of telecommunications, the only way of linking one telephone with another was by fixed cables. Links between continents relied on cables under the sea. The invention of radio brought the first wireless communications, but because the surface of the Earth is curved these signals could not travel far.

Satellites changed everything. They sit at an exact height above the Earth's equator (usually around 35,000 km/22,000 miles) and they rotate at the same speed as the Earth spins. This means that they stay in a fixed position. Telephone signals can be sent to the satellites and bounced back to Earth. Everywhere on the planet can be covered by only five or six satellites, except for the poles and surrounding areas, which are out of their range.

Cables under the sea

Soon after telegraph cables came into use in the 1840s, attempts were made to lay them across rivers and between islands and mainlands. Most didn't work. In 1850 the first cable was laid across the English Channel. It had to resist attack by salt water, ocean currents and water pressure, so had a thick, water-resistant, steel cover. Inside were copper wires that carried the power and signal.

Technical improvements and the demand for faster communications led to cables being laid over ever greater distances. Several attempts to lay them across the Atlantic failed when the cables snapped, but one was completed in 1858. To mark the occasion, Queen Victoria sent a telegraph message to President Buchanan in the USA. It took almost 18 hours. Attempts were made to increase the pace by raising the voltage, but this burned out the cable. In 1865 the world's largest ship at the time, the *Great Eastern*, laid the first continuous cable across the Atlantic.

During the 20th century, telegraph cables, which transmitted Morse code were steadily replaced by telephone cables, which could transmit voices. Hundreds of thousands of kilometres of underwater cables were laid across the world's oceans and seas. These have been replaced by fibre-optic cables, which offer faster transmission and many more connections.

Telecom timeline

1700s

1793 Word "telegraph" first used (in France)

1837 Charles Wheatstone and William Cooke set up first electric telegraph in London

1843 Morse code inventor Samuel Morse (USA) sends first telegraph message between Washington and Baltimore

1850 Telegraph cable laid between England and France across English Channel, but fails; 19,312 km (12,000 miles) of telegraph line in USA

1851 Thomas Crampton lays successful Dover-Calais cable

1852 First telegraph line in India; there are now 37,015 km (23,000 miles) of telegraph line in USA

1854 First Australian telegraph line (Melbourne to Williamstown)

1858 First transatlantic telegraph cable laid, but fails

1861 First USA transcontinental telegraph

1862 51,500 km (32,000 miles) of telegraph line and more than 5 million messages sent in USA

1867 First theory suggests using radio waves for telecommunication

1876 Alexander Graham Bell patents the telephone – beating his rival Elisha Gray by a matter of hours. He makes his historic first call to his assistant, Thomas Watson, who is in the next room: "Mr Watson, come here, I want to see you." The invention is demonstrated at the Centennial Exposition, Philadelphia, USA where Emperor Don Pedro of Brazil hears Bell recite the "To be or not to be" speech from *Hamlet* over the phone.

1877 Bell makes the first long-distance call between Boston and Salem, Massachusetts, 22.5 km (14 miles) away

1878 Bell demonstrates his telephone to Queen Victoria at Osborne House on the Isle of Wight. She becomes the first European monarch to use a phone

1884 First telephone handset is launched

1889 First coin-in-the-slot public phone, USA

1891 France and England are connected by telephone cable

Alexander Graham Bell making the first telephone call between New York and Chicago

Telephone Bell

Alexander Graham Bell (1847–1922) is often called the father of the telephone. He was born in Edinburgh, Scotland, moved to Canada in 1870, and later to the USA. He became an expert on the science of speech and his first inventions helped deaf people to hear sounds. During his research, Bell developed a method of transmitting voice messages along a wire. In 1876 he patented the device, which he called the harmonic telegraph. This was the first telephone.

Countries with most mobile phones

China	720,000,000
India	506,044,156
USA	271,000,000
Russia	190,000,000
Brazil	169,800,000
Indonesia	140,200,000
Japan	107,490,000
Germany	107,000,000
UK	75,750,000
World total	4,017,294,000

2000s

1894 Guglielmo Marconi invents wireless telegraphy

1897 There are seven phones per 1,000 people in the USA

1901 Marconi sends a radio signal across the Atlantic

1902 The trans-Pacific telephone cable connects Canada, New Zealand and Australia

1907 There are an estimated 1,653,356 km (1,027,348 miles) of land telecommunications lines and 376,302 km (233,823 miles) of submarine cable worldwide

1914 The first radio message is sent to an aircraft; the first transcontinental telephone call is made in the USA

1919 Rotary dial telephones are invented

1945 British writer Arthur C. Clarke proposes putting communications satellites in orbit above the Earth, which move at the same speed as the Earth spins; this means they stay in a fixed position, and communication with the ground is not interrupted

1956 The first transatlantic telephone cable is laid

1965 Intelsat I (*Early Bird*), the first commercial telecommunications satellite, is launched

1967 The first cordless telephones go on sale

1975 The first handheld mobile phones are sold

1988 The first transatlantic fibre optic cable is laid

2004 There are 1.2 billion telephone lines around the world: 538,981,500 in Asia, 327,657,500 in Europe, 295,292,700 in North and South America, 25,929,800 in Africa and 13,773,000 in Oceania

2005 Mobile phone users now number more than 2 billion worldwide

2006 US company Western Union ends its telegraph service after 150 years, as e-mails replace telegrams

2009 The 3G iPhone has sold 21.17 million worldwide

2010 Google launches its Nexus One smartphone using its Android operating system

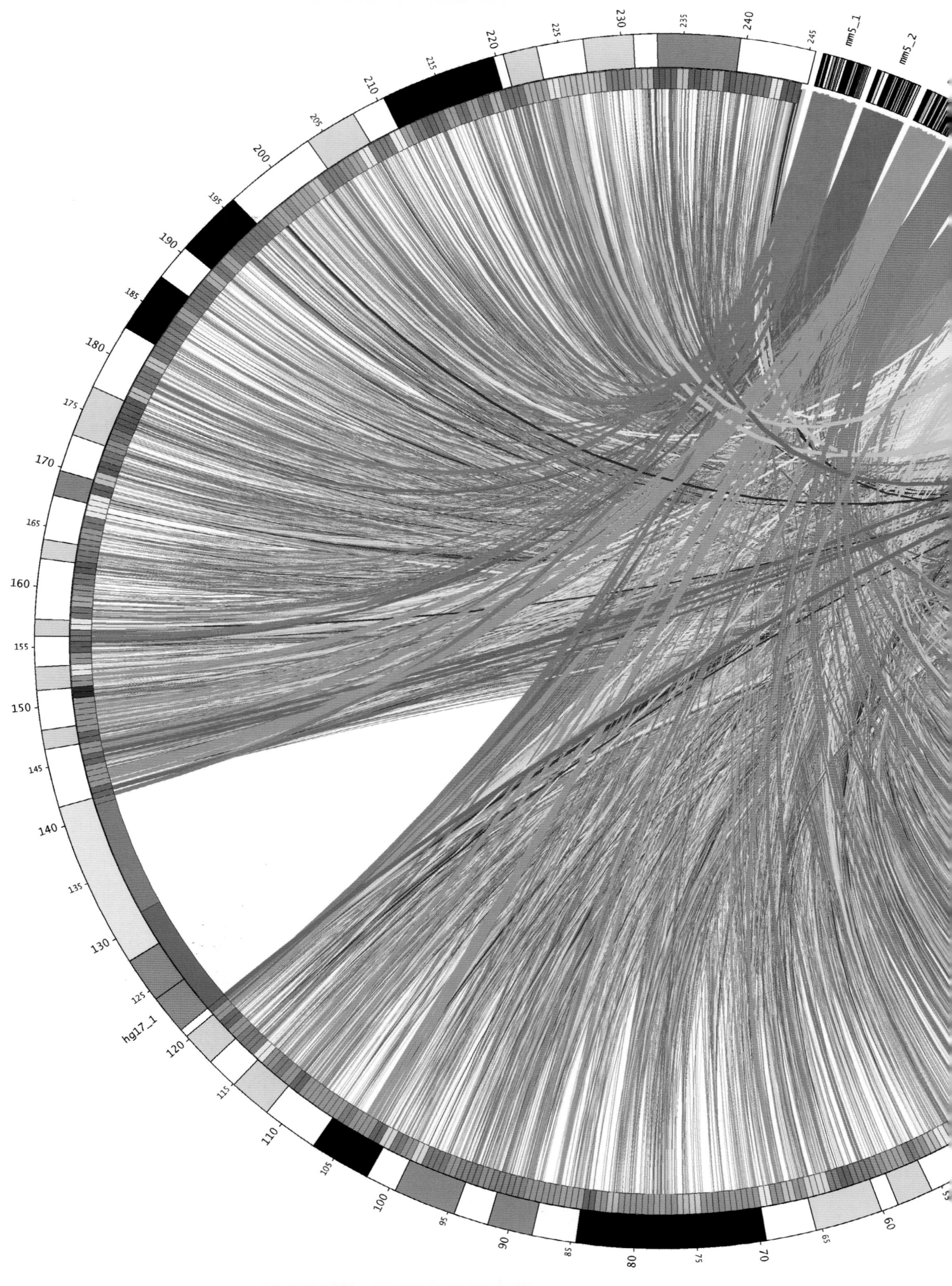
mm5_1
mm5_2
245
240
235
230
225
220
215
210
205
200
195
190
185
180
175
170
165
160
155
150
145
140
135
130
125
hg17_1
120
115
110
105
100
95
90
85
80
75
70
65
60

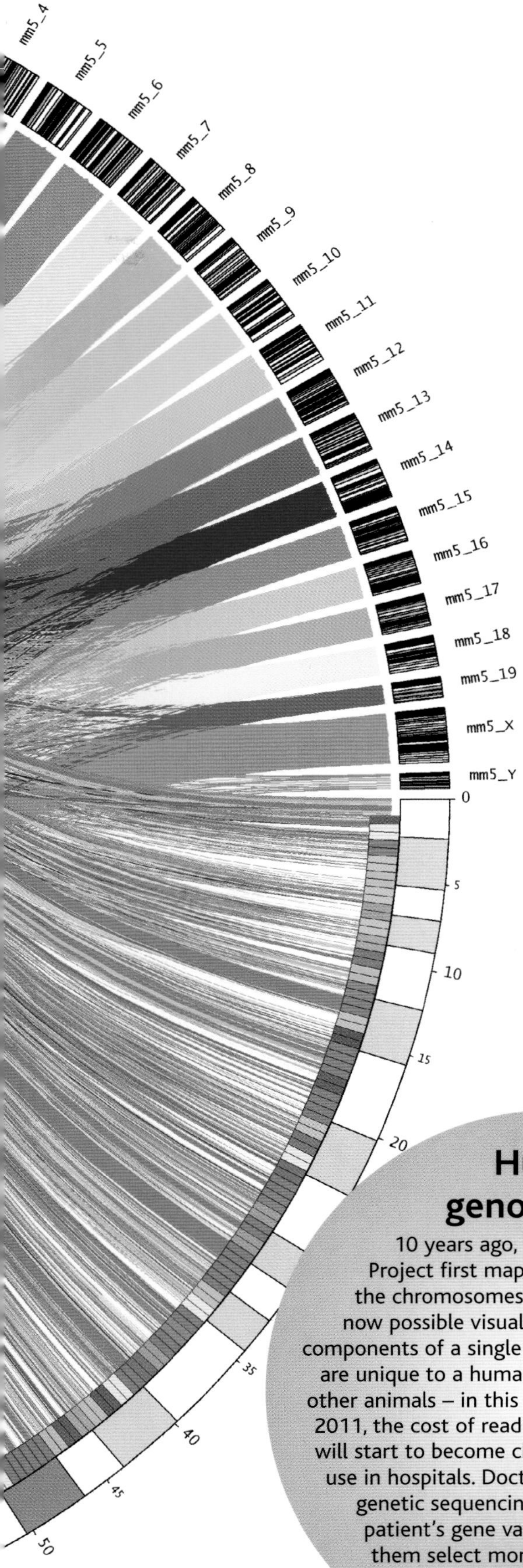

Human Body

Human genome map

10 years ago, the Human Genome Project first mapped the genes found in the chromosomes of the human body. It is now possible visually to compare the genetic components of a single chromosome, revealing which are unique to a human and which are shared with other animals – in this diagram, those of a mouse. In 2011, the cost of reading a person's whole genome will start to become cheap enough for mainstream use in hospitals. Doctors will soon be able to use genetic sequencing machines to identify a patient's gene variants, which could help them select more effective methods of providing treatment and combating diseases.

Your amazing body

Blood
An adult man's body contains about 5 l (10.5 pt) of blood. A woman's contains about 4.3 l (9.1 pt). The blood travels along 100,000 km (62,137 miles) of blood vessels. It contains 25,000,000,000 to 30,000,000,000 red cells. The life span of red cells is only about 120 days, and 1,200,000 to 2,000,0000 of them are made every second.

Breathing
The average person inhales 6 l (12.6 pt) of air per minute, or 8,640 l (18,260 pt) a day. You take 13–17 breaths a minute when sitting still and up to 80 during vigorous exercise.

Cells
There are 50 trillion cells in your body and 3 billion of them die every minute (4,320,000,000,000 a day). Most of these are replaced. You make 10 billion new white blood cells each day. You have a total of 1,000,000,000,000 white cells, which help fight germs and infections.

Chemicals
There is enough carbon in your body to fill 900 pencils, enough fat to make 75 candles, enough phosphorus to make 220 match heads and enough iron to make a 7.5 cm (3 in) nail.

Digestive system
Your stomach produces up to 2 l (4.2 pt) of hydrochloric acid a day. It does not damage the stomach walls because 500,000 cells in your stomach lining are replaced every minute. The small intestine is about 5 m (16.4 ft) long. The large intestine is thicker, but only about 1.5 m (4.9 ft) long.

Eyes
You blink about 20,000 times a day.

Gas
On average, you release 2 l (4.2 pt) of gases from your intestines as burps or farts.

Hair
Hair grows about 0.5 mm (0.02 in) a day.

Heartbeats
Your heart pumps 13,640 l (28,800 pt) of blood around your body in a day. An average heartbeat rate of 70 beats a minute adds up to more than 100,000 beats a day.

Mouth
You will produce 37,800 l (79,900 pt) of saliva in your life.

Nerves
Your body has about 13,000,000,000,000 nerve cells, transmitting messages at speeds of 290 km/h (180 mph).

Sweat
You lose about 0.5 l (1.1 pt) of water a day through 3,000,000 sweat glands. In hot climates you may lose as much as 13.5 l (28.5 pt) a day.

Urine
You will pass 400 to 2,000 ml (0.8 to 4.2 pt) of urine every day, depending on your age, your size and outside conditions, especially temperature.

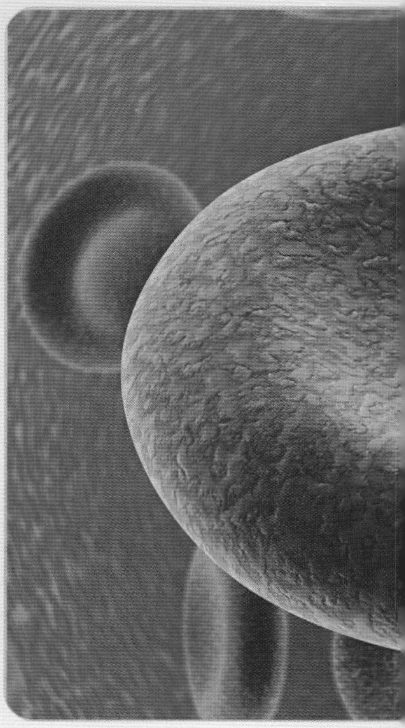

Highly magnified image of red blood cells

Brain power

- A newborn baby's brain weighs about 350–400 g. By the time it is a year old, it may weigh as much as 1,000 g. From baby to adult, it more than triples in weight.
- If 'ironed out', the surface area of the brain would be 2,090 sq cm (324 sq in), equivalent to that of a small table.
- The brain represents less than 2% of body weight but uses 20% of its oxygen intake, 20% of calories and 15% of blood supply.
- 750–1,000 millilitres of blood flow through the brain every minute
- There are as many as 100 billion neurons – the nerve cells that transmit information through electrical impulses – in the human brain.
- As much as 78% of the brain is composed of water.

Einstein's brain

Soon after his death in 1955, the brain of physicist Albert Einstein was removed and studied by researchers. Its weight of 1,230 g was actually below average, but although some details of its structure have been claimed to have been unusual, no conclusions have yet been reached as to what made him a genius.

What's your body made of?

Most of the human body is made up of water, or H_2O, which is a combination of hydrogen and oxygen. As much as 99 per cent of the body is made up of oxygen, carbon, hydrogen, nitrogen, calcium and phosphorus. There are also small amounts of other elements.

Element	Avg. in 70 kg (154 lb) person g (oz)
Oxygen	43,000 (1,1517)
Carbon	16,000 (564)
Hydrogen	7,000 (247)
Nitrogen	1,800 (64)
Calcium	1,200 (42)
Phosphorus	780 (28)
Sulphur	140 (5)

Element	Avg. in 70 kg (154 lb) person g (oz)
Potassium	110–140 (4–5)
Sodium	100 (3.5)
Chlorine	95 (3.35)
Magnesium	25 (0.8)
Iron	4 (0.1)
Zinc	2.3 (0.08)
Silicon	1 (0.03)

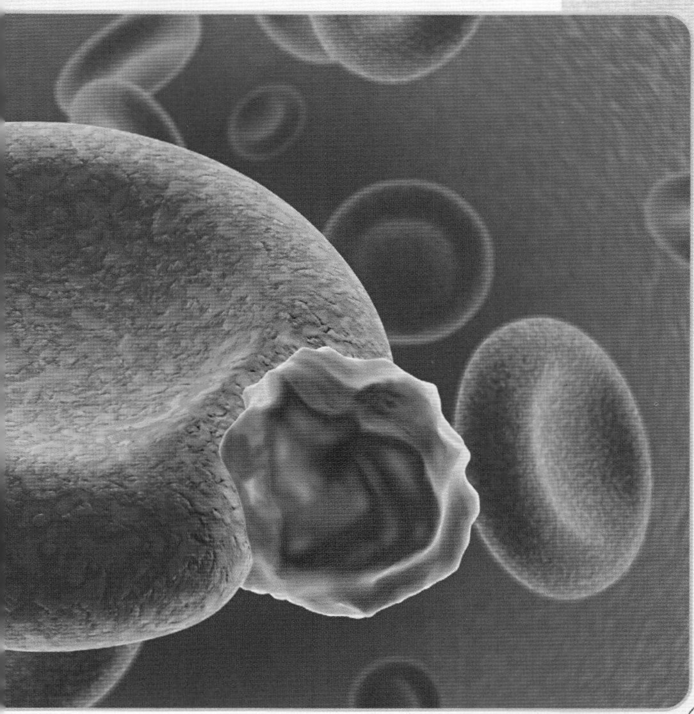

Human skeleton

The skeleton is the body's framework. The bones of the skeleton support the body, protect the internal organs such as the heart and lungs, and allow you to move.

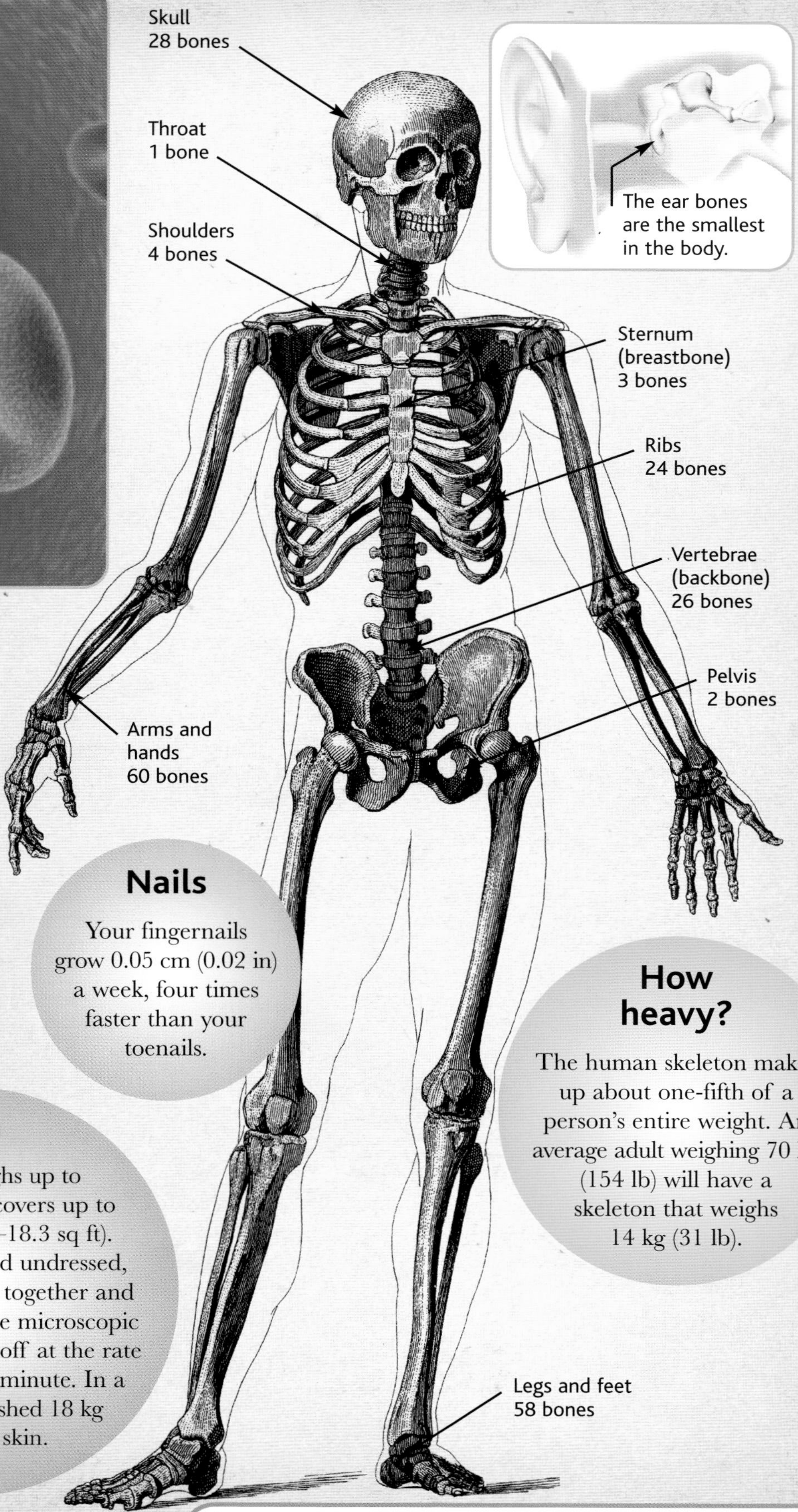

The ear bones are the smallest in the body.

Longest bones in the body

These are the average measurements of the longest bones of an adult male. The same bones in the female skeleton are usually 6–13 per cent smaller, except the breastbone which is almost the same.

Femur (thighbone, upper leg) 50.50 cm (19.88 in)
Tibia (shinbone, inner lower leg) 43.03 cm (16.94 in)
Fibula (outer lower leg) 40.50 cm (15.94 in)
Humerus (upper arm) 36.46 cm (14.35 in)
Ulna (inner lower arm) 28.20 cm (11.10 in)
Radius (outer lower arm) 26.42 cm (10.40 in)
7th rib 24.00 cm (9.45 in)
8th rib 23.00 cm (9.06 in)
Hipbone (one half of pelvis) 18.50 cm (7.28 in)
Sternum (breastbone) 17.00 cm (6.69 in)

Nails

Your fingernails grow 0.05 cm (0.02 in) a week, four times faster than your toenails.

Skin

Your skin weighs up to 4 kg (8.8 lb) and covers up to 1.3–1.7 sq m (14–18.3 sq ft). Getting dressed and undressed, rubbing body parts together and even breathing cause microscopic flakes of skin to fall off at the rate of 50,000 flakes a minute. In a lifetime you will shed 18 kg (39.7 lb) of skin.

How heavy?

The human skeleton makes up about one-fifth of a person's entire weight. An average adult weighing 70 kg (154 lb) will have a skeleton that weighs 14 kg (31 lb).

www.innerbody.com search

Weighty wonder

Daniel Lambert (1770–1809) was one of the heaviest British people of all time. At his largest, he weighed 330 kg (727.5 lb) and measured 2.8 m (9.2 ft) round his body and 94 cm (37 in) round his leg. Lambert used to charge visitors to his house a shilling (five pence) just to look at him.

When he died in 1809, it took 34 m (111.5 ft) of elm planking to make his coffin, which looked like a gigantic packing case. A window and part of the wall of his house had to be removed to get the coffin out, and it had to be mounted on wheels to trundle it to the cemetery.

Daniel Lambert

Body records

Longest beard
Hans Langseth (1846–1927) had a beard that measured 5.33 m (17 ft 6 in). It has been in the Smithsonian Institution, Washington DC, USA, since 1967.

Hans Langseth

Longest nails
Shridhar Chillal of Pune, India (1937–) has not cut the nails on his left hand since 1952. By 2000 the total length of his nails on that hand was over 600 cm (236 in).

Longest moustache
Kalyan Ramji Sain of Sundargath, India, holds the record. His moustache is 3.29 m (11 ft 11.5 in) from tip to tip.

Longest hair
Swami Pandarasannadhi was the head of a monastery in Madras, India. When his hair was measured in 1949 it was 7.9 m (26 ft) long.

Longest sneezing bout
Donna Griffiths of Pershore, Worcestershire, started sneezing on 13 January 1981 and continued for 978 days.

Maths genius
When he was only eight years old, American Zerah Colburn (1804–40) worked out how many seconds had elapsed since the birth of Christ. He did this in his head within seconds. When Zerah was asked whether 4,294,967,297 was a prime number (one that cannot be divided evenly by another number), he instantly replied that it was not – it is equal to 641 times 6,700,417.

Longest hiccuping
Charles Osborne of Anthon, Iowa, USA, hiccuped from 1922 to 1990.

Infant prodigy
By the age of four, Kim Ung-Yong of Korea (1963–) could speak fluent Korean, English, Japanese and German, and could solve calculus problems.

Memory
Gon Yang-ling of Harbin, China, has memorized more than 15,000 telephone numbers.

World's oldest people

Below is a list of the world's longest-living people, or supercentenarians. It includes only those for whom there are accurate records of their birth and death dates.

Although Christian Mortensen is ninth in the list, he is the world's oldest man. The others in the list are women.

Jeanne Calment (1875–1997), France: 122 years and 164 days
Sarah DeRemer Knauss (1880–1999), USA: 119 years and 97 days
Lucy Hannah (1875–1993), USA: 117 years and 248 days
Marie-Louise Meilleur (1880–1998), Canada: 117 years and 229 days
María Esther Heredia Lecaro de Capovilla (1889–2006) Ecuador: 116 years and 347 days
Tane Ikai (1879–1995), Japan: 116 years and 175 days
Elizabeth Bolden (1890–2006) USA: 116 years and 118 days
Maggie Barnes (1882–1998), USA: 115 years and 319 days
Christian Mortensen (1882–1998), Denmark/USA: 115 years and 252 days
Charlotte Hughes (1877–1993), UK: 115 years and 228 days

Oldest living person

Eugénie Blanchard (France) was born on 16 February 1896 and, at 114, became the oldest living person in 2010.

Tom Thumb and friends

American showman Phineas T. Barnum first met Charles Sherwood Stratton (USA, 1838–83) when he was four years old. He was 61cm (24 in) tall and weighed 6.8 kg (15 lb). Barnum persuaded Charles's parents to allow him to exhibit their son for a fee of $3 a week. He was advertised as "General Tom Thumb, a dwarf eleven years of age, just arrived from England". By the time he died, he had grown to 1 m (3 ft 3 in) and weighed 32 kg (70 lb). Lavinia Warren (USA, 1841–1919) was 79 cm (31 in) tall. Her first husband was Tom Thumb.

"Commodore" Nutt (USA, 1844–81) was 74 cm (29 in) tall. Like Tom Thumb he was exhibited by Phineas T. Barnum.

Human endurance records

Under water
On 5 August 1926 escapologist Harry Houdini was lowered into the swimming pool of the Hotel Shelton, New York, inside a sealed iron coffin. Despite having no breathing apparatus, he survived being submerged for 1 hour 31 minutes before he escaped.

Without sleep
In 2007 Tony Wright of Penzance, UK, stayed awake for 266 hours to claim the record for the longest period anyone has stayed awake, However, some people believe Toimi Soini, of Hamina, Finland had already set a record of 276 hours in 1964, while others think Maureen Weston, of Peterborough, UK, stayed awake for an amazing 449 hours in a rocking chair marathon in 1977.

Swimming the Atlantic
In 2009 Jennifer Figge (USA) became the first woman to swim the Atlantic. She swam 3,219 km (2,000 miles) from the Cape Verde Islands to Trinidad inside a 6 m x 4 m (19 x 14 ft) cage to protect her from sharks. It took her 24 days.

Multi-marathons
In 1983, Wally Herman of Ontario, Canada, became the first person to run a marathon in each of the 50 US states and Washington DC – a total distance of 2,152 km (1,337 miles). His feat has since been repeated by over 400 runners and new records have been set, such as running a marathon in each of 100 countries around the world, or, as Ricardo Abad of Spain did in 2009, running a marathon every day for 150 days.

Tallest real giants
These are the most reliable records. All are men, except Trijntje Keever and Jeng Jinlian.

Robert Pershing Wadlow (1918–40), USA: 2.72 m (8 ft 11.1 in)
John William Rogan (1868–1905), USA: 2.68 m (8 ft 9.8 in)
John Aasen (1887–1938), USA: 2.67m (8 ft 9.8 in)
John F. Carroll (1932–69), USA: 2.64 m (8 ft 7.6 in)
Al Tomaini (1918–62), USA: 2.55 m (8 ft 4.4 in)
Trijntje Keever (1616–33), Netherlands: 2.54 m (8 ft 3.3 in)
Edouard Beaupre (1881–1904), Canada: 2.50 m (8 ft 2.5 in)
Bernard Coyne (1897–1921), USA: 2.49 m (8 ft 1.2 in)
Don Koehler (1925–81), USA: 2.49 m (8 ft 1.2 in)
Jeng Jinlian (1964–82), China: 2.48 m (8 ft 1.1 in)
Väinö Myllyrinne (1909–63), Finland: 2.48 m (8 ft 1.1 in)
Sultan Kosen (1982–), Turkey: 2.47m (8 ft 1 in)
Louis Moilanen (1885–1913), Finland/USA: 2.46 m (8 ft 1 in)
Gabriel Estavo Monjane (1944–90), Mozambique: 2.46 m (8 ft 0.75 in)

Life expectancy
Life expectancy is the average number of years people in different countries are likely to live. Conditions can improve or sometimes get worse, so life expectancy can get higher or lower.

The country with the highest life expectancy is Andorra at 82.36 years. The country with the lowest life expectancy is Swaziland with 31.84 years. People who live in the UK and the USA have an average life expectancy of 79.16 years and 78.24 years respectively.

Commodore Nutt, Miss Warren, normal-sized man and Tom Thumb

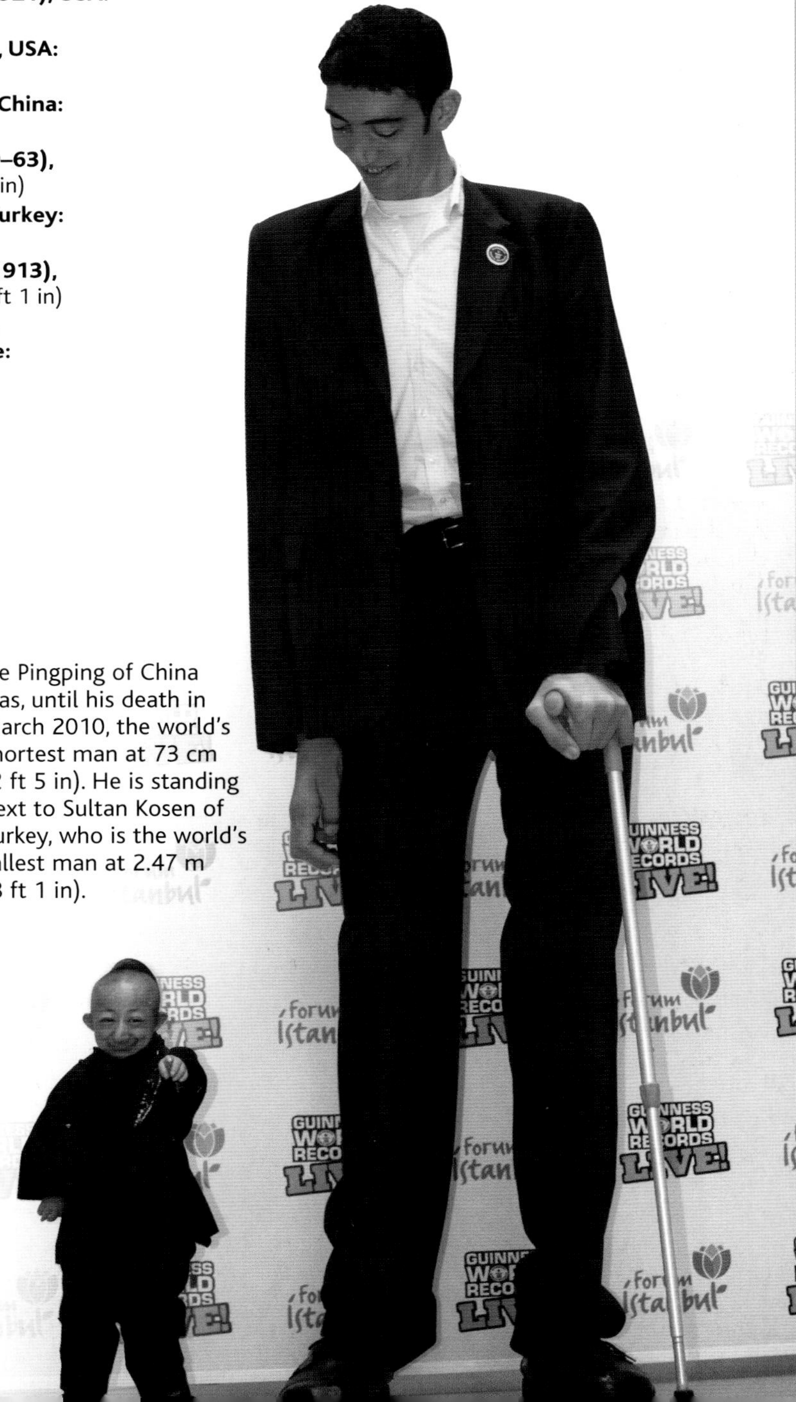

He Pingping of China was, until his death in March 2010, the world's shortest man at 73 cm (2 ft 5 in). He is standing next to Sultan Kosen of Turkey, who is the world's tallest man at 2.47 m (8 ft 1 in).

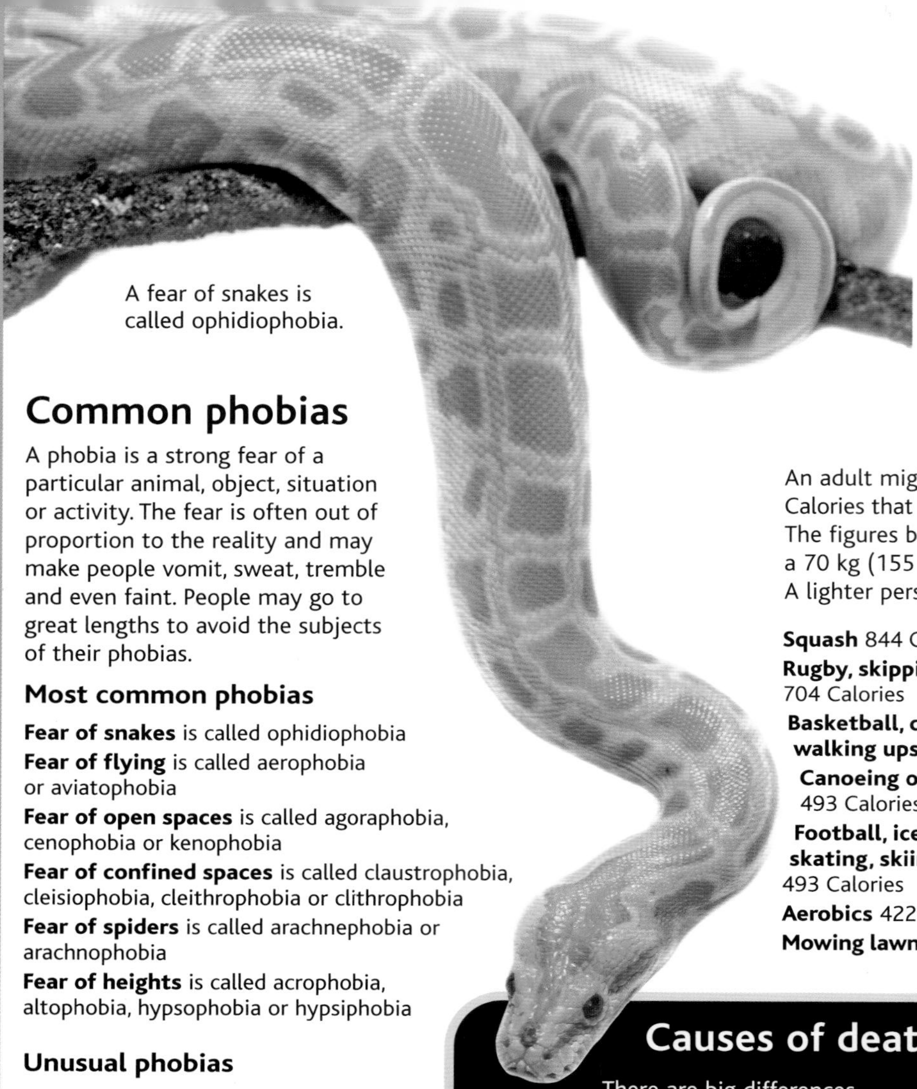
A fear of snakes is called ophidiophobia.

Calorie counts

A Calorie (with a capital C) is a unit that measures the amount of energy in foods. It is also known as a kilocalorie and is equal to 1,000 calories (with a small c). A calorie is the amount of heat needed to raise the temperature of 1 gram (0.035 oz) of water by 1°C (1.8°F).

An adult might eat up to 3,000 Calories a day. Eating too many Calories that the body does not use for energy may make you fat. The figures below are based on the average number of Calories a 70 kg (155 lb) adult burns when doing an activity for one hour. A lighter person uses fewer Calories; a heavier person more.

Squash 844 Calories
Rugby, skipping, swimming 704 Calories
Basketball, cycling, running, walking upstairs 563 Calories
Canoeing or rowing 493 Calories
Football, ice skating, roller skating, skiing, tennis 493 Calories
Aerobics 422 Calories
Mowing lawn 387 Calories
Cricket (batting or bowling), gardening, skateboarding 352 Calories
Dancing 317 Calories
Golf, table tennis 281 Calories
Housework, walking dog 246 Calories
Frisbee, surfing 211 Calories
Playing piano 176 calories
Standing 120 calories
Sitting 90 calories
Sleeping 65 calories

Common phobias

A phobia is a strong fear of a particular animal, object, situation or activity. The fear is often out of proportion to the reality and may make people vomit, sweat, tremble and even faint. People may go to great lengths to avoid the subjects of their phobias.

Most common phobias

Fear of snakes is called ophidiophobia
Fear of flying is called aerophobia or aviatophobia
Fear of open spaces is called agoraphobia, cenophobia or kenophobia
Fear of confined spaces is called claustrophobia, cleisiophobia, cleithrophobia or clithrophobia
Fear of spiders is called arachnephobia or arachnophobia
Fear of heights is called acrophobia, altophobia, hypsophobia or hypsiphobia

Unusual phobias

Fear of beards is called pogonophobia
Fear of chickens is called alektorophobia
Fear of dancing is called chorophobia
Fear of dolls is called pediophobia
Fear of fish is called ichthyophobia
Fear of frogs is called batrachophobia
Fear of hair is called chaetophobia
Fear of mirrors is called eisoptrophobia
Fear of the number 13 is called triskaidekaphobia
Fear of string is called linonophobia
Fear of teeth is called odontophobia

Causes of death worldwide

There are big differences between the causes of death in developing countries and in developed countries. In developing countries, many more deaths are caused by infectious diseases and illnesses spread by insects such as malaria.

In developed countries more people become ill from being overweight and eating rich diets. There are about 57,029,000 deaths a year worldwide.

Heart diseases 16,733,000 per year
Cancers 7,121,000 per year
Respiratory infections 3,963,000 per year
Lung diseases 3,702,000 per year
HIV/AIDS 2,777,000 per year
Digestive diseases 1,968,000 per year
Diarrhoeal diseases 1,798,000 per year
Tuberculosis 1,566,000 per year
Malaria 1,272,000 per year
Road traffic injuries 1,192,000 per year
Neuropsychiatric disorders 1,112,000 per year

Medical milestones 100 BC

c. 460 BC The first medical studies were carried out by Hippocrates (Greece)
AD 1543 Accurate anatomical drawings were made by Andreas Vesalius (Belgium)
1628 Blood circulation was discovered by William Harvey (UK)
1683 Bacteria were first described by Antonie van Leeuwenhoek (the Netherlands)
1796 The first smallpox vaccination was carried out by Edward Jenner (UK)
1805 Morphine was used as a painkiller by Friedrich Sertürner (Germany)
1810 Homeopathy was used by Samuel Hahnemann (Germany)
1816 The stethoscope was invented by René Laënnec (France)
1818 The first blood transfusion was carried out by Thomas Blundell (UK)
1842 Ether was administered as an anaesthetic by Crawford Long (USA)
1844 Nitrous oxide (laughing gas) was used as an anaesthetic by Horace Wells (USA)
1846 Ether vapour was used as an anaesthetic by William Morton (USA)
1847 Chloroform was used as an anaesthetic by John Bell/James Simpson (UK)
1864 The Red Cross was founded by Henri Dunant (Switzerland)
1867 Antiseptic was used before surgery by Joseph Lister (UK)
1885 Rabies vaccine was developed by Louis Pasteur (France)
1895 X-rays were discovered by William von Röntgen (Germany)
1895 Psychoanalysis was used by Sigmund Freud (Austria)
1898 Aspirin was made by Felix Hoffman (Germany)
1901 Blood groups were identified by Karl Landsteiner (Austria)

Dentistry

Some basic dentistry – treating and extracting decayed teeth and medicines to cure gum disease – was practiced in ancient times, but developed little until the early 19th century.

- False teeth were once made of animal teeth, hippopotamus or walrus ivory (US president George Washington had teeth made of hippopotamus tusks, not wood as is commonly claimed).
- Sometimes false teeth were created using the teeth taken from dead people, often from soldiers killed in warfare, so they were sometimes called 'Waterloo Teeth' after the battle fought there.
- In England in the 1820s, Claudius Ash began making dentures out of porcelain that looked natural and were set in gold, later vulcanite, a type of rubber.
- Since then new inventions such as the use of x-rays and anaesthetics and improved equipment, drills and filling and repairing materials have resulted in great advances in treating tooth and gum problems, preserving, whitening and straightening teeth.

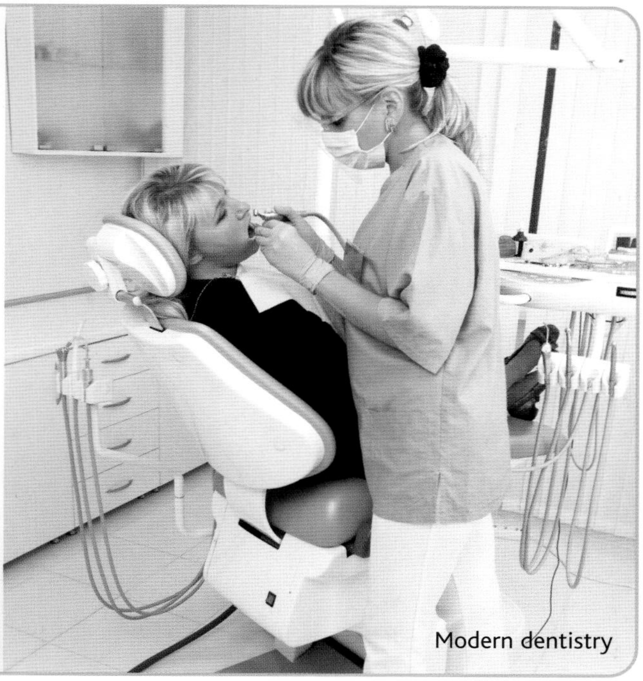
Modern dentistry

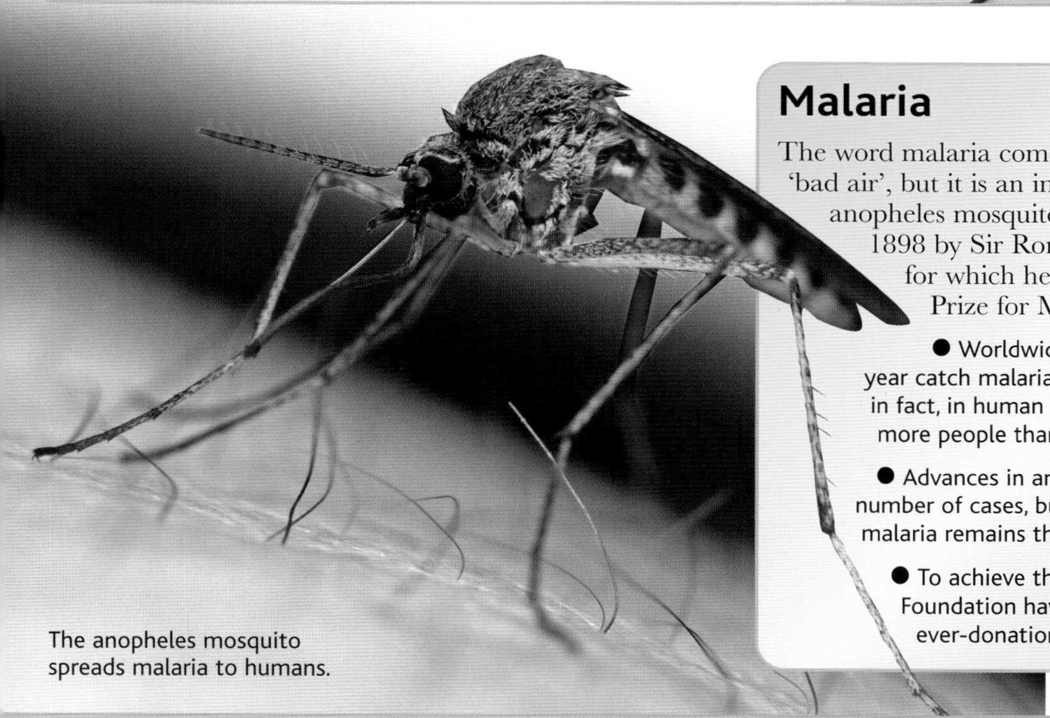
The anopheles mosquito spreads malaria to humans.

Malaria

The word malaria comes from the medieval Italian for 'bad air', but it is an infectious disease transmitted by the anopheles mosquitoes. This connection was proved in 1898 by Sir Ronald Ross, a British doctor in India, for which he received the second-ever Nobel Prize for Medicine, 1902.

- Worldwide, as many as 500 million people a year catch malaria, more than one million dying from it – in fact, in human history, malaria has probably killed more people than any other disease.
- Advances in anti-malarial drugs have reduced the number of cases, but a vaccine to combat and eradicate malaria remains the world's goal.
- To achieve this, the Bill and Melinda Gates Foundation have pledged $35 billion, the largest ever-donation to medical research.

2000s

1906 Vitamins were discovered by Frederick Hopkins (UK)
1922 Insulin was used to treat diabetes by Frederick Banting and John Macleod (Canada) and Charles Best (USA)
1927 Iron lung was invented by Philip Drinker (USA)
1928 Penicillin was discovered by Alexander Fleming (UK)
1940 Penicillin was first used by Howard Florey (Australia) and Ernest Chain (UK)
1952 The first artificial heart valve was used by Charles Hufnagel (USA)
1953 DNA structure was identified by Francis Crick (UK) and James Watson (USA)
1955 Kidney dialysis machine was invented by Willem J. Kolff (the Netherlands/USA)
1957 First heart pacemaker was used by Clarence Lillehie (USA)
1967 The first human heart transplant was performed by Christiaan Barnard (S. Africa)
1970 First artificial heart was used by Robert Jarvik (USA)
1978 First test-tube baby (Louise Brown) was born after procedure perfomed by Patrick Steptoe (UK)
1980 Smallpox was eradicated by World Health Organization
1984 Genetic fingerprinting was invented by Alec Jeffreys (UK)
1984 AIDS virus was first identified by Centers for Disease Control (USA)
1996 First mammal was cloned (Dolly, a sheep) by Ian Wilmut, Roslin Institute (UK)
2000 Human DNA genome sequence was completed
2006 Robot heart surgery was performed by Carlo Pappone (Italy)
2007 DNA testing allows checking for genetic disorders
2009 Stem cell research approved in US offers hope that paralyzed people may walk.

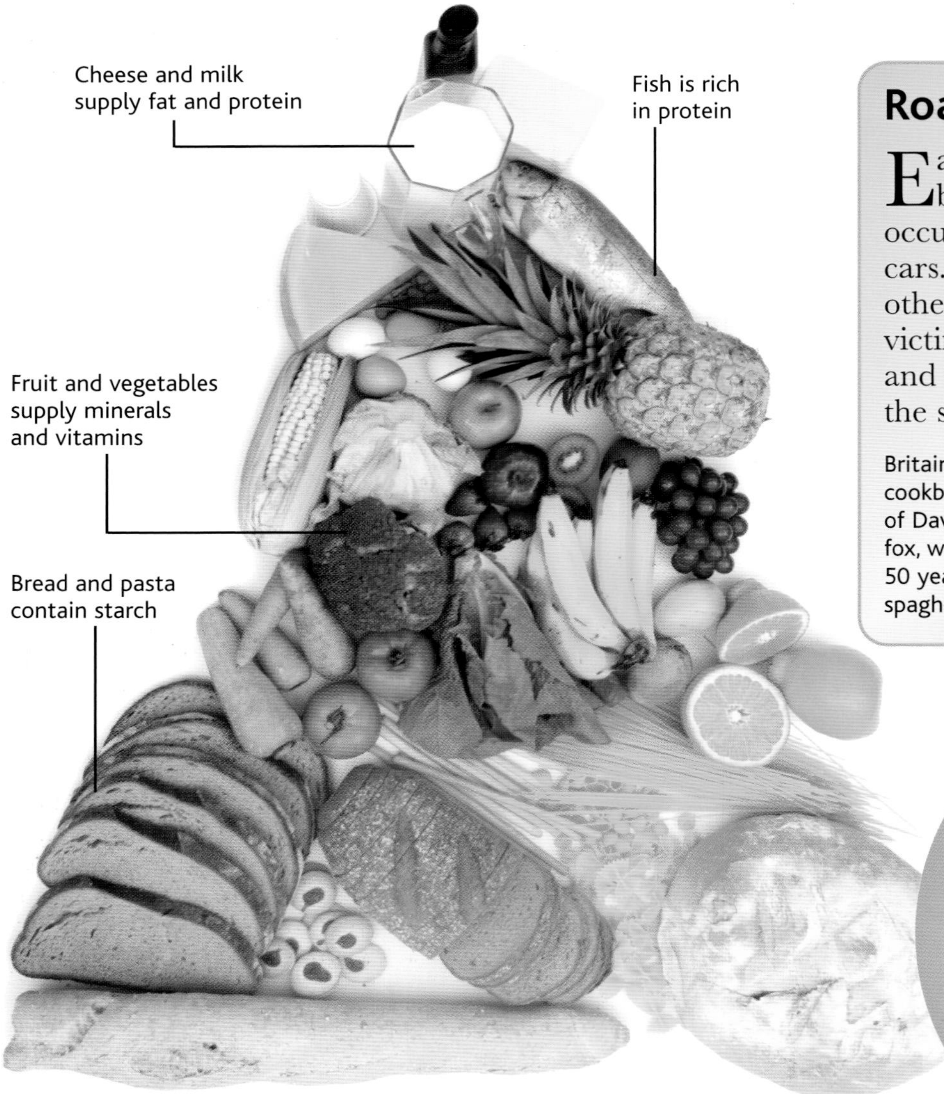

Roadkill recipes

Eating roadkill (animals that have been killed on the road) has occurred ever since there have been cars. In the USA, where deer and other large animals are common victims, a number of recipe books and websites have been devoted to the subject.

Britain's first "flattened fauna" (squashed animals) cookbook was announced in 2006 by Arthur Boyt of Davidstow, Cornwall, who has included badger, fox, weasel and bat among his meals over the past 50 years. His roadkill recipes include one for spaghetti with hedgehog.

Eating a zoo

During the Franco-Prussian War of 1870, the inhabitants of Paris were under siege and starving, so after eating all the horses, dogs, cats and rats they could find in the city, they decided to eat the contents of the Paris Zoo, including two elephants called Castor and Pollux, along with a yak, zebra and other animals.

What we eat

A family food survey is carried out in the UK every year. The latest figures for what we eat in the home (not including takeaways and eating out) show that the average person will consume more than 50 tonnes of food and drink in an 80-year lifespan. These are some of the main items in the survey, and the amounts each of us can expect to eat in our lives:

Milk and cream (including yoghurt, etc) 8,253 kg (18,195 lb)
Soft drinks 7,014 kg (15,463 lb)
Vegetables 4,742 kg (10,453 lb)
Fresh fruit 3,557 kg (7,842 lb)
Potatoes 3,249 kg (7,163 lb)
Alcoholic drinks 3,211 kg (7,079 lb)
Bread 2,816 kg (6,274 lb)
Cereals and cereal products 2,230 kg (4,916 lb)
Fruit juice 1,414 kg (3,117 lb)
Poultry 1,044 kg (2,302 lb)
Fats 753 kg (1,660 lb)
Fish 686 kg (1,512 lb)
Biscuits 678 kg (1,495 lb)
Cakes and pastries 661 kg (1,457 lb)
Sweets 537 kg (1,184 lb)
Sugar and preserves (jam, etc) 520 kg (1,146 lb)
Cheese 495 kg (1,091 lb)
Bacon and ham 453 kg (999 lb)
Eggs 399 kg (880 lb)
Pasta 383 kg (844 lb)
Beverages (tea, coffee, etc) 233 kg (514 lb)
Mutton and lamb 229 kg (505 lb)
Flour 225 kg (496 lb)

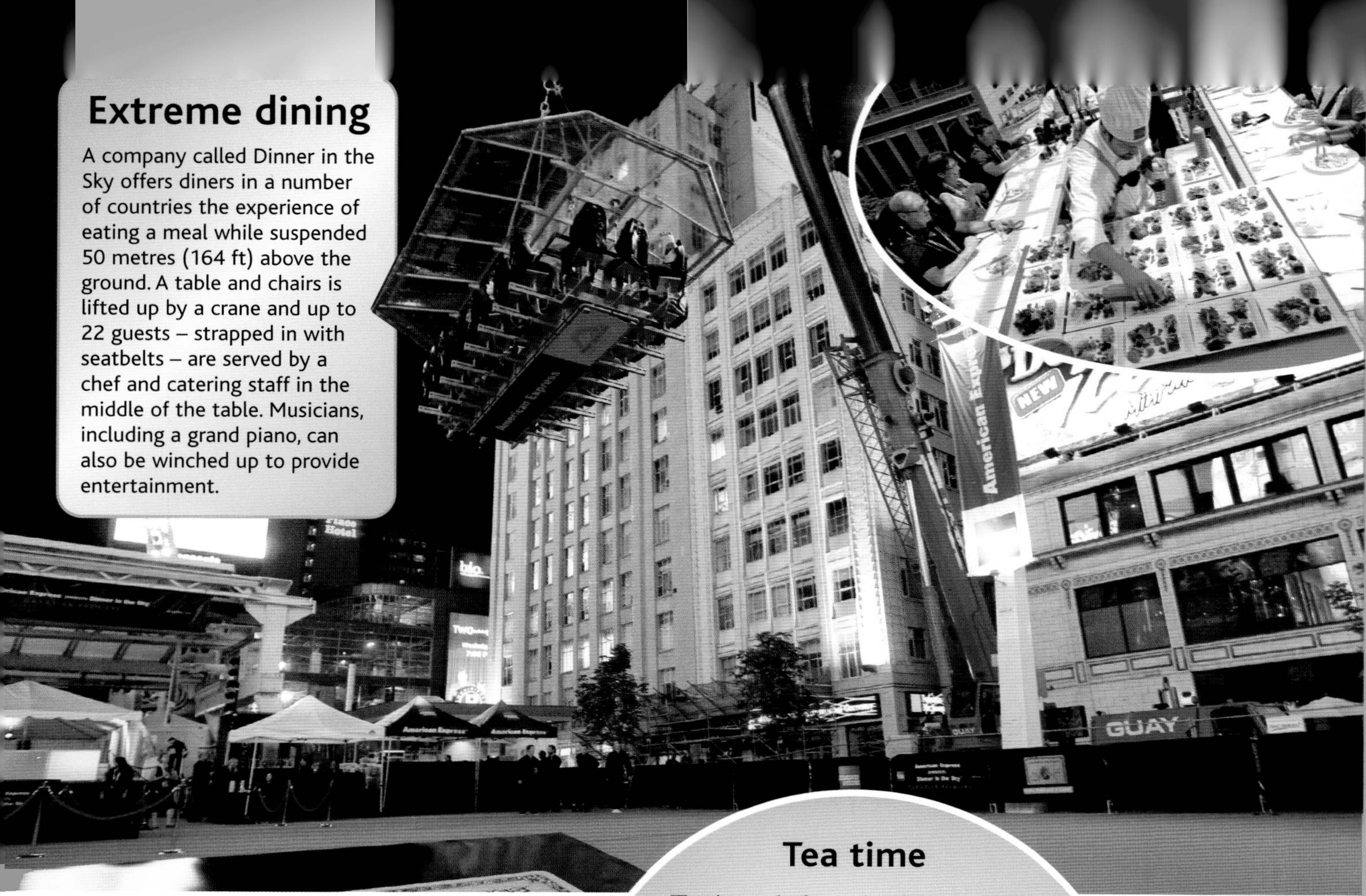

Extreme dining

A company called Dinner in the Sky offers diners in a number of countries the experience of eating a meal while suspended 50 metres (164 ft) above the ground. A table and chairs is lifted up by a crane and up to 22 guests – strapped in with seatbelts – are served by a chef and catering staff in the middle of the table. Musicians, including a grand piano, can also be winched up to provide entertainment.

The drinks we drink

Soda water

Carbonated water – water with carbon dioxide forced into it to make it sparkling – was invented by Dr William Brownrigg of Whitehaven, UK, in 1741. One of the most famous manufacturers was German-born scientist Jean Jacob Schweppe who moved to London in 1792. By the 1870s the company he founded was also making ginger ale and Indian Tonic Water, by adding quinine to sweetened soda water, after the style of the British in India who drank it as an antidote to malaria.

Bottled water

Drinking mineral water from natural springs has been done since Roman times and became fashionable in the 18th century when people went to spa towns to bathe and undergo medical treatments. It is claimed that water from Malvern, UK, was bottled as early as 1622, while French mineral water became especially popular, including Evian (1826), Badoit (1838), Vittel (1882) and Perrier (1898). Perrier's club-shaped bottles were designed to resemble the Indian clubs used for exercise by the spa's British owner William Albert St John Harmsworth.

Carbonated drinks

The first Coca-Cola was served in Jacob's Pharmacy, in Atlanta, Georgia, on 8 May 1886. It was the creation of pharmacist Dr John Stith Pemberton. It was first served in bottles in 1894 (although its distinctive bottle design was not introduced until 1915) and in cans in 1955. Its rival Pepsi dates from 1898, when it was named 'Brad's Drink' after its inventor Caleb Bradham. It was trademarked as Pepsi-Cola in 1903.

Tea time

Tea is made from the dried leaves of a plant. It has been drunk in China since ancient times, but was not known in Europe until the early 17th century. It is mainly grown in tropical countries such as India and Turkey, but some varieties can be cultivated in cooler climates. Paper tea bags became popular in the USA in the 1920s, but were not sold in the UK until 1952. Tea time, a light meal taken in the later afternoon, became a cultural activity in Britain, where tearooms became common in the 18th and 19th centuries.

Tea picker in India

WHITAKER'S WORLD OF FACTS

World History

Remembering 9/11

2011 marks the 10th anniversary of the events of 11 September 2001, when a series of terrorist attacks on the USA killed almost 3,000 people. Al-Qaeda terrorists flew planes into the twin towers of the World Trade Center, which collapsed, and the Pentagon in Washington DC. Another plane crash landed in the Pennsylvania countryside. Each year on this date, the New York sky is lit up by 88 searchlights in an art installation called the Tribute of Light.

Prehistoric ages

Prehistory is the time before events were written down and recorded. Human prehistory is usually divided into three periods.

Stone Age

The period when stone was used for tools. It is divided into two parts: Palaeolithic (Old Stone) from about 2 million to 10,000 BC and Neolithic (New Stone) from about 10,000 to 3300 BC.

Bronze Age (c. 3300–c. 2500 BC)

The period when people began to make things with bronze, which was more reliable and hardwearing than stone.

Iron Age (c. 1200 BC–c. AD 50–1000)

The period when iron was used for making tools. Bronze is a better material, but iron was more widely available, so cheaper.

Neolithic burial place, called a dolmen, in Portugal

Historical periods

History is usually divided into different periods to make it easier to study and talk about. The following are the main periods in the history of the Western world since the fall of the Roman empire.

The early Middle Ages (Dark Ages)

This period came after the fall of the Roman empire in AD 476, when so-called barbarians (Germanic tribes) took over areas that had been under Roman control. It became known as the Dark Ages because there was very little writing, science or culture during this time. The lack of writing also means that we do not know much about what happened. The early Middle Ages came to an end after the Norman Conquest when there was a revival in learning.

The Middle (Medieval) Ages

This was a very religious time. Most people believed in an all-powerful God, responsible for bringing order and prosperity. The Church was very influential and wealthy, and many great cathedrals and monasteries were built during this period. It was a great age of learning, and the first universities were founded in Parma and Bologna, then Paris and Oxford. Chartres Cathedral in France was built and the writings of Dante and Chaucer were published.

The Renaissance

The Renaissance began in Italy during the 14th century, and spread to northern Europe in the 16th century. The name Renaissance comes from the French word for rebirth; people looked back to Greek and Roman ideals in arts such as architecture and sculpture at this time. These ideas spread with the help of printing, which was invented by German Johannes Gutenberg in the mid-15th century. The Renaissance was marked by people's belief in progress and personal achievement. The playwright William Shakespeare and the artist Leonardo da Vinci lived and worked during this time.

The Reformation

In 16th-century Europe most people belonged to the Roman Catholic Church, which was headed by the Pope. Some were concerned that the Church was too involved with power and money. Leaders such as Erasmus and Martin Luther wanted people to reject the priests and return to the roots of Christianity and the Bible. This led to the start of Protestantism and its split from the Roman Catholic Church.

The age of colonialism

In 1492 Christopher Columbus discovered the Americas. This encouraged many European countries to invade and conquer other smaller or weaker countries so they could use their resources, trade with them or use them as stopping points for their ships. Portugal gained control of what is now Brazil, and Spain took most of Latin America, as well as large parts of what is now the USA. The Dutch gained the Indonesian islands and the French took Canada. Britain was the most powerful colonizing power. It gained 13 colonies in North America, plus Australasia, some Caribbean islands and vast tracts of Africa and Asia, including India. European colonization continued throughout the 19th century and up to the First World War (1914–18). After the War, the victors divided many of the territories of the losers.

Extent of European colonialism 1815–1914

The Industrial Revolution

The Industrial Revolution began with the invention of steam power and steam-driven machinery (mainly used in the textile industry) in 18th-century Britain. During the following century inventions such as steam-powered ships and railways spread throughout the world. This revolution led thousands of people to leave the countryside and move to crowded slum towns where there were large factories employing huge numbers of workers. The new industries needed better transport to bring supplies and deliver finished goods, so a huge network of roads and canals was built during the 18th century, followed by railways in the 19th. The Industrial Revolution also led to a growth in child labour and a widening divide between rich and poor people.

The modern age

During the 20th century advances in technology led to great changes in society and global politics. New weapons and military techniques changed the way wars were fought. Huge numbers of people died during World Wars I and II. During the Cold War between the USA and the USSR there was no fighting, but both sides were afraid of the nuclear weapons they were developing.

Air travel, television and, most recently, the Internet have all enabled more people to experience the world beyond their own country. At the same time, cheap domestic appliances such as washing machines and dishwashers allow people more time to spend on activities such as entertainment and shopping.

Modern living

In the 20th century, factories began to mass-produce cars that ordinary people could afford. This allowed them to live further from their work places and led to the building of suburbs all over the Western world.

Apple's i-Pad

View down an elevator inside a shopping centre

www.schoolshistory.org.uk search

Romulus and Remus, the founders of Rome, nursed by a she-wolf

753 BC Rome founded

According to legend, Rome was founded by Romulus and Remus, the twin sons of the god Mars and priestess Rhea Silvia. The city is named after Romulus, who killed his brother and ruled as Rome's first king. Rome was the capital of the Roman empire, which controlled the entire Mediterranean region and far beyond by 44 BC.

1789 French Revolution

The French people had many complaints against their system of government, especially the power of the monarchy and the land-owning aristocracy. These erupted in a revolution in which the Bastille prison was seized. The violent period that followed became known as the Reign of Terror, and King Louis XVI and many other members of the ruling class were executed.

Napoleonic Wars

After the French Revolution, a series of battles on land and sea in the period 1803–15, in which French troops under Napoleon fought against Britain and her allies, left up to 2.5 million soldiers and sailors and 1 million civilians dead before Napoleon was captured and exiled. Britain emerged from the conflict as the world's major industrial power, with a large army and navy and an extensive empire, and prospered for the next 100 years.

The Statue of Liberty in New York has a tablet in her left hand which reads July 4 1776.

1776 US Independence

The Declaration of Independence was prepared after years of tension between Britain and the American colonies over matters such as taxation. It listed the colonies' complaints and expressed the determination of the people of America to separate themselves from their British rulers. The declaration was signed on 4 July 1776. The armed conflict that followed ended with America's victory in 1781. In 1783 the Treaty of Paris recognized the country's independence.

History timeline

1000s

1600s

753 BC Rome founded
221 BC Qin Shihuangdi becomes first Emperor of China
about AD 33 Jesus crucified
43 Emperor Claudius invades Britain
79 Pompeii in Italy destroyed by the eruption of Vesuvius volcano
476 Roman empire ends when Goths invade
632 Death of Muhammad, founder of Islam
1066 Battle of Hastings; William the Conqueror becomes king of England
1086–7 Domesday Book records all land in England
1096–99 First Crusade – European Christians attempt to recover Jerusalem and the Holy Land from Muslim control
1215 King John signs Magna Carta, granting rights to English citizens
1347–80s Black Death kills 75 million in Asia and Europe
1337–1453 100 Years War between England and France; France eventually wins
1415 Henry V of England defeats the French at Agincourt and goes on to conquer Normandy
1431 17-year-old French patriot Joan of Arc leads an army and defeats the English (1429), but is burned at the stake
1455–85 Wars of the Roses (civil war in England)
1476 Caxton begins printing in London
1478 Spanish Inquisition begins the persecution of non-Catholics
1492 Columbus sails from Palos, Spain, to Americas
1517 Reformation starts when Martin Luther publishes protests against Catholic Church
1519-22 Ferdinand Magellan's expedition circumnavigates the globe
1588 Spanish Armada defeated by the English fleet, fireships and storms
1618–48 Thirty Years War (Catholic v Protestant) in Europe
1620 The Pilgrim Fathers sail from Plymouth for America and found a new colony
1642–49 English Civil War
1649 King Charles I executed
1660 Restoration of the monarchy; Charles II becomes king
1664–65 The Great Plague kills 70,000 in London
1666 Great Fire of London
1707 Act of Union – Scotland and England unite
1776 US Declaration of Independence
1776–83 American War of Independence

Lenin addressing a crowd of workers

1917 Russian Revolution

The rule of the Russian royal family led by the tsar ended with the February Revolution in 1917. The revolution was triggered by problems such as food shortages and Russia's involvement in World War I. The October Revolution followed later that year, when Soviet forces seized control. They murdered the tsar and his family and attempted to create a Communist state under the leadership of Lenin. A civil war followed from 1918 to 1922. Soviet rule lasted until 1991.

1989 Fall of Berlin Wall

After World War II, control of the East German city of Berlin was split between West Germany (with American, British and French troops) and Soviet East Germany. In 1961 the East Germans built the Berlin Wall to stop its inhabitants fleeing to the West, and 192 people were shot while trying to defect. The wall was a symbol of the divide between the Soviet Union and the West. When the Soviet Union collapsed, the wall was torn down and East and West Germany were reunited, with Berlin as the new capital city.

2011 Centenaries

1511
Baracoa, the first European settlement on the island of Cuba, was founded.

1611
William Shakespeare's *The Winter's Tale* and *The Tempest* were first performed.

1711
The tuning fork was invented by trumpeter John Shore (UK).

1811
The element iodine was discovered by French chemist Bernard Courtois.

1911
- The first Monte Carlo Rally and first Indianapolis 500 auto race were held.
- Leonardo da Vinci's painting, the *Mona Lisa*, was stolen from the Louvre Museum, Paris, but recovered in 1913.
- Anglo-American author Frances Hodgson Burnett published her popular children's book, *The Secret Garden*.
- Marie Curie received the Nobel Prize for Chemistry. She had previously won the Nobel Prize for Physics in 1903.
- The lost Inca city of Machu Picchu, Peru, was discovered by US explorer Hiram Bingham III.
- The Lewis machine gun, later used by fighter aircraft, was patented.
- The horse-drawn bus service in London ended.

See also
Lost Cities: page 119
Leonardo da Vinci: page 80

2000s

1783 First balloon flight (Montgolfier brothers, France)
1788 First European settlers arrive in Australia
1789 French Revolution
1793 Louis XVI of France executed
1815 Battle of Waterloo; Wellington defeats Napoleon
1825 World's first public railway, Stockton to Darlington
1833 Slavery abolished in the British empire
1853–56 Crimean War
1860–65 American Civil War
1863 First underground railway, London
1869 Suez Canal opens
1869 US transcontinental railway completed
1876 Alexander Graham Bell invents telephone
1901–10 Peak decade for immigration into USA (8.8 million immigrants)
1903 First aeroplane flights (Wright brothers, USA)
1903 Henry Ford begins mass production of cars
1914–18 World War I – 8,545,800 military deaths
1917 Russian Revolution establishes Soviet Union
1929–33 Great Depression (world economic crisis)
1939–45 World War II – 15,843,000 military deaths
1945 Atom bombs dropped on Hiroshima and Nagasaki, Japan
1945–90 Cold War between USSR and the West
1950–53 Korean War
1959–75 Vietnam War (USA involved 1961–73)
1961 First man in space (Yuri Gagarin, USSR)
1961 Berlin Wall built, separating East and West Germany
1963 US President John F. Kennedy assassinated
1969 Neil Armstrong becomes first man on the Moon
1989 Fall of the Berlin Wall triggers the end of the Soviet Union
1994 Nelson Mandela becomes president of South Africa
2001 World Trade Center, New York, destroyed by terrorists; USA retaliates by invading Afghanistan
2003 Iraq War and Saddam Hussein overthrown; elections later held but violence continues
2006 Saddam Hussein executed
2008 Global financial crisis and recession begin with the collapse of banks and other businesses
2009 Barack Obama inaugurated as 44th US President, watched by 1.8 million spectators

Mesopotamia/Sumeria

Mesopotamia was a region around the Tigris and Euphrates rivers, which is now part of Turkey, Syria and Iraq. The area was controlled by several different peoples, beginning with the Sumerians in around 3500 BC. They set up a number of city-states that constantly battled to control land and trade routes until they were united under one ruler in 2350 BC. They finally became absorbed into other races around 2000 BC.

Ancient Egypt

Egypt is an area in the Nile valley which was ruled as a single state from about 3200 BC. There were 30 dynasties, led by pharaohs who were both kings and gods. The pyramids were built during the fourth dynasty (2575–2467 BC) as tombs for the pharaohs of that time. The Great Pyramid of Giza was the world's tallest building for 4000 years, and it is the only wonder of the world that still stands. Like other powerful empires, ancient Egypt was weakened by invasions, until it was taken over by Alexander the Great in 332 BC.

Ancient Greece

Ancient Greece was called Hellas. The civilization was at its strongest in 500–400 BC, after Greece colonized Cyprus, parts of Italy, Ukraine and the South of France. This era was known as the Golden Age. Some city-states, such as Athens and Sparta, became great centres of art, learning and politics. Many famous thinkers lived in Athens during this period, including Aristotle, Plato, Socrates and Aristophanes. The ancient Greeks also created the idea of democracy: its citizens were encouraged to debate and then vote on issues. The Golden Age ended in wars between the city-states, which paved the way for King Philip of Macedonia to invade Greece, followed later by his son Alexander.

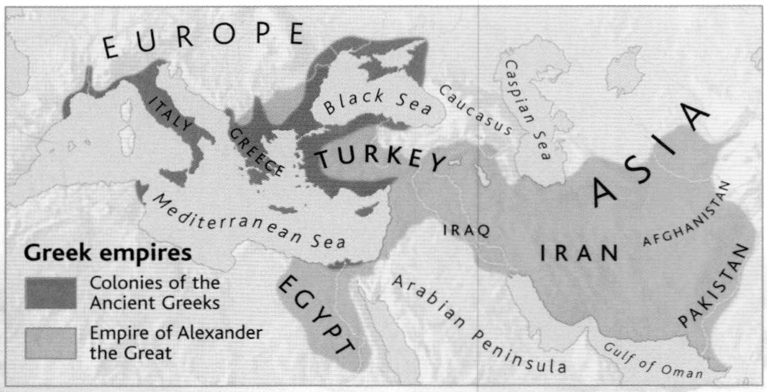

Alexander the Great's empire

Alexander III of Macedonia lived for only 33 years, from 356 to 323 BC. In that short time he built an empire covering Persia (modern Iraq, Iran, Syria and Turkey), Egypt, Greece and Babylon. It was difficult to keep this huge empire together, and it collapsed soon after his death. Alexander ended the Achaemenid Persian Empire that had been established in 550 BC when Cyrus the Great conquered the Median Empire. Persia became part of the Selucid Empire but rose again as the Parthian Empire under Mithridates I and the Sassanid Empire that ruled for over 400 years, until the Islamic conquest of AD 651.

Chinese empire

China was one of the first places where people are known to have lived. From 1600 BC it was made up of many small kingdoms which all united in 221 BC under one leader or emperor. Various dynasties ruled the empire, starting with the Qin dynasty. During this time, the Great Wall of China was built to keep invaders out. China was an extremely learned civilization, ahead of Europe in the arts and sciences by up to 200 years. The empire finally fell apart under the Han dynasty in AD 220 as a result of corruption and poverty.

Roman empire

The Roman empire was formed in 31 BC under the leadership of Caesar Augustus, who ruled over every aspect of Roman life. Caesar Augustus brought peace, prosperity and culture. The empire expanded so much that by the 2nd century AD Rome had colonies which stretched from the Middle East to Spain, and from Great Britain to North Africa. The sheer size of the empire brought problems. There was not enough money to pay for an army spread across the world, which made the empire vulnerable to enemies. Constant attacks by German barbarians eventually defeated the army, and the empire fell in AD 476. The influence of ancient Rome is staggering: Roman roads still cross Europe, the Roman legal system is still the model for countries in Europe and Latin America, and its language, Latin, is the basis of many languages spoken today.

The Great pyramid of Giza (seen here in the centre), also called the Pyramid of Khufu, stands near the smaller pyramids of Khafre and Menkaure.

Mayan pyramid in Tikal, once the capital of the Mayan empire

Mayan empire

The Mayan empire was made up of city-states that stretched across southern Mexico and northern Central America. There have been Mayan people since 2000 BC but their greatest period was from AD 300 to 900, when architectural wonders such as Palenque and Uxmal were built. These structures and many others show that the Mayans had an advanced knowledge of mathematics. The Mayan empire gradually declined after 900, and the Spanish invaded the area in the 15th century.

Inca empire

The Incas had a great empire that stretched 900,000 sq km (350,000 sq miles) across South America, including Colombia, Bolivia and Argentina, with a capital, Cuzco, in Peru. It lasted from around 1200 until 1533. Inca society was very organized: every person was told which job they had to do and where to do it. In return, they were looked after by the state. Like the Aztecs, the Incas were brutally repressed by Spanish conquistadors in the 15th century.

Aztec empire

The Aztecs arrived in Mexico in 1325 and founded the city of Tenochtitlán, home to about 90,000 people. It showed the Aztecs' skill in engineering and included a system of drainage that was far ahead of any in Europe. The Aztecs conquered neighbouring city-states and extended their empire until it stretched from the Pacific to the Gulf of Mexico into Guatemala. The empire ended when the Spanish, led by Hernán Cortés, invaded between 1519 and 1522.

Ottoman empire

The Ottoman empire was an Islamic state from the 13th to 20th centuries and the most powerful empire in the world during the 1500s and 1600s. It covered Turkey, parts of southwest Asia, southeast Europe and North Africa. The capital was Constantinople (now Istanbul). The empire began to decline because its rulers refused to modernize and they lost lands in several wars. It allied with Germany in World War I. Defeated, its remaining lands were divided among the victors.

The Taj Mahal in Agra, India

Mogul empire

The Mogul empire was founded in 1526 in northern India by a descendent of Genghis Khan. This was a hugely wealthy civilization and the Moguls greatly valued education, culture and art. The Taj Mahal was built by Moguls from 1632–53. This beautiful mausoleum was made for Emperor Shah Jahan's favourite wife, Mumtaz Mahal, and is built of marble with exquisite inlaid decoration. The empire's Muslim leaders wanted the people to keep Muslim ways, but many of its subjects were Hindu. In 1691 the empire was torn apart by bloody battles between Muslims and Hindus. The Mogul empire was finally overthrown by the British in 1857.

British empire

At the beginning of the 20th century, about a quarter of the world's people lived under British rule. The British had been expanding their empire since the 15th century, and by 1900 its lands included South Africa, Kenya, Egypt, Hong Kong, India, Iraq, Nepal, Singapore, Malta, Australia, New Zealand and Canada. Most of Britain's former colonies have now won or been granted independence. Many belong to the Commonwealth, which is a voluntary association of independent states founded in 1931 (see map on pages 102–103).

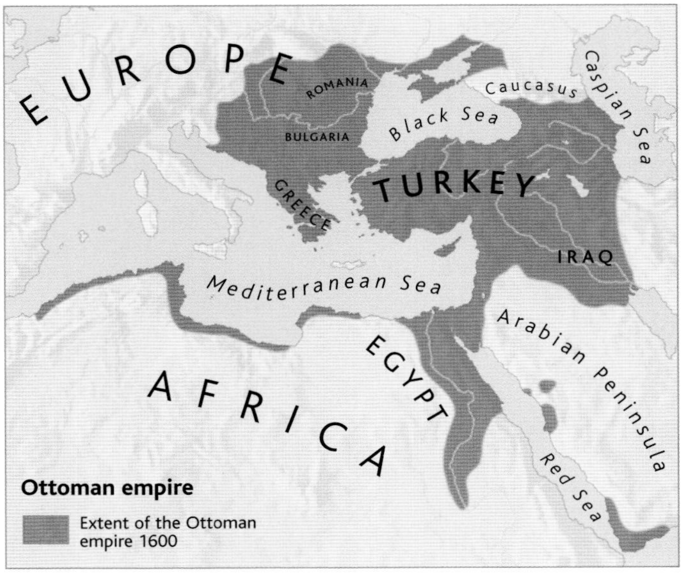

US presidents

US presidents are elected for a term of four years. George Washington was the first president of the USA and he served two terms. Only Franklin Delano Roosevelt served three terms. He died shortly after he was elected for a fourth term.

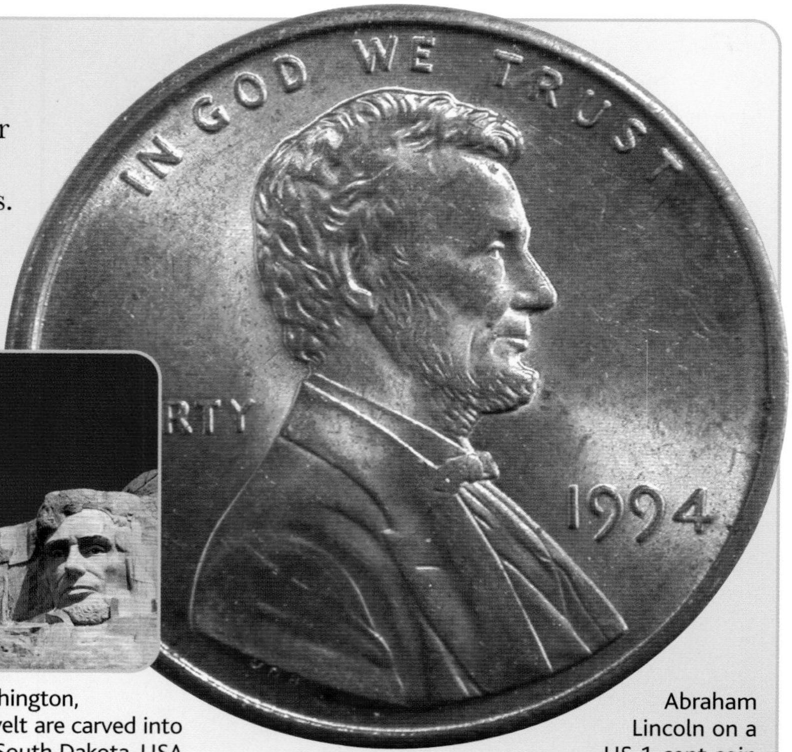

Abraham Lincoln on a US 1-cent coin

In 1951 the 22nd Amendment to the US Constitution ruled that two terms are the most any president may serve. The two main political parties in the USA today are the Democratic Party and the Republican Party. The dates in the list below are when the Presidents were inaugurated.

The heads of presidents Washington, Jefferson, Lincoln and Roosevelt are carved into the face of Mt Rushmore in South Dakota, USA.

1 George Washington (Federalist party) 1789
2 John Adams (Federalist party) 1797
3 Thomas Jefferson (Dem-Rep party) 1801
4 James Madison (Dem-Rep party) 1809
5 James Monroe (Dem-Rep party) 1817
6 John Quincy Adams (Dem-Rep party) 1825
7 Andrew Jackson (Democratic party) 1829
8 Martin Van Buren (Democratic party) 1837
9 William Henry Harrison (Whig party) 1841
10 John Tyler (Whig party) 1841
11 James Knox Polk (Democratic party) 1845
12 Zachary Taylor (Whig party) 1849
13 Millard Fillmore (Whig party) 1850
14 Franklin Pierce (Democratic party) 1853
15 James Buchanan (Democratic party) 1857
16 Abraham Lincoln (Republican party) 1861
17 Andrew Johnson (Democratic party) 1865
18 Ulysses Simpson Grant (Republican party) 1869
19 Rutherford Birchard Hayes (Republican party) 1877
20 James Abram Garfield (Republican party) 1881
21 Chester Alan Arthur (Republican party) 1881
22 Grover Cleveland (Democratic party) 1885
23 Benjamin Harrison (Republican party) 1889
24 Grover Cleveland (Democratic party) 1893
25 William McKinley (Republican party) 1897
26 Theodore Roosevelt (Republican party) 1901
27 William Howard Taft (Republican party) 1909
28 Woodrow Wilson (Democratic party) 1913
29 Warren Gamaliel Harding (Republican party) 1921
30 Calvin Coolidge (Republican party) 1923
31 Herbert Clark Hoover (Republican party) 1929
32 Franklin Delano Roosevelt (Democratic party) 1933
33 Harry S. Truman (Democratic party) 1945
34 Dwight David Eisenhower (Republican party) 1953
35 John Fitzgerald Kennedy (Democratic party) 1961
36 Lyndon Baines Johnson (Democratic party) 1963
37 Richard Milhous Nixon (Republican party) 1969
38 Gerald Rudolph Ford (Republican party) 1974
39 Jimmy Carter (Democratic party) 1977
40 Ronald Reagan (Republican party) 1981
41 George Bush (Republican party) 1989
42 Bill Clinton (Democratic party) 1993
43 George Walker Bush (Republican party) 2001
44 Barack Hussein Obama (Democratic party) 2009

World monarchies

A monarchy is a country where the head of state is a king, queen or other hereditary ruler – someone who inherits the throne from a family member. In some countries, such as Malaysia, the monarch is elected.

Bahrain Shaikh Hamad bin Isa al-Khalifa succeeded to the throne in 1999

Belgium King Albert II succeeded to the throne in 1993

Bhutan Jigme Khesar Namgyel Wangchuck succeeded to the throne in 2006 (he was crowned in 2008)

Brunei Sultan Haji Hassanal Bolkiah succeeded to the throne in 1967

Cambodia King Norodom Sihamoni succeeded to the throne in 2004

Denmark Queen Margrethe II succeeded to the throne in 1972

Japan Emperor Akihito succeeded to the throne in 1989

Jordan King Abdullah II succeeded to the throne in 1999

Kuwait Shaikh Sabah al-Ahmad al-Sabah succeeded to the throne in 2006

Lesotho Letsie II became king in 1990 but stepped down in 1995. He succeeded to the throne again when his father was killed in 1996.

Liechtenstein Prince Hans Adam II succeeded to the throne in 1989

Amazing monarchs

Oldest monarch to ascend the British throne
William IV (ruled 1830–37) was 64 when he was crowned.

British monarchs with the most children
Edward I had 16 children (6 sons and 10 daughters). Both George III and James II had 15.

Most-married British monarch
Henry VIII had six wives who suffered various fates. They were: Catherine of Aragon (divorced), Anne Boleyn (beheaded), Jane Seymour (died 1537), Anne of Cleves (divorced), Catherine Howard (beheaded) and Catherine Parr, who survived Henry.

Youngest British monarchs
Henry VI was just eight months old when he became king on 1 September 1422 after the death of his father, Henry V. When his grandfather, Charles VI, died 50 days later on 21 October 1422, Henry also became king of France.

Shortest-reigning British monarchs
Queen Jane (Lady Jane Grey), ruled for only nine days in 1553, before being sent to the Tower of London. She was executed the following year. Edward V ruled for 75 days. He was one of the Princes in the Tower, who were allegedly murdered on the orders of their uncle, Richard III. Edward VIII abdicated (gave up the throne) on 11 December 1936, before his coronation. He had ruled for just 325 days.

Longest-reigning world monarch
King Louis XIV of France became king at the age of five. He ruled for 72 years, from 1643–1715.

Longest-reigning British monarch
Queen Victoria was 18 years old when she became queen in 1837 and she ruled for 63 years.

Richest world ruler
King Bhumibol Adulyadej of Thailand has been claimed to have a fortune of $30 billion.

Monarchies with the most rulers
Japan's monarchy dates from 40 BC. Since then, it has had 125 rulers.

Henry VIII

Most subjects
Monarchies (countries with a king or queen or other hereditary ruler as head of state) contain about 1/12th of the world's population. The largest is the British Commonwealth, consisting of the UK plus 15 other countries, with a total population of 132,645,981 (2011 estimate), with Queen Elizabeth II at its head since 1952. The largest single-country monarchy is Japan (126,475,664), ruled by Emperor Akihito since 1989. Mainland Europe's largest monarchy is Spain (40,560,943), ruled by Juan Carlos I since 1975, and the world's smallest is Monaco, with a population of 32,224, under the rule of Prince Albert II since 2005.

See also
Types of government: pages 110–111

Henry VII was the first Tudor. He devised the Tudor Rose to symbolize unity between the House of York (white rose) and the House of Lancaster (red rose).

Luxembourg Grand Duke Henri succeeded to the throne in 2000
Malaysia Sultan Mizan Zainal Abidin succeeded to the throne in 2006
Monaco Prince Albert II succeeded to the throne in 2005
Morocco King Mohammed VI succeeded to the throne in 1999
Nepal King Gyanendra Bir Bikram Shah Dev succeeded to the throne in 2001
Netherlands Queen Beatrix succeeded to the throne in 1980
Norway King Harald V succeeded to the throne in 1991
Oman Sultan Qaboos Bin Said al-Said succeeded to the throne in 1970
Qatar Shaikh Hamad bin Kaalifa al-Thani succeeded to the throne in 1995
Saudi Arabia King Abdullah ibn Abdul Aziz al-Saud succeeded to the throne in 2005
Spain King Juan Carlos I succeeded to the throne in 1975
Swaziland King Mswati III succeeded to the throne in 1986
Sweden King Carl XVI Gustaf succeeded to the throne, 1973
Thailand King Bhumibol Adulyadej succeeded to the throne in 1946
Tonga George Tupou V succeeded to the throne in 2006
United Kingdom Queen Elizabeth II succeeded to the throne in 1952

Votes for women

The Isle of Man was the first place to give women the vote, in 1880, but the island is part of the UK and not a separate country. Until 1920 the only European countries that allowed women to vote were Sweden (1919) and Czechoslovakia (1920).

In the USA women were granted the vote in 1920, although some states allowed it earlier. Women could not vote in France or Italy until 1945, in Switzerland until 1971 or in Liechtenstein until 1984. Women were granted the right to vote in Kuwait for the first time in 2005, but they are still not allowed to vote in Brunei, Saudi Arabia and the United Arab Emirates. There are other countries where women have no vote – but neither do men.

1 The first country to give women the vote was New Zealand in 1893.
2 Australia followed suit in 1902 although women had the vote in South Australia in 1894 and in Western Australia in 1898 before the separate states were united in 1901.
3 Finland (then a Grand Duchy under the Russian Crown) granted women the vote in 1906.
4 Norway gave some women the vote in 1907. It was not until 1913 that all women over 25 could vote.
5 Denmark and Iceland (a Danish dependency until 1918) allowed women to vote in 1915.
6 The Netherlands and the USSR both gave women the vote in 1917.
8 Austria, Canada, Germany, Poland, Great Britain and Ireland all gave women the vote in 1918. (In Ireland, part of the UK until 1921, only women over 30 got the vote in 1918. This was lowered to 21 in 1928.)

www.rulers.org search

British poster demanding votes for women

Types of government

There have been many different types of government around the world throughout history. Many of the names for them end in the term -cracy, from a Greek word meaning power.

Aristocracy
Rule by a small group of members of a privileged class.

Autocracy
Government by one person with unrestricted power; also known as despotism and dictatorship.

Fidel Castro was President of Cuba for almost 50 years before handing power to his brother Raúl.

Communist
Government of a classless state in which private ownership is abolished and the state controls all means of production, as in China and Cuba.

Democracy
Government by the people directly or through elected representatives, as in the UK and USA.

Magna Carta

The Magna Carta or Great Charter is a document that established the rights of the subjects of the British monarch, including their agreement to be bound by the country's laws, the right of habeas corpus (Latin for 'have the body'), which prevents people from being imprisoned unlawfully, and limiting the power of the ruler. The original Magna Carta was prepared by the leading barons of England and was sealed, rather than signed, by King John at Runnymede, Surrey, on 15 June 1210. It was later revised, but many of the principles it set have remained in force for almost 800 years and have been used in defining the rights of citizens in other countries, including the United States. Early copies of the Magna Carta are displayed in Hereford and Salisbury Cathedrals and in other collections in Britain and overseas.

Women in parliament

As at 1 January 2010, there were 59 countries with at least 20 per cent of their parliament made up of women – but a number of countries still do not have any women representatives at all.

Based on the most recent general election results, these countries have the highest percentages of women in parliament: Rwanda 56.3 per cent, Sweden 46.4 per cent, South Africa 44.5 per cent, Cuba 43.2 per cent, Iceland 42.9 per cent, Netherlands 42.0 per cent.

Meritocracy
Government by leaders selected according to their ability.

Monarchy
Government in which power is held by a king (or queen, emperor or empress) who can pass power on to their heirs.

Oligarchy
Government by a small group of people.

Plutocracy
A government or state in which wealthy people rule.

Theocracy
Government ruled by or subject to religious authority.

Major international organizations

A number of international organizations have been set up to deal with issues that concern the world in general, rather than the interests of individual countries. These organizations are not linked to political parties but often become involved in political matters.

Flags flying outside the United Nations, New York

United Nations

The UN was founded in 1945. Most countries of the world – a total of 192 – are members. The General Assembly of the UN makes decisions about peacekeeping and human rights.

Amnesty International (AI)
Amnesty International is a charitable organization set up in 1961. It campaigns for human rights throughout the world and against the detention of political prisoners.

International Monetary Fund (IMF)
The IMF was established in 1944 and promotes world trade. It has 185 member countries.

International Red Cross and Red Crescent Movement
These organizations help the victims of such events as warfare and natural disasters.

Organization for Economic Co-operation and Development (OECD)
The OECD was formed in 1961. It aims to encourage economic and social development in industrialized countries and provide aid to developing countries.

United Nations Children's Fund (UNICEF)
UNICEF was set up in 1947. It works to improve the health and welfare of children and mothers in developing countries.

United Nations Educational, Scientific and Cultural Organization (UNESCO)
UNESCO was set up in 1946. It encourages countries to get together on matters such as education, culture and science.

World Bank
The World Bank was founded in 1944 and has 185 member countries. It helps developing countries by giving loans.

World Health Organization
The WHO is part of the UN. It promotes health matters worldwide and aims to raise medical standards and monitor diseases.

World Trade Organization (WTO)
The Swiss-based WTO has 151 member countries. It establishes trade agreements between countries.

World Wildlife Fund (WWF)
The WWF was set up in 1961 and is the world's largest conservation organization. Its main aims are to protect endangered animals and the places where they live.

NATO
The North Atlantic Treaty Organization (NATO) was founded in 1949. Ten countries signed a defence treaty that committed them to helping each other in the event of attack. There are now 26 country members, and the NATO headquarters are based in Belgium.

G20

The G20 is a group of finance ministers from the world's 19 major economies and the European Union who meet to discuss global economic issues. Together, they control more than 80 per cent of the world's production and trade.

Countries of the World

New countries, 2010

After many years of discussion and a series of referendums, on 10 October 2010 the five Caribbean islands that made up the Netherlands Antilles were dissolved as a federation. Curaçao and St Maarten became self-governing countries within the Kingdom of the Netherlands. Meanwhile, the islands of Saba (seen here), Bonaire and St Eustatius became cities with the new status of 'Kingdom Islands', with their legal and other aspects of their government under the control of the Netherlands.

Key to numbered countries

Europe
1 Netherlands
2 Luxembourg
3 Andorra
4 Monaco
5 Lichtenstein
6 Vatican City State
7 San Marino
8 Slovenia
9 Boznia-Herzegovina
10 Serbia
11 Macedonia
12 Montenegro
13 Kosovo

Africa
14 Republic of Congo

Asia
15 Singapore

ARCTIC OCEAN
Svalbard (NORWAY)
Barents Sea
Kara Sea
Arctic Circle
RUSSIA
NORWAY
SWEDEN
FINLAND
Baltic Sea
ESTONIA
LATVIA
LITHUANIA
Russia
North Sea
DENMARK
POLAND
BELARUS
UKRAINE
BELGIUM
GERMANY
CZECH REP
SLOVAKIA
AUSTRIA
HUNGARY
SWITZ
FRANCE
MOLDOVA
ROMANIA
CROATIA
ITALY
ALBANIA
BULGARIA
Black Sea
Corsica (FRANCE)
Sardinia (ITALY)
Mallorca (SPAIN)
GREECE
MALTA
TUNISIA
Mediterranean Sea
CYPRUS
LEBANON
ISRAEL
TURKEY
GEORGIA
ARMENIA
AZERBAIJAN
Caspian Sea
KAZAKHSTAN
Aral Sea
UZBEKISTAN
TURKMENISTAN
KYRGYZSTAN
TAJIKISTAN
MONGOLIA
Sea of Okhotsk
Sea of Japan
NORTH KOREA
SOUTH KOREA
JAPAN
CHINA
SYRIA
IRAQ
JORDAN
IRAN
AFGHANISTAN
PAKISTAN
KUWAIT
BAHRAIN
QATAR
SAUDI ARABIA
UNITED ARAB EMIRATES
OMAN
YEMEN
NEPAL
BHUTAN
INDIA
BANGLADESH
MYANMAR
LAOS
THAILAND
CAMBODIA
VIETNAM
TAIWAN
Philippine Sea
PHILIPPINES
South China Sea
PACIFIC OCEAN
Tropic of Cancer
ALGERIA
LIBYA
EGYPT
Red Sea
NIGER
CHAD
SUDAN
ERITREA
DJIBOUTI
ETHIOPIA
SOMALIA
NIGERIA
TOGO
BENIN
CAMEROON
CENTRAL AFRICAN REPUBLIC
EQUATORIAL GUINEA
SÃO TOMÉ & PRÍNCIPE
GABON
DEMOCRATIC REPUBLIC OF CONGO
UGANDA
KENYA
RWANDA
BURUNDI
TANZANIA
Angola
ANGOLA
ZAMBIA
MALAWI
MOZAMBIQUE
ZIMBABWE
NAMIBIA
BOTSWANA
SWAZILAND
LESOTHO
SOUTH AFRICA
MADAGASCAR
COMOROS
SEYCHELLES
MAURITIUS
MALDIVES
SRI LANKA
Arabian Sea
Bay of Bengal
MALAYSIA
BRUNEI
PALAU
MICRONESIA
MARSHALL ISLANDS
Equator
NAURU
KIRIBATI
INDONESIA
PAPUA NEW GUINEA
EAST TIMOR
SOLOMON ISLANDS
TUVALU
Coral Sea
VANUATU
SAMOA
FIJI
New Caledonia (FRANCE)
TONGA
INDIAN OCEAN
AUSTRALIA
Tropic of Capricorn
Tasman Sea
NEW ZEALAND
SOUTHERN OCEAN
Antarctic Circle
Antarctica
1
2
3
4
5
6
7
8
9
10
11
12
13
14
15

Montreal, Canada's second largest city

Largest countries

These figures are based on total land area, including inland water, such as rivers and lakes. If the water area was not taken into account, China would be second largest, at 9,326,410 sq km (3,600,947 sq miles), the USA third with 9,161,923 sq km (3,537,439 sq miles) and Canada fourth at 9,093,507 sq km (3,511,023 sq miles).

Largest countries

Country	Area sq km (sq miles)
Russia	17,075,200 (6,592,772)
Canada	9,984,670 (3,855,103)
USA	9,826,630 (3,794,083)
China	9,596,960 (3,705,407)
Brazil	8,511,965 (3,286,488)
Australia	7,686,850 (2,967,910)

Smallest countries

Country	Area sq km (sq miles)
Vatican City	0.44 (0.17)
Monaco	2 (0.77)
Nauru	21 (8)
Tuvalu	26 (10)
San Marino	61 (24)
Liechtenstein	160 (62)

Biggest landlocked countries

A landlocked country has no coastline. This means that it has no direct access to the sea and fishing. Also, people and goods travelling to and from the country must go through another country. This may be difficult or expensive.

There are more than 40 landlocked countries in the world. The largest, Kazakhstan, has a coast on the Caspian Sea – which is a landlocked sea. The largest landlocked European country is Hungary (92,300 sq km [35,637 sq miles]). Europe also contains the world's smallest landlocked countries – Andorra, Liechtenstein, San Marino and Vatican City. All are less than 500 sq km (193 sq miles) in size. Liechtenstein and Uzbekistan are both double-landlocked. This means that they are surrounded by other landlocked countries.

Kazakhstan 2,717,300 sq km (1,049,155 sq miles)
Mongolia 1,564,116 sq km (603,908 sq miles)
Chad 1,284,000 sq km (495,755 sq miles)
Niger 1,267,000 sq km (489,191 sq miles)
Mali 1,240,000 sq km (478,766 sq miles)
Ethiopia 1,127,127 sq km (435,186 sq miles)
Bolivia 1,098,580 sq km (424,164 sq miles)

Longest and shortest frontiers

A country's frontier is made up of the combined length of all its land borders.

Longest
China 22,117 km (13,743 miles)
Russia 20,097 km (12,488 miles)
Brazil 16,885 km (10,488 miles)
India 14,103 km (8,763 miles)
USA 12,034 km (7,478 miles)

Shortest
Vatican City 3.2 km (2.0 miles)
Monaco 4.4 km (2.7 miles)
Cuba 29.0 km (18 miles)
San Marino 39.0 km (24 miles)
Qatar 60 km (37 miles)

Biggest and smallest populations

In most countries, more people are born every day than die, so population figures are going up all the time. China has the biggest population, but India is catching up fast.

Biggest population

Country	Population
China	1,329,111,520
India	1,187,125,055
USA	309,473,626
Indonesia	231,749,876
Brazil	197,289,533
Pakistan	155,360,000
Nigeria	154,622,507
Bangladesh	147,243,324
Russia	140,728,754
Japan	128,240,609

Smallest population

Country	Population
Vatican City	541
Tuvalu	9,981
Nauru	10,175
Palau	20,945
San Marino	30,509
Monaco	34,028
Liechtenstein	35,870
Saint Christopher and Nevis	50,388
Marshall Islands	54,185
Dominica	70,509

Most neighbourly countries

Most island countries have no neighbours (although some, such as Indonesia, do), and many countries, such as Canada (with the USA) and the UK (with Ireland) have only a single border with another. Excluding dependencies and other territories, these countries have the most neighbours:

Country	No. of neighbours	Country	No. of neighbours
Russia	16	Zambia	8
China	14	Afghanistan	7
Brazil	10	Algeria	7
Dem. Rep. of Congo	9	Hungary	7
Germany	9	India	7
Sudan	9	Mali	7
Austria	8	Niger	7
France	8	Poland	7
Serbia	8	Saudi Arabia	7
Tanzania	8	Ukraine	7
Turkey	8		

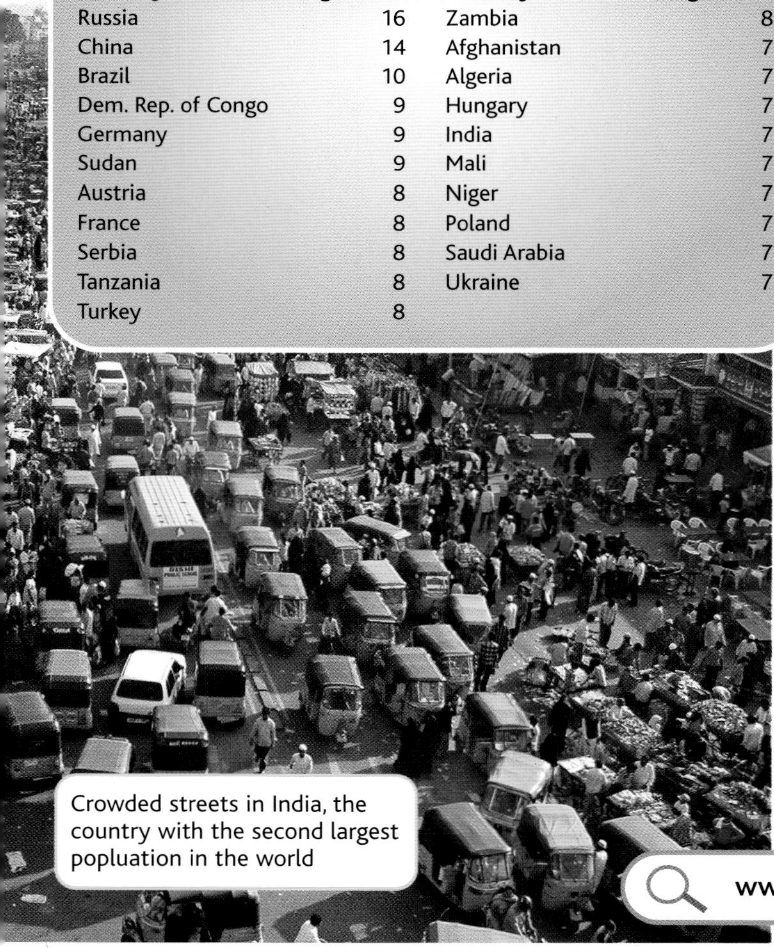

Crowded streets in India, the country with the second largest popluation in the world

Population density

In densely populated countries, lots of people live on a small amount of land, usually in cities. The least densely populated countries are usually difficult for people to live in. The climate may be very cold or very hot, or there may be large areas of mountain, desert or forest.

Most densely populated countries

	people per sq km	sq ml
Monaco	17,450	45,195
Singapore	8,145	21,095
Malta	1,288	3,336
Vatican City	1,230	3,186
Bahrain	1,191	3,085
[**UK**	253.0	655.3]

Least densely populated countries

	people per sq km	sq ml
Mongolia	1.73	4.48
Namibia	2.69	6.97
Australia	2.69	6.97
Mauritania	3.04	7.87
Iceland	3.14	8.13

Monaco

www.census.gov/main/www/popclock.html search

Changing names

Many cities change their names after the countries they are in become independent. Others are renamed after political changes, such as those ending the former Soviet Union. Some changes come from variations in the way in which foreign languages are translated from one alphabet to another.

Old name/country	**New name (since)**
Batavia, Indonesia	**Jakarta** (1949)
Bombay, India	**Mumbai** (1995)
Calcutta, India	**Kolkata** (2001)
Christiana, Norway	**Oslo** (1924)
Byzantium/Constantinople, Turkey	**Istanbul** (1930)
Danzig, Poland	**Gdansk** (1945)
Leningrad, USSR	**St Petersburg**, Russia (1991)
Léopoldville, Belgian Congo	**Kinshasa**, D.R. Congo (1960)
New Amsterdam, America	**New York**, USA (1664)
Pretoria, South Africa	**Tshwane** (2005)
Rangoon, Burma	**Yangon**, Myanmar (1989)
Saigon, Vietnam	**Ho Chi Minh City** (1975)
Salisbury, Rhodesia	**Harare**, Zimbabwe (1980)
Santa Isabel, Equatorial Guinea	**Malabo** (1973)
Tsaritsyn/Stalingrad, USSR	**Volgograd**, Russia (1961)

Cities with the most people*

1 Tokyo, Japan	37,730,064
2 Mexico City, Mexico	23,610,441
3 New York, USA	23,313,036
4 Seoul, South Korea	22,692,652
5 Mumbai (Bombay), India	21,900,967
6 São Paulo, Brazil	20,831,058
7 Manila, Philippines	20,654,307
8 Jakarta, Indonesia	19,231,919
9 Delhi, India	18,916,890
10 Shanghai, China	18,572,816

*Estimated figures for city and adjoining populated areas 2009. This calculation applies throughout this section.
Source: World Gazetteer.

www.citypopulation.de/cities.html search

Highest towns and cities

Some towns and cities are in surprisingly high places. The Chinese city of Wenchuan, founded in 1955, is at more than half the height of Everest. Even the towns and cities at the bottom of this list are at more than a third the height of Everest.

1 Wenchuan, China – 5,099 m (16,729 ft)
2 Potosí, Bolivia – 3,976 m (13,045 ft)
3 Oruro, Bolivia – 3,702 m (12,146 ft)
4 Lhasa, China – 3,684 m (12,087 ft)
5 La Paz, Bolivia – 3,632 m (11,916 ft)
6 Cuzco, Peru – 3,399 m (11,152 ft)
7 Huancayo, Peru – 3,249 m (10,659 ft)
8 Sucre, Bolivia – 2,835 m (9,301 ft)
9 Tunja, Colombia – 2,820 m (9,252 ft)
10 Quito, Ecuador – 2,819 m (9,249 ft)

La Paz, the world's highest capital city

What is a city?

A city is a large town. In some countries, a city has a special status. In the UK it may have been given a royal charter. In the USA it is an urban area with its own government.

A town is a densely populated area with a defined boundary and its own government. A town is smaller than a city and larger than a village.

A village is a small group of houses and other buildings in a country area.

A hamlet is a small village or a cluster of houses in a country area. In the UK a village is a hamlet if it does not have a church.

A settlement is a small group of inhabited buildings, or a small countryside community, such as a ranch or farm with a few dwellings.

The rediscovered city of Troy

Lost cities

There are some cities that were very famous in the past but have since been destroyed or abandoned.

Angkor, Cambodia
Angkor was once the largest city in the world and more than a million people lived there. The city had an area of more than 78 sq km (30 sq miles) and was surrounded by a water-filled moat. It was abandoned in about AD 1100. Frenchman Henri Mouhot was the first westerner to discover the city, in 1861.

Nuclear ghost town

The Ukrainian town of Pripyat, built in 1970 and once home to nearly 50,000 people, was evacuated after the Chernobyl nuclear accident of 1986 and is now completely deserted. Abandoned homes, schools, a hospital and cinema are gradually collapsing and becoming overgrown, while a Ferris wheel in the amusement park stands rusting amid the devastation.

Machu Picchu, Peru

See also
World civilizations and empires: pages 106–107

Atlantis
Some people believe that there was a city and island of Atlantis, perhaps in the Mediterranean, that was destroyed by an earthquake and flooding almost 12,000 years ago. No one knows exactly where it was or even whether it really existed.

Chichén Itzá, Mexico
Chichén Itzá was once the centre of the Mayan empire. It was built in about AD 400 and had many buildings used in Mayan rituals. The city was abandoned in AD 1200.

Cliff Palace (Mesa Verde), Colorado, USA
This Native American Indian city was built on a cliff side, but was abandoned during a long drought in the late 13th century. It lay unknown until 18 December 1888, when Richard Wetherill, a local farmer, spotted it while looking for stray cattle.

Machu Picchu, Peru
The fortified Inca city on top of a mountain was stumbled on in 1911 by American explorer Hiram Bingham. He was searching for Vilcabamba, another lost Inca city.

Pompeii, Italy
The entire city was buried by volcanic ash when Mount Vesuvius erupted in AD 79. Nearby Herculaneum was buried at the same time. Excavations began in 1748, and many treasures have been uncovered, including beautifully preserved murals (wall paintings). Plaster casts have been made of the bodies of inhabitants who were buried beneath the debris.

Troy, Turkey
Troy was once thought to have existed only in legends, but its site was discovered in the 1870s.

Ur, Iraq
Ur was once one of the greatest cities in the world, but was abandoned in the 4th century BC. Its magnificent royal tombs and other sites were excavated by archaeologists in 1922–34 and many treasures discovered.

Banff National Park, Alberta, Canada

Canada

Canada is the second largest country in the world, after Russia. Almost half of Canada's land area is covered by forest and it exports more timber, pulp and newsprint than any other country. Canada also has a successful fishing industry and lots of natural resources, such as minerals and metals. Its varied landscape attracts millions of tourists each year. Famous Canadian landmarks include Niagara Falls and the Rocky Mountains.

Area 9,984,670 sq km (3,855,103 sq miles)
Country population 32,812,518
Capital city (pop) Ottawa (1,177,673)
Official languages French/English
Currency Canadian dollar

United States

The USA is made up of 50 states (including Alaska and Hawaii) and the District of Columbia, which contains the capital city, Washington. It includes a huge variety of landscapes, from hot deserts to snow-covered mountains. The country was once a colony under British rule but has been independent since 1776. It is now the world's wealthiest country and a great economic and military superpower.

Area 9,826,630 sq km (3,794,083 sq miles)
Country population 309,473,626
Capital city (pop) Washington DC (8,400,990)
Language English
Currency US dollar

Mexico

Some of the world's oldest civilizations have lived in Mexico, such as the Aztecs and Mayans. Nowadays, many tourists visit and it has plenty of natural resources. However, almost half the people are very poor and many try to cross the border into the USA every year. Some of them are arrested by border patrols.

Area 1,972,550 sq km (761,606 sq miles)
Country population 109,561,057
Capital city (pop) Mexico City (23,610,441)
Official language Spanish
Currency Peso

Guatemala

Guatemala is one of Central America's most beautiful countries, with a dramatic landscape of forests, lakes and volcanoes. It is also one of the poorest and most violent. The country is still suffering from the after-effects of a long civil war (1960–96). Two-thirds of Guatemalan children live in poverty.

Area 108,890 sq km (42,043 sq miles)
Country population 14,964,785
Capital city (pop) Guatemala City (3,681,309)
Official language Spanish
Currency Quetzal

Honduras

Honduras lies in Central America between the Caribbean Sea and the Atlantic Ocean. It is one of the world's poorest countries, although it has valuable stocks of timber. In 1998 Hurricane Mitch caused four billion dollars' worth of damage.

Area 112,090 sq km (43,278 sq miles)
Country population 8,249,574
Capital city (pop) Tegucigalpa (2,317,902)
Official language Spanish
Currency Lempira

El Salvador

The tiny country of El Salvador is on Central America's Pacific coast. It often suffers hurricanes and earthquakes. Coffee is a major crop, but El Salvador relies heavily on aid money from other countries.

Area 21,040 sq km (8,124 sq miles)
Country population 7,446,545
Capital city (pop) San Salvador (1,950,604)
Official language Spanish
Currency US dollar

Nicaragua

Nicaragua is the largest country in Central America. It is one of the poorest countries in the Western world and half its people are very poor indeed. In 1998, Hurricane Mitch caused great damage and left 20 per cent of Nicaraguans homeless.

Area 129,494 sq km (49,998 sq m)
Country population 5,495,369
Capital city (pop) Managua (1,837,921)
Official language Spanish
Currency Córdoba

Panama

Panama is a narrow strip of land stretching between North and South America. It has coastlines on the Atlantic Ocean and the Pacific Ocean and has a canal, which connects the two oceans. Panama receives money from the many ships that use the canal each year and has other successful industries, but nearly 40 per cent of the people are poor.

Area 78,200 sq km (30,193 sq miles)
Country population 3,582,256
Capital city (pop) Panama City (1,272,599)
Official language Spanish
Currency Balboa

Costa Rica

Costa Rica is one of the most successful Central American countries and has a good standard of living. Its landscape is beautiful, with many mountains and tropical forests, and tourism is increasing. However, the country is also becoming more and more involved in the illegal drugs trade.

Area 51,100 sq km (19,730 sq miles)
Country population 4,707,751
Capital city (pop) San José (1,724,403)
Official language Spanish
Currency Costa Rican colón

St Christopher and Nevis

The Caribbean islands of St Christopher (also known as St Kitts) and Nevis became independent of the UK in 1983. Most of the people are descended from slaves brought from West Africa to work on the islands. Sugar has always been the islands' main crop, but tourism and financial services are now important industries.

Area 261 sq km (101 sq miles)
Country population 50,388
Capital city (pop) Basseterre (13,360)
Official language English
Currency East Caribbean dollar

The Bahamas

The Bahamas are made up of more than 700 islands, which lie southeast of Florida in the Atlantic Ocean. The islands were ruled by the British, but became independent in 1973. Queen Elizabeth II is still the head of state. About 40 per cent of people work in tourism, but banking and finance are also important.

Area 13,940 sq km (5,382 sq miles)
Country population 342,708
Capital city (pop) Nassau (241,207)
Official language English
Currency Bahamian dollar

Jamaica

The Caribbean island of Jamaica became independent of the UK in 1962, but has remained in the Commonwealth. Tourism is its main industry, but many visitors are put off by the island's poverty and violence. Jamaica has one of the world's highest murder rates.

Area 10,991 sq km (4,244 sq miles)
Country population 2,708,552
Capital city (pop) Kingston (948,683)
Official language English
Currency Jamaican dollar

Dominican Republic

The Dominican Republic makes up the eastern two-thirds of the island of Hispaniola, sharing it with Haïti. It is the oldest European settlement in the Americas. The Dominican Republic is one of the Caribbean's poorest countries, but it is now very popular with tourists.

Area 48,730 sq km (18,815 sq miles)
Country population 10,005,587
Capital city (pop) Santo Domingo (3,512,391)
Official language Spanish
Currency Dominican Republic peso

Belize

Belize was a British colony called British Honduras, but became independent in 1981. Queen Elizabeth II is still the head of state. The coral reef off the coast is the world's second largest after Australia's Great Barrier Reef. Belize is now popular with tourists.

Area 22,966 sq km (8,867 sq miles)
Country population 343,493
Capital city (pop) Belmopan (21,794)
Official language English
Currency Belize dollar

Antigua and Barbuda

The Caribbean islands of Antigua and Barbuda were settled by the Spanish, the French and the British before becoming independent in 1981. They are still part of the Commonwealth and Queen Elizabeth II is the head of state. The islands are popular with tourists.

Area 443 sq km (171 sq miles)
Country population 87,883
Capital city (pop) St John's (22,215)
Official language English
Currency East Caribbean dollar

Haïti

Haïti shares the island of Hispaniola with the Dominican Republic. In 1804, Haïti was the first Caribbean state to become independent. Now Haïti is the poorest country in the Americas, after years of dictatorship and violence. An earthquake in January 2010 destroyed much of its capital city, and initiated one of the biggest international rescue and aid missions in history.

Area 27,750 sq km (10,714 sq miles)
Country population 8,820,901
Capital city (pop) Port-au-Prince (1,786,783)
Official languages Haïtian Creole/French
Currency Gourde

Cuba

Cuba is 150 km (93 miles) south of Florida and is the largest island in the Caribbean. It has a Communist government, which was led by Fidel Castro from 1959 to 2008, and is now led by his brother Raúl. Cuba attracts more and more tourists, but the collapse of the Soviet Union and trade restrictions put on Cuba by the USA have caused financial problems.

Area 110,860 sq km (42,803 sq miles)
Country population 11,260,368
Capital city (pop) Havana (2,605,022)
Official language Spanish
Currency Cuban peso

A street in Havana, Cuba

St Vincent and the Grenadines

This Caribbean nation includes 33 small islands. It became independent from Britain in 1979, but it is still a member of the Commonwealth. Bananas are the main crop. Many tourists visit the islands.

Area 389 sq km (150 sq miles)
Country population 100,369
Capital city (pop) Kingstown (16,531)
Official language English
Currency East Caribbean dollar

Boats moored near the island of St Vincent

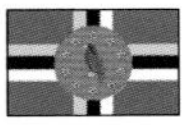

Dominica

This tropical, mountainous Caribbean island was once under British rule. It became independent in 1978. Dominica's main exports are bananas and fruit juices, but the crops are often destroyed by hurricanes.

Area 754 sq km (291 sq miles)
Country population 70,509
Capital city (pop) Roseau (13,436)
Official language English
Currency East Caribbean dollar

Barbados

This Caribbean island became an independent state in 1966, but it remains part of the Commonwealth. Queen Elizabeth II is the head of state. The main industries are tourism and sugar manufacturing.

Area 431 sq km (166 sq miles)
Country population 283,224
Capital city (pop) Bridgetown (94,197)
Official language English
Currency Barbados dollar

Grenada

Grenada lies between the Caribbean Sea and the Atlantic Ocean, north of Trinidad and Tobago. Nearly 400,000 tourists visit Grenada every year. The island exports spices, and about a quarter of the world's nutmeg come from here.

Area 344 sq km (133 sq miles)
Country population 107,850
Capital city (pop) St George's (5,242)
Official language English
Currency East Caribbean dollar

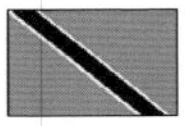

Trinidad and Tobago

The Caribbean islands of Trinidad and Tobago lie northwest of Venezuela. They have large reserves of oil and natural gas and are among the richest of all Caribbean nations. Tobago is quieter than Trinidad. Both islands are popular with tourists.

Area 5,128 sq km (1,980 sq miles)
Country population 1,362,640
Capital city (pop) Port of Spain (50,260)
Official language English
Currency Trinidad and Tobago dollar

St Lucia

This mountainous island lies between the Atlantic Ocean and the Caribbean Sea. It is famous for its two large, cone-shaped peaks known as the Pitons. Bananas are the island's main crop, but banking and tourism are also important.

Area 616 sq km (238 sq miles)
Country population 173,907
Capital city (pop) Castries (9,469)
Official language English
Currency East Caribbean dollar

South America

Argentina

Argentina was once ruled by Spain, but it became independent in 1816. This South American country is famous for its beef and has large mineral deposits.

Area 2,766,890 sq km (1,068,302 sq miles)
Country population 40,724,269
Capital city (pop) Buenos Aires (14,598,065)
Official language Spanish
Currency Peso

Venezuela

Venezuela is a land of great natural beauty in northern South America. Angel Falls is the world's highest waterfall, and Maracaibo is the largest lake in South America. Venezuela has large reserves of oil, coal and gold, but almost half of Venezuelans live in poverty.

Area 912,050 sq km (352,145 sq miles)
Country population 30,102,382
Capital city (pop) Caracas (4,478,851)
Official language Spanish
Currency Bolívar

Suriname

This is the smallest independent nation in South America. It was governed by the Netherlands but became independent in 1975. Suriname has large amounts of timber as well as bauxite and gold, but 70 per cent of the people are still very poor.

Area 163,270 sq km (63,039 sq miles)
Country population 530 ,431
Capital city (pop) Paramaribo (241,297)
Official language Dutch
Currency Surinamese dollar

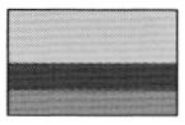

Colombia

Colombia is in the northwest of South America. The main crops are coffee, bananas and sugar, and the country has oil and mineral reserves. Colombia is also the world's leading producer of cocaine.

Area 1,138,910 sq km (439,736 sq miles)
Country population 45,469,397
Capital city (pop) Bogotá (8,423,837)
Official language Spanish
Currency Colombian peso

Uruguay

Uruguay is the second smallest country in South America. It is wealthier than most South American nations because of its livestock, tourism and banking industries. It has a good welfare system and its people are well educated.

Area 176,220 sq km (68,039 sq miles)
Country population 3,447,569
Capital city (pop) Montevideo (1,892,802)
Official language Spanish
Currency Uruguayan peso

Ecuador

Ecuador lies on the Equator and stretches across the Andes Mountains. The country's main exports are fish, bananas, cocoa and coffee. Oil was discovered there in 1972.

Area 283,560 sq km (109,483 sq miles)
Country population 14,333,771
Capital city (pop) Quito (1,650,034)
Official language Spanish
Currency US dollar

Bolivia

The Andes mountain range crosses Bolivia. The Bolivian capital La Paz is in the Andes and is the highest capital city in the world. Bolivia is one of only two landlocked countries in South America.

Area 1,098,580 sq km (424,164 sq miles)
Country population 10,907,778
Capital city (pop) La Paz (2,363,886)
Official languages Spanish/Quechua/Aymara
Currency Boliviano

Peru

Peru lies on South America's Pacific coast. It has been home to famous ancient civilizations, including the Inca Empire. Peru has important natural resources, including gold and oil, but the wealth they create is shared very unequally amongst the population, leaving much of the population in poverty.

Area 1,285,220 sq km (496,226 sq miles)
Country population 27,403,473
Capital city (pop) Lima (8,000,111)
Official languages Spanish/Quechua
Currency New sol

Paraguay

The Republic of Paraguay is landlocked. It has one of the smallest populations in South America. Alfredo Stroessner, the region's longest-ruling dictator, was overthrown in 1989, but Paraguay is still struggling with political and financial problems.

Area 406,750 sq km (157,047 sq miles)
Country population 6,608,137
Capital city (pop) Asunción (2,329,061)
Official languages Spanish/Guaraní
Currency Guaraní

Guyana

Guyana is the only country in South America where English is the official language. Its natural resources include gold and diamonds, but it is very poor and has political problems. The country has many fascinating animals and plants and is popular with tourists interested in nature.

Area 214,970 sq km (83,000 sq miles)
Country population 790,153
Capital city (pop) Georgetown (141,305)
Official language English
Currency Guyana dollar

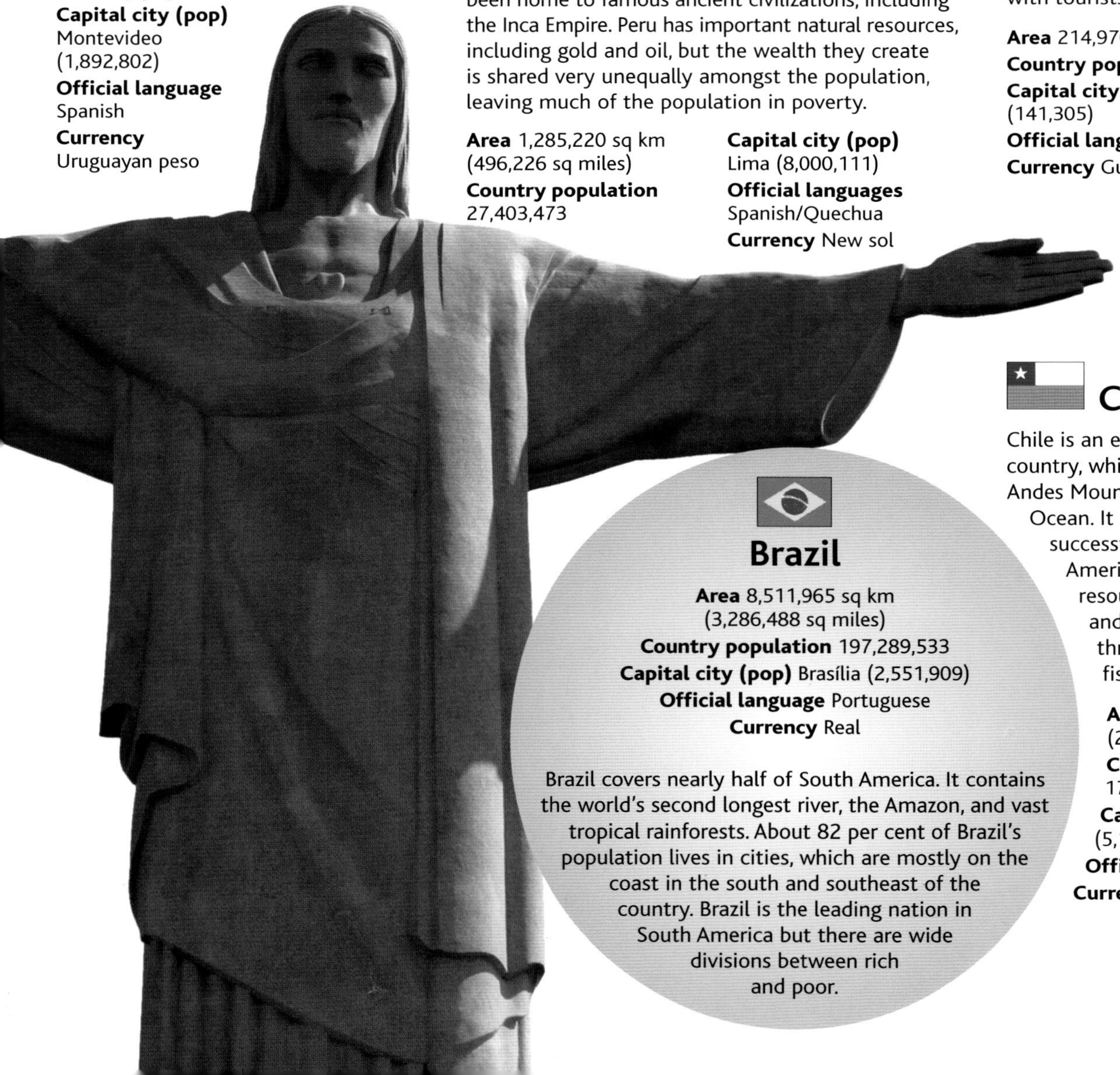

Statue of Christ, Rio de Janeiro, Brazil

Chile

Chile is an extremely long, narrow country, which lies between the Andes Mountains and the Pacific Ocean. It is one of the most successful nations in South America and has many natural resources, including minerals and timber, as well as thriving agriculture and fishing industries.

Area 756,950 sq km (292,260 sq miles)
Country population 17,569,945
Capital city (pop) Santiago (5,196,846)
Official language Spanish
Currency Chilean peso

Brazil

Area 8,511,965 sq km (3,286,488 sq miles)
Country population 197,289,533
Capital city (pop) Brasília (2,551,909)
Official language Portuguese
Currency Real

Brazil covers nearly half of South America. It contains the world's second longest river, the Amazon, and vast tropical rainforests. About 82 per cent of Brazil's population lives in cities, which are mostly on the coast in the south and southeast of the country. Brazil is the leading nation in South America but there are wide divisions between rich and poor.

Norway

Norway is famous for its fjords. The population is small and has a very good standard of living, thanks to the country's plentiful natural resources. Only Russia and Saudi Arabia export more oil than Norway.

Area 323,802 sq km (125,021 sq miles)
Country population 4,856,464
Capital city (pop) Oslo (900,017)
Official language Norwegian
Currency Krone

Oil rig supply boat in Bergen harbour, Norway

Ireland

Ireland was divided in the 1920s, when 26 counties in the south gained independence from the United Kingdom. Since then there has been conflict in Northern Ireland between those who want to remain part of the United Kingdom and those who want a united, independent Ireland. Since Ireland joined the European Community in 1973 it has become a modern, high-tech nation with successful industry. It began using the Euro in January 2002, along with ten other nations.

Area 70,200 sq km (27,135 sq miles)
Country population 4,493,457
Capital city (pop) Dublin (1,069,861)
Official languages Irish/English
Currency Euro

Denmark

Denmark shares a border with Germany and is the smallest, most southerly Scandinavian nation. It is a wealthy, high-tech country and has all the oil and natural gas it needs. The standard of living is high. Denmark is a monarchy and the kingdom includes the Faeroe Islands and Greenland.

Area 43,094 sq km (16,639 sq miles)
Country population 5,503,988
Capital city (pop) Copenhagen (1,080,638)
Official language Danish
Currency Danish krone

Luxembourg

Luxembourg is landlocked by Belgium, Germany and France. Its inhabitants have an amazingly high standard of living. Steel was once the main industry, but financial services have now become more important.

Area 2,586 sq km (999 sq miles)
Country population 469,412
Capital city (pop) Luxembourg (75,185)
Official languages French/German/Luxembourgish
Currency Euro

Finland

Since the end of World War II, Finland has changed from being a rural country covered with dense forest into a modern nation. It has very successful industries and an excellent welfare system. Finland joined the European Union in 1995 and started using the Euro as its currency in 2002.

Area 338,145 sq km (130,559 sq miles)
Country population 5,309,813
Capital city (pop) Helsinki (575 570)
Official languages Finnish/Swedish
Currency Euro

Sweden

Sweden is a rich country with a high standard of living. Swedes have one of the world's longest life expectancies. The country has many natural resources including iron ore, lead, granite, zinc and forests. Forests cover about half the land and there are important timber and paper industries.

Area 449,964 sq km (173,732 sq miles)
Country population 9,212,929
Capital city (pop) Stockholm (1,768,177)
Official language Swedish
Currency Swedish krona

Brandenburg Gate, Berlin, Germany

Germany

Germany was divided after World War II. The Soviet Union and Poland claimed the East, and the USA, UK and France controlled the West. The East became a Communist state and the West became a democracy. Thousands of East Germans fled to the West. The Berlin Wall was built in 1961 to close the border and stop the flow of people. The decline of the USSR led to the fall of the Berlin Wall in 1989 and Germany was reunited in 1990. Today, 80 per cent of Germany's people live in the West, and the effects of Communism are still felt in the East.

Area 357,021 sq km (137,847 sq miles)
Country population 81,848,867
Capital city (pop) Berlin (5,076,511)
Official language German
Currency Euro

People bathing in the Blue Lagoon, Iceland

Iceland

Iceland is a volcanic island and is the most westerly country in Europe. Its capital city is the furthest north in the world. Iceland is a wealthy country, with low inequality and a good welfare system. Fishing provides 70 per cent of its exports, which could cause problems as fish stocks decline.

Area 103,000 sq km (39,769 sq miles)
Country population 323,192
Capital city (pop) Reykjavík (208,448)
Official language Icelandic
Currency Icelandic króna

The Netherlands

The Netherlands is a low-lying country and much of it has been reclaimed from the sea. Nearly a quarter of the land lies below sea level, which makes it vulnerable to flooding, despite coastal defences and a network of dykes and canals. Banking, shipping and fishing all are important industries. The Netherlands is the sixth largest exporter in the world.

Area 41,526 sq km (16,033 sq miles)
Country population 16,479,744
Capital city (pop) Amsterdam (760,949)
Official languages Dutch/Frisian
Currency Euro

Belgium

Belgium is divided into Flanders (in the northwest), and Wallonia (in the southeast). Brussels is the headquarters of the European Union. This has brought wealth to the country as multinational companies have settled in the city. Belgium is well known for its fine chocolates and beer – and Tintin!

Area 30,528 sq km (11,787 sq miles)
Country population 10,729,253
Capital city (pop) Brussels (2,227,246)
Official languages Flemish/French/German
Currency Euro

France

France is the largest country in Western Europe and a key member of the European Union. It has a varied landscape ranging from coastal plains to the Alps in the southeast. Farms and forests cover a large proportion of the country, and agricultural products – particularly wine and liqueurs – are major exports. France once had one of the world's largest empires. Most of its former colonies are now independent, but French Guiana, Guadeloupe, Martinique, Réunion, Mayotte, St Pierre and Miquelon, French Polynesia, New Caledonia, Wallis and Futuna and the Southern and Antarctic Territories are all still part of France.

Area 547,030 sq km (211,209 sq miles)
Country population 62,751,344
Capital city (pop) Paris (11,949,824)
Official language French
Currency Euro

United Kingdom

The United Kingdom is made up of Great Britain (England, Scotland and Wales) and Northern Ireland. Although it is a small country, the UK has had a huge influence on the world because of its cultural, military and industrial strengths. At one time, it controlled a vast empire of lands across the globe and was the world's leading industrial nation. Traditional manufacturing industries are now less important. In the 21st century the UK's main industries are technology, tourism and services such as banking, and it is still an important economic power.

Area 244,820 sq km (94,526 sq miles)
Country population 61,762,815
Capital city (pop) London (7,744,942)
Language English
Currency British pound

Monaco

Monaco is a principality – it is ruled by a prince. It is surrounded by France and is the second smallest independent state in the world. It has no income tax and low business taxes so rich people flock there to escape taxes.

Area 2 sq km (0.77 sq miles)
Country population 34,028
Capital city (pop) Monaco (34,028)
Official language French
Currency Euro

Plaza de España in Seville, Spain

Spain

Spain covers most of the Iberian peninsula. The country has many cultures. Basque, Catalan, Galician and Valencian are spoken in different regions, but Castilian Spanish is the official language. There are 19 regions with their own elected authorities. There is a campaign for independence by the Basque country in the north, which has caused ongoing problems for the government. Spain is the world's second most popular tourist destination (after France) and has more than 50 million visitors every year. The fishing industry is one of the biggest in Europe, but unemployment is high.

Area 504,782 sq km (194,897 sq miles)
Country population 47,208,363
Capital city (pop) Madrid (6,380,913)
Official language Castilian Spanish
Currency Euro

Portugal

Portugal lies to the west of Spain on the Iberian peninsula. It is one of the European Union's least developed countries and has the highest number of people working on the land. Portugal's economy has grown rapidly since it joined the European Union in 1986. Tourism is one of its fastest growing industries. Portugal once had a vast empire, stretching across the Americas, Africa and Asia. Over 177 million people worldwide speak Portuguese.

Area 92,391 sq km (35,672 sq miles)
Country population 10,720,868
Capital city (pop) Lisbon (2,641,704)
Official language Portuguese
Currency Euro

Malta

Malta, which includes the neighbouring island of Gozo, used to be under British rule. It became independent in 1964, but remains a part of the Commonwealth. Malta became the European Union's smallest new member in 2004. Tourism is the island's most important industry and Malta has more than a million visitors every year.

Area 316 sq km (122 sq miles)
Country population 405,980
Capital city (pop) Valletta (254,728)
Official languages Maltese/English
Currency Euro

Vatican City State

The Vatican City is the smallest country in the world, both in area and population. It is surrounded by the city of Rome. The Vatican is home to the Pope and it is the spiritual centre of the Roman Catholic Church. It depends on contributions from Roman Catholics all over the world for its income, and the sale of souvenirs and publications.

Area 0.44 sq km (0.17 sq miles)
Country population 541
Capital city (pop) Vatican City (541)
Official language Latin
Currency Euro

San Marino

San Marino is entirely surrounded by Italy and it is the third smallest state in Europe. The tiny republic attracts about three million tourists every year. San Marino's inhabitants (known as Sammarinese) enjoy the world's sixth highest income per person.

Area 61 sq km (24 sq miles)
Country population 30,509
Capital city (pop) San Marino (4,441)
Official language Italian
Currency Euro

Andorra

Andorra is a small principality (a state ruled by a prince), which dates from 1278. It lies in the mountains between France and Spain. Tourism is its main industry, but financial services are also becoming important.

Area 468 sq km (181 sq miles)
Country population 91,023
Capital city (pop) Andorra la Vella (25,917)
Official language Catalan
Currency Euro

Estonia

The small Baltic state of Estonia regained its independence in 1991 when the Soviet Union collapsed. It was one of the Eastern European nations that joined the European Union in 2004.

Area 45,226 sq km (17,462 sq miles)
Country population 1,331,934
Capital city (pop) Tallinn (393,013)
Official language Estonian
Currency Kroon

Italy

Italy is a long, narrow country reaching into the Mediterranean Sea. It includes the islands of Sicily and Sardinia among others. Italy can be divided into two: the wealthy, industrial north, and the poorer south, where most people work on the land and around 20 per cent of the population is unemployed. About 40 million foreign tourists visit Italy every year, many of them to see its beautiful cities, which include Rome, Venice and Florence.

Area 301,230 sq km (116,306 sq miles)
Country population 59,983,205
Capital city (pop) Rome (4,022,723)
Official language Italian
Currency Euro

Austria

Austria is a small mountainous country. It is landlocked by the Czech Republic, Slovakia, Italy, Slovenia, Hungary, Germany, Switzerland and Liechtenstein. It was once the centre of the powerful Austro-Hungarian empire, until its defeat in World War I. It was occupied by Nazi Germany and then by the Allies after World War II. Since the war Austria has flourished, and it is now a popular holiday spot.

Area 83,870 sq km (32,382 sq miles)
Country population 8,397,949
Capital city (pop) Vienna (2,134,108)
Official language German
Currency Euro

Czech Republic

The Czech Republic was part of Czechoslovakia until it split from Slovakia in 1993. It now attracts investment from other countries and has a thriving tourism industry. The country joined the European Union in 2004.

Area 78,866 sq km (30,450 sq miles)
Country population 10,340,367
Capital city (pop) Prague (1,384,676)
Official language Czech
Currency Koruna

Switzerland

Switzerland is the most mountainous country in Europe. The Alps occupy 60 per cent of its land area. It has a very high income per person, low unemployment and its people have a long life expectancy. Switzerland was not involved in either World War and has not joined the European Union.

Area 41,290 sq km (15,942 sq miles)
Country population 7,801,127
Capital city (pop) Bern (123,022)
Official languages German/French/Italian/Romansch
Currency Swiss franc

Belarus

Belarus became independent when the Soviet Union collapsed in 1991. It continues to have close ties with Russia. The country still suffers from the effects of nuclear fallout from the 1986 Chernobyl accident, which took place in neighbouring Ukraine.

Area 207,600 sq km (80,155 sq miles)
Country population 9,544,020
Capital city (pop) Minsk (1,763,899)
Official languages Belarusian/Russian
Currency Belarusian rouble

Poland

Poland is the largest nation in Central Europe and has the highest population. It was devastated by World War II, when more than six million people died – more than in any other country. In 1989 Poland was the first Eastern European nation to topple its Communist leaders. In May 2004 it joined the European Union.

Area 312,685 sq km (120,729 sq miles)
Country population 38,019,451
Capital city (pop) Warsaw (2,260,396)
Official language Polish
Currency Zloty

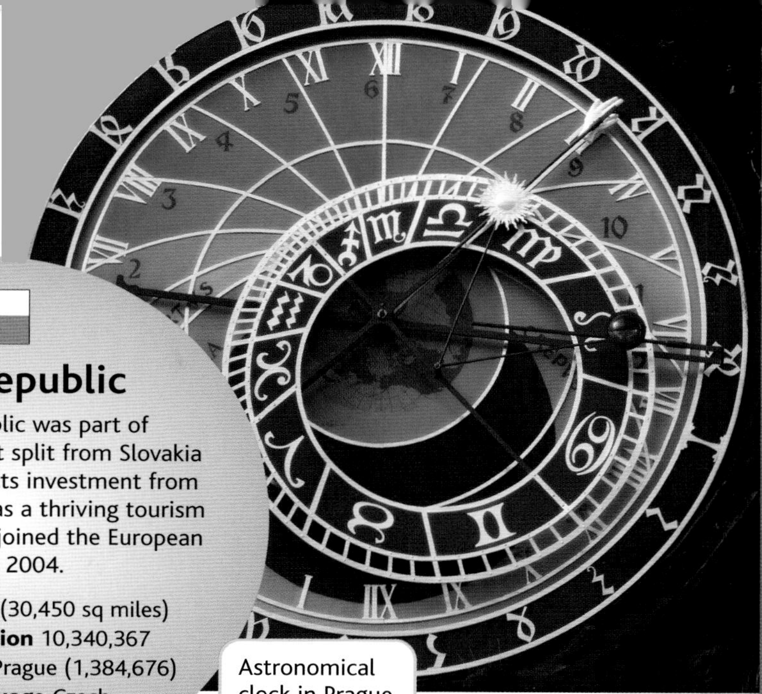

Astronomical clock in Prague, Czech Republic

Latvia

Latvia is bounded by the Baltic Sea, Estonia, Lithuania, Belarus and Russia. It became independent of the Soviet Union in 1991 and in 2004 it was accepted into the European Union.

Area 64,589 sq km (24,938 sq miles)
Country population 2,241,149
Capital city (pop) Riga (786,506)
Official language Latvian
Currency Lats

Lithuania

Lithuania became independent of the Soviet Union in 1991. It used to depend on Russia, but more recently it has developed trade links with the West. It joined the European Union in 2004.

Area 65,200 sq km (25,174 sq miles)
Country population 3,327,188
Capital city (pop) Vilnius (542,947)
Official language Lithuanian
Currency Litas

Liechtenstein

Liechtenstein is the sixth smallest country in the world. Its low taxes have encouraged extraordinary economic growth, and thousands of foreign companies have bank accounts there.

Area 160 sq km (62 sq miles)
Country population 35,870
Capital city (pop) Vaduz (5,125)
Official language German
Currency Swiss franc

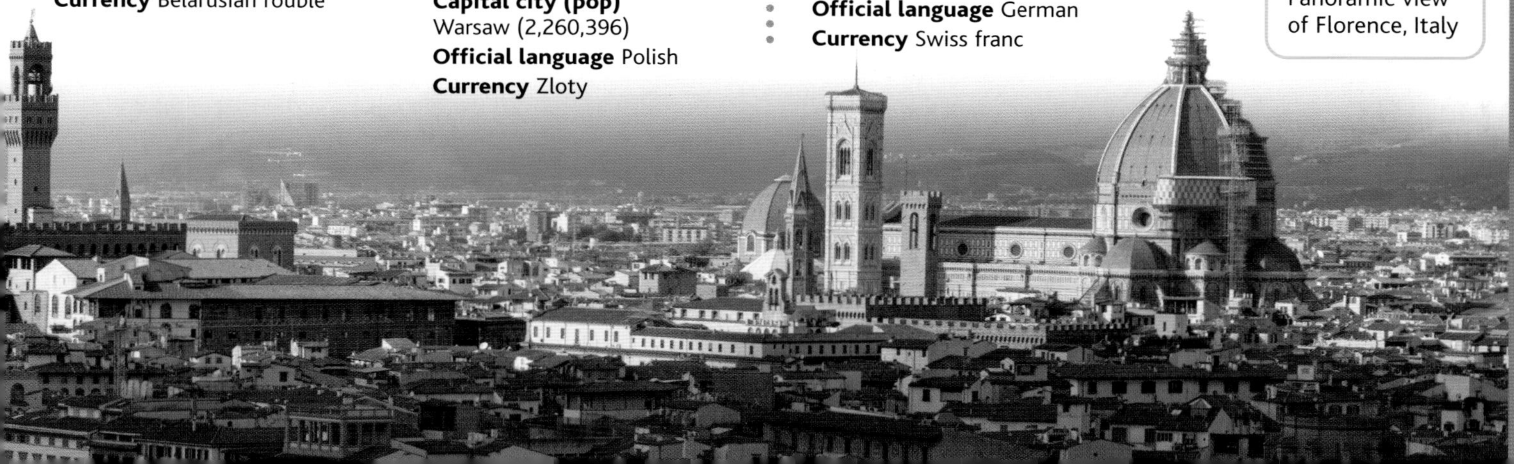

Panoramic view of Florence, Italy

View of Rovinj, Croatia

Croatia

Croatia was one of Yugoslavia's most advanced and prosperous areas, and declared its independence in 1991. The country borders the Adriatic Sea and its coast was popular with tourists. The Yugoslavian conflict of 1991–95 threw the country into turmoil, but visitors are now returning.

Area 55,542 sq km (21,831 sq miles)
Country population 4,449,966
Capital city (pop) Zagreb (706,353)
Official language Croatian
Currency Kuna

Bulgaria

Bulgaria was Communist until 1990, when it became a democracy. It has now joined the European Union, despite organized crime, corruption, inflation and unemployment. Bulgaria is becoming popular with tourists, especially the historic capital city of Sofia.

Area 110,910 sq km (42,823 sq miles)
Country population 7,418,091
Capital city (pop) Sofia (1,205,412)
Official language Bulgarian
Currency Lev

Bosnia and Herzegovina

Bosnia and Herzegovina was recognized as an independent state in 1992 after Yugoslavia collapsed in 1991. Since then clashes between Bosnia's Croats, Serbs and Muslims have caused civil war, which is still not resolved. Despite this, more tourists are beginning to visit the country again.

Area 51,129 sq km (19,741 sq miles)
Country population 3,885,424
Capital city (pop) Sarajevo (420,724)
Official languages Bosnian/Croatian/Serbian
Currency Convertible marka

Slovakia

Slovakia is landlocked and mountainous. It became independent in 1993, when Czechoslovakia divided into the Czech Republic and Slovakia. It joined the European Union in 2004.

Area 48,845 sq km (18,859 sq miles)
Country population 5,396,753
Capital city (pop) Bratislava (422,696)
Official language Slovak
Currency Euro

Moldova

Moldova is Europe's poorest country. It has no natural resources and imports all its energy supplies from Russia, from which it became independent in 1991.

Area 33,843 sq km (13,067 sq miles)
Country population 3,477,920
Capital city (pop) Chisinau (676,126)
Official language Moldovan
Currency Moldovan leu

Hungary

Hungary became Communist after World War II. In the 1990s, it defied the Soviet Union and began some free trade with the West. This central European country has flourished since the Soviet Union's collapse and it entered the European Union in 2004.

Area 93,030 sq km (35,919 sq miles)
Country population 10,042,311
Capital city (pop) Budapest (2,567,975)
Official language Hungarian
Currency Forint

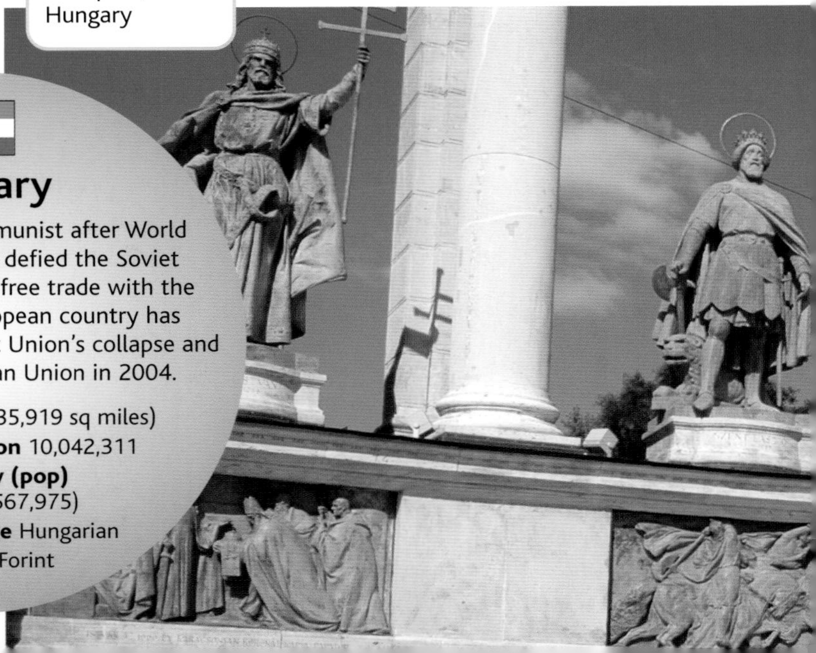

The Millennium Monument in Budapest, Hungary

Ukraine

Ukraine is a vast area between Poland and Russia. It became independent after the collapse of the Soviet Union. In 1986 it was the scene of the world's worst nuclear disaster, when a reactor at the Chernobyl nuclear plant exploded.

Area 603,700 sq km (233,090 sq miles)
Country population 46,017,580
Capital city (pop) Kiev (2,982,115)
Official language Ukrainian
Currency Hryvna

Albania

Albania depends mostly on farming, and its main crops are wheat, maize, sugar beet, potatoes and fruit. It has borders with Montenegro, Kosovo, Macedonia and Greece.

Area 28,748 sq km (11,100 sq miles)
Country population 3,192,932
Capital city (pop) Tirana (570,837)
Official language Albanian
Currency Lek

Georgia

Georgia lies in a key position east of the Black Sea between Russia and Turkey. It has coal deposits, but they have not yet been exploited. The country relies on farming – particularly grapes from which wine is made.

Area 69,700 sq km (26,911 sq miles)
Country population 4,662,077
Capital city (pop) Tbilisi (1,314,713)
Official language Georgian
Currency Lari

Slovenia

About half of Slovenia is covered in forest, making it the third most forested country in Europe. Slovenia became independent from Yugoslavia in 1991 and joined the European Union in 2004. Its people now have a reasonably good standard of living.

Area 20,273 sq km (7,827 sq miles)
Country population 2,031,721
Capital city (pop) Ljubljana (257,673)
Official language Slovene
Currency Euro

Greece

The ancient country of Greece lies in an important position between Europe, Asia and Africa. It includes about 2,000 islands as well as the mainland. About 14 million tourists visit Greece every year. However, it has few natural resources and relies on money from the European Union.

Area 131,940 sq km (50,942 sq miles)
Country population 11,278,730
Capital city (pop) Athens (3,876,931)
Official language Greek
Currency Euro

A typical seafront scene on a Greek island

Azerbaijan

Azerbaijan regained its independence from the Soviet Union in 1991. The country has rich mineral resources as well as oil and natural gas. However, conflict and corruption have kept it from developing a healthy economy.

Area 86,600 sq km (33,436 sq miles)
Country population 9,043,357
Capital city (pop) Baki/Baku (2,275,927)
Official language Azerbaijani
Currency Manat

Macedonia

Macedonia's full name is the Former Yugoslav Republic of Macedonia (FYROM), not to be confused with the Greek region of Macedonia. Macedonia became independent in 1991. Since then there have been clashes between the country's large Albanian minority and its Macedonian majority.

Area 25,333 sq km (9,781 sq miles)
Country population 2,058,611
Capital city (pop) Skopje (625,671)
Official language Macedonian
Currency Denar

Armenia

Armenia was the first country formally to adopt Christianity in AD 301. This mountainous country is bordered by Azerbaijan, Georgia, Iran and Turkey. Its key position between Europe and Asia led to invasions by the Persian, Ottoman, Roman and Byzantine empires, among others.

Area 29,800 sq km (11,506 sq miles)
Country population 3,260,476
Capital city (pop) Yerevan (1,373,079)
Official language Armenian
Currency Dram

Romania

The mountainous Republic of Romania is the largest Balkan nation. The Communist regime was overthrown in 1989 when the dictator Nicolae Ceausescu was executed. The country is still very poor, with almost half of Romanians living in poverty. It is now a member of the European Union.

Area 237,500 sq km (91,699 sq miles)
Country population 21,430,643
Capital city (pop) Bucharest (1,918,256)
Official language Romanian
Currency Leu

Cyprus

The Mediterranean island of Cyprus has been divided since Turkey invaded the north of the island in 1974. The Turkish Republic of Northern Cyprus is recognized only by Turkey. Greek Cyprus attracts many tourists and was accepted into the European Union in 2004. The Turkish part depends heavily on loans from Turkey.

Area 9,250 sq km (3,571 sq miles)
Country population 1,148,826
Capital city (pop) Nicosia (217,606)
Official languages Greek/Turkish
Currency Cyprus pound

Serbia

This landlocked country was formerly part of Yugoslavia but is now independent.

Area 77,498 sq km (29,992 sq miles)
Country population 7,380,626
Capital city (pop) Belgrade (1,099,352)
Official language Serbian
Currency Serbian dinar

Kosovo

Area 10,887 sq km (4,203 sq miles)
Country population 2,144,280
Capital city (pop) Pristina (212,791)

Montenegro

Montenegro was a former part of Yugoslavia and became independent from Serbia in 2006. It is now a full member of the United Nations and, although not a member of the European Union, it has adopted the Euro as its national currency.

Area 14,026 sq km (5,415 sq miles)
Country population 627,775
Capital city (pop) Podgorica (146,674)
Official languages Serbian/Montenegrin
Currency Euro

Morocco

Morocco is in northwestern Africa. The country was divided between Spanish and French rule, but gained independence in 1956. It has rich mineral deposits and nearly three-quarters of the world's phosphate. Tourism is becoming increasingly important, but almost half the population work on the land.

Area 446,550 sq km (172,414 sq miles)
Country population 31,587,385
Capital city (pop) Rabat (1,819,812)
Official language Arabic
Currency Dirham

Algeria

Algeria became independent from France in 1962. Throughout the 1990s the country was torn apart by civil war, in which 100,000 people are thought to have died. Algeria is still struggling to control its religious militants.

Area 2,381,740 sq km (919,595 sq miles)
Country population 35,539,444
Capital city (pop) Algiers (2,239,613)
Official language Arabic
Currency Algerian dinar

Tunisia

The North African country of Tunisia shares borders with Algeria and Libya and has a Mediterranean coastline. About one-fifth of the people live by farming and fishing.

Area 163,610 sq km (63,170 sq miles)
Country population 10,531,767
Capital city (pop) Tunis (2,102,517)
Official language Arabic
Currency Tunisian dinar

Cape Verde

Cape Verde is made up of the Windward Islands and the Leeward Islands in the Atlantic Ocean off the west coast of Africa. Their main exports are bananas and coffee.

Area 4,033 sq km (1,557 sq miles)
Country population 516,733
Capital city (pop) Praia (132,042)
Official language Portuguese
Currency Cape Verdean escudo

Ethiopia

Ethiopia is Africa's oldest independent country. It has suffered many droughts and famines. These, combined with civil war and a border dispute with Eritrea, have made Ethiopia one of Africa's poorest nations. Its natural resources are underdeveloped, and 85 per cent of the people still depend upon the land for a living.

Area 1,127,127 sq km (435,186 sq miles)
Country population 83,269,332
Capital city (pop) Addis Ababa (3,315,108)
Official language Amharic, one of 70 languages spoken in the country
Currency Ethiopian birr

Eritrea

Eritrea is in eastern Africa and has had violent border disputes with Ethiopia since 1998. The conflict has affected Eritrea's economy, but the government continues to improve the country's roads, schools and transport systems. Its Red Sea ports are an important source of income.

Area 121,320 sq km (46,842 sq miles)
Country population 5,112,117
Capital city (pop) Asmara (1,304,382)
Official languages No official language; Arabic, Tigrinya and English are the main working languages. Italian is also spoken.
Currency Nakfa

Libya

Libya has large oil reserves, but its economy has suffered from sanctions imposed by the United Nations. These were in response to the bombing of an airliner over Lockerbie in Scotland in 1988. Sanctions have now been lifted and Libya's leader, Colonel Gaddafi, has promised to bring his country back into the international community.

Area 1,759,540 sq km (679,362 sq miles)
Country population 6,100,818
Capital city (pop) Tripoli (1,025,244)
Official language Arabic
Currency Libyan dinar

Camel and rider near the Great Pyramid in Egypt

Egypt

Egypt lies in a key position. It has a coastline on both the Mediterranean and Red Seas, and borders with the Sudan, Libya, Israel and the Gaza Strip. Egypt also controls the vital Suez Canal. This allows about 15,000 ships each year to travel between the Mediterranean and the Indian Ocean without sailing around Africa. Famous landmarks include the pyramids.

Area 1,001,450 sq km (386,662 sq miles)
Country population 77,665,621
Capital city (pop) Cairo (8,105,071)
Official language Arabic
Currency Egyptian pound

Fortified town of Aït Benhaddou in the High Atlas mountains, Morocco

Somalia

Somalia is one of the world's poorest countries and there has been conflict between different groups. The north declared independence under the name Somaliland, but is not recognized by any foreign government.

Area 637,657 sq km (246,201 sq miles)
Country population 13,183,884
Capital city (pop) Mogadishu (1,579,041)
Official languages Somali/Arabic
Currency Somali shilling

Mauritania

Mauritania is mainly desert. It became independent from France in 1960. There is conflict between the country's African and Arab peoples. Mauritania has rich mineral deposits, but these have not yet been exploited.

Area 1,030,700 sq km (397,955 sq miles)
Country population 3,148,992
Capital city (pop) Nouakchott (822,207)
Official language Arabic
Currency Ouguiya

Sudan

Sudan is the biggest country in Africa. It has large oil reserves, which have been exploited since 1999. However, the country has suffered from civil war since its independence in 1956. This war has been going on longer than any other war in Africa. Since 2003 fighting has been particularly severe in the western region of Darfur, which is one of the poorest parts of the country. The United Nations has described this as the world's worst humanitarian crisis.

Area 2,505,810 sq km (967,499 sq miles)
Country population 39,128,332
Capital city (pop) Khartoum (10,082,702)
Official language Arabic
Currency Sudanese pound

Djibouti

Djibouti lies in a key position between Ethiopia and the Red Sea. The country provides refuelling facilities for ships and operates a free port, which bring money into Djibouti.

Area 23,000 sq km (8,880 sq miles)
Country population 893,938
Capital city (pop) Djibouti (c. 400,000)
Official languages Arabic/French
Currency Djibouti franc

Senegal

Senegal is almost divided into two by The Gambia. It became independent from France in 1960. It is now popular with tourists, but has few natural resources, high unemployment and more than half its people live in poverty.

Area 196,190 sq km (75,749 sq miles)
Country population 11,743,259
Capital city (pop) Dakar (2,583,028)
Official language French
Currency CFA franc

Guinea

Guinea has been placed under great strain by thousands of refugees from its war-torn neighbours, Liberia and Sierra Leone. Guinea has natural resources, including iron ore, gold and diamonds.

Area 245,857 sq km (94,926 sq miles)
Country population 10,683,113
Capital city (pop) Conakry (2,007,310)
Official language French
Currency Guinean franc

Niger

Niger is the largest nation in West Africa. It is also one of the hottest and poorest countries in the world. Niger borders the Sahara Desert and droughts often kill much of the country's vital livestock. It has one of the world's lowest literacy rates.

Area 1,267,000 sq km (489,191 sq miles)
Country population 14,861,804
Capital city (pop) Niamey (980,478)
Official language French
Currency CFA franc

Gambia

The Gambia is a sliver of land and the smallest country in mainland Africa. About 80 per cent of Gambians work on the land. It is becoming increasingly popular as a tourist destination.

Area 11,300 sq km (4,363 sq miles)
Country population 1,622,271
Capital city (pop) Banjul (32,921)
Official language English
Currency Dalasi

Dogon people from Mali dancing on stilts

Mali

Mali's first democratically elected government came to power in 1992 after more than 20 years of dictatorship. This West African nation is one of the world's poorest countries. About 80 per cent of the people depend on farming for a living.

Area 1,240,000 sq km (478,766 sq miles)
Country population 13,277,905
Capital city (pop) Bamako (2,306,662)
Official language French
Currency CFA franc

Nigeria

Nigeria has the biggest population of any African country. It is the leading oil producer south of the Sahara. However, about 60 per cent of Nigerians live in poverty because of corruption, unequal distribution of money and a rapidly growing population.

Area 923,768 sq km (356,668 sq miles)
Country population 154,622,507
Capital city (pop) Abuja (1,352,679)
Official language English
Currency Naira

Guinea-Bissau

Guinea-Bissau is one of the poorest countries in the world. A civil war in 1998-9 destroyed many of its roads, schools and hospitals, and ruined its economy. Most people live by fishing and farming. Cashew nuts are the main crop.

Area 36,120 sq km (13,946 sq miles)
Country population 1,578,012
Capital city (pop) Bissau (395,954)
Official language Portuguese
Currency CFA franc

Burkina Faso

Burkina Faso is an inland country in West Africa that was called Upper Volta. About 90 per cent of people work on the land. It has the lowest literacy rate in the world.

Area 274,200 sq km (105,869 sq miles)
Country population 15,084,452
Capital city (pop) Ouagadougou (1,411,869)
Official language French
Currency CFA Franc

Ghana

Ghana was a British colony, but in 1957 it became the first African country to win independence from foreign rule. It contains Lake Volta, the world's largest artificial lake, and it is one of the world's top ten gold producers.

Area 239,460 sq km (92,456 sq miles)
Country population 24,603,548
Capital city (pop) Accra (2,449,922)
Official language English
Currency Cedi

Liberia

The West African country of Liberia was founded by freed American slaves. It has been independent since 1847. Its president is Africa's first elected female head of state.

Area 111,370 sq km (43,000 sq miles)
Country population 3,591,365
Capital city (pop) Monrovia (2,056,529)
Official language English
Currency Liberian dollar

Benin

The African country of Benin became fully independent from France in 1960. It now has a thriving tourist industry, which provides much-needed money.

Area 112,620 sq km (43,483 sq miles)
Country population 8,509,040
Capital city (pop) Porto Novo (258,975)
Official language French
Currency CFA Franc

Transporting dried grasses by river in Chad

Chad

The Sahara desert covers much of Chad. Since gaining independence from France in 1960, it has suffered conflict with its neighbour Libya. Oil has been found in Chad and is now being exported. Most of its people work on the land.

Area 1,284,000 sq km (495,755 sq miles)
Country population 9,372,504
Capital city (pop) N'Djaména (1,579,246)
Official languages Arabic/French
Currency CFA Franc

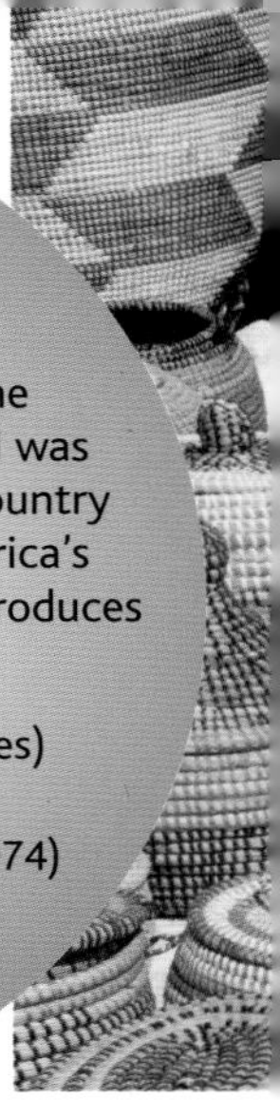

Republic of Congo

The region of Middle Congo became independent from France in 1960 and was renamed the Republic of Congo. The country has large oil deposits and is one of Africa's largest producers of petroleum. It also produces zinc, lead, gold and diamonds.

Area 342,000 sq km (132,047 sq miles)
Country population 3,845,224
Capital city (pop) Brazzaville (1,252,974)
Official language French
Currency CFA franc

Cameroon

Cameroon in West Africa became an independent republic in 1972. It has good natural resources, including bauxite and aluminium, and grows crops such as cocoa, coffee and rubber.

Area 475,440 sq km (183,568 sq miles)
Country population 19,988,219
Capital city (pop) Yaoundé (2,298,174)
Official languages French/English
Currency CFA Franc

Côte d'Ivoire

Côte d'Ivoire became independent from France in 1960. It was a peaceful, prosperous African country until its first military coup in 1999. Trouble then began between rebels and the government which is still going on.

Area 322,460 sq km (124,502 sq miles)
Country population 21,377,030
Capital city (pop) Yamoussoukro (234,788)
Official language French
Currency CFA Franc

Sierra Leone

Sierra Leone became independent from Britain in 1961. Between 1991–2002 the country was in a state of civil war. Many thousands of people were killed and thousands more were forced to move from their homes. Sierra Leone has diamond and gold deposits, but its political problems have made it one of the world's poorest countries, along with Somalia and East Timor. Unemployment is high and about three-quarters of its people live on less than US $2 a day.

Area 71,740 sq km (27,698 sq miles)
Country population 5,360,883
Capital city (pop) Freetown (836,574)
Official language English
Currency Leone

Traditional woven baskets from the Republic of Congo

Central African Republic

The Central African Republic is a landlocked country in central Africa. It became independent from France in 1960. Since then there have been almost constant political problems and it is now a very poor country. It exports some timber and diamonds, but most people work on the land.

Area 622,984 sq km (240,536 sq miles)
Country population 3,426,494
Capital city (pop) Bangui (770,753)
Official language French
Currency CFA Franc

Togo

Togo was the French territory of Togoland until it became independent in 1960. More than half the people work on the land. Cotton, coffee and cocoa are the main exports. Nearly a third of the people are very poor.

Area 56,785 sq km (21,924 sq miles)
Country population 5,837,017
Capital city (pop) Lomé (848,428)
Official language French
Currency CFA franc

Equatorial Guinea

Equatorial Guinea is made up of five islands and part of the African mainland. It became independent from Spain in 1968 and is one of the smallest countries in Africa. Many people work on the land, but gas and oil have been found and so the country is becoming wealthier.

Area 28,051 sq km (10,831 sq miles)
Country population 1,170,308
Capital city (pop) Malabo (179,273)
Official languages Spanish/French
Currency CFA franc

São Tomé and Príncipe

The islands of São Tomé and Príncipe lie on the Equator in the Gulf of Guinea and make up Africa's smallest country. Cocoa is the main crop, but São Tomé and Príncipe has other potential sources of income, such as newly discovered oil.

Area 1,001 sq km (387 sq miles)
Country population 163,544
Capital city (pop) São Tomé (65,468)
Official language Portuguese
Currency Dobra

Gabon

Gabon has a small population and good oil and mineral reserves. It is one of Africa's richest nations. However, many of its people are very poor because its wealth has been mismanaged and is unequally distributed.

Area 267,667 sq km (103,346 sq miles)
Country population 1,822,791
Capital city (pop) Libreville (753,550)
Official language French
Currency CFA franc

Democratic Republic of Congo

The Democratic Republic of Congo, which was called Zaïre, is Africa's third largest country. In 2003 a five-year struggle between government forces and rebels ended and since then it has been fairly peaceful. The country has good natural resources but has been very poor since the war.

Area 2,345,410 sq km (905,567 sq miles)
Country population 67,149,684
Capital city (pop) Kinshasa (8,900,721)
Official language French
Currency Congolese franc

Rare mountain gorilla in the Democratic Republic of Congo

Sand dune in the Namib desert

Namibia

Namibia became independent from South Africa in 1990. The country often suffers from drought so much of its food has to be imported from other countries. Namibia is an important producer of diamonds, but the wealth from this is unevenly distributed. Half of all Namibians are living in poverty.

Area 825,418 sq km (318,696 sq miles)
Country population 2,220,035
Capital city (pop) Windhoek (315,932)
Official language English
Currency Namibian dollar

Rwanda

Rwanda is a densely populated country in Central Africa. It is still suffering the effects of a civil war that began in 1990 and lasted for four years. At least 60 per cent of the people live in poverty.

Area 26,338 sq km (10,169 sq miles)
Country population 9,171,893
Capital city (pop) Kigali (1,029,384)
Official languages Kinyarwanda/French/English
Currency Rwanda franc

Angola

Angola became independent from Portugal in 1975. Since then, there has been a civil war almost all the time. The country has valuable oil and diamond deposits, but has many financial problems.

Area 1,246,700 sq km (481,354 sq miles)
Country population 17,747,679
Capital city (pop) Luanda (2,644,318)
Official language Portuguese
Currency Kwanza

Uganda

Uganda is a landlocked West African nation on the shores of Lake Victoria. It is now a fairly peaceful country, after a devastating civil war and a military dictatorship. The land is fertile and it has natural resources, but Uganda is still being held back by a large international debt.

Area 236,040 sq km (91,136 sq miles)
Country population 29,600,217
Capital city (pop) Kampala (1,857,324)
Official language English
Currency Uganda shilling

Burundi

Burundi gained independence in the 1960s. Since then it has been devastated by fighting between the two main tribes, the Hutus and the Tutsis. Burundi lies between the politically troubled countries of Rwanda and the Democratic Republic of Congo, and is being held back by uncertainty over its future.

Area 27,830 sq km (10,745 sq miles)
Country population 9,180,801
Capital city (pop) Bujumbura (374,766)
Official languages Kirundi/French
Currency Burundi franc

Malawi

In 1964, the British territory of Nyasaland in southeastern Africa became Malawi, which is an independent republic. The country has had many natural disasters and depends on aid from other countries. About 15 per cent of the adult population has HIV or AIDS, and Malawi now has one of the world's lowest life expectancies.

Area 118,480 sq km (45,745 sq miles)
Country population 13,656,346
Capital city (pop) Lilongwe (723,576)
Official languages Chichewa/English
Currency Kwacha

Zambia

The landlocked country of Zambia in Central Africa has a small population. Copper is its chief export, but demand for copper has fallen and Zambia is now one of the world's poorest countries. Over 60 per cent of its people live on less than US $1 dollar a day.

Area 752,614 sq km (290,586 sq miles)
Country population 13,166,392
Capital city (pop) Lusaka (3,024,830)
Official language English
Currency Kwacha

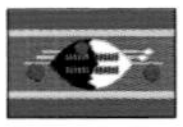

Swaziland

Swaziland is one of the world's few absolute monarchies – political parties were banned by the king in 1973. The country relies on South Africa for trade. About 40 per cent of the people live on less than US $1 a day. It has one of the highest levels of HIV/AIDS in the world and the world's lowest life expectancy.

Area 17,363 sq km (6,704 sq miles)
Country population 961,338
Capital city (pop) Mbabane (61,794)
Official languages English/Swazi
Currency Lilangeni

Lesotho

The Kingdom of Lesotho was once called Basutoland and became independent from the UK in 1966. It is entirely surrounded by South Africa. Lesotho has diamond mines but few other resources. Most people work on the land or in South African mines.

Area 30,355 sq km (11,720 sq miles)
Country population 1,896,174
Capital city (pop) Maseru (253,887)
Official languages Sotho/English
Currency Loti

Tanzania

Tanzania is made up of the country that used to be called Tanganyika on the eastern African mainland, and the island of Zanzibar, which is in the Indian Ocean just off the coast of Tanganyika. The two nations joined in 1964 after becoming independent. The country contains Lake Victoria, Mount Kilimanjaro and Serengeti National Park.

Area 945,087 sq km (364,900 sq miles)
Country population 42,047,263
Capital city (pop) Dodoma (179,757)
Official languages Swahili/English
Currency Tanzanian shilling

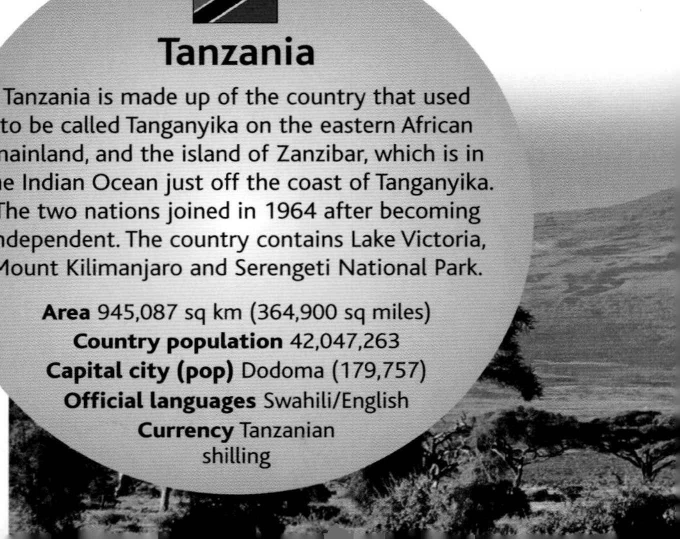

Botswana

Botswana used to be called the British Protectorate of Bechuanaland, but in 1966 it became an independent Commonwealth republic. It is now one of the wealthiest countries in Africa. Botswana has many natural resources and is one of the world's largest producers of diamonds. However, around one-third of the population has HIV/AIDS.

Area 600,370 sq km (231,804 sq miles)
Country population 1,982,226
Capital city (pop) Gaborone (236,992)
Official language English
Currency Pula

Zimbabwe

Zimbabwe was previously the British colony of Rhodesia. It used to be a fairly well-off country, but since 2000 has suffered a series of political problems and upsets. Zimbabweans now have an extremely low standard of living: one-third have HIV/AIDS and 70 per cent live in poverty.

Area 390,580 sq km (150,804 sq miles)
Country population 12,595,593
Capital city (pop) Harare (3,252,529)
Official language English
Currency Zimbabwe dollar

Madagascar

Madagascar is in the Indian Ocean off the coast of Africa. It is the fourth largest island in the world. More than 80 per cent of people work on the land. The country has often suffered natural disasters. In 2000 most of its rice crop was destroyed by cyclones.

Area 587,040 sq km (226,657 sq miles)
Country population 19,541,930
Capital city (pop) Antananarivo (1,783,031)
Official languages Malagasy/French/English
Currency Ariary

Mauritius

Mauritius is a group of islands in the Indian Ocean. It has a stable government, and Mauritians have high incomes. The country exports sugar cane and has a thriving tourist industry. It is home to some of the world's rarest plants and animals.

Area 2,040 sq km (788 sq miles)
Country population 1,280,251
Capital city (pop) Port Louis (156,720)
Official language English
Currency Mauritius rupee

Dancing Masai women, Kenya

Kenya

Kenya lies on the Equator on the east coast of Africa. It has some of the most fertile land in Africa, and 75 per cent of the people work in farming. It is also one of Africa's most popular tourist destinations.

Area 582,650 sq km (224,962 sq miles)
Country population 36,359,464
Capital city (pop) Nairobi (3,246,384)
Official languages Swahili/English
Currency Kenya shilling

Mozambique

Mozambique used to be a Portuguese colony. It gained independence in 1975, became a republic in 1990, and held its first free elections in 1994. About 70 per cent of its people live in poverty. But since the beginning of the 21st century, things have begun to improve and other countries have started to invest in Mozambique.

Area 801,590 sq km (309,496 sq miles)
Country population 21,971,712
Capital city (pop) Maputo (2,123,971)
Official language Portuguese
Currency Metical

South Africa

South Africa lies on the southern tip of the continent. Until 1994 the country was ruled by its white minority and had an apartheid policy. This segregated the races – kept black and white apart – and denied black citizens the vote. Because of this many other countries refused to trade with South Africa. The African National Congress won South Africa's first inclusive elections in 1994, and it has been in power ever since.

Area 1,219,912 sq km (471,011 sq miles)
Country population 49,461,575
Capital city (pop) The seat of government is Tshwane (Pretoria) (2,426,056); the seat of the legislature is Cape Town (5,083,934); the seat of the judiciary is Bloemfontein (609,046)
Official languages 11 official languages: Afrikaans, English, Ndebele, Pedi, Sotho, Swazi, Tsonga, Tswana, Venda, Xhosa, Zulu
Currency Rand

Mount Kilimanjaro, Tanzania, is the highest mountain in Africa.

Yemeni women in traditional veils

Israel

After World War II, Israel was created in Palestine as a homeland for Jews. When Britain left the area in 1948 the State of Israel was proclaimed, and there was immediate conflict between the Jewish settlers and the Arabs who were living there. The State of Israel gained a great deal of land in the conflict, and many Palestinians were made homeless. There have been many attempts to make peace between the two sides, but the conflict continues.

Area 20,770 sq km (8,019 sq miles)
Country population 7,562,250
Capital city (pop) Jerusalem (768,229) Jerusalem is the seat of government but is not recognized as the capital by the UN because East Jerusalem is part of the Occupied Territories captured in 1967. The UN considers Tel Aviv (1,112,738) to be the capital.
Official languages Hebrew/Arabic
Currency Shekel

Yemen

In 1990 North and South Yemen were formally joined as the Republic of Yemen after years of conflict. Yemen is a poor country, affected by drought, political problems and a fast-growing population.

Area 527,970 sq km (203,850 sq miles)
Country population 23,003,454
Capital city (pop) Sana'a' (2,079,158)
Official language Arabic
Currency Riyal

Turkey

Turkey is in a key position between Europe and Asia. The territory west of the Bosphorus strait is in Europe, while the much larger area to the east is in Asia. Turkey is popular with tourists, and between seven and ten million people every year visit its coastline and the historic city of Istanbul.

Area 780,580 sq km (301,384 sq miles)
Country population 72,613,728
Capital city (pop) Ankara (3,848,440)
Official language Turkish
Currency Turkish lir

Syria

Syria has been home to some of the world's oldest civilizations, and Damascus is probably the oldest city in the world. Syria became independent from France in 1946. Its people come from many ethnic groups and religions, including Arabs, Kurds, Assyrians and Armenians, and different Muslim and Christian groups.

Area 185,180 sq km (71,498 sq miles)
Country population 20,960,588
Capital city (pop) Damascus (2,831,738)
Official language Arabic
Currency Syrian pound

Kazakhstan

Kazakhstan is an enormous, landlocked nation almost four times the size of Texas. It was part of the former Soviet Union. Kazakhstan is rich in minerals and fossil fuels, including oil, coal, natural gas, gold, silver and lead.

Area 2,717,300 sq km (1,049,155 sq miles)
Country population 15,800,526
Capital city (pop) Astana (407,908)
Official languages Kazakh/Russian
Currency Tenge

United Arab Emirates

The UAE is a group of seven Middle Eastern states and is one of the wealthiest countries in the region. It used to be a very poor country where most people lived by fishing, but is now the Gulf's third largest oil producer.

Area 83,600 sq km (32,278 sq miles)
Country population 4,067,178
Capital city (pop) Abu Dhabi (599,773)
Official language Arabic
Currency UAE dirham

The Burj Al Arab hotel in Dubai, United Arab Emirates

Kuwait

Kuwait has large oil reserves that make up more than eight per cent of the world's total. The country's economy was almost destroyed when Iraqi forces invaded in 1990 and burned oil wells as they retreated. The Kuwaiti government has spent billions of dollars on repairs, and oil production is now higher than it was before the invasion.

Area 17,820 sq km (6,880 sq miles)
Country population 3,205,199
Capital city (pop) Kuwait City (2,662,633)
Official language Arabic
Currency Kuwaiti dinar

Jordan

Jordan shares borders with Syria, Israel, the West Bank, Saudi Arabia and Iraq. Despite the problems of its neighbours the country is relatively peaceful. It doesn't have many natural resources, and its vital supplies of Iraqi oil were halted by the Iraq war of 2003.

Area 92,300 sq km (35,637 sq miles)
Country population 6,321,252
Capital city (pop) Amman (1,206,266)
Official language Arabic
Currency Jordanian dinar

Saudi Arabia

Saudi Arabia is a monarchy. It is ruled by the sons and grandsons of Abdul Aziz ibn Saud, who founded the kingdom. Saudi Arabia is one of the richest countries in the Middle East. It has the largest reserves of petroleum in the world and exports more than any other country. It is about the same size as Western Europe and includes an area called the Empty Quarter, the world's largest sand desert. Saudi Arabia is a Muslim country and includes the city of Makkah (or Mecca). This was the birthplace of the Prophet Muhammad and millions of Muslims make a pilgrimage there every year.

Area 2,149,690 sq km (830,000 sq miles)
Country population 25,699,143
Capital city (pop) Riyadh (4,878,473)
Official language Arabic
Currency Saudi riyal

Iran

Iran is a mountainous Middle Eastern country. Until 1935 it was known as Persia. It shares borders with several of the world's most troubled nations, including Iraq, Afghanistan and Pakistan. This discourages investment from other countries and tourism, and Iran's economy depends on oil.

Area 1,648,000 sq km (636,297 sq miles)
Country population 72,764,589
Capital city (pop) Tehran (13,236,489)
Official language Farsi
Currency Rial

Iraq

Iraq has had a violent recent history. From 1979 to 2003, Iraq was controlled by the dictator President Saddam Hussein. The USA, supported by countries including the UK, Spain, Australia, Poland and Denmark, removed Hussein from power in 2003. Hussein was executed in 2006, but conflict continues in Iraq.

Area 437,072 sq km (168,754 sq miles)
Country population 37,027, 692
Capital city (pop) Baghdad (5,402,486)
Official language Arabic
Currency New Iraqi dinar

Lebanon

Lebanon is a small country bordering the Mediterranean Sea. It became independent from France in 1943. Since Lebanon's civil war of 1975–91 huge sums have been spent on rebuilding the country and it is heavily in debt.

Area 10,400 sq km (4,015 sq miles)
Country population 4,690,325
Capital city (pop) Beirut (2,025,123)
Official language Arabic
Currency Lebanese pound

The GUM department store, Moscow, Russia

Russia

The Russian Federation is the largest country in the world, almost twice the size of the United States. It stretches from Europe to Asia and covers 13 per cent of the world's total land area. Russia was the chief republic of the former Soviet Union, which in 1991 was split into 15 separate republics. Oil, natural gas, timber and metals make up more than 80 per cent of its exports. The country is still held back by poor transport and other systems. It also suffers from violent conflict in the Chechnya region.

Area 17,075,200 sq km (6,592,772 sq miles)
Country population 140,728,754
Capital city (pop) Moscow (14,926,656)
Official language Russian
Currency Rouble

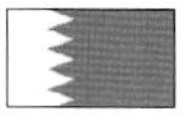

Bahrain

The island state of Bahrain is 32 km (19.9 miles) off the east coast of Saudi Arabia. Oil is its main source of income, but the country is also a centre for offshore banking.

Area 665 sq km (257 sq miles)
Country population 826,344
Capital city (pop) Manama (157,474)
Official language Arabic
Currency Bahraini dinar

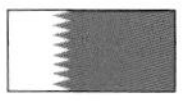

Qatar

Qatar became independent from Britain in 1971 and has changed from being a poor country dependent on pearl fishing to one of the Gulf's richest states. It has large reserves of oil and gas, which have brought great wealth.

Area 11,437 sq km (4,416 sq miles)
Country population 1,015,249
Capital city (pop) Doha (812,156)
Official language Arabic
Currency Qatar riyal

Oman

Oman borders Yemen, Saudi Arabia and the United Arab Emirates so is in a key position for the transportation of oil. Oil makes up more than 80 per cent of Oman's exports, but the government wants to encourage tourism and information technology.

Area 212,460 sq km (82,031 sq miles)
Country population 2,865,504
Capital city (pop) Muscat (1,211,776)
Official language Arabic
Currency Omani rial

Kyrgyzstan

Kyrgyzstan is a picturesque country of mountains, glaciers and lakes. It became independent from the former Soviet Union in 1991. Since then it has seen many political changes.

Area 198,500 sq km (76,641 sq miles)
Country population 5,379,432
Capital city (pop) Bishkek (945,892)
Official languages Kyrgyz/Russian
Currency Som

Tajikistan

Tajikistan lies west of China in Central Asia. It was part of the former Soviet Union. About 50,000 people died in the civil war of 1992–97 and the country is still violent and unsettled.

Area 143,100 sq km (55,251 sq miles)
Country population 7,648,351
Capital city (pop) Dushanbe (975,444)
Official language Tajik
Currency Somoni

Afghanistan

Afghanistan is a mountainous country in Central Asia. It has been through more than 20 years of political upheaval. The country was controlled by the Taliban from 1996 until 2001, when the Taliban was overthrown by an alliance led by the US military. At present many people are involved in the drugs trade and over one million of the population may be close to starvation.

Area 647,500 sq km (250,001 sq miles)
Country population 24,913,215
Capital city (pop) Kabul (2,971,403)
Official languages Dari (Persian)/Pashto
Currency Afghani

Mongolia

Mongolia is a landlocked nation between Russia and China. It is three times the size of France and is a land of deserts, grasslands, forests and mountains. Temperatures range from summer highs of 40˚C (104°F) in the Gobi Desert to -40˚C (-40°F) during the winter. More than half the population are nomads – they move from place to place with their livestock. Gers (moveable tent-like huts) are the most common form of shelter, even in cities.

Area 1,564,116 sq km (603,908 sq miles)
Country population 2,703,161
Capital city (pop) Ulaanbaatar (865,648)
Official language Khalkha Mongolian
Currency Tugrik

India

India is the largest democratic country in the world. It became independent from the UK in 1947 when it was divided into India and Pakistan. This division has led to three wars. India has the world's largest population, after China. In 1999 its population passed the one billion mark. Most people still live by farming and around 70 per cent of the population live in rural areas. India has a booming information technology industry and one of the most successful film industries in the world.

Area 3,287,590 sq km (1,269,346 sq miles)
Country population 1,187,125,055
Capital city (pop) New Delhi (18,916,890)
Official languages Hindi/English
Currency Indian rupee

Bhutan

The mountainous kingdom of Bhutan lies between Tibet (China) and India in the eastern Himalayas. Its main exports are rice, machinery and diesel oil, but tourism is also important.

Area 47,000 sq km (18,147 sq miles)
Country population 696,183
Capital city (pop) Thimphu (93,179)
Official language Dzongkha
Currency Ngultrum

Turkmenistan

Turkmenistan borders the Caspian Sea in Central Asia. About 90 per cent of its land is desert. It has the fifth largest oil and natural gas reserves in the world, but is crippled by debt to other countries.

Area 488,100 sq km (188,456 sq miles)
Country population 7,586,280
Capital city (pop) Ashgabat (947,221)
Official languages Turkmen
Currency Manat

Pakistan

Pakistan was created in 1947 as a home for Indian Muslims. It was divided into Pakistan and Bangladesh in 1971. The country is in dispute with India over ownership of the state of Kashmir. This has led to fears of an arms race, as both countries are believed to have nuclear weapons.

Area 803,940 sq km (310,403 sq miles)
Country population 176,242,949
Capital city (pop) Islamabad (689,249)
Official language Urdu
(Punjabi is the most commonly used language, and English is used in business, government and higher education)
Currency Pakistan rupee

Sri Lanka

Sri Lanka was called Ceylon until 1972, having become independent from the UK in 1948. It is a tropical island in the Indian Ocean, only 20 km (12 miles) from the south coast of India. The country has textile, food processing and telecommunications industries. It is held back, however, by nearly 20 years of conflict between some of its people, the Tamils, who want independence, and the government.

Area 65,610 sq km (25,332 sq miles)
Country population 20,648,412
Capital city (pop) Colombo (2,647,631)
Official language Sinhala
Currency Sri Lankan rupee

Nepal

Nepal is home to Everest, the world's highest mountain, and tourism brings vital money into the country. In 2001, Nepal's Crown Prince murdered ten members of the royal family before taking his own life.

Area 147,181 sq km (56,827 sq miles)
Country population 28,026,128
Capital city (pop) Kathmandu (1,765,416)
Official language Nepali
Currency Nepalese rupee

Yak train making its way over the Khumbu glacier, Nepal

China

China is one of the oldest civilizations in the world and has the oldest continuously used language system. It also is home to the world's largest population. The economy of China is growing rapidly, and in 2009 it became the world's largest exporter. Tourism has also become a major industry.

Area 9,596,960 sq km (3,705,407 sq miles)
Country population 1,329,111,520
Capital city (pop) Beijing (12,522,839)
Official language Mandarin Chinese
Currency Renminbi (also known as the yuan)

Taiwan

The island of Taiwan lies 150 km (93 miles) from mainland China. Taiwan has a thriving electronics industry. It is one of the world's leading producers of computer technology. China claims that Taiwan is part of its territory.

Area 35,980 sq km (13,892 sq miles)
Country population 23,287,909
Capital city (pop) Taipei (2,655,972)
Official language Mandarin Chinese
Currency New Taiwan dollar

Uzbekistan

Uzbekistan has the largest population in Central Asia. It has been independent of the Soviet Union since 1991. It is the third largest exporter of cotton in the world and has mineral deposits. However, its people are poor because the wealth is distributed unequally.

Area 447,400 sq km (172,742 sq miles)
Country population 28,091,362
Capital city (pop) Tashkent (3,221,614)
Official language Uzbek
Currency Som

Bangladesh

Bangladesh was divided from Pakistan in 1971. About 70 per cent of the people work in farming and the country produces all its own food. The main industries include cotton, tea, leather, sugar and natural gas, and its leading export is clothing.

Area 144,000 sq km (55,599 sq miles)
Country population 147,243,324
Capital city (pop) Dhaka (14,327,157)
Official language Bengali
Currency Taka

North Korea

North Korea is one of the world's few remaining Communist states. As many as three million North Koreans have probably died of starvation because of famine and financial mishandling, while the regime spends money on military equipment. North Korea's nuclear programme threatens the international food aid that keeps the population going at present.

Area 120,540 sq km (46,541 sq miles)
Country population 24,102,269
Capital city (pop) Pyongyang (3,270,582)
Official language Korean
Currency Won

South Korea

The Korean peninsula was effectively divided after World War Two. In 1950 North Korea attacked the South with Chinese support, and a three-year civil war began. South Korea is a democratic country and has a thriving, high-tech economy and a growing tourism industry.

Area 98,480 sq km (38,023 sq miles)
Country population 48,595,924
Capital city (pop) Seoul (22,692,652)
Official language Korean
Currency Won

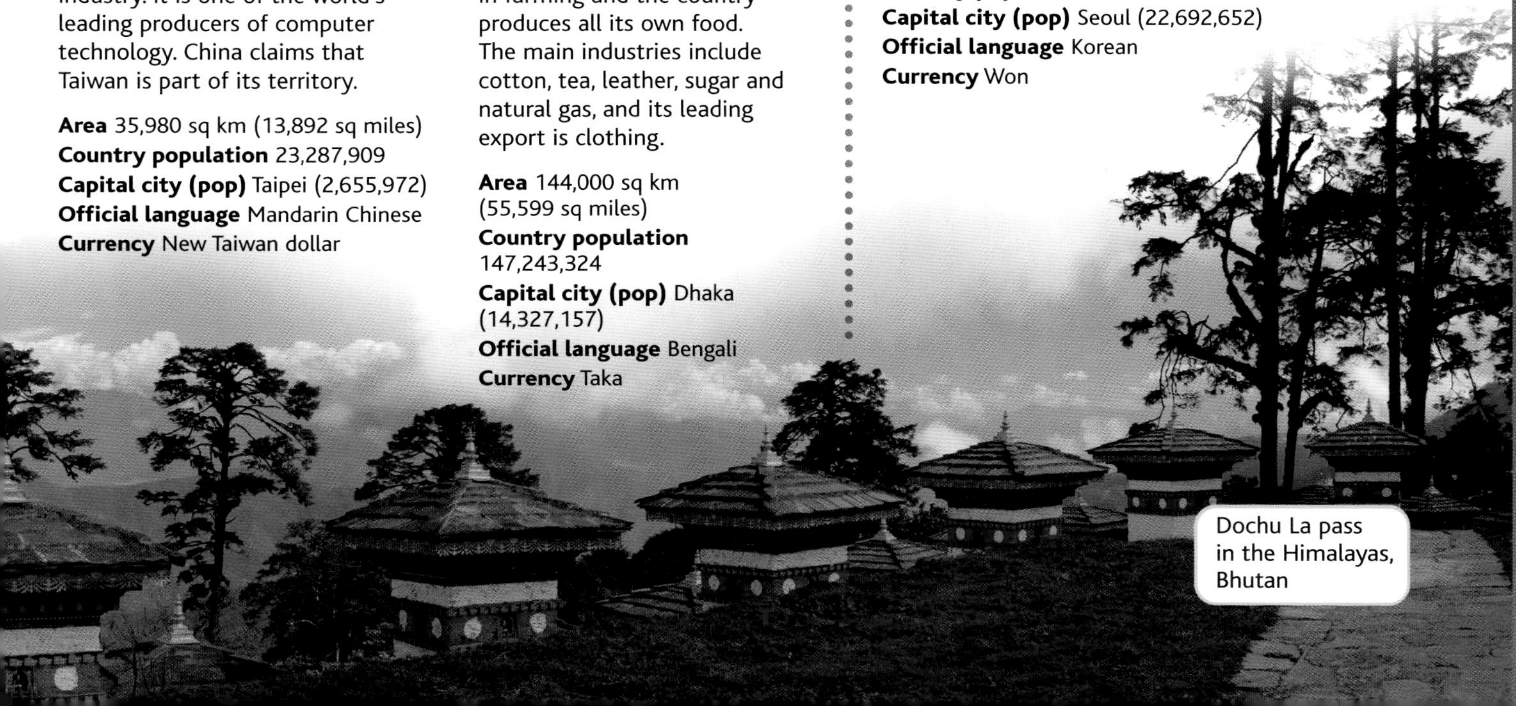

Dochu La pass in the Himalayas, Bhutan

Tokyo skyline

Japan

Japan is made up of four large islands and many smaller islands. This mountainous and volcanic country is one of the world's most densely populated places, and there are more people in Tokyo than any other city in the world. Japan is a wealthy country and a world leader in the electronics, robotics and car production industries.

Area 377,835 sq km (145,882 sq miles)
Country population 128,240,609
Capital city (pop) Tokyo (37,730,064)
Official language Japanese
Currency Yen

The Philippines

The Philippines is made up of more than 7,000 islands in Southeast Asia. More than 80 per cent of the population is Roman Catholic – the Philippines is the only Asian nation that is mainly Christian. It suffers from natural disasters, such as volcanic eruptions and typhoons, as well as a very high birth rate. Many Filipinos go to work abroad and their country depends on the US $6–7 billion they send home each year.

Area 300,000 sq km (115,831 sq miles)
Country population 93,897,444
Capital city (pop) Manila (11,248,470)
Official languages Filipino/English
Currency Philippine peso

Myanmar

Myanmar used to be called Burma. The country is ruled by an undemocratic military government and has been accused by foreign governments of severe human rights abuses. It is also a major producer of heroin. These things have led the European Union and the USA to limit trade with the country.

Area 678,500 sq km (261,970 sq miles)
Country population 58,782,355
Capital city (pop) Naypyidaw (930,000)
Official language Burmese
Currency Kyat

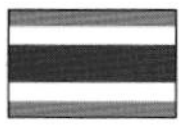

Thailand

Until 1939, Thailand was called Siam. It is the only country in Southeast Asia never to have been under the control of a European power. About ten million tourists visit Bangkok and the country's beautiful coasts each year. Farming is important and about half the people still work on the land.

Area 514,000 sq km (198,456 sq miles)
Country population 64,339,590
Capital city (pop) Bangkok (5,831,835)
Official language Thai
Currency Baht

Laos

Laos is a landlocked, mountainous country bordered by China, Vietnam, Cambodia, Thailand and Myanmar. It is one of the world's last remaining Communist states. Laos is popular with adventurous tourists, but it is extremely primitive. There are few paved roads and no railways.

Area 236,800 sq km (91,429 sq miles)
Country population 6,113,660
Capital city (pop) Vientiane (237,300)
Official language Lao
Currency Kip

Malaysia

Malaysia is made up of two regions, separated by about 1,030 km (640 miles) of the South China Sea. The country used to rely on farming and exports of raw materials, but it is now a leading producer and exporter of high-tech, electronic merchandise.

Area 329,750 sq km (127,317 sq miles)
Country population 29,005,448
Capital city (pop) Kuala Lumpur (8,063,230)
Official language Bahasa Malaysia (Malay)
Currency Malaysian dollar (Ringgit)

Singapore

The city state of Singapore in Southeast Asia is one of the richest nations in the world. Its people have one of the world's highest standards of living. Singapore's thriving manufacturing industry includes shipbuilding and electronics.

Area 693 sq km (267 sq miles)
Country population 5,560,904
Official languages Malay/Mandarin/Tamil/English
Currency Singapore dollar

Vietnam

North and South Vietnam were rejoined in 1976 after 30 years of war. At first the war was between the Communists and the French colonialists, and later between the Communist North Vietnam and the South, which was supported by the USA. Nearly four million people died and much of Vietnam's landscape was destroyed. There is now a Communist socialist government. Vietnam is now one of the world's leading rice exporters, and the country's oil production has increased.

Area 329,560 sq km (127,243 sq miles)
Country population 88,271,591
Capital city (pop) Hanoi (2,749,634)
Official language Vietnamese
Currency Dông

Villamendhoo Island in the Maldives

East Timor

East Timor became independent from Indonesia in 2002. It is Southeast Asia's youngest nation and the world's second-newest democracy. East Timor is a very poor country and often suffers floods.

Area 15,007 sq km (5,794 sq miles)
Country population 981,208
Capital city (pop) Dili (171,449)
Official languages Portuguese/Tetum
Currency US dollar

Brunei

Brunei gained full independence from Britain in 1984. It is ruled by the Sultan, whose family have reigned for six centuries. Brunei is enormously wealthy because of its natural gas and oil fields.

Area 5,770 sq km (2,228 sq miles)
Country population 428,519
Capital city (pop) Bandar Seri Begawan (33,677)
Official language Malay
Currency Brunei dollar

The Comoros

The Comoros is a group of volcanic islands between Madagascar and Mozambique. It is one of the world's poorest countries. The Comoros has few natural resources. It exports vanilla, cloves and essential oils, but depends on aid from other countries.

Area 2,170 sq km (838 sq miles)
Country population 648,247
Capital city (pop) Moroni (48,543)
Official languages Arabic/French/Comoran
Currency Comorian franc

Seychelles

The Seychelles is made up of 155 islands in the Indian Ocean, east of mainland Africa. It became independent from Britain in 1976. About 90 per cent of the islands' people live on the main island of Mahé and are reasonably well off, thanks to successful tourism and tuna fishing industries.

Area 455 sq km (176 sq miles)
Country population 87,786
Capital city (pop) Victoria (21,680)
Official languages English/French/Creole
Currency Seychelles rupee

Traditional wayang golek wooden puppets from Indonesia

Indonesia

Indonesia includes more than 17,000 islands. The world's largest Muslim population lives on about 6,000 of these. Indonesia is rich in minerals, and it exports petroleum, textiles, timber, natural gas and rubber. There are frequent natural disasters.

Area 1,919,440 sq km (741,100 sq miles)
Country population 231,749,876
Capital city (pop) Jakarta (19,231,919)
Official language Bahasa Indonesian
Currency Rupiah

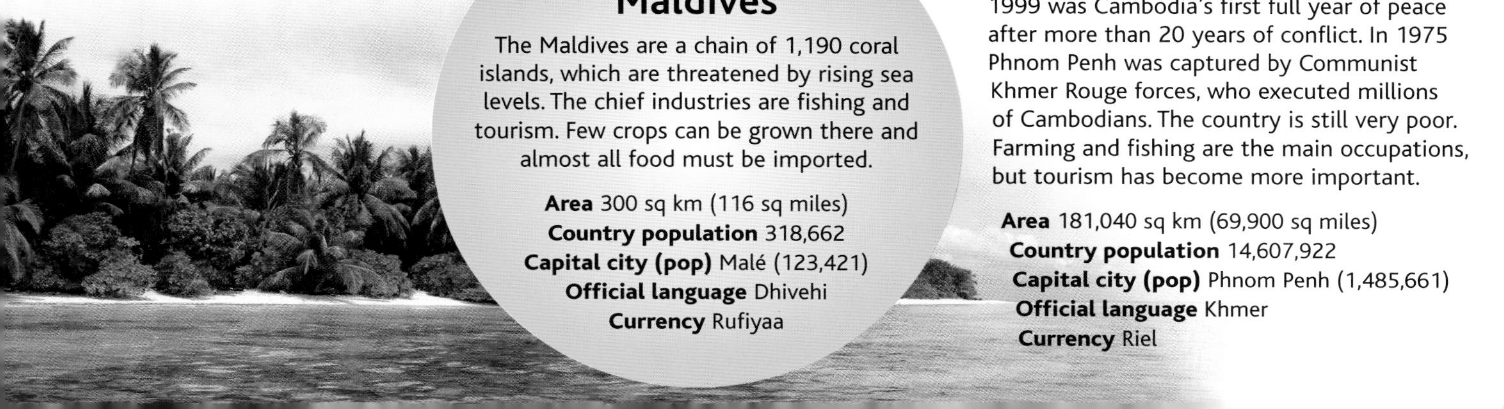

Maldives

The Maldives are a chain of 1,190 coral islands, which are threatened by rising sea levels. The chief industries are fishing and tourism. Few crops can be grown there and almost all food must be imported.

Area 300 sq km (116 sq miles)
Country population 318,662
Capital city (pop) Malé (123,421)
Official language Dhivehi
Currency Rufiyaa

Cambodia

1999 was Cambodia's first full year of peace after more than 20 years of conflict. In 1975 Phnom Penh was captured by Communist Khmer Rouge forces, who executed millions of Cambodians. The country is still very poor. Farming and fishing are the main occupations, but tourism has become more important.

Area 181,040 sq km (69,900 sq miles)
Country population 14,607,922
Capital city (pop) Phnom Penh (1,485,661)
Official language Khmer
Currency Riel

Papua New Guinea

Papua New Guinea is made up of many small islands and one half of New Guinea, the world's second largest island. It has mineral deposits such as gold and copper, as well as oil and natural gas. It has been difficult to use these to the full because the country lacks good roads and transport, and there are large areas of rainforest.

Area 462,840 sq km (178,704 sq miles)
Country population 6,740,586
Capital city (pop) Port Moresby (307,103)
Official language English
Currency Kina

Solomon Islands

The Solomon Islands include several densely forested volcanic islands in the South Pacific. People live by farming, forestry and fishing, but since 1998 there has been conflict between different groups in the population. Law and order has broken down, and the islanders' average income has been halved. A peacekeeping force led by Australia arrived in 2003.

Area 28,450 sq km (10,985 sq miles)
Country population 530,735
Capital city (pop) Honiara (63,343)
Official language English
Currency Solomon Islands dollar

Kiribati

Kiribati is made up of 33 islands in the Pacific Ocean, halfway between Hawaii and Australia. Kiribati's main exports are coconuts and fish.

Area 811 sq km (313 sq miles)
Country population 100,062
Capital city (pop) Tarawa (47,946)
Official languages English/Kiribati
Currency Australian dollar

The Olgas, natural rock formations in Australia

Palau

The Republic of Palau is made up of 340 islands in the Pacific Ocean, southeast of the Philippines. It became independent in 1994 and is one of the world's youngest nations. The islands rely mainly on tourism. The waters around Palau are rich in marine life, and visitors come to snorkel and scuba-dive. The islands also export fish, shellfish and coconuts.

Area 458 sq km (177 sq miles)
Country population 20,945
Capital city (pop) Koror (9,266)
Official languages Palauan/English
Currency US dollar

Micronesia

The Federated States of Micronesia is a group of more than 600 islands in the North Pacific Ocean. It gained independence from the USA in 1986, but the USA has kept the right to have military bases on the islands. This agreement brings Micronesia billions of dollars of financial aid.

Area 702 sq km (271 sq miles)
Country population 108,452
Capital city (pop) Palikir (7,523)
Official language English
Currency US dollar

New Zealand

New Zealand lies in the Pacific Ocean, about 1,600 km (994 miles) east of Australia. It is made up of two main islands and several smaller ones. The capital, Wellington, lies further south than any other capital city. New Zealand is mountainous and relatively unspoilt, and is becoming more and more popular with tourists from all over the world.

Area 268,680 sq km (103,738 sq miles)
Country population 4,217,585
Capital city (pop) Wellington (369,393)
Official languages English/Maori
Currency New Zealand dollar

A view of the city of Auckland in New Zealand

Australia

Australia was discovered by Captain James Cook in 1770. It became independent in 1931, but it is part of the British Commonwealth and Queen Elizabeth II is the head of state. Australia is the world's sixth largest country. It has important mineral resources and vast areas are given over to sheep and cattle farming. Some famous landmarks include the Great Barrier Reef and Uluru.

Area 7,686,850 sq km (2,967,910 sq miles)
Country population 20,638,212
Capital city (pop) Canberra (334,276)
Official language English
Currency Australian dollar

Tonga

Tonga is a group of 169 islands in the southern Pacific Ocean. It is the only country in the Pacific ruled by a monarchy. The islands have no natural resources and people rely on farming. Tonga exports products such as coconuts, vanilla and yams. Around half of the Tongan people live abroad, particularly in the USA and Australasia.

Area 748 sq km (289 sq miles)
Country population 102,368
Capital city (pop) Nuku'alofa (24,310)
Official languages Tongan/English
Currency Pa'anga

Traditional Polynesian canoe on a beach in Tonga

Vanuatu

Vanuatu is a chain of 83 volcanic islands in the South Pacific Ocean, between Hawaii and Australia. About 65 per cent of the people work on the land, but offshore banking and tourism are growing industries. However, the islands sometimes suffer earthquakes, tsunamis and cyclones, which may limit the growth of tourism.

Area 12,200 sq km (4,710 sq miles)
Country population 248,935
Capital city (pop) Port Vila (47,510)
Official languages Bislama/English/French
Currency Vatu

Fiji

Fiji is made up of more than 300 volcanic islands in the South Pacific Ocean, about 1,770 km (1,100 miles) north of New Zealand. Fiji's main export is sugar cane, and it has a flourishing tourism industry. However, political problems from time to time have discouraged other countries from investing in the islands.

Area 18,270 sq km (7,054 sq miles)
Country population 841,387
Capital city (pop) Suva (85,754)
Official languages English/Fijian/Hindustani
Currency Fiji dollar

Nauru

The island of Nauru lies 53 km (33 miles) south of the Equator in the Pacific Ocean. It is the smallest independent republic in the world. Its people once had one of the highest incomes per head in the world, thanks to the export of phosphates (fertilizer). However, Nauru's phosphate reserves are running low, and it has few other resources.

Area 21 sq km (8 sq miles)
Country population 10,175
Capital city (pop) no official capital
Official languages Nauruan/English
Currency Australian dollar

Samoa

Samoa is a group of islands in the South Pacific Ocean. Samoa's beaches and rainforests have led to a booming tourism industry. This now brings in a quarter of the islands' income.

Area 2,944 sq km (1,137 sq miles)
Country population 181,718
Capital city (pop) Apia (36,440)
Official languages Samoan/English
Currency Tala

Tuvalu

Tuvalu was a British colony until 1978. It is a group of nine coral atolls in the South Pacific Ocean. It is the second lowest country in the world and is under threat from rising sea levels. Tuvalu has the world's second smallest population. The country has no known natural resources, and has fewer than 1,000 tourists a year. The islanders rely on exporting fish, stamps and handicrafts, as well as the money sent home from Tuvaluans working abroad.

Area 26 sq km (10 sq miles)
Country population 9,981
Capital city (pop) Funafuti (5,145)
Official languages Tuvaluan/English
Currency Australian dollar

Marshall Islands

The Marshall Islands lie in the central Pacific. The islands were occupied by the USA after World War II until 1986, and were used for nuclear weapons testing. About half the people work in farming. Coconut oil is the main export.

Area 11,854 sq km (4,576 sq miles)
Country population 54,185
Capital city (pop) Majuro (20,144)
Official languages Marshallese/English
Currency US dollar

Jin Jiyane
Jiyane
Nekuje

People

Women of the world

Turkish women at an International Women's Day rally in Istanbul, Turkey. Held annually on 8 March, the event celebrates its centenary in 2011. It was originally associated with protests against women's working conditions, but today is a celebration of women's achievements in political, economic, social and other areas. It is an official national holiday in certain countries, and has become merged with Mother's Day in others. It is marked by special events and the giving of gifts.

Princes Harry and William: Their names are now two of the favourite boys' names in England and Wales.

Surnames around the world

Surnames were not used in Britain until after the Norman Conquest in 1066. Until then, most people were known only by their first name. People started to add extra names in order to be able to tell one William from another.

Some surnames came from where a person lived or the person's father's name – so the son of someone called John was known as Johnson. Others were based on a person's occupation (a blacksmith would be called Smith) or their appearance (a brown-haired person might be called Brown). The origins of some surnames have been forgotten.

Popular first names

First name fashions change – especially those for girls. Some traditional names remain popular but new names come into use. Olivia was not in the Top 10 in the UK until 1999 or in the USA until 2001, but has kept its popularity. These are the most popular names now and 100 years ago in England and Wales and USA.

	UK Girls/Boys	USA Girls/Boys	England & Wales (1914) Girls/Boys	USA (1911) Girls/Boys
1	Olivia/Jack	Emma/Jacob	Mary/John	Mary/John
2	Ruby/Oliver	Isabella/Michael	Margaret/William	Helen/William
3	Emily/Thomas	Emily/Ethan	Doris/George	Margaret/James
4	Grace/Harry	Madison/Joshua	Dorothy/Thomas	Dorothy/George
5	Jessica/Joshua	Ava/Daniel	Kathleen/James	Ruth/Robert
6	Chloe/Alfie	Olivia/Alexander	Florence/Arthur	Anna/Joseph
7	Sophie/Charlie	Sophia/Anthony	Elsie/Frederick	Elizabeth/Charles
8	Lily/Daniel	Abigail/William	Edith/Albert	Mildred/Frank
9	Amelia/James	Elizabeth/Christopher	Elizabeth/Charles	Marie/Edward
10	Evie/William	Chloe/Matthew	Winifred/Robert	Frances/Thomas

A very long name

Anna Pepper was born in Derby, England, on 19 December 1882. She was given 26 first names, one for each letter of the alphabet, in alphabetical order: Anna Bertha Cecilia Diana Emily Fanny Gertrude Hypatia Inez Jane Kate Louisa Maud Nora Ophelia Prudence Quince Rebecca Starkey Teresa Ulysis Venus Winifred Xenophon Yetty Zeus Pepper.

Most common surnames

	China	Denmark	England	France	Germany	India	Ireland	Japan
1	Wáng	Jensen	Smith	Martin	Müller	Singh	Murphy	Sato
2	Li	Nielsen	Jones	Bernard	Schmidt	Kumar	Kelly	Suzuki
3	Zhang	Hansen	Taylor	Dubois	Schneider	Sharma/Sarma	O'Sullivan	Takahashi
4	Liú	Pedersen	Brown	Thomas	Fischer	Patel	Walsh	Tanaka
5	Chén	Andersen	Williams	Robert	Meyer	Shah	Smith	Watanabe
6	Yáng	Christensen	Wilson	Richard	Weber	Lal	O'Brien	Ito
7	Huáng	Larsen	Johnson	Petit	Schulz	Gupta	Byrne	Yamamoto
8	Zhào	Sørensen	Davies	Durand	Wagner	Bhat	Ryan	Nakamura
9	Zhou	Rasmussen	Robinson	Leroy	Becker	Rao	Fitzgerald	Kobayashi
10	Wú	Jørgensen	Wright	Moreau	Hoffmann	Reddy	O'Connor	Saito

Known by one name

Some people are so famous they are instantly recognizable by just one name.

Another long name!

In the late 19th century, the Reverend Ralph William Lyonel Tollemache of Grantham, Lincolnshire gave his 15 children very long names. These included Lyulph Ydwallo Odin Nestor Egbert Lyonel Toedmag Hugh Erchenwyne Saxon Esa Cromwell Orma Nevill Dysart Plantagenet Tollemache-Tollemache (1876–1961). The initial letters of his first names spell 'Lyonel the Second'.

Aaliyah US singer/actress Aaliyah Haughton, 1979–2001
Banksy UK, graffiti artist, true identity unknown
Beyoncé US singer Beyoncé Knowles, 1981–
Björk Icelandic singer/actress Björk Gudmundsdóttir, 1965–
Bono Irish rock band U2 singer Paul Hewson, 1960–
Canaletto Italian painter Giovanni Antonio Canale, 1697–1768
Cher US singer Cherilyn Sarkasian, 1946–
Colette French writer Sidonie-Gabrielle Colette, 1873–1954
Dido UK singer Dido Armstrong, 1971–
Eminem US rap singer Marshall Mathers, 1972–
Enya Irish singer Eithne ní Bhraonáin, 1961–
Evita Argentinean politician Eva Peron, 1919–52
Flea US Red Hot Chili Peppers bass guitarist Michael Peter Balzary, 1962–
Hergé Belgian Tintin cartoonist Georges Rémi, 1907–83
Houdini US magician Erich Weiss, 1874–1926
Lulu UK singer Marie McDonald McLaughlin, 1948–
Madonna US singer Madonna Louise Ciccone, 1958–
Meatloaf US singer Marvin/ Michael Lee Aday, 1947–
Michelangelo Italian painter Michelangelo Buonarroti, 1475–1564
Moby US musician Richard Melville Hall, 1965–
Nelly Cornell Haynes Jr, US rapper, 1974–
Pelé Brazilian footballer Edson Arantes Nascimento, 1940–
Pink US singer Alecia Moore, 1979–
Ronaldo Brazilian footballer Ronaldo Luiz Nazario de Lima, 1976–
Seal UK singer Seal Samuel, 1963–
Shaggy Jamaican singer Orville Richard Burrell, 1968–
Sting UK singer Gordon Matthew Sumner, 1951–
Twiggy Lesley Hornby, British model, 1949–
Usher Usher Raymond IV, US singer-songwriter, 1978–

Initial impressions

These famous people are known by their initials and surnames, rather than their full first names.

Early Heinz wagon from about 1900

W.H. (Wystan Hugh) Auden was a poet
Rev. W. (Wilbert) Awdry wrote *Thomas the Tank Engine*
P.T. (Phineas Taylor) Barnum was a circus proprietor
J.M. (James Matthew) Barrie was the author of *Peter Pan*
T.S. (Thomas Stearns) Eliot wrote the book on which the musical *Cats* was based
W.C. (William Claude) Fields was a film actor
W.G. (William Gilbert) Grace played cricket
H.J. (Henry John) Heinz manufactured food
k.d. (Kathryn Dawn) Lang is a singer
D.H. (David Herbert) Lawrence was a writer
T.E. (Thomas Edward) Lawrence was a soldier/writer (Lawrence of Arabia)
C.S. (Clive Staples) Lewis wrote *The Lion, the Witch and the Wardrobe*
A.A. (Alan Alexander) Milne wrote *Winnie the Pooh*
E. (Edith) Nesbit wrote *The Phoenix and the Carpet*
J.K. (Joanne Kathleen) Rowling is the author of *Harry Potter*
O.J. (Orenthal James) Simpson was a footballer
R.L. (Robert Lawrence) Stine wrote the *Goosebumps* series
J.R.R. (John Roland Ruel) Tolkien wrote *Lord of the Rings*
J.M.W. (Joseph Mallord William) Turner was a painter
H.G. (Herbert George) Wells was a science-fiction author
E.B. (Elwyn Brooks) White wrote *Charlotte's Web* and *Stuart Little*
F. W. (Frank Winfield) Woolworth was a retailer

Russia	Scotland	Spain	Sweden	USA	Wales
1 Smirnov	1 Smith	1 García	1 Johansson	1 Smith	1 Jones
2 Ivanov	2 Brown	2 Fernández	2 Andersson	2 Johnson	2 Williams
3 Kuznetsov	3 Wilson	3 González	3 Karlsson	3 Williams	3 Davies
4 Popov	4 Robertson	4 Rodríguez	4 Nilsson	4 Brown	4 Evans
5 Sokolov	5 Thomson	5 López	5 Eriksson	5 Jones	5 Thomas
6 Lebedev	6 Campbell	6 Martínez	6 Larsson	6 Miller	6 Roberts
7 Kozlov	7 Stewart	7 Sánchez	7 Olsson	7 Davis	7 Lewis
8 Novikov	8 Anderson	8 Pérez	8 Persson	8 García	8 Hughes
9 Morozov	9 Scott	9 Martín	9 Svensson	9 Rodríguez	9 Morgan
10 Petrov	10 Murray	10 Gómez	10 Gustafsson	10 Wilson	10 Griffiths

Puritan names

Protestant extremists of the 16th and 17th-century known as Puritans often gave their children religious slogans as names. They included some we still use, such as Faith, Hope and Prudence, but also many strange ones, like Praise-god, Hate-evil, Joy-in-sorrow and Safe-on-high.

Who's who in the family?

We all know who's who in our immediate family – our mothers, fathers, grandparents, aunts and uncles, sisters and brothers. But who is a second cousin or a cousin once removed?

Nephew
Son of your sister or brother

Niece
Daughter of your sister or brother

Cousin, or first cousin
Child of your aunt and uncle

Second cousin
Child of your first cousin. Second cousins have the same great-grandparents as you, but not the same grandparents. Third cousins have the same great-great-grandparents, and so on.

Removed
A child of your first cousin is called "once removed". Removed means a different generation. Once removed is one generation, twice removed is two generations, and so on.

Step
Stepmother, stepfather, stepsister, stepbrother, stepson or stepdaughter is a person who is related to you only by the remarriage of someone in your immediate family after death or divorce. For example, if a woman marries again, her new husband will be her children's stepfather but he has no blood relationship with them.

Half
A half-sister or half-brother has either the same mother or father as you, but not both.

Weddings and divorces around the world

The number of people marrying every year varies from country to country. Some are tropical islands and countries that are popular with tourists who travel there for a romantic wedding.

Others have cultures that place a specially high value on marriage. The number of divorces varies greatly from country to country, according to the legal system and religion.

Number of marriages per 1000 per year*

High rates
China 35.9
Cook Islands 32.8
Barbados 13.1
Cyprus 12.9

Medium rates
USA 7.8
Australia 5.4
UK 5.1
Canada 4.7

Low rates
Venezuela 3.3
Argentina 3.2
Armenia 3.2
Saudi Arabia 3.2

Number of divorces per 1000 per year*

High rates
Russia 5.30
Aruba 5.27
USA 4.19
Ukraine 3.79

Medium rates
Australia 2.85
UK 2.58
Canada 2.24

Low rates
Guatemala 0.12
Belize 0.17
Mongolia 0.28

* In those countries for which data available

Underwater wedding

In some countries, such as Indonesia and Thailand, holiday resorts offer underwater weddings. They are popular with scuba divers, but the guests also have to be divers, the wedding photographer has to use an underwater camera and the wedding certificate must be waterproof.

An underwater wedding, like this one in Hong Kong's Ocean Park, can be very expensive!

www.sog.org.uk search

Till death do us part...

Longest marriages

- Sir Temulji Bhicaji Nariman and Lady Nariman of Mumbai (Bombay), India were married in 1853 at five years old. They stayed married for 86 years until Sir Temulji's death in 1940.
- Lazarus Rowe and Molly Weber were allegedly married in Greenland, New Hampshire, USA, in 1743. They remained married for 86 years until 1829 when Lazarus died.

According to the Bible, King Solomon had 700 wives as well as 300 concubines.

Most marriages

- King Mongkut of Siam (1804–68) had 39 wives and 82 children. His life inspired the musical *The King and I* and the film *Anna and the King* (1999).
- American Glynn "Scotty" de Moss Wolfe (1908–97) was married 29 times, which is a US record. His 29th and last wedding was on 20 June 1996 to Linda Essex. It was her 23rd wedding – another US record.
- US asbestos millionaire Tommy Manville (1894–1967) was married 13 times.

Seventh time lucky
In the UK, Sir Francis Ferdinand Maurice Cook (1907–78) was married seven times.

Family history is increasingly popular

Family history

Genealogy is the study of family connections, while family history includes additional information about family members, such as their education, work and homes. Both have long been popular pastimes among people keen to discover more about their ancestors and to locate living relatives. The Internet has enabled anyone to carry out online research and contact family members around the world and share information. Special computer software now makes it easy to organize records and create family trees.

- In the past, families often kept records of births, marriages and deaths in their family bibles. Sometimes it was the only book in the household, and was treasured and passed on through generations, along with other information such as photographs and diaries.
- The main official sources are records of births, marriages and deaths. In England and Wales these have been compulsory since Queen Victoria came to the throne in 1837, and from 1855 in Scotland. In the USA and Canada they are kept by individual states. For earlier years, back to the 16th century in some places, the registers of churches that recorded baptisms, marriages and burials are valuable to researchers, alongside a wide range of other sources such as wills, professional and military archives and immigration and emigration records.
- Censuses have been held in the UK every 10 years since 1841. Those up to 1911 are available online to researchers who can gain valuable information about family members, their birthplaces, occupations and addresses. A US census has been held every 10 years since 1790 – those up to 1930 are available online.
- In recent years, genetic genealogy – the use of DNA tests –has become a useful way of establishing an individual's relationship to other family members.

Anniversary gifts

There is a very old tradition of celebrating wedding anniversaries by presenting special types of gift. For example, for a 25th anniversary people give gifts made of silver. In the UK and USA most people celebrate only the milestone anniversaries: the 25th, 30th, 40th, 50th and 60th.

The 75th anniversary was traditionally the diamond but few married couples live long enough to celebrate it. Since Queen Victoria's Diamond Jubilee was held to mark her 60 years on the throne, the 60th wedding anniversary has become the diamond celebration.

1st Cotton (UK); paper (US)
2nd Paper (UK); cotton, calico (US)
3rd Leather
4th Fruit, flowers (UK); linen, silk (US)
5th Wood
6th Sugar, sweets, iron
7th Wool, copper
8th Bronze
9th Pottery, willow
10th Tin, aluminium
11th Steel
12th Silk, linen
13th Lace
14th Ivory
15th Crystal, glass
20th China
25th Silver
30th Pearls
35th Coral, jade
40th Rubies
45th Sapphires
50th Gold
55th Emeralds
60th Diamonds
70th Platinum
75th Diamonds (again)

Tourists photograph themselves at the Gandhi memorial, Delhi, where his body was cremated after his assassination in 1948.

Mahatma Gandhi

(1869–1948) Indian

Gandhi began his career as a lawyer but became a great and spiritual leader. He led the peaceful civil disobedience of Indians against British rule in India and negotiated with the British government until 1947, when India was granted independence. Gandhi became the first icon of a people's struggle against oppression. His simple lifestyle and his belief in religious tolerance have made him a symbol of decency and peace ever since.

Christopher Columbus

(1451–1506) Italian

Christopher Columbus is one of the most famous of all explorers. He believed he could reach Asia by sailing west across the Atlantic Ocean and in 1492 he set sail in the *Santa Maria* to prove his theory. Instead, he landed on the islands now known as the West Indies. His discoveries led to the European exploration and settlement of the Americas.

William Shakespeare

(1564–1616) English

William Shakespeare is generally agreed to be the greatest playwright in the English language. He began as an actor and wrote at least 154 love poems and 37 plays, including *King Lear*, *Hamlet*, *Romeo and Juliet* and *Macbeth*. Shakespeare also probably introduced more than 1,700 new words to the English language.

A US stamp commemorating the 400th anniversary of Shakespeare's birth in 1964

Charles Darwin

(1809–82) English

Naturalist Charles Darwin established the theory of evolution. He began forming his ideas when he served as official naturalist on a world voyage on *HMS Beagle* (1831–36) and spent the rest of his life back in England developing them. When his famous book *The Origin of Species by Means of Natural Selection* was published in 1859 there were violent reactions against it. Darwin challenged the Bible's account of creation, and explained that human beings are descended from an ape-like ancestor. Another English naturalist, Alfred Russel Wallace, independently developed very similar ideas at the same time as Darwin.

Emmeline Pankhurst

(1858–1928) English

Emmeline Pankhurst was the most famous of the women who campaigned for the right to vote in the UK. From 1905 she fought for the vote by any means possible and was frequently arrested and imprisoned. She died in 1928 shortly before her aims were realized and every woman over 21 years old was granted the vote.

Emmeline Pankhurst, 1914

Karl Marx

(1818–83) German

Karl Marx's ideas on economic history and sociology changed the world. Marx was a social philosopher who attacked the state and predicted a future in which everyone was equal. He explained his theories in the *Communist Manifesto* (compiled with Friedrich Engels and published in 1848) and *Das Kapital* (1867–94). His ideas eventually led to the Russian Revolution and communism. By 1950 almost half of the world's people lived under communist regimes.

Albert Einstein

(1879–1955) German/American

Einstein was one of the greatest of all physicists and his name has become a symbol of genius. When his most famous work, *The General Theory of Relativity*, was proven in 1919, Einstein became the most celebrated scientist in the world, and he won the Nobel Prize for Physics in 1921. Einstein was a firm believer in pacifism, but his scientific theories helped his adopted country, the USA, to develop the atomic bomb. A week before he died Einstein wrote to Bertrand Russell, a British philosopher and leading anti-nuclear campaigner, asking to put his name to a manifesto urging all countries to give up their nuclear weapons.

Adolf Hitler

(1889–1945) Austrian
Adolf Hitler was Germany's leader from 1933 to 1945, during which time he led the world into the most devastating war in history. Hitler's hatred of Jewish people and his desire for a blue-eyed, blond-haired master race led to the murder of six million people during World War II; most died in concentration camps in Eastern Europe.

Nelson Mandela

(1918–) South African
Nelson Mandela dedicated his life to the fight against apartheid – a policy which kept black and white South Africans apart and denied black citizens the vote. He was imprisoned in 1964 for his aggressive opposition to South Africa's racist government and was held for 26 years. In 1990, after his release, Mandela was elected president of the African National Congress. In 1993 he won the Nobel Peace Prize for his work to end apartheid.

See also
History timeline: page 105

Bill Gates

(1955–) American
Bill Gates created his first computer program while still at high school, co-founded Microsoft in 1977, and by 1993 was the richest man on Earth. In 2000 Gates and his wife formed the Bill & Melinda Gates Foundation, which is the largest charity in the world. One of its aims is to rid the developing world of polio and other deadly diseases.

James Watson (1928–) American and Francis Crick

(1916–2004) English
American biologist James Watson and English scientist Francis Crick discovered the molecular structure of DNA, using theories already written by Maurice Wilkins. Their theory helps to explain how DNA carries hereditary information and their discoveries have revolutionized our understanding of genetics and the study of disease.

Martin Luther King, Jr

(1929–68) American
Martin Luther King was a Baptist minister who campaigned against the segregation of blacks in the southern states of the USA. He was influenced by Gandhi and believed in peaceful protest. He won the Nobel Peace Prize in 1964. King was assassinated in 1968, but will always be remembered for his dignified, passive resistance to an unjust society.

Mao Zedong/Mao Tse-tung/ Chairman Mao

(1893–1976) Chinese
Mao Zedong was one of the founders of the Chinese Communist Party and the first chairman of the People's Republic of China in 1949. He had an enormous influence on his country and was greatly admired for founding the Chinese republic and for changes in the early years of his rule. During his rule, Mao's image was displayed everywhere – in every school, home, factory and workplace.

The charity co-founded by Bill Gates (right) supports important medical research

Women adventurers

These are just some of the intrepid women who went where no other woman – in some cases, no man – had gone before.

Amelia Earhart in the cockpit of her plane

- French novelist Jules Verne's novel *Around the World in 80 Days* inspired American journalist Nellie Bly (real name Elizabeth Cochrane, 1864–1922) to beat this time. She set out in 1889, and returned to New York on 25 January 1890 – a record round-the-world trip of 72 days, 6 hours, 11 minutes and 14 seconds.
- Amelia Earhart (USA, 1898–1937) became the first woman to fly solo across the Atlantic in 1932.
- Cosmonaut Valentina Tereshkova (USSR, 1937–) was the first woman in space. She went into orbit on 16 June 1963.
- Sheila Scott (UK, 1927–88) was the first woman to fly round the world solo, in 1971. She was also the first woman to pilot a plane over the North Pole.
- Clare Francis (UK, 1946–) became the first woman to sail solo across the Atlantic in 1973.
- Ellen MacArthur (UK, 1978–) set a world record for the fastest single-handed, round-the-world voyage of 71 days 14 hours 18 minutes 33 seconds, on 7 February 2005.

Polar exploration firsts

The North and South Poles are two of the most difficult places on Earth to reach and so have been great challenges for explorers. These are some of the people who reached the poles by one means or another.

First to reach the North Pole

American adventurer Frederick Cook (1865–1940) claimed that he and two Inuit reached the North Pole on 21 April 1908, but he probably faked his journey. Another American, Robert Edwin Peary (1856–1920), his companion Matthew Alexander Henson (1866–1955) and four Inuit were said to have first reached the pole on 9 April 1909. The first corroborated overland journey was that of a team led by Wally Herbert (UK) that arrived at the pole on 6 April 1969 - 60 years after Peary's claimed expedition.

First to reach the South Pole

Norwegian explorer Roald Amundsen (1872–1928) and four companions reached the South Pole on 14 December 1911. They just beat British explorer Robert Falcon Scott and his team, who got there on 17 January 1912 but died on their return journey.

First pole-to-pole journey

British explorer Sir Ranulph Fiennes and his partner Charles Burton were the first people to walk from pole to pole. They crossed the South Pole on 15 December 1980 and reached the North Pole on 10 April 1982.

First solo overland journey to the North Pole

Japanese explorer Naomi Uemura reached the North Pole on 1 May 1978. He travelled by dog sled, but was then picked up by an aircraft. Frenchman Jean-Louis Etienne made the first solo journey without dogs, reaching the pole on 11 May 1986.

First woman to reach the South Pole solo

Norwegian Liv Arnesen trekked to the South Pole unaided in 50 days, arriving at the pole on 25 December 1994.

First swim at the North Pole

British swimmer Lewis Gordon Pugh swam 1 km in gaps between ice at the North Pole, 15 July 2007.

First manned descent to North Pole seabed

On 2 August 2007, two Russian *MIR* submarines placed a Russian flag on the seabed beneath the North Pole.

Solar circumnavigation

Bertrand Piccard of Switzerland, who with Brian Jones was the first man to fly round the world in a balloon, is planning to repeat his feat in 2012 in *Solar Impulse*, a solar-powered aircraft.

First round the world

Since the first voyage round the world, almost 500 years ago, people have been looking for different ways of circumnavigating (travelling right round) the planet by land, sea or air.

First circumnavigation
Juan Sebastian de Elcano and his crew of 17 on *Vittoria* sailed from Spain in 1519 and returned 1,079 days later. The expedition was led by Ferdinand Magellan, but he was murdered in the Philippines on 27 April 1521.

First British circumnavigation
Sir Francis Drake and a crew of 50 left Plymouth, England in 1577 on the *Golden Hind* and returned on 26 September 1580.

First solo sailing
Canadian-born sailor Captain Joshua Slocum (1844–1910) sailed round the world alone in *Spray*, an oyster boat he built himself. He left the USA on 24 April 1895 and returned on 27 June 1898.

First walk
George Matthew Schilling (USA) claimed to have walked round the world between 1897 and 1904, but his journey has not been verified. David Kunst (USA) made the first confirmed journey from 20 June 1970 to 5 October 1974. He wore out 21 pairs of shoes during his 23,250 km (14,446 miles) walk.

Explorers and travellers

Today there are few places that have not been explored, but this was not always the case. America was unknown to Europeans until little over 500 years ago, and Australia was scarcely known by the rest of the world until the late 18th century. These are some of the people who made Europeans aware of the rest of the world.

Marco Polo (c. 1254–1324)
Italian traveller Marco Polo was one of the first Europeans to visit China and other Far Eastern territories. His reports were not believed, but he encouraged the idea of trading with the East.

John Cabot (1450–98)
Italian-born explorer John and his son Sebastian Cabot were employed by British merchants to seek a western route to Asia. During their travels they discovered parts of the northeast coast of America.

Christopher Columbus (1451–1506)
Italian explorer Christopher Columbus discovered North, Central and South America and the islands of the West Indies.

Vasco da Gama (c. 1460–1524)
Portuguese explorer Vasco da Gama travelled round the Cape of Good Hope and up the East coast of Africa. He discovered a trade route to India.

Ferdinand Magellan (1480–1521)
Magellan was a Portuguese explorer who led the first voyage round the world. He discovered the Strait of Magellan, near the tip of South America.

Abel Tasman (1603–59)
Abel Tasman, a Dutchman, explored Australia. In 1642 he discovered Van Diemens Land (later called Tasmania) and New Zealand.

Henry Hudson (c. 1550–1611)
Henry Hudson was an English navigator who searched for a Northwest Passage (a route to the East by travelling north of America). He discovered Hudson Bay.

James Cook (1728–79)
British Captain James Cook led several major expeditions. He explored the coasts of Australia, New Zealand and North America.

David Livingstone (1813–73)
Livingstone was a Scottish missionary and explorer of Africa. He discovered and named the Victoria Falls after Queen Victoria.

Sir Richard Burton (1821–90)
Burton was one of the first Europeans to travel to Arabia. With John Hanning Speke he discovered Lake Tanganyika in Africa.

John Hanning Speke (1827–64)
Speke discoverered Lake Tanganyika with Burton. He also discovered Lake Victoria, believed to be the source of the River Nile.

Sir Henry Morton Stanley (1841–1904)
Stanley was a British explorer of Africa and was involved in the search for Livingstone.

Youngest solo voyage

Jessica Watson of Australia became the youngest person to sail solo round the world when she completed her journey on 15 May 2010, 3 days before her 17th birthday. Her voyage from and to Sydney, Australia, in 10.23-metre (34-ft) *Ella's Pink Lady* took 6 months and 27 days.

Steve Fossett in *Virgin Atlantic Global Flyer*

First non-stop flight
USAF B-50A bomber *Lucky Lady II* piloted by Capt. James Gallagher flew from Fort Worth, Texas on 26 February 1949. The journey took 94 hours 1 minute and the plane was refuelled four times in mid-air.

First underwater
US Navy nuclear submarine *Triton* travelled round the world underwater between 16 February and 25 April 1960.

First non-stop solo voyage
British yachtsman Robin Knox-Johnston sailed from and returned to Falmouth, UK, in *Suhali* between 14 June 1968 and 22 April 1969.

First in a wheelchair
Rick Hansen (Canada) went round the world in a wheelchair between 21 March 1985 and 22 May 1987. He travelled through 34 countries.

First balloon flight
Brian Jones (UK) and Bertrand Piccard (Switzerland) made a round-the-world voyage in the *Breitling Orbiter 3*. They left on 1 March 1999 and their journey took three weeks.

First solo flight
On 7 March 2005 Steve Fossett (USA) achieved the first solo round-the-world flight without refuelling in *Virgin Atlantic Global Flyer*. He covered 36,818 km (22,878 miles) in a flight time of 67 hours, 2 minutes and 38 seconds. On 1 February 2006 he once again took off from the USA to fly around the world. This time he carried on to Bournemouth, UK, making this voyage the longest ever solo, non-stop, round-the-world flight. He travelled a distance of 36,912.68 km (22,936.5 miles) in 76 hours, 42 minutes and 55 seconds.

Apollo 8 astronauts James Lovell, William Anders and Frank Borman, 1968 "people of the year"

In the news

Every year the editors of *Time* magazine nominate a person of the year – the individual or group who has most influenced world events during the year. The winner may not always have had a good influence – Adolf Hitler was nominated in 1938.

Nominees may be a man, a couple (Chinese leaders General and Madame Chiang Kai-shek in 1937), a woman (Queen Elizabeth II in 1952), a group of people (three astronauts in 1968), even a machine (a computer in 1982). Here are just some of the winners.

2009 Ben Bernanke, economist
2008 Barack Obama (incoming US President)
2007 Vladimir Putin (Russian president)
2006 You
2005 Bill and Melinda Gates/Bono
2003 The American Soldier
1999 Jeff Bezos (founder of Amazon.com)
1994 Pope John Paul II
1992/98 Bill Clinton (US president)
1987/89 Mikhail Gorbachev (Soviet leader)
1966 Young people
1963 Martin Luther King, Jr (civil rights campaigner)
1961 John F. Kennedy (US president)
1949 Winston Churchill (British prime minister)
1930 Mohandas Gandhi (Indian leader)

http://s9.com search

Late success

As people live longer, many continue to work well into what was once thought of as extreme old age. These are all people who made great achievements in their eighties and beyond.

Alice Porlock, British writer, published her first book at 102 years old.
Ichijirou Araya, Japanese climber, climbed Mount Fuji aged 100 years.
George Burns, US actor, appeared in *Radioland Murders* (1994) at 98.
Dimitrion Yornanidis, Greek athlete, ran a marathon at 98.
Pablo Casals, Spanish musician, conducted the Israel Festival Youth Orchestra when he was 96.
Michelangelo, Italian artist, produced his Rondandini *Pietà* sculpture at the age of 88.
Claude Monet, French painter, completed his water-lily paintings when he was 84 years old.

Against the odds

All these people triumphed over disability or illness to achieve fame.

Lance Armstrong
(1971–) US cyclist, contracted cancer that affected his brain and lungs. He recovered and went on to win the gruelling Tour de France cycle race a record seven times in a row, 1999–2005.

Douglas Bader
(1910–82) became a British war hero and flying ace, despite losing both his legs in a plane crash.

Lord Horatio Nelson

(1758–1805) was a British admiral. He lost an arm and an eye in battle, but won many naval victories, including the Battle of Trafalgar in 1805.

Stephen Hawking

(1942–) a British physicist and celebrated author of *A Brief History of Time*, suffers from motor neurone disease. He is confined to a wheelchair and speaks with the aid of a voice synthesizer.

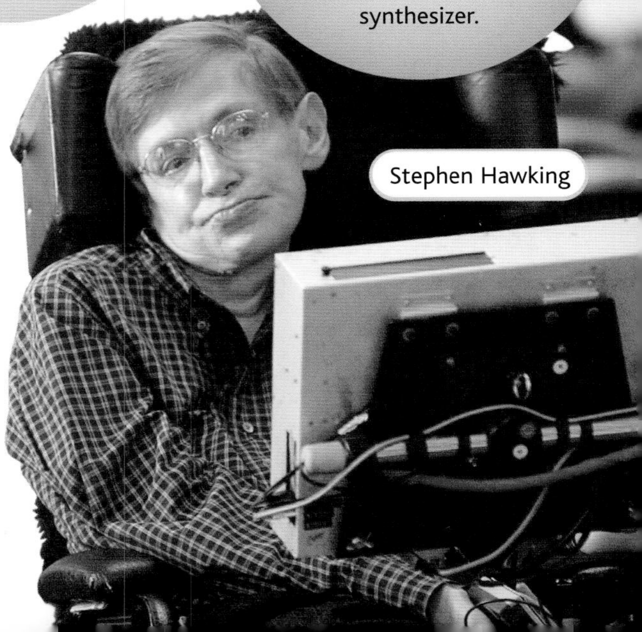

Stephen Hawking

William Gladstone, British politician, became prime minister for the fourth time when he was 82 years old.

Benjamin Franklin, American statesman, helped write the US Constitution when he was 81 years old.

George Cukor, US film director, directed *Rich and Famous* (1981) at 81 years old.

One and only

At the age of 82, Irish playwright George Bernard Shaw won an Oscar® for Best Screenplay for *Pygmalion* (1938). He had already won the Nobel Prize for Literature in 1925, so became the only person ever to win both a Nobel and an Oscar®.

Ludwig van Beethoven

(1770–1827) was one of the world's greatest composers. He continued to compose music even after he became totally deaf in 1817.

Sarah Bernhardt

(1844–1923) French actress, lost a leg in 1914 but continued acting.

Andrea Bocelli

(1958–) an Italian opera singer who was blinded at the age of 12. He went on to achieve international singing success.

Louis Braille

(1809–1852) was blind and invented the Braille system of printing with raised dots to enable blind people to read.

Terry Fox

(1958–81) Canadian athlete, lost a leg to cancer. He took up long-distance running, and through this he raised money for a cancer charity.

Frank Gardner

(1952–) British television reporter, was paralysed in 2004 from a gun attack while working in Saudi Arabia. He later resumed work with the BBC.

Evelyn Glennie

(1965–) Scottish percussionist, overcame profound deafness to become a world-class musician.

Mark Inglis

(1959–) In 2006, the New Zealander became the first double amputee to reach the top of Everest.

Helen Keller

(1880–1968) was a famed author and lecturer despite being blind and deaf.

Awards

Awards are presented in almost every area of achievement. The ones that receive the most attention in newspapers and on television are those given to famous film stars, writers, artists and singers. Among the best known are the following.

Academy Awards (Oscars®)
These are the most famous of all film awards. The Oscar® presentations are now watched on television by more than a billion people worldwide. The Academy Awards – also called the Oscars® after the statuette that winners receive – were first presented in 1929. In 2010, *The Hurt Locker* won Oscars in six categories, including Best Film.

BAFTA Awards
The British Academy of Film and Television Arts awards began in 1947. In 2009 *Slumdog Millionaire* won the Best Film award.

Booker Prize
This British book prize was set up in 1968 and is awarded each year for a novel published in the previous 12 months. It is now known as the Man Booker Prize.

BRIT Awards
The BRITs are British popular music awards which started in 1977. Robbie Williams is the most successful solo artist, with 11 wins. In 2010, Lady Gaga won three BRIT awards.

Cannes Film Festival
This annual international film festival is held in Cannes in the South of France. Its most important award is the Palme d'Or (Golden Palm), which dates back to 1955.

Golden Globe Awards
These US film awards began in 1943. Julia Roberts has been nominated six times and won three awards, and Tom Hanks has won four of the six awards for which he was nominated.

Grammy Awards
The US music awards have been presented since 1959. The classical awards have been dominated by conductor Sir Georg Solti, who won 38 Grammys. Beyoncé won six awards in 2010, the most by a female artist in one ceremony, while Taylor Swift (20) was the youngest to receive the Grammy Award for Album of the Year.

MTV Video Music Awards
The music television channel MTV established its awards in 1984. Madonna is the most successful MTV artist, with 70 nominations and 21 awards.

Nobel Prize
These international awards are named after Alfred Nobel, the inventor of dynamite, and were first presented in 1901. There are now six categories – Physics, Chemistry, Medicine, Literature, Peace and Economics. Famous winners include Winston Churchill (Literature, 1953) and Mother Theresa (Peace, 1979). US President Barack Obama won the Nobel Peace Prize in 2009.

Pulitzer Prizes
These US awards are given for achievements in journalism, writing (fiction, non fiction and poetry) and music. They are named after publisher Joseph Pulitzer and began in 1917.

Turner Prize
This British art prize is named after landscape painter J.M.W. Turner and was established in 1984. The winning works are often controversial, and usually not conventional paintings. Damien Hirst is a notorious winner.

Golden Raspberry awards

The Golden Raspberries, founded in 1980, are joke awards presented to the worst films and actors! Madonna was a notable winner. She also received the Razzies award for worst actress of the 20th century. At the 30th annual ceremony in 2010, Sandra Bullock won the Worst Actress award for *All About Steve* – which she collected in person. The next day, she won the Best Actress Oscar for her role in *The Blind Side*.

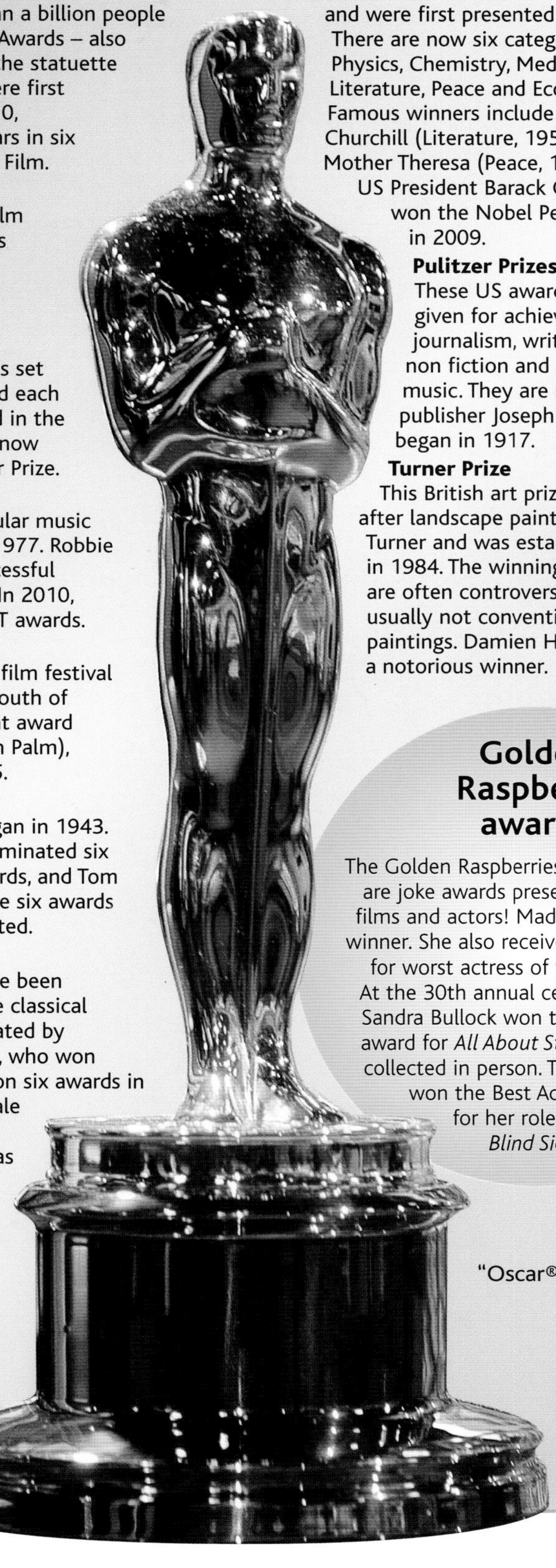

"Oscar®"

Where are the children?

In countries such as India, where people have large families and relatively short lives, there are more children than older people. In the USA and UK there are more middle-aged and older people than children. Most people have smaller families so there are fewer young people. In the UK there are 10,056,003 children.

No. of children aged 0–14 yrs*

India	352,866,393
China	235,097,526
Indonesia	67,144,054
Nigeria	63,541,220
Pakistan	63,531,222
USA	62,889,723
Bangladesh	53,681,543
Brazil	53,399,691
Ethiopia	42,058,330

* Estimated for 2011

Schoolchildren in India taking part in a physical education class

World's youngest billionaire

Albert Maria Lamoral Miguel Johannes Gabriel, 12th Prince of Thurn and Taxis (born 24 June 1983), inherited his father's fortune when he was aged seven. In 2009, the prince, who studied economics and theology at Edinburgh University and is a racing car driver with the Reiter Engineering team, was estimated to be worth $2.1 billion, including large amounts of land, works of art and the Thurn and Taxis palace, Regensburg, Germany, which is open to the public.

Young populations

Countries with a lot of people under 15 usually have high birth rates and high death rates. In countries where families have many children who are too young to work and adults die relatively young, there are not enough people of working age to earn money to feed and take care of the families. As a result, these countries tend to be among the world's poorest.

Population under 15 years old*

	Country	Percentage under 15
1	**Uganda**	49.9
2	**Niger**	49.6
3	**Mali**	47.3
4	**Ethiopia**	46.3
5=	**Burundi**	46.0
=	**Chad**	46.0
7	**Burkina Faso**	45.8
	World average	26.3

The USA, UK and Canada have a lower than average proportion of children.

USA	20.1
UK	16.4
Canada	15.7

* Estimated for 2011

Young fame

Miley Cyrus, the daughter of country singer Billy Ray Cyrus, was born on 23 November 1992.

At the age of 14 she became the star of the TV series *Hannah Montana* in 2006, appearing in the dual role of the pop star title character and Miley Stewart. By the time she was 16 she had released US No.1 albums, earning a reputed $25 million in 2008, and appeared in films, including *Hannah Montana: The Movie* (released in 2009).

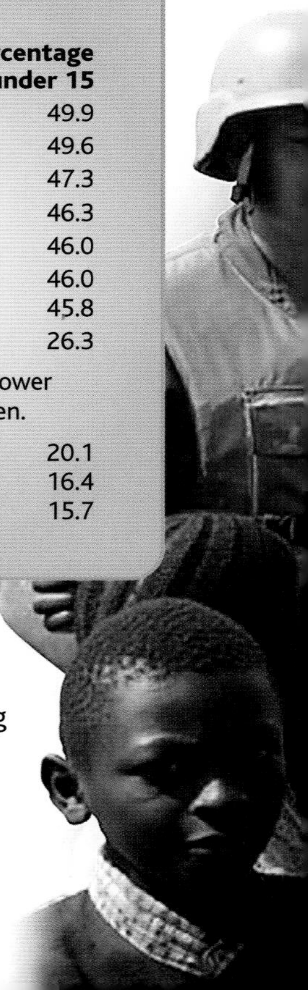

Hollywood star Angelina Jolie visiting a refugee camp in her role as Goodwill Ambassador for the United Nations High Commissioner for Refugees

The UN Convention on the Rights of the Child

The United Nations issued its Declaration on the Rights of the Child in 1959 to try to relieve the suffering of children in poor and war-torn countries. It came into force as a convention in 1990. 193 countries are parties to the Convention: Somalia and the USA are not.

All the signaturies agree to make sure that children under 18 have certain basic rights, such as housing and medical care. Recent optional additions include one that children will not have to serve in military action.

The Convention on the Rights of the Child states that all children have the right to:

- a name and nationality
- affection, love, understanding and material security
- adequate nutrition, housing and medical services
- special care if disabled – physically, mentally or socially
- be among the first to receive protection and relief in all circumstances
- be protected against all forms of neglect, cruelty and exploitation
- full opportunity for play and recreation and equal opportunity to free and compulsory education, to enable the child to develop his/her individual abilities and to become a useful member of society
- develop his/her full potential in conditions of freedom and dignity
- be brought up in a spirit of understanding, tolerance, friendship among peoples, peace and universal brotherhood
- enjoy these rights regardless of race, colour, sex, religion, political or other opinion, national or social origin and property, birth or other status.

International youth organizations

Scouts and Cub Scouts

Sir Robert Baden-Powell (1857–1941), a former general in the British army, launched the scouting movement in 1907. Today there are scouts in 216 countries and territories with a total worldwide membership of more than 28 million. There are 3,994,638 in the USA and 446,557 in the UK, but the leading scouting country is Indonesia, with almost nine million members. Scouting is forbidden in some countries, including Cuba and North Korea. The junior division for boys under 11 is called the Cub Scouts (formerly Wolf Cubs in the UK) and was founded in 1930.

Girl Guides/Girl Scouts and Brownies

The Girl Guide Movement was started in 1910 by Sir Robert Baden-Powell and his younger sister Agnes (1858–1945). From then on, Girl Guides and Girl Scouts organizations were established around the world – the Girl Scouts of the United States of America dates from 1912 and the junior group, the Brownies, was set up in 1914. A century after the foundation, of the movement, there are Guides in 145 countries, with a total worldwide membership of more than 10 million.

YMCA and YWCA

The YMCA (Young Men's Christian Association) was founded by George Williams in the UK in 1844 and in the USA in 1851. Its aim was to provide shelter and other support for young men who came into cities to find work. The YMCA now has branches in 135 countries. The YWCA (Young Women's Christian Association), was founded in the UK in 1855 and in the USA in 1858.

www.unicef.org.uk/worldexplorers search

Beliefs & Ideas

Sagrada Familia

One of the longest-ever major building projects reached a milestone in 2010 when part of the Sagrada Familia cathedral in Barcelona, Spain, was scheduled to open for worship in September, and then be consecrated by the Pope in November. The striking design is by Spanish architect Antoni Gaudí (1852–1926). Construction started in 1882 and is unlikely to be completed before 2026. It has undergone many changes in its 128-year construction with new elements being incorporated and the latest building methods applied. More than 2 million tourists a year visit the cathedral.

Gods and goddesses

In most of the world's major religions today only one god is worshipped. But in many ancient religions, followers worshipped a group of gods. Each god had special characteristics and responsibilities, and some could appear in a variety of forms.

The myths and legends of ancient cultures and the range of gods worshipped often changed over thousands of years as different gods and goddesses rose or fell in importance. Those listed on these pages are a selection of the most revered and long-standing gods of some of the world's ancient cultures.

Chinese gods

The Chinese worshipped a large range of gods for more than 4,000 years, up to the coming of Chinese communism in the 20th century. Some Chinese people continue to worship these gods – often in secret – today.

Dragon Kings Ao-shin (North), Ao-chin (South), Ao-kuang (East) and Ao-jun (West), the gods of rain, rivers and seas
Fu-xi god of arts and creativity
Guan-yin god and goddess of compassion
Guan-yu god of war
Meng-po goddess of the underworld
Nu-guawas serpent goddess of creation
Pan-gu giant creator god
Qi-yu god of the rain (half bull, half giant)
Three Pure Ones supreme trinity of Yuan-shi-tian-zong, Ling-bao-tian-song and Lao-jun
Xi-he goddess of light
Xi-wangmu goddess of immortality
Yi-di god of wine
Zao-jun god of the household

Ancient Egyptian gods

Egyptian religion dates back about 5,000 years and lasted until the coming of Christianity and Islam. Its huge range of gods and goddesses were believed to control almost every aspect of people's lives.

Amun-Ra king of the gods
Anubis jackal god of death and Egyptian mummies
Aten god of the sun-disc
Bast/Bastet cat goddess of fertility
Bes lion-like domestic god
Hathor cow-headed goddess of happiness
Horus falcon-headed sky god
Isis wife of Osiris, mother of Horus, goddess of motherhood and royalty
Month falcon-headed god of war
Nefertum god of the sacred blue lotus and the rising sun
Osiris god of the underworld and agriculture
Ptah creator god and patron of craftsmen
Ra Sun-god, ancient Egypt's most important god
Reshef god of war and thunder
Sekhmet/Sakhmet lion-headed goddess of war and destruction
Seth god of storms and violence
Thoth ibis-headed god of the Moon, arts and sciences

Ancient Egyptian falcon-headed god Horus depicted on a mummy mask

See also
World civilizations and empires: pages 106–107
Time: pages 14–16

Greek and Roman gods

The ancient Greeks had 12 major gods and goddesses. They believed the gods all lived on Mount Olympus and influenced the well-being of all humans. As the Greek civilization declined and the Roman empire grew, the Romans renamed the Greek gods and took them as their own.

Greek/Roman
Hera/Juno chief goddess – marriage
Aphrodite/Venus goddess of beauty
Artemis/Diana goddess of hunting
Athena/Minerva goddess of wisdom
Demeter/Ceres goddess of the harvest, nature
Hestia/Vesta goddess of the hearth
Zeus/Jupiter chief god – sky and air
Apollon/Apollo god of poetry, music, Sun
Ares/Mars god of war
Hephaistos/Vulcan god of blacksmiths
Hermes/Mercury messenger of the gods
Poseidon/Neptune god of the sea

The 12 Norse gods

The Norse people lived in ancient and medieval Scandinavia (modern Norway, Sweden, Finland, Iceland and Denmark).

The 12 Norse, or Scandinavian, gods were together called the Aesir, and their homeland was Asgard. There was also a second group of gods called the Vanir, who fought the Aesir. Later some Vanir gods, including Frey and his sister Freya, became Aesir.

- Odin, or Woden, chief god in Norse mythology
- Thor, red-haired and bearded son of Odin and Jord, god of war (his name gave us Thursday – Thor's day)
- Tyr, Tiu or Tiw, another son of Odin, god of warfare and battle (his name is commemorated in Tuesday)
- Balder or Baldur, god of sunlight
- Brag or Bragi, god of poetry
- Vidar, god of silence, stealth and revenge
- Hoder the blind
- Hermód or Hermoder the Brave, Odin's son and his messenger
- Hönir or Hoenir, a minor god
- Odnir, husband of Freya
- Loki, god of strife or mischief, capable of changing shape and performing tricks
- Vali, Odin's youngest son by Rind, a giantess. He slew Hod, who had murdered his brother Balder

Aztec gods

The Aztecs were based in central Mexico. They flourished from the 14th century until their conquest by Spanish invaders in 1522. They sacrificed humans to the gods, who were believed to control daily life and agriculture.

Chalchiuhtlicue goddess of lakes and streams, youth and beauty
Cinteotl god of maize
Coyolxauhqui goddess of the Moon
Ehecatl god of the wind and weather
Huehueteotl god of the hearth, the fire of life
Huitzilopochtli war god
Ilamatecuhtli goddess of the Earth, death and the Milky Way
Itztlacoliuhqui god of stone and the Morning Star
Mayahuel goddess of alcohol and the maguey plant (from which alcoholic drinks were made)
Mictlantecuhtli god of death
Quetzalcoatl creator god – and bringer of chocolate!
Tepeyollotl god of caves and earthquakes
Tezcatlipoca god of night and death
Tlahuizcalpantecuhtli god of dawn
Tonacatecuhtli god of food
Xipe-totec god of spring and agriculture, patron of goldsmiths
Xochipilli god of love, flowers, singing and dancing
Xochiquetzal goddess of love

Statue of the Aztec god Xochipilli, made between the 14th and 16th centuries

Inca gods

The Inca people lived in the part of South America that is now Peru from about 1200 to 1533. Inca gods were thought to influence natural events.

Apocatequil god of lightning
Apu Illapu god of thunder
Ilyap'a weather god
Inti Sun god
Kon god of rain and the southern wind
Mama Oello mother goddess, daughter of Inti and Mama Quilla
Mama Quilla Moon goddess, daughter of Viracocha and wife of Inti
Manco Capac creator god, Sun and fire
Pachacamac Earth god
Punchau Sun god
Vichaama god of death
Viracocha god of creation

Mayan gods

The Mayan civilization and neighbouring Olmec culture date back 3,000 years. Descendants of the Mayans still live in southern Mexico, Belize and Guatemala.

Bacabs gods of the four directions – Mulac (north), Cauac (south), Kan (east) and Ix (west)
Balu-chabtan god of war and sacrifice
Chak god of rain, fertility and agriculture
Hunahau god of death
Itzamna reptile creator god
Ix-chel Moon goddess
Kinichi-ahau Sun god
Kukulcan feathered serpent god
Xbalanque god of the jaguar
Yum-kaax corn god

The five pillars of Islam

The following are the five most important aspects of the Muslim faith.

1 ash-Shahada – profession of faith in Allah and his prophet Muhammad
2 salat – prayer five times a day, facing Makkah
3 zakat – giving alms to the poor and needy
4 sawm – fasting between dawn and dusk during Ramadan
5 hajj – pilgrimage to Makkah, at least once in one's lifetime

Jihad, meaning holy war, is sometimes added as an extra pillar.

Religious buildings

- Abbey – a building occupied by monks or nuns and run by an abbot or abbess
- Basilica – a type of early Christian church
- Cathedral – the main church in an area and the seat of the bishop
- Chapel – a place of worship within a larger building, or a nonconformist Christian religious building
- Church – a building used for public worship by Christians
- Convent or nunnery – the home of a community of nuns
- Dagoba – a Buddhist shrine
- Friary – home to friars, members of a religious order
- Meeting house – a place where certain religious groups, such as Quakers, gather
- Monastery – the home to a religious community of monks
- Mosque – a Muslim place of worship
- Pagoda – an Eastern temple
- Priory – a religious house run by a prior; it may be under the control of an abbey

Major religions*

Christianity 2,173,816,023
Islam 1,358,290,337
Hinduism 872,921,745
Chinese folk-religions 379,843,528
Buddhism 378,724,109
Ethnic religions 259,917,388
Sikkhism 22,782,827

* followers worldwide

The Golden Temple, Amritsar, India

Holy places

A holy place is somewhere that is especially revered by the followers of a religion. Examples include the birthplace of the founder of a religion, shrines and places of pilgrimage. There has been conflict in some of these holy places when members of other religions have claimed or attacked the sites.

Amritsar, India
This city is the Sikh religion's spiritual centre. The Golden Temple is the main shrine.

Athos, Greece
This is a holy mountain for the Greek Orthodox Church where there are many monasteries. Women are forbidden to go on to the mountain.

Benares, India
This Hindu holy city is dedicated to the god Shiva.

Bethlehem, Israel
The birthplace of Jesus

Canterbury, UK
The city was once England's most important pilgrimage centre.

Ganges, India
The Ganges river is sacred to Hindus, who bathe here and scatter the ashes of their dead in its waters.

Jerusalem, Israel
A holy city for Christians, Muslims and Jews. Sites include the Western Wall, Dome of the Rock and Church of the Holy Sepulchre.

Karbala, Iraq
This city is the centre of Shi'a Islam and contains the shrine of the prophet Muhammad's grandson al-Husain.

- Shrine – a place of worship connected with a sacred person or saint. It may contain sacred objects or relics
- Synagogue – a building for Jewish religious services
- Tabernacle – a house or tent used for worship, named after the tent used by the Israelites to cover the Ark of the Covenant
- Temple – a place of worship dedicated to a particular god or gods. Also sometimes used instead of synagogue

Gate of a Shinto shrine in Miyajima, Japan

Holy cows

Visitors to India are often amazed by the number of cows wandering in the streets (one theory as to why they congregate in busy traffic is that the exhaust fumes kill the flies). Gau Mata, or Mother Cow, has long been an important part of the Indian economy, its milk providing nourishment and its dung used for fuel, but it is also the most revered animal in the Hindu religion and features in many myths and legends; the phrase 'sacred cow' is even used in non-Hindu cultures. Gaudan, the act of presenting cows to Brahmin priests, is highly regarded, while killing a cow is prohibited and beef is never eaten (McDonalds restaurants in India serve vegetarian burgers). Once a cow has ceased to produce milk, it is often released to roam freely in the certain knowledge that devout Hindus will not let it starve.

Gods of the Vedas (sacred books)

Indra is the thunder god of battle.
Varuna is the guardian of order.
Agni is the god of fire.
Surya is the sun deity.

Other Hindu gods

Brahma is the creator.
Vishnu is the preserver, who has ten incarnations:
- Matsya, the fish
- Kurma, the tortoise
- Varah, the boar
- Nrisinha, half-man, half-lion
- Vamana, the dwarf
- Parasurama, Rama with the axe
- Ramachandra, Rama with bow and arrows
- Krishna, god of the Bhagavadgita
- Buddha, teacher
- Kalki, "the one to come".

Shiva is the god of destruction.
Ganesh is the elephant-headed god.
Hanuman is the monkey warrior god.

Hindu goddesses

Durga or Amba is the warrior god.
Parvati is the wife of Shiva.
Kali is the goddess of destruction.
Lakshmi is the wife of Vishnu, goddess of beauty, wealth and fortune.
Saraswati is the goddess of learning, arts and music.

The cow is revered in India

Lhasa, Tibet (China)
The centre of Tibetan Buddhism. The monastery here was once the home of the Dalai Lama.

Lourdes, France
In 1858 Bernadette Soubirous (later St Bernadette) saw visions of the Virgin Mary in a grotto at Lourdes. Since then Catholics have made pilgrimages there, seeking cures for their illnesses.

Makkah (Mecca), Saudi Arabia
Every year, millions of Muslims go on pilgrimage to this city. They also turn to face Makkah when they pray.

Medina, Saudi Arabia
This is the site of the tomb of the prophet Muhammad.

Olympus, Greece
The ancient Greeks believed the mountain to be the home of Zeus and other gods.

Salt Lake City, Utah, USA
The headquarters of the Church of Latter-Day Saints (Mormons)

Santiago de Compostela, Spain
In the 9th century a tomb believed to belong to the apostle James the Greater was discovered here. Christians make pilgrimages to a shrine made on the site.

Mount Shasta, California, USA
A dormant volcano and a sacred site for Native Americans

Vatican City
The city-state in Rome, Italy, is the centre of the Roman Catholic faith.

www.adherents.com search

The Koran

Allah is the Islamic name for God. Muslims believe that He revealed His wishes for the world to a man called Muhammad. These messages were later collected together as the Koran (also written Qur'an). Muslims believe that the words of the Koran are the exact words of Allah. It is said that it has not been altered since it first appeared in AD 632. The Koran is written in Arabic, the language which Muhammad spoke, and it contains the main teachings of Islam.

The Cairo Koran, made for the Sultan of Morocco in the 18th century

Boy reading from the Torah at a bar mitzvah ceremony

The Torah

The Torah is Judaism's most sacred text. It includes the first five books of the Bible, also known as the Pentateuch. These include the laws that God revealed to Moses on Mount Sinai. The Jewish scriptures also include the books of the prophets, historical writings and the Talmud. The Talmud contains instructions for following a Jewish way of life and understanding Jewish laws.

Sacred books

The Vedas

The four books of the Vedas contain the earliest Hindu beliefs and they have also influenced Buddhism, Sikhism and Jainism. The *Rig Veda* is the oldest of the Vedas. It was composed about 1500 BC, although it was not written down until around 300 BC. The Vedas include rituals and hymns that give us a glimpse of life in ancient India. Another important Hindu text is the *Bhagavad Gita*, or Song of the Lord. This is one section of a very long epic poem called the *Mahabharata*. The *Bhagavad Gita* is about 700 verses long and sets out Hindu philosophy, explaining the importance of selflessness, duty, devotion and meditation.

The Pali Canon

The Pali Canon is a collection of sacred texts followed by the Theravada school of Buddhism. The teachings of the Buddha were first passed on through the spoken word and were not written down until the 1st century BC. The Pali Canon is written in the Pali language, and is also known as the Tripitaka, meaning three baskets. The texts are divided into three sections which were originally written on palm leaf scrolls and kept in three different baskets. They include rules for Buddhist monks and nuns, tales of the Buddha's life and teachings, stories and philosophical arguments.

Guru Granth Sahib

Sikhs believe that the Guru Granth Sahib is the supreme spiritual authority and head of the Sikh religion, rather than any living person. The original version was compiled by Guru Arjan Dev, the fifth Sikh guru, in 1604. He collected the compositions of previous gurus over a number of years. The text includes almost 6,000 hymns and poems composed at different times and in different languages, which makes it very difficult to translate. It also includes Hindu and Muslim writings, reflecting the religious tolerance of the gurus.

The Bible

The Christian sacred book is called the Bible. It is made up of two parts – the Old Testament and the New Testament. The Old Testament describes the history of the Israelites and contains books of history, law, poetry and wisdom. It was written by different people, probably between 1100 and 200 BC. The New Testament describes the story of Jesus's life and his importance for Christians, and also contains writings by some important early Christians. It was probably written between AD 50 and 150. Passages from the Bible are read at Christian church services, and Christians also see the Bible as containing a code to live by and guidance in following their faith.

The original 12 disciples

1 Andrew: a fisherman and brother of Simon Peter; crucifed in Achaia, Greece; the patron saint of Scotland and Russia (30 November)
2 Bartholomew (24 August)
3 James the Great: son of Zebedee and brother of John; martyred by Herod Agrippa (25 July)
4 James the Less (3 May)
5 John: son of Zebedee and younger brother of James the Great; also known as John the Evangelist; said to have written the Gospel that bears his name (27 December)
6 Judas Iscariot: the disciple who betrayed Jesus in return for 30 pieces of silver; he later hanged himself
7 Jude: known as Judas, son of James; said to have been martyred in Persia with Simon (28 October)
8 Matthew: originally a tax collector before he became a disciple; author of the first Gospel (21 September)
9 Peter: a fisherman from Capernaeum; according to tradition he was crucified upside-down; usually depicted holding the keys to heaven; considered to have been the first pope (29 June)
10 Philip (3 May)
11 Simon: also called Peter; a Galilee fisherman (28 October)
12 Thomas: known as Didymus, "the twin"; the patron saint of Portugal (21 December)

See also
Bestsellers: page 230

Noah's Ark

Noah's Ark, seen here in a painting by American artist Edward Hicks, is one of the Bible's best-known stories. It appears in the first book, Genesis, and tells how Noah was instructed by God to build an ark to save his family and pairs of animals from a terrible flood that engulfed the world. The story also appears in the myths of other cultures and many people believe it to be true. Some have calculated the size of the ark, built replicas and launched expeditions to find archaeological evidence of its existence.

Noah's Ark, painted by Edward Hicks in 1846

The Ten Commandments

The commandments are the divine law handed down to Moses by God on Mount Sinai.

They are key to both Christian and Jewish religions. The commandments appear in the books of Exodus and Deuteronomy in the Old Testament of the Bible, but are also described by Jesus in Matthew's Gospel in the New Testament, where he shortens them to just two – Love God, Love your neighbour.

1. Thou shalt have no other gods before me
2. Thou shalt not make unto thee any graven image
3. Thou shalt not take the name of the Lord thy God in vain
4. Remember the sabbath day, to keep it holy
5. Honour thy father and thy mother
6. Thou shalt not kill
7. Thou shalt not commit adultery
8. Thou shalt not steal
9. Thou shalt not bear false witness against thy neighbour
10. Thou shalt not covet thy neighbour's house, thou shalt not covet thy neighbour's wife, nor his manservant, nor his maidservant, nor his ox, nor his ass, nor any thing that is thy neighbour's (Exodus xx.3)

Animals in the Bible

There are many animals mentioned in the Bible. Sheep and lambs are referred to most often, probably because they were important for their meat and wool.

The lion appears because it is a symbol of power, strength and wisdom.

Animal	OT*	NT*	Total
1 Sheep	155	45	200
2 Lamb	153	35	188
3 Lion	167	9	176
4 Ox	156	10	166
5 Ram	165	0	165
6 Horse	137	27	164

* Occurrences in verses in the King James Bible
OT: Old Testament, NT: New Testament

Longest-serving popes

Popes are usually chosen from among senior cardinals. They rarely live long enough to serve more than about 20 years. However, Pope Benedict IX is said to have been only 12 years old when he was elected in 1033!

Pius IX was the longest-serving pope. He was 85 years old when he died. Leo XIII was even older at 93. The shortest-serving pope was Urban VII, who died of malaria 12 days after his election in 1590.

Pius IX was in office for 31 years (16 June 1846 to 7 February 1878).
John Paul II was in office for 26 years (16 October 1978 to 2 April 2005).
Leo XIII was in office for 25 years (20 February 1878 to 20 July 1903).
Pius VI was in office for 24 years (15 February 1775 to 29 August 1799).
Adrian I was in office for 23 years (1 February 772 to 25 December 795).
Pius VII was in office for 23 years (14 March 1800 to 20 August 1823).
Alexander III was in office for 21 years (7 September 1159 to 30 August 1181).

Pope Benedict XVI celebrates Easter Mass at St Peter's, Vatican City

The Vatican

The Holy See is the name given to the religious government of the Roman Catholic church. It is based in the Vatican or Vatican City, which operates as a state within a state (Italy), with its own laws and government. It occupies just 44 hectares, making it one of the world's smallest countries, and in 2009 had a resident population of just 541, including members of the church and 101 Swiss Guards, a security force that wears uniforms and carries weapons dating from the 16th century. At the heart of the Vatican, St Peter's Basilica, which contains the tombs of 91 popes, is a place of pilgrimage for Roman Catholics. The Basilica itself can hold 60,000, while from a balcony the Pope addresses large crowds in the square below. Over four million tourists a year visit the Vatican and its museum, which contains the Sistine Chapel and many treasures. The Vatican has its own railway, just 330 m (1,083 ft) long, a newspaper, radio and TV station and its own Internet domain, .va.

Largest Christian populations

1 **USA** 245,930,675
2 **Brazil** 170,213,252
3 **Russia** 114,510,266
4 **China** 101,997,935
5 **Mexico** 99,945,687
6 **Philippines** 75,520,618
7 **India** 64,226,200

Christianity timeline

c. 6-4 BC Birth of Jesus Christ, Bethlehem

AD c. 33 Christ crucified

c. 60-100 Gospels written

c. 64 Persecution of Christians by Roman Emperor Nero

312 Emperor Constantine converts to Christianity, leading to it becoming sole religion in the Roman Empire

300s

324 Building of St Peter's Basilica, Vatican, Rome, begun on site of Circus of Nero

c. 380 Final agreement on which books should be in the Christian Bible

635 Jerusalem and most of Middle East conquered by Muslims

999 Most of Europe converted to Christianity

1000s

1054 Christian church splits into Western (Catholic) and Eastern (Orthodox)

1095–1272 Crusades (series of wars by Christians to take holy sites in Middle East away from Muslim control)

1187 Jerusalem captured by Saladin

1209 Franciscan order of monks started

1382 John Wycliffe translates Bible into English

1456 First printed Bible (Johannes Gutenberg, Germany)

1479 Spanish Inquisition begins to persecute heretics

1517 Martin Luther begins Protestant Reformation, Germany

Patron saints

A patron saint is a saint chosen to be the protector of a particular person or group of people, or associated with a particular problem or situation.

Many more saints are called upon for help with problems than are linked with pleasant events. For example, at least 26 saints are connected with difficult marriages, but only one (Saint Valentine) with happy marriages.

Patron saints for special problems

Appendicitis Erasmus
Arthritis/rheumatism James the Greater
Broken bones Drogo+
Cold weather Sebaldus
Coughs Blaise+
Dog bites Vitus
Earache Cornelius+
Famine Walburga
Floods Christopher+
Headaches Acacius+
Insect bites Felix+
Knee problems Roch+
Lost articles Anne+
Natural disasters Agatha
Poisoning Benedict+
Shipwreck Anthony of Padua
Snake bites Hilary of Poitiers+
Storms Scholastica+
Toothache Apollonia+
\+ More than one saint

Patron saints of professions and groups

Accountants Matthew the Apostle
Actors Genesius of Rome+
Air travellers Joseph of Cupertino
Ambulance drivers Michael the Archangel
Architects Barbara+
Artists Luke the Apostle+
Astronauts Joseph of Cupertino
Athletes Sebastian
Authors Francis de Sales
Bakers Elizabeth of Hungary+
Beekeepers Ambrose of Milan+
Booksellers John of God+
Boys John Bosco+
Bricklayers Stephen of Hungary
Broadcasters Gabriel the Archangel
Cab drivers Christopher+
Carpenters Joseph+
Children Nicholas of Myra+
Comedians Vitus+
Cooks Martha+
Dentists Apollonia
Doctors Cosmas+
Farmers Isidore the Farmer+
Fathers Joseph
Firefighters Florian+
Fishermen Andrew the Apostle+
Gardeners Adelard
Girls Agnes of Rome+
Hairdressers Cosmas+
Librarians Jerome+
Mathematicians Barbara
Mothers Monica+
Motorcyclists Our Lady of Grace
Musicians Cecilia+
Nurses Agatha+
Plumbers Vincent Ferrer
Poets David+
Police officers Michael the Archangel+
Postal workers Gabriel the Archangel
Printers Augustine of Hippo+
Prisoners Dismas
Sailors Francis of Paola+
Scientists Albertus Magnus+
Sculptors Claude de la Columbiere+
Soldiers George+
Teachers Catherine of Alexandria+
\+ More than one saint

The real Father Christmas

Saint Nicholas was an early Christian bishop who lived in Greece *c.*270–346. Legends about him often told of the gifts he secretly gave to the poor. As well as becoming the patron saint of sailors, of countries such as Russia and of many cities, including Liverpool and Aberdeen in the UK, he is the patron saint of children and in European countries became identified with Father Christmas. The Christmas stocking that Saint Nicholas/Santa Claus fills on Christmas Eve is part of this tradition in numerous countries. The remains of Saint Nicholas were taken to Bari in Italy and his tomb there became a shrine for pilgrims. When they were examined by scientists, they discovered that he was just 1.5m (5ft) tall.

1800s **2000s**

1534 Henry VIII breaks with Rome; leads to the founding of the Church of England
1610–1795 Baptist, Congregationalist, Presbyterian, Quaker (Society of Friends) and Methodist Churches founded
1611 King James Bible published
1800–1900 The Age of the Mission. Western Churches send missionaries to every country in the world. Number of Christians doubles by the end of the century
1830 Church of the Latter-Day Saints (Mormons) founded, Fayette, New York, USA
1872 Jehovah's Witnesses founded by Charles Taze Russell, USA
1878 Salvation Army founded by William Booth, UK
1910 International Missionary Conference marks first attempt in nearly 1,000 years to reunite churches
1962–65 Second Vatican Council radically reforms the Catholic Church worldwide
1992 Church of England votes to allow women priests
2007 Boris Yeltsin's Russian Orthodox funeral is the first of a head of state in Russia since 1894
2010 Pope Benedict XVI travels to the UK, the first papal visit for 28 years

See also
History timeline: page 104

Buddhist festivals

There are a number of Buddhist traditions, and Buddhists in different countries have their own festivals on different dates. These are the most important Buddhist festivals.

- Wesak, held on the full moon in May, is the most important Buddhist festival and celebrates the birth of Buddha.
- Dharma Day celebrates Buddha's teaching and is held on the full moon of July. On Dharma Day there are readings from Buddhist scriptures, and people spend time reflecting on what they mean.
- Sangha Day is held on the full moon in November and celebrates the spiritual Buddhist community. Buddhists traditionally give presents on this day.
- Parinirvana Day, also known as Nirvana Day, marks the death of Buddha. Celebrations vary from place to place, but generally Buddhists go to temples or monasteries on this day, or meditate.

Losar

Losar is a Tibetan Buddhist festival. It is held in February and marks the New Year. The festival lasts for three days, when people go to monasteries, visit friends and family and exchange gifts.

Tibetan monks blowing horns to celebrate the Buddhist festival of Losar

Christian festivals

Epiphany (also known as Twelfth Night)

6 January (18 January in Russia; 1 February in Ethiopia). The Epiphany (Epiphaneia: Greek for manifestation) celebrates three events that are all thought to have happened on this day: Jesus's appearance as a newborn to the Magi (three wise men); Jesus's baptism, when God acknowledged his son; Jesus's first public miracle, when he turned water to wine in Galilee.

Ash Wednesday

The first day of Lent (see below). Ash Wednesday is a day of repentance for Christians, when they make amends for the year's sins before the fasting of Lent. Anglican and Roman Catholic churches hold ceremonies at which churchgoers' foreheads are marked with crosses using ash.

Lent

The 44 days before Good Friday (including Sundays). Lent is a period of fasting when Christians identify with Jesus Christ's suffering. The day before the start of Lent is known as Shrove Tuesday or "Fat Tuesday" (Mardi Gras), when Christians traditionally eat up any leftover animal products (often in the form of pancakes), as these cannot be eaten during Lent.

Palm Sunday

The Sunday before Easter Sunday and the first day of Holy Week. Palm Sunday commemorates Jesus's arrival in Jerusalem, when the crowd threw palm leaves in front of his donkey. Later that week, many in the cheering crowd were calling for Christ's execution.

Maundy (or Holy) Thursday

The Thursday before Easter Sunday. Maundy Thursday commemorates the Last Supper, which established the ceremony of Holy Communion, when bread and wine became identified with Jesus's body and blood. It was also the day when Jesus washed the feet of his disciples. At Roman Catholic church services on Maundy Thursday the priest ceremonially washes 12 people's feet.

Good Friday

The Friday before Easter Sunday. Good Friday ("good" meant "holy" in Early Modern English) commemorates the day when Jesus Christ was crucified. The symbol of the cross is an important part of church services on Good Friday, and churchgoers read the psalms and the gospels to remember Christ's experience.

Easter Sunday

The Sunday that follows the first full moon after the 21 March (the spring equinox). Easter always falls between 22 March and 25 April in the Western calendar. Easter is up to two weeks later in Orthodox Churches. Easter Sunday is the most important day in the Christian calendar, as it celebrates Jesus's resurrection from the dead. Easter Sunday is a day of joy for Christians.

Pentecost/Whitsunday

Fifty days after Easter Sunday. Pentecost celebrates the day the Holy Spirit entered the Apostles, enabling them to speak many new languages and spread the word of God. This event is considered by most Christians to mark the birth of the Church.

Christmas

Christmas is the celebration of the birth of Jesus on 25 December (6 January in Russia and 17 January in Ethiopia). It comes in midwinter, a time of the year when many faiths hold festivities.

Jewish festivals

The main Jewish festivals celebrate the great events in the history of the people of Israel. The Jewish month in which they fall is given here, with an approximate equivalent in the Gregorian calendar.

Tishri (September/October)
Rosh Hashana: New Year
Yom Kippur: Day of Atonement
Sukkoth: Feast of Tabernacles
Shemini Atzeret: 8th Day of the Solemn Assembly
Simhat Torah: Rejoicing of the Law
Kislev (November/December)
Hanukkah: Feast of Dedication
Adar (February/March)
Tanrit Esther: Fast of Esther
Purim: Feast of Lots
Nisan (March/April)
Pesach (Passover)
Holocaust Remembrance Day
Iyar (April/May)
Lag B'Omer: Counting Day of Barley Sheaves
Sivan (May/June)
Shavuoth: Feast of Weeks
Tammuz (June/July)
Shiva Asar be-Tammuz: Fast of 17th Tammuz
Av (July/August)
Tisha be-Av: Fast of 9th Av

Muslims at the Grand Mosque in Makkah before pilgrimage (Hajj) month

Islamic festivals

Most Islamic festivals (see below) commemorate events in the life of the Prophet Muhammad. New Year's Day, for example, marks the day on which he set out from Makkah to Medina in the year 622. The month of the Islamic calendar in which the festival falls is given.

Every month starts approximately on the day of a new moon, or when a crescent is first seen after a new moon, so the calendar shifts and these festivals fall at different times every year according to the Gregorian calendar.

Sky lanterns lit up in India for the Divali festival

Islamic festival dates

New Year's Day 1 Muharram
Birthday of Muhammad, AD 572 12 Rabi I
Night of Ascent (of Muhammad to Heaven) 27 Rajab
Month of fasting during daylight hours 1 Ramadan
Night of Power (sending down the Koran to Muhammad) 27 Ramadan
Feast of Breaking of the Fast (Eid Ul Fitr) 1 Shawwal (end of Ramadan)
Pilgrimage (Hajj) **month** 8–13 Dhu-al-Hijja ceremonies at Makkah
Feast of the Sacrifice 10 Dhu-al-Hijja

Hindu festivals

These are the main Hindu festivals, held in honour of gods as well as to celebrate important events in mythology and in the heavens. The Hindu month in which they fall is given, with an approximate equivalent in the Gregorian calendar.

Chaitra (March/April)
Ramanavami: Birthday of Lord Rama
Asadha (June/July)
Rathayatra: Pilgrimage of the Chariot at Jaggannath
Sravana (July/August)
Jhulanayatra: Swinging the Lord Krishna
Rakshabandhana: Tying on Lucky Threads
Bhadrapada (August/September)
Janamashtami: Birthday of Lord Krishna
Asvina (September/October)
Durga-puja: Homage to Goddess Durga
Navaratri: Festival of Nine Nights
Lakshmi-puja: Homage to Goddess Lakshmi
Diwali, Dipavali: String of Lights
Magha (January/February)
Sarasvati-puja: Homage to Goddess Sarasvati
Maha-sivaratri: Great Night of Lord Shiva
Phalguna (February/March)
Holi: Festival of Fire
Dolayatra: Swing Festival

www.interfaithcalendar.org search

The Labours of Hercules

The Greek hero Hercules killed his wife Megara and some of their children after being driven mad by his stepmother, the goddess Hera.

As a punishment he had to perform 12 dangerous tasks or labours. When he succeeded in all of them, he was granted immortality.

1 Slay the Nemean lion (its skin resisted weapons, so he strangled it)
2 Kill the Hydra (a many-headed monster) of Lerna
3 Catch the Arcadian stag
4 Destroy the giant Erymanthian boar
5 Clean the Augean stables
6 Destroy the cannibal birds of the Lake Stymphalis
7 Capture the fire-breathing Cretan bull
8 Catch the horses of the Thracian king Diomedes
9 Seize the girdle of Hippolyta, Queen of the Amazons
10 Capture the oxen of the monster Geryon
11 Obtain the golden apples of the Hesperides
12 Bring Cerberus from Hades (hell)

Statue of Hercules fighting with the Cretan bull

Unicorns

A unicorn has the body of a horse, a lion's tail, a goat's beard, an antelope's legs and a single, often twisted, horn growing from its forehead. The unicorn is a popular subject in medieval stories; it is ferocious but good, and can purify water – or neutralize poison – by dipping its horn into it. The way to catch a unicorn is to use a young girl as bait, as a unicorn will lie down peacefully next to a maiden.

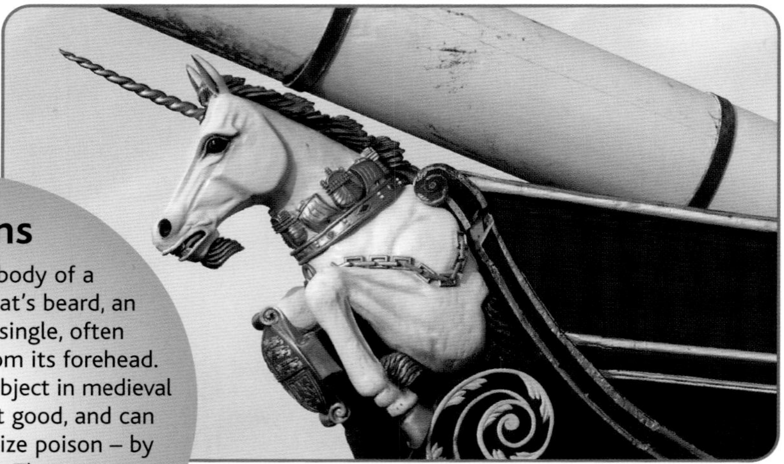

Figurehead of *The Unicorn*, a former warship

Mythical creatures

Almost every culture on Earth has legends of imaginary beasts. Some are like humans with supernatural powers; some are part human, part animal; while others are unlike anything we know.

Giants
Giants or ogres are enormous human-shaped creatures. They are usually seen as fearsome but stupid monsters that feed on human flesh. Famous giants include Goliath in the Bible, and Cyclops, Atlas and the Titans in Greek mythology.

Leprechauns
Leprechauns are small Irish fairies who bring good luck. They are helpful creatures, usually shown wearing green clothes, with an apron, buckled shoes and a red cap. Their fun-loving nature means that leprechauns are fond of alcohol, music and sport, but they are also mischievous and love practical jokes. Other "little people", including elves, dwarfs, gnomes and pixies, appear in many European fairy stories.

Centaurs
A centaur is half-horse and half-man, with the head and arms of a man and the body of a horse. It is one of the best known of all Greek mythological creatures and is said to have come from Thessaly in northern Greece. The myth may have arisen because of the skilful horsemanship of the people there.

Fairies
Fairies also feature in many tales. They are usually sweet, kindly creatures. In the Middle Ages, however, people believed that fairies stole children and replaced them with fairy beings known as changelings.

Heroes of legend

King Arthur
Legend says that Arthur, king of the Britons, won the throne by pulling a sword – the famous Excalibur – from a stone. This was a feat that only the true king was able to achieve. Arthur ruled during a period of peace and prosperity in Britain. Some folk tales say that if Britain is in danger, Arthur will return with his knights to defend the nation.

Beowulf
Beowulf was a Scandinavian warrior and the hero of *Beowulf*, the oldest poem in the English language. Beowulf was loyal to his king and also extremely brave. He killed Grendel the ogre, Grendel's mother and finally a fearsome dragon, which cost him his own life.

Paul Bunyan
The lumberjack Paul Bunyan is a famous character in American folklore. It is said that he was so enormous, he created the Grand Canyon by dragging his pick behind him, and his giant footsteps formed the lakes of Minnesota. The legend came from stories told by the lumberjacks of the northern United States.

El Cid
El Cid really did exist and many legends have grown up around him. He was also known as El Cid Campeador (meaning my lord, the champion). His real name was Rodrigo Díaz de Vivar and he was a Spanish nobleman who was born in about 1040 and died in 1099. El Cid is a national hero in Spain because he is seen as a brave and accomplished warrior who fought to take control of

Dragons
Dragons appear in the myths of many cultures, especially China, where the dragon was a symbol of the emperor. A typical dragon has a serpent-like body covered with scales, large wings, and can breathe fire. In legends, dragons often guard a cave of treasure.

Vampires
Vampires are the "undead" who drink the blood of the living to survive. Ideas about vampires include the belief that plunging a wooden stake through a vampire's heart can destroy it. Some people also think that you can protect yourself against vampires with garlic, holy water, crosses and bibles, and that a vampire cannot enter a home unless invited.

Werewolves
Werewolves, or lycanthropes, are mythical creatures in the folk tales of many cultures. They usually appear as men by day, but may turn into wolves on the night of a full moon. The werewolf is bloodthirsty and ruthless. It devours its prey and shows none of the remorse that it might have felt in human form.

Trolls
Trolls are grotesque, malicious, rather dim-witted creatures in Scandinavian folklore. They are said to steal sleeping children, sometimes replacing them with one of their own. Trolls have poor eyesight, and are active only at night because sunlight turns them to stone.

Mermaids
Mermaids are beautiful creatures with the head and body of a woman and the tail of a fish. The first mermaid legend is thought to have been the story of Atargatis, a Syrian moon goddess of about 1000 BC. Atargatis had a child with a human. She then killed her lover, abandoned the child and jumped into a lake, where she took the form of a mermaid.

See also
Movie monsters: page 272

This *Little Mermaid* illustration was created in 1895

Spain from the Muslims. Legend suggests that El Cid fought for both sides at different times.

St George
St George was a soldier for the Roman Empire who refused to take part in the Empire's persecution of Christians. He was executed for treachery and became a Christian martyr. Later, King Edward III made him the patron saint of England. St George is the hero of a legend in which he slays a man-eating dragon that was guarding a city's water supply. The city's inhabitants were so grateful that they converted from paganism to George's Christianity.

Heracles/Hercules
According to Greek and Roman mythology, Hercules was born with superhuman strength. By the time he reached adulthood he had killed a lion. Hercules had a jealous stepmother, who drove him to madness. While in this state, Hercules killed his wife and children. In order to regain his honour, Hercules had to perform 12 difficult tasks (see p. 170).

Robin Hood
The Robin Hood of folklore was an English nobleman whose land was seized while King Richard the Lionheart was away fighting in the Crusades (1188–92). He became an outlaw in Sherwood Forest and led a band of Merry Men (and Maid Marian, his true love). They robbed the nobility who travelled through the forest and passed on the valuables they stole to the poor and needy. Robin Hood was a master of disguise and many stories describe how he dressed as somebody else in order to trick his enemies or rescue his friends.

Good and bad luck signs

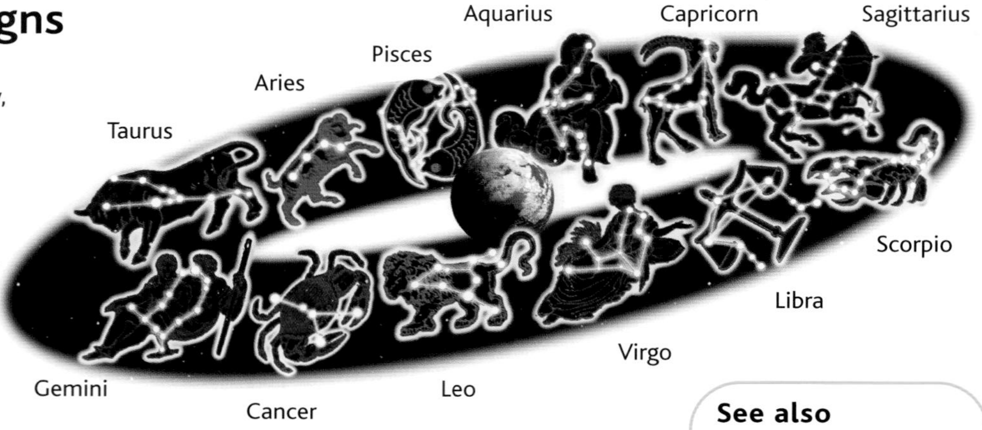

Black cats

In the UK, people think black cats are lucky, particularly if they cross your path. The opposite is true in the USA and several European countries, where a black cat is seen as a bad omen. In the USA a white cat is very good luck, while in the UK it is a sign of bad luck.

Horseshoes

A horseshoe is a piece of metal fixed to a horse's foot. Some people think that if you find a horseshoe and the open space is facing you it will bring you luck. Traditionally, people also hang horseshoes above the doorway of their home to bring good luck. In many European countries, the horseshoe is hung downwards – that's believed to let the luck flow out into the house. In Britain and Ireland, the shoe must be hung with the opening at the top to keep the good fortune.

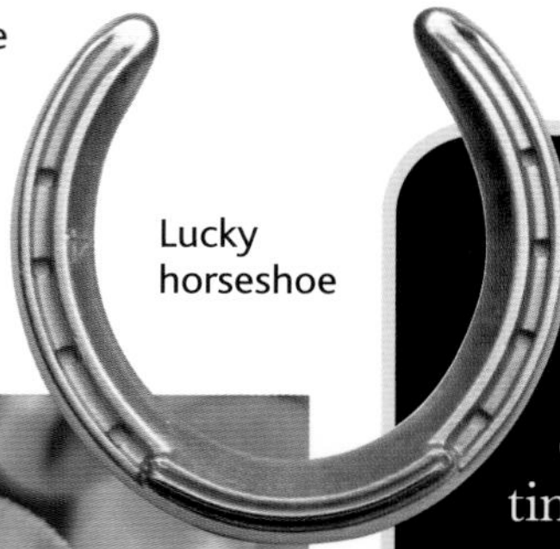
Lucky horseshoe

See also
Constellations: page 21

Clovers

Four-leaf clovers are very rare. Anyone who finds one is said to be able to recognize evil influences and avoid them.

Ladders

A ladder leaning against a wall forms a triangle. Some believe it is disrespectful, and unlucky, to walk underneath one because triangles symbolize the Holy Trinity. The bad luck is warded off by crossing the fingers or making a wish while under the ladder.

Magpies

Magpies are generally thought to be unlucky. This belief is said to come from the Bible, as the magpie was the only bird that refused to enter Noah's Ark. In China, however, the magpie is a good omen, and should never be killed.

Mirrors

Breaking a mirror is said to bring seven years' bad luck. This idea may come from the old belief that your reflection is an image of your soul, so anything that changes the reflection may bring evil. The length of the period of bad luck may come from the Roman belief that life renews itself every seven years.

Spilling salt

Salt was once valuable and spilling it was thought to cause bad luck, unless the person who spills it throws a pinch over their left shoulder. In his painting of the Last Supper, Leonardo da Vinci shows Jesus's betrayer Judas knocking over the salt cellar.

The signs of the zodiac

In Western astrology the zodiac has 12 parts. Each is named after a constellation and corresponds to a different time of year. Astrologists believe that the movements of the planets influence what happens on Earth, and that people born under the different signs have certain characteristics.

Aries, the ram
21 March–19 April
Creative, impatient, masculine, competitive, warrior-like, independent, outspoken

Taurus, the bull
20 April–20 May
Determined, resourceful, materialistic, touchy, ruthless, entrepreneurial

Gemini, the twins
21 May–21 June
Intellectual, shallow, inquisitive, selfish, talkative, witty, indecisive, irritable

Cancer, the crab
22 June–22 July
Emotional, sympathetic, moody, sensitive, home-loving, romantic, loyal, tactless

Leo, the lion
23 July–22 August
Generous, creative, broad-minded, patronising, bossy, extroverted, idealistic, arrogant

Virgo, the virgin
23 August–23 September
Diligent, intelligent, modest, conservative, overcritical, pedantic, affectionate, methodical

Libra, the scales
24 September–23 October
Charming, sociable, gullible, flirtatious, attractive, objective, artistic

Scorpio, the scorpion
24 October–22 November
Forceful, passionate, jealous, obsessive, secretive, intense, outspoken, extreme, rebellious

Sagittarius, the archer
23 November–21 December
Optimistic, honest, philosophical, careless, irresponsible, energetic, adventurous

Capricorn, the goat
22 December–20 January
Disciplined, economical, patient, reserved, pessimistic, serious, organized, rational

Aquarius, the water bearer
1 January–19 February
Inventive, friendly, independent, unpredictable, serious, intelligent, eccentric

Pisces, the fishes
20 February–20 March
Imaginative, compassionate, vague, gentle, sensitive, creative, spiritual, easygoing

Number 13

The belief that the number 13 is unlucky is very ancient. The Romans believed the number 13 was a symbol of death and destruction. Norse legends claimed that the thirteenth guest at a banquet is the spirit of evil.

The Christian belief that the number brings bad luck is often said to come from the Last Supper, when Christ sat down with his 12 disciples – making 13 people. Some people think that the first person to leave a dinner table at which there are 13 diners will die before the end of the year.

Unlucky for some?

- The thirteenth *Apollo* space mission was known as *Apollo 13*. On 13 April 1970, there was an explosion on board and the spacecraft began to leak oxygen. This happened two days after it took off at 13:13 (1:13pm). The spacecraft only just made it back to Earth.
- On Friday, 13 September 1928, a hurricane killed 2,000 people in Puerto Rico, Florida and the Virgin Islands, and caused approximately $25 million in damage.
- There is no building in Paris that bears the number 13.
- Italy omits the number 13 from its national lottery.
- The 13th of the month costs the USA about $1 billion a year through cancellations on trains and planes, absenteeism from work, and reduced business activity.

Lucky for others?

- The number 13 was sacred for the Mayans and Aztecs of Central America, and it is traditionally a lucky number in China.
- Buddhists pay homage to 13 Buddhas, and the orthodox Jewish prayerbook holds 13 principles of faith.

See also
The Last Supper: page 165

Crystal balls

Magicians traditionally claimed they could see into the future by gazing or 'scrying' into crystal balls. Queen Elizabeth I's astrologer Dr John Dee used a crystal ball that can still be seen in the British Museum, London, which also has his scrying mirror. It is made of obsidian, a hard black crystal, and had been used by Aztec sorcerers. It is claimed that in 1605 Dee's magic mirror foretold the Gunpowder Plot.

Palmistry

Palmistry is the art of telling the future from the lines on the palms of your hands. The lines are unique to each person and are said to show the person's character and what will happen in the future. Palmistry began in India thousands of years ago as a form of counselling.

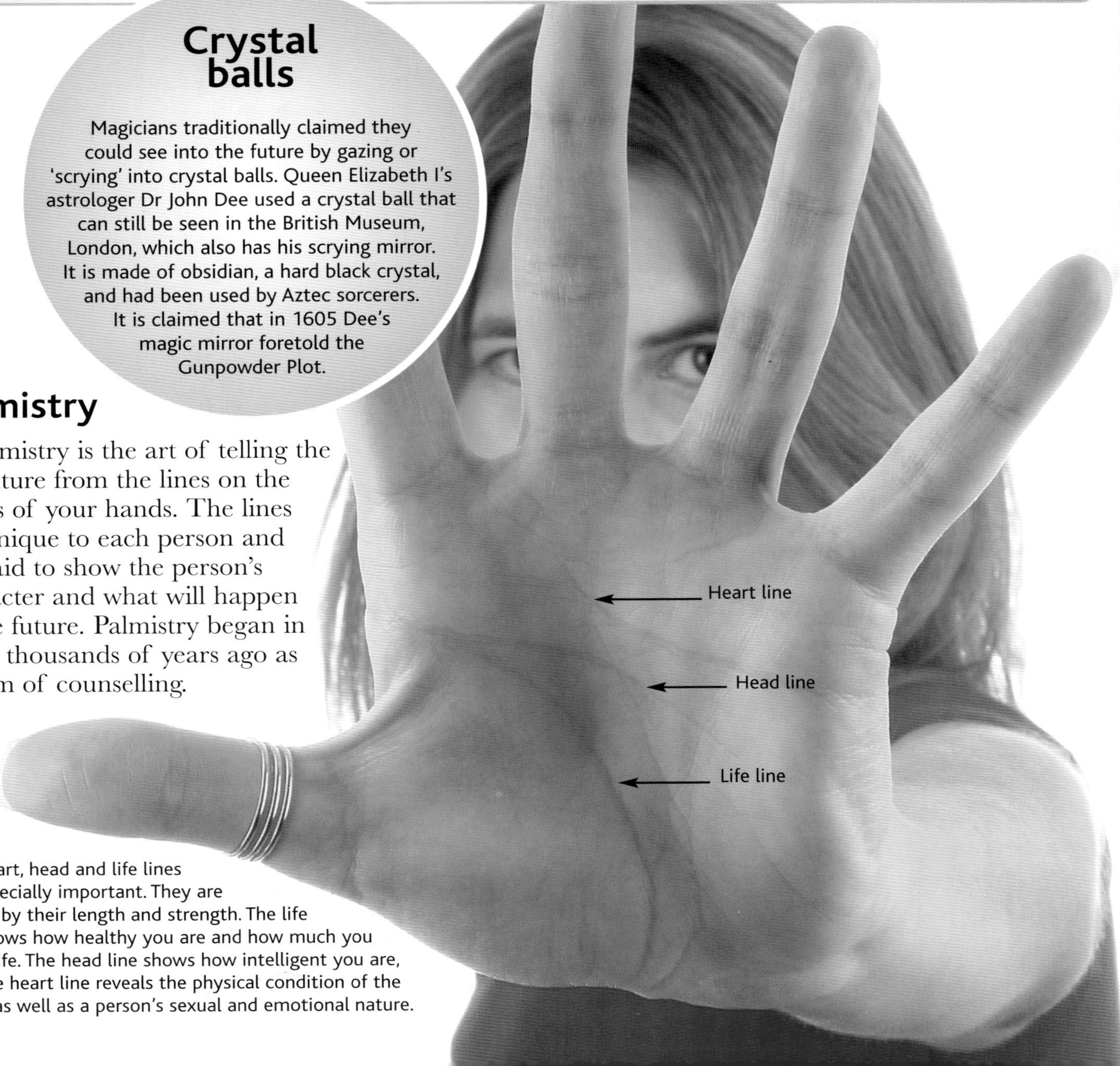

The heart, head and life lines are especially important. They are judged by their length and strength. The life line shows how healthy you are and how much you enjoy life. The head line shows how intelligent you are, and the heart line reveals the physical condition of the heart, as well as a person's sexual and emotional nature.

Mysterious places

The Nazca Lines

The Nazca Lines are enormous drawings on the ground (called geoglyphs) that stretch across the Nazca Desert in southern Peru. They show more than 300 geometric patterns, spirals and animals. The lines are so vast (one extends 65 km [40 miles]) that they can only be seen properly from a height of about 300 m (1,000 ft). Most experts agree that they were made by the Nazca Indians who lived in the region between 300 BC and AD 800, but there are many questions yet to be answered about them. For example, why were the pictures made and how are they so precise if their makers had no means to view them from the sky?

Easter Island

Easter Island (or Rapa Nui) lies in the South Pacific between Chile and Tahiti, and is one of the most isolated islands in the world. By the 16th century, Easter Island had nearly 10,000 inhabitants, who made huge statues known as *moai*. The 887 *moai* were carved from the island's volcanic rock and have long, angular faces. Some have eyes made from coral. The average *moai* was about 4 m (13 ft) tall and weighed over 14 tonnes, so they would have been extremely difficult for the islanders to transport. Archaeologists believe that the statues symbolize the spirits of Easter Island's most important inhabitants.

Teotihuacán

In AD 600 Teotihuacán in Mexico was the sixth largest city in the world and about 200,000 people lived there. Just 150 years later, Teotihuacán was almost deserted, and plants had begun to grow over the city's huge pyramids. Nobody knows why Teotihuacán was abandoned, but it may have been devastated by a huge fire in AD 650.

The Bermuda Triangle

The Bermuda Triangle is an area of the Atlantic Ocean off the coast of Florida. It is famous for being the supposed site of many unexplained disappearances. The points of the triangle are Miami, Bermuda and San Juan in Puerto Rico. In the 15th century, Christopher Columbus claimed to have seen a "great flame of fire" falling into the ocean in the area. The Bermuda Triangle first began to attract attention in 1945, when Flight 19, a training mission of five US bombers, vanished off the Florida coast. The plane that was sent to find them also disappeared, and around 100 boats and aircraft have been lost there. Explanations include magnetic fields, sea monsters and abduction by aliens, but most experts agree the disappearances are due to bad navigation and/or extreme weather conditions.

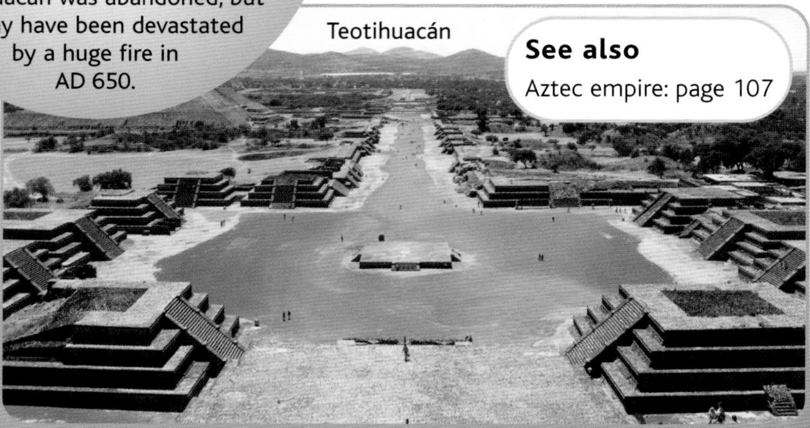
Teotihuacán

See also
Aztec empire: page 107

Stonehenge

Stonehenge is a circle of 17 upright stones called sarsens which stand on Salisbury Plain in southwest England. The stones weigh up to 50 tonnes and have other stones, called lintels, laid across the top. There is also an inner circle of smaller bluestones weighing up to 4 tonnes each. Stonehenge is the only stone circle in the world with lintels across the top of the stones, and experts think it was completed in about 1500 BC. They believe that the sarsen stones were transported from 32 km (20 miles) away and the bluestones came from an incredible 250 km (155 miles) away. At least 600 men would have been needed to move each sarsen stone on some of the steepest parts of the journey. Nobody knows exactly why Stonehenge was built, but it may have been a druids' temple or even a kind of astronomical calendar.

Stonehenge

Crop circles

Crop circles are complicated geometric patterns, usually in wheat fields. Some people believe that the patterns are left by the imprint of an extra-terrestrial craft, or that they are a message from extra-terrestrials themselves.

Another theory is that natural forces such as tornadoes, heat or strong winds create the patterns by flattening the crops, but the regular shapes of most crop circles makes this unlikely. The most likely explanation is that the circles are made by people as a hoax. They gradually build up a design by flattening the wheat, using very basic equipment such as rope and planks of wood.

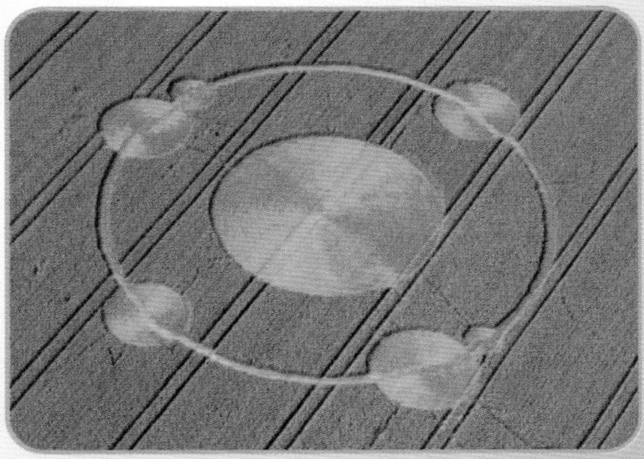

Crop circles in Slovenia

Mysterious monsters

The Loch Ness Monster

The Loch Ness Monster, nicknamed Nessie, is said to live in Loch Ness in Scotland. The monster is generally thought to be a long-necked creature with flippers, like a prehistoric reptile. Many people have reported seeing Nessie, and in 2006 it was claimed that it might have been a circus elephant swimming in the Loch! However, there is no real evidence that the creature exists.

Yeti

The Yeti, also called the Abominable Snowman, is believed to live in the Himalayan mountains. People say this legendary creature measures up to 1.4 m (8 ft), is covered in long brown hair, and walks upright like a human being. Everest mountaineers, including Sir Edmund Hillary and Sherpa Tenzing Norgay, have reported seeing mysterious footprints in the snow.

Bigfoot

Another legendary creature is said to live in the northwest of North America. People who claim to have seen Bigfoot say it is a large hairy creature that walks upright like the Yeti. There is no firm evidence that Bigfoot exists, but there are some fuzzy photos and videos that are supposed to show this mystery monster.

On the Moon, or is this photo a fake?

Conspiracy theories

Many people believe that certain well-known historical events have been manipulated by governments and other secret organizations to conceal the truth. Some of the better-known beliefs are:

- A secret society called the Illuminati controls the world. This shadowy organization features in Dan Brown's novel *Angels and Demons*. Other powerful secret societies, including Opus Dei and the Priory of Sion, feature in his bestselling *The Da Vinci Code*.
- Sinister groups were responsible for plotting the deaths of US President Abraham Lincoln, civil rights leader Martin Luther King, musician John Lennon and Princess Diana. Some people claim that the Mafia were responsible for assassinating US President John F. Kennedy. Others believe it was the work of Russian spies.
- Inventions have been hushed up by big businesses and oil companies who fear loss of income if new technologies become available. These include light bulbs that last for ever and ways of running cars on water.
- Aliens from other planets have crashed on Earth at Roswell, New Mexico. Their bodies and spacecraft have been secretly examined in a place in Nevada, USA, known as Area 51, and the US government has acquired advanced weapon and space travel technology from them.
- Photographs of the *Apollo* Moon landings (20 July 1969) were faked by NASA in a TV studio. Conspiracy theorists have produced "evidence" such as the wrong sort of shadows and a lack of stars in the photographs, which were supposedly taken on the Moon's surface. They have even suggested that some astronauts were killed as part of the cover-up.

UK UFOs

For over 50 years, the UK Ministry of Defence operated a hotline so that members of the public could report sightings of Unidentified Flying Objects, or UFOs, which were then investigated. On 1 December 2009, after receiving some 12,000 calls and e-mails, the service abruptly closed. Conspiracy theorists claimed that this was an attempt to cover up actual sightings of alien spacecraft.

Conflict & Crime

Withdrawal from Afghanistan

US Marines patrol an opium poppy field in Helmand province, Afghanistan. US, British and other NATO troops have been in the country for 10 years, since 2001. The total force numbered over 250,000 in 2010. They are scheduled to begin withdrawal in 2011 as newly-formed local forces take over the security operation combating Al-Qaeda terrorists and Taliban insurgents and preventing the trade in illegal drugs.

Weapons named after people

- **Big Bertha**

Big Bertha was a 144-tonne cannon used by the German army to shell Paris from a distance of 122 km (76 miles) during World War I. The name came from Bertha Krupp von Bohlen und Halbach (1886–1957), who inherited the German Krupp armaments business from her father.

- **Browning pistol**

Invented in America in 1896 by John Moses Browning (1855–1926), the Browning was an automatic pistol used by both civilians and military.

- **Gatling gun**

In 1862, Dr Richard Jordan Gatling (1818–1903) patented the hand-cranked machine gun with a fire rate of up to 350 rounds per minute. It appeared too late to be widely used in the American Civil War, and it was soon overtaken by more efficient weapons. The slang term "gat" for any gun derives from the name.

- **Kalashnikov**

This machine gun is named after its inventor, Russian Mikhail Kalashnikov (1919–). More than 70 million have been made.

- **Lüger**

Gunmaker Georg Lüger (1849–1923) pioneered the P-08 pistol that bears his name in 1898. It was adopted by the German army and was widely used during both World Wars.

- **Mauser**

The Mauser bolt-action rifle was developed in 1898 by German brothers Wilhelm (1834–82) and Peter Paul Mauser (1838–1914). They also invented an automatic pistol.

- **Maxim gun**

American (later British) inventor Sir Hiram Maxim (1840–1916), who was also an aviation pioneer, made this machine gun in 1884.

- **Molotov cocktail**

This was a crude but effective bomb made with a petrol-filled bottle and fuse. It was given its name by the Finns in about 1940 who used it during the war against Russia. They called it a cocktail for Molotov. Vyacheslav Mikhailovich Molotov (1890–1986) was the Soviet prime minister at the time.

- **Shrapnel**

This name was given to exploding shells invented by British officer Henry Shrapnel (1761–1842). Fragments of bombs are now also called shrapnel.

- **Tommy gun**

The Thompson sub-machine gun was invented by American army general John Taliaferro Thompson and US Navy commander John N. Blish. It became known as the Tommy gun and was popular with gangsters during the 1920s.

Nuclear explosion

Weird weapons

Combined gun and plough

This was patented by C.M. French and W.H. Fancher of Waterloo, New York in 1862. It was designed to be used by farmers so they could quickly turn their ploughs into powerful guns if they were attacked while ploughing.

Hard cheese

In 1865 during a war between Uruguay and Brazil, a Uruguayan ship ran out of cannon balls. Instead they fired stale Dutch cheeses, one of which dismasted an enemy vessel and killed two sailors.

Boomerang bullets

These bullets were invented in the USA in 1870, and were designed to fire in a curved line. The danger was that if they travelled in a complete circle, they could kill the person who fired them.

Countries with nuclear weapons

The world's arsenal of nuclear warheads peaked at about 65,000 in 1985, and has been declining ever since. Precise figures are secret, but these are the best estimates and ranges:

Russia: 14,237–17,237
USA: approx 9,914
France: approx 350
Israel: 75–200
China: 100–200
UK: fewer than 160
India: up to 100
Pakistan: up to 60

World total: up to 28,221

Weapons milestones

1500s

500,000 BC Spears
250,000 BC Stone axes
25,000 BC Boomerang-like weapons (Poland) and knives
15,000 BC Spear-throwers
3000 BC Bows and arrows, shields and war chariots
2000 BC Armour and swords
865 BC Battering rams and other siege engines (Assyria)
3rd C BC Galleys, Crete
397 BC Catapults propelling darts
332 BC Catapults throwing stones
7th century Gunpowder (China)
8th century Viking longships
11th century Chain mail and crossbows
1150 Longbows
1221 Bombs (China)
1242 English monk Roger Bacon first describes gunpowder
1288 First guns (China)
1324 Cannon used at Battle of Metz
1346 Cannon (siege of Calais)
1370s Arbalests (crossbows)
1492 Leonardo da Vinci invents giant siege crossbows
1514 Man-of-war
1515 Wheel-lock muskets
1590 Bayonets made at Bayonne, France
1776 Submarine torpedoes
1784 Shrapnel shells
1835 Revolvers, Samuel Colt (US)
1838 Breech-loading rifles
1847 Guncotton, invented by Christian Friedrick Schönbein
1847 Nitroglycerine (explosive) invented by Ascanio Solaro
1850 Battleships
1860 Repeating rifle invented by Christopher Spencer (US)
1861 Metal gun cartridges and sea mines
1862 Gatling machine guns and Winchester repeating rifles
1866 Dynamite invented by Alfred Nobel (Sweden)
1872 Automatic pistols
1884 Maxim machine guns
1897 Dum-dum bullets (banned 1908)
1898 Lüger pistols
1901 Modern submarines

Largest armed forces

The number of personnel in the armed forces listed below are all active forces, but some countries have many reserves who can be called for service if needed. South Korea may have as many as 4.7 million reserve forces, Vietnam may have 5 million and China 800,000.

1 China 1,600,000 army, 255,000 navy and 330,000 airforce personnel. Total: 2,185,000

2 USA 632,245 army, 339,453 navy and 340,530 airforce personnel. Total: 1,539,587

3 India 1,100,000 army, 55,000 navy and 120,000 airforce personnel. Total: 1,281,200

4 North Korea 950,000 army, 46,000 navy and 110,000 airforce personnel. Total: 1,106,000

5 Russia 360,000 army, 142,000 navy and 195,000 airforce personnel. Total: 1,027,000

Some totals include other forces

Biological warfare

The aim of biological warfare is to infect enemies with deadly diseases. It is a modern form of warfare. However, in the Middle Ages the rotting carcasses of animals were catapulted into enemy castles to infect the inhabitants. In 1500 Leonardo da Vinci suggested using bombs containing saliva from mad dogs or pigs, or the venom of animals such as toads and spiders.

Gunner on a US army Black Hawk helicopter

2000s

1902 Armoured cars
1911 Aircraft carriers and bombers
1914 Zeppelin airships and large multi-engined aircraft able to carry heavy bombs used in aerial warfare
1914 Flechéttes first used – steel darts, designed to be dropped from aircraft on the enemy beneath
1915 Aircraft machine gun invented by German manufacturer Anthony Fokker
1915 Poisonous gases, such as mustard gas, chlorine, and tear gas, first used by German army at Ypres. Gas masks invented to combat them
1915 Rifles with periscopic sights (allowing users to remain hidden) invented by an Australian soldier
1917 Water-cooled Browning machine guns invented by John Browning. Tanks introduced as a way of getting through enemy barbed wire, and increasingly as a battlefield weapon
1936 Nerve gas (Tabun) and Spitfire fighter aircraft
1939 Military helicopters
1940 Bazookas and radar
1942 Napalm and V2 rockets
1942 Dam-buster bombs
1943 Jet bombers and fighters
1945 Atomic bomb
1952 Hydrogen bomb
1955 Nuclear submarines
1960 Harrier jump jets
1970 Exocet missiles
1982 Air-launched cruise missiles
1984 Stun guns
1988 Stealth bombers
1988 IMINT (Imagery Intelligence) satellites
2001 Heckler and Koch MP7 submachine guns
2003 Multiple JDAM (Joint Direct Attack Munition) air-launched smart bombs
2009 Boeing YAL–1 Airborne Laser (ABL) system, capable of shooting down missiles, tested
2009 North Korea claimed to have undertaken an underground nuclear test

World War I

World War I (1914–18) was the worst conflict the world had ever known, with a total of about 16 million civilian and military deaths and a further 21 million wounded.

Countries suffering the most casualties

	Country	Mobilized*	Wounded	Missing/PoW#	Dead
1	Germany	11,000,000	4,216,058	1,152,800	1,773,700
2	Russia	12,000,000	4,950,000	2,500,000	1,700,000
3	France	8,410,000	4,266,000	537,000	1,375,800
4	Austria-Hungary	7,800,000	3,620,000	2,200,000	1,200,000
5	British Empire	8,904,467	2,090,212	191,652	908,371
6	Italy	5,615,000	947,000	600,000	650,000
7	Rumania	750,000	120,000	80,000	335,706
8	Turkey	2,850,000	400,000	250,000	325,000
9	USA	4,355,000	234,300	4,526	126,000
10	Bulgaria	1,200,000	152,390	27,029	87,500

* Total at peak strength
# Prisoner of war

World War I firsts

The war saw the introduction of many new weapons, among them:

First heavy bomber
On 10 December 1914 the Imperial Russian Air Force formed the first ever bomber squadron with a fleet of Ilya Muromets aircraft, the world's first four-engined bomber.

First aerial bombardment
The first time civilians were bombed from the air was on 19 January 1915 when German Zeppelin airships dropped bombs on Great Yarmouth and other East Coast UK towns. The first air raid on London occurred on 31 May 1915. A total of 558 people in the UK were killed by bombing in World War I.

First plastic surgery
Plastic surgery techniques to reconstruct faces damaged by shrapnel were pioneered during World War I.

First tank
The first tank used in battle was a British Mark I D1 at Delville Wood, France, on 15 September 1916. For secrecy, the new weapon was described as a 'water tank', hence its name.

Gas warfare

Although tear gas was used earlier, the first use of lethal gas in battle was on 22 April 1915 when the German army released chlorine during the Second Battle of Ypres, Belgium. When even deadlier gases were used, troops were issued with gas masks, but it is estimated that 88,498 soldiers died in gas attacks, with 1,240,853 injured, many of them suffering the effects for the rest of their lives.

Gas victims in World War I

Major wars

1600s

431–404 BC Peloponnesian War
Sparta v Athens
264–146 BC Punic Wars
Rome v Carthage
1095–1291 Crusades
Christians v Muslims
1337–1543 Hundred Years War
England v France
1455–85 Wars of the Roses
York v Lancaster

1618–48 Thirty Years War
Catholic v Protestant forces in Europe
1642–51 English Civil War
Crown v Parliament
1701–14 War of the Spanish Succession
France v Grand Alliance (of other European countries)

1740–48 War of the Austrian Succession
France, Spain, Bavaria, Prussia v Britain, Netherlands, Savoy
1756–63 Seven Years War
Austria, Russia, France, Sweden, Poland v Prussia, Britain, Portugal
1775–83 American War of Independence
America v Britain

1792–1815 Napoleonic Wars
Britain, Austria, Russia, Sweden, Naples v France
1812–15 War of 1812
USA v Britain
1846–48 Mexico-American War
Mexico v USA
1853–56 Crimean War
Russia v Turkey, Britain, France, Sardinia

www.militaryhistoryonline.com search

Trafalgar

On 21 October 1805, during the Napoleonic Wars, the British fleet under Lord Nelson won this sea battle against the French, although Nelson was killed.

The Battle of Trafalgar, painted by John Callow, 1875

Great sea battles

Salamis, 20 October 480 BC (Greco-Persian Wars)
The Greeks overcame a Persian fleet, saving Greece from conquest.

Aegosopotami, 405 BC (Peloponnesian War)
In this battle 180 Athenian triremes were faced with 170 Peloponnesian ships. The Athenians were conquered, and the Peloponnesian War ended.

Actium, 2 September 31 BC (Wars of the Second Triumvirate)
Mark Antony and the Egyptian fleet were defeated by the Romans during this battle.

Lepanto, 7 October 1571 (Cyprus War)
The Spanish force defeated the Turkish fleet, which lost 25,000 sailors in 250 galleys.

Spanish Armada, 29 July 1588 (Anglo-Spanish War)
In July 1588, 130 Spanish ships with 2,500 guns and 30,000 troops set out to attack England. The English fleet badly damaged the Spanish ships with their guns, and the rest of the fleet was destroyed by bad weather.

Jutland, 31 May 1916 (World War I)
During this engagement the Royal Navy took on the German fleet, which withdrew.

Guadalcanal, 9 August–30 November 1942 (World War II)
This series of six naval engagements between the USA and Japanese resulted in heavy losses on both sides.

Coral Sea, 8 May 1942 (World War II)
The US Navy took on the Japanese in the first major battle fought using aircraft from carriers.

Leyte Gulf, 22–27 October 1944 (World War II)
USA defeated Japan in this battle. The Japanese lost three battleships, four aircraft carriers, ten cruisers and nine destroyers.

Child soldiers

'Red Hand Day', commemorated around the world on 12 February each year, is part of a global campaign to eradicate the use of child soldiers. Although expressly forbidden under the Optional Protocol to the Convention on the Rights of the Child, which has been signed by 126 countries, Organizations such as the United Nations and Human Rights Watch report that some 15 countries and territories continue to use children as soldiers.

1900s

1861–65 American Civil War
North v Confederate (Southern) states

1870–71 Franco-Prussian War
France v Germany

1894–95 Chinese-Japanese War
China v Japan

1898 Spanish-American War
Spain v USA

1899–1902 Boer War
Boers (South Africa) v Britain

1904–05 Russo-Japanese War
Russia v Japan

1914–18 World War I
Allies v Germany and others

1931–33 Chinese-Japanese War
China v Japan

1936–39 Spanish Civil War
Nationalists v Republicans

1937–45 Chinese-Japanese War
China v Japan

1939–45 World War II
Allies v Germany and others (Axis powers)

1950–53 Korean War
North Korea (with Chinese aid) v South Korea (supported by USA)

1957–75 Vietnam War
North Vietnam v South Vietnam (with US aid)

1982 Falklands War
Argentina v Britain

2000s

1983– The Sri Lanka Civil War is an ongoing conflict between the Sri Lankan government and Tamil Tigers with some 80,000 killed.

1991 Gulf War
Iraq v Allied forces

2001– "War on Terror"
USA and allies v al-Qaeda, Taliban in Afghanistan

2003 Iraq War
USA and allies v Iraq

Legal language

Accessory – someone who assists a criminal
Accomplice – a criminal's partner in crime
Acquit – to free or release from a charge, find not guilty
Affidavit – a written statement
Arson – deliberately setting a building on fire
Assault – is inflicting harm on another person
Bail – a sum of money paid to ensure a person appears in court. The money is forfeited if they fail to appear
Battery – unlawful assault
Blackmail – attempting to obtain money by threats
Burglary – breaking into a building to commit theft
Capital crime – a crime for which the penalty is death (abolished in the UK in 1965)
Civil law – disputes between individuals
Criminal law – deals with acts considered harmful to the community
Damages – money paid as compensation for injury or loss
Defamation – harming a person's reputation by libel or slander
Evidence – information presented to a court to prove or disprove a legal issue, such as a defendant's guilt or innocence
Fraud – deception to gain money, etc
Homicide – the unlawful killing of another person
Indictment – a written accusation
Kidnap – illegally carrying off a person, for example, to obtain ransom payment
Libel – defamation in writing, such as in a newspaper article
Manslaughter – taking another person's life without deliberate intent
Murder – the deliberate killing of another person
Oath – a promise to tell the truth in court, often sworn on a holy book such as the Bible
Perjury – a false statement made while under oath in a court
Probation – placing an offender under the supervision of a probation officer
Receiving – taking goods knowing that they are stolen
Robbery – theft with force or threat of violence
Slander – defamation of a person in spoken language
Sue – to bring legal proceedings against a person, organization, etc
Summons – an official order to attend court
Trespass – illegal entry of another person's property
Trial – the examination of a case in a court of law
Vandalism – deliberate damage to another's property
Verdict – the outcome of a trial, ie whether the accused is guilty or not guilty
Warrant – a legal document allowing for someone's arrest, the search of their property, etc

Law courts

This is the court system in England and Wales. The system differs in Scotland. Some countries follow the English system, but most have their own procedures. In many court rooms in the UK and elsewhere there is an image of justice as a woman, which dates from Roman times.

It traditionally shows her holding scales in one hand, to show that she is impartial, and a sword to represent the power of the law. Sometimes she is blindfolded to show that justice cannot be influenced.

County Court
Civil (non-criminal) cases are heard by a judge in a County Court.

Magistrates' Court
Criminal and civil cases are held before Justices of the Peace or District Judges, without a jury. There are limits on the sentences and fines they can impose. Youth Courts are part of Magistrates' Courts and hear cases involving young people between 10 and 17 years of age.

Crown Court
These hold trials by judge and jury for more serious criminal cases.

High Court
The High Court tries civil cases and hears appeals in criminal cases.

Court of Appeal
These hear appeals against civil and criminal cases following High Court and Crown Court convictions.

House of Lords
The House of Lords is the highest court in the land and hears appeals against judgements of the Court of Appeal.

Coroners' Courts
Coroners' courts investigate violent and unnatural deaths or sudden deaths in which the cause is unknown.

A statue of justice holding scales and sword on the roof of the Old Bailey, the Central Criminal Court in London

Scottish law

Scottish law differs from English law in a number of ways. The Procurator Fiscal presents the case for the prosecution in Sheriff Courts and in District Courts (where minor cases are tried). Advocates, instead of barristers, appear in Scottish courts. In Scottish law, if a person is charged with a criminal offence, they must be brought to trial within 110 days. If that does not happen, they are set free. In English courts juries can only find defendants guilty or not guilty, but in Scotland they may find a case "not proven".

Execution methods

Capital punishment is the legal killing of a person, usually those found guilty of murder or other serious crimes, although execution for minor offences or for political motives has occurred throughout history. These are some of the most common methods.

Hanging

Hanging has been used in Britain since the Saxon period. The bodies of highwaymen and other criminals were often hung in iron frames called gibbets to warn other would-be criminals. The last public hanging on mainland Britain was in 1868 and the last within a prison in 1964. Capital punishment was abolished in the UK in 1965. Hanging is still used in some countries and as an alternative to lethal injection in two US states.

Burning at the stake

Many famous people were burned at the stake, including the French patriot Joan of Arc in 1431 and Protestant martyrs in England. In Germany up to 100,000 people accused of witchcraft and other crimes were burned during the 16th, 17th and 18th centuries. In 1589 133 people were burned in a single day. Witches were rarely burned in England, and never in America, where hanging was the usual punishment.

Beheading

Capital punishment literally means removing the head. In the UK it was the main execution method for aristocrats and members of the royal family. Heads of victims were often placed on spikes on the entrances to London as a warning. Beheading is still used in some countries, such as Saudi Arabia.

Firing squad

Execution by firing squad is common in warfare and for heads of state such as Emperor of Mexico Maximilian I, who was shot in 1867. In England, traitors and spies were shot at the Tower of London, the last in 1941. The firing squad is an optional method in three US states.

Electric chair

The electric chair's first victim was William Kemmler at Auburn Prison, New York, USA, on 6 August 1890. The chair remains an optional method in nine US states.

Gas chamber

Introduced in Nevada, USA, in 1924, the gas chamber is optional in five US states, with lethal injection an alternative.

Lethal injection

Texas was the first US state to use lethal injection with the execution of Charles Brooks Jr on 7 December 1982. It is now authorized in 35 of the 50 US states.

French Queen Marie Antoinette beheaded by guillotine, 1793

Guillotine

Devices for beheading people with a machine rather than an axe or sword were known in England (the Halifax Gibbet) as early as 1286 and in Ireland in 1307. The guillotine became used in France during the French Revolution after Dr Joseph-Ignace Guillotin invented an improved version which was used to execute King Louis XVI and Queen Marie Antoinette. It was last used in public in 1939.

Strange laws

- It is forbidden to beat a carpet or touch a pelican in a London royal park.
- In Wisconsin, USA, restaurants may not serve apple pie without also serving cheese.
- Since 1540, it has been illegal for barbers in the City of London to practice surgery – but they are allowed to pull teeth out.
- Flying or landing flying saucers in French vineyards is not allowed.
- In Spokane, Washington, USA, buying a radio on a Sunday is permitted – but not a television.
- Any whale caught in England is the property of the monarch. At one time, the head was sent to the king and the tail to the queen.
- A law in Denver, Colorado, USA, prevents people from lending a vacuum cleaner to their next-door neighbour.
- Llamas may not be grazed in Canadian national parks.
- In Australia, reading tarot cards is considered witchcraft and is illegal.
- Treading on money is illegal in Thailand.
- Until 1976, London taxi drivers had to carry a bale of hay to feed their horses.
- You may not drive geese down Cheapside, London, unless you are a freeman of the City.
- According to a law dating from the Middle Ages, all Englishmen over 14 must practice shooting a longbow for two hours a week.

www.oldbaileyonline.org search

Punishments

In most countries people who break the law are either fined or imprisoned, but through the ages there have been many other forms of punishment.

Alcatraz, in the bay of San Francisco, is no longer used as a prison.

Flogging
Whipping or flogging was once common: mutinous sailors were whipped with a cat-o'-nine-tails or keelhauled (dragged beneath a ship on the end of a rope). Flogging was widely used in the USA. The last state to abolish it was Delaware – but not until 1972!

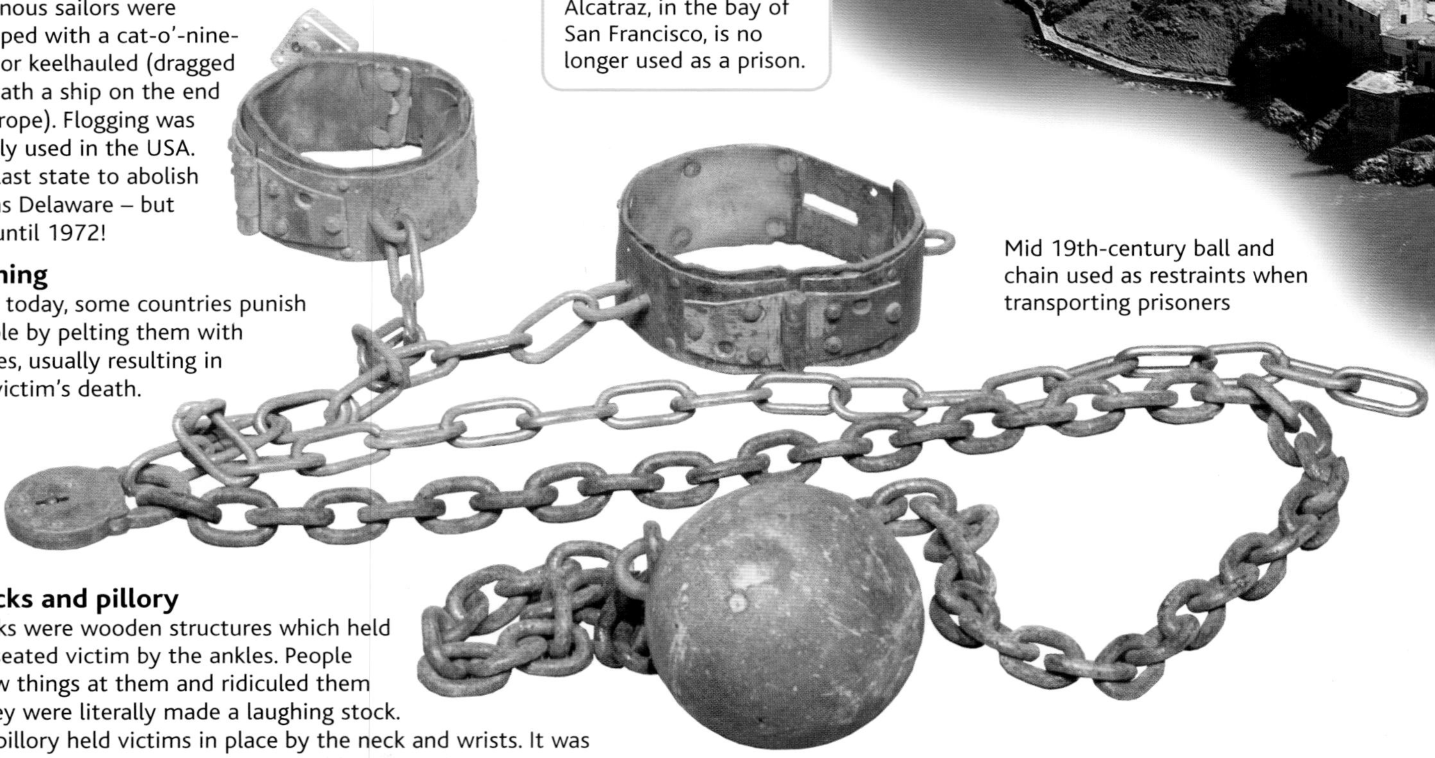

Mid 19th-century ball and chain used as restraints when transporting prisoners

Stoning
Even today, some countries punish people by pelting them with stones, usually resulting in the victim's death.

Stocks and pillory
Stocks were wooden structures which held the seated victim by the ankles. People threw things at them and ridiculed them – they were literally made a laughing stock.
The pillory held victims in place by the neck and wrists. It was worse than the stocks as people could not use their hands to protect their faces from things thrown at them, and could be blinded or even killed. The last person to be pilloried in England was Peter James Bossy in London on 22 June 1830. A Chinese version, a sort of heavy wooden collar, was known as the Winged Tiger.

Ducking stool
This punishment was used in England and America. The victims were usually women. They were strapped into a special chair and plunged into a river or pond. The last person to be punished this way in England was Jenny Pipes in Leominster, Herefordshire, in 1809.

Chain gang
Chain gangs, in which prisoners were chained together as they did heavy labour, such as breaking rocks, were used across the USA until 1955. In recent years they have been reintroduced in some prisons.

The Iron Maiden
The torture device known as the Iron Maiden was a metal cabinet with spikes on the inside, used in the 18th century. Victims were strapped inside it standing up and threatened with the spiked door being slowly closed on them unless they confessed to the crime of which they were accused.

Great robberies

Mona Lisa
Leonardo da Vinci's famous painting was stolen from the Louvre Museum, Paris, on 21 August 1911 by Vicenzo Peruggia. He kept it for two years, but when he tried to sell it he was caught and jailed.

Art theft
On 18 March 1990 two thieves disguised as policemen stole 12 works of art by Rembrandt, Degas, Vermeer and others from the Isabella Stewart Gardner Museum, Boston. The paintings were valued at $300 million and have never been recovered.

Dunbar Armored robbery
Believed to be the USA's biggest cash robbery, an estimated $8.9 million was stolen in an armed hold-up at the Dunbar Armored facility in Los Angeles, California, on the night of 13 September 1997. The gang leader was caught and jailed for 24 years, but most of the money has not been found.

Iraq Central Bank
In March 2003, just before the USA-led invasion of Iraq, President Saddam Hussein removed almost $1 billion in cash from the Iraq Central Bank. About $650 million was later discovered in his palace, but the rest has never been located.

Securitas depot robbery
On 22 February, 2006, Britain's biggest ever robbery took place at the Securitas depot, Tonbridge. The gang kidnapped the family of the depot manager and got away with £53,116,760 in cash. Following a series of police raids, some of the cash was recovered and several people were arrested.

Science and crime detection

Modern detectives use a wide range of scientific techniques to help them identify and catch criminals.

Fingerprinting
Fingerprints have been used for more than 100 years to prove whether someone was at a crime scene or held a weapon. Experts dust areas for hidden prints, which can also be revealed under special lights or on contact with certain chemicals. Faint prints can be improved by laser image enhancement.

DNA testing
Now forensic scientists use DNA testing or genetic fingerprinting to prove or disprove a suspect's connection with a crime. Everyone's DNA is unique and even the smallest samples – a single hair or a trace of saliva – can provide evidence.

Psychological profiling
Experts prepare profiles that suggest certain features of the killer, based on the nature of their murders. The profile may give likely age, background and habits. This builds a portrait of the criminal and helps detectives track him or her down.

Ballistics
All guns have a unique "fingerprint" – the marks made on a bullet as it leaves the barrel. Ballistics specialists examine these with microscopes and compare bullets used in crimes with those fired from a suspect's gun to find out whether they are identical.

Identikit
The Identikit system, which was developed in the USA in the 1940s, used transparent layers to build up a picture of a suspect's face. Witnesses' descriptions of eye colour, hair styles, etc, were laid over a basic face shape. Modern developments include Photofit and computerised E-fit (Electronic Facial Identification Technique).

Surveillance
Crime-fighters increasingly use electronic methods to spy on suspects. They can plant bugs (hidden microphones and video cameras) and intercept telephone calls and computer data.

50 years for whistling!

As French queen Marie Antoinette took her seat at a Paris theatre in 1786, Marie-Augustin, Marquis de Pélier, whistled at her, and was promptly arrested and jailed in the Bastille. The queen was executed in 1793 during the French Revolution, and Marie-Augustin was forgotten, until 1834 when, aged 72, and 50 years after he was imprisoned, he was released and his property restored to him.

Famous prisons

Newgate
This was once London's most notorious prison. Public hangings took place outside its gates, and it features in several of Charles Dickens's novels. Newgate was finally demolished in 1902. The Central Criminal Court (Old Bailey) was built on the site of the prison.

Dartmoor
Dartmoor was first used for prisoners of war during the Napoleonic Wars and has served as a high-security, long-term prison ever since. The prison is miles from anywhere on a bleak Devon moor so if prisoners escape, they are usually recaptured quickly.

Guantánamo Bay
Since 2002, the detention camp on the US Navy base at Guantánamo Bay, Cuba, has held hundreds of suspected al-Qaeda and other prisoners captured in Afghanistan and elsewhere. Following his inauguration in 2009, President Obama announced that the camp would be closed within the year.

Alcatraz
This island in San Francisco Bay, California, USA, is often known as The Rock, but was originally called Isla de los Alcatraces (Isle of the Pelicans). It was first used as a military prison, but then became a prison for the country's most dangerous criminals, among them Al Capone. Robert Stroud, a bird expert who became famous as the Birdman of Alcatraz, spent many years there.

Sing Sing
This New York prison was named after the Sin Sinck Native Americans who originally lived there. It was built from 1825 to 1828, and from 1891 onwards many murderers were electrocuted in the electric chair at Sing Sing. In 1969 the prison was renamed Ossining Correctional Facility.

Most wanted

Since 1950, the FBI (Federal Bureau of Investigation) in the USA, has issued a list of its "ten most wanted" criminals. Osama bin Laden, the international terrorist and al-Qaeda leader, is currently at the top of the list. There is a $50 million (£34.6 million) reward to anyone who provides information that leads to his capture.

www.institutions.org.uk/prisons search

Work & Home

Earth Hour

During Earth Hour on the last Saturday of March, homes, businesses and public buildings are encouraged to turn off their lights, along with street lights and other electrical appliances, for one hour to raise awareness of the impact of climate change. Earth Hour was established in Sydney, Australia, by the World Wide Fund for Nature in 2007. Five years on, it now takes place in 126 countries around the world. Here in Vilnius, Lithuania, supporters of the campaign spell out the Earth Hour '60' logo in candles.

The first vacuum cleaner

In 1901, Englishman Hubert Cecil Booth invented the first successful vacuum cleaner. The machine worked well and was popular with rich people. It was also used in places such as Westminster Abbey, Buckingham Palace and Windsor Castle. Booth's cleaner was so large that it had to be pulled along by a horse, and six people were needed to operate it. The machines were only hired out, never sold.

The upright vacuum cleaner was invented by an American named James Murray Spangler in 1907. Spangler realized that his asthma was made worse by dust, and wanted to find a more effective way of sweeping. He made the first upright vacuum cleaner with the help of a pillowcase tied to a broom handle and an electrical pump. Spangler sold the patent to his cousin William H. Hoover, who improved the invention and started a very successful business selling vacuum cleaners.

At the table

In Europe before the 17th century, the normal way of eating one's food was by cutting it with a knife and using the fingers, perhaps sharing a spoon with other diners. Forks were used for lifting food to a piece of wood or stale bread known as a trencher (hence the word 'trencherman', a greedy eater). In the 18th century, china plates were introduced along with forks. Originally they had two prongs or 'tines', and later three or four. Eating was less messy as a result, so napkins, once the size of towels, became much smaller.

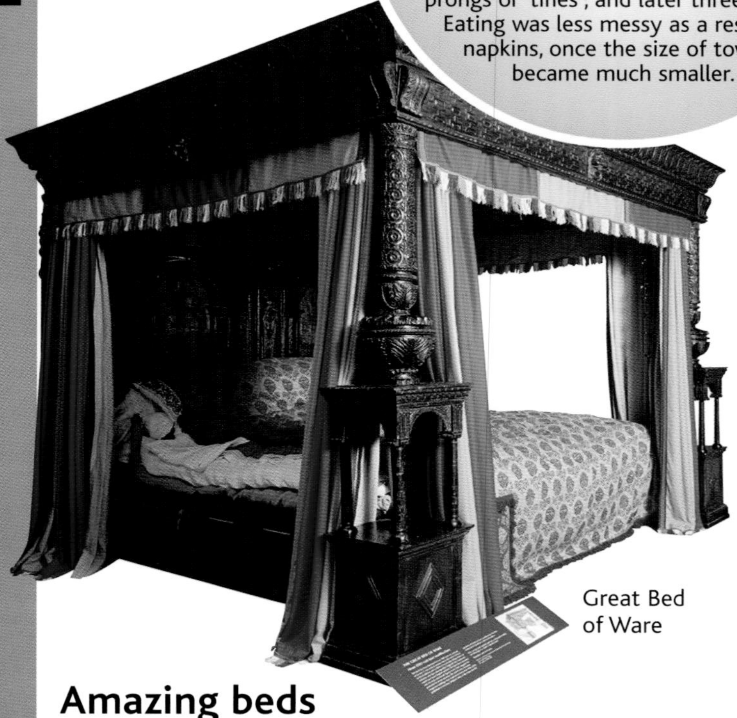
Great Bed of Ware

Amazing beds

One of the largest beds in the world is the Great Bed of Ware. It is 3.26 m (10 ft 8.5 in) wide, 3.38 m (11 ft 1 in) long and was made in about 1580. The bed is mentioned by Shakespeare in *Twelfth Night*. It is now in the Victoria and Albert Museum in London.

In 1882 an Indian maharajah had a bed made of solid silver. At each corner there was a life-sized statue of a naked woman holding a fan. When the maharajah lay on the bed, his weight started a mechanism that made the women wave their fans.

Toilet paper

- Before the invention of toilet paper, people improvised with many different things. The rich used wool or lace, but the poor used anything they could find, including wood shavings, grass, stone, sand, leaves, corn cobs, moss, seashells, water or snow, as well as their hands. Later people began to use newspapers or telephone directories as toilet paper.

Hot and cold

Cookers

• Cooking was done over open fires until ranges with iron ovens came into use in the 1780s.

• American-born scientist Benjamin Thompson, Count Rumford, invented a new metal oven in 1798.

• Gustaf Dalen, a blind Swedish scientist, invented the Aga cooker in 1929.

• The late 19th century saw the introduction of gas and electric cookers in the home.

• The first microwave ovens were sold in the 1950s, but were very expensive. The first for home use appeared in the 1970s – today 92 per cent of homes in the UK and 97 per cent in the USA have a microwave oven.

Refrigerators

• In the 17th century some homes had ice houses – ice was collected from lakes in the winter and used to keep food fresh in the hotter months.

• Ice boxes and primitive fridges were introduced in the 19th century, but the first practical electric models for the home were not widely used until the 1920s. Today 67 per cent of homes worldwide and over 99 per cent in the UK and USA have a fridge.

• In Labrador in 1912–15, American naturalist Clarence Birdseye observed the Inuit preserving fish with ice. He developed the method commercially, creating the frozen food industry. The first frozen foods went on sale in 1930 and the first frozen meals in 1939.

• Frozen food became popular from the 1940s, as increasing numbers of people had home freezers. Today, 22 per cent of the world's households own a freezer, 98 per cent in the UK, but only 36 per cent in the USA.

1903 advertisement for refrigerators

Home accidents

We think of our homes and gardens as safe places, but a surprising number of accidents are caused by everyday things. These UK figures record the number of people in a year who needed hospital treatment after accidents at home.

Sport/leisure items

Footballs and basketballs 13,695
Swings 6,528
Slides 5,801
Climbing frames 3,743
Bouncy castles 3,690
Rollerblades 2,874
Skateboards 2,643
Cricket bats 621
Cricket balls 461
Golf balls 355

Containers/packaging

Boxes 8,764
Glass bottles 8,249
Plastic bottles 2,448
Corned beef tins 2,147
Plastic bags 2,111
Aerosols 1,348
Tubes 745
Ring pulls 621
Lollipop sticks 160
Paper bags 8

Animals

Dogs 66,915
Cats 16,126
Bees and wasps 11,123
Rabbits, hamsters, etc 3,264
Wild birds 745
Pet birds 692
Snakes and other reptiles 426
Pet fish 106

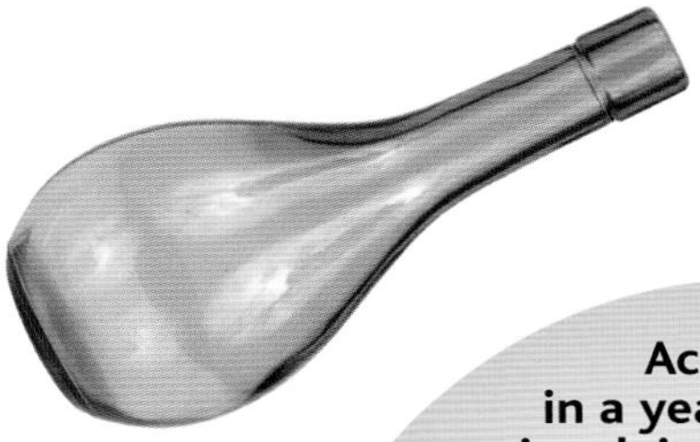

Accidents in a year in the UK involving clothing or personal effects

Trainers 60,830
Slippers 60,493
Jewellery 13,695
Socks, tights, etc 11,726
Wellington boots 4,364
Trousers 3,885
Shirts/T-shirts 1,472
Coats 1,401
Hairbrushes 1,224
Toothbrushes 763
False teeth 532

Toilet fact file

● In medieval Europe people used chamber pots which they emptied out of the window. In castles there would be a garderobe – a small cupboard with a hole that let waste out into the moat.

● Throwing waste out of the windows into the street or rivers that provided drinking water, spread disease. The worst epidemic was the Black Death in the 14th century, which killed about a quarter of the people in Europe.

● In London a gigantic cesspit was built under 200,000 houses and it often overflowed into them. Cesspits in London were abolished in 1847 and every home had to have a lavatory. However, sewage was still diverted into the River Thames, which resulted in the "Great Stink" in the summer of 1858 – the worst smell in the city's history.

● Europe's major cities and the biggest cities in the USA started building sewers in the 19th century. Many of these early systems are still in use today. "Sewer tours" are popular in Paris, France, and in Brighton, UK. The systems are such amazing works of engineering that people travel to these cities just to visit them!

● Today, Japan makes the most advanced toilets. Known as "washlets", they have control panels, water jets, heated seats, driers and telephones. More improvements are being developed, including voice-activated toilets and some that can do medical tests.

Elizabethan toilet

In 1596 John Harington 1561–1612), a member of Queen Elizabeth I's court, wrote a book called *The Metamorphosis of Ajax* in which he included a design for a flushing toilet. He is said to have installed one for the Queen in Richmond Palace, but she complained that it was noisy, and it was almost 300 years before most homes in Britain had one.

● Chinese emperors used toilet paper in the 14th century, but the first commercial toilet paper was produced in 1857 by Joseph Gayetty, an American businessman. Gayetty's paper was sold as individual sheets with his name on them.

● Every person in the UK spends an average of £16.00 on toilet paper every year, compared with the average American's £12.50. The world average is £2.40 per person.

www.geffrye-museum.org.uk/kidszone search

Valuable toys

Some wealthy collectors prize rare toys, especially those that are in good condition – in their original box, and never played with. These are just some of the toys that may have cost very little when they were made, but now sell for high prices.

- G.I. Joe prototype was sold by Heritage Galleries & Auctioneers of Dallas, Texas for $200,000 (£126,580) in 2003.
- Titania's Palace, a doll's house with 2,000 items of furniture, was sold at Christie's, London, in 1978 for £135,000 ($258,728).
- Dingley Hall, a doll's house dating from 1877, was sold at Christie's, London, in 2003 for £124,750 ($211,938).
- A 1906 train set made by German toymaker Märklin was sold at Christie's, London, in 2001 for £113,750 ($165,290).
- 'Teddy Girl', a teddy bear made by the German manufacturer Steiff in 1904, was sold at Christie's, London, on 5 December 1994 for a record £110,000 ($171,600). Yoshiro Sekiguchi, a Japanese collector bought the bear for his teddy bear museum near Tokyo.
- A black mohair Steiff teddy bear, made in about 1912, was sold at Christie's, London, in 2000 for £91,750 ($132,157). It was one of only 494 black Steiff bears made as a mark of respect after the sinking of the *Titanic*. They are known as "mourning teddies".
- A tinplate clockwork motorcycle with Mickey Mouse and Minnie from about 1930, was sold at Christie's, London, in 1997 for £51,000 ($83,650).
- In 2007 the Stephen and Marilyn Steckbeck collection of nearly 500 mechanical banks (toy money boxes) was sold in the USA for a record total of $7.7 million (£3.7 million). One, a whale from which the Biblical Jonah emerges when money is inserted, made $414,000 (£200,000).
- In 2008 a box of six Dinky toy vans was sold by Vectis of Stockton-on-Tees, UK, for £35,000 and a rare single van for £20,000.

The first Barbie dolls, in the Barbie Museum, Palo Alto, California

Birth of Barbie

The first Barbie doll appeared in February 1959. It was made by Ruth and Elliot Handler, co-founders of American toy manufacturers Mattel, and they named the doll after their daughter Barbara. The doll was dressed in a black and white striped swimsuit, with sunglasses, high heels and gold hoop earrings. In the first year a total of 351,000 Barbies were sold at $3 (£1) each. The doll went on to become one of the bestselling toys of all time.

Marque make his mark

In Atlanta, USA, on 15 July 2009, a doll made by French sculptor Albert Marque (1872–1939), dating from 1914 and dressed in a costume worn by the Ballet Russe, a Russian ballet company, set a new auction record of $263,000, beating the previous record of $215,000, which was also for a doll by Marque.

Toy-buying countries

Forecast sales of traditional toys (eg construction toys, model vehicles, indoor games, dolls and teddy bears) and video games in 2009 are estimated to average £14.40 ($20) for every person on the planet. There are huge differences between countries: North Americans spend the most and people in African countries the least per child.

Children and adults ride the ferris wheel inside a Toys 'Я' Us store in New York, USA

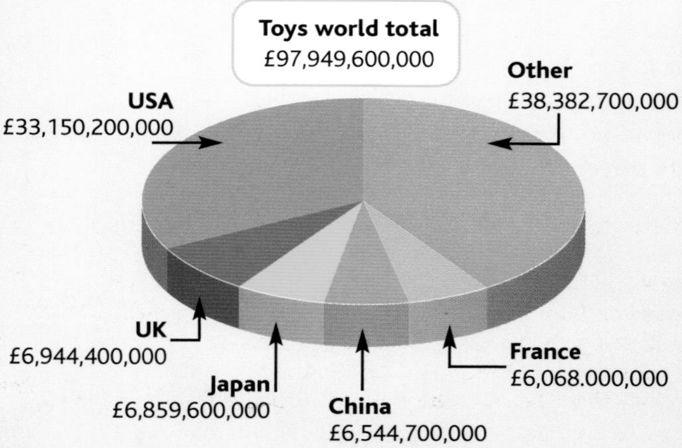

Wii

Wii, a 7th generation games console made by Japanese manufacturer Nintendo, was launched in 2006. Originally codenamed 'Revolution', the name 'Wii' was chosen because it is easy to remember and pronounce in most languages, in English it sounds like 'we', suggesting that it is for all, and the two lowercase 'i' characters standing side by side are said to represent two players.

In addition to buttons, the controller, the Wii Remote, allows users to point at the screen and make hand and arm movements to control the on-screen action. Many of the games available for the Wii, especially those involving sports and keep-fit, appeal to a wider age group than traditional computer game players. It has been one of the most successful entertainment products of the 21st century, with worldwide sales of over 50 million.

The Wii Series of games includes:

- Wii Sports – baseball, bowling, boxing, golf and tennis; over 40.5 million have been sold.
- Wii Play – includes billiards, laser hockey, shooting range and table tennis; over 21 million have been sold.
- Wii Fit – aerobics, balance games, strength training and yoga, used in conjunction with the Wii Balance Board; over 14 million have been sold.
- Wii Chess – as with other games, it offers the ability to play online.
- Wii Music – launched in 2008; 66 different instruments can be played.
- Wii Sports Resort – launched in 2009, it is used with the Wii MotionPlus accessory.

Nintendo also produces games such as Mario Kart Wii, played with the Wii Wheel, over 13.7 million of which have been sold. A large range of software has been produced by other manufacturers. Total world sales of Wii games to the end of 2008 was estimated at 312.22 million.

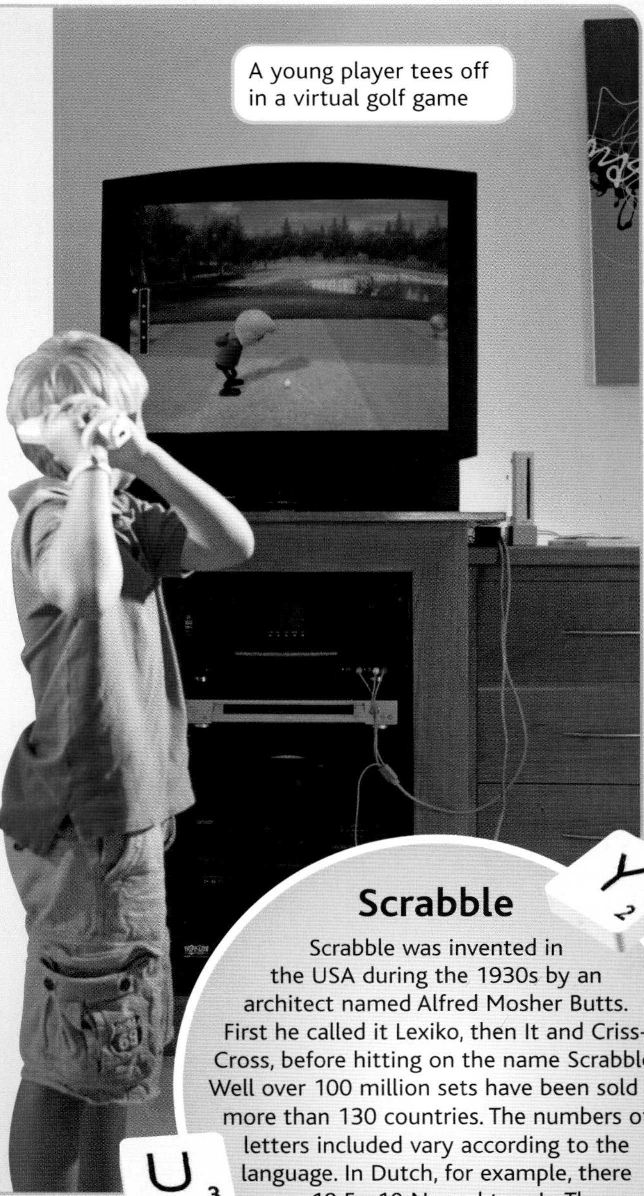

A young player tees off in a virtual golf game

Scrabble

Scrabble was invented in the USA during the 1930s by an architect named Alfred Mosher Butts. First he called it Lexiko, then It and Criss-Cross, before hitting on the name Scrabble. Well over 100 million sets have been sold in more than 130 countries. The numbers of letters included vary according to the language. In Dutch, for example, there are 18 Es, 10 Ns and two Js. The Slovak version has 41 different letters – more than any other version.

Monopoly®

Monopoly was invented in 1934 by an unemployed engineer called Charles Darrow, who lived in Philadelphia, USA. In his first version of the game he used street names from Atlantic City in New Jersey because he dreamed of going there, but could not afford the fare. The game was so successful that Darrow became a millionaire and spent the rest of his life travelling and growing rare orchids.

There are many national and local versions around the world, as well as specialized versions including those for animal lovers, Birdopoly, Dogoploy and Horse-opoly, based on films such as James Bond and Shrek, as well as Bible-opoly and Elvis Monopoly. Parkers, the US manufacturers of the game, print more Monopoly money than the US Treasury prints dollars.

Monopoly® around the world

Country	City*	Mayfair becomes
Australia	Canberra + state capitals	Kings Avenue
Canada	Vancouver, etc	Robson Street
China	Hong Kong	Victoria Peak
Egypt	Cairo	Shari Qasr El Nil
France	Paris	Rue de la Paix
Germany	Munich	Schlossallee
Ireland	Dublin	Shrewsbury Road
Netherlands	Amsterdam	Kalverstraat
New Zealand	Auckland	Queen Street
Portugal	Lisbon	Rossio
Russia	Moscow	Arbat
Singapore	Singapore	Queen Astrid Park
South Africa	Johannesburg	Eloff Street/Eloffstraat
Spain	Madrid	Paseo Del Prado
Switzerland	Zurich, etc	Paradeplatz
US	Atlantic City	Boardwalk

* Some feature streets from more than one city

Russian Monopoly board

Jobs then and now

At the time of the 1911 UK Census the most common occupations in were domestic service (1.3 million people), agriculture (1.2 million), coal mining (1 million) and building (800,000). The most recent estimates show that 22.4 million people are now employed in service trades (shop and office work and other businesses), including 3.4 million in health and social work, 2.4 million in education and 1.68 million in hotels and restaurants. There are 2.9 million in manufacturing, 1.3 million in construction, 240,000 in agriculture and fishing and 60,000 in mining and quarrying.

Countries with the most workers

Less than half the world's population (about 3.134 billion people) are in paid employment. The rest are too young, students, retired or too old, unemployed or unable to work, or stay at home to look after children. Based on the number of people aged 15 to 64 who are currently employed, these countries have the most workers:

Country		% unemployed	Workers (2009)
1	China	4.3	812,700,000
2	India	9.5	467,000,000
3	USA	9.4	154,500,000
4	Indonesia	7.7	113,200,000
5	Brazil	7.4	95,210,000
6	Russia	8.9	75,810,000
7	Bangladesh	2.5	72,500,000
8	Japan	5.6	65,970,000
9	Pakistan	15.2	55,880,000
10	Vietnam	6.5	47,660,000

Dirty work

Many unpleasant jobs of the past no longer exist. Among these are:

Climbing boy

Small boys were employed by chimney sweeps to climb inside with brushes. It was extremely dangerous and they were often trapped or injured. Even though it was banned in 1840, many boys continued in this work well into the 19th century.

Oakum picker

Oakum is tarry old rope used from ships. Picking it apart by hand was an early recycling process. The strands were sent back to shipyards for sealing gaps in ships' planks. This messy job was carried out by inmates of workhouses – places where unemployed people were put to work in return for a small amount of food and a bed for the night.

Burlak

Before they were motorized, barges on canals and rivers in England and other countries were drawn by horses, but in Russia human haulers called burlaks were employed in this backbreaking task.

Gong farmer

Gong farmers or gong scourers were the men who took away the contents of toilets and cesspits, usually at night. They were often killed by the fumes.

Pure collector

'Pure' was the name given to dog droppings. They were collected from the streets by young girls or old women for use in the leather tanning industry.

State-owned Indian Railways is one of the world's largest employers

Biggest employers

The American store WalMart employs some 1.8 million workers worldwide, while Indian Railways has about 1.6 million employees and China National Petroleum, the country's state-owned energy company, over 1 million. Various state organizations, such as the British National Health Service and the military forces of large countries also employ hundreds of thousands of people.

Money facts

The first coins Coins made from gold and silver were used in Lydia, an ancient Middle Eastern kingdom, in about 687–652 BC.

Smallest coins The silver quarter-jawa was made in Nepal in about 1740 and weighed only 0.002 g (0.00007 oz).

Largest coins Swedish 10-daler copper coins (made in 1644) weighed 19.71 kg (43.45 lb).

US coins made The US mint issued more than 3.5 million coins in 2009, more than half of them 1-cent coins.

Banknotes Paper money was first made in China in the 13th century. The first European notes were made in Sweden in 1548. Banknotes were issued in 1690 in America and 1695 in England.

Smallest banknotes Romanian 10-bani notes of 1917 had a printed area of just 27.5 x 38 mm (1.08 x 1.5 in) – not much bigger than a postage stamp.

Largest banknotes One-guan Chinese notes from the late 14th century measured 22.8 x 33 cm (9 x 13 in) – bigger than a page of this book.

Cheques The first cheque was issued in London on 22 April 1659. It was for £10 and made payable to the bearer by Nicholas Vanacker. It was drawn on the bank of Clayton &

Film stuntmen and women are in one of the riskiest professions

Dangerous jobs

There are many jobs that have a higher than average risk of being killed at work, including:

Bomb disposal and mine clearance expert
Deep sea diver
Deep sea fisherman
Construction worker
Oil platform worker
Professional stuntman
Steeplejack

Unemployment

In countries with economic problems, unemployment tends to increase. In turn, more people become dependant on the state and the output and demand for goods and services fall, so the economy worsens. These are the countries in which more than half the people who are available to work do not have paid jobs:

	Country	% of labour force unemployed
1	Nauru	90.0
2	Liberia	85.0
3	Zimbabwe	80.0
4	Burkina Faso	77.0
5	Turkmenistan	60.0
6	Djibouti	59.0
7=	East Timor	50.0
=	Zambia	50.0

Countries with most children who work

In many countries children traditionally work to help their families in agriculture. In some countries children are employed to work in often dangerous conditions in factories and mines, for example. They are paid low wages and the work prevents them from attending school. The United Nations and International Labor Organization are attempting to eradicate child labour around the world. More than half the children aged 7–14 work in some African countries:

	Country	% of children who work
1	Mali	70.9
2	Guinea-Bissau	67.5
3	Sierra Leone	65.0
4	Ethiopia	56.0
5	Burkina Faso	50.0

Child labour is common in many countries

Morris. The original cheque was sold for £1,200 ($2,160) at Sotheby's, London in 1976.

Credit cards The first credit card was invented by Frank X. McNamara in the USA and issued in 1950 by Diner's Club. Holograms were first used for security on Visa cards in the US in 1984. Smart cards (cards with built-in microchips) were introduced in France in 1975. There are 165.4 million payment cards in the UK, including 67.3 million credit cards, 5.7 million charge cards and 71.6 million debit cards.

ATM The world's first ATM (Automated Teller Machine, or cashpoint) began operation on 27 June 1967 at Barclays Bank, Enfield, London.

Euro The new European currency was introduced in 1999 and was taken up by most European Union countries on 1 January 2002.

Lewes Pound In 2008, Lewes, the county town of East Sussex, issued its own currency, the Lewes Pound. It is designed to encourage people to pay for goods and services within the town and encourage local businesses.

www. royalmint.com search

Top energy users

These countries guzzle more energy than any others in the world. The figures below show the amount of gas, coal or other power needed to produce the same amount of energy as a tonne of oil. This is the standard way of comparing energy produced and consumed from different sources.

Country	Oil	Gas	Coal	Nuclear	HEP*	Total
1 USA	884.5	600.7	565.0	192.0	56.7	2,299.0
2 China	375.7	72.6	1,406.3	15.5	132.4	2,005.5
3 Russia	130.4	378.2	101.3	36.9	37.8	684.6
4 Japan	221.8	84.4	128.7	57.0	15.7	507.5
5 India	135.0	37.2	231.4	3.5	26.2	433.3
6 Canada	102.0	90.0	33.0	21.1	83.6	329.8
7 Germany	118.3	73.8	80.9	33.7	4.4	311.1
8 France	92.2	39.8	11.9	99.6	14.3	257.9
9 South Korea	103.3	35.7	66.1	34.2	0.9	240.1
10 Brazil	105.3	22.7	14.6	3.1	82.3	228.1
UK	*78.7*	*84.5*	*35.4*	*11.9*	*1.1*	*211.6*

Energy consumption
2008 World total
Oil *3,927.9* Gas *2,726.1* Coal *3,303.7* Nuclear *619.7* HEP* *717.5*
Total *11,294.9*
* Hydroelectric power

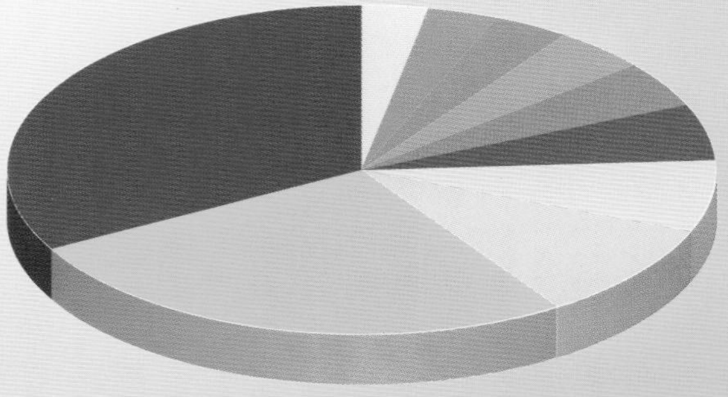

Peak oil

● The world uses over 85 million barrels of oil a day, 31 billion a year. Increased usage by countries such as China has led to some experts predicting that consumption will rise to 100 million or more barrels a day.

● If we continue to use oil at the current rate, a point will come when world output will reach a peak, then decline until it is completely exhausted. Around the world, this is occurring at different rates according to the size and production of oilfields: some counties have passed their peak – the USA in 1970 and UK in 1999 – while some, such as Saudi Arabia, Kuwait and Iraq, have not yet reached theirs.

● At the same time, new discoveries of oil and improved extraction methods mean that, despite increasing global consumption, total world reserves have actually increased and are now more than one-third greater than the trillion barrels identified in the early 1990s.

● As many of the world's economies shrink and people consume less energy or use it with greater efficiency – such as insulating homes, using energy efficient lightbulbs and not leaving electronic equipment on standby – and as car manufacturers become more fuel-conscious and the use of renewable energy sources increases, both peak oil and its final exhaustion may be more distant than has been predicted.

How much oil is left?

Oil is the world's most important single source of energy. It is used for the production of electricity and most motor vehicles run on petrol or diesel that are refined from oil. The world's estimated reserves – the amount that is left under ground or under the sea – are:

Country	2009 reserves (barrels*)
1 Saudi Arabia	264,100,000,000
2 Iran	137,600,000,000
3 Iraq	115,000,000,000
4 Kuwait	101,500,000,000
5 Venezuela	99,400,000,000
6 United Arab Emirates	97,800,000,000
7 Russia	79,000,000,000
8 Libya	43,700,000,000
9 Kazakhstan	39,800,000,000
10 Nigeria	36,200,000,000
USA	*30,500,000,000*
Canada	*28,600,000,000*
UK	*3,400,000,000*
World total	*1,408,700,000,000*

* A barrel of crude oil is equivalent to 159 litres (40 US gallons)

An oil and natural gas drilling platform

See also
Pollution fact file: page 70

Wind farm in California, USA

Wind energy

Windmills were used in Persia (now Iran) in the 7th century, and in Europe since the 12th century, but they were first used for making electricity in the late 19th century. Today, California, USA, is the world's leading area for wind-generated electricity. Tehachapi Wind Resource, California, produces as much wind energy as the rest of the USA combined.

The world's energy sources

A century ago, few homes had electricity and cars were a rare sight. Today, much of the world's energy is turned into electricity for homes, to power equipment in factories and to fuel our cars and other forms of transport. Some energy sources will always be available, but carbon-based fuels and nuclear power will eventually run out, so it is important that the use of renewable sources continues to increase in the future.

Renewable energy

Hydropower

Flowing water has been used as a power source since the Middle Ages. Modern hydropower uses water flowing through turbines in dams to produce electricity.

Solar energy

The Sun's warmth can be stored to produce energy. Mirrors and glass were used to collect heat in ancient times, but the first houses to use solar heating were not built until 1955. Solar energy is becoming more popular and the technology is getting better all the time. The world's largest solar energy generating plants are in the Mohave Desert, California, USA. They are designed to use the Sun's rays to heat oil which drives a generator. Each produces enough electricity to power a small town.

Tidal energy

Using waves and marine currents to release energy is expensive and as yet small-scale. The first and largest tidal power station on the Rance river, St Malo, France, was completed in 1967. It can produce enough energy every year to supply power to 120,000 households.

Non-renewable energy

Oil

The first oil wells were drilled less than 150 years ago but oil, and petroleum which comes from it, has become the most important energy source. Almost 33 per cent of the world's energy supply comes from oil. Most oil is found in the Middle East and has to be taken by tankers or pipelines to places where it is used around the world.

Coal

Coal is the world's second most important source of energy. It makes up over 29 per cent of the total. Coal is a fossil fuel and is made from plants that lived and died 300 million years ago. The world's coal reserves will last about another 121 years. This is more than twice as long as gas (60 years) and more than three times as long as oil (41 years).

Natural gas

The third main source of power comes from gas that occurs naturally beneath the Earth's surface. It accounts for 24 per cent of the world total. The gas is mainly methane, with some ethane, propane and other gases. It is collected and taken to where it is needed by pipelines.

Nuclear power

Nuclear power makes up just over 5 per cent of the world total. A nuclear reaction releases huge amounts of heat which in turn heats water or other liquid and drives a turbine to produce electricity. The first nuclear power station to produce electricity for public use was Calder Hall, UK, which opened in 1956.

Solar energy collectors concentrate the sun's rays

Buildings & Structures

Strata SE1

Nicknamed 'The Razor', this building in the Elephant and Castle district of London is a 147-m (482-ft) 43-storey residential skyscraper with shops underneath. It was completed in 2010 and is one of the most environmentally-friendly structures ever built. It was designed to maximise the use of natural light and ventilation and recycled rainwater, uses low-energy lighting and heating and has low CO_2 emissions. It is also a world first in having three 9-m (29.5-ft) wind turbines built into the roof. These supply enough electricity to light the common parts of the building.

Western architecture

Below are the main styles of Western architecture, from prehistory to the present day and famous examples of each. Styles did not stop and start abruptly; one style blended into another, so all dates are approximate.

Before the Renaissance most buildings had several architects or the architect's name was not recorded. The names of the architects of more recent buildings are given in brackets.

Prehistoric
Wooden post buildings, simple stone buildings, stone circles
Stonehenge, Wiltshire, UK

Ancient 3000–337 BC
Ancient Egyptian pyramids, tombs and temples
Great Pyramid, Giza, Egypt

Etruscan 700–200 BC
Alatri Temple, Villa Giulia, Rome, Italy

Greek 600–100 BC
Parthenon, Athens, Greece

Roman 100 BC–AD 370
The Baths of Caracalla, Rome, Italy
The Pantheon, Rome, Italy
The Colosseum, Rome, Italy
Maison Carrée, Nîmes, France

Byzantine 330–1450
Hagia Sophia, Istanbul, Turkey
St Mark's, Venice, Italy

Pre-Columbian 300–1540
Mayan, Aztec, Inca South and Central American
Mayan temples at Tikal, Guatemala

Carolingian 751–987
Chapel Palatine (now part of cathedral), Aachen, Germany

Romanesque 800 to 1200
St James, Santiago de Compostela, Spain
Tournai Cathedral, Belgium

Moorish/Islamic from 8th century
Great Mosque, Cordoba, Spain

Norman 1045–1180
Durham Cathedral, Durham, UK
Ely Cathedral, Ely, UK

Gothic 1140–1534
Cologne Cathedral, Cologne, Germany
Notre Dame Cathedral, Paris, France
Chartres Cathedral, Chartres, France
Salisbury Cathedral, Salisbury, UK

Renaissance 1400–1600
Hampton Court Palace, London, UK
Little Moreton Hall, Cheshire, UK
Florence Cathedral, Florence, Italy (Filippo Brunelleschi)
Ducal Palace, Urbino, Italy (Luciano Laurana)
Château de Chambord, France (Domenico da Cortona)

Baroque 1585–1750
St Paul's Cathedral, London, UK (Sir Christopher Wren)
Versailles Palace, France (Louis Le Vau and Jules Hardouin Mansart)
Greenwich Hospital (Royal Naval College), London, UK (Inigo Jones and Sir Christopher Wren)
Blenheim Palace, Oxfordshire, UK (Sir John Vanbrugh)

American Colonial 1600–1780
Governor's Palace, Williamsburg, Virginia, USA (rebuilt 1930)

Jacobean 1618–25
Ham House, Twickenham, Middlesex, UK
Blickling Hall, Norfolk, UK

Rococo 1650–1790
Vierzehnheiligen Church, Banz, Germany (Johann Balthasar Neumann)

Georgian 1714–1837
The Circus, Bath, UK (John Wood, Sr and Jr)
Charlotte Square, Edinburgh, UK (Robert Adam)

Neoclassical/Federalist US 1750–1880
Panthéon, Paris, France (Germain Soufflot)
Brighton Pavilion, Brighton, UK (John Nash)
University of Virginia, Charlottesville, Virginia, USA (Thomas Jefferson)

Greek

The Parthenon, Athens, Greece, 447–438 BC. Doric is the first and simplest classical Greek building style and this is the finest Doric building still standing. When it was first built, the Parthenon was decorated with marble sculptures painted in bright colours. Some of these, known as the Elgin Marbles, were removed and are now in the British Museum, London.

See also
Mysterious places: page 174

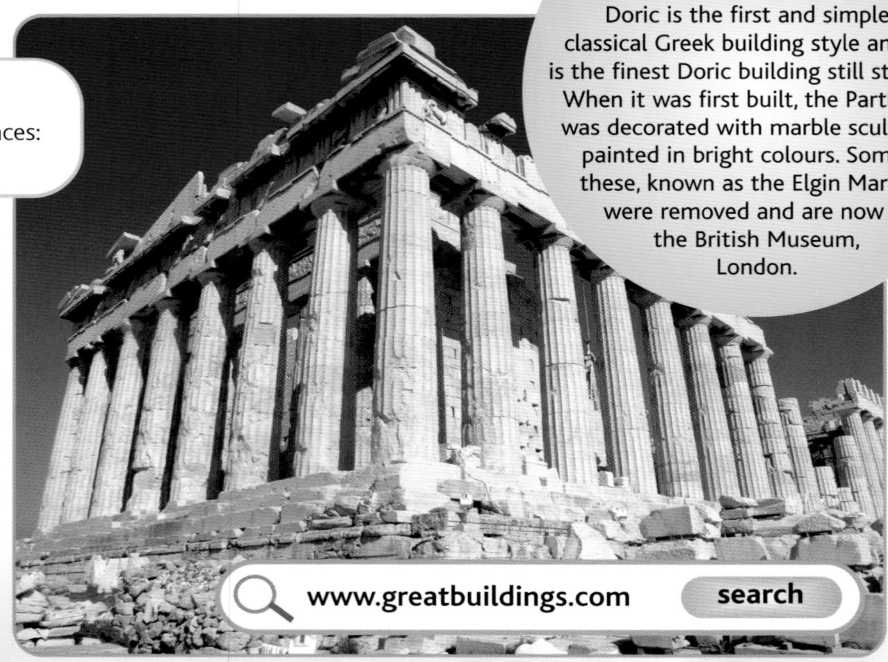
The Parthenon

www.greatbuildings.com search

Skyline of Chicago, USA, with skyscrapers and other modern buildings

Victorian 1837–1901
Houses of Parliament, London, UK (Sir Charles Barry and A.W.N. Pugin)
Crystal Palace, London, UK (Joseph Paxton)
American Surety Building, New York, USA (Bruce Price)

Arts and crafts 1860–1900
The Red House, Kent, UK (Philip Webb)

Art Nouveau 1890–1905
Glasgow Art School, Glasgow, UK (Charles Rennie Macintosh)
Paris Metro stations (Hector Guimard)
La Sagrada Familia, Barcelona, Spain (Antonio Gaudí)
Secession Building, Vienna, Austria (Joseph Maria Olbrich)

Art Deco 1925–35
Chrysler Building, New York, USA (William Van Alen)

Bauhaus 1919–37
Bauhaus, Dessau, Germany (Walter Gropius)

International modernism 1920–50
Fallingwater, Pennsylvania, USA (Frank Lloyd Wright)

Brutalism 1950s
Unité d'Habitation, Marseilles, France (Le Corbusier)
Seagram Building, New York, USA (Mies van der Rohe)

High-tech 1970s–
Centre Georges Pompidou, Paris, France (Richard Rogers and Renzo Piano)
Swiss Re Building (The Gherkin), London, UK (Norman Foster)

Post-modern 1970s
Staatsgalerie, Stuttgart, Germany (James Stirling)

Deconstruction 1990s–
Guggenheim Museum, Bilbao, Spain (Frank Gehry)

Art Deco
Chrysler Building, New York, USA, 1930.
The Chrysler is one of the best-known Art Deco buildings. The gleaming metal spire was based on the Chrysler cars of the time and skyscrapers are still a key feature of the New York skyline.

High-tech
Bahrain World Trade Center, 2004.
The 240-m (787-ft) twin towers have three powerful wind turbines on the skybridges between them. They are able to supply up to one-sixth of the power required to run the lighting, air conditioning, computers and lifts in the buildings.

Japanese architecture
Eastern countries, such as Japan, had their own strong traditions of architecture. The Katsura Palace in Kyoto was built in the early 17th century, at the time of baroque and Jacobean architecture in Europe. It is a simple, elegant building and one of the most perfect examples of traditional Japanese architecture.

American Colonial
Governor's Palace, Williamsburg, Virginia, USA, 1722
European settlers in the New World used architectural ideas from their home countries. The historic district of Williamsburg in Virginia has some of the most famous colonial buildings, dating from before the War of American Independence. The Governor's Palace is one of the finest.

Great religious buildings

The world's major religions, including Christianity, Islam, Judaism, Buddhism, Hinduism and Sikhism, have inspired many of the world's greatest buildings. Some are shrines to the religion's founders. Others are places of pilgrimage. Several are among the world's largest structures. These are the tallest churches.

1 The Chicago Methodist Temple*
Chicago, USA, built 1924, 173 m (568 ft)
2 Ulm Cathedral
Ulm, Germany, built 1890, 161 m (528 ft)
3 Notre Dame de la Paix
Yamoussoukro, Côte d'Ivoire, built 1989, 158 m (519 ft)
4 Cologne Cathedral
Cologne, Germany, built 1880, 156 m (513 ft)
5 Rouen Cathedral
Rouen, France, built 1876, 148 m (485 ft)

* Built on top of a 25-storey, 100 m (328 ft) building

Largest churches
Salt Lake Temple, Utah, USA (1893) has a floor area of 23,506 sq m (253,015 sq ft). St Peter's in the Vatican (1612), the centre of the Roman Catholic Church, is 218.7 m (717.5 ft) long and covers an area of 23,000 sq m (247,572 sq ft). It was the largest Christian cathedral in the world until 1989, when it was overtaken by the 30,000 sq m (322,917 sq ft) basilica in Yamoussoukro, Côte d'Ivoire.

Tallest mosques
The Great Hassan II Mosque, Casablanca, Morocco (1993) is the tallest mosque at 210 m (689 ft). The Saddam Mosque, Baghdad, Iraq was designed to be the largest in the Middle East, with a record-breaking 280 m (919 ft) minaret, but it has not been completed.

Largest mosque
The Masjid al Haram is the holy mosque of Makkah (formerly Mecca), the birthplace of the prophet Muhammad. Millions of Muslim pilgrims visit the mosque every year. The mosque covers 82,000 sq m (882,640 sq ft) and the surrounding yards cover another 985,000 sq m (10,602,442 sq ft). Together they can accommodate up to 1.2 million worshippers.

Largest Buddhist temple
The largest Buddhist temple in the world is Borobudur (many Buddhas), near Yogyakarta, Java, Indonesia. It was built between AD 750 and 842. The temple covers 60,000 sq m (645,834 sq ft) and contains 56,634 cu m (2 million cu ft) of stone.

Largest Hindu temple
Angkor Wat, Cambodia, built between 879 and 1191, is the largest religious structure in the world. The complex of buildings inside its walls and moat covers 83,110 sq m (894,588 sq ft).

Largest synagogue
The world's largest synagogue is Temple Emanu-El, New York City, USA. It opened in 1929 and occupies an area of 3,523 sq m (37,921 sq ft).

The Great Hassan II Mosque, Casablanca, Morocco was built in 1993

Big structues

Tallest chimney
Ekibastuz GRES-2 power station in Kazakhstan (1987) has the world's tallest chimney, 419.7 m (1,377 ft) high, which is taller than the Empire State Building.

Biggest sphere
The 74-m (243-ft) high Biosphère, Montreal, Canada, was designed for Expo '67 by the architect Buckminster Fuller. It is now a museum of the environment.

Tallest dam
The Itaipú Dam on the Paraná River between Brazil and Paraguay (1984) is 7,235 m (23,737 ft) long and 225 m (738 ft) high.

Biggest particle accelerator
CERN's Large Hadron Collider (2008) on the France/Switzerland border, is 27 km (17 miles) in circumference.

See also
Holy places: page 162

The O_2 (formerly the Millennium Dome), London, UK

Biggest domes and roofs

In 1434, the Duomo Cathedral in Florence, Italy, had the largest dome in the world. It was 45.5 m (149.3 ft) across and was still the world's largest dome 400 years later.

The diameter of the O_2 is almost eight times greater, thanks to modern building techniques and materials. Some of the domes in the list below are supported by struts and cables, others are free-standing. Some can even be opened.

The O_2 (formerly the Millennium Dome), London, UK, was completed in 1999. It measures 358 m (1,175 ft) in diameter. The span is supported by steel masts that project through the dome.

Wembley Stadium, London, UK, was completed in 2007. It has the largest single-span roof in the world (supported only at the sides). It measures 315 m (1,033 ft) in diameter.

The Georgia Superdome, Atlanta, Georgia, USA was completed in 1992 with a diameter of 256 m (840 ft). It has the world's largest cable-supported fabric roof.

The Fantasy Entertainment Complex, Kyosho, Japan, was completed in 2002. It has a diameter of 216 m (710 ft).

The Houston Astrodome, Houston, Texas, USA, was completed in 1966. It measures 216 m (710 ft) in diameter.

The Louisiana Superdome, New Orleans, Louisiana, USA, was completed in 1975. It measures 207 m (680 ft) in diameter.

SkyDome, Toronto, Canada, was completed in 1989 with a diameter of 205 m (674 ft). It has the world's largest retractable roof.

The Multi-Purpose Arena, Nagoya, Japan, was completed in 1997. It measures 187 m (614 ft) in diameter.

Tacoma Dome, Tacoma, Washington, USA, was completed in 1983 with a diameter of 162 m (532 ft).

The Superior Dome, Marquette, Michigan, USA, was completed in 1991 and has a diameter of 160 m (523 ft).

Obelisks and columns

Obelisks are stone columns made in ancient Egypt almost 4,000 years ago. Some were taken as trophies by invading armies and are now in cities such as Istanbul, Rome, London, Paris and New York. More recently, people have built memorials based on the design of obelisks.

- A column commemorating the battle of San Jacinto (1836) near Houston, Texas, USA, is the world's tallest monument at 174 m (570 ft). It was completed in 1939.
- The Washington Monument, Washington DC, USA, was completed in 1884. It is 169 m (555 ft) tall, made of 36,491 stone blocks on an iron frame and weighs 82,421 tonnes. It was the world's tallest structure for five years until it was overtaken by the Eiffel Tower in 1889.
- The Wellington Monument in Dublin, Ireland is a stone obelisk made to celebrate the victories of the Duke of Wellington. It was completed in 1861 and is Europe's tallest obelisk at 63 m (206 ft).
- The Monument in London commemorates the Great Fire of London in 1666. It was built in 1667 and is 62 m (202 ft) tall.
- Nelson's Column in Trafalgar Square, London, was completed in 1842 to celebrate Britain's great naval commander. The column is 44 m (145 ft) high and has a 5 m (17 ft) statue of Nelson on top.
- The tallest Egyptian obelisk is in the Piazza San Giovanni in Laterano, Rome, Italy. It measures 32 m (106 ft). The tallest still in Egypt is in Karnak and is 30 m (97 ft) tall. The ancient Egyptian obelisk in New York is 22 m (73 ft) and the London obelisk, Cleopatra's Needle, is 21 m (69 ft).

Modern pyramids

The ancient Egyptian pyramids are the best known, but this style of building has also been used in modern times.

"Mad Jack" Fuller's tomb, Brightling, East Sussex. Jack Fuller, an eccentric landowner and Member of Parliament, had his own 8 m (25 ft) pyramid tomb built in 1811. It is said that his body is inside, wearing a top hat!

Louvre Museum Pyramid, Paris, France The architect I.M. Pei designed the 22 m (71 ft) glass pyramid which was built in 1989 as the main entrance to the Louvre Museum, Paris, France.

Christa McAuliffe Planetarium, Concord, New Hampshire, USA Christa McAuliffe was killed in the *Challenger* space shuttle disaster. The pyramid-shaped planetarium named after her opened in 1990.

Luxor Hotel and Casino, Las Vegas, Nevada, USA This was opened in 1993. It is 107 m (350 ft)-tall and at its entrance is a sphinx that shoots laser beams from its eyes.

Rainforest Pyramid, Galveston, Texas, USA This 38 m (125 ft)-tall pyramid, finished in 1993, houses one of the world's largest indoor rainforests.

Tallest skyscrapers over the last 100 years

New York's 119.2 m (391 ft) Park Row Building was the tallest office or apartment building in the world when it was completed in 1899. Since then it has been overtaken many times by the progressively taller skyscrapers on this list. The latest world record-holder, the Burj Dubai, is almost seven times as tall as the Park Row Building.

	Building	Year completed	Floors	Height m/ft*	
1	Burj Dubai, Dubai, UAE	2009	162	818.0	2,684.0
2	Taipei 101, Taipei, Taiwan	2004	101	509.2	1,670.6
3	Petronas Tower, Kuala Lumpur, Malaysia	1996	88	451.9	1,482.6
4	Sears Tower, Chicago, USA	1974	108	442.0	1,450.1
5	One World Trade Center, New York, USA#	1972	110	417.0	1,368.1
6	Empire State Building, New York, USA	1931	102	381.0	1,250.0
7	Chrysler Building, New York, USA	1930	77	318.8	1,045.9
8	The Trump Building, New York, USA	1929	71	282.5	926.8
9	Woolworth Building, New York, USA	1913	59	241.4	792.0
10	Metropolitan Life, New York, USA	1909	50	213.4	700.1

* Excluding masts, etc

Destroyed in terrorist attack of 11 September 2001

See also
Art Deco: page 199

Buildings that never were

Architects have often come up with exciting plans for fantasy buildings that in reality were too big, too difficult, too expensive, or often just too crazy ever to be built.

- In 1829 Thomas Willson announced his plans for a giant Pyramid to be built in London. It was to be taller than St Paul's' cathedral and bigger than the Great Pyramid in Egypt, but it was to contain not one, but 5,167,104 tombs, to relieve the pressure on London's cemeteries. It was never built.
- In 1956 American architect Frank Lloyd Wright designed The Illinois, a mile-high (1,731.1-m/5,680 -ft) skyscraper with 528 floors to be built in Chicago.

- In the 1980s, the US company Domino's Pizza commissioned a design for a 30-storey office skyscraper that deliberately sloped at 15 degrees. It was never built, but was immediately nicknamed 'The Leaning Tower of Pizza'.
- X-Seed 4000 designed in Tokyo, Japan, in 1995, was a single building shaped like a volcano and bigger than Mount Fuji, at 4,000 m (13,123 ft) high, with 800 floors rising from the sea. It was so large that it would function as a city of up to a million people.

Chrysler Building

The Chrysler Building in New York held the record as the world's tallest for just 338 days, from 28 May 1930 to 1 May 1931, when the Empire State Building overtook it. Since the destruction of the twin towers of the World Trade Center in 2001, the two buildings were again the city's tallest and second tallest, but in 2009 the Chrysler Building was pushed into third place with the completion of the 366-m (1,200-ft) Bank of America Tower.

What is a skyscraper?

There is no official definition of 'skyscraper', other than it has to be habitable by humans, so masts, towers, chimneys and tombs do not qualify. The Equitable Life Building in New York, USA, built in 1870 and destroyed by fire in 1912, was only 40 m (130 ft) high - a third of that of the Great Pyramid – but is considered the world's first skyscraper.

Tallest masts and towers

The world's tallest mast (a metal antenna supported by steel guy ropes, rather than a freestanding structure like a skyscraper) is the 629-m (2,063-ft) KVLY-TV mast in Blanchard, North Dakota, USA, which has stood since 1963. In 1974, it was overtaken by the Warsaw, Poland, radio mast which was the world's tallest structure at 646 m (2,121 ft) until it collapsed on 8 August 1991, since when the KVLY-TV mast has once again held the record. The tallest tower (a self-supporting structure, but not habitable) is the 553-m (1,815-ft) CN Tower in Toronto, Canada, completed in 1976 and with an observation deck at 342 m (1,122 ft). While it was being built, it overtook the 540-m (1,772 ft) Ostankino Tower, Moscow, Russia, which had held the record from 1967–75.

A view of the skyscrapers of Hong Kong from Victoria's Peak

The Empire State Building

New York's tallest building is the Empire State Building, which stands on Fifth Avenue, New York, between 33rd Street and 34th Street. It was built on the site of the Waldorf-Astoria Hotel and took 410 days at a rate of 4½ floors a week to complete. The building was opened on 1 May 1931 by remote control, when President Herbert Hoover pressed a button in Washington DC.

The Empire State Building towers 381 m (1,250 ft) above ground – and measures 443.2 m (1,454.1 ft) to the top of the TV tower. A further 16.7 m (54.8 ft) is below ground. The spire on top was designed as an airship mooring mast, but after a German airship, the *Hindenburg*, burned at its mooring mast in New Jersey in 1937, the mast was never used. For more than 40 years, the Empire State held the record as the world's tallest office or apartment building, until the twin towers of the World Trade Center were completed. Since their destruction in 2001, it is once again New York's tallest. More than 2.5 million tourists a year go up to the observatories on the 86th and 102nd floors.

- The workforce – 3,400 at its peak – took seven million man-hours to complete the building.
- The cost was $40,948,900 including the land (the building cost only $24,718,000).
- It weighs 331,122 tonnes, including a 54,431-tonne steel frame, 10 million bricks and 662 tonnes of aluminium and stainless steel.
- The Empire State is served by 73 lifts and contains 3,194,547 light bulbs, 80 km (49.7 miles) of radiator pipes and 113 km (70.2 miles) of water pipes.
- The lightning conductor was struck 68 times in the building's first ten years.
- In 2003 Australian runner Paul Crake broke his own record for racing up the 1,575 steps to the 86th floor in 9 min 33 sec.
- On 28 July 1945, a B-25 bomber crashed in fog between the building's 78th and 79th floors, killing the pilot and 13 other people. It happened on a Saturday so most offices were empty, or the casualties would have been higher.
- On St Valentine's Day, couples can marry on the 80th floor.
- The building's coloured lights are changed for seasonal celebrations. They are red, white and blue on Independence Day and green on St Patrick's Day. The lights are turned off when birds are migrating to avoid confusing them.

Bridge types

Arch An arch bridge is a very strong curved structure made of stone, concrete or steel. It is firmly supported on both sides.

Bascule A bascule bridge has a central section that opens to allow tall ships to pass. London's Tower Bridge is one of the most famous bascule bridges.

Beam A beam bridge is supported by the shore at both ends. This is the simplest and oldest type of bridge – a log across a stream is a very simple beam bridge. It is not very strong and may need to be strengthened by supports underneath.

Cantilever This type of bridge has two long arms held in place at the ends by anchors. Some can swing to let large ships through. Cantilever bridges are closest in length to suspension bridges.

Suspension This bridge is supported by steel cables fixed to high towers on the banks. All the world's longest bridges are suspension bridges because they are very strong.

Swing A swing bridge can be swung to one side to allow ships through. The Gateshead Millennium Bridge across the Tyne is a unique swing bridge, which rotates upwards to allow boats to pass beneath.

Arch bridge

Bascule bridge

Beam bridge

Cantilever bridge

Suspension bridge

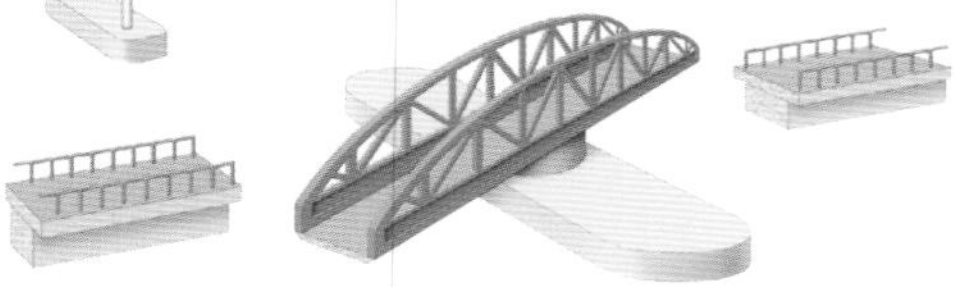

Swing bridge

Famous bridges

Pont d'Avignon, France
This bridge was built in the 12th century. It was made famous by the song "Sur le Pont d'Avignon" (On Avignon Bridge).

Bridge of Sighs, Venice, Italy
The Bridge of Sighs was designed in 1560. It connects the Doge's Palace with the city jail, and prisoners who had been sentenced to death had to cross the bridge to reach the jail. Its name is said to come from their sighs of despair.

Pont Neuf, Paris, France
Pont Neuf was completed in 1604. The bridge is in two halves and links the Right and Left Banks of the River Seine to Ile de la Cité, the island on which Notre Dame Cathedral stands.

Kintai-Kyo Bridge, Iwakuni, Japan
This wooden arch bridge was built across the Nishiki River in 1673. It has been damaged and rebuilt many times.

Iron Bridge, Shropshire
The Iron Bridge was completed in 1781 and was the first bridge built of iron.

Longest bridges 200 BC

All these bridges were the world's longest when they were built. Today's longest, the Akashi-Kaikyo in Japan, is nearly 54 times longer than the Martorell bridge in Spain.

† No longer standing

217 BC Martorell, Spain
A stone arch bridge with a span of 37 m (121 ft)

27 BC Augustus, Narni, Italy
A stone arch bridge with a span of 43 m (142 ft)

AD 104 Trajan, Danube, Romania
A timber arch bridge with stone piers and a span of 52 m (170 ft)

1371 Trezzo, Adda, Italy †
A stone arch bridge with a span of 72 m (236 ft)

1757 Schaffhausen, Switzerland †
A timber bridge with a span of 119 m (390 ft)

1816 Schuylkill Falls, Philadelphia, USA †
A suspension bridge with a span of 124 m (407 ft)

1820 Union/Tweed, Berwick, UK
An iron chain suspension bridge with a span of 137 m (449 ft)

1826 Menai Strait, Anglesey, UK
A chain suspension bridge with a span of 177 m (580 ft)

1834 Fribourg, Switzerland †
Wire-cable suspension bridge with a span of 273 m (896 ft)

1849 Wheeling, West Virginia, USA
A suspension bridge with a span of 308 m (1,010 ft) long

1851 Lewiston-Queenston, Niagara, USA
A suspension bridge with a span of 318 m (1,043 ft)

The Millau Viaduct, France, is the world's tallest bridge

Road and rail tunnels

The first tunnel built specially for passenger trains was the 766 m (2,513 ft) Tyler Hill Tunnel in Kent, UK. It opened on 4 May 1830. The first underwater rail tunnel was the Thames Tunnel, London, UK, which opened in 1869.

Some of the most amazing tunnels are made under the sea. The Seikan tunnel was built to link the Japanese islands of Honshu and Hokkaido; 23.3 km (14.5 miles) is below the sea bed. The Channel Tunnel has 38 km (23.6 miles) under the sea. The tunnels listed are all for railways.

Longest tunnels

1 Gotthard Base Tunnel (Alp Transit Link) Switzerland, 2018* will be 57.07 km (35.46 miles)
2 Seikan Japan, 1988 is 53.85 km (33.46 miles)
3 Channel Tunnel France/England, 1994 is 50.45 km (31.35 miles)
4 Moscow Metro (Serpukhovsko-Timiryazevskaya line) Russia, 1983 is 38.90 km (24.17 miles)
5 Lötschberg Base Tunnel Switzerland, 2007 is 34.58 km (21.49 miles)
6 Guadarrama Spain, 2007 is 28.38 km (17.63 miles)
7 Taihang China, 2008 is 27.9 km (17.4 miles)
8 London Underground (East Finchley/Morden, Northern Line) UK, 1939 is 27.84 km (17.29 miles)
9 Hakkoda Japan, 2010* will be 26.46 km (16.44 miles)
10 Iwate Japan, 2002 is 25.81 km (16.04 miles)
* Still being built

Kintai-Kyo Bridge

The bridge, which crosses the Nishiki River at Iwakini, Japan, is one of the world's oldest surviving wooden bridges, although it has been damaged by flooding and restored many times. It has five arches mounted on stone piers and a total length of 175 m (574 ft).

Iron Bridge, Shropshire
The Iron Bridge was completed in 1781 and was the first bridge built of iron.

Tower Bridge, London
Tower Bridge was completed in 1894. It opens and lifts in the middle to allow tall ships to pass underneath.

Brooklyn Bridge, New York, USA
After many setbacks, Brooklyn Bridge was finally opened in 1883. For a short time it was the world's longest bridge.

Sydney Harbour Bridge, Sydney, Australia
Sydney Harbour Bridge was built in 1932 to carry road and rail traffic across the harbour. It is a famous feature of the Sydney harbour skyline.

Kintai-Kyo Bridge, Japan

1990s

1867 The Cincinnati-Ohio River, Covington, USA
A suspension bridge with a span of 322 m (1,057 ft)

1869 Niagara-Clifton, Niagara, USA/Canada †
A suspension bridge with a span of 387 m (1,268 ft)

1883 Brooklyn, New York
A suspension bridge with a span of 486 m (1,596 ft)

1890 Firth of Forth Rail, Scotland
A cantilever bridge with a span of 521 m (1,710 ft) long

1917 Quebec Rail, Canada
A cantilever bridge with a span of 549 m (1,800 ft)

1929 Ambassador, Detroit, USA/Windsor, Canada
A suspension bridge with a span of 564 m (1,850 ft) long

1931 George Washington, New York
A suspension bridge with a span of 1,067 m (3,500 ft)

1937 Golden Gate, San Francisco, USA
A suspension bridge with a span of 1,280 m (4,200 ft)

1964 Verazzano Narrows, New York, USA
A suspension bridge with a span of 1,298 m (4,260 ft)

1980 Humber Estuary, Hull, UK
A suspension bridge with a span of 1,410 m (4,626 ft)

1997 East Bridge, Denmark
A suspension bridge with a span of 1,624 m (5,328 ft)

1998 Akashi-Kaikyo, Japan
A suspension bridge with a span of 1,991 m (6,532 ft)

See also
Rail Transport: pages 214–15

The Seven Wonders of the ancient world

Early Greek writers drew up lists of the most important buildings in the world they knew. Of these only the Great Pyramid survives, but we know about the others from writers' accounts and archaeologists.

The Great Pyramid of Giza
The Great Pyramid of Giza, Egypt, is the oldest, and the only one of the Seven Wonders to survive. It was made as a tomb for King Khufu, who ruled Egypt from about 2551 to 2528 BC, and it is the largest stone structure ever built. Its sides are 230 m (754 ft) long and it covers an area the size of 200 tennis courts.

The Hanging Gardens of Babylon
The legendary gardens of King Nebuchadnezzar II may not have existed. Some people believe they were created in about 600 BC in Babylon, 88 km (55 miles) south of present-day Baghdad, the capital of Iraq. "Hanging" suggests that they were a series of terraces made of bricks, some glazed and brightly coloured.

The Statue of Zeus at Olympia
This was an enormous statue of the Greek god, carved by the sculptor Phidias. It was inside the Temple of Zeus, built about 466–456 BC. The statue was 13 m (43 ft) high and one of the largest indoor sculptures ever made. Today little remains of the temple and nothing of the statue.

The Temple of Artemis
The Temple of Artemis at Ephesus, Turkey, was built to honour the Greek goddess of hunting and nature. The temple was completed in 550 BC. It was the largest of all ancient Greek buildings and measured 114 by 55 m (375 x 180 ft). Archaeologists have found the foundations and some columns of this ancient wonder.

The Mausoleum at Halicarnassus
This was the tomb of Persian ruler Mausolus, who ruled part of the Persian empire from 377 to 353 BC. Halicarnassus (modern-day Bodrum) in Turkey was his capital. After his death his widow built this magnificent tomb, which measured 105 by 242 m (344 x 794 ft) and was 43 m (140 ft) high. It was damaged by an earthquake and demolished in 1522. The word mausoleum has come to mean any great tomb.

The Colossus of Rhodes
The huge statue of sun god Helios stood in Rhodes harbour, Greece. In 305–304 BC warrior king Demetrius Poliorcetes attacked the city of Rhodes. When he abandoned his siege, the people built the giant statue as an offering to the god Helios. It took 12 years to build and stood 33 m (110 ft) high, but in 226 BC it was destroyed by an earthquake.

See also
Chinese Empire: page 106

The Great Wall of China can be seen from space.

The Great Pyramid of Giza and the Sphinx

The Pharos of Alexandria

This was a lighthouse off the coast of the city of Alexandria. Work started on it in about 299 BC and it took about 20 years to build. It was 124 m (407 ft) tall – the tallest lighthouse ever made. It was damaged by earthquakes and in 1375 toppled into the sea. A few remains have been found.

Seven modern wonders

There are many candidates for this list and here is a selection.

Hoover Dam, USA
When it was built in 1936, the 221 m (725 ft) high Hoover Dam was the largest in the world. A record 3.63 million m^3 (128.19 million ft^3) of concrete were used to make the structure, which controls the flooding of the Colorado River.

Deltawerken flood barrier, Netherlands
After a disastrous flood in 1953, engineer Johan van Veen designed the Delta Project, or Deltawerken. This is a series of interconnected dams that forms a movable sea barrier while preserving the habitat and sea life within it.

Kansai International Airport, Japan
This airport was opened in 1994. It stands on a 4 x 1.2 km (2.5 x 0.75 miles) island which is entirely man-made. It was built with 48,000 huge blocks, made from earth excavated by flattening three mountains, and designed to withstand typhoons and earthquakes. Its terminal building was designed by Italian architect Renzo Piano.

Channel Tunnel, England/France
Work on the second longest underwater rail tunnel in the world began in 1987. It took seven years and 15,000 workers to create the 50.45 km (31.35 miles) tunnel (38 km [23.6 miles] under sea), which opened in 1994. The tunnel links Folkestone in England to Sangatte, France.

Guggenheim Museum, Bilbao, Spain
The Guggenheim was built in 1997 to the design of Canadian-born architect Frank Gehry. It houses a collection of modern art in a striking, ultra-modern setting. The structure combines limestone blocks of varied shapes, curved sections covered in panels of titanium (a light, strong metal) and large areas of glass.

The Eden Project, Cornwall, UK
About 1.8 million tonnes of earth were moved to make the foundations for the world's largest greenhouses. These are a series of domes, each devoted to a particular type of climate, and housing 100,000 plants. The Eden Project was designed by Nicholas Grimshaw and opened in 2001. It is one of the UK's most popular tourist attractions.

Panama Canal, Panama
It took 34 years, from 1880 to 1914, to build the ship canal that connects the Atlantic and Pacific Oceans. The 77-km (48-mile) canal was a remarkable feat of engineering, but cost the lives of up to 27,500 workers.

Leaning Tower of Pisa

The Seven Wonders of the medieval world

People have never been able to agree on the Seven Wonders of the medieval world, and this is just one of several lists that have been made. It includes the Leaning Tower of Pisa (pictured right). In 2007, an organization produced a new list of Seven Wonders, according to a voting system, that included the Colosseum and the Great Wall of China, along with the Taj Mahal, India, Chichén Itzá, Mexico, Macchu Picchu, Peru, Petra, Jordan and the statue of Christ the Redeemer, Rio de Janeiro, which was completed as recently as 1931.

Stonehenge
The circle of huge stones was built in stages from about 3000 BC. The origin of the stones, how they were transported and the purpose of the site remain a mystery. It was possibly some sort of ancient observatory.

The Great Wall of China
This was a defensive wall designed to protect China from its warlike neighbours to the north. It was built in stages after 220 BC, using a huge labour force of as many as 300,000 workers. The main part is 3,460 km (2,150 miles) long and wide enough for an army to march along it ten abreast.

The Colosseum, Rome, Italy
This amphitheatre was opened in AD 80 with a huge spectacle lasting 100 days. It is oval and measures 48 m (157 ft) high, 188 m (617 ft) long and 156 m (512 ft) wide. It could hold up to 50,000 spectators and could be flooded for re-enactments of sea battles.

The Catacombs of Alexandria (Kom El Shoqafa), Egypt
These Roman tombs beneath the city of Alexandria, Egypt, were discovered in 1900 when a donkey fell into them. The beautifully preserved, carved catacombs had been made in solid rock during the 2nd century AD.

Hagia Sophia, Istanbul, Turkey
Hagia Sophia (Holy Wisdom), Istanbul, Turkey, was originally built in AD 360 by the Emperor Constantius. It was later rebuilt as one of the world's finest churches, with many mosaics and ornate details. In 1453 the church was converted into an Islamic mosque.

The Porcelain Pagoda of Nanking, China
The Porcelain Pagoda was built in about 1412 by Emperor Yung-lo. It was an eight-sided structure covered in glazed tiles, and soared to 79 m (260 ft). It was destroyed during a rebellion in 1853.

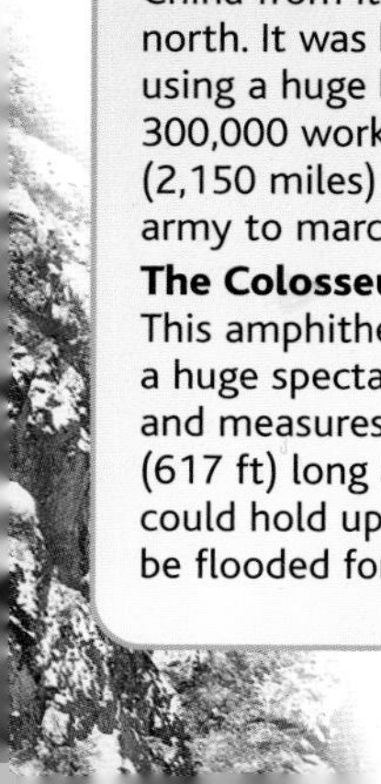

Leaning Tower of Pisa

Building began on the bell tower of Pisa Cathedral, Italy, in 1173. Soon the foundations began to sink on one side. The design was adjusted, but by the time the tower had reached its full height of 55 m (179 ft) it was leaning sharply. The tilt increased over the centuries and it is amazing that the 14,000-tonne structure is still standing.

Transport & Travel

Electric car

Hailed by *Time* magazine as one of the 50 Best Inventions of 2009, carmaker Nissan's LEAF, which stands for '**L**eading, **E**nvironmentally **F**riendly, **A**ffordable, **F**amily Car' went into production in 2010. It is a 5-seater all-electric hatchback with a range of over 160 km (100 miles) and a top speed of 140 km/h (87 mph). It is powered by batteries that can be recharged from a household electric supply and produces zero emissions.

Types of ship

There are many different types of passenger and commercial ships:

Barge
This name is used for various types of ship, ranging from a slow canal boat to a small sailing cargo boat or a decorated rowing boat used by royalty.

Clipper
A 19th-century sailing ship with a large sail area designed to transport cargo long distances at speed.

Container ship
A cargo ship designed to carry standard-sized containers, making it easy to load and unload.

Ferry
A ship that takes passengers and vehicles from one port to another.

Galleon
A medieval sailing ship. The word was first used in 1529.

Galley
An ancient warship driven by oars. Biremes have oars on two levels, and triremes on three.

Hydrofoil
A boat with a special device to lift its hull out of the water, so increasing speed.

Junk
A high-sterned (the stern is the aft or back end), flat-bottomed, Chinese or Japanese sailing ship with two or three masts.

Liner or cruise ship
An ocean-going ship once used to take passengers on long journeys, such as across the Atlantic. Cruise ships are luxury liners designed to take people on pleasure cruises.

Oil tanker
A large vessel that carries oil from oil fields to refineries in other countries.

Yacht
A sailing or engine-powered ship used for pleasure cruises or racing.

Catamarans

Racing catamarans are very fast – in 2005, French yachtsman Bruno Peyron and a 13-man crew sailed the 36.8-m (120.7-ft) catamaran *Orange II* round the world in a record time of 50 days 16 hours 20 minutes, winning the Jules Verne Trophy for the fastest circumnavigation.

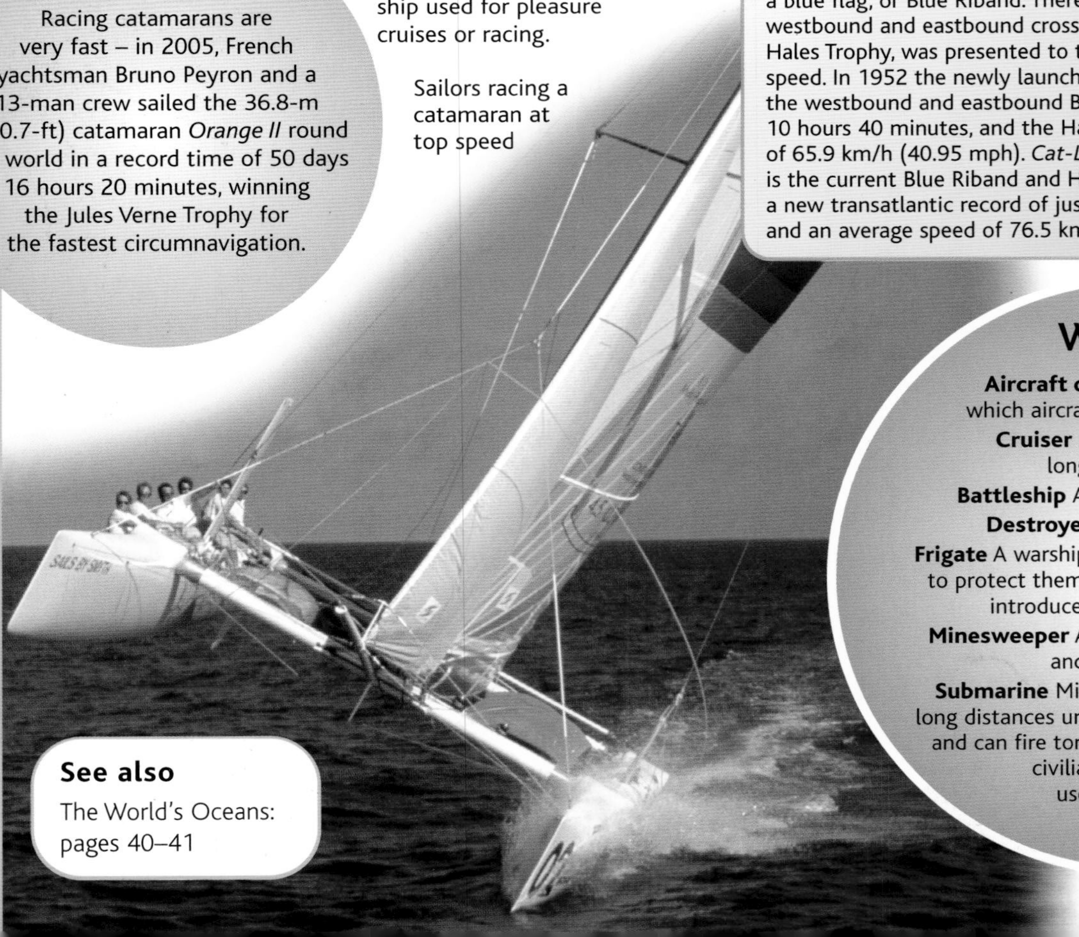

Sailors racing a catamaran at top speed

Top speeds

Rowing eight
The Oxford and Cambridge Boat Race is rowed annually on the River Thames, London, and covers 6.8 km (4.25 miles). The Cambridge crew won in 1998 in a record time of 16 minutes 19 seconds, equivalent to a speed of 25 km/h (15.5 mph).

Aircraft carrier
The US Navy's Nimitz class nuclear-powered aircraft carriers can travel at more than 56 km/h (34.8 mph).

Submarine (submerged)
Russian Alfa class nuclear submarines could probably travel at 83.4 km/h (51.8 mph), but these are no longer in use. US Navy Los Angeles class subs are said to achieve 74 km/h (46 mph), but the precise figures are military secrets.

Sailing vessel
During the 19th century clippers could average 36.63 km/h (22.76 mph). The modern sailing yacht record is held by Simon McKeon and Tim Daddo of Australia. On 26 October 1993 they sailed their yacht *Yellow Pages Endeavour* at 86.21 km/h (53.57 mph).

Car ferry
The catamaran *Luciano Federico L* (1997) carries 52 cars and 446 passengers between Buenos Aires, Argentina, and Montevideo, Uruguay, at a top speed of 107 km/h (66.5 mph).

Hovercraft
On 25 January 1980 a US Navy Bell SES-1008 experimental vehicle achieved a speed of 170 km/h (105.6 mph).

Hydroplane
These super-fast racing motor boats are capable of great speeds: Dave Villwock set a record average speed of 343.5 km/h (213.4 mph) in *Miss Budweiser* at Oroville, California, USA, on 13 March 2004.

Ocean liners
Steam ships began carrying passengers across the Atlantic between Europe and the USA in 1838. In the early years, the journey (about 4,828 km [3,000 miles]) could take 18 days or longer. Shipping companies competed with each other and the fastest ship carried a blue flag, or Blue Riband. There were separate Blue Ribands for westbound and eastbound crossings, and after 1934 an award, the Hales Trophy, was presented to the ship with the fastest average speed. In 1952 the newly launched liner *SS United States* won both the westbound and eastbound Blue Riband with a time of 3 days 10 hours 40 minutes, and the Hales Trophy with an average speed of 65.9 km/h (40.95 mph). *Cat-Link V*, a Danish catamaran ferry, is the current Blue Riband and Hales Trophy holder. In 1998, it set a new transatlantic record of just 2 days, 20 hours and 9 minutes, and an average speed of 76.5 km/h (47.5 mph).

Warships

Aircraft carrier A warship from which aircraft can take off and land.

Cruiser A medium-sized, fast, long-range warship.

Battleship A large armoured warship.

Destroyer A small fast warship.

Frigate A warship that escorted cargo convoys to protect them from attack by submarines, introduced during World War II.

Minesweeper A naval ship designed to find and destroy mines.

Submarine Military submarines can travel long distances under water to avoid detection, and can fire torpedoes and missiles. Special civilian submarines are used for undersea research.

See also
The World's Oceans: pages 40–41

Biggest ships

All the ships listed here held the record as the biggest ship in the world when they were launched. The first purpose-built Atlantic steamship, the *Great Western*, was less than 1/5 the length and 1/164 the tonnage of the newly-launched *Oasis* class ships. Other record holders have also been overtaken by a large margin – the *Titanic*, for example, was less than 1/5 the tonnage, despite being almost 3/4 the length, of the giant *Oasis* cruise ships. Some of these ships are still sailing, but many have been scrapped. The *Titanic* and *Lusitania* sank with the loss of many lives.

Great Western (launched in1838) gross tonnage*: 1,340
President (1840) gross tonnage: 2,360
Great Britain (1845) gross tonnage: 3,448
Great Eastern (1858) gross tonnage: 18,914
Oceanic (1899) gross tonnage: 17,274
Baltic (1904) gross tonnage: 23,884
Lusitania (1907) gross tonnage: 31,550
Mauretania (1907) gross tonnage: 31,938
Titanic (1912) gross tonnage: 46,232
Bismarck/Majestic/Caledonia†, (1922) gross tonnage: 56,621
Normandie/Lafayette† (1935) gross tonnage: 79,301
Queen Elizabeth (1938) gross tonnage: 83,673
Voyager of the Seas (1999) gross tonnage: 137,276
Explorer of the Seas (2000) gross tonnage: 137,308
Navigator of the Seas (2002) gross tonnage: 138,279
Queen Mary 2 (2003) gross tonnage: 142,200
Liberty of the Seas (2007) gross tonnage: 160,000
***Oasis* class** (2009–) gross tonnage: 220,000

* Weights given are the weight of the ship when empty, without cargo, crew, supplies or passengers.
† Renamed

Oasis of the Seas is the largest cruise ship afloat

World's biggest ship

Twin *Oasis* class ships *Oasis of the Seas* (launched 2008, maiden voyage 2009) and *Allure of the Seas* (scheduled for completion in 2010) are the biggest cruise ships ever. Built in Finland, they are 16 decks high and 360 m (1,181 ft) long. They carry 5,400 passengers and have such facilities as gardens, four swimming pools, a basketball court and a golf course.

Famous ships

Some ships, such as the *Titanic*, are famous because they sank, but here are some famous ships that are celebrated for a variety of other reasons.

Niña, Pinta and Santa Maria
The three ships on Christopher Columbus's voyage of 1492 to America.

Mayflower
The ship that took the settlers known as the Pilgrim Fathers from Plymouth to America in 1620.

Endeavour
Captain James Cook's ship on his exploration of Australia and New Zealand in 1768–71.

Bounty
The crew of this British ship mutinied against Captain William Bligh in 1789.

Victory
Captain Horatio Nelson's flagship at the Battle of Trafalgar, 1805. It is now on display in Portsmouth.

Beagle
The research ship on which British scientist Charles Darwin visited the Galápagos Islands in 1835.

Cutty Sark
A tea clipper (a sailing ship designed to bring tea from China as fast as possible) launched in 1869. The ship is preserved in dry dock at Greenwich, London and was seriously damaged by fire in 2007.

Replica of the *Mayflower*, moored in Plymouth, Massachusetts

Great Eastern
This ship was designed by Isambard Kingdom Brunel and launched in 1858. It laid the first transatlantic cable in 1866, but was scrapped in 1888.

Marie Celeste
A US ship found abandoned in the Atlantic in 1872. The fate of its crew remains a mystery.

Kon-Tiki
A balsawood raft on which Norwegian anthropologist Thor Heyerdahl sailed from South America across the Pacific to Polynesia in 1947. He made the voyage to prove his theory that Polynesian people came from South America.

Famous cars

● Mercedes
The German luxury car manufacturer was a brand of the Daimler company, later called Mercedes-Benz. It has used its familiar 3-pointed star logo since 1909.

● Rolls-Royce
British car enthusiasts Henry Royce and Charles Rolls joined forces to form Rolls-Royce in 1906 and set new standards for a luxury vehicle. The company's engines are also used in many of the world's aircraft.

● Model T Ford
The first Model T Ford, nicknamed the Tin Lizzie, was made in the USA in 1908 by the Ford Motor Company, which was founded in 1903 by Henry Ford. By 1927, when production finished, a total of 16,536,075 had been built. At one point, more than half the new cars in the world were Model Ts.

● Aston Martin
This luxury sports car has been made in the UK since the 1920s. It became one of the most featured and gadget-laden cars in the James Bond films.

● Bugatti Royale
Only six Bugatti Royales (1926) were ever made. The Royale was designed by Italian Ettore Bugatti and was one of the largest vehicles of all time. It was 6.7 m (22 ft) long with a 12.7 litre (777 in^3) engine originally designed for aircraft. In 1980 one of these rare vehicles set a new world record price when it was sold for $15 million (£9.1 million).

● Volkswagen Beetle
The Volkswagen Beetle was designed by Ferdinand Porsche and first manufactured

James Bond's Aston Martin

Top vehicle-owning countries

There are so many cars today that there is one car for every 9.9 people in the world. In the USA there are 2.2 people per car and in the UK 2.0, but in some countries the ratio is amazingly high. In Myanmar, for example, there are more than 5,777 people per car!

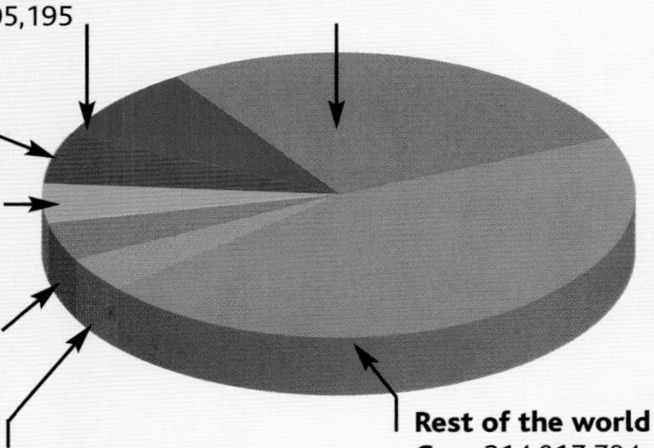

Car timeline

1800s

1883 First experimental petrol-driven car (France)
1886 Karl Benz and Gottlieb Daimler (Germany) build first cars
1892 First US car built by Charles and Frank Duryea
1893 Rudolf Diesel patents engine
1894 First cars in UK
1895 First car race, Paris-Bordeaux-Paris, France, 1,178 km (732 miles)
1895 First car show in UK
1895 Michelin (France) makes first pneumatic car tyres
1896 First car theft (France)
1896 First motoring death (UK)
1897 First woman driver in UK, Minnie Palmer
1898 First woman driver in USA, Genevra Mudge
1899 Jacob German arrested for speeding in New York (12 mph/ 19.3 km/h)
1900 8,000 vehicles on the road in USA

1900s

1903 First driving licences issued, Paris, France
1903 Registration plates in UK
1903 National speed limit in UK 20 mph (32 km/h)
1903 30,204 vehicles made in France, 11,235 USA, 9,437 UK
1904 28,842 vehicles in UK
1907 First Rolls-Royce made, the Silver Ghost (UK)
1908 First Model T Ford made (USA)
1909 143,000 vehicles in UK
1910 468,500 vehicles in USA
1912 First petrol station built (USA)
1915 Headlamp dipping and stoplights introduced (USA)
1919 Mechanical windscreen wipers developed (USA)
1921 First autobahn (high speed road or motorway) built in Germany
1922 A survey shows there are 12,588,949 motor vehicles in the world, of which 10,506,660 (83%) are in the USA.

in Germany in 1937. When production ended in 2003 a total of 21,529,464 Beetles had been made, the last of them in Brazil and Mexico. A new version of the Beetle was introduced in 1998. By its 10th anniversary in 2008, more than 1 million had been sold.

- **MINI**

The MINI was launched in the UK in August 1959, when it cost just under £500 ($1,400). It was designed by Alec Issigonis (1906–88). More than 6 million MINIs, including 1.4 million of the new model, launched in 2001, were sold up to its 50th anniversary in 2009.

Car name origins

Audi (1909) – it was founded by August Horsch, whose surname means 'hark', which in Latin is *audi*.

BMW (1916) – Bayerische Motoren Werke (Bavarian Motor Works).

Edsel (1957) – a car produced by Ford, named after founder Henry Ford's son Edsel Bryant Ford (1893–1943).

Mercedes (1901) – after Mercédès Jellinek (1889–1929), the daughter of Daimler car company director Emil Jellinek.

Volkswagen (1937) – from the German for 'people's car'.

Fastest car

ThrustSSC is the most powerful car ever built. It uses two Rolls-Royce engines from Phantom fighter aircraft. In 1997, driven by Royal Air Force fighter pilot Andy Green, *Thrust* set a new land speed record of 1,227.986 km/h (763.035 mph). It was also the first road vehicle to break the sound barrier.

See also
ThrustSSC: page 15

Amazing vehicles

- **Biggest dumper trucks**

The General Motors Terex Titan 33-19 mine truck, first made in 1974, can carry 317.5 tonnes. An average truck carries about 5 tonnes.

- **Biggest fire engines**

Fire trucks made by the Oshkosh Truck Corporation of Wisconsin, USA for airports have eight wheels, 860-horsepower engines and weigh 60 tonnes.

- **Longest limos**

The current record-holder, built by Jay Ohrberg of California, measures 30.5 m (100 ft) and has 26 wheels. It is so long that it has to be hinged in the middle to enable it to turn corners.

- **Biggest bus**

The articulated Super City Train Buses used in the Democratic Republic of Congo are 32.2 m (105.7 ft) long. They can carry 110 seated passengers and 140 standing in the first part, and 60 seated and 40 standing in the second, a total of 350 people.

- **Fastest electric car**

The *White Lightning Electric Streamliner* holds the official record for the fastest electric vehicle. In 1999, driven by Patrick Rummerfield (USA), it went at a speed of 395.133 km/h (245.524 mph). It is powered by two 200 horse-power motors and a 420 volt battery pack.

- **Biggest tyres**

The largest road vehicle tyres are 3.82 m (12.5 ft) in diameter. They are made by the Bridgestone Corporation, Tokyo, Japan, for giant dumper trucks. Normal car tyres are 60 cm (23.6 in) in diameter.

White Lightning

2000s

1930 First traffic light installed in New York
1933 First drive-in cinema built (USA)
1935 First parking meters installed in Oklahoma City, USA
1935 Driving tests introduced in UK
1939 3,148,000 vehicles in UK
1940 32,453,200 vehicles in USA
1955 Highway Code issued in UK
1958 First motorway built in UK (Preston by-pass)
1960 8,512,000 vehicles in UK
1960 73,868,600 vehicles in USA
1962 200 millionth car produced in USA
1969 Czechoslovakia becomes first country to make seat belts compulsory
1970 Unleaded fuel introduced in USA
1978 Bosch (Germany) patents first satellite navigation
1980 155,796,000 vehicles in USA
1980 19,199,000 vehicles in UK
1983 Seat belts made compulsory in UK
1985 Seat belts made compulsory in New York
2005 The Bugatti Veyron 16.4 is the fastest, most powerful and most expensive car ever built
2007 Tesla Roadster electric cars capable of 400 km (250 miles) on a single charge
2009 The Tata Nano, the world's cheapest car (£1,600/$2,500) goes on sale in India
2010 World motor vehicle production is cut and sales fall as a result of economic downturn

www.beaulieu.co.uk/motormuseum search

Types of train

Not all trains are the same: these are just some of the variations around the world.

Rubber-tyred metro
These electric trains run along a tracked roadway. They are quiet, can accelerate quickly and tackle slopes. They first ran in Paris in the 1950s and have been introduced in other French cities and Santiago, Chile, Mexico City, and Montreal, Canada.

Maglev
The name Maglev comes from the words magnetic and levitation. These trains do not run on a track, but float above it by means of magnetic repulsion. They can travel very smoothly at high speeds (up to 650 km/h (400 mph) – and use little energy. A new 160 km (99.4 miles) Maglev line is being built between Shanghai and Hangzhou, China – the first inter-city Maglev service.

Cog railway
Cog or rack-and-pinion railways are used in mountains. The train has a rotating cog wheel that meshes with a rack rail, so the train can climb steep slopes. Mount Pilatus in Switzerland, has the world's steepest. The Snowdon Mountain Railway in Wales is the only one of this type in the UK.

Monorail
A monorail train runs on a single rail, instead of on a track or two rails. It is either suspended from the rail or straddles it. The Tokyo Monorail in Japan carries 100 million passengers a year. There are also monorails in Malaysia, Australia and the USA.

Funicular

Funiculars (from the Latin *funiculus*, a thin rope) are designed to go up and down steep hills or mountains. Cars are drawn up by cables and descend by gravity. Funiculars are used in mountain and other resorts, and in hilly parts of cities, such as Montmartre in Paris, and Montjuic in Barcelona. The steepest passenger funicular is the Katoomba Scenic Railway in New South Wales, Australia.

Wellington Cable Car, a funicular railway in Wellington, New Zealand, opened in 1902 and was rebuilt in 1979

The Ghan on its first journey across Australia

One and only

The only time a train has been powered by fish was during a coal shortage in Turkestan in 1919. Dried fish, caught in the Aral Sea, were used as fuel. A total of almost 9,000 tonnes were used to stoke the train's boilers.

Famous trains

Orient Express
The Orient Express began trips from Paris, France, to Bulgaria on 5 October 1883 and from 1889 went as far as Constantinople (now Istanbul), Turkey. It was the first trans-European train and travelled a total of 2,736 km (1,700 miles) across six countries. It stopped running in 1977, but was re-launched five years later.

20th Century Limited
The luxurious 20th Century Limited ran between New York and Chicago from 1902 to 1967.

Trans-Siberian Express
The Trans-Siberian Express travels 9,297 km (5,777 miles) between Moscow and Vladivostok. The line opened in 1914 and is the world's longest continuous rail line.

Flying Scotsman
The Flying Scotsman provided a luxurious non-stop journey from King's Cross, London to Edinburgh, Scotland. It ran for 40 years, from 1923 until 1963.

Golden Arrow
From 1929 to 1971, the Golden Arrow ran from Victoria, London to Dover on the south coast of England. From there passengers could sail across the Channel and then take the French Flèche d'Or to Paris.

Blue Train
This is one of the world's most luxurious trains and it has operated between Cape Town and Tshwane (Pretoria), South Africa since 1939. The train, carriages and decor are mainly blue – hence the name.

Underground railways

An underground railway is an urban train line that runs mostly, or completely, underground. The world's first underground system was the London Metropolitan Line, opened between Bishop's Road, Paddington, and Farringdon Street, in 1863.

Steam trains were used on this and London's Circle Line, completed in 1884. They had a device to absorb smoke so that passengers were not suffocated in their gas-lit carriages. During the 1890s, several inventions made deep tunnelling, electric motors, electric lights and lifts or escalators possible. After that, underground railways in London and other countries were electrified.

First underground railways

London, UK opened 10 January 1863
Budapest, Hungary opened 2 May 1896
Glasgow, UK opened 14 December 1896
Boston, USA opened 1 September 1897
Paris, France opened 19 July 1900

Longest underground rail networks

City (stations)	Total track length km (miles)
London, UK (268)	408 (254)
New York, USA (468)	368 (229)
Madrid, Spain (231)	294 (183)
Moscow, Russia (177)	293 (182)
Seoul, South Korea (266)	287 (179)
Shanghai, China (162)	228 (142)
Paris, France (300)	214 (133)

Busiest underground systems

Annual passengers
Tokyo, Japan 2,916,000,000
Moscow, Russia 2,529,000,000
Seoul, South Korea 1,654,000,000
New York, USA 1,563,000,000
Mexico City, Mexico 1,417,000,000

Longest rail networks

These countries all have more than 10,000 km (6,214 miles) of railway. At the other end of the scale, Puerto Rico, Saint Christopher and Nevis, Paraguay and Nicaragua have less than 100 km (62 miles). Some countries have none at all.

USA: 226,612 km (140,810 miles)
Russia: 87,157 km (54,157 miles)
China: 75,438 km (46,875 miles)
India: 63,221 km (39,284 miles)
Germany: 48,215 km (29,959 miles)
Canada: 48,068 km (29,868 miles)
Australia: 38,550 km (23,954 miles)
Argentina: 31,902 km (19,823 miles)
France: 29,370 km (18,250 miles)
Brazil: 29,295 km (18,203 miles)
Japan: 23,474 km (14,586 miles)
Poland: 23,072 km (14,336 miles)
Ukraine: 22,473 km (13,964 miles)
South Africa: 20,872 km (12,969 miles)
Italy: 19,460 km (12,092 miles)
Mexico: 17,665 km (10,977 miles)
UK: 16,567 km (10,294 miles)
Spain: 14,974 km (9,304 miles)
Kazakhstan: 13,700 km (8,513 miles)
Sweden: 11,528 km (7,163 miles)
Romania: 11,385 km (7,074 miles)
World total: 1,370,782 km (851,764 miles)

Bullet Train
Japanese bullet trains (shinkansen) are the world's fastest scheduled rail services. They were introduced in 1964 to coincide with the Tokyo Olympic Games.

TGV
The French TGV (Train à Grande Vitesse, or high speed train) was launched in 1981 and is an electric train service between Paris and Lyon. A specially modified TGV, the Atlantique, set a world speed record of 515.3 km/h (320.2 mph) on 18 May 1990.

Eurostar
The Eurostar service was launched on 14 November 1994 to carry passengers between London, Paris and Brussels through the Channel Tunnel. It can reach speeds of 300 km/h (186 mph). In its first ten years it carried a total of 59 million passengers.

Ghan
The Ghan is the first rail service from Adelaide to Darwin on the north–south route across Australia. It was named after the camel trains that were once the only way to cross the desert. The first train ran in 2004. It had 43 carriages, measured more than 1 km (3,280 ft) in length, and carried 330 passengers.

www.nrm.org.uk search

Aviation firsts

First flight
Orville Wright (USA, 1871–1948) made the first ever flight, a distance of approximately 37 m (121 ft) at Kitty Hawk, North Carolina, USA, on 17 December 1903.

First Channel crossing
On 25 July 1909 Louis Blériot (France, 1872–1936) became the first person to fly across the English Channel, in a time of 37 minutes.

First flight in the UK
American-born showman and aviator Samuel Franklin Cody made the first flight in Britain, a distance of 424 m (1,360 ft), at Farnborough, Hampshire, on 16 October 1908. He was killed in a plane crash in 1913.

First non-stop Transatlantic flight
On 14–15 June 1919 John Alcock (UK, 1892–1919) and Arthur Whitten Brown (1886–1948) completed the first ever non-stop flight across the Atlantic, from Newfoundland to Ireland.

First solo Transatlantic flight
In his aircraft, *The Spirit of St Louis*, Charles Lindbergh (USA, 1902–74) became the first pilot to fly solo across the Atlantic, from New York to Paris, on 20–21 May 1927.

First non-stop US coast-to-coast flight
US pilots Oakley G. Kelly and John A. Macready flew a Fokker T-2 monoplane from New York to California, landing on 3 May 1923 after a 4,034-km (2,521-mile) flight lasting 26 hours 50 minutes.

First to fly over Mount Everest
In an expedition led by Douglas Douglas-Hamilton (then Lord Clydesdale, UK, 1903–73), two open-cockpit Westland biplanes flew over Everest on 3 April 1933.

First non-stop round-the-world
Dick Rutan (USA, 1938–) and Jeana Yeager (USA, 1952–) flew the *Voyager* aircraft round the world, a distance of 40,211 km (24,986 miles), on 14–23 December 1986.

Concorde

Concorde fact file

Concorde, the only passenger aircraft ever to fly faster than the speed of sound, was first named in a speech by General de Gaulle on 13 January 1963. The Anglo-French project began the following year.

- The first prototype Concorde was shown at the Toulouse Air Show on 11 December 1967.
- The first French flight took place on 2 March 1969.
- The first British flight took place on 9 April 1969.
- The first landing at London Heathrow was on 13 September 1970.
- The first Concorde landing in the USA was at Dallas-Fort Worth on 20 September 1973.
- The only Concorde crash was near Paris, 25 July 2000, when 109 passengers and crew and four people on the ground died.
- Concorde's last flight took place on 24 October 2004. All surviving BA and Air France Concordes are on public display in museums and airports in the USA, UK, France, Germany and Barbados.

Rocket man

On 26 September 2008 Swiss pilot and inventor Yves Rossy, nicknamed FusionMan, became the first ever to fly a jet-powered wing across the English Channel. He took off from an aircraft above Calais, France, and landed in Dover, UK, a distance of 35 km (miles), 13 minutes later, reaching a top speed of 299 km/h (186 mph) and landing by parachute.

Rocket man, Yves Rossy, crossing the English Channel

See also
Steve Fossett: page 153

Breaking the sound barrier

Charles "Chuck" Yeager became the first person to break the sound barrier on 14 October 1947. His Bell X-1 rocket plane was dropped from a carrier aircraft above Muroc Dry Lake, California. At 12,800 m (42,000 ft) he reached a speed of 1,078 km/h (670 mph). He did not break the air speed record because only aircraft that take off and land under their own power are eligible. The speed of sound is not fixed and varies according to height and air conditions. In dry air at sea level the speed of sound is 1,229 km/h (763.67 mph), but at high altitudes, where air density is less, it is lower.

High-level railway

The Qingzang railway from Beijing, China, to Lhasa, once the world's highest capital city, climbs to 5,072 m (16,640 ft) across the Tanggula Pass where the altitude is so thin that passengers are supplied with oxygen. The Fenghuoshan tunnel on this line is the world's highest at 4,905 m (16,093 ft) above sea level, which is higher than Mont Blanc, Europe's tallest mountain.

www.flyingmachines.org search

First manned balloon flights

The first balloons worked on the principle that when air is heated, it rises. They were filled with hot air by burning things under them, such as paper, straw and wool – and even old shoes and rotten meat!

The balloons often caught fire and once the air cooled, they quickly came down. Soon after the first hot-air flights, people realized that the gas hydrogen could be used instead. Hydrogen is the lightest of all elements – almost 15 times lighter than air. Gas balloons can also be filled with helium, which is not as light as hydrogen but does not catch fire so easily. Most balloons today use hot air made by burning propane gas.

The first hot-air balloon flight

The Montgolfier brothers, Joseph and Etienne, tested their first unmanned hot-air balloon on 5 June 1783. On 21 November 1783, François Laurent, Marquis d'Arlandes and Jean-François Pilâtre de Rozier took off from the Bois de Boulogne, Paris, in a Montgolfier hot-air balloon. They travelled about 9 km (5.6 miles) in 23 minutes.

First hydrogen balloon flight

On 1 December 1783, Jacques Alexandre César Charles and Nicholas-Louis Robert made the first flight in a hydrogen balloon. They took off from the Tuileries, Paris, watched by a crowd of 400,000, and travelled 43 km (27 miles) north to Nesle in about two hours. Charles then took off again alone, so was the first ever solo pilot.

First British flight

On 27 August 1784 James Tytler, a doctor and newspaper editor, took off in a home-made balloon from Comely Gardens, Edinburgh. He reached an altitude of 107 m (350 ft) in a 0.8 km (0.5 miles) hop.

First Channel crossing

On 7 January 1785 Jean-Pierre Blanchard made the first Channel crossing in a balloon with Dr John Jeffries (the first American to fly). They also carried the first airmail letter. As they lost height, they had to reduce weight, so they threw almost everything overboard – including their clothes!

First flight in the USA

On 9 January 1793 in Philadelphia, Blanchard made the first balloon flight in America. He took a small black dog with him as a passenger. The flight was watched by George Washington, who gave Blanchard a passport permitting his flight, which was the first pilot's licence and America's first airmail document.

First hot-air balloon flight

First non-stop solo flight

US adventurer Steve Fossett made the first non-stop solo and fastest round-the-world balloon flight, 19 June to 3 July 2002.

Shipwrecks

Shipping disasters as a result of collisions, storms, fires, explosions or military action are among the most famous of human tragedies. Some wrecks were carrying treasure that has since been recovered.

The *Mary Rose*, which sank in 1545

Mary Rose
This Tudor galleon sank in 1545 as Henry VIII watched from the shore. She was found in 1968, raised in 1982, and is exhibited in Portsmouth, UK.

Spanish Armada
Between August and October 1588 military action and storms combined to destroy the Spanish fleet off the British coast. About half the 130 ships that set out were wrecked, killing about 4,000 men.

St George, Defence and Hero
On 4 December 1811 these three British warships were stranded off the Jutland coast. More than 2,000 people died.

Tek Sing
This Chinese junk carrying 2,000 passengers and 350,000 pieces of porcelain sank in 1822. It was found in 1999 and its treasures sold for high prices.

Sultana
On 27 April 1865, the *Sultana*, a steamboat on the Mississippi River near Memphis, USA, was destroyed by a boiler explosion. This was the USA's worst ever marine accident and a total of 1,547 people died.

Princess Alice
On 3 September 1878 the pleasure steamer *Princess Alice* was taking people down the Thames in London. She collided with the *Bywell Castle* and 786 people died.

Titanic
On the night of 14 April 1912, the "unsinkable" *Titanic* struck an iceberg on its maiden voyage and sank the next day, killing 1,517. The wreck was discovered and explored by Robert Ballard in 1986.

Lusitania
The British liner was torpedoed off the Irish coast by a German U-boat on 7 May 1915, with the loss of 1,198 lives.

Wilhelm Gustloff
The German liner, laden with refugees, was torpedoed off Gdansk, Poland, on 30 January 1945 by a Soviet submarine, S-13. Between 5,348 and 7,800 people died, making this the worst ever marine disaster.

Dona Paz
The *Donna Paz* sank off the Philippines on 20 December 1987, killing up to 3,000 people. This was the world's worst passenger ferry disaster.

Kursk
This Russian nuclear submarine sank in the Barents Sea on 12 August 2000, with the loss of all 118 crew.

Rail disasters

Rail travel is one of the safest ways of journeying from place to place, taking into account the large numbers of passengers carried and distances travelled. But there have been accidents.

World's worst
At Telwatta, Sri Lanka, on 26 December, 2004, the *Queen of the Sea* train was struck by the Indian Ocean tsunami. The exact number killed is unknown, but is estimated to be between 1,700 and 2,000.

UK
On 22 May 1915 a troop train crashed head-on into another at Quintinshill near Gretna Green, Scotland. The wreckage was then struck by an express. The crashes and fire that followed left 227 dead and 246 injured.

USA
Two USA accidents resulted in 101 deaths. On 10 August 1887 a bridge at Chatsworth, Illinois caught fire and collapsed as a train was passing over. 101 people were killed and as many as 372 were injured. The second accident happened on 9 July 1918 at Nashville, Tennessee, when two trains collided head-on.

Underground
On 28 October 1995, at Baku, Azerbaijan, an underground train caught fire one evening killing more than 300 people.

British underground
Britain's worst tube disaster was on 8 March 1943 at Bethnal Green, London. About 173 people who were trying to enter the station during an air raid were killed in the crush.

American underground
America's worst subway accident was on 1 November 1918 at Brooklyn, New York. A train was derailed in the Malbone Street tunnel, leaving 97 dead.

Road disasters

Many people are killed and injured on the roads – more than 40,000 a year in the USA – but accidents involving more than a few drivers or pedestrians are rare.

Worst road disaster On 3 November 1982 a petrol tanker collided with a Soviet army truck and exploded in the 2.7 km (1.7 miles) Salang Tunnel in Afghanistan. At least 2,000, and perhaps as many as 3,000, people died as a result of the explosion, fire and fumes.

US road disaster The worst US road disaster took place on 15 December 1967. The Silver Bridge across the Ohio River from Kanauga, Ohio, to Point Pleasant, West Virginia, collapsed during heavy pre-Christmas rush hour traffic. About 60 vehicles plunged into the river and 46 people died.

British road accident On 27 May 1975 a coach crashed near Grassington, North Yorkshire, killing 33.

The Royal Tar

The paddle steamer Royal Tar was sailing off the coast of Maine, USA, on 25 October 1836 when it caught fire. As well as its crew of 21, it carried 70 passengers and a travelling circus of animals, including an elephant, lions, camels and snakes. In the chaos, lifeboats and a makeshift raft were launched, but as passengers attempted to board the raft the elephant jumped over the side, capsizing it. Some were rescued by another ship, but 32 died, along with all the animals.

Two hijacked planes crash into the World Trade Center, New York

Air disasters

Worst ever
Two terrorist attacks on the twin towers of the World Trade Center, New York, on 11 September 2001, killed everybody on both hijacked planes (92 on one and 65 on the other). More than 2,000 people also died in the buildings.

On the ground
On 27 March 1977, two Boeing 747s collided on the runway of Los Rodeos airport in Tenerife in the Canary Islands. The aircraft were carrying 614 passengers and 30 crew between them. A total of 61 people managed to escape.

Single-aircraft disaster
On 12 August 1985 a JAL Boeing 747 on an internal flight from Tokyo to Osaka crashed, killing 520.

Mid-air collision
At Charkhi Dadri, India, on 12 November 1996, a Saudi Airways Boeing 747 collided with a Kazakh Airlines Ilyushin IL-76 cargo aircraft. A total of 349 people died.

Miracle on the Hudson

On 15 January 2009, as a US Airways Airbus A320 took off from LaGuardia airport, New York, it struck a flock of geese and lost power to both engines. The aircraft's captain Chesley Sullenberger managed to ditch it in the Hudson River, where all 155 passengers and crew were rescued.

History of tourism

People have been travelling from place to place since ancient times. Nomadic people moved about to graze their livestock. Later people travelled to trade, or to seek their fortunes in gold rushes, and millions emigrated to other countries to escape persecution or to seek better lives.

Apart from a few historical examples, tourism – travelling for pleasure – is a relatively modern idea. Today, people spend more than $944 billion a year on tourism.

Most visited cities

City/country	Millions*
Paris, France	15.6
London, UK	14.8
Bangkok, Thailand	10.8
Singapore	10.1
New York, USA	9.5
Hong Kong, China	7.9
Istanbul, Turkey	7.0
Dubai, United Arab Emirates	6.9
Shanghai, China	6.7
Rome, Italy	6.1

* In latest year for which figures are available

Taking the waters
The Romans placed great value on bathing. They settled in many places with natural springs and developed cities as spas (the name comes from Spa in Belgium). In the 18th century, it became fashionable to visit these spas to "take the waters" – drinking and bathing as cures for various illnesses. Bath in England is a well-known Roman spa.

Package tours
On 5 July 1841, British travel pioneer Thomas Cook took 570 members of the Temperance Society (an organization opposed to drinking alcohol) on the newly opened railway from Leicester to Loughborough. This was the first package tour, and the beginning of what was to become the world's best-known travel company. When the Paris Exhibition opened in 1851, Cook took "excursionists" abroad for the first time. By the time Thomas Cook died in 1892, he had made travel possible for the masses.

Exhibitions
During the 19th and 20th centuries, major exhibitions in Europe and the USA brought millions of people to the big cities of the world. Many had never travelled before. The Great Exhibition in London in 1851 had more than 6 million visitors. A century later, the 1951 Festival of Britain attracted 8.5 million. The Paris Exposition of 1889, for which the Eiffel Tower was built, had 28 million visitors, and more than 51 million visited the New York World's Fair of 1964–65.

The Roman baths in Bath, England

Festivals
The world's major arts and music festivals receive millions of visitors. The annual Texas State Fair in the USA attracts as many as 3 million, and many other North American fairs receive 1 million or more. Festivals such as the carnival held in Rio De Janeiro, Brazil, and Mardi Gras in New Orleans, USA, are attended by large crowds.

Sport tourism
Winter sports such as skiing, water sports and adventure sports such as white-water rafting have become very popular. When the Olympic Games is held, the host country can expect a huge boost to its tourist industry.

Amusement parks
The world's most-visited amusement park is Disney World, Florida, USA, which attracts 17.06 million visitors a year. The total number of visitors at all Disney attractions around the world is 115 million a year. Britain's leading amusement park is Blackpool Pleasure Beach, with almost 6 million visitors a year.

Sleeping Beauty's Castle, Disneyland, Paris

See also
Countries of the World: pages 116-117

Northeast Greenland National Park

Northeast Greenland National Park

The world's largest national park, it measures 972,0000 sq km (375,291 sq miles) – which makes it larger than 163 of the world's countries. It was established in 1974 and is largely uninhabited, but is home to a wide range of Arctic animals, including polar bears, seals and musk ox.

National parks

National parks are established by governments to preserve areas of land and the plants and animals they contain. Yellowstone National Park in the USA, set up in 1872, was the first. There are more than 1,200 national parks in over 100 countries. Including protected places, a total of more than 6,500 such areas have been designated worldwide.

Everglades (founded 1934; 5,929 sq km/ 2,289 sq miles) The Everglades, USA is the only subtropical park in North America. Many different types of creatures live in its swamps, including alligators.

Great Barrier Reef (founded 1979; 343,800 sq km/ 132,742 sq miles) Australia's Great Barrier Reef, off the coast of Queensland, is the world's largest coral reef system, supporting many rare marine animals and plants.

Galápagos Islands (founded 1986; 6,937 sq km/ 2,678 sq miles) These volcanic islands off the coast of Ecuador are home to birds, seals and unique creatures including giant turtles and marine iguanas.

Lake District (founded 1951; 2,292 sq km/ 885 sq miles) The largest and most visited of Britain's national parks. The parks receive a total of 100 million visitors a year.

Wood Buffalo (founded 1922; 44,807 sq km/ 17,300 sq miles) This area of Canada contains forests, plains and many lakes. It has the largest herd of wild buffalo anywhere on Earth as well as many rare species such as the whooping crane.

Wrangell-St Elias (founded 1980; 33,820 sq km/ 13,057 sq miles) This national park in Alaska is the largest in the USA. It contains the most glaciers and peaks higher than 4,880 m (16,010 ft) in North America, as well as many wild animals, including bears, wolves and moose.

Yellowstone (founded 1872; 8,991 sq km/ 3,471 sq miles) This area of the Rocky Mountains in the USA is famed for its hot springs and geysers. Most famous is the Old Faithful geyser which sprays steam and water up to 56 m (184 ft) high.

Xingu (founded 1961; 22,000 sq km/ 8,494 sq miles) This large area of Brazilian rainforest is teeming with tropical wildlife. It is also inhabited by tribes of indigenous peoples who have little contact with outsiders.

Top tourist countries

In 2008, one in seven people in the world travelled as tourists to another country – a total of 922 million. Of these, almost half visited the top ten destinations below. By the year 2020 the number of international tourists is likely to more than double to 1.5 billion.

Country	Visitors	% of world total
1 France	79,300,000	8.6
2 USA	58,030,000	6.3
3 Spain	57,316,000	6.2
4 China	53,049,000	5.6
5 Italy	42,734,000	4.6
6 UK	30,182,000	3.3
7 Ukraine	25,392,000	2.8
8 Turkey	24,994,000	2.7
9 Germany	24,886,000	2.7
10 Mexico	22,637,000	2.5
Top 10 total	418,520,000	45.4

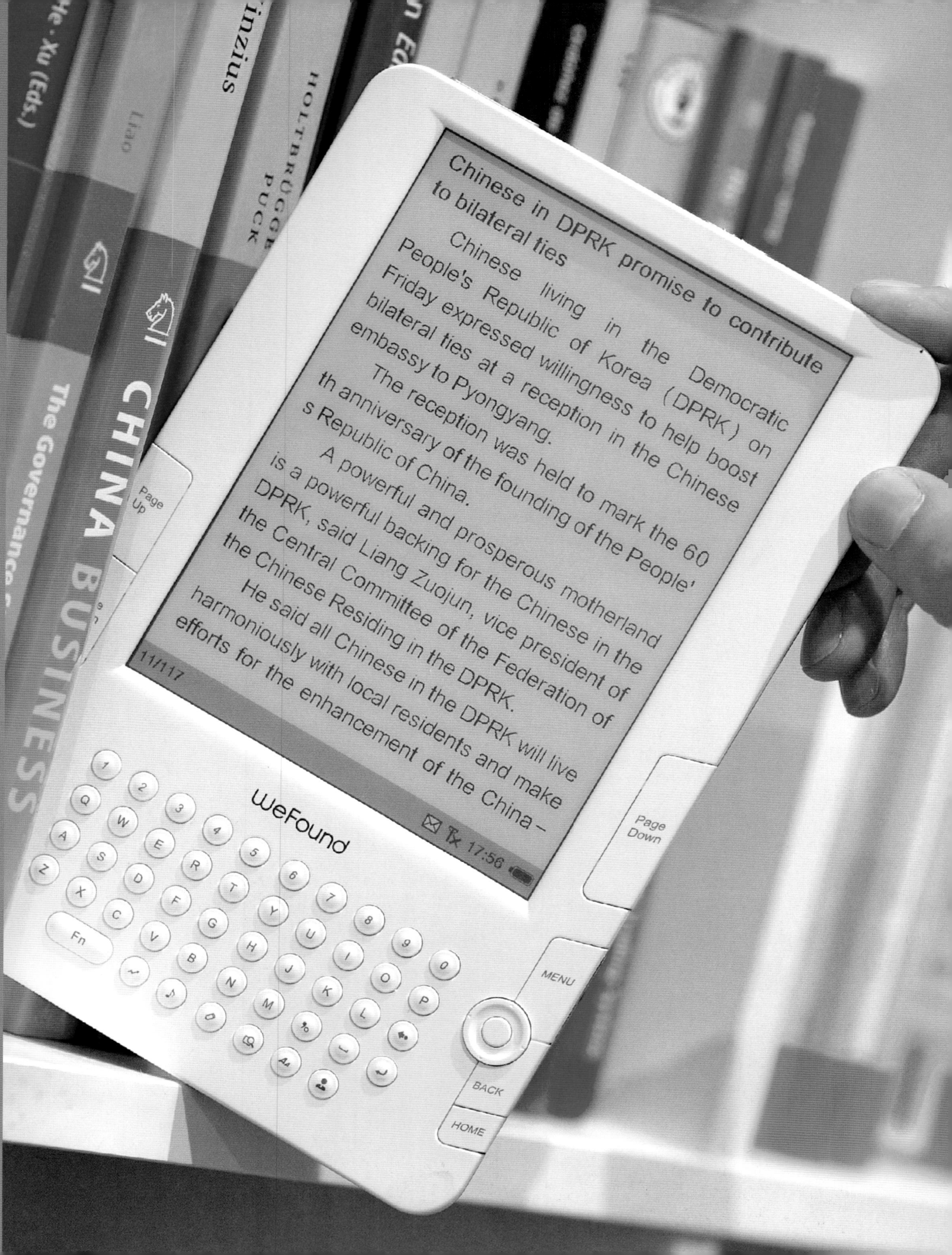
Chinese in DPRK promise to contribute to bilateral ties
Chinese living in the Democratic People's Republic of Korea (DPRK) on Friday expressed willingness to help boost bilateral ties at a reception in the Chinese embassy to Pyongyang.
The reception was held to mark the 60th anniversary of the founding of the People's Republic of China.
A powerful and prosperous motherland is a powerful backing for the Chinese in the DPRK, said Liang Zuojun, vice president of the Central Committee of the Federation of the Chinese Residing in the DPRK.
He said all Chinese in the DPRK will live harmoniously with local residents and make efforts for the enhancement of the China-
11/117
17:56
Page Up
Page Down
WeFound
MENU
BACK
HOME

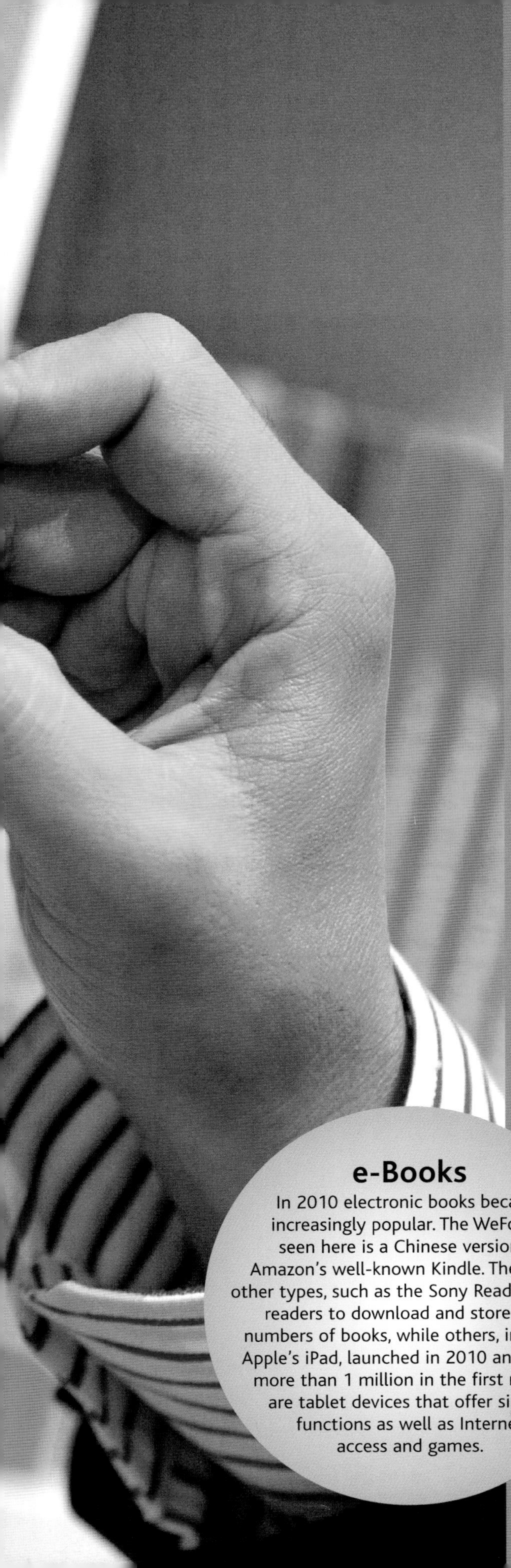

Language & Literature

e-Books

In 2010 electronic books became increasingly popular. The WeFound seen here is a Chinese version of Amazon's well-known Kindle. These and other types, such as the Sony Reader, enable readers to download and store large numbers of books, while others, including Apple's iPad, launched in 2010 and selling more than 1 million in the first month, are tablet devices that offer similar functions as well as Internet access and games.

Most spoken languages

Chinese (Mandarin)
Approximately 885,000,000 speakers. Chinese has many dialects, but about two-thirds of the people speak Mandarin. Wu is the next most common dialect, with approximately 77 million speakers. At least 30 million people around the world are learning Mandarin Chinese because China is becoming an important economic power.

Spanish
Approximately 332,000,000 speakers. Spanish is one of the most widely used of all languages. It is spoken not only in Spain but also in South America, the west coast of Africa and the USA.

English
Approximately 328,000,000 speakers. Far fewer people have English as their main language than Chinese, but millions more know at least some English and it is spoken in every corner of the globe. The USA dominates cinema, television, pop music, technology (Internet) and business and this has increased the importance of the English language. At least 800 million people use the Internet and about 35 per cent of them communicate in English. There are probably more than one billion people worldwide learning English.

Arabic
Approximately 246,000,000 speakers. Arabic is the official language of 17 countries and it is also the language of the Muslim religion. As a result, many millions of Muslims in other countries have some knowledge of the language.

Hindustani
Approximately 182,000,000 speakers. Hindustani includes Hindi and Urdu, which are almost the same language. Hindustani is the official language of Pakistan, where it is written in modified Arabic script and called Urdu. It is also the official language of India, but there it is written in the Devanagari script and called Hindi.

Portuguese
Approximately 178,000,000 speakers. Portuguese is spoken as a first language by the people of Portugal and also by many of the inhabitants of Brazil, Angola and other former colonies in Africa and elsewhere. These stretch from the Caribbean to Macau, China.

Last Cornish speaker

Once spoken by nearly 40,000 people, the Cornish language died out with Dolly Pentreath (c.1692–1777), who claimed to be its last native speaker. Since then it has been revived and today children learn Cornish at some schools in the county.

Other major languages

Bengali
Approximate number of speakers: 189,000,000

Russian
Approximate number of speakers: 170,000,000

Japanese
Approximate number of speakers: 125,000,000

German (standard)
Approximate number of speakers: 95,450,000

Chinese (Wu)
Approximate number of speakers: 77,200,000

French
Approximate number of speakers: 77,000,000

A stop sign in English and Inuktituk (the language of the Inuit people)

Dying languages

Many of the world's 6,912 languages are spoken only by a few elderly people. As they die, the languages vanish – it is believed that up to 90 per cent will be extinct by 2050.

Alphabets

An alphabet is the basis of a system of writing, using letters or characters to represent sounds or words. These are some of the oldest and most important alphabets.

Greek
The Greek alphabet is the oldest surviving European alphabet. The early Greek alphabet was written from right to left, but by about 500 BC it was written from left to right. The Greeks introduced an upper case (capital letters) and a lower case (small letters).

Cyrillic
The Cyrillic alphabet was invented in the 9th century by two Greek missionaries, St Cyril and his brother St Methodius. It is used for Slavonic languages such as Russian, Bulgarian and Ukrainian. The Russian Cyrillic alphabet originally had 43 letters, but the number was reduced to 33 after the Russian Revolution of 1917. Like the Greek alphabet, Cyrillic also has upper case and lower case versions of the alphabet.

Hebrew
Hebrew is written horizontally from right to left. Also, sometimes the letters are used as numerals.

Arabic
Arabic evolved from Aramaic in the 4th century, and is written from left to right. It consists of 28 consonants. Vowels are shown by marks placed above or below the consonants but are not always used. Arabic letters are

Reading the dots

Braille is widely used on products such as medicine packaging to enable visually-impaired and blind people to identify it, but increasingly electronic texts on computers are used instead.

Braille

Braille is a system of raised dots that allows blind people to read by touch. It was invented in the 19th century by a blind Frenchman named Louis Braille. The dots are embossed on to paper, either by hand or using a machine. They are read by moving the fingers across the top of the dots.

Writing in Braille

The reader uses both hands – the right works out the message while the left feels ahead for the beginning of the next line. A skilled Braille reader can understand up to 150 words a minute, which is about half the speed of a sighted person reading ordinary text.

written differently depending upon where they appear in a word. The positions of characters are known as final (end), medial (middle), initial (beginning) and isolated (on its own).

Chinese and Japanese

These are logographic writing systems. This means that each symbol represents a word, or part of a word, instead of a sound. The Chinese system has 40–50,000 characters and the Japanese system has 18,000, but you need to know only about 2,000 and 1,850 respectively to get by in these languages. In 1966 the Chinese language changed quite dramatically, when books and newspapers were printed with the characters running horizontally from left to right rather than vertically from right to left. There is now a phonetic alphabet known as pin-yin, made up of 25 letters taken from the Roman alphabet.

Most Chinese characters are made up of eight basic strokes. These are all in the character for eternity. Words in a Chinese dictionary are in order of the number of strokes they contain. Chinese verbs and adjectives usually contain only one character or syllable, but nouns often consist of two characters or more. The examples below show how some compound words are made up.

木	林	森
tree	woodland (2 trees)	forest (3 trees)

Chinese symbol in the background means eternity

Phonetic alphabet

You may have heard pilots and soldiers on television and in films using the phonetic alphabet in radio messages. The alphabet is used to spell out parts of a message that might be difficult to recognize in unclear radio transmissions. The version generally used was developed in the 1950s.

It is known as the NATO (North Atlantic Treaty Organization) Phonetic Alphabet and was designed to be understood and easily pronounced by all NATO members. They chose words that were used in lots of different languages and could not be confused with other common words or those used for another letter. Aircraft and ship crews also use the phonetic alphabet. For example, in the phonetic alphabet "over and out" becomes Oscar Victor Echo Romeo Alpha November Delta Oscar Uniform Tango.

A Alpha
B Bravo
C Charlie
D Delta
E Echo
F Foxtrot
G Golf
H Hotel
I India
J Juliet
K Kilo
L Lima
M Mike
N November
O Oscar
P Papa
Q Quebec
R Romeo
S Sierra
T Tango
U Uniform
V Victor
W Whiskey
X X-ray
Y Yankee
Z Zulu

See also
Brainchildren: young inventors: page 81

Hieroglyphics on the pillars of Habu Temple in Luxor, Egypt

Hieroglyphics

The simplest of all writing systems use pictures. These are called pictograms and look like the things they describe – just like many road signs and computer icons today.

Writing or carving pictograms is very slow and a lot of work, so people began to use simpler versions of images, such as hieroglyphics. Ancient Egyptian hieroglyphics were used on obelisks, wall paintings, tombs and papyri (documents on a type of paper made from reeds). They are symbols that represent an object, a sound or an idea. They are not a code: you cannot simply convert an Egyptian hieroglyph into a letter and read it as we read words in a book. People stopped using hieroglyphics in the 1st century AD. From then on, no one could understand them until 1822 when French scholar Jean François Champollion worked out how to translate the text of the Rosetta Stone in the British Museum.

Semaphore

In 1791 French inventor Claude Chappe (1763–1805) and his brothers invented a new way of signalling called a semaphore. They used two wooden arms which could both be set to seven positions. This gave a total of 196 combinations, each representing a letter or other symbol. By mounting it on a high building, it could be seen from a distance by an operator viewing it through a telescope from the next semaphore station. The following year a system linked Paris to Lille, and eventually covered most of France, and by 1796 a British version connected London to the navy's dockyard at Portsmouth. From this, developed the use of human arms and flags at sea to send messages from ship to ship. It continued to be used up to the 1960s, even after the electric telegraph had replaced land-based semaphore signalling systems and radio was commonly used at sea.

Morse code

By using Morse code you can send a signal in a series of dots and dashes. The signal can be sent by sound or by flashing lights. There are five parts to the code: a dot, a dash, a short gap or pause (between letters), a medium gap (between words) and a long gap (between sentences).

Morse was created by and named after American artist and inventor Samuel Finley Breese Morse (1791–1872). He sent the first Morse code message from Washington DC, to Baltimore, Maryland, on 24 May 1844. It read "What hath God wrought!" An international version of Morse code became widely used to send telegrams by wire. Once people could send messages by radio transmissions they still used Morse code in situations such as warfare, when clear voice signals were not always possible.

A ·-	**N** -·	**0** -----	**5** ·····
B -···	**O** ---	**1** ·----	**6** -····
C -·-·	**P** ·--·	**2** ··---	**7** --···
D -··	**Q** --·-	**3** ···--	**8** ---··
E ·	**R** ·-·	**4** ····-	**9** ----·
F ··-·	**S** ···		
G --·	**T** -		
H ····	**U** ··-		
I ··	**V** ···-		
J ·---	**W** ·--		
K -·-	**X** -··-		
L ·-··	**Y** -·--		
M --	**Z** --··		

A Morse key for sending messages

Communications milestones 3500 BC

A variety of ways of communicating between people without speaking have been devised, some dating back thousands of years. These are just some of the important steps in this history.

3500 BC First writing

1700–1450 BC Minoans of Crete use Linear A and Linear B scripts for writing

100 BC Roman alphabet with 23 letters

AD 105 Chinese make paper

150 Parchment books replace scrolls

400–1400 Monks produce copies of manuscripts

1034 First moveable type (made of clay) in China

1450 First printing presses in Europe

1476 William Caxton prints first books in London

1588 Beacons used in England to warn of invasion by Spanish Armada

1702 *The Daily Courant* was the first daily newspaper in the UK

1783 *The Pennsylvania Evening Post and Public Advertiser* was the first daily newspaper published in America

1791 Optical telegraph invented by Claude Chappe (France)

1839 First commercial telegraph (London)

Postal factfile

First stamps
The first adhesive stamps were Penny Blacks, issued in the UK in 1840.

Largest stamps
In 1913, Chinese express delivery stamps were issued that measured 248 x 70 mm (9.75 x 2.75 inches).

Smallest stamps
In 1863 10 cent and 1 peso stamps of the Colombian State of Bolivar were 9.5 x 8 mm (5/16 x 3/8 inch).

Upside-down stamp
Because they are rare, stamps with printing mistakes are prized by collectors. In 2005 a block of four 1918 US 24 cent stamps with a biplane upside-down was sold for $2.7 million (£1.5 million).

Letter boxes
The first letter boxes in the UK date from 1852. India is the country with the most letter boxes, a total of 655,581. India also has the most post offices – 155,035.

Letters
Despite the increasing use of e-mail, people in the USA send and receive more letters than any country in the world, a total of more than 200 billion a year out of a worldwide total of 433 billion.

Oldest American post office
The Post Office and Customs House in Galena, Illinois, dates from 1858 and has been preserved as a perfect example of a working mid-19th century American post office.

Papal post
The Vatican sends the most letters per person of any country, 6,973, but this is because people in Rome use the Vatican's postal service as it is more reliable than the Italian post.

Pony Express
Started in the USA in 1860, the Pony Express carried mail by a network of riders galloping between towns on horses. The famous cowboy and showman Buffalo Bill was once a Pony Express rider. It closed in 1861 as the telegraph made it possible to send messages instantaneously.

Pigeon post
Carrier pigeons have been used to carry messages since ancient times, especially in wartime: microfilm was first used to send messages out of Paris when it was under siege by the German army in 1870–71, and from the trenches in World War I.

Post office railway
A 10-km (6.5-ml) underground railway with driverless electric trains once carried four million letters and parcels a day across London. It ran from 1927 until it was closed in 2003.

Text messaging is one of the world's most widely used communication methods

Texting abbreviations

Texting is also known as SMS (Short Message service) as there is a limit to the number of characters. Because of this and to save time in composing messages, abbreviations are commonly used.

Word or Phrase	Abbreviation(s)
at the moment	atm
be right back	brb
by the way	btw
don't worry	dw
got to go	g2g, gtg
later	L8er
laugh out loud	lol
message	msg
no problem	np
see you/see you later	cya, cu, cya, cul8er, l8a
text (me) back	tb, tmb
to be honest	tbh
tomorrow	2moz, 2moro
whatever	wateva

Early air mail

During the Prussian Siege of Paris in 1870, hydrogen balloons were used to carry messages out of the city.

2000s

1867 Sending messages by flashing signal lamps, invented by Philip Colomb, adopted by the British Navy

1867 The first commercially successful typewriter invented by Christopher Scholes (USA)

1876 The heliograph for signalling using sunlight reflected by a mirror patented by Sir Henry Mance (UK)

1888 The Telautograph, an early version of the fax machine, invented by Elisha Gray (USA) – the modern fax machine was developed in the 1970s

1943 *Colossus*, an early computer, was built in the UK to decode messages encoded by the German *Enigma* machine

1960 The first international telex service enabled electronic transmission of text messages

1971 The "@" sign became standard in e-mail addresses; email began to be used from 1972 onwards

1972 Ceefax, the first TV text information service, was launched in the UK

1993 Although there are earlier claims, it is probable that the first SMS (text) messages were sent

2006 Twitter, a 'micro-blog' service, was started in the USA

2010 Visual Voicemail, which converts phone messages to text, offered on some mobile phones

Unusual libraries

Around the world, there are some unusual ways of carrying books to readers. In Kenya, there is a camel-drawn library: one camel carries 500 books, another carries a tent which is set up as a mobile library. In Alaska, a bookboat carries library books to children who travel with their parents to summer fishing grounds.

The main reading room at the Library of Congress in Washington DC

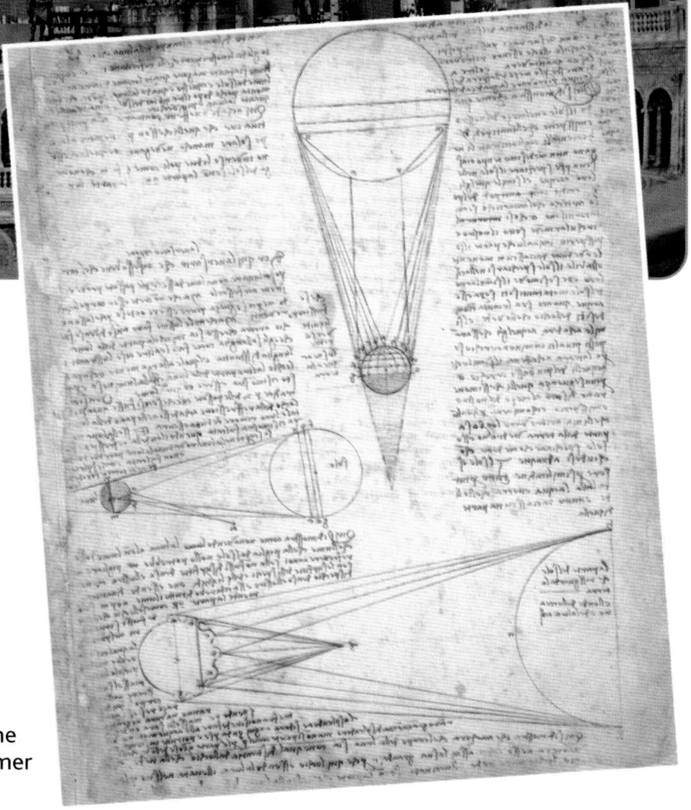

Page from the Codex Hammer

Largest libraries

A library is a collection of books and other printed material. The word library can also be used to describe the building where a collection of books is kept, as well as manuscripts, maps, periodicals and photographs. Below are the world's largest libraries, each containing over 15 million books.

The Library of Congress, Washington DC, USA was founded in 1800 and holds 32,124,001 books.

The British Library*, London, UK was founded in 1753 and holds 29,000,000 books.

Library of the Russian Academy of Sciences, St Petersburg, Russia was founded in 1714 and holds 20,500,000 books.

National Library of Canada, Ottawa, Canada was founded in 1953 and holds 19,500,000 books.

Deutsche Bibliothek, Frankfurt, Germany was founded in 1990 and holds 22,200,000 books.

The Russian State Library, Moscow, Russia was founded in 1862 and holds 17,000,000 books.

Harvard University Library, Cambridge, Massachusetts, USA was founded in 1636 and holds 15,826,570 books.

* Founded as part of the British Museum, 1753; became independent in 1973

Valuable books and manuscripts

- The Codex Hammer (previously called the Codex Leicester) was sold in New York, USA, in 1994 for $28,800,000 (£18,643,190). It was bought by Bill Gates, the billionaire founder of Microsoft. The Codex is one of Leonardo da Vinci's notebooks and includes many of his scientific drawings and diagrams.
- A rare copy of the Gutenberg Bible, one of the first books ever printed, was sold in New York, USA, in 1987 for $5,390,000 (£3,264,688).
- One of the first-ever printed books was Geoffrey Chaucer's *The Canterbury Tales* (c. 1477). A copy was sold in London in 1998 for £4,621,500 ($7,570,941).
- A "first folio" (early edition) of the works of William Shakespeare dating from 1623 was sold in London in 2001 for £4,156,947 ($6,166,000).
- John James Audubon's *The Birds of America* (1827–38) was sold in New York, USA in 2000 for $8,000,000 (£5,187,731), making it the most expensive printed book. Its giant pages feature more than 400 hand-coloured engravings of birds.
- J.K. Rowling's *The Tales of Beedle the Bard* handwritten book, sold in 2007 for £1.95 million ($3.98 million) to aid a children's charity.

Types of book

Almanac
This is an annual calendar of dates and events. It originally contained astronomical facts and figures, but now includes useful statistics and other information. Almanac is sometimes spelled almanack.

Anthology
A collection of writings by one author or on a theme, such as an anthology of animal poems.

Atlas
A book of maps.

Autobiography
An account of a person's life written by himself or herself. Sometimes a "ghost" writer may help someone write an autobiography.

Bibliography
A list of books or sources on a particular subject.

Biography
A book about someone's life written by another person.

Chronology
A dictionary of dated events.

Dictionary
An alphabetical list of words and their meanings. There are also dictionaries on a single subject, for example *Dictionary of Art*.

Dictionary of quotations
A listing of interesting remarks or extracts from the writings of famous people.

Directory
An alphabetical list of names and addresses of people or organizations.

Encyclopedia
A book of articles on many subjects, arranged alphabetically. Encyclopedias are often published in many volumes or, today, on CD-ROM or on the Internet.

Gazetteer
A book that lists and describes places (countries, cities, etc).

Glossary
A list of words and phrases used in a particular subject area, for instance *A Glossary of Computer Terms*.

Language dictionary
A dictionary that gives translations of words and phrases to and from other languages, for example a *French-English/English-French Dictionary*.

Monograph
A book on a specialized subject, such as the work of a particular artist.

Novel
A work of fiction, usually involving imaginary people. A historical novel may be about real historical characters.

Novella
A short work of fiction.

Phrasebook
A book for travellers, with translations of words and phrases into and from a foreign language.

Pop-up book
A book, usually for children, made so that pictures stand up or move when the pages are opened.

Thesaurus
A book organized to show words with similar meanings.

Travel guide
A book of information about a particular country or area.

Who's who or biographical dictionary
Alphabetical summaries of the lives of famous people, living or dead, sometimes by their subjects (such as a *Dictionary of Scientists*).

Yearbook
An annual reference book with information about the events of the previous year. Yearbooks containing statistical information about a country are often called *Abstracts*.

Book firsts and records

First printed books
Books were printed in China in the 8th century using woodblocks, and in 14th-century China and Korea using movable type.

First books printed in English
In 1474 William Caxton printed the first book in English, *Recuyell of the Historyes of Troye*. It was printed in Bruges, Flanders. Chaucer's *Canterbury Tales* was probably the first book in English to be printed in England, in about 1477.

First books printed in America
Massachusetts Bay Colony: The Oath of a Free-Man (1638) and *An Almanack for the Year of Our Lord* (1639) are the first two books known to have been printed in the new American colonies.

First American novel
The Power of Sympathy (1789) was the first novel published in America. It was published anonymously, but is believed to have been written by William Hill Brown.

First sequel
Daniel Defoe wrote *The Farther Adventures of Robinson Crusoe* in 1719, after the success of *Robinson Crusoe* earlier that year.

Longest novel
A science-fiction novel by French writer Georges-Jean Arnaud, *La Compagne des Glaces* (1980–92), runs to 62 volumes and has about 11,000 pages.

First detective story
Murders in the Rue Morgue, by American author Edgar Allan Poe, was first published in *Grahame's Magazine* in 1841.

Smallest book
This was produced by a German typographer Josua Reichertand called *The World's Smallest Book*. It measures 2.4 x 2.9 mm (0.09 x 0.1 in) – the size of a match head.

Largest book
The largest book was published in 2003. It is a collection of photos called *Bhutan: A Visual Odyssey Across the Last Himalayan Kingdom*. When opened out it measures 2.1 x 1.5 m (7 x 5 ft) – almost the size of a table-tennis table! It costs $15,000 (£30,000) a copy.

Apple iPad
As well as allowing users to listen to music and watch films, the iPad tablet computer launched by Apple in 2010 enables readers to download the text of books and magazines and has a function to read them aloud. Some publishers have predicted that 10 per cent of their sales in 2011 will be downloads, rather than printed books.

Steve Jobs of Apple at the launch of the iPad

Famous diaries

People have kept personal diaries for more than 500 years. Most were written as personal records about the times the writers lived through or events that happened to them, and they are often fascinating to read.

Samuel Pepys (1633–1703)

Pepys kept a diary for nearly ten years from 1660. He lived in London and wrote about events such as the Great Plague and Great Fire of London. He wrote in a special code, which was not translated until the 19th century. Pepys' original diaries are kept in the library of Magdalene College, Cambridge.

Anne Frank (1929–1945)

Anne Frank was forced to hide with her family in Amsterdam, Netherlands, during World War II, when Jewish people were being persecuted by the Nazis. Anne kept her diary while she was in hiding, but left it behind when she and her family were found. She was deported and died in a German concentration camp. Her father survived and edited her diary, which was published after the war. *The Diary of Anne Frank* became a bestseller and was translated into more than 55 languages. It has also been made into an award-winning play and a film. The house in which the Frank family hid is now a museum.

Adolf Hitler (1889–1945)

In 1993, the German magazine *Stern* paid 10 million marks (£4.0 million) to journalist Gerd Heidemann to publish extracts from what were claimed to be the diaries of the German dictator Adolf Hitler. The diaries were soon discovered to have been forgeries written by Konrad Kujau. He and Heidemann were imprisoned for their deception.

Bestsellers

These are some of the bestselling books ever. But the Bible has outsold them all. It is believed to have sold more than six billion copies in hundreds of versions and translations.

- One of the bestselling books of all time is a collection of quotations by Chinese leader Mao Zedong, known as his *Little Red Book*. Between 1966 to 1971 every Chinese adult had to own a copy and 900 million were printed.
- J.R.R. Tolkien's *The Lord of the Rings* trilogy was first published in 1954–55. It has sold well over 100 million and its sales received a further boost when the films based on the books were released between 2001 and 2003.
- *The American Spelling Book* by Noah Webster (1783) was used in American schools for generations. It has sold nearly 100 million copies.
- *The Common Sense Book of Baby and Child Care* by American doctor Benjamin Spock came out in 1946. Since then more than 50 million copies have been sold.
- British crime writer Agatha Christie has sold at least one billion copies of her novels in English and another billion in 45 foreign languages. In 1935 her novel *The Mysterious Affair at Styles* was one of the first Penguin paperbacks ever published.
- American author Margaret Mitchell's only book, *Gone With the Wind* (1936), has sold around 30 million copies. It is one of the bestselling novels ever.

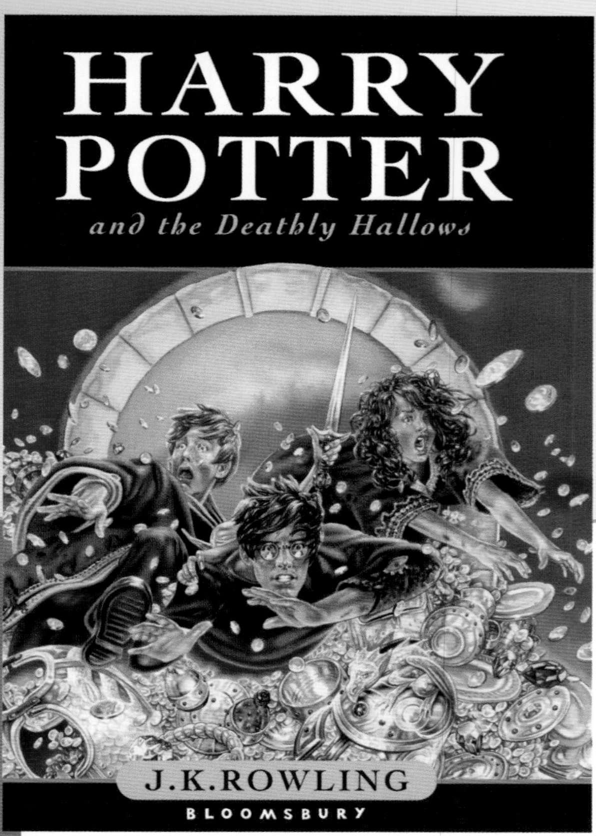

Covers for two *Harry Potter* books

J.K. Rowling

J.K. Rowling was born on 31 July 1965 as Joanne Rowling (she later borrowed the name Kathleen from her grandmother to create a middle initial). Her first Harry Potter book, *Harry Potter and the Philosopher's Stone*, was published in 1997. It has been followed by six more books with sales now over 400 million copies in 67 languages. If all Harry Potter books ever sold were placed end to end, they would stretch 80,000 km (49,710 miles) – twice the distance round the Equator! Earnings from the book sales and films have made J.K. Rowling the richest author ever, and the first to make more than $1 billion (£509 million) from writing. She has given large amounts to charities. The final book, *Harry Potter and the Deathly Hallows*, was published on 21 July 2007.

Translations

These are the ten most translated authors in the world, according to UNESCO's *Index Translationum* (1979–2009).

Agatha Christie	6,453	Barbara Cartland	3,403
Jules Verne	4,185	Danielle Steel	2,858
William Shakespeare	3,603	Hans Christian Andersen	2,811
V. I. Lenin	3,516	Stephen King	2,696
Enid Blyton	3,495	Jakob Grimm	2,448

Official sequels

After a popular author's death, sequels to their novels are often written by others in their style to fulfil the continuing public demand for their books. Where the original writer's work is in copyright, they must be licenced by his or her literary estate, and so are considered 'official' sequels. If the author is out of copyright, such as Lewis Carroll's *Alice in Wonderland* or the Sherlock Holmes stories of Arthur Conan Doyle, there is nothing legally to prevent anyone from writing a sequel. Among the official sequels published in recent years are:

Scarlett (1991), Alexandra Ripley's sequel to Margaret Mitchell's *Gone With the Wind* (1936)

Peter Pan in Scarlet (2006), Geraldine McCaughrean's sequel to J.M. Barrie's *Peter and Wendy* (1911)

Devil May Care (2008), Sebastian Faulks's sequel to Ian Fleming's James Bond books (1953–66)

And Another Thing... (2009), Eoin Colfer's sequel to Douglas Adams's *Hitchhiker's Guide to the Galaxy* series (1973–92)

Return to the Hundred Acre Wood (2009), David Benedictus's sequel to A.A. Milne's Winnie-the-Pooh books (1926–28), is a notable example of a modern sequel to a classic book

J.K. Rowling
Photograph
© Richard Young

Nobel Prize for Literature

Nobel prizes have been given every year since 1901 for achievements in different fields, including literature. Nobel Prize winners for literature include poets, playwrights and authors from all over the world. Below are some of the best known winners.

2009 Herta Müller (Germany, 1953–)
2008 J.M.G. Le Clézio (France, 1940–)
2007 Doris Lessing (UK, 1919–)
2006 Orhan Pamuk (Turkey, 1952–)
2005 Harold Pinter (UK, 1930–2008)
2003 J.M. Coetzee (South Africa, 1940–)
2001 V.S. Naipaul (UK, 1932–)
2000 Gao Xingjian (China, 1940–) first win by a Chinese writer
1999 Günter Grass (Germany, 1927–)
1995 Seamus Heaney (Ireland, 1939–)
1993 Toni Morrison (USA, 1931–)
1991 Nadine Gordimer (South Africa, 1923–)
1983 William Golding (UK, 1911–93) author of *The Lord of the Flies*
1973 Patrick White (Australia, 1912–90)
1970 Alexander Solzhenitsyn (Russia, 1918–2008)
1962 John Steinbeck (USA, 1902–68) author of *The Grapes of Wrath*
1958 Boris Pasternak (Russia, 1890–1960) author of *Doctor Zhivago*
1954 Ernest Hemingway (USA, 1899–1961)
1953 Winston Churchill (UK, 1874–1965) British prime minister and writer
1948 T.S. Eliot (US-born, UK, 1888–1965) author of the book that inspired the musical *Cats*
1938 Pearl Buck (USA, 1892–1973)
1932 John Galsworthy (UK, 1867–1933) author of *The Forsyte Saga*
1925 George Bernard Shaw (UK, 1856–1950)
1923 William Butler Yeats (Ireland, 1865–1939)
1907 Rudyard Kipling (UK, 1865–1936) author of *The Jungle Book*
1901 Sully Prudhomme (France, 1839–1907) the first winner

http//www.jkrowling.com **search**

Children's firsts

First children's book
The first English children's book for entertainment (not a school book) was a collection of rhymes called *A Booke in Englyssh Metre, of the Great Merchante Man called Dives Pragmaticus, very preaty for Children to reade*. It was printed in London in 1563.

First children's book printed in the USA
John Cotton's *Milk for Babies* was printed in Cambridge, Massachusetts, America, in 1641–45.

First children's encyclopedia
Pera Librorum Juvenilium (Collection of Juvenile Books) was compiled in Germany by Johann Christoph Wagenseil in 1695.

First story for children
The History of Little Goody Two-Shoes was published by John Newbery in London in 1765. Some experts believe it was written by the famous British poet and playwright Oliver Goldsmith.

First nursery rhyme book
Tommy Thumb's Pretty Song Book was published in London in 1744. It contained well-known rhymes such as "London Bridge is falling down", "Hickory, dickory dock" and "Sing a song of sixpence".

First children's library
The Bingham Library for Youth was set up in Salisbury, Connecticut, USA, in January 1803 when Caleb Bingham, who came from the town, donated 150 books. In 1862 Britain's first library for children was created – an area set aside just for them inside the Campfield Reference Library, Manchester.

First children's book to win Whitbread Book of the Year Award (now Costa Book of the Year Award)
In 2001, British writer Philip Pullman won the Whitbread Children's Book of the Year Award and the Book of the Year Award for his novel *The Amber Spyglass* from *His Dark Materials* trilogy. It was the first time a children's book had won the overall prize.

Aesop's Fables

Aesop's Fables, a collection of tales involving animals, each of which ends with a moral lesson, is one of the best known of all books, having been in print in many versions for over 500 years. The first-ever edition was issued by English printer William Caxton on 26 March 1486. The identity of Aesop remains a mystery, but he is popularly believed to have been a slave in Greece who lived in about 620–560 BC.

Fairy tale authors

Fairy tales are fantastic stories for children that do not always involve fairies. They are traditional tales that were retold from generation to generation. The writers below collected the stories and wrote or re-wrote them in books that became hugely popular all over the world. Many fairy tales have been made into films – especially animated films by Disney.

Charles Perrault
French writer Charles Perrault (1628–1703) put together a collection of stories with the help of his son Pierre (1678–1700). Their collection contained *Cinderella*, *Little Red Riding-Hood*, *Sleeping Beauty* and *Puss in Boots*. The stories were translated into English in 1729. Later editions had the French title, *Contes de ma mère l'Oye*, or *Mother Goose's Tales*.

Brothers Grimm
German brothers Jacob Ludwig Carl Grimm (1785–1863) and Wilhelm Carl Grimm (1786–1859) were the authors of *Grimm's Fairy Tales*, which were first published for Christmas 1812. This was a collection of traditional stories, re-written for a young audience. It included many famous fairy tales, such as *Hansel and Gretel*, *Rumpelstiltskin* and *Snow White and the Seven Dwarfs*. They were translated into English in 1823 and became a worldwide bestseller.

Hans Christian Andersen
Danish author Andersen (1805–75) wrote 156 fairy tales, including *The Little Mermaid*, *The Emperor's New Clothes* and *The Ugly Duckling*. His stories first appeared in English in 1846.

Aesop's fable *The Frog and the Ox*, illustrated by Charles Henry Bennett, 1875

Children's Laureate

Since 1999, a leading children's writer or illustrator has been appointed Children's Laureate to promote literature for young people. The Laureates so far have been:

Quentin Blake	1999–2001
Anne Fine	2001–03
Michael Morpurgo	2003–05
Jacqueline Wilson	2005–07
Michael Rosen	2007–09
Anthony Browne	2009–11

Multi-million sellers

J.K. Rowling (UK, 1965–)
At the end of 2008, the seven Harry Potter books had sold more than 400 million copies worldwide. In 2007, *Harry Potter and the Deathly Hallows* sold 2,652,656 copies in the UK on its first day of release – the biggest one-day sale ever recorded.

Enid Blyton (UK, 1897–1968)
Enid Blyton wrote more than 700 children's books. Total sales of her works are more than 400 million. She was the bestselling English-language author until the arrival of J.K. Rowling.

René Goscinny (France, 1926–77) and Albert Uderzo (France, 1927–)
René Goscinny and Albert Uderzo created the comic-strip character Astérix the Gaul in 1959. They jointly produced 24 books, and Underzo went on to create 9 more after Goscinny's death. Their total worldwide sales are more than 330 million copies.

R.L. Stine (USA, 1943–)
The 138 books in R.L. Stine's *Goosebumps* series and its sequels have sold over 330 million copies worldwide. *Goosebumps HorrorLand* (2008–09) is Stine's latest series.

Hergé (Belgium, 1907–83)
Georges Rémi was the author-illustrator who wrote under the pen-name Hergé. He created the comic-strip character Tintin in 1929. The boy detective's adventures have appeared in book form since 1948 onwards and have been translated into about 45 languages and

The Cat in the Hat, a character from one of Dr Seuss' most popular books

Famous illustrators

Below are some of the artists who have produced the best-loved illustrations for children's books. Some, such as Beatrix Potter, also wrote the books they illustrated.

Honor C. Appleton (American, 1879–1951) *Josephine and Her Dolls*

Quentin Blake (British, 1932–) Illustrated Roald Dahl's books and others

Raymond Briggs (British, 1934–) *The Snowman* and *Father Christmas*

Jean de Brunhoff (French, 1899–1937) *Babar the Elephant* series

Hergé (Belgian, 1907–83) the *Tintin* books

Tove Jansson (Finnish, 1914–2001) the *Moomin* series

Arnold Lobel (American, 1933–87) the *Frog and Toad* books

Henriette Willebeek Le Mair (Dutch, 1889–1966) *Our Old Nursery Rhymes*

Tintin by Hergé

Beatrix Potter (British, 1866–1943) the *Peter Rabbit* books and others

Arthur Rackham (British, 1867–1939) illustrated classics

William Heath Robinson (British, 1872–1944) illustrated classics

Maurice Sendak (American, 1928–) *Where the Wild Things Are* and others

Ernest Shepard (British, 1879–1976) *The Wind in the Willows*, *Winnie the Pooh*

Dr Seuss (Theodor Seuss Geissel; American, 1904–91) *The Cat in the Hat* and many others

Jessie Willcox Smith (American, 1863–1935) *The Water Babies*

Albert Uderzo (French, 1927–) the *Astérix* books

Chris Van Allsburg (American, 1949–) *Jumanji*, *The Polar Express*

Book into film

Popular illustrated children's books have long been a source of animated and live-action films, but this has become increasingly so in the 21st century with Dr Seuss's *The Cat in the Hat* (2003), Maurice Sendak's *Where the Wild Things Are* and Roald Dahl/Quentin Blake's *Fantastic Mr Fox* (2009), with A.A. Milne/Ernest Shepard's *Winnie the Pooh* and Ricky Gervais/Rob Steen's *Flanimals*, scheduled for release in 2011.

dialects. Total sales are over 200 million.

Beatrix Potter (UK, 1866–1943)
The Tale of Peter Rabbit (1901) and her other books have sold more than 150 million copies in 30 languages.

Lewis Carroll (UK, 1832–98)
There are no world figures for sales of Lewis Carroll's books, *Alice in Wonderland* and *Alice Through the Looking Glass*, but these two books have never been out of print. They have appeared in hundreds of editions and in many languages.

Dr Seuss (USA, 1904–91)
Green Eggs and Ham, one of Dr Seuss' most popular books, has sold more than 8 million in the USA alone. Worldwide, he has sold more than 100 million copies of his books.

Rev. W. Awdry (UK, 1911–97)
Rev. Awdry began writing his *Thomas the Tank Engine* books in 1946. The books have sold more than 90 million copies.

Mark Twain (USA, 1835–1910)
Book sales in the USA were not accurately recorded before 1895. *The Adventures of Tom Sawyer* (1876) and *The Adventures of Huckleberry Finn* (1884) have probably each sold more than 20 million copies worldwide.

http://www.ukchildrensbooks.co.uk search

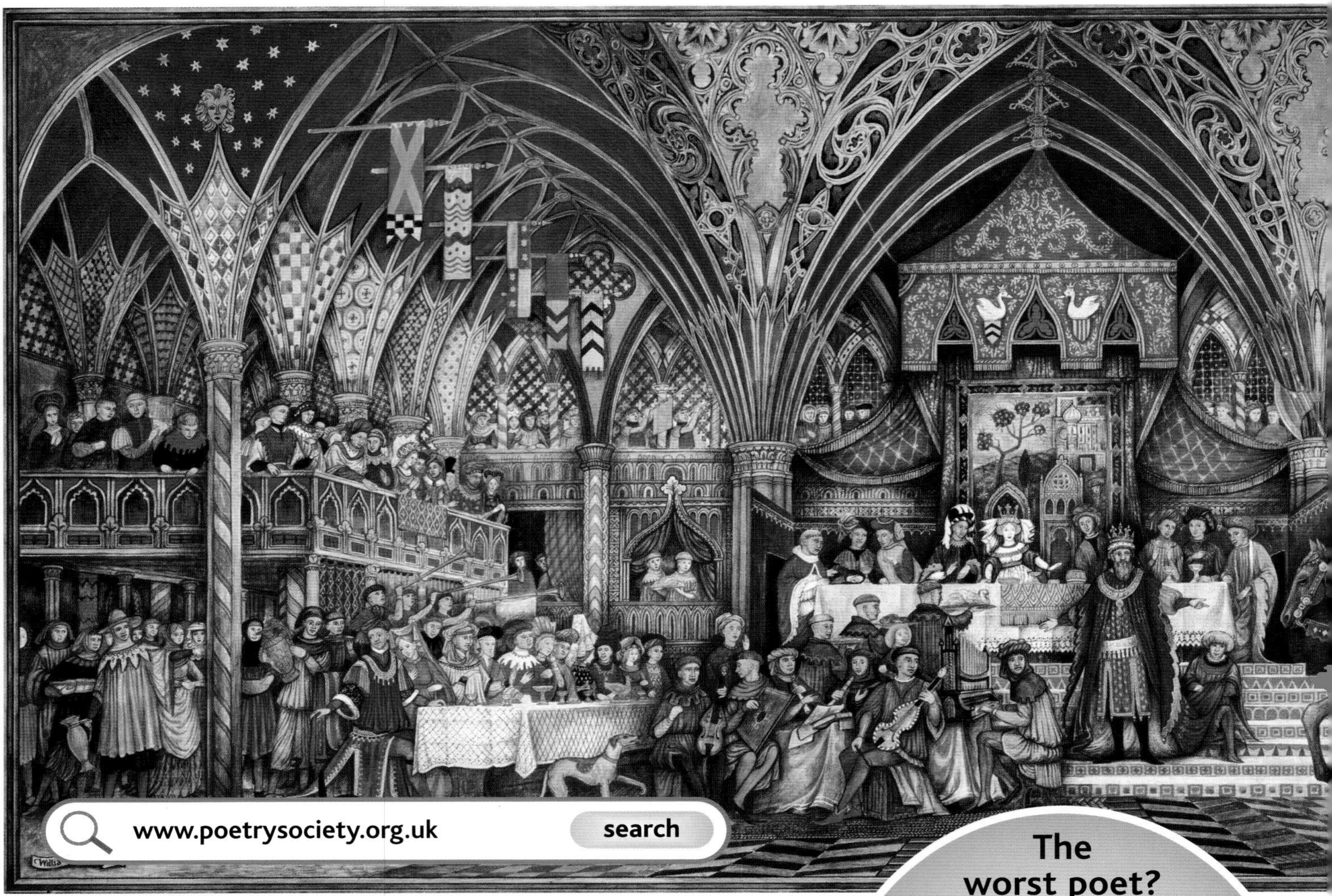

www.poetrysociety.org.uk search

The worst poet?

Scottish poet William Topaz McGonagall (1825–1902) is considered by many to be the worst poet of all time. His poems often did not rhyme properly, or contained verses that were unintentionally funny, such as:

ALAS! Lord and Lady Dalhousie are dead, and buried at last,

Which causes many people to feel a little downcast.

Ancient poems

Before stories and poems were written down they were passed on orally. Some of the most famous long narrative, or story, poems were passed on this way for hundreds of years before being written down by the poet who is now known as the author.

The Iliad – Homer

This Greek poem dates from 850 BC and tells the story of the final year of the war between the Greeks and the Trojans. It describes the great battle and the story of how beautiful Helen left her husband Menelaus for the Trojan prince Paris. It also tells us about the interference of the gods and their quarrels about the action on the battlefield below them.

The Odyssey – Homer

This describes Odysseus' journey home from the Trojan war. Odysseus features briefly in the *Iliad*. Again, human characters work side by side with the gods, who are given human characteristics. Although they are so powerful, the gods bear grudges, seek revenge and are very proud. The word odyssey has now come to mean any long, hard journey. The poem has strongly influenced other works of literature – most famously the novel *Ulysses* by the Irish writer James Joyce.

Rubáiyat

Omar Khayyám was a Persian writer, mathematician and astronomer who lived in the 11th and early 12th centuries. His *Rubáiyat* was introduced to the rest of the world in 1859, when it was translated by Edward Fitzgerald. Each verse contains a complete thought.

Beowulf

An epic poem of almost 3,200 lines written in Old English (or Anglo-Saxon). This is an early form of the English language that modern readers find hard to understand. The main theme is the struggle of the hero Beowulf with the water monster Grendel. Details of the poem's exact date and author are not known, but it may have been written in the 8th century by more than one person.

Sir Gawain and the Green Knight

This poem was written by a monk from the northwest of England during the second half of the 14th century. Its 2,530 lines describe events in King Arthur's court and the testing of Sir Gawain, a model knight. There are many opportunities for the character to fail, but he does not.

An illustration by William McLaren for *Sir Gawain and the Green Knight*

Famous poets and poems

Most poets write many poems. Below are some of the most famous poets and their best-known works.

Charles Baudelaire (1821–67), France, wrote *Les Fleurs du Mal*

William Blake (1757–1827), England, wrote *The Tyger; London*

Matsuo Basho (1644–94), Japan, wrote numerous haiku

Elizabeth Barrett Browning (1806–61), England, wrote *How Do I Love Thee?*

Robert Burns (1759–96), Scotland, wrote *Tam o' Shanter*

Lord Byron (1788–1824), England, wrote *Don Juan*

Geoffrey Chaucer (c. 1343–1400), England, wrote *The Canterbury Tales*

Samuel Taylor Coleridge (1772–1834), England, wrote *Kubla Khan; The Rime of the Ancient Mariner*

Dante Alighieri (1265–1321), Italy, wrote *The Divine Comedy*

Emily Dickinson (1830–86), USA, wrote *Because I Could Not Stop for Death*

T.S. Eliot (1888–1965), USA/England, wrote *The Waste Land*

Robert Frost (1874–1963), USA, wrote *Stopping by Woods on a Snowy Evening; The Road Not Taken*

Seamus Heaney (1939–), Ireland, wrote *Death of a Naturalist*

Homer (c. 8th century BC), Greece, wrote *The Iliad*; *The Odyssey*

John Keats (1795–1821), England, wrote *Ode to a Nightingale*; *La Belle Dame Sans Merci; To Autumn*

Rudyard Kipling (1865–1936), England, wrote *If*

Mikhail Lermontov (1814–41), Russia, wrote *The Novice*

Li Po (701–762), China, wrote *Drinking Alone Under the Moon*

John Milton (1608–74), England, wrote *Paradise Lost*; *Paradise Regained*

Pablo Neruda (1904–71), Chile, wrote *Canto General*

Nezami (1140–c. 1217), Iran, wrote *Khamseh* (or *The Quinary*)

Ovid (43 BC–AD 17), ancient Rome, wrote *Metamorphoses*

Sylvia Plath (1932–63), USA, wrote *Ariel*

Arthur Rimbaud (1854–91), France, wrote *Une Saison en Enfer* (or *A Season in Hell*)

Christina Rossetti (1830–94), England, wrote *Remember*

William Shakespeare (1564–1616), England, wrote *Sonnet 18* (or *Shall I Compare Thee to a Summer's Day*)

Percy Bysshe Shelley (1792–1822), England, wrote *Ozymandias*

Edmund Spenser (1552–99), England, wrote *The Faerie Queene*

Alfred Tennyson (1809–92), England, wrote *In Memoriam* and *The Lady of Shalott*

Dylan Thomas (1914–53), Wales, wrote *Fern Hill*

Virgil (70–19 BC), ancient Rome, wrote *The Aeneid*

Walt Whitman (1819–92), USA, wrote *Song of Myself*

William Wordsworth (1770–1850), England, wrote *The Prelude* and *Daffodils*

William Butler Yeats (1865–1939), Ireland, wrote *Sailing to Byzantium*; *The Lake Isle of Innisfree*

Sylvia Plath

Lord Byron was as famous for his adventurous life as for his poems

Sonnets

A sonnet, from the Italian for 'little song', is a type of 14-line poem dating from the 13th century that became widely known through the works of William Shakespeare. His *Sonnet XVIII*, which begins 'Shall I compare thee to a summer's day?', is one of the most popular English poems. Poets of the Romantic period of the late 18th and early 19th centuries, such as John Keats, wrote numerous sonnets and Seamus Heaney and other modern poets have kept the style alive.

Poets Laureate

The word laureate means crowned with laurel. The expression dates back to ancient Rome, where a successful person was traditionally crowned with a wreath of laurel leaves.

In Britain, the position of Poet Laureate was created as a royal office in 1668 with the appointment of John Dryden by King Charles II. The position was traditionally held for life, but is now restricted to ten years. When it becomes vacant the prime minister has a list of names drawn up and the monarch chooses a new Laureate. The Poet Laureate's main task is to write odes to celebrate royal birthdays, marriages and important state occasions. Poets Laureate receive a salary of £70 per annum – the same as in the 17th century! Some famous Poets Laureate in the UK include William Wordsworth, Sir John Betjeman and Ted Hughes. Andrew Motion was Poet Laureate from 1999–2009, when Carol Ann Duffy became the first ever woman Poet Laureate.

In the United States the first Poet Laureate (Joseph Auslander) was appointed in 1937. A new Laureate is appointed every year. He or she serves from October to May and is paid $35,000 (£17,500).

Most valuable comics

Copies of American comic books with the first appearances of superheroes Superman and Batman are the most valued by collectors. On 29 March 2010, the previous record for *Action Comics* No. 1 published in June 1938, with the first Superman story, was shattered when one changed hands for $1.5 million (£975,500), and five days later *Detective Comics* No. 27 (May 1939), in which Batman made his debut, was sold for $1,075,000 (£705,000).

Captain America

All about comics

Comic strips

A comic strip is a story told in a series of pictures published in a newspaper. The New York *Daily Graphic* was the first newspaper to feature a comic strip. It started on 11 September 1875 with *Professor Tigwissel's Burglar Alarm*. The first regular strip was The Yellow Kid, which began in a supplement of the New York World on 5 May 1895. A syndicated comic strip is one that appears in more than one newspaper. Some appear in hundreds of papers all over the world.

Comics

In the UK, weekly collections of cartoon strips and jokes began to appear in the 1880s and 1890s. Comics such as *Dandy* (1937) and *Beano* (1938) are still published today. From the 1890s in the USA, series of cartoon strips began to appear in newspapers and were syndicated nationwide. *Katzehjammer Kids*, which was first published in 1897, still appears in many newspapers and magazines.

Comic books

The first American comic book was called *Funnies on Parade* and came out in 1933. The first to be published regularly was *Famous Funnies* in 1934. Many comic books were about the adventures of a single superhero, such as Batman or Superman, who used special powers to fight crime and defeat evil villains.

Computer-generated comics

The first comic entirely produced by computer was *Shatter*, an American science-fiction comic published in March 1985. Since then, illustrators have increasingly used digital technology to create comic strips. This method allows writers and illustrators in different locations to work together.

See also
Book firsts and records: page 229

Newspaper fact file

First newspapers

From 59 BC onwards Roman emperor Julius Caesar had handwritten reports on news posted in public places in Rome. China had newspapers from about AD 713. The first European printed newspapers appeared in Germany in 1609.

The first daily newspaper, *Einkommende Zeitungen*, also started in Germany, in 1650. Britain's first daily paper was the *Perfect Diurnall*, published in London in 1660. America's first successful newspaper was the *Boston News-Letter*, which appeared in 1704.

Smallest

Newspaper publishers sometimes produce miniature editions for publicity purposes. The smallest regular publication was the *Daily Banner*, published in 1876 in Oregon, USA. It measured just 9.5 x 7.6 cm (3.75 x 3 in).

Largest

The edition of the Belgian newspaper *Het Volk* published on 14 June 1993 had pages measuring 142 x 99.5 cm (55.9 x 39.2 in), which is more than six times the area of an ordinary broadsheet (large page size) newspaper.

First appearances

Some comic strip and comic book characters are older than you might think. Below is a list of some famous comic characters' first appearances.

Rupert Bear appeared as a strip in the *Daily Express* (UK) on 8 November 1920
Tintin *Le Vingtième Siècle* (Belgium) on 10 January 1929
Popeye appeared as a strip in *Thimble Theatre* (USA) on 17 January 1929
Dick Tracy appeared as a strip in the *Chicago Tribune* (USA) on 4 October 1931
Flash Gordon appeared as a syndicated strip (USA) on 7 January 1934
Desperate Dan *Dandy* (UK) on 4 December 1937
Superman *Action Comics* No. 1 (USA) in June 1938
Batman *Detective Comics* No. 27 (USA) in May 1939
Captain Marvel *Whiz Comics* No. 1 (USA) in Febrruary 1940
The Green Lantern *All American Comics* No. 16 (USA) in July 1940
The Flash *Flash Comics* No. 1 (USA) in January 1940
Robin (Batman's assistant) *Detective Comics* No. 38 (USA) in April 1940
Wonder Woman *All-Star Comics* No. 8 (USA) in December 1941
Captain America *Captain America Comics* No. 1 (USA) in March 1941
Dan Dare *Eagle* (UK) on 14 April 1950
Peanuts appeared as a syndicated strip (USA) on 2 October 1950
Dennis the Menace (USA) appeared as a syndicated strip (USA) on 12 March 1951
Dennis the Menace (UK) *Beano* (UK) on 17 March 1951
Astérix the Gaul *Pilote* (France) on 29 October 1959
Supergirl *Action Comics* No. 252 (USA) in May 1959
Spiderman *Amazing Fantasy* No. 15 (USA) in August 1962
The Incredible Hulk* *Hulk* (USA) in March 1962
X-Men *The X-Men* (USA) in September 1963
Daredevil *Daredevil* (USA) in June 1964

* The Hulk had grey skin in March 1962, but became The Incredible Hulk, with green skin, in the May issue two months later.

Magazine fact file

First-ever popular magazine
Mercure Galant, a gossip magazine, was first published in Paris in March 1672.

First women's magazine
The Ladies' Mercury was first published in London on 27 June 1693.

First American magazine
The American Magazine, published in Philadelphia, probably began on 13 February 1741.

First children's magazine
The *Lilliputian Magazine* appeared in the UK in June 1751 and ran for just over a year. The first in the USA was the *Children's Magazine*, published in January 1789.

First fashion magazine
The Paris magazine *Le Cabinet des Modes* was first published in 1785.

Longest-running US magazine
Scientific American was launched on 28 August 1845 and is the longest continuously published magazine in the USA. At first, it was a four-page newspaper and included features on science and technology as well as topics such as religion and poetry. Later it began to focus on science and is now the world's most popular scientific journal.

First photograph in a magazine
Each copy of the June 1846 issue of the *Art Union* (UK) contained a photograph by Henry Fox Talbot, one of the inventors of photography.

Heaviest

The Sunday edition of the *New York Times* for 14 September 1987 contained 1,612 pages and weighed 5.4 kg (12 lb). At one time 127 hectares (314 acres) of forest containing almost 63,000 trees had to be chopped down to make one edition of the paper. Nowadays, much of the paper used for newspapers is recycled.

Top selling

The *Yomuri Shimbun* (Japan) sells more than 10 million copies a day. *Bild-Zeitung* (Germany) is the highest-circulation newspaper outside Japan, selling more than 3.5 million copies a day. *The Times of India* and *The Sun* (UK) each sell over 3.1 million copies a day, making them the top-selling English-language newspapers in the world.

First online newspapers

The *Mercury Center*, of San Jose, California, was the first online newspaper, made available to America Online subscribers in May 1993. Britain's first online national newspaper was the *Electronic Telegraph*, launched in November 1994.

WHITAKER'S WORLD OF FACTS

Education & the Arts

Education for all

Schoolchildren in India celebrate Independence Day, an annual event that takes place on 15 August. India has 134 million children aged between 5 and 14, many of whom will benefit from a new law that came into force in 2010 making free primary schooling compulsory for all. Many Indian children leave education to help their parents at home or work to raise money for their families. Girls in particular often fail to complete their education, and the Indian National Commission for Protection of Children's Rights calculates that about a quarter of girls drop out of school between the ages of 6 and 10 and up to half of girls aged between 10 and 13.

Oldest schools

School	Founded	School	Founded
Shishi Middle School, Chengdu, China	143–141 BC	Gymnasium Carolinum in Osnabrück, Germany	804
The King's School, Canterbury, UK	597	Warwick School, UK	914
The King's School, Rochester, UK	604	St Alban's School, UK	948
St Peter's School, York, UK	627	The King's School, Ely, UK	970
Beverley Grammar School, UK	700	Menntaskólinn í Reykjavík, Iceland	1056
Gymnasium Paulinum, Münster, Germany	797	Salisbury Cathedral School, UK	1091

King's School Canterbury and Canterbury Cathedral

USA grade system

American children have 12 years of schooling. They start at five and the first year at school is called kindergarten. The grade system begins in the second year with first grade (six year olds) and continues to twelfth grade (18 year olds). In high schools, years have names instead of numbers: ninth grade is known as the freshman year, tenth as the sophomore year, eleventh as the junior year and twelfth as the senior year.

Education timeline 3000 BC

3000 BC The Sumerians pioneer the idea of teaching. Education available only to those who could afford to pay a teacher for each lesson.

590 BC The city of Athens becomes the first to offer public education to all men for a small fee. Free education available to the sons of war veterans.

597 King's School in Canterbury opens – the first school in the UK

859 The world's first university still in existence is founded in Fez, Morocco

1064 The first European university is founded in Parma, Italy

1160 Oxford University becomes the first university in England

1538 The first university of the New World opens in Santo Domingo (now the Dominican Republic)

1635 The first publicly funded high school in the USA opens in Boston

1636 Harvard University becomes the first university in the USA

1760 The first school for deaf children opens in Paris. Pupils are taught an early version of sign language

1781 The first nursery school is opened in Scotland for parents who have to go to work

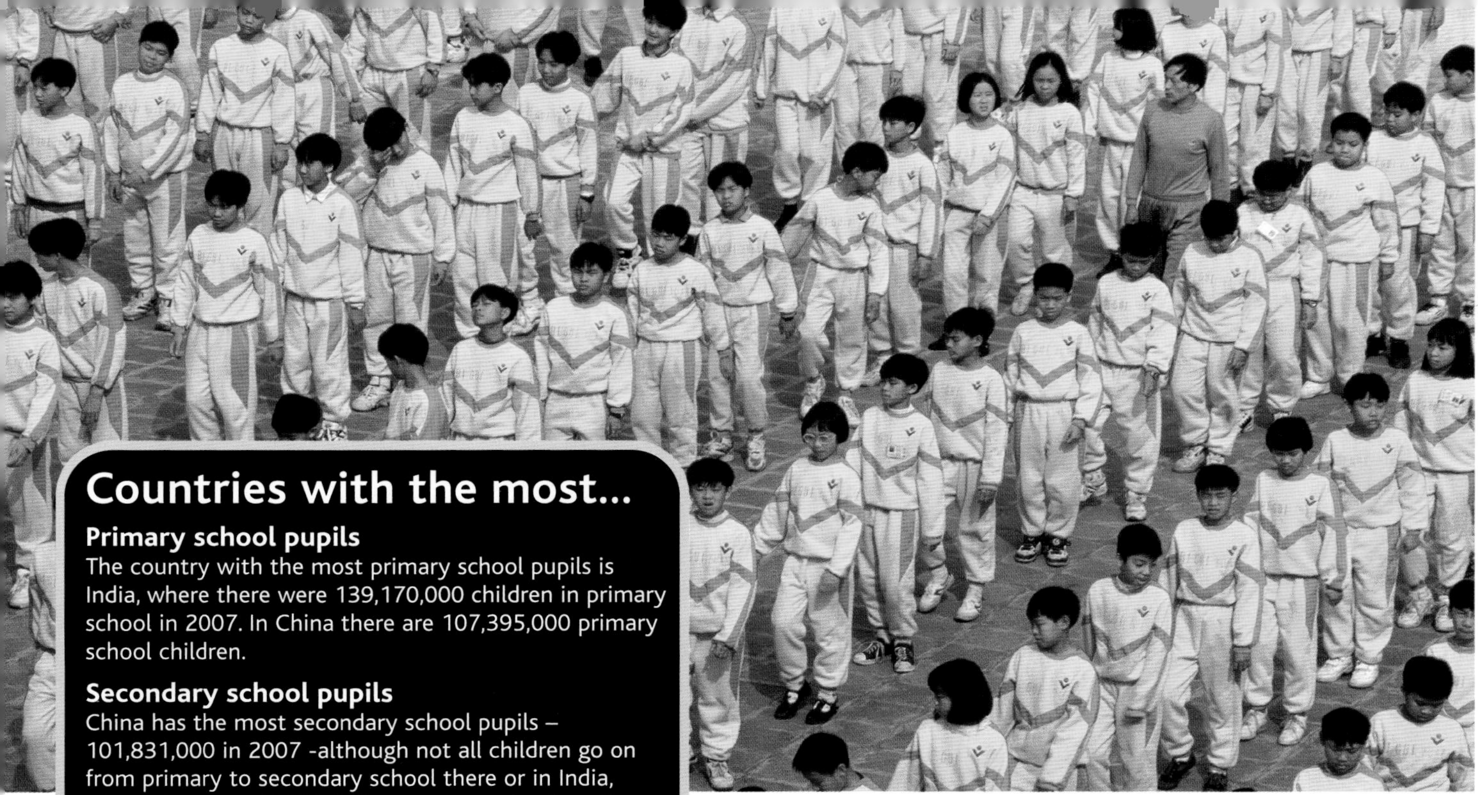

Children at a Chinese boarding school doing their morning exercises

Countries with the most...

Primary school pupils

The country with the most primary school pupils is India, where there were 139,170,000 children in primary school in 2007. In China there are 107,395,000 primary school children.

Secondary school pupils

China has the most secondary school pupils – 101,831,000 in 2007 -although not all children go on from primary to secondary school there or in India, where there are 91,529,000 secondary school pupils.

University students

China has 25,346,000 students at university compared with the USA's 17,759,000. There are 12,853,000 at university in India and 9,370,000 in Russia.

Pupils per teacher at primary school

Primary school children in some African nations are taught in classes of more than 50 – there are 142 pupils per teacher in Liberia and up to 49 in Benin. At the other end of the scale, there are 22 per class in the UK, 16 in the USA and only 6 per class in Iceland.

Pupils per teacher at secondary school

In secondary schools in Eritrea, there are as many as 49 pupils for each teacher. Schools in Greece have 8, Portugal 7 and Bermuda 6 in each class. The UK and USA both have an average of 15.

See also
Largest countries: page 116

Schooling around the world

Time spent at school

- School children in China spend more time at school than children in any other country. They have 251 schooldays a year – 59 days more than British children, and 71 more than American children.
- In the United Kingdom, the United States, France, Canada, Germany, Belgium, the Netherlands, Australia and New Zealand children have 10, 11 or 12 years of education. In most African countries and parts of South America children spend just five or six years at school. Only two African countries, Gabon and Tunisia, have ten years of compulsory schooling.
- In Italy and China, children can legally finish school at the age of 14. In Myanmar, Angola and Pakistan, children are allowed to finish at the age of nine, after only four or five years at school. In several European countries, including Croatia, Denmark, Sweden and Switzerland, parents don't have to send their children to school until they are seven years old – two years later than in many other countries.

Largest school

The largest school in the world is the City Montessori school in Lucknow, northern India; it has more than 31,000 pupils.

2000s

1783 Poland becomes the first country to ban corporal punishment in schools
1784 The first school for blind children is started in Paris
1841 Oberlin College becomes the first university in the USA to award degrees to women
1871 A school in New York introduces the first distance-learning courses for young people who live too far away from schools to travel to them
1878 London University becomes the first UK university to award degrees to women
1987 Corporal punishment is banned in all UK state schools
1999 Corporal punishment is banned in all independent schools in the UK
2007 UK confirms intention to raise school leaving age to 18 years old in 2013

Most remote school

The world's most remote school is Kiwirrkurra Remote Community School in Australia. It is a 25-hour road journey from the nearest major town. The 100 pupils and seven teachers at another school in the region, Oombulgurri Remote Community School, can only get to school by light aircraft or by barge. The aircraft takes just 35 minutes, but the barge can take up to 12 hours.

The *Mona Lisa* by Leonardo da Vinci

The theft of the *Mona Lisa*

One of the world's most famous paintings, Leonardo da Vinci's *Mona Lisa*, was stolen from the Louvre Museum, Paris, on 21 August 1911 by an employee of the museum, Vincenzo Peruggia (1881–1947). He hid overnight in a broom cupboard in the Louvre, removed it from the wall when it was empty and walked out with the painting under his clothing. He kept it in his apartment for two years, but when he attempted to sell it he was caught and jailed.

Western art styles

Medieval
Paintings, mosaics and miniatures in manuscripts, mostly of religious subjects.

Renaissance
The word means rebirth – the Renaissance art of the 15th and 16th centuries replaced medieval styles and revived the art of the Greek and Roman period.

Mannerism
A style of 16th-century Italian art, which uses bright colours and distorts scale and perspective.

Baroque/rococo
An ornate style that was popular in Italy during the 17th and 18th centuries.

Neoclassicism
A style of the 18th century modelled on classical (Greek and Roman) art.

Romanticism
This late 18th/early 19th-century style explores emotion and shows nature in its untamed state.

Realism/naturalism
19th-century style that showed real life, including its unpleasant side such as poverty.

Pre-Raphaelitism
This short-lived style, inspired by medieval history and myths, was invented in 1848. The aim was to go back to the simplicity of painting before Raphael.

Impressionism
This style of painting developed in France and was named in 1874. The aim was to convey an impression of what the eye sees rather than what the mind knows is there.

Symbolism
An attempt by late 19th-century artists to link the real and the spiritual worlds in their work.

Post-Impressionism
A development from Impressionism, which includes the Pointillism (dot painting) of Seurat and others. In Pointillism, small dots of colour are applied to the canvas. These appear to fuse when seen from a distance.

Art Nouveau
A flowing ornamental style of the late 19th/early 20th centuries, which influenced architects and furniture makers and painters.

Expressionism/abstract expressionism
Early 20th-century styles in which the emotions of the painter are powerfully expressed.

Cubism
An abstract style which is mostly about shape and colour.

Art Deco
An angular, decorative style popular in the 1920s and 1930s.

Surrealism
A style that emerged between the World Wars, in which artists explore dreams and fantasy.

Abstract art
Non-naturalistic art in which shapes, lines and colour are more important than the objects they represent.

Pop art
Style conceived in the 1950s, using images from popular culture such as comics and advertising.

Environmental art
Art in which the landscape is decorated or altered. The artist uses natural objects such as stones to create his work.

Britart
Modern art by a group of young British artists. The movement began in 1988.

Giant eggs decorate the Dali museum in Rosas, Spain.

Famous artists

Artist	Famous work
Fra Angelico (c. 1400–55) Italian	*Deposition of Christ*
Sandro Botticelli (1445–1510) Italian	*Birth of Venus*
Hieronymus Bosch (c. 1450–1516) Flemish	*Garden of Earthly Delights*
Leonardo da Vinci (1452–1519) Italian	*Mona Lisa*
Albrecht Dürer (1471–1528) German	*Four Apostles*
Michelangelo (1475–1564) Italian	Sistine Chapel ceiling
Raphael (1483–1520) Italian	*Madonna*
Hans Holbein (1497–1543) German	*Sir Thomas More*
El Greco (1541–1614) Greek	*Burial of Count Orgaz*
Sir Peter Paul Rubens (1577–1640) Flemish	*Descent from the Cross*
Rembrandt Van Rijn (1606–69) Dutch	*The Night Watch*
Jan Vermeer (1632–75) Dutch	*Girl with a Pearl Earring*
Antonio Canaletto (1697–1768) Italian	*The Grand Canal and the Church of the Salute, Venice*
Sir Joshua Reynolds (1723–92) British	*The Family of the Duke of Marlborough*
Thomas Gainsborough (1727–88) British	*Blue Boy*
Francisco Goya (1746–1828) Spanish	*Maja Nude/Clothed*
J.M.W. Turner (1775–1851) British	*Rain, Steam, and Speed*
John Constable (1776–1837) British	*The Haywain*
Dante Gabriel Rossetti (1828–82) British	*Proserpine*
Sir John Everett Millais (1829–96) British	*Ophelia*
Sir Edward Burne-Jones (1833–98) British	*The Golden Stairs*
Edgar Degas (1834–1917) French	*The Rehearsal*
James McNeill Whistler (1834–1903) American	*Symphony in White*

Art terms

acrylic
Quick-drying plastic-based paint

cartoon
A preliminary sketch for a painting

chiaroscuro
Light and shade in painting

collage
A work made from pieces of paper and other materials stuck on to a background

composition
The arrangement of the elements and colour within a work

fresco
A painting on a freshly plastered wall

gouache
Water-based paint

icon
A portrait of a religious subject, such as a saint

impasto
Thickly applied paint

landscape
A painting of the natural world

medium
The material used to create a work of art

montage
Cut-out objects mounted on a surface

palette
The surface used by an artist for mixing paints, but also used to refer to the selection of colours

pastel
Coloured pigments in stick form used for drawing

still-life
A painting of an object or a group of objects

tempera
Pigments mixed with egg yolk and oil or water

trompe l'oeil
A painting that plays tricks on the eye to look as if it is three-dimensional

watercolour
Coloured pigments mixed with water

Most expensive paintings

Jackson Pollock's *No. 5, 1948*, was sold privately in New York in 2006 for a price believed to have been about $140 million (£75.7 million), making it the most expensive painting not sold at auction. Among the highest prices paid at auction are:

- Pablo Picasso, *Nude, Green Leaves and Bust*, $106.5 million (£70.2 million), May 2010
- Pablo Picasso, *Boy with a pipe*, $104.2 million (£58 million), May 2004
- Pablo Picasso, *Dora Maar with Cat*, $95.2 million (£53.6 million), May 2006
- Gustav Klimt, *Portrait of Adele Bloch-Bauer II*, $87.9 million (£47.4 million), November 2006
- Francis Bacon, *Triptych*, $86.3 million (£44.2 million), May 2008
- Vincent van Gogh, *Portrait du Dr Gachet*, $82.5 million (£49 million), May 1990

Most expensive sculpture

In 2010, Swiss sculptor Alberto Giacometti's life-sized bronze statue *L'homme Qui Marche I* (*The Man Who Walks I*) was sold in London for £65 million ($104.3 million), making it the most expensive sculpture ever sold at auction. The previous record was held by *The Guennol Lioness*, a 7.6-cm (3-in) high statue dating from *c.*3000 BC and sold in New York in 2007 for $57.2 million (£27.7 million).

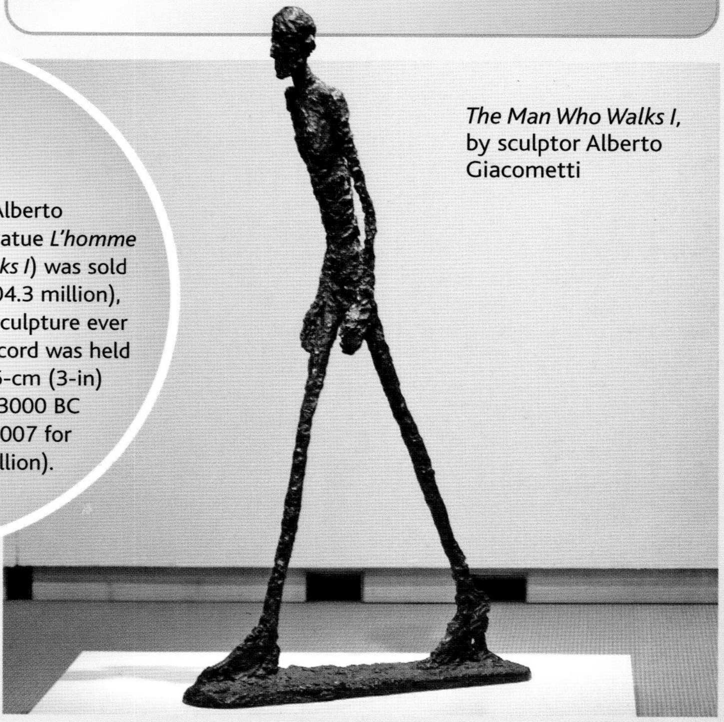

The Man Who Walks I, by sculptor Alberto Giacometti

www.artcyclopedia.com search

Artist	Famous work
Paul Cézanne (1839–1906) French	*Large Bathers*
Claude Monet (1840–1926) French	*Waterlilies*
Berthe Morisot (1841–95) French	*The Cradle*
Pierre Renoir (1841–1919) French	*Luncheon of the Boating Party*
Mary Cassatt (1844–1926) American	*The Bath*
Paul Gauguin (1848–1903) French	*Nevermore*
Vincent van Gogh (1853–90) Dutch	*Sunflowers*
Georges Seurat (1859–91) French	*Sunday Afternoon on the Island of La Grand Jatte*
Henri de Toulouse-Lautrec (1864–1901) French	*Aristide Bruant* (poster)
Henri Matisse (1869–1954) French	*The Dance*
Piet Mondrian (1872–1944) Dutch	*Broadway Boogie Woogie*
Pablo Picasso (1881–1973) Spanish	*Guernica*
Salvador Dali (1904–89) Spanish	*The Persistence of Memory*
Francis Bacon (1909–92) British	*Study after Velazquez's Portrait of Pope Innocent X*
Jackson Pollock (1912–56) American	*Number One 1948*
Lucien Freud (1922–) British	*Girl with Roses*
Roy Lichtenstein (1923–97) American	*Whaam!*
Jasper Johns (1930–) American	*Flag*
Andy Warhol (1930–89) American	*Marilyn Monroe*
David Hockney (1937–) British	*A Bigger Splash*
Jeff Koons (1955–) American	*Balloon Flower – Magenta*
Tracey Emin (1963–) British	*My Bed*
Damien Hirst (1965–) British	*Golden Calf*

Art exhibitions and world fairs

Major art exhibitions and world fairs have been held for more than 200 years. Art exhibitions focus on a particular artist or style. World fairs promote the trade or image of a country and display new inventions.

Great Exhibition, London, 1851
This was a showpiece of the arts and industries of the world and the first exhibition of its kind in the UK. It was seen by 6,039,195 visitors.

First Impressionist Exhibition, Paris, France, 1874
Many Impressionist painters, including Claude Monet, first showed their work at this exhibition, which was shocking to many people.

Philadelphia Centennial Exposition, Philadelphia, USA, 1876
This first major show in the USA was held to celebrate the 100th anniversary of the Declaration of Independence. It was seen by 9,910,966 people. Inventor Alexander Graham Bell first demonstrated the telephone at the Exposition.

Exposition Universelle, Paris, 1889
The Eiffel Tower was built as a temporary exhibit for this show, which commemorated 100 years since the French Revolution. It attracted 28,121,975 visitors.

World's Columbian Exposition, Chicago, USA, 1893
This show celebrated the 400th anniversary of Columbus' discovery of America and had more than 27.3 million visitors. Many Americans experienced electricity and hand-held cameras for the first time.

Armory Show, New York, 1913
This was the first exhibition of modern art in the United States and included the work of Picasso. It influenced American artists, collectors and museums.

Exposition Internationale des Arts Décoratifs et Industriels Modernes, Paris, 1925
This exhibition of art marked the beginning of Art Deco style and attracted 5,852,783 visitors.

Crazy Horse Memorial with model in foreground

World's Fair, Flushing Meadow Park, Queens, New York, 1939–40
The fair had 44,932,978 visitors and first introduced television to the public.

Festival of Britain, London, 1951
This was a celebration of post-war life, held 100 years after the Great Exhibition. It attracted 8.5 million visitors.

Treasures of Tutankhamen, British Museum, London, 1972–73
This was one of the most popular exhibitions of all time and attracted 1,694,117 visitors. The show went to New York in 1978–79, where it was seen by 1,226,467 people.

Expo 2005, Japan
22 million people visited the show, themed "Nature's Wisdom". All the exhibition pavilions were built from recycled materials.

Museum fact file

First museum open to the public
Uffizi Gallery, Florence, Italy, 1591.

First museum in England
The Ashmolean Museum, Oxford, opened in 1683 to display the collection of natural history exhibits, coins, weapons and other items belonging to the collector and antiquary Elias Ashmole (1617–92).

The first national museum
The British Museum, London, opened to the public in 1759.

First public museum in the USA
Charleston Museum, Charleston, South Carolina, opened 1773.

First open-air museum
Skansen, Stockholm, Sweden, opened in 1891.

First children's museum
Brooklyn, New York, USA, opened 1899 and was the first of more than 300 children's museums worldwide.

First interactive museum
The Exploratorium, San Francisco, California, USA, opened in 1969 and has hundreds of hands-on exhibits.

Largest museum complex
The Smithsonian Institution, Washington DC, USA, consists of 16 museums with a total of more than 140 million items in their collections.

Crazy Horse Memorial

Started in 1948 by Polish-American sculptor Korczak Ziolkowski and continued after his death in 1982 by his widow and children, this gigantic equestrian statue of the 19th-century native American warrior Crazy Horse is being carved out of Thunderhead Mountain, South Dakota, USA. It is 172 m (563 ft) high and 195 m (641 ft) long and is not expected to be completed for several years, but will be the world's largest sculpture.

The world's tallest monuments

Many giant monuments around the world proudly celebrate the achievements of countries or their people. They also serve as memorials to – or the tombs of – their rulers and leaders.

Monument/location/year	m	ft
Gateway Arch, St Louis, Missouri, USA (1965)	192	630
San Jacinto Monument, La Porte, Texas, USA (1939)	174	570
Crazy Horse Memorial, Thunderhead Mountain, South Dakota, USA (under construction)	172	563
Juche Tower, Pyongyang, North Korea (1982)	170	558
Washington Monument, Washington, DC, USA (1884)	169	555
Cruz de los Caidos, San Lorenzo de El Escorial, Spain (1956)	150	492
Victory Monument, Moscow, Russia (1995)	142	465
Pyramid of Khufu, Giza, Egypt (2560BC)	139	455
National Monument, Jakarta, Indonesia (1975)	137	449
Pyramid of Khafre, Giza, Egypt (2532BC)	136	448

Gateway Arch
The Gateway Arch, St Louis, Missouri, is part of a national memorial commemorating the westward expansion of the United States. Visitors can travel up inside it in a specially-designed tram car and look out from an observation deck.

Abu Simbel, Egypt
The four huge statues, each standing 20 m (66 ft) high, used to guard a temple. They were moved in 1966 when the Aswan High Dam was built and the area flooded.

Statues of Abu Simbel

Unusual museums

Cockroach Hall of Fame, Plano, Texas, USA
Record-breaking cockroaches, and insects dressed as famous people

Colman's Mustard Museum, Norwich, Norfolk, UK
Tells the fascinating history of mustard

The Museum of Dog Collars, Leeds Castle, Maidstone, Kent, UK
A collection of dog collars, some of them from the Middle Ages

Gallery of Also-Rans, Norton, Kansas, USA
A collection celebrating people who came second or lost political campaigns and other contests

The Lawnmower Museum, Trerice, Cornwall, UK
Mechanical lawnmowers through the ages

The Medieval Crime Museum, Rothenburg, Germany
Medieval crime, punishment and torture implements

National Wool Museum, Geelong, Australia
The only museum devoted to wool, opened in 1988

Nut Museum, Old Lyme, Connecticut, USA
Nut carvings, 2.4 m (7.9 ft)-long nutcrackers and other nut-related exhibits

Philips Mushroom Museum, Kennett Square, Pennsylvania, USA
A museum focusing on all types of mushrooms and other fungi

The Piggy Bank Museum, Amsterdam, Netherlands
Displays 12,000 piggy banks from all periods

Porter Thermometer Museum, Onset, Massachusetts, USA
More than 3,000 devices for taking temperatures

Amazing collectors

Louis XIV
The French king owned a collection of 413 ornate beds. He kept them in different places all over France, so wherever he travelled, he could sleep in his own bed.

The Schlumpf brothers
French factory owners Hans and Fritz Schlumpf built up one of the world's largest car collections. They had 427 vehicles, including 120 rare Bugattis. These are now on public display at the National Auto Museum of France in Mulhouse.

Sir Thomas Phillips
Eccentric English book collector Sir Thomas Phillips (1792–1872) wanted to own a copy of every book ever printed – and he almost succeeded. He acquired more than 50,000 books and 100,000 manuscripts. His collection plunged his family into debt, but he rescued many priceless treasures from destruction. Sales from his collection have continued almost every year since his death.

Robert Opie
Robert Opie began his collection in 1963 with the wrapper from a packet of sweets. He now owns the world's largest collection of British packaging and advertising material, a total of more than 500,000 items.

Henry Holt
Lancashire collector Henry Holt built up the world's largest collection of bricks. When he died in 1996 he left 7,000 of them to the local museum, stacked up in various locations. The museum has been puzzling over what to do with them ever since.

In 2005, George Barris the "King of Customizers" auctioned his film and television cars, including this one he made for Elvis Presley.

Unusual auction items

- In 1888 a cemetery containing 300,000 mummified cats was found in Egypt. Almost 20 tonnes of the mummies were shipped to Liverpool, UK, and sold at auction for £4 ($19.50) per tonne.
- A burnt loaf from the Great Fire of London, 1666, was sold at Sotheby's, London, in 1996 for £322 ($500).
- A pair of Queen Victoria's underpants were sold at Sotheby's, London, in 1996 for £253 ($395). A pair of Victorian rollerblades dating from c. 1860 was sold at the same sale for £575 ($900).
- A dish containing a sample of penicillium mould prepared by penicillin inventor Alexander Fleming in 1935 was sold by Christie's, London, in 1997 for £14,950 ($23,770). At the same sale a box of 300 glass eyes was sold for £2,760 ($4,390).
- At a sale in London in 2010, two Daleks from *Dr Who* made a total of £36,000.
- More than 2,000 items that had belonged to the singer Elvis Presley were sold at an auction in Las Vegas in 1999. These included clothing as well as letters, one of Elvis's school report cards and 29 dry-cleaning bills made out to Elvis.
- Several pairs of spectacles belonging to John Lennon of the Beatles have sold for up to $1.5 million (£750,000).
- In April 2009 more than 2,000 items belonging to Michael Jackson were offered at a four-day auction in Beverly Hills, California. Among his possessions was property from his Neverland Ranch – furniture, stage costumes and crystal gloves, music awards, paintings, his tour bus, and even a life-sized waxworks figure of Jackson himself. The catalogue of the sale was in five volumes, and the complete set cost $100, but the sale was cancelled.
- In 2008, a light sabre that appeared in *Star Wars* and *The Empire Strikes Back* was auctioned in California for $240,000 (£160,000).

Young enthusiasts sorting a collection of baseball cards

Who collects what?

As soon as someone starts to collect something a word is invented to describe the collector. Most end in -ist, which means a person who does something (as a motorist is someone who drives a car or a violinist someone who plays a violin). Another ending is -phile or -philist, which means a lover of something.

Collectable	Collector
airmail	**aerophilatelist**
autographs	**philographist**
badges and patches	**scutelliphilist**
banknotes	**notaphilist**
beer bottle labels	**labeorphilist**
beer mats	**tegestologist** or **tegetologist**
book plates	**ex-librist**
books	**bibliophile** or **bibliophilist**
butterflies and moths	**lepidopterist**
cigar bands	**brandophilist** or **cigrinophilist**
coins, money, medals	**numismatist**
corkscrews	**helixophile**
dolls	**plangonologist**
eggs	**oologist** (illegal in many countries)
egg-cups	**pocillovist**
flags and banners	**vexillologist**
gramophone records	**discophilist**
keyrings	**copoclephilist**
keys	**cagophilist**
maps	**cartomaniac**
match books	**phillumenist**
matchboxes	**cumyxaphilist**
money boxes	**argyrothecologist**
postcards	**deltiologist**
prints and book illustrations	**iconophilist**
shells	**conchologist**
stamps	**philatelist**
sugar packets	**sucrologist**
teddy bears	**arctophilists**
telephone cards	**fusilatelist**
transport tokens	**vecturist**

Collecting picture postcards

Picture postcards appeared in Switzerland in the 1870s, but were prohibited by the postal services of many countries. Once they were permitted, by the Royal Mail in the UK on 1 September 1894 and the United States Postal Service on 19 May 1898, they became one of the most common ways in which people communicated with their families and friends, especially when they were on holiday, with millions of cards posted every year. Picture postcard collecting, known as deltiology, also became popular. Card collectors often find a subject that interests them and concentrate on that, for example:

- **Place** – also called 'topographical': cards with photographs showing places, particular countries or towns, or themes within them, such as castles or shops.
- **Subject** – comic seaside postcards are very popular, as are specific themes such as transport (ships, railways, cars, aircraft), famous people (including actors and royalty), animals (birds, dogs, etc), advertising, sports such as golf or the Olympic games, exhibitions, music, military, political and scenes showing everyday life.
- **Artist** – certain illustrators, such as comic artist Donald McGill, Louis Wain, who specialized in cards featuring cartoon cats, or Mabel Lucie Attwell, who featured children and babies, are prized by collectors.
- **Publisher** – some card manufacturers produced ranges of cards, or cards of a particular style, and some collectors aim to find an example of each.

A collection of picture postcards

http://kids.si.edu/collecting search

A collection of shells

Music & Performance

The saxophone

170 years ago Adolphe Sax, a Belgian musician, invented the saxophone. He wanted to create an instrument that would be the most powerful and vocal of the woodwinds and the most adaptive of the brass, to fill the vacant middle ground between the two sections. In 1841 he showed his new creation to Hector Berlioz. The composer was so impressed by the unique instrument that he gave it its debut in an 1844 concert. The saxophone gained greater popularity in the 1920s, when it began to be used in jazz bands, a role it is perhaps best known for today.

Musical instrument records

Double bass
A double bass 4.26 m (14 ft) long and weighing 590 kg (1,300 lb) was built by Arthur K. Ferris of Ironia, New Jersey, USA, in 1924.

Organ
The world's largest cathedral organ was built in St Stephen's Cathedral, Passau, Germany, in 1928. It has 17,774 pipes.

Guitar
A giant version of a Gibson guitar 11.63 m (38.2 ft) long was made in 1991 by students at Shakamak High School, Jasonville, Indiana, USA. Large stringed instruments that are bigger than the span of human hands are difficult or even impossible to play.

Pianos
In 1935 in London, Charles H. Challen built a piano which is probably the largest in the world. It weighs 1.25 tonnes and is 3.55 m (11.6 ft) long. One of the lightest pianos ever made was a baby grand weighing just 180 kg (397 lb). It was made mostly of aluminium covered in yellow pigskin. Made by the Blüthner company of Germany for the airship *Hindenburg*, it was destroyed when the airship exploded in 1937.

Tuba
In 1896 John Philip Sousa, who is the American inventor of the sousaphone, played a 2.28 m (7.48 ft) tuba on a world tour. This is the largest brass instrument ever made and had 11.8 m (38.7 ft) of tubing.

See also
Inventions: pages 80–81

Big Bertha
The University of Texas Longhorn Band has a drum nicknamed Big Bertha which is 7.6 m (24.9 ft) in circumference.

Valuable instruments

Guitars
In 2002 two guitars owned by Grateful Dead guitarist Jerry Garcia were sold in New York: 'Tiger' for £657,850 ($957,500) and 'Wolf' for £542,425 ($789,500). A Fender Stratocaster signed by over 20 famous rock guitarists has been sold twice at auctions in aid of a charity to help tsunami victims, raising a total of £2.1 million ($3.7 million).

Violins
A Stradivarius violin made in 1707 and named 'The Hammer' after its former owner, Christian Hammer, was sold at auction in New York in 2006 for a record £1,873,878 ($3,544,000).

Upright piano
John Lennon's Steinway Model Z upright piano, on which he wrote such songs as *Imagine*, was sold to singer George Michael in 2000 for £1,450,000 ($2,105,472).

Recording timeline

1800s

1877 Thomas Alva Edison first recorded a human voice (singing "Mary Had a Little Lamb") on a tinfoil cylinder phonograph
1878 Edison is granted phonograph patent
1885 "Graphophone" with wax cylinders is invented by Alexander Graham Bell and Charles Tainter
1888 "Gramophone", with 7-inch (17.8 cm) flat disk, is patented by Emile Berliner
1895 First spring-driven phonograph is sold by Edison
1896 Improved gramophone produced by Eldridge Johnson
1897 Shellac discs introduced
1898 First magnetic recorder, with steel wire, patented by Valdemar Poulsen
1904 First mass-produced, double-sided discs are sold in Germany
1925 First electrically-recorded discs make it possible to record entire orchestral works. Sound recordings for films are introduced.
1927 First coin-operated juke box is produced
1931 Stereo recording introduced
1934 First hi-fi (high-fidelity sound) records are made
1935 "Magnetophone" (tape recorder) is demonstrated in Berlin

Musical terms

Many musical terms are derived from Italian words. Here are the meanings of some common ones.

Musical tempos

Tempo	Meaning
Larghissimo	As slow as possible
Largo	Very slow and solemn
Largementa	Slow, broad
Larghetto	Slightly less slow
Lento	Slow
Adagissimo	Very slow
Adagio	Slow
Adagietto	Slightly faster
Andante	Moderately slow
Andantino	Slightly slower than andante
Moderato	At a brisk walking pace
Allegretto	Fairly lively
Allegramente	Lightly
Allegro	Lively, fast (from the Italian for cheerful)
Vivace	Fast
Vivacissimo	Very quick
Presto	Very fast
Prestissimo	Extremely fast

Other musical terms

Term	Meaning
Agitato	Agitated or excited
Brillante	Sparkling, brilliant
Brio	Spirit or vigour
Crescendo	Gradual increase in volume
Dolce	Sweet, soft and gentle
Dolente	Sad
Forte	Loud or strong
Fortissimo	Very loud
Grave	Slow and serious
Legato	Smoothly and evenly
Molto	Much or very
Pianissimo	Very soft
Piano	Soft
Ritenuto	Slowing in tempo
Scherzo	Lively
Sotto voce	Quiet and subdued
Tutti	All the players

National anthems

Most countries have a national anthem, a patriotic song, often based on a hymn or a poem about the country that is sung on special occasions.

The Dutch anthem *Het Wilhelmus*, which dates from the 1570s, is considered the world's oldest. Britain's anthem, *God Save The Queen*, which is also sung, with variations, in some British Commonwealth countries, has been sung to the same tune since 1744. The tune is also used for the anthems of other countries, including Liechtenstein and Norway. The French *Marseillaise* was officially adopted in 1795. In the USA *The Star-Spangled Banner*, although written in 1814, did not become the national anthem until 1931.

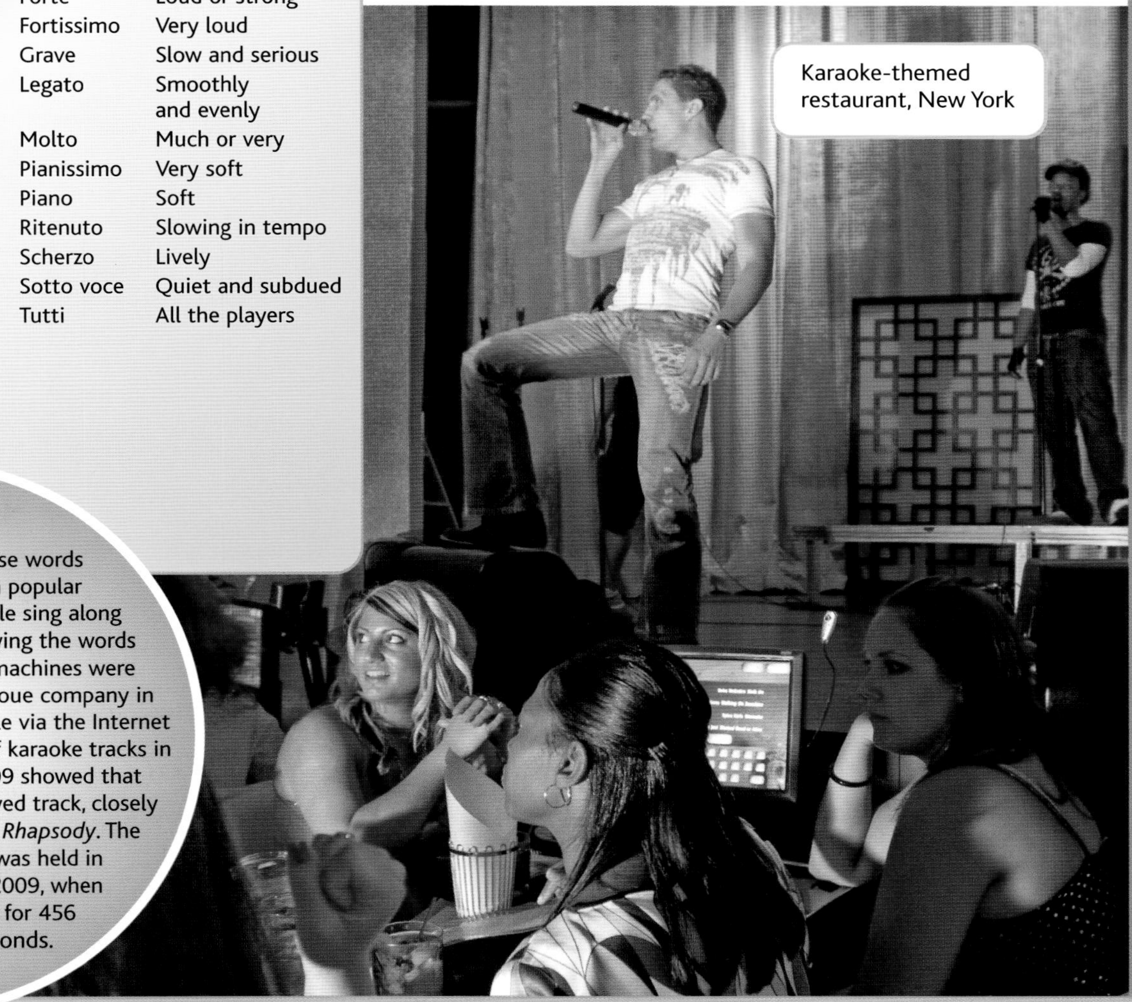

Karaoke-themed restaurant, New York

Karaoke

Karaoke, from the Japanese words for 'empty orchestra', is a popular entertainment in which people sing along to a music track, usually following the words on a screen. The first karaoke machines were made in Japan by the Daisuke Inoue company in the 1970s. Karaoke is now available via the Internet and on mobile phones. A survey of karaoke tracks in the UK in the period 1993–2009 showed that Abba's *Waterloo* is the most-played track, closely followed by Queen's *Bohemian Rhapsody*. The longest karaoke marathon was held in Chanchung City, China, in 2009, when 1,300 singers performed for 456 hours 2 minutes 5 seconds.

2000s

1948 First 12-inch (30.5 cm) 331/3 rpm, micro-groove LP vinylite record is produced, with 23-minute capacity per side
1949 First 7-inch (17.8 cm), 45 rpm, micro-groove EP (Extended Play) vinylite record and player is introduced
1958 First stereo LPs are sold
1963 First compact audio cassette is produced
1969 Dolby Noise Reduction is introduced
1979 First Sony Walkman portable audio cassette players are sold
1982 First CDs are sold
1987 DAT (Digital Audio Tape) players are launched
1992 Mini-discs are introduced
1997 MP3 format is launched
2001 Apple's iPod is launched
2006 MSI launches the solar-powered MP3 player
2007 It is estimated that 200 billion CDs have been sold since the format was launched 25 years ago
2009 98% of UK singles and 12.5% of album sales are downloads
2012 Album downloads predicted to overtake CD sales

www.recording-history.org search

Strings

Violin

Viola

The viola is larger and deeper-voiced than the violin, and is played in the same way.

Cello

Double bass

Harp

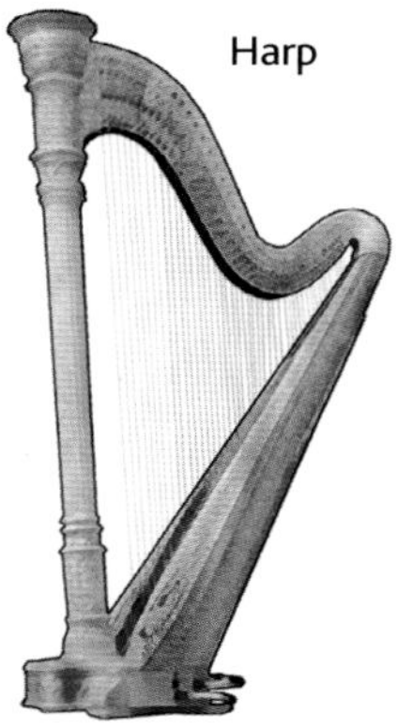

The violin has a hollow wooden body which resonates when the violinist pulls a bow over the four strings. There may be 30 or more violins in a modern orchestra.

The cello's full name is the violoncello. It is the third-largest member of the violin family and is played sitting down.

The largest and deepest stringed instrument in an orchestra is the double bass. Double bass players usually stand to play, pulling a bow across the strings, or plucking them.

The orchestral harp has 48 strings of different lengths, attached to the top and side, and seven pedals at the base.

Opera terms

aria
A song for a single voice

comic opera
Opera with a comic plot

finale
The ending, when the whole cast often sing together

libretto
The text of an opera, from the Italian for little book

operetta
A light (rather than serious) opera, usually with an amusing story

prima donna
First lady (from the Italian) – the main female singer, or diva

recitative
A part in an opera that is spoken rather than sung

Instruments of the orchestra

The range and number of instruments in a modern orchestra varies enormously. There may be as many as 100 or more, and less familiar instruments are brought in for special performances. The ones illustrated here are the most common instruments.

Brass

Trumpet

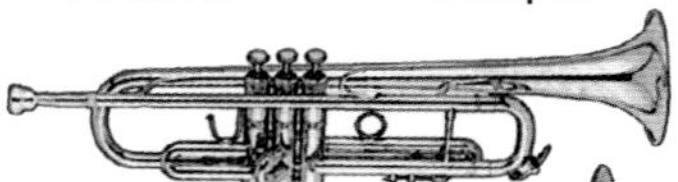

A trumpet is a tightly coiled metal tube with a cone called the bell at one end. Trumpets have three small buttons called valves which make different notes when pressed.

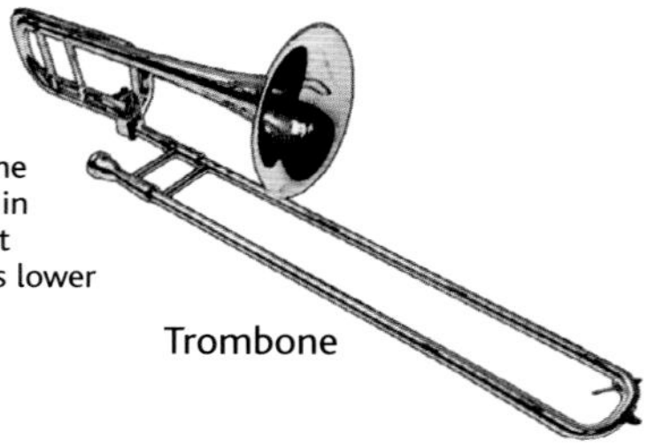

Trombone

The trombone is also made from coiled metal and has a section called the slide, which players move in and out to create different notes. The trombone plays lower notes than the trumpet.

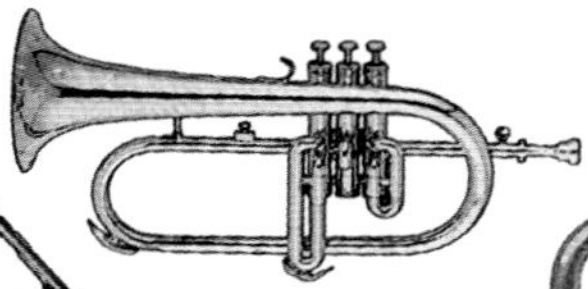

Flugelhorn

French horn

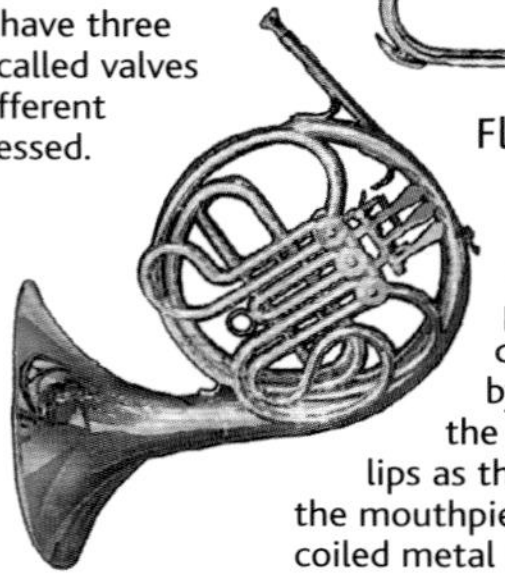

French horn players make different notes by changing the shape of their lips as they blow into the mouthpiece of this coiled metal tube.

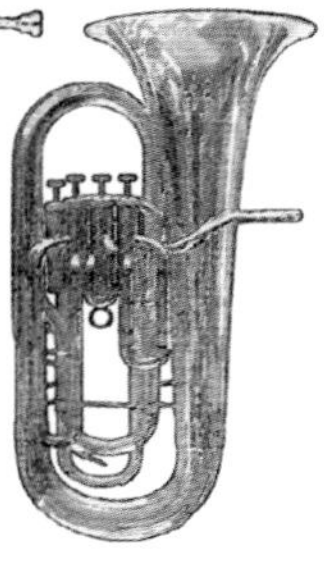

Euphonium

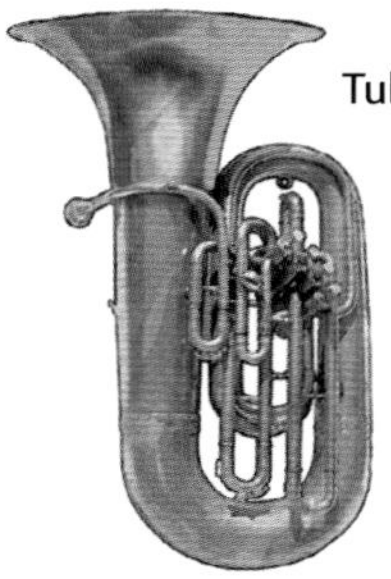

Tuba

There is usually just one tuba in an orchestra. It plays the lowest notes of all the brass instruments.

Singing parts

Name	Female voices
Soprano	The highest female voice
Mezzo soprano	Between a soprano and a contralto
Contralto	The lowest female voice
	Male voices
Alto	The highest male voice, traditionally sung by choirboys
Tenor	A high male voice. A countertenor voice is very high
Baritone	A voice higher than a bass, but lower than a tenor
Bass	The lowest male voice. Basso profundo is the lowest possible voice
Falsetto	An unnaturally high voice sung by tenors and basses

Woodwind

Piccolo

Flute

The concert flute is played through a blow hole at one end. Alto and bass flutes are larger versions which play lower notes. The piccolo is half the size of the concert flute and plays the highest notes in the orchestra.

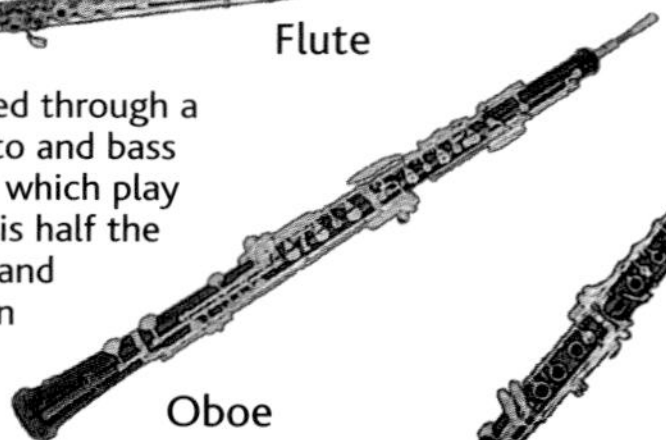

Oboe

Oboe players blow through a double reed made from two small slices of cane tied together and inserted into the mouthpiece of the instrument.

Clarinet

The clarinet is also played through a reed. There are several different types of clarinet. B flat and A are played most often.

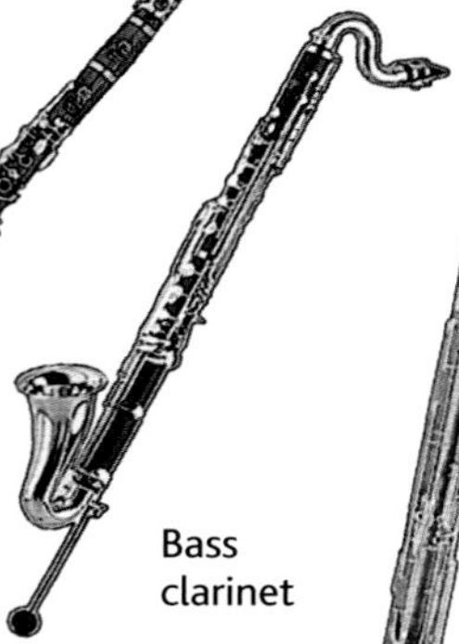

Bass clarinet

Bassoon

The bassoon plays the lowest notes of the woodwind instruments. It is a doubled-up wooden tube with a curved metal crook at one end, which holds the reed.

Cor anglais

Aïda performed at Luxor, Egypt

Grandest grand opera

The opera *Aïda* has often been performed on a grand scale, with a huge cast including elephants and other animals. It has been staged at the pyramids, Egypt, and in the year 2000 was performed in a football stadium in Shanghai, China, with a cast of 3,000 and an audience of 45,000.

Opera facts

Most-performed operas

Puccini's *La Bohème* is the most-performed opera in London and New York. It has been staged 969 times since 1897 at London's Royal Opera House, and 1,200 times at the Metropolitan Opera House in New York. *Aïda* and *Carmen* are the closest runners-up in both places.

Largest opera venues

The two largest opera houses where operas are regularly performed are in Italy and America. They are the Arena di Verona in Verona, which holds 16,663 people, and the Municipal Opera Theatre in St Louis, USA, which holds 11,745. The Teatro alla Scala, Milan, Italy, which has 3,600 seats, is one of the world's largest indoor opera theatres, although several US opera houses come close in size.

Longest operas

Richard Wagner's *Gotterdämmerung* is the longest regularly performed opera. The opera can last up to six hours, including intervals.

Dame Nellie Melba

The real name of Australian opera singer Dame Nellie Melba (1881–1931) was Helen Mitchell. She was a great food-lover and inspired the famous chef Escoffier to create several new dishes for her at the Savoy Hotel, London. These included Peach Melba (a raspberry and redcurrant sauce poured over peaches and ice cream), Melba Toast (crisp dried bread) and Melba Garniture (chicken, truffles and mushrooms stuffed into tomatoes).

Percussion

Timpani/Kettledrums

Orchestras usually have three or four timpani or kettledrums. They are made of copper with a plastic skin stretched over the top.

Triangle

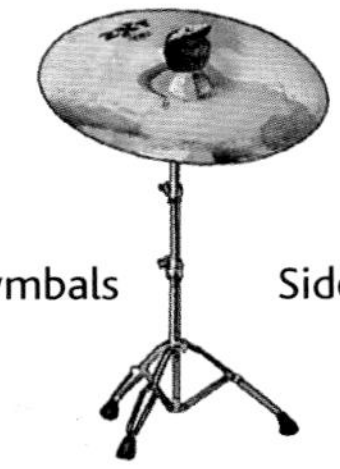

Cymbals

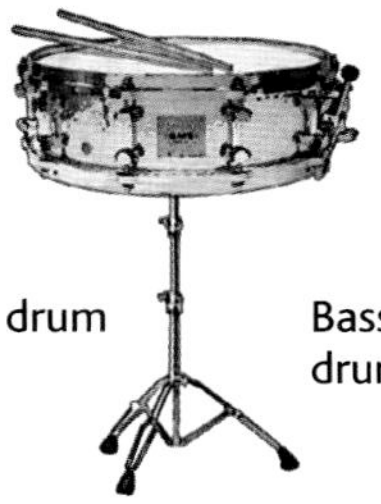

Side drum

Bass drum

Various other instruments are sometimes played in orchestras, including keyboards (piano, organ, celesta, etc), bells, castanets, glockenspiels, gongs, marimbas, rattles, tambourines, wind machines, wood blocks, xylophones, guitars, mandolins and saxophones.

Top singles of all time *

The numbers of singles sold outside the USA and some European countries have only been recorded fairly recently, so world sales here are estimates.

White Christmas was the world's bestselling single for more than 50 years until it was overtaken by Elton John's tribute to Princess Diana in 1997.

Artist/single/year	Estimated world sales (millions)
Elton John, *Candle in the Wind* (1997)/ *Something about the Way You Look Tonight* (1997)	37
Bing Crosby, *White Christmas* (1945)	30
Elvis Presley, *It's Now or Never* (1960)	28
Bill Haley and His Comets, *Rock Around the Clock* (1954)	25
USA for Africa, *We Are the World* (1985)	20
The Beatles, *I Want to Hold Your Hand* (1963)	12
Céline Dion, *My Heart Will Go On* (1998)	12

* These figures are only for singles sung in the English language.

Downloads fact file

- In 2004 British rock band Arctic Monkeys released their songs only on the Internet.
- In 2004 download charts were published in the UK. Westlife had the first No. 1 downloaded single with *Flying Without Wings*.
- By January 2005, digital downloads outsold physical singles in the UK for the first time. The official singles chart now included both downloads and sales of singles.
- In 2006, *Keep Tryin'* by Utada Hikaru (Japan) set a new record for 2.5 million downloads.
- Flo Rida's *Low* (2007) became the bestselling digital single in the USA, with sales of more than 4 million. In 2009 Flo Rida's *Right Round* set a record of 636,000 downloads in a single week.
- In February 2010, Apple announced that 10 billion songs had been downloaded from its iTunes Store since its 2003 launch.

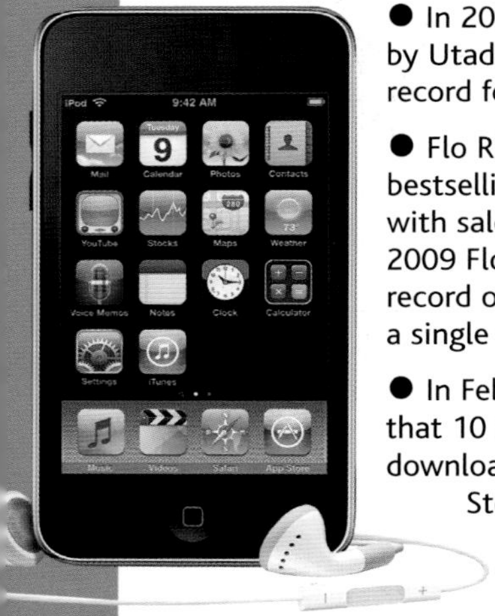

Apple's iPod Touch

iTunes all-time downloads

1 *I Gotta Feeling*, Black Eyed Peas
2 *Poker Face*, Lady Gaga
3 *Boom Boom Pow*, Black Eyed Peas
4 *I'm Yours*, Jason Mraz
5 *Viva la Vida*, Coldplay
6 *Just Dance*, Lady GaGa & Colby O'Donis
7 *Low*, Flo Rida (featuring T-Pain)
8 *Love Story*, Taylor Swift
9 *Bleeding Love*, Leona Lewis
10 *Tik Tok*, Ke$ha

Black Eyed Peas

Popular music styles

Blues Blues music began in the USA in the 1860s, when it grew out of work songs (songs sung by people working to a rhythm, such as picking crops) and spirituals.

Country Country, country and western, bluegrass and related types of music began in the south-western states of the USA. Nashville, Tennessee, is the home of the Country Music Hall of Fame. Its foremost male performer, Garth Brooks, is one of the bestselling artists of all time, having sold nearly 130 million albums.

Electronic Electronic music emerged in the 1950s as the technology to record and synthesize sounds became available to musicians. Electronic equipment is used to create both classical and popular music, with such branches as techno – a popular dance genre.

Folk Folk music includes the popular songs and dances that are passed from generation to generation in a country. In modern times, artists such as Bob Dylan have based many of their songs on their national folk tradition.

Hip hop Hip hop is a style of music that emerged in New York in the 1970s. It is often used to mean rap music, although rap is strictly a style of lyrics involving rhyming and wordplay to a rhythmic beat that originated earlier and remains one of the most widely popular styles today.

Jazz Jazz music originated in New Orleans, USA, in the 1890s and became so popular in the 1920s that the period is sometimes known as the 'Jazz Age'.

Pop Pop music is the general name given to the type of music that became popular in the 1950s with the arrival of artists such as Elvis Presley. Its rebellious spirit, energy and volume were designed to appeal to a young audience.

Reggae Reggae is a style of music that grew out of 1950s Jamaican

Major rock events

The following are among the best-attended rock events ever. The Live Aid concerts (13 July 1985) and Live 8 concerts (2 July 2005) had smaller audiences split over several venues but were reckoned to have had the greatest TV audiences of all time.

About 1.5 billion people, or a quarter of the world's population, watched Live Aid on television. The figure for Live 8 was over 2 billion.

Event/date	Est. audience
Rod Stewart, Copacabana Beach, Rio de Janeiro, Brazil, 31 December 1994	3,500,000
Golden Jubilee Concert, Buckingham Palace, London, 3 June 2002	over 1,000,000
Live 8, 10 free concerts in nine countries, 2 July 2005	over 1,000,000
(The largest single audience was 200,000 in Hyde Park, London.)	
Garth Brooks in Central Park, New York, USA, 7 August 1997	750,000
Summer Jam, Watkins Glen, New York, 28 July 1973	600,132
Simon and Garfunkel in Central Park, New York, USA, 19 September 1981	500,000
Rolling Stones Free Concert, Hyde Park, London, 5 July 1969	up to 500,000
Molson Canadian Rocks for Toronto, Toronto, Canada, 30 July 2003	489,176
Woodstock Festival, Bethel, New York, USA, 15–17 August 1969	over 400,000
The Spice Girls, O2 Arena, London, UK, 15 Dec 2006–22 Jan 2007	256,647
U2, Croke Park, Dublin, Ireland, 24–27 July 2009	243,198

Bono of U2

Top albums of all time worldwide

The USA has always led the world in album sales. Total worldwide sales are less easy to find, but using the best estimates available these albums can claim to be world-beaters. Michael Jackson's *Thriller* album had a surge in sales following the singer's death, selling 1.27 million copies in the USA alone in 2009.

	Total sales (million)	
Album/performer/year	**USA**	**World**
Thriller, Michael Jackson (1982)	29	100
Back in Black, AC/DC (1980)	22	49
The Dark Side of the Moon, Pink Floyd (1973)	15	45
Bat Out of Hell, Meat Loaf (1977)	14	43
Their Greatest Hits (1971-1975), Eagles (1976)	29	42
Dirty Dancing, Various Artists (1987)	11	42
The Bodyguard, Whitney Houston/ Various Artists (1992)	17	42
Rumours, Fleetwood Mac (1977)	19	40
Saturday Night Fever, Various Artists (1977)	15	40
Millennium, Backstreet Boys (1999)	13	40

ska and in turn influenced British pop music. Its most famous performer was Bob Marley.

Rhythm and blues Rhythm and blues, or R&B, developed in the USA from blues and pop music, with Bo Diddley and Chuck Berry among its most famous performers.

Rock Recorded by Bill Hailey and His Comets, Rock Around the Clock (1954) was the first commercially successful rock and roll record. During the 1960s, many of the world's leading bands, including the Beatles and Rolling Stones, established rock music as the most popular of all musical styles.

Soul Combining gospel, blues and jazz, soul music is an often highly emotional style of music. It was especially popular in the 1960s when its leading exponent was Aretha Franklin.

www.theofficialcharts.com search

Treasures of rock

Fans of rock music often like to buy items that belonged to their favourite singers and bands. The more successful the artist, the higher the price.

- The bass drum skin that appears on the front cover of The Beatles' *Sgt Pepper's Lonely Hearts Club Band* album (1967) was sold in London on 10 July 2008 for £541,250 ($1.068,000). At the same auction, John Lennon's handwritten lyrics for *Give Peace a Chance* (1969) were sold for £421,250 ($831,200). The record price for Beatles memorabilia is the £600,000 ($1,047,300) paid in London on 28 July 2005 for Lennon's handwritten lyrics for *All You Need is Love*.
- "Blackie" Fender Stratocaster guitar owned by Eric Clapton. Sold in New York, USA, on 25 June 2004 for £528,068 ($959,500).
- Bernie Taupin's handwritten lyrics for the re-written "Candle in the Wind", sung by Sir Elton John in Westminster Abbey at the funeral of Diana, Princess of Wales. Sold in Los Angeles, USA, on 11 February 1998 for £278,512 ($400,000).

John Lennon's Rolls-Royce

See also
Tom Thumb: page 95

Canadian circus troupe Cirque du Soleil (French for "Circus of the Sun")

A quick history of circus

Open air circuses with acrobats, chariot races, bareback riders and comedy acts were popular in ancient Rome. In the 18th century fixed buildings were used, and in the early 19th century travelling circuses appeared in Europe and America. Troupes moved from place to place, setting up a large tent, or "big top". The most famous American circus proprietor was Phineas T. Barnum (1810–91).

His shows were spectacular, with trick riding, juggling, trapeze acts, tightrope walking, strong men, and wild-cat tamers. They also featured "human oddities", or freak shows, in which Siamese twins, giants or bearded ladies were often paraded before the curious crowd. Since the 20th century, all-human Chinese and Russian circus companies have toured the world, as well as alternative circus troupes such as Circus Oz, Ra Ra Zoo and Archaos, whose acts have included juggling with chainsaws and jumping over blazing motorbikes.

Famous playwrights and their famous plays

Aeschylus (Greek, c. 525–546 BC) – *The Oresteia*
J.M. Barrie (Scottish, 1860–1937) – *Peter Pan*
Samuel Beckett (Irish, 1906–89) – *Waiting for Godot*
Anton Chekhov (Russian, 1860–1904) – *The Cherry Orchard*
Noël Coward (English, 1899–1973) – *Private Lives*
Euripides (Greek, c. 484–406 BC) – *The Trojan Women*
Federico García Lorca (Spanish, 1898–1936) – *Blood Wedding*
Oliver Goldsmith (English 1728–74) – *She Stoops to Conquer*
David Hare (English, 1947–) – *Plenty*
Henrik Ibsen (Norwegian, 1828–1906) – *Hedda Gabler*
Ben Jonson (English, 1572–1637) – *The Alchemist*
Christopher Marlowe (English, 1564–93) – *Doctor Faustus*
Arthur Miller (American, 1915–2005) – *The Crucible*
Molière (French, 1622–73) – *Tartuffe*
John Osborne (English, 1929–94) – *Look Back in Anger*
Harold Pinter (English, 1930–) – *The Birthday Party*
Peter Shaffer (English, 1926–) – *Amadeus*
William Shakespeare (English, 1564–1616) – *Hamlet*
George Bernard Shaw (Irish, 1856–1950) – *Pygmalion*
Richard Brinsley Sheridan (English, 1751–1816) – *The Rivals*
Neil Simon (American, 1927–) – *Plaza Suite*
Sophocles (Greek, c. 496–405 BC) – *Antigone*
Tom Stoppard (Czech, 1937–) – *Rosencrantz and Guildenstern are Dead*
J.M. Synge (Irish, 1871–1909) – *The Playboy of the Western World*
John Webster (English, 1580–1625) – *The Duchess of Malfi*
Oscar Wilde (Irish, 1854–1900) – *The Importance of Being Earnest*
Tennessee Williams (American, 1911–83) – *A Streetcar Named Desire*

Theatre records

First actor
Thespis was the first performer ever recorded. He was an actor in Greece in 534 BC. At this time, Greek actors used masks, and Thespis was the first to use stage make-up.

World's oldest theatres
The oldest indoor theatre in the world is the Teatro Olimpico, Vicenza, Italy, which opened on 3 March 1585. London's oldest theatre is the Theatre Royal, Drury Lane, which opened on 7 May 1663. It burnt down in 1672 and was rebuilt by Sir Christopher Wren. In 1800 it became the world's first theatre to have safety curtains. The oldest surviving theatre in the USA is the Walnut Street Theatre in Philadelphia, Pennsylvania.

World's biggest theatres
The National People's Congress Building Theatre, Beijing, China was built in 1959 and can hold audiences of 10,000. The Perth Entertainment Centre, Australia (1976) has up to 8,500 seats, the Chaplin (originally Blanquetta), Havana, Cuba (1949) has 6,500 and Radio City Music Hall, New York, USA, has 6,200. The 3,483-seater Hammersmith Odeon is the largest theatre in Britain, but the Royal Albert Hall in London can hold up to 7,000, depending on the event and how the seating is organized.

The Teatro Olimpico in Vicenza, Italy

Worst disasters at a theatre

Fires, in which people were burned or trampled to death, have caused the worst disasters at theatres. The worst ever was at Canton (now Guangzhou), China, in 1845 when 1,670 died. Europe's worst was at the Ring Theatre, Vienna, Austria, in 1881, which killed at least 620 people. The worst in the USA was at the Iroquois Theatre, Chicago, in 1903, which left 602 dead. These are the worst single-building (rather than city or forest) fires in history.

Longest-running shows

The Golden Horseshoe Revue (Disneyland, California, 1955–86) 47,250
The Mousetrap (London, 1952–) *23,888
La Cantatrice Chauve (The Bald Soprano) (Paris, 1957– *17,527
The Fantasticks (New York, 1960–2002) 17,162
Shear Madness (Boston, 1980–) *12,679
Les Misérables (London, 1985–) *10,130
Shear Madness (Washington DC, 1987–) *9,986
The Phantom of the Opera (London, 1986–) *9,795
The Mousetrap (Toronto, 1977–2004) 9,648
The Drunkard (Los Angeles, 1933–59) 9,477
Perfect Crime (New York, 1987–) *9,379
The Phantom of the Opera (New York, 1988–) *9,251
Blood Brothers (London, 1988–) *9,035
Cats (London, 1981–2002) 8,949
The Woman in Black (London, 15 Feb 1989–) *8,525
Tubes (New York, 1991–2005) *8,454
Shear Madness (Chicago, 1982–2007) 7,697

* Still running, total as at 31 March 2010

Short runs

A play is expensive to stage, so everyone involved hopes that it will run for long enough to earn back the money spent on it. Shows that run for years earn back their initial investment many times over, but some fail on their first night, or even earlier!

- On 18 December 1816 the one and only performance of J.R. Ronden's *The Play Without an A* took place at the Paris Théâtre des Variétés. It was written with words without the letter "a", which made it very hard to perform and understand. The audience rioted and did not allow the play to finish.
- In 1888, at London's Shaftesbury Theatre, *The Lady of Lyons* failed to make its first night when the safety curtain jammed.
- The *Intimate Revue* opened and closed at the Duchess Theatre, London, on 11 March 1930. It was a disaster from start to finish. The scenery changes took so long that seven scenes were abandoned to allow the long-suffering audience to go home before midnight.
- *Little Johnny Jones*, a musical starring Donny Osmond, opened and closed at the Alvin Theater, New York, on 21 March 1982.
- *Carrie* closed in New York on 17 May 1988 after struggling through five performances. It is said to have cost the Royal Shakespeare Company, who performed it, $7 million.

The Mousetrap

Crime novelist Agatha Christie's murder mystery has been running in London since 25 November 1952, a world record for a play. It reached its milestone 10,000th performance on 17 December 1976 and its 24,000th on 1 July 2010.

Oberammergau

Oberammergau is a town in Bavaria, Germany, where a Passion play (a play dealing with the crucifixion of Christ) is performed. The first play was put on in 1634 after an outbreak of plague in the town. The people vowed to repeat the play every ten years from then on. More than 2,000 people take part in the play, nearly all of them from Oberammergau, and the performance lasts six hours.

Scene from the Singapore production of *Les Misérables*

www.theatremuseum.org.uk search

John Travolta in *Saturday Night Fever*, 1977

Highest-earning dance films

The most successful dance film of all time is *Saturday Night Fever*. It starred John Travolta as a talented disco dancer and has earned nearly $300 million around the world. Below are some of the other highest-earning dance films in the world.

1	*Saturday Night Fever* (1977)	$285.4 million
2	*The Full Monty* (1997)	$257.9 m.
3	*Dirty Dancing* (1987)	$214.0 m.
4	*Shall We Dance* (2004)	$170.1 m.
5	*Step Up 2 the Streets* (2008)	$148.4 m.
6	*Save the Last Dance* (2001)	$131.7 m.
7	*Staying Alive* (1983)	$127.6 m.
8	*Step Up* (2006)	$114.2 m.
9	*Coyote Ugly* (2000)	$113.9 m.
10	*Billy Elliot* (2000)	$109.3 m.

Girl breakdancing

Dance spectaculars

American choreographer Busby Berkeley (1895–1976) staged the most spectacular dance films ever made. He used his knowledge of organizing military parades during World War I to create dance numbers with casts of hundreds.

They were often photographed from cranes high above them, on huge sets and sometimes with giant mirrors so that they formed geometrical patterns apparently vanishing into infinity. His films included *42nd Street* (1933) and *Gold Diggers of 1933* (1933), which was hit by an earthquake during filming in Los Angeles. The quake cut all power and nearly collapsed the set.

Breakdancing

Breakdancing began in New York in the late 1970s and early 1980s. Some of its movements came from martial arts such as kung fu and from gymnastics. It became a feature of hip-hop culture.

Popular dances

Ballroom dancing
Ballroom dancing has a long history and gained an international following through the popularity of competitive dancing on television. In recent years, TV shows such as *Strictly Come Dancing* and *Dancing with the Stars*, in which celebrities dance with professionals, have revived interest in this style of dancing.

Barn dances
These developed from traditional Scottish dancing. They were popular in the USA in the 1890s when they were held to celebrate the building of a barn on a farm. Barn dances are still held today in country areas.

Belly dance
The popular name of a style of dance that originated in the Middle East, especially Egypt. It was originally danced only by women, and men were not permitted to watch.

The Charleston
The Charleston was named after the city in South Carolina, USA and was one of the most popular dances of the 1920s.

The conga
People dance the conga in a line, each dancer holding on to the person in front. The conga began in Latin American carnivals and spread to the USA in the 1930s.

The hula
The hip-swaying hula is danced by Polynesian islanders who settled in Hawaii. It was banned by Christian missionaries for a while, but became popular again in the late 19th century.

The limbo
This competitive dance comes from Trinidad. Dancers lean back to pass under a bar, which is placed lower and lower. The winner is the dancer who passes under the lowest bar.

Lindy Hop
The Lindy Hop was a version of the Charleston and another dance called the Breakaway. It was named after US aviator Charles Lindbergh (nicknamed Lindy). In 1927 he became the first person to fly solo across the Atlantic.

Morris dancing
This is a traditional English folk dance. Dancers wear special costumes with bells, and hold sticks, handkerchiefs and swords.

The polka
The polka was originally a Czech peasant dance which developed in Bohemia in the 1830s. It became popular in Paris in the 1840s and eventually spread worldwide.

Salsa
Salsa derives from rhythmic dances such as the mambo, cha cha cha and rumba. It has its roots in Spanish-speaking

Dance marathons

Dance marathons began in New York in 1923, when Alma Cummings won a contest by dancing for 27 hours with six different partners. Marathons were popular during the Depression years of the 1930s, when unemployed people danced non-stop for many days to win money.

The last couple standing won. Dancers were allowed only very short breaks and partners pinched and kicked each other to stay awake or tied themselves together to prevent one from falling down. Dance marathons were banned in many places because they were so dangerous for people's health.

Mike Ritof and Edith Boudreaux danced from 29 August 1930 to 1 April 1931 at the Merry Garden Ballroom, Chicago, USA, to win a prize of $2,000. They danced for a total of 5,154 hours 28 minutes 30 seconds (215 days) with only short rest breaks.

Lindy Hop

The Lindy Hop, which combines elements of the Charleston and other dances such as the Breakaway, was invented to celebrate the first solo flight across the Atlantic by US aviator Charles Lindbergh (who was nicknamed 'Lindy') in 1927.

Dancers perform the Lindy Hop

Tap dancing

Tap dancing became popular as a stage act in which dancers wear special shoes and dance on a hard surface to produce a distinctive sound. It became a feature of many popular musicals of the 1930s onwards with such stars as Fred Astaire and Gene Kelly, famed for his dance routine in *Singin' in the Rain* (1952). *42nd Street*, a stage show first performed in 1980, features large numbers of tap dancers. The animated film *Happy Feet* 2006) brought this style of dancing back to public attention.

and parts of the USA, with many local variations.

The twist
The twist started when Hank Ballard recorded the song of this name in 1959. It became popular when Chubby Checker performed his cover version on US television on 22 October 1961. A woman called Ra Denny holds the twist record. She twisted for 100 hours at Christchurch, New Zealand, in March 1962.

The waltz
The waltz began in Austria in the late 18th century. Its name comes from a German word meaning to revolve. Many people were shocked by the dance when it first came to England in 1812 because it involved men and women dancing close to each other.

www.streetswing.com/histmain.htm search

Most-performed ballets

These are the ballets most often performed by the Royal Ballet at the Royal Opera House, Covent Garden, from 1946 to 2008.

Ballet	Choreographer	First performance at ROH	Perfs.
Swan Lake	Marius Petipa, Lev Ivanov	19 Dec 1946	917
The Sleeping Beauty	Marius Petipa	20 Feb 1946	818
Giselle	Jules Perrot, Jean, Coralli, Marius Petipa	12 Jun 1946	524
Romeo and Juliet	Kenneth MacMillan	9 Feb 1965	418
Cinderella	Frederick Ashton	23 Dec 1948	383
Les Sylphides	Michel Fokine	16 May 1946	352
La Fille Mal Gardée	Frederick Ashton	28 Jan 1960	323

Modern dance companies and choreographers

Choreographers and dance teachers have established many of the most famous modern dance companies and created some of the most memorable performances of the past 100 years, among them:

Isadora Duncan (1877–1927), an American dancer who was regarded as the founder of modern dance

Sir Frederick Ashton (1904–88), British dancer and choreographer of works including *The Tales of Beatrix Potter*

George Balanchine (1904–83), Russian choreographer who worked with the New York City Ballet

Pina Bausch (1940–2009), German choreographer, winner of the Goethe Prize and Laurence Olivier Award in 2006

Twyla Tharp (1941–), American dancer and chorographer, winner of a Tony Award in 2003

Merce Cunningham (1919–2009), American choreographer whose dance company was founded in 1927

Alvin Ailey (1931–89), whose American Dance Theater, founded in 1958, promoted African-American dancers

Alonzo King (birth date unknown), choreographer and founder of LINES Ballet, and LINES Ballet School, 2001

Ballet terms

arabesque
Position in which the dancer stands on one leg, with arms extended, the body bent forwards and the other leg stretched back

ballerina
A female ballet dancer

barre
The bar dancers hold on to while they practise, to help them balance

choreographer
The person who works out the steps and movements in a ballet

corps de ballet
Chorus of dancers (not those dancing solo)

entrechat
Rapid crossing and uncrossing of the feet during a jump

fouetté
A turn in which one leg is whipped round

glissade
A gliding movement

jeté
A jump from one foot to the other

pas
A dance step

pas de deux
A dance for two (usually the principal male and female dancers in the company)

pas seule
A solo dance

pirouette
A complete turn on one leg

plié
A knee-bending movement

pointes
On the tips of the toes. Dancers wear special point shoes with blocks in the toes to help them stand on their toes

positions
A range of five positions that are the basis of ballet dancing

prima ballerina
The leading ballerina in a company

tutu
The stiff skirt worn by ballerinas performing classical ballet

Dancers perform Alonzo King's *Three Stops on the Way Home*

Darcey Bussell of the Royal Ballet performing at the Royal Opera House, London, UK

Famous ballet dancers

Carlos Acosta (Cuban, 1973–) Trained in Cuba and became a principal dancer with the Royal Ballet in London. He has also staged his own show.

Mikhail Baryshnikov (Russian, 1948–) One of the greatest male dancers. He began with the Kirov in Russia but later joined the American Ballet Theatre.

Matthew Bourne (British, 1960–) Began as a dancer and became a famous choreographer and director. He is best known for his production of *Swan Lake*, in which all the swans are played by male dancers.

Darcey Bussell (British, 1969–) Became a principal dancer with the Royal Ballet at the age of 20. She is one of their most popular soloists, and in 1995 she was awarded an OBE for her work in dance. She retired in 2007.

Michael Clark (British, 1962–) Danced with the Royal Ballet and Merce Cunningham companies before becoming a choreographer and starting his own company. He is best known for his very original shows and for using music such as punk in his work.

Sir Anton Dolin (British, 1904–83) Originally danced with Diaghilev's Ballets Russes. He founded the London Festival Ballet (now English National Ballet).

Sir Anthony Dowell (British, 1943–) He was principal dancer with the Royal Ballet for many years and was Director of the Royal Ballet for 15 years from 1986.

Dame Margot Fonteyn (British, 1919–91) Royal Ballet prima ballerina, she is most famous for her long-term partnership with Rudolf Nureyev.

Dame Beryl Grey (British, 1927–) Prima ballerina at the Sadler's Wells Ballet, London and the first English ballerina to perform with the Bolshoi.

Sylvie Guillem (French, 1965–) Principal guest artist with the Royal Ballet, she is a versatile and athletic dancer, famous for her extraordinarily high leg extensions.

Dame Alicia Markova (British, 1910–2004) She danced with Anton Dolin and they are most famous for their *Giselle*. Dolin and Markova formed a ballet company.

Rudolf Nureyev (Russian, 1938–93) Former Kirov star who defected to the West and became the most popular male dancer of his generation.

Anna Pavlova (Russian, 1881–1931) Became the most famous ballerina of her generation through her world tours.

Dame Marie Rambert (Polish/British, 1888–1982) Dancer and teacher whose dance company promoted many new works.

Maria Taglioni (Swedish/Italian, 1804–84) One of the first ballet stars, famous for her role in *La Sylphide*.

Vaslav Nijinsky (Russian, 1890–1950) One of most famous of all male dancers. He was a leading dancer with the Ballets Russes and best known for his performance in Stravinsky's *Rite of Spring*.

Carlos Acosta

Ballet firsts and records

First ballet
In the late 16th century, performances that included dancing, music and acting were given at the French court of Henri II and Catherine de Médici. The *Ballet Comique de La Reine* (1581) was the first recorded.

First tutu and first on points
Ballerina Maria Taglioni (1804–84) wore a muslin dress known as a tutu when she danced in *La Sylphide* at the Paris Opéra on 12 March 1832. The dress allowed more freedom of movement so became popular in classical ballet. In the same ballet she danced on points without support – the first time any dancer had done so.

First ballet in the USA
On 7 February 1827 Francisquy Hutin performed a ballet in the play *The Deserter* at the Bowery Theatre, New York. The women in the audience were so shocked by it that they fled from the theatre.

Most curtain calls for a ballet performance
In October 1964 Margot Fonteyn and Rudolf Nureyev received 89 curtain calls after their performance in *Swan Lake* at the Staatsoper, in Vienna, Austria.

First *entrechat douze*

The first dancer to perform *entrechat dix* – crossing and uncrossing the legs five times, a total of ten movements during a single leap, was Russian dancer Rudolf Nureyev. The first to perform *entrechat douze* – crossing and uncrossing six times, or twelve movements – was British dancer Wayne Sleep on 7 January 1973. He was in the air for just 0.71 seconds. Wayne Sleep later became famous for dancing on stage with Princess Diana.

www.ballet.co.uk search

Film, TV & Radio

Pirates set sail again

After three international blockbuster hits with *Pirates of the Caribbean: The Curse of the Black Pearl* (2003), which earned $654.3 million worldwide, *Pirates of the Caribbean: Dead Man's Chest* (2006; $1066.2 million) and *Pirates of the Caribbean: At World's End* (2007, $961.0 million), the Disney series returns to the screen in 2011 with *Pirates of the Caribbean: On Stranger Tides*, again starring Johnny Depp as Jack Sparrow.

Top feature film-producing countries

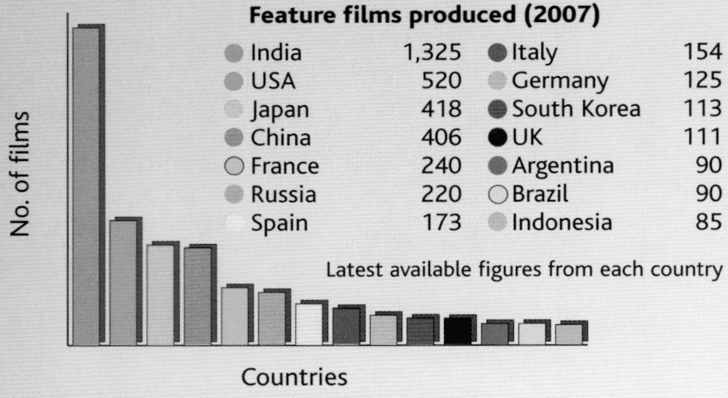

Casts of thousands

About 200,000 of the extras in *Gandhi* were volunteers, but another 94,560 were paid a small fee. They appeared in the scene showing Gandhi's funeral, which lasted just two minutes and five seconds after editing.

In *Around the World in 80 Days* (1956), there were animal extras too – 3,800 sheep, 2,448 buffalos, 950 donkeys, 800 horses, 512 monkeys, 17 bulls, 15 elephants, 6 skunks and 4 ostriches. In recent films, such as the *Lord of the Rings* trilogy, scenes with thousands of people were computer-generated, so huge numbers of extras were not needed.

Film	Extras
Gandhi (UK, 1982)	294,560
Kolberg (Germany, 1945)	187,000
Monster Wangmagwi (South Korea, 1967)	157,000
War and Peace (USSR, 1968)	120,000
Ilya Muromets (*The Sword and the Dragon*) (USSR, 1956)	106,000
Dun-Huang (Ton ko) (Japan, 1988)	100,000
Razboiul Independentei (*The War of Independence*) (Romania, 1912)	80,000
Around the World in 80 Days (USA, 1956)	68,894
Intolerance (USA, 1916)	60,000
Dny Zrady (*Days of Betrayal*) (Czechoslovakia, 1973)	60,000

Actress Angelina Jolie filming *The Tourist* on location in Paris, France

Top cinema-goers*

1 USA and Canada 1,364,000,000
2 France 200,900,000
3 China 195,800,000
4 Mexico 178,000,000
5 UK 173,500,000
6 India 160,500,000
7 Japan 160,500,000
8 South Korea 150,800,000
9 Germany 146,300,000
10 Russia 138,500,000
11 Italy 111,200,000
12 Spain 110,800,000

* per annum, latest available figures

Who does what in a film?

Director The director controls everything, gives orders to the cast and crew and makes sure that the script is followed.

Producer(s) There can be more than one producer, who is responsible for raising the money to make the film and for other important activities, such as casting and controlling the costs.

Cast The actors and actresses who appear in the film.

Screenplay writer The person who writes the script. This gives the actors and actresses their lines and explains how the action takes place.

Extras The people who appear in crowd scenes but do not have speaking parts.

Animatronic engineer The person who makes the robotic creatures used in science-fiction and fantasy films.

Art director The art director coordinates the costumes, sets and make-up to set the overall style of the film.

Best boy The deputy electrician, assistant to the gaffer.

Casting director The person who chooses the actors for each role in the film.

Caterer The caterer supplies meals so that the cast and crew can work all day.

Cinematographer The person who directs the lighting and films the action, originally called the cameraman.

Clapper loader Details of each scene are written on a special board called a clapper board. The clapper loader snaps it shut in front of the camera as filming begins to record what is being filmed.

Film budgets

The production budgets of a film include the salaries paid to the director, writer(s), stars and crew, the designing and building of sets, costumes, the transport and location costs (filming away from the studio) and the cost of making and editing the film. Other costs include P & A (Prints and Advertising) – making thousands of copies of the film, distributing them to cinemas, and advertising the film in the press, on television and on the Internet.

An average Hollywood feature film takes eight weeks to film. It may cost $5 million or more a week, depending on how lavish the production is and how expensive the stars are. *Titanic* (1997) held the record for the largest production budget ($200 million) until it was equalled by *Spider-Man 2* (2004) and then broken by *King Kong* (2005) at $207 million. It has since been overtaken by *Superman Returns* (2006) at $232 million, *Spider-Man 3* (2007) at $258 million and *Pirates of the Caribbean: At World's End* (2007) with $300 million.

Top box office countries

Country	Box office revenue ($US)
1 USA	10,665,000,000
2 Japan	1,515,000,000
3 UK	1,343,000,000
4 France	1,281,000,000
5 Germany	1,054,000,000
World total (including countries not in top 5):	26,530,000,000

Below: costs and income of a typical big-budget Hollywood film, *Spider-Man 2* (2004)

COSTS

Estimated cost ($US million)	
Actors	
Toby Maguire	17
Kirsten Dunst	7
Alfred Molina	3
Rest of cast	3
Director (Sam Raimi)	10
Story rights	20
Screenplay	10
Producers	15
Production costs	45
Special effects	65
Music	5
Total production budget	**200**
Prints and advertising	75
Income	
US box office	374
Rest of world	410
Home video/DVD sales and rentals	58.5
TV broadcast rights	15.0
Total	**784**
Profit	**509**

Video and DVD sales and rentals and TV broadcast rights would also add to the total income

La Géode cinema stands in the Parc de la Villette, Paris. Inside the enormous dome is a giant screen measuring 1,000 sq m (10,764 sq ft).

Composer The composer writes the music or adapts an existing score as a backing track for the film.

Costume designer The costume designer is responsible for designing and supplying the clothing worn by the cast.

Editor The editor cuts and connects the best versions of each section of film to create the final version.

Gaffer The chief electrician, who is responsible for lighting the set. The word may come from slang for grandfather – a senior person respected by everyone. Gaffer tape is the heavy-duty tape used on sets to secure cables and almost anything else.

Key grip A grip is responsible for moving the sets and for laying the tracks on which the camera runs. The key grip is in charge of all the other grips.

Make-up artist He or she applies the cosmetics which alter or improve an actor's looks under the studio lights.

Sound engineer This engineer makes sure that the dialogue and other sounds heard on the film are properly recorded and synchronized with the action.

Special-effects coordinator This person is responsible for creating spectacular scenes with photographic, mechanical and computer methods.

Stunt man/woman Specialists who perform the actions that are too difficult or dangerous for an actor. Stunt doubles are stunt men or women made up to look like the actors so it looks as though the actors have performed a feat themselves.

Wardrobe mistress The wardrobe mistress (or master) is in charge of the costumes, making sure they fit, are in good condition and available when they are needed for a scene.

Transformers (2007) made $708.3 million worldwide and its 2009 sequel, *Transformers: Revenge of the Fallen*, $836.3 million

Highest-earning films

These films have made the most money at the box office.

Film	World total ($US million)
Avatar (2009)	2,713.4
Titanic (1997)	1,848.8
The Lord of the Rings: The Return of the King (2003)	1,133.0
Pirates of the Caribbean: Dead Man's Chest (2006)	1,066.2
The Dark Knight (2008)	1,001.9
Harry Potter and the Sorcerer's Stone (2001)	985.8
Pirates of the Caribbean: At World's End (2007)	961.0
Harry Potter and the Order of the Phoenix (2007)	938.5
Harry Potter and the Half-blood Prince (2006)	934.0
The Lord of the Rings: The Two Towers (2002)	926.3
Star Wars: Episode I - The Phantom Menace (1999)	924.3
*Shrek 2** (2004)	920.7
Jurassic Park (1993)	914.7
Harry Potter and the Goblet of Fire (2005)	896.0
Spider-Man 3 (2007)	890.9
*Ice Age: Dawn of the Dinosaurs** (2009)	884.8
Harry Potter and the Chamber of Secrets (2002)	879.0
Alice in Wonderland (2010)	875.0
The Lord of the Rings: The Fellowship of the Ring (2001)	871.4
*Finding Nemo** (2003)	864.6
Star Wars: Episode III – Revenge of the Sith (2005)	850.0
Transformers: Revenge of the Fallen (2009)	836.3
Spider-Man (2002)	821.7
Independence Day (1996)	817.0
*Shrek the Third** (2007)	799.0
Star Wars: Episode IV - A New Hope (1977)	797.9
Harry Potter and the Prisoner of Azkaban (2004)	795.5
E.T. the Extra-Terrestrial (1982)	792.9
Indiana Jones and the Kingdom of the Crystal Skull (2008)	786.6
Spider-Man 2 (2004)	784.0
*The Lion King** (1994)	783.8
2012 (2009)	769.7
The Da Vinci Code (2006)	758.2
The Chronicles of Narnia: The Lion, The Witch and The Wardrobe (2005)	745.0
The Matrix Reloaded (2003)	738.6
The Twilight Saga: New Moon (2009)	709.7
Transformers (2007)	708.3

* animated film

Musicals

Musicals – films in which songs sung by the characters are part of the story – date back 80 years.

Soon after the end of the silent era and the introduction of sound to films, one of the earliest musicals, *The Broadway Melody* (1929), featured eight songs and was the first sound film to win a Best Picture Oscar. The 1930s was regarded as the 'Golden Age' of film musicals, while those of the 1950s and 1960s, such as *The King and I* (1956) and *The Sound of Music* (1965) were often based on successful stage shows. After a decline in the 1980s and 1990s, the 2000s have seen a revival of musicals, with *Mamma Mia!* becoming the most successful musical and one of the 50 highest-earning films ever.

Film	World total ($US million)
Mamma Mia! (2008)	609.8
Grease (1978)	394.6
Chicago (2002)	306.8
Saturday Night Fever (1977)	285.4
High School Musical 3: Senior Year (2008)	252.9
Hairspray (2007)	200.6
Moulin Rouge! (2001)	177.7
The Sound of Music (1965)	163.2
The Phantom of the Opera (2004)	154.6
Sweeney Todd; The Demon Barber of Fleet Street (2007)	152.5
Evita (1996)	141.0
The Rocky Horror Picture Show (1975)	139.9
Staying Alive (1983)	127.6

Computer games and films

Computer games are big business and a number of recent blockbuster films have been based on some of the most popular games.

These include *Max Payne* (video game 2001, film 2008), *Lara Croft: Tomb Raider* (game 1992, film 1995) and *Mortal Kombat* (game 1992, film 1995).

The link between films and games also works the other way, with games based on live-action and animated films – for example, *Quantum of Solace* (film and game 2008), *The Incredibles* (2004) and *The Lord of the Rings: Battle for Middle Earth* (2004) – a game based on *The Lord of the Rings* trilogy (2001–2003).

James Bond films

Including the latest, *Quantum of Solace*, Ian Fleming's 12 James Bond books have been made into 22 official and two unofficial films, the original *Casino Royale* (1967), a comedy starring David Niven, and *Never say Never Again* (1983), with Sean Connery as Bond, which was a remake of *Thunderball*.

Daniel Craig as James Bond in *Quantum of Solace*

Film	Bond actor	World total ($US million)
Casino Royale (2006)	Daniel Craig	594.2
Quantum of Solace (2008)	Daniel Craig	586.1
Die Another Day (2002)	Pierce Brosnan	432.0
The World is Not Enough (1999)	Pierce Brosnan	390.0
GoldenEye (1995)	Pierce Brosnan	352.2
Tomorrow Never Dies (1997)	Pierce Brosnan	339.3
Moonraker (1979)	Roger Moore	210.3
For Your Eyes Only (1981)	Roger Moore	195.3
The Living Daylights (1987)	Timothy Dalton	191.2
Octopussy (1983)	Roger Moore	187.5
The Spy Who Loved Me (1977)	Roger Moore	185.4
Licence to Kill (1989)	Timothy Dalton	156.2
A View to a Kill (1985)	Roger Moore	152.4
Thunderball (1965)	Sean Connery	141.2
Live and Let Die (1973)	Roger Moore	126.4
Goldfinger (1964)	Sean Connery	124.9
Diamonds Are Forever (1971)	Sean Connery	116.0
You Only Live Twice (1967)	Sean Connery	111.6
The Man with the Golden Gun (1974)	Roger Moore	97.6
From Russia with Love (1963)	Sean Connery	78.9
On Her Majesty's Secret Service (1969)	George Lazenby	64.6
Dr No (1963)	Sean Connery	59.6

Will Bond be back?

Daniel Craig first appeared as James Bond in *Casino Royale* (2006) and again in *Quantum of Solace* (2008). In 2010, plans for a 23rd Bond film, also starring Craig, were put on hold.

See also
All about comics: page 236

Top films based on comic books

Comic book characters have been popular subjects for film makers ever since the 1930s. The characters are already familiar, so are immediately appealing to audiences. The exploits of superheroes such as Superman and Batman are perfect for exciting action films, many of which have been hugely successful.

Film	Comic first published	Film released	World total ($US million)
The Dark Knight	1939	2008	1001.9
Spider-Man 3	1962	2007	890.9
Spider-Man	1962	2002	821.7
Spider-Man 2	1962	2004	784.0
Men in Black	1990	1997	589.4
Iron Man	1963	2008	582.0
X-Men: The Last Stand	1963	2006	459.3
300	1998	2007	456.1
Men in Black II	1990	2002	441.8
Batman	1939	1989	413.4
X2: X-Men United	1963	2003	407.6
Superman Returns	1938	2006	391.1

The American Film Institute's top films

The American Film Institute has listed greatest films in a number of categories, based on the views of a panel of 1,500 film experts.

Greatest American movies of all time

1 *Citizen Kane* (1941)
2 *Casablanca* (1942)
3 *The Godfather* (1972)
4 *Gone with the Wind* (1939)
5 *Lawrence of Arabia* (1962)
6 *The Wizard of Oz* (1939)
7 *The Graduate* (1967)
8 *On the Waterfront* (1954)
9 *Schindler's List* (1993)
10 *Singin' in the Rain* (1952)

Funniest films

1 *Some Like It Hot* (1959)
2 *Tootsie* (1982)
3 *Dr Strangelove, or: How I Learned to Stop Worrying and Love the Bomb* (1964)
4 *Annie Hall* (1977)
5 *Duck Soup* (1933)
6 *Blazing Saddles* (1974)
7 *M*A*S*H* (1970)
8 *It Happened One Night* (1934)
9 *The Graduate* (1967)
10 *Airplane!* (1980)

Love stories

1 *Casablanca* (1942)
2 *Gone With the Wind* (1939)
3 *West Side Story* (1961)
4 *Roman Holiday* (1953)
5 *An Affair to Remember* (1957)
6 *The Way We Were* (1973)
7 *Doctor Zhivago* (1965)
8 *It's a Wonderful Life* (1946)
9 *Love Story* (1970)
10 *City Lights* (1931)

Thrillers

1 *Psycho* (1960)
2 *Jaws* (1975)
3 *The Exorcist* (1973)
4 *North by Northwest* (1959)
5 *The Silence of the Lambs* (1991)
6 *Alien* (1979)
7 *The Birds* (1963)
8 *The French Connection* (1971)
9 *Rosemary's Baby* (1968)
10 *Raiders of the Lost Ark* (1981)

Science fiction film *Alien* was voted one of the greatest-ever thrillers

What is an Oscar?

The Academy Awards or "Oscars" have been presented since 1929. The award is a gold-plated statuette made of tin, copper and antimony. It is 34.3 cm (13.5 in) high and weighs 3.8 kg (8.4 lb). Winning an Oscar is important because it encourages more people to see the film and helps the individual winners' careers.

Why is it called an Oscar?

According to legend, Academy librarian Margaret Herrick named it when she declared that the statuette looked like her Uncle Oscar!

Who decides who wins?

Members of the US Academy of Motion Picture Arts & Science members, including previous nominees and winners, vote to create a shortlist of five nominees in each of 24 categories, other than special, honorary and technical awards.

Who can win an Oscar?

The main categories are Best Picture, Best Director, Best Actor, Best Actress, Best Supporting Actor and Best Supporting Actress. There are other awards eg screenplay, cinematography, soundtrack, documentary, animated feature, foreign film.

Oscar® winners

These are the Best Picture, Best Actor and Best Actress winners for the last 25 years. The date given is the date of release. Oscars are awarded the following year.

Year	Best Picture	Best Actor	Best Actress
2009	*The Hurt Locker*	Jeff Bridges	Sandra Bullock
2008	*Slumdog Millionaire*	Sean Penn	Kate Winslet
2007	*No Country for Old Men*	Daniel Day-Lewis	Marion Cotillard
2006	*The Departed*	Forest Whitaker	Helen Mirren
2005	*Crash*	Philip Seymour Hoffman	Reese Witherspoon
2004	*Million Dollar Baby*	Jamie Foxx	Hilary Swank
2003	*The Lord of the Rings: The Return of the King*	Sean Penn	Charlize Theron
2002	*Chicago*	Adrien Brody	Nicole Kidman
2001	*A Beautiful Mind*	Denzel Washington	Halle Berry
2000	*Gladiator*	Russell Crowe	Julia Roberts
1999	*American Beauty*	Kevin Spacey	Hilary Swank
1998	*Shakespeare in Love*	Roberto Benigni	Gwyneth Paltrow
1997	*Titanic*	Jack Nicholson	Helen Hunt
1996	*The English Patient*	Geoffrey Rush	Frances McDormand
1995	*Braveheart*	Nicholas Cage	Susan Sarandon
1994	*Forrest Gump*	Tom Hanks	Jessica Lange
1993	*Schindler's List*	Tom Hanks	Holly Hunter
1992	*Unforgiven*	Al Pacino	Emma Thompson
1991	*The Silence of the Lambs*	Anthony Hopkins	Jodie Foster
1990	*Dances With Wolves*	Jeremy Irons	Kathy Bates
1989	*Driving Miss Daisy*	Daniel Day-Lewis	Jessica Tandy
1988	*Rain Man*	Dustin Hoffman	Jodie Foster
1987	*The Last Emperor*	Michael Douglas	Cher
1986	*Platoon*	Paul Newman	Marlee Martin
1985	*Out of Africa*	William Hurt	Geraldine Page
1984	*Amadeus*	F. Murray Abraham	Sally Field
1983	*Terms of Endearment*	Robert Duvall	Shirley MacLaine

Highest-earning actors and actresses

	Estimated 2009 earnings ($US million)
Daniel Radcliffe	41
Ben Stiller	40
Tom Hanks	36
Tyler Perry*	32.5
Adam Sandler*	31.5
Denzel Washington	31
Emma Watson	30
Owen Wilson	29
Nicolas Cage	28
Russell Crowe	28
Cameron Diaz	27
Steve Carell	25
Johnny Depp	25

* Including earnings as director or produce

Sandra Bullock won an Oscar for her role in *The Blind Side* (2009)

AFI's Top ten film songs

Song	Film
1 Over the Rainbow	*The Wizard of Oz* (1939)
2 As Time Goes By	*Casablanca* (1942)
3 Singin' in the Rain	*Singin' in the Rain* (1952)
4 Moon River	*Breakfast at Tiffany's* (1961)
5 White Christmas	*Holiday Inn* (1942)
6 Mrs Robinson	*The Graduate* (1967)
7 When You Wish Upon a Star	*Pinocchio* (1940)
8 The Way We Were	*The Way We Were* (1973)
9 Stayin' Alive	*Saturday Night Fever* (1977)
10 The Sound of Music	*The Sound Of Music* (1965)

See also
Awards: page 155

Most wins
These three films have each won 11 Oscars, including Best Picture: *Ben-Hur* (1959), *Titanic* (1997) and *The Lord of the Rings: The Return of the King* (2003).

A no-win situation
The Turning Point (1977) and *The Color Purple* (1985) had 11 nominations each but neither of them won a single Oscar. *Gangs of New York* (2002) received 10 nominations, also without winning anything.

Long and short
Gone with the Wind (1939) was the longest film (238 minutes) and the first colour film to win Best Picture. *Marty* (1955) was the shortest Best Picture winner at 91 minutes.

Black and white
Marty was also one of the last black and white films to win Best Picture. *The Apartment* (1960) and *Schindler's List* (1993) are the only black and white films to have won since.

First appearances

These are the films in which some of the most famous animated characters made their first appearances.

Mickey Mouse *Plane Crazy* (1928)
Plane Crazy was Walt Disney's first Mickey Mouse cartoon and was silent. Two months later Mickey appeared in Disney's *Steamboat Willie*, the first Mickey Mouse cartoon with sound. Mickey starred in *Fantasia* (1940), and his *Lend a Paw* won an Oscar® in 1941.

Popeye *Popeye the Sailor with Betty Boop* (1933)
Popeye was born in 1929 as a newspaper comic strip by Elzie Crisler Segar. Animator Max Fleischer adapted it for the screen. Popeye cartoons were made for cinema and TV until the 1980s.

Donald Duck *The Wise Little Hen* (1934)
Clarence Nash was the voice of Donald Duck for 50 years. The Donald Duck anti-Hitler film *Der Fuehrer's Face* (1942) won an Oscar.

Bugs Bunny *Porky's Hare Hunt* (1938)
A Wild Hare (1940) was the first cartoon in which Bugs Bunny said "Eh, what's up, Doc?" but he was not named until *Elmer's Pet Rabbit* (1941). *Knighty-Knight Bugs* (1958) won an Oscar.

Tom and Jerry *Puss Gets The Boot* (1940)
The very first Tom and Jerry cartoon was nominated for an Oscar. The characters also appeared in the 1992 film *Tom and Jerry: The Movie*. This full-length film is the only one in which they speak.

Casper the Ghost *The Friendly Ghost* (1945)
Casper starred in more than 50 cartoons and in a part live action/part computer animated feature film in 1995, which earned nearly $300 million around the world.

The Flintstones *The Flintstone Flyer* (1960)
This was the first episode of *The Flintstones* to be broadcast on TV. It went on to become the longest-running cartoon series until it was overtaken by *The Simpsons*. The live-action film *The Flintstones* (1994) was one of the top-earning films of the year.

Simpsons *Simpsons Roasting on an Open Fire* (1989)
Matt Groening's hugely successful animated series began in 1987 as short episodes screened on the Tracey Ullman Show. It was developed into longer weekly episodes and has become the longest-running and most successful cartoon series ever.

Walt Disney's first animated features

Walt Disney (1901–66) produced short animated films, including Mickey Mouse cartoons, before making main features. *Snow White* was Hollywood's first full-length animated feature film and earned Disney an honorary Oscar. The film made $188 million in the USA alone.

Film	First released in cinemas
1 *Snow White and the Seven Dwarfs*	21 December 1937
2 *Pinocchio*	7 February 1940
3 *Fantasia*	12 November 1940
4 *Dumbo*	23 October 1941
5 *Bambi*	9 August 1942

Walt Disney in his studio

Types of animation

The word animation comes from the Latin *animatus*, meaning filled with life. Even before the invention of cinema, people realized that if the human eye sees a series of images that change at a rate of at least 24 frames a second, the brain can be tricked into thinking it is seeing a live moving image. 19th-century optical toys such as zoetropes worked on this principle.

A zoetrope – when the viewer spins the zoetrope and looks through a slit, the pictures inside appear to be moving.

Traditional animation
Individual frames of a story are hand drawn on cels – transparent sheets of plastic. They are then photographed as a sequence against painted backgrounds.

Cut-out
In this type of animation, two-dimensional drawings are placed on a fixed background. These are moved and photographed to create the impression of movement.

CGI
CGI (Computer Generated Imagery) has been used since the 1970s, originally for short films. The 1989 film *The Abyss* used some CGI visual effects, but the hugely successful

Avatar

A large proportion of the record $237 million production budget of *Avatar* was spent on computer generated imagery, which comprises two-thirds of the film. This and its revolutionary 3-D visual effects captured the public imagination and within four months of its December 2009 release it had broken every box office record, generating box office income of over $700 million in the USA and almost $2 billion in the rest of the world.

Most expensive animated films

Making animated films has become more and more expensive. In 1937 *Snow White and the Seven Dwarfs* cost $1.49 million – a record-breaking sum at the time. *Tarzan* (1999) and *The Polar Express* (2004) are the costliest films ever made and were more than 100 times as expensive as *Snow White*.

Film	Year	Budget ($US million)
A Christmas Carol	2009	190
WALL-E	2008	180
UP	2009	175
The Polar Express	2004	170
Shrek the Third	2007	160
Bee Movie	2007	150
Beowulf	2007	150
Bolt	2008	150
Madagascar: Escape 2 Africa	2008	150
Ratatouille	2007	150
Shrek 2	2004	150

Toy Story (1995), from the Disney and Pixar Animation Studio, was the first CGI feature film. Another development known as 3D motion capture has been used in films such as *Beowulf* (2007), a $150 million budget film with Ray Winstone in the title role, in which the movements of the actors are converted into computer images.

Stop motion

This type of animation is created by moving three-dimensional figures and other objects a tiny amount between shots. This method has been used since 1925, but the best-known modern examples of this technique are the *Wallace & Gromit* films by Aardman Animation.

Beowulf was filmed by the motion capture process

Highest-earning animated films

Film	Year	Earnings ($US million)
Shrek 2	2004	920.7
Ice Age: Dawn of the Dinosaurs	2009	884.8
Finding Nemo	2003	864.6
Shrek the Third	2007	799.0
The Lion King	1994	783.8
Up	2009	731.3
Ice Age: The Meltdown	2006	655.4
Kung Fu Panda	2008	631.7
The Incredibles	2004	631.4
Ratatouille	2007	623.7
Madagascar: Escape 2 Africa	2008	603.9
Madagascar	2005	532.7
The Simpsons Movie	2007	527.1
Monsters, Inc.	2001	525.4
WALL-E	2008	521.3
Aladdin	1992	504.1
Toy Story 2	1999	485.0
Shrek	2001	484.4
Cars	2006	462.0

Casablanca (1942), in which screen legends Humphrey Bogart and Ingrid Bergman both starred

Top 10 screen legends

This is the Top 10 of the American Film Institute's list of the greatest American screen legends.

	Actor	Actress
1	Humphrey Bogart	Katharine Hepburn
2	Cary Grant	Bette Davis
3	James Stewart	Audrey Hepburn
4	Marlon Brando	Ingrid Bergman
5	Fred Astaire	Greta Garbo
6	Henry Fonda	Marilyn Monroe
7	Clark Gable	Elizabeth Taylor
8	James Cagney	Judy Garland
9	Spencer Tracy	Marlene Dietrich
10	Charlie Chaplin	Joan Crawford

Stars whose films have earned most

These are the stars who have appeared in the most films that have made more than $100 million at the US box office. A number of less well-known actors who have supplied their voices to animated films have made as many or even more high-earning films.

Star	Films	$100 m+ films
Tom Hanks	42	18
Tom Cruise	34	16
Eddie Murphy	35	13
Morgan Freeman	49	13
Will Smith	20	12
Harrison Ford	37	12
Robin Williams	54	12
Samuel L. Jackson	78	12
Stan Lee	14	11
Jim Carrey	27	11
Mel Gibson	36	11
John Travolta	41	11

The vampires are coming!

Following the success of TV's *Buffy the Vampire Slayer* series, vampires have become big business at the film box office, with the *Blade* and *Underworld* series and especially the first two *Twilight* films, *Twilight* (2008) and *The Twilight Saga: New Moon* (2009), becoming the highest-earning vampire films of all time, making a total of more than $1 billion worldwide between them.

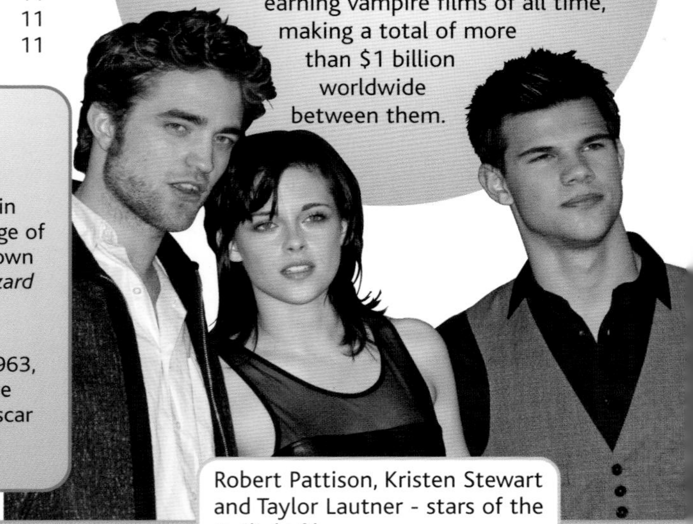

Robert Pattison, Kristen Stewart and Taylor Lautner - stars of the *Twilight* films

Child stars

Shirley Temple
An American dancer and singer, Shirley Temple (born 1928) began appearing in films at the age of four and became the world's most famous child star. After retiring from show business, she became a diplomat, serving as US Ambassador to Ghana and Czechoslovakia.

Georgie Henley
The British actress (born 9 July 1995) plays Lucy in *The Chronicles of Narnia* series. At the age of 10 she won a Phoenix Film Critics Award for her role in *The Lion, the Witch and the Wardrobe*.

Judy Garland
The American actress (1922–69) appeared in her first role at the age of seven. She is best known as Dorothy in *The Wizard of Oz* (1939).

Tatum O'Neal
Born in the USA in 1963, Tatum O'Neal became the youngest-ever Oscar winner for her role in *Paper Moon* (1973).

Movie monsters

Ever since cinema began, film-makers have played on everyone's fear of monsters. These are some of the most popular monster films.

Aliens
Hundreds of films have been made about alien monsters attacking Earth. The most successful of these was *Independence Day* (1996).

Dinosaurs
One of the first cartoons was *Gertie* (1914). It featured a drawing of a brontosaurus that comes to life. Dinosaur films *Jurassic Park* (1993) and its two sequels, *The Lost World: Jurassic Park* (1997) and *Jurassic Park III* (2001), are among the biggest blockbusters of all time.

Frankenstein's monster
Frankenstein is the name of the creator of the monster, not the monster itself. The original story was written in 1816 by English writer Mary Shelley. It was first made into a silent film in 1910 by the inventor Thomas Edison and has been remade many times since. *Mary Shelley's Frankenstein* (1994) is the highest-earning of all the versions.

Egyptian mummies
The Mummy (1932) featured an Egyptian mummy that comes to life and attacks people. *The Mummy* was remade in 1999 and its sequel, the comedy-adventure *The Mummy Returns* (2001), has made more than $433 million.

Funny monsters
Some of the most successful cartoon monsters are those in *Monsters, Inc.* (2001). The monsters are led by Sulley, whose secret is that the monsters are scared of children!

Stage names

Actors and actresses choose stage names for a variety of reasons. Their real names may be the same as or similar to those of other people, or they may be difficult to spell or pronounce.

Here are some famous performers who decided to change their names.

Film name	Real name
Woody Allen	Allan Stewart Konigsberg
Jennifer Aniston	Jennifer Linn Anastassakis
Mel Brooks	Melvin Kaminsky
Nicolas Cage	Nicholas Kim Coppola
Michael Caine	Maurice Joseph Micklewhite
Jackie Chan	Chan Kong-sang
Tom Cruise	Thomas Cruise Mapother IV
Kirk Douglas	Issur Danielovitch Demsky
Whoopi Goldberg	Caryn Elaine Johnson
Cary Grant	Archibald Alexander Leach
Richard E. Grant	Richard Grant Esterhuysen
Goldie Hawn	Goldie Jean Studlendegehawn
Hulk Hogan	Terry Gene Bollea
Angelina Jolie	Angelina Jolie Voight
Ben Kingsley	Krishna Bhanji
Queen Latifah	Dana Elaine Owens
Jet Li	Li Lian Jie
Marilyn Monroe	Norma Jean Baker
Demi Moore	Demetria Gene Guynes
Natalie Portman	Natalie Hershlag
Winona Ryder	Winona Horowitz
Susan Sarandon	Susan Abigail Tomalin
Christian Slater	Christian Michael Leonard Hawkins
Sigourney Weaver	Susan Weaver

Poster for the original horror-adventure film *King Kong* (1933); the film has been remade twice, most recently in 2005

Killer creatures
Giant ape King Kong is one of the most famous animal monsters and the star of the film *King Kong* (1933, 1976 and 2005). Giant spiders have featured in films such as *Arachnophobia* (1990) and *Eight Legged Freaks* (2002). Harry Potter also meets an army of huge spiders in *Harry Potter and the Chamber of Secrets* (2002). Other famous killer creatures include sharks (*Jaws*, 1977 and its three sequels, 1978–87), alligators (*Lake Placid*, 1999) and snakes (*Anaconda*, 1997 and *Snakes on a Plane*, 2006). A giant worm terrorizes a town in *Tremors* (1990) and mythical creatures such as the Kraken, a giant sea monster, appear in *Clash of the Titans* (2010).

Vampires
Irish writer Bram Stoker's vampire novel *Dracula* was published in 1897 and was first filmed in the silent era, along with others, such as German *Nosferatu* (1921). Bram Stoker's *Dracula* (1992), *Van Helsing* (1994) and *Interview with the Vampire* (2004) led the way for a 21st-century revival of interest in vampire films.

Zombies
Zombies are the "undead" – bodies that come out of their graves and terrorize the living. They have been the subject of many films, including the most successful, *Dawn of the Dead* (2004) and comedy spoofs such as *Shaun of the Dead* (2004). This was billed as the first "Rom-Com-Zom" (Romantic Comedy Zombie film).

See also
Mythical creatures: pages 170–71

www.afi.com search

Video and DVD fact file

- The terms video recording and videotape were first used in the early 1950s, but only among TV professionals.
- The abbreviation VCR (video cassette recorder) was first used in the UK and USA in 1971.
- The first domestic video cassette recorders were sold in 1974, but both machines and tapes were very expensive and few people bought them.
- The VHS (video home system) was launched in 1976 in the US and 1978 in Europe.
- By 1980 about 7,687,000 homes had video recorders; by 1996 the global figure was put at 400,976,000.
- DVD (digital video disc or digital versatile disc) players and discs were launched in Japan and the USA in 1997.
- Worldwide, sales of DVDs overtook video sales in 2002.
- By 2003 almost one in three UK households had a DVD player. In 2007 the figure increased to over 83 per cent, with sales of discs over £2.3 billion.
- In 2007, most major film studios stopped releasing films on video. In 2008 Blu-Ray was adopted as the standard format for HD (High Definition) DVD. Although blank tapes are still produced, by 2009 the production of pre-recorded VHS tapes had ended.

TV-owning countries

Country	TV households*	Country	TV households*
China	384,288,600	Germany	39,326,500
USA	120,233,800	Mexico	27,971,900
India	87,514,100	UK	27,409,500
Indonesia	63,287,100	France	26,804,500
Brazil	54,853,200	Italy	23,997,100
Russia	51,323,500		
Japan	50,578,900		

* Households with colour TVs, 2011 forecast

TV viewing

- In the average US home, the TV is switched on for 7 hours 40 minutes a day.
- US children aged 2 to 17 watch an average of 19 hours 40 minutes' TV every week. That is 1,023 hours a year compared with 900 hours a year in school.
- In the UK children aged 8 to 15 spend an average of 2 hours 13 minutes a day watching TV and adults over 16 spend an average of 2 hours 23 minutes.

A 1950s US magazine advertisement for TVs

First countries to have television*

The BBC's first broadcasts used Baird's mechanical television system. In this, spinning disks were used to scan images.

This was later dropped in favour of US inventor Philo Taylor Farnsworth's electronic system. Electronic television did not rely on moving parts, was more reliable and gave a better picture.

Country	Year
UK	1936
USA	1939
USSR	1939
France	1948
Brazil	1950

* High-definition regular public broadcasting service

TV milestones 1900s

1922
18 October, BBC (British Broadcasting Company) founded

1929
First transmissions of Scottish inventor John Logie Baird's experimental mechanical television system and, in the USA, Philo T. Farnsworth's electronic TV system

1936
22 November, BBC opens the world's first regular high-definition television service, from Alexandra Palace, London

1937
21 June, Wimbledon Tennis Championships first broadcast

1938
30 April, television coverage of the FA Cup Final
31 May, first BBC TV panel game, *Spelling Bee*

1939
1 September, BBC television service is suspended throughout World War II
30 April, Franklin D. Roosevelt is the first president to appear on TV, opening the World's Fair in New York
10 June, the first king and queen on TV in the USA are King George VI and Queen Elizabeth, seen visiting the World's Fair

1941
1 July, the first ever TV commercial, for a Bulova clock, is broadcast by WNBT New York, during a game between the Brooklyn Dodgers and the Philadelphia Phillies

1946
1 June, first TV licences are issued in the UK (cost £2)
7 June, BBC television broadcasts resume
7 July, first British children's TV programme, *For the Children*, is broadcast

1947
21 February, America's first regular daytime serial, or soap opera, *A Woman to Remember*, begins its run

1948
29 July, London Olympic Games is televised

1951
24 December, in the USA *Amahl and The Night Visitors* becomes the world's first commercial colour broadcast

1953
2 June, the coronation of Queen Elizabeth II is watched live by about 20 million people in the

Radio milestones

1896
2 June, Italian inventor Guglielmo Marconi applies for first British "wireless" patent
1906
24 December, first radio programme (music and speech) broadcast by Professor Reginald Fessenden from the US coast and received by ships.
1920
15 June, Marconi broadcasts a concert by opera singer Dame Nellie Melba
1922
18 October, BBC (British Broadcasting Company) founded. The first BBC broadcast was made on 14 November – the six o'clock news read by Arthur Burrows
1923
26 April, first daily weather forecast by the BBC
1926
24 January, launch of *The Week's Good Cause*, the BBC's longest-running programme
1933
28 August, first BBC woman announcer, Sheila Borrett
1939–45
During World War II the BBC provides information and stirring speeches from Winston Churchill and other wartime leaders
1951
1 January, launch of *The Archers*, longest-running BBC radio serial
1964
Pirate radio stations broadcast from ships to UK, encouraging the BBC to launch a pop music station (Radio 1, 30 September 1967)
1993
First Internet radio broadcasts
1995
First experimental DAB (digital audio broadcasting) in UK. DAB gives listeners better quality reception, easy tuning and text information
2002
BBC launches five new DAB channels
2005
BBC radio begins to make programmes available as podcasts that can be downloaded to computers, MP3 and DAB players
2007
Internet radio becomes available to mobile phones
2009
More than 1,800 US radio stations use HD radio technology that allows high quality digital and analogue signals and text data to be broadcast simultaneously.

www.bbc.co.uk search

The Archers

Billed as 'an everyday story of country folk', *The Archers*, a BBC radio programme that focuses on the lives of the Archers, a farming family, and their neighbours in the fictitious village of Ambridge, was first broadcast on 1 January 1951 and passed its 16,000th episode in 2010, making it the world's longest-running radio soap opera.

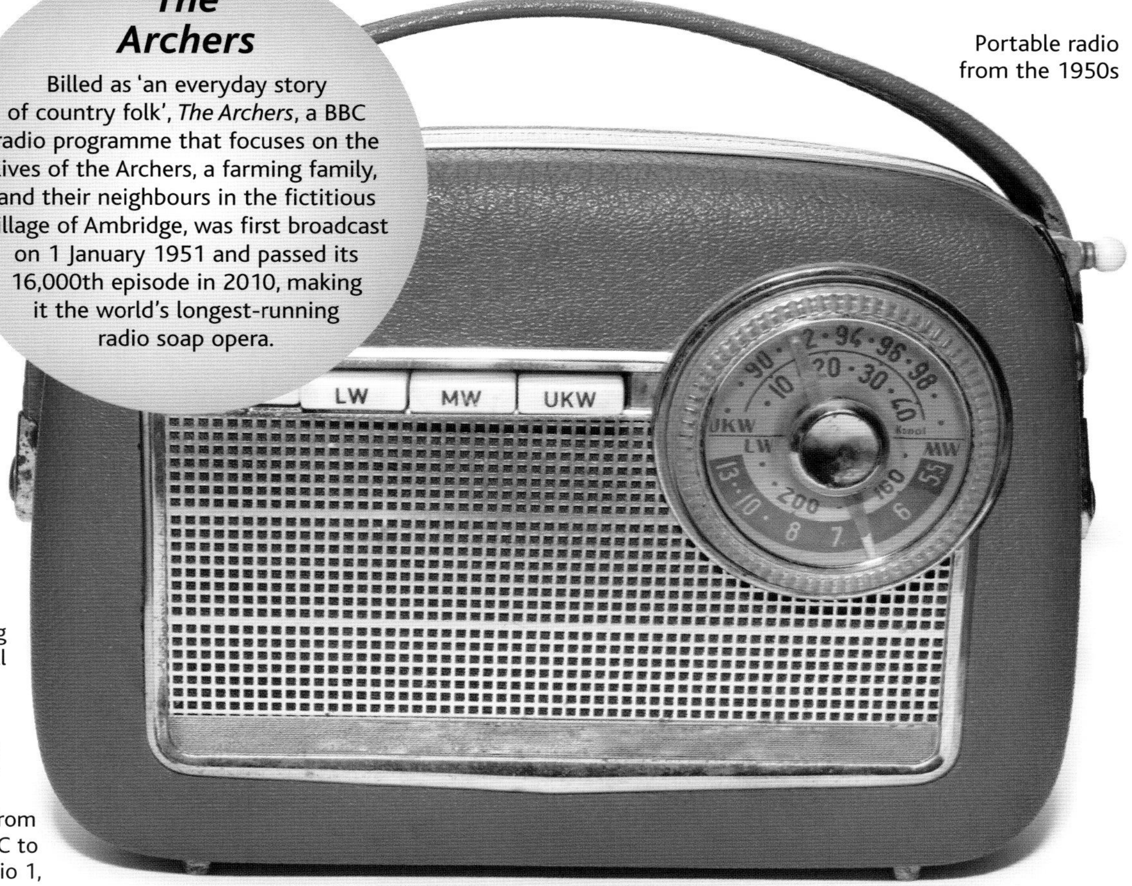

Portable radio from the 1950s

UK and 200 million worldwide
21 November, current affairs programme Panorama is launched; goes on to become the longest-running programme on British TV
1954
1 January, the *Tournament of Roses* parade at Pasadena, California, USA, becomes the first programme ever broadcast coast-to-coast
11 January, first TV weather forecast in the UK
9 April, Britain's first TV soap opera, *The Grove Family*
1955
22 September, first TV advert in the UK, for Gibbs SR toothpaste
1957
13 May, first schools programmes broadcast in UK
25 December, the Queen's first TV Christmas message broadcast
1958
16 October, *Blue Peter* starts, and becomes the longest-running children's programme
1969
21 July, first live broadcasts from the Moon (*Apollo XI*)
15 November, BBC1 and ITV start broadcasting in colour
1981
1 August, MTV launched; The Buggles' *Video Killed the Radio Star* the first music video to be broadcast
1989
5 February, Sky begins satellite broadcasting in the UK
1997
9 November, BBC1 begins broadcasting 24 hours a day, seven days a week (previously, TV closed down at night)
2000
18 July, UK launch of *Big Brother* starts a fashion for reality TV
2006
High Definition television (HDTV) becomes available in the UK and other countries
2008
SED (Surface-conduction electron-emitter display) high definition televisions go on sale
2009
Switchover from analogue to digital TV in USA
2012
Switchover to digital in UK completed

adidas
New Zealand
SEVENS
GILBERT

Sports

Rugby World Cup

The Rugby World Cup was first held in 1987 in Australia and New Zealand, with New Zealand the winners, and has been staged every four years since. It took place in the UK, France and Ireland in 1991 (won by Australia), South Africa in 1995 (won by South Africa), Wales in 1999 (won by Australia), Australia in 2003 (won by England) and France in 2007 (won by South Africa). New Zealand, seen here playing in a rugby sevens tournament, will host the next competition in September–October 2011.

Teams and competitors

Team sizes

These are the number of players allowed on a pitch at any one time. The full team can also include some substitutes. In American football, for example, there are 45 full-time team members. Different players come on the pitch for defensive and offensive moves.

Sport	Team on pitch
Australian Rules football	18
Gaelic football, hurling, Rugby Union	15
Rugby League	13
Canadian football, korfball, women's lacrosse	12
American football, bandy, cricket, field hockey, soccer, speedball	11
Men's lacrosse, slow-pitch softball	10
Baseball, rounders, fast-pitch softball	9
Tug-of-war	8
Team handball, netball, water polo	7
Ice hockey, volleyball	6
Basketball, roller hockey	5
Polo	4

Most competitors

- The Boston Marathon centenary race in 1996 attracted a record 38,706 competitors, the most ever for a marathon.
- The Athens Olympic Games (2004) had 11,099 competitors, the most of any Olympics.
- The world's biggest road race is the 12 km (7.5 miles) Bay to Breakers race in San Francisco, USA. It has been held every year since 1912. The 1988 race had a record 78,769 official entries, but the total number of people taking part was probably about 110,000, many of them in fancy dress.
- In 1929 the Grand National horse race had a record 66 runners, but only nine reached the finish line.

Most-watched sporting event

The 2008 Beijing Olympics was the most-watched sporting event ever with an estimated 4.7 billion watching on television. Approximately 7 million tickets, for watching events live, were sold.

Sporting sizes

	Dimensions and distances
Blade of an ice skate (width)	33 mm (1.3 in)
Tenpin height	38 cm (15 in)
Parallel bars in gymnastics (distance between)	42 cm (16.5 in)
Dartboard diameter	45 cm (17.7 in)
Tennis net height (at centre)	91 cm (35.8 in)
Hurdles height (men's 400 m)	91.4 cm (36 in)
Cricket bat (maximum)	96.52 x 10.8 cm (38 x 4.3 in)
Water polo pool depth (minimum)	1.8 m (6 ft)
Women's javelin length (minimum)	2.2 m (7.2 ft)
Soccer goal height	2.44 m (8 ft)
Men's javelin length (minimum)	2.6 m (8.5 ft)
Table tennis table	2.74 x 1.52 m (9 x 5 ft)
Rugby goal crossbar height	3.05 m (10 ft)
Snooker table (full size)	3.66 x 1.86 m (12 x 6.1 ft)
Boxing ring	6.1 x 6.1 m (20 x 20 ft)
Soccer goal width	7.32 m (24 ft)
Marathon distance	42.195 km (26 miles 385 yd)
Australian Rules football pitch (oval)	135–185 x 110–155 m (442.9–607 x 360.9–508.5 ft)
Polo pitch	275 x 183 m (902.2 x 600.4 ft)
Formula One Grand Prix (Brazilian Grand Prix circuit)	306 km (190.1 miles)
Isle of Man TT motorcycle race (longest, 1957)	485.8 km (301.9 miles)
Longest course in majors golf (Torrey Pines, San Diego 2008)	6,989 m (7,643 yards)
Hazeltine National, 2009 US PGA Championship	7,017 metres (7,674 yards)
Iditarod dog sled race, Alaska north route (even-numbered years)	1,790 km (1,112 miles)
south route (odd-numbered years)	1,820 km (1,131 miles)
Le Mans 24 Hour race (greatest distance covered in the time, 1971)	5,333.7 km (3,314.2 miles)
Tour de France cycle race (record longest, 1926)	5,745 km (3,569.8 miles)
Tour d'Afrique, Cairo to Cape Town (longest cycle race)	11,900 km (7,394 miles)
Around alone (solo round-the-world yacht race)	46,276.7 km (28,754.6 miles)

Marathon sprint!

If a 100-metres sprinter ran at the same speed as the fastest-ever marathon runner, it would take him 17.63 seconds to cover the distance.

Sport origins

Early days of boxing

The first record of a boxing contest in England was in 1681 and in 1719 James Figg beat Ned Sutton to become the first boxing champion. Boxers fought without gloves and there were no regulations governing the length or number of rounds – a round ended when a fighter was knocked down. But that all changed in 1865 when the 9th Marquess of Queensberry drew up his famous rules of boxing and introduced the three-minute round rule, with a one-minute break in between. Gloved fighting replaced bare-knuckle contests, with the last bare-knuckle world heavyweight championship fought in 1889.

Origins of golf

Many countries lay claim to being the founders of golf, including the French, Dutch and Belgians who all played a version of the sport in the Middle Ages, but Scotland's claim seems to be the strongest. In 1457 the playing of 'gouf' was banned in Scotland following an Act of Parliament. But monarchs, including James IV and Mary Queen of Scots, both enjoyed playing the game. Scotland can certainly claim the world's oldest golf club, the Honourable Company of Edinburgh Golfers, founded in 1744.

US golfer, Phil Mickelson, winner of the 2010 US Masters Tournament, putts during the final round of the competition

Sport top speeds

Sport	km/h	mph
Competition rifle bullet	3,787	2,353
Longbow arrow	547	340
Drag racer (0.4 km [0.25 miles] from standing start)	535	332
Free-fall skydiver	531	330
Pelota (jai-alai) ball	302	188
Indy 500 racing car (record, 1990)	299	186
Golf ball (leaving tee)	273	170
Downhill skier (record)	248	154
Squash ball (record, 1988)	243	151
Tennis serve (record, 2004)	249	155
Racing car (Formula One)	238	148
Water skiing (record, 1983)	230	143
Isle of Man TT race (record, 2009)	212	132
Snowboarding (record)	202	126
Ice hockey puck	190	118
Ski-bob (record, 2003)	202	125
Table tennis ball	170	106
Baseball (pitched)	162	101
Cricket bowl (record, 2003)	161	100
Luge	137	85
Frisbee	119	74
Cyclist (record, 2008)	132	82
Skateboard (record, 1998)	101	63
4-man bobsleigh	90	56
Racehorse	72	45
Greyhound	67	42
100-m sprinter	59	37
Boxing punch	56	35
Karate chop	51	32

Longest events

- In Formula One motor racing, the 19-race season (2010) was spread over eight months.
- The Tour d'Afrique cycle race includes 100 days of cycling and 20 days of rest.
- The Tour de France lasts 22 days (with rest days).
- The Iditarod dog sled race, held in Alaska, lasts nine days.
- The 10th Volvo Ocean Race (formerly the Whitbread Round the World Race) started from Alicante (Spain) in October 2008 and ended eight and a half months later at St Petersburg, Russia, after a total of 36,995 nautical miles.
- The longest boxing match with gloves was a 110-round fight between Andy Bowen and Jack Burke (both USA). It started at 9.15 pm on Thursday, 6 April 1893 and finished at 4.34 am on Friday, 7 April – a total of 7 hours 19 minutes.

Oldest sporting events

Doggett's Coat and Badge Race is the world's oldest continuous sporting event. It is a rowing contest held on the River Thames in England and has been held every year since 1715. The Newmarket Town Plate horse race is even older, but the race was discontinued for a while.

Event	First held
Newmarket Town Plate horse race	1665
Doggett's Coat and Badge Race (rowing)	1715
Real Tennis Championship	1740
St Leger horse race	1776
Epsom Derby horse race	1780
County Cricket Championship	1827
Oxford and Cambridge Boat Race	1829
Grand National steeplechase	1836
Henley Regatta	1839
British Open golf championship	1860
Melbourne Cup horse race	1861
America's Cup yachting series	1870
Football Association Challenge Cup	1872
Kentucky Derby horse race	1875
Test Match cricket	1877
Wimbledon Lawn Tennis Championships	1877

Event	First held
Football League championship (England)	1888
Stanley Cup ice hockey competition	1893
US Open golf championship	1895
Davis Cup tennis tournament	1900
Baseball World Series	1903
Tour de France cycle race	1903
Ryder Cup golf tournament	1927
FIFA Soccer World Cup	1930
Formula One World Championship	1950
Super Bowl (US football championship)	1967
Cricket World Cup	1975
Athletics World Cup	1977
World Athletics Championships	1983
Breeders' Cup horse race series	1984
Rugby Union World Cup	1987
Cricket World Twenty20 Cup	2007

Grand National steeplechase (19th century)

Top sporting events

These are the leading events in the world's most popular sports, in addition to the Olympic Games.

American football Super Bowl
Athletics IAAF (International Athletics Association Federations) World Championship
Grand Prix Auto racing (US) Indianapolis 500
Baseball World Series
Basketball NBA (National Basketball Association) Final
Cycling Tour de France
Golf British Open, US Open, Ryder Cup (every two years)
Horse racing Epsom Derby, Grand National, Breeders' Cup, Kentucky Derby
Ice hockey Stanley Cup
Motor racing World Formula One Championship
Rallying Dakar Rally
Rugby League Challenge Cup, Super League
Rugby Union Six Nations Tournament, World Cup (every four years)
Soccer UEFA Champions League, FIFA World Cup (every four years)
Tennis Wimbledon Championships, US Open
Motor cycling MotoGP world championship

See also
Major rock events: page 255

Sports timeline

Experts argue about the exact origins of many sports. The dates here are generally agreed to be when these sports were first played or contested on an organized basis.

Athletics	3800 BC	Soccer	1848	Basketball	1891
Horse racing	AD 1540	Tenpin bowling	1850	Rugby League	1895
Boxing	1681	Show jumping	1864	Darts	1896
Rowing	1715	Cycling	1867	Motor cycling	1896
Ice skating	1742	Badminton	1873	Speedway	1902
Cricket	1744	Lawn tennis	1873		
Golf	1744	American football	1874		
Swimming	1791	Hockey (field)	1875		
Baseball	1839	Hockey (ice)	1887		
Rugby Union	1839	Motor racing	1887		

Bare-knuckle boxing match (1820)

Wembley Stadium

The new Wembley Stadium was completed in 2007, nearly four years after the demolition of the old stadium. The largest stadium in the UK with a capacity of 90,000 and all seats under cover, it cost £800 million to build. Chelsea, the last team to win the FA Cup at the old Wembley, beat Manchester United 1–0 in the first FA Cup final at the new stadium.

Wembley Stadium

Biggest crowds

In the past, more than 100,000 people at a time crammed into American football's Rose Bowl, the old Wembley Stadium and other venues across Europe to watch sport. Today, there are laws which limit the number of people allowed in a sports stadium. Outdoor events such as the New York City Marathon and the Tour de France now draw the biggest crowds. They are held over open roads and people don't have to pay to watch them.

- About 2.5 million people watch the New York Marathon – the biggest crowd for a single day at a sporting event. As many as 15 million people turn out to see the Tour de France during its three weeks.
- The record crowd for a golf tournament was set at the US Open, Flushing Meadows, 2009, which was attended by 721,059 people.
- In horse racing, more than 60,000 watch the Grand National and about 120,000 go to the Epsom Derby every year.
- Cricket attracts big crowds. More than 400,000 people watched the India v Pakistan Test match in Calcutta in 1998–99.
- The biggest crowd for a baseball game was at the Los Angeles Memorial Coliseum in 2008 when 115,300 watched an exhibition game between Los Angeles Dodgers and Boston Red Sox.
- The biggest crowd at a boxing match was in 1941 when more than 135,000 watched the Tony Zale vs. Billy Pryor middleweight non-title fight at Juneau Park, Milwaukee, USA. The contest was organised by the Fraternal Order of Eagles and admission was free. The biggest paying crowd was the 120,757 for the Gene Tunney vs. Jack Dempsey world heavyweight title fight in 1926.

Underwater hockey

Also known as Octopush, underwater hockey was first played by members of the Southsea Sub-Aqua Club, Hampshire, UK, in 1954. Each team consists of eight members per side and the puck is projected by a small hand-held stick. The sport is now popular worldwide and holds a world championship every two years.

Oldest World Championships

The first-ever world champion in any sport was a Frenchman called Clergé, the greatest exponent of Real Tennis, who held the world title from *c.*1740 to 1750.

c.1740	Real Tennis
1820	Rackets
1860	Boxing (First world title bout)
1863	Sculling
1870	Billiards
1886	Chess (Unofficial World Championship from 1851)
1897	Shooting
1889	Speed Skating
1893	Cycling
1896	Figure Skating
1898	Weightlifting
1903	Cross Country
1903	Gymnastics
1920	Ice Hockey
1923	Ten Pin Bowling
1925	Nordic Skiing
1926	Table Tennis
1927	Snooker
1930	Association Football

The first world championships of other selected sports are:

Athletics	1983
Bowls	1966
Cricket	1975
Darts	1978
Golf (World Cup)	1953
Motor cycling	1949
Motor racing	1950
Rugby League (World Cup)	1954
Rugby Union (World Cup)	1987
Speedway	1936
Swimming	1973

Summer Olympics

The modern Olympic Games have been held every four years since 1896, except during World Wars I and II. Over this time the numbers of competitors, events and nations taking part have all increased dramatically.

Winter Paralympic events for athletes with disabilities have been held since 1976. The Summer Paralympics began in 1960 and were first held in conjunction with the regular Summer Olympics in 1988.

Year/City/country	Competitors	No. of nations	Events	Most golds	Most medals
1896 Athens, Greece	245	14	43	USA 11	Greece 47
1900 Paris, France	1,225	26	95	France 26	France 95
1904 St Louis, USA	687	13	91	USA 79	USA 245
1906 Athens, Greece	884	20	76	France 15	France 40
1908 London, UK	2,035	22	110	UK 54	UK 138
1912 Stockholm, Sweden	2,547	28	102	USA 25	Sweden 64
1920 Antwerp, Belgium	2,669	29	154	USA 41	USA 95
1924 Paris, France	3,092	44	126	USA 45	USA 99
1928 Amsterdam, Netherlands	3,014	46	109	USA 22	USA 56
1932 Los Angeles, USA	1,408	37	117	USA 41	USA 103
1936 Berlin, Germany	4,066	49	129	Germany 33	Germany 89
1948 London, UK	4,099	59	136	USA 38	USA 84
1952 Helsinki, Finland	4,925	69	149	USA 40	USA 76
1956* Melbourne, Australia	3,342	72	145	USSR 37	USSR 98
1960 Rome, Italy	5,348	83	150	USSR 43	USSR 103
1964 Tokyo, Japan	5,140	93	163	USA 36	USA 90
1968 Mexico City, Mexico	5,531	112	172	USA 45	USA 107
1972 Munich, West Germany	7,123	121	195	USSR 50	USSR 99
1976 Montreal, Canada	6,028	92	198	USSR 49	USSR 125
1980 Moscow, USSR	5,217	80	203	USSR 80	USSR 195
1984 Los Angeles, USA	6,797	140	221	USA 83	USA 174
1988 Seoul, South Korea	8,465	159	237	USSR 55	USSR 132
1992 Barcelona, Spain	9,367	169	257	EUN† 45	EUN 112
1996 Atlanta, USA	10,744	197	271	USA 44	USA 101
2000 Sydney, Australia	10,651	199	300	USA 39	USA 97
2004 Athens, Greece	11,099	202	301	USA 35	USA 103
2008 Beijing, China	11,028	204	302	China 51	USA 110

* The equestrian events in 1956 were held in Stockholm, Sweden, from 10–17 June, because of quarantine restrictions in Australia at the time.

† The Unified Team (EUN) was made up of the former Soviet republics of Russia, Ukraine, Kazakhstan and Uzbekistan.

Sport changes London 2012

Baseball and softball have both been dropped from the Olympic programme for London 2012. There are no new sports scheduled for 2012 but there are changes to the men and women's cycling events and the inclusion of a mixed doubles tennis competition. Rugby sevens and golf will both be added to the Olympics in Rio de Janeiro in 2016.

All-time medal table

Country	Medals: gold	silver	bronze	Total
1 USA	929	728	647	2,304
2 Soviet Union	395	319	296	1,010
3 Great Britain	207	255	252	714
4 France	191	212	233	636
5 Germany	163	163	203	529
6 Italy	190	158	174	522
7 Sweden	142	160	173	475
8 Hungary	159	141	159	459
9 Australia	131	137	164	432
10 East Germany	153	129	127	409
11 China	163	117	106	386

Based on all medals won at all Summer Olympics 1896–2008, not including those awarded at the Intercalated Games of 1906 which the IOC do not recognise as official medals.

The Olympic Oath

The Olympic Oath was written by Baron de Coubertin, the founder of the modern Olympics, and is taken by a competitor representing the host nation. It was first taken at the 1920 Antwerp Olympics and states: "In the name of all competitors, I promise that we shall take part in these Olympic Games, respecting and abiding by the rules that govern them, in the true spirit of sportsmanship, for the glory of sport and the honour of our teams."

Beijing records

At Beijing in 2008, 43 new world records were set and 132 new Olympic records established. A record 87 countries won a medal. Afghanistan, Bahrain, Mauritius, Sudan, Tajikistan and Togo all won their first ever Olympic medals.

Olympic firsts 1800s

1896 First modern Olympics. Doves released to symbolize peace

1896 First American gold medal winner, James Connolly (triple jump)

1896 First British gold medal winner, Launceston Elliot (weightlifting)

1900 First women competitors. First woman to win a gold medal, Charlotte Cooper from Great Britain for tennis

1908 First parade of athletes with national flags

1908 First athlete to win ten gold medals (in four Olympics, 1900, 1904, 1906 and 1908), Ray Ewry (USA)

1912 Electronic timing and photo-finish equipment first used

1920 Olympic oath, "We swear that we will take part in the Olympic Games in a spirit of chivalry, for the honour of our country and for the glory of sport", first taken, by Belgian fencer Victor Boin

1920 Olympic flag first raised

1924 First Olympics with more than 100 women competitors (there were 136 women and 2,956 men)

1924 First live radio transmissions of events

1928 First Olympic flame, large results display board first used

Sir Chris Hoy

At Beijing in 2008, Chris Hoy became the first Briton to win three golds at one Games since swimmer Henry Taylor in 1908. He is also the most decorated British Olympic cyclist of all time with four golds and one silver between 2000–08. He was created a Knight in 2009.

Top medal winners

These athletes have won the most medals in the history of the Summer Olympics from 1896–2008.

Athlete	Sport	Years	Gold	Silver	Bronze	Total
Larissa Latynina (USSR)	Gymnastics	1956–64	9	5	4	18
Michael Phelps (USA)	Swimming	2004-08	14	0	2	16
Nikolai Andrianov (USSR)	Gymnastics	1972–80	7	5	3	15
Boris Shakhlin (USSR)	Gymnastics	1956–64	7	4	2	13
Edoardo Mangiarotti (Italy)	Fencing	1936–60	6	5	2	13
Takashi Ono (Japan)	Gymnastics	1952–64	5	4	4	13
Paavo Nurmi (Finland)	Athletics	1920–28	9	3	0	12
Sawao Kato (Japan)	Gymnastics	1968–76	8	3	1	12
Alexei Nemov (Russia)	Gymnastics	1996–2000	4	2	6	12

Athlete Ray Ewry (USA) won only ten medals but they were all gold! He still holds the record for the most individual gold medals. Ewry won his medals between 1900 and 1908 in the standing jump events: high jump, long jump and triple jump. Amazingly, Ewry had suffered polio as a child, but overcame his illness to become one of the greatest athletes ever.

The spectacular opening ceremony at the 2008 Beijing Olympics

2000s

1928 First women competitors in track and field events

1932 First Olympic logo, three-tier victory stand, national anthem played and flag raised for winner

1936 Introduction of Olympic torch relay (from Olympia, Greece, to Berlin, Germany)

1936 Games televised for the first time

1956 Athletes enter closing ceremony together to symbolize unity

1956 First games in the southern hemisphere (Melbourne, Australia)

1960 First Summer Paralympics, held in Rome, Italy

1960 Worldwide TV coverage for the first time

1984 Professionals allowed to compete for the first time

2004 Women competed in freestyle wrestling for first time Ukraine, Japan and China all won gold medals

2004 First Olympics broadcast over the Internet

2008 BMX cycling events introduced

2012 Rugby sevens will be staged for the first time

www.olympic.org/en search

Cuban high jumper Javier Sotomayor

Leaps and bounds

It took 25 years for Ralph Boston to break Jesse Owens' world long jump record of 8.13 m (26.7 ft) in 1960. Once Boston broke it, the record steadily got pushed up to 8.35 m (27.4 ft) by 1967.

But a year later, at the Mexico Olympics, Bob Beamon shattered the record by an astonishing 55 cm (1.8 ft). Like Owens' record, it was felt it could never be bettered. It took 23 years to do so, but eventually it was broken, by Mike Powell in 1991.

Flo-Jo's remarkable run

When East Germany's Marlies Oelsner knocked 13/100ths of a second off the women's 100 metres world record in 1977, it was the biggest improvement in the record for 42 years and the first time the distance was run in under 11 seconds. By the time the US Olympic trials came around in July 1988, Evelyn Ashford had reduced the record to 10.76 seconds but then came one of the most amazing runs in track and field history when Florence Griffith-Joyner (USA) lowered the record by 27/100ths of a second. Over 22 years later, her record still stands. She also broke the 200 metres world record later in the year at the Seoul Olympics – a record that also still stands.

Marathon

The race takes its name from a place called Marathon in Greece, which was the scene of a battle between Athenian and Persian troops in 490 BC.

The Athenians won and supposedly sent a messenger named Pheidippides from Marathon to Athens to spread the news – a distance of about 25 miles (40.23 km). It is said that Pheidippides dropped dead after delivering his message! The current marathon distance of 26 miles 385 yards (42.195 km) was first used at the 1908 Olympics in Britain. It was worked out so that the race from Windsor would finish in front of the Royal Box at the White City Stadium. This distance has been the standard for all marathons since 1924.

Marathon fact file

Hundreds of marathon races are held all over the world every year. There is an Antarctica Marathon, a Sahara Marathon and even a night-time marathon, run in Marburg, Germany. The following are some of the biggest and most popular events.

Boston Marathon
This race has been held since 1897 and is run on Patriots' Day every April. It is the oldest marathon in the USA and one of the world's most important road races. Kenya's Robert Kipkoech Cheruiyot won the race in 2003, 2006, 2007 and 2008.

New York City Marathon
First held in 1970, the race goes through all five boroughs of New York and finishes in Central Park. It is usually held on the first Sunday in November. In 2009, a world record 43,659 competitors finished the race.

Chicago Marathon
The Chicago Marathon began in 1977. It was originally called the Mayor Daley Marathon after Chicago mayor Richard J. Daley, who died in office in 1976. Khalid Khannouchi of Morocco won the men's race a record four times between 1997 and 2002.

Track and field records

These are the current world records for major track and field events as at 1 January 2010. Most events have both male and female record holders. A few events are contested by only men or women.
For country name abbreviations, please refer to the list on page 318.

Event		Time (min:sec)	Record holder	Date
100 m	(m)	9.58	Usain Bolt (Jam)	2009
	(w)	10.49	Florence Griffith-Joyner (USA)	1988
200 m	(m)	19.19	Usain Bolt (Jam)	2009
	(w)	21.34	Florence Griffith-Joyner (USA)	1988
400 m	(m)	43.18	Michael Johnson (USA)	1999
	(w)	47.60	Marita Koch (GDR)	1985
800 m	(m)	1:41.11	Wilson Kipketer (Den)	1997
	(w)	1:53.28	Jarmila Kratochvílová (Cze)	1983
1500 m	(m)	3:26.00	Hicham El Guerrouj (Mar)	1998
	(w)	3:50.46	Qu Yunxia (Chn)	1993
1 mile	(m)	3:43.13	Hicham El Guerrouj (Mar)	1999
	(w)	4:12.56	Svetlana Masterkova (Rus)	1996
5,000 m	(m)	12:37.35	Kenenisa Bekele (Eth)	2004
	(w)	14:11.15	Tirunesh Dibaba (Eth)	2008
10,000 m	(m)	26:17.53	Kenenisa Bekele (Eth)	2005
	(w)	29:31.78	Wang Junxia (Chn)	1993
3,000 m steeplechase	(m)	7:53.63	Saaeed Shaheen (Qat)	2004
	(w)	8:58:81	Gulnara Galkina-Samitova (Rus)	2008
110 m hurdles	(m)	12.87	Dayron Robles (Cub)	2008
100 m hurdles	(w)	12.21	Yordanka Donkova (Bul)	1988
400 m hurdles	(m)	46.78	Kevin Young (USA)	1992
	(w)	52.34	Yuliya Pechonkina (Rus)	2003
4 x 100 m relay	(m)	37.10	Jamaica	2008
	(w)	41.37	GDR	1985
4 x 400 m relay	(m)	2:54.20	USA	1998
	(w)	3:15.17	USSR	1988
		Ht/lgth (m)		
High jump	(m)	2.45	Javier Sotomayor (Cub)	1993
	(w)	2.09	Stefka Kostadinova (Bul)	1987
Pole vault	(m)	6.14	Sergey Bubka (Ukr)	1994
	(w)	6.06	Yelena Isinbayeva (Rus)	2009
Long jump	(m)	8.95	Mike Powell (USA)	1991
	(w)	7.52	Galina Chistyakova (USSR)	1988
Triple jump	(m)	18.29	Jonathan Edwards (GBR)	1995
	(w)	15.50	Inessa Kravets (Ukr)	1995
Shot	(m)	23.12	Randy Barnes (USA)	1990
	(w)	22.63	Natalya Lisovskaya (USSR)	1987
Discus	(m)	74.08	Jürgen Schult (GDR)	1986
	(w)	76.80	Gabriele Reinsch (GDR)	1988
Hammer	(m)	86.74	Yuriy Sedykh (USSR)	1986
	(w)	77.96	Anita Wlodarczyk (Pol)	2009
Javelin	(m)	98.48	Jan Zelezny (Cze)	1996
	(w)	72.28	Barbara Spotakova (Cze)	2008

Usain Bolt, the world's fastest runner

World's fastest

The world's fastest man is Usain Bolt of Jamaica who ran the 100 metres in 9.58 seconds during the World Championships at Berlin on 16 August 2009.

The world's fastest woman was Florence Griffith-Joyner (USA), who died in 1998. She ran the 100 m in 10.49 seconds in Indianapolis in 1988. The fastest living woman is Carmelita Jeter (USA). She ran the 100 metres in 10.64 seconds in Shanghai in 2009.

London Marathon
Dionico Cerón (Mexico), António Pinto (Portugal) and Martin Lel (Kenya) have each won the men's race a record three times. Ingrid Kristiansen (Norway) won the women's race four times between 1984 and 1988.

Marathon record holders
The current male record holder, Haile Gebreselassie (Ethiopia), ran the Berlin Marathon in 2 hours 3 minutes 59 seconds on 28 September 2008. The female record is held by Paula Radcliffe (GB), who ran the London Marathon on 13 April 2003 in 2 hours 15 minutes 25 seconds.

See also
Ancient Greece: page 106

www.gbrathletics.com search

Yankees All-Star Alex Rodriguez

Baseball World Series

Major League baseball started in the USA when the National League was formed in 1876. The rival American League was started in 1901, and in 1903 the World Series, a best-of-nine game event, was held between the winners of each league's championship. In the first series the Boston Red Sox beat the Pittsburgh Pirates 5–3. The World Series has been a best-of-seven games series since 1905, except in 1919–21 when it went back to a nine-game series.

Most wins American League: New York Yankees – 27 between 1923 and 2009; National League: St Louis Cardinals – 10 between 1926 and 2006

Most consecutive wins New York Yankees – 5 (1949–53)

Baseball

Baseball is one of the most popular sports in the USA and is also played in Japan, Mexico, Cuba and a number of South American countries. It is played by two teams of nine players each.

Medieval manuscripts show ball games with bats, and a game called "base-ball" appears in a picture published in London in 1744. The game of rounders was first described in 1828, and this or a similar game was known among British settlers in America. The first rules were drawn up in 1845 by Alexander Joy Cartwright Jr and the first match under these rules played on 19 June 1846.

Golf majors

The four big competitions in golf are known as the majors. They are the US Masters, British Open, US Open and US PGA Championship, and are played in that order every year.

The Masters, founded in 1934, is the only one of the four played on the same course each year, at Augusta National in Georgia, USA. The oldest of the majors is the British Open, which was first held in 1860. It is also the only one played outside the USA. The US Open was first played in 1895 and the US PGA in 1916.

Players with most professional major wins

Jack Nicklaus (USA) 18: 3 British Open; 4 US Open; 5 US PGA; 6 Masters

Tiger Woods (USA) 14: 3 British Open; 3 US Open; 4 US PGA; 4 Masters

Walter Hagen (USA) 11: 4 British Open; 2 US Open; 5 US PGA

Ben Hogan (USA) 9: 1 British Open; 4 US Open; 2 US PGA; 2 Masters

Gary Player (S Africa) 9: 3 British Open; 1 US Open; 2 US PGA; 3 Masters

Tom Watson (USA) 8: 5 British Open; 1 US Open; 2 US Masters

Bobby Jones

Bobby Jones is the greatest amateur golfer of all time. He won a total of 13 majors, seven of them professional majors. In 1930 he completed golf's most remarkable Grand Slam when he won the professional and amateur titles of both the USA and Great Britain, making him the only man ever to win four majors in one year.

Basketball

Basketball is hugely popular in the USA and is now played in other parts of the world, as well as at the Olympics. The game is played by two teams of five players each, usually on an indoor court.

Players score points by shooting the ball through the basket. The National Basketball Association (NBA) in the USA was formed in 1949. It contains 30 teams divided into two conferences, Eastern and Western. At the end of the season the two conference winners meet in a best-of-seven series for the NBA Championship.

Rugby World Cup finals

1987 New Zealand beat France 29–9
1991 Australia beat England 12–6
1995 South Africa beat New Zealand 15–12
1999 Australia beat France 35–12
2003 England beat Australia 20–17
2007 South Africa beat England 15–6

Rugby

The game of rugby probably started in 1823 at Rugby School in England, when William Webb Ellis picked up a football and ran with it. The first rules were drawn up in 1848 and the Rugby Football Union (RFU) was formed by Edwin Ash in 1871.

Today's game of Rugby Union is played between two teams of 15 players. The two biggest events are the International Championship and the World Cup. The International Championship began in 1884 and was originally played by four teams: England, Ireland, Scotland and Wales. France joined in 1910 and Italy in 2000, making it a six-nation tournament. The Rugby World Cup was launched in 1987 and has been held every four years since then. In 2007, 20 teams took part and over 2.25 million people watched the 48 live matches at an average of 47,150 per game.

Rugby League

Rugby League dates from 29 August 1895, when 21 major clubs in the north of England formed a league outside the RFU. They were protesting against the RFU's refusal to pay players who had to take time off work. To make Rugby League less like Rugby Union they changed various rules, including reducing the team size from 15 to 13. Rugby League is now played professionally in Great Britain, Australia, New Zealand, France and Papua New Guinea. One of the major events in Rugby League is the Challenge Cup, open to British, French and Russian teams. There is also a Rugby League World Cup, which was last won by New Zealand in 2008.

Gaelic sports

The Gaelic Athletic Association was established in 1884 with the aim of promoting Gaelic sports such as camogie, handball, rounders and the two best known, hurling and Gaelic football. These latter two are very popular sports and over 80,000 attend the All-Ireland finals of the respective sports at Dublin's Croke Park every September.

The winners of the All-Ireland Gaelic football championship receive the coveted Sam Maguire Cup. Kerry won it a record 36 times between 1903–2009. The winners of the All-Ireland hurling final receive the Liam McCarthy Cup, which Kilkenny won a record 32 times in 1904–2009.

www.cricinfo.com search

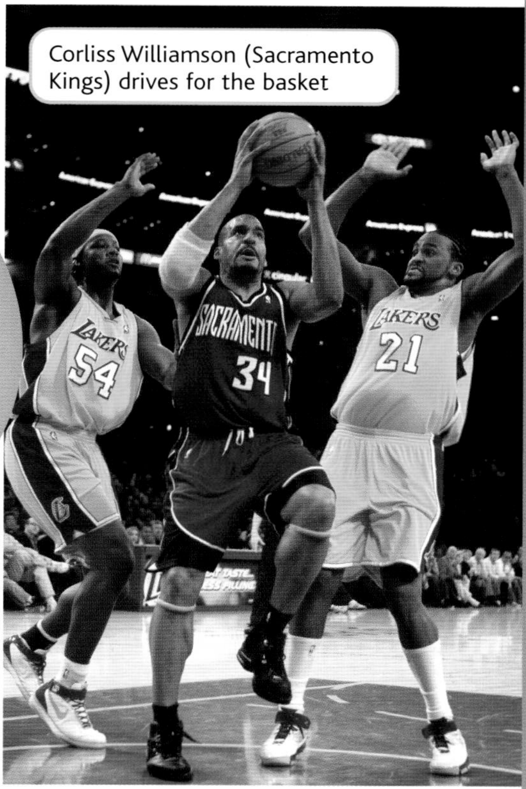

Corliss Williamson (Sacramento Kings) drives for the basket

Test cricket

Cricket is a bat and ball game played between two teams of 11 players. The aim is to score more runs than the opposing team. Among the major competitions are the Test matches, which are normally played over five days.

They are called Test matches because they were started as a test of the relative skills of the two sides. Test matches are played between teams representing their countries. There are currently ten countries that play Test cricket, Bangladesh in 2000 being the most recent.

Twenty20 cricket

Twenty20 is a new form of cricket that was launched in 2003 as an inter-county tournament in England. Both teams bat for a single innings of 20 overs, which encourages big hitting and quick scoring. It has proved to be very popular with fans – games are often much shorter than in conventional versions of the sport. Since its launch, Twenty20 has become popular worldwide and international tours normally take in a mini-Twenty20 series alongside Test Matches. In 2010 England beat Australia in the Twenty20 World Cup, played in the Caribbean.

The World Cup

The first soccer World Cup was played in 1930 in Uruguay. Thirteen teams took part and the hosts beat Argentina 4–2 in the final in Montevideo.

They won the Jules Rimet trophy, named after the president of FIFA (Fédération Internationale de Football Association) when the competition began. Brazil were allowed to keep the trophy after winning it for the third time in 1970 and it was replaced by the FIFA World Cup trophy. The World Cup final takes place every four years.

The 2010 World Cup was the first to be played on the African continent when South Africa won the right to stage the tournament. It ran from 11 June with the final played at Soccer City, Johannesburg on 11 July.

Winning country	Year	Winning country	Year
Uruguay	1930	Brazil	1970
Italy	1934	West Germany	1974
Italy	1938	Argentina	1978
Not held	1942	Italy	1982
Not held	1946	Argentina	1986
Uruguay	1950	West Germany	1990
West Germany	1954	Brazil	1994
Brazil	1958	France	1998
Brazil	1962	Brazil	2002
England	1966	Italy	2006

The Italian team that won the 2006 World Cup

World Cup facts

- Lothar Matthäus (Germany) played a record 25 games in the World Cup 1982–98.
- Ronaldo (Brazil) is the World Cup's leading scorer with 15 goals in 1998–2006. When Daniel Xuereb of France came on as a substitute in 1986, it meant that players' surnames beginning with every letter of the alphabet had appeared since the tournament began in 1930.

Worst World Cup record

El Salvador have the worst World Cup record, having won none of their six matches and scoring just one goal (in a 10–1 World Cup record defeat by Hungary in 1982), conceding a total of 22 goals.

International caps

On 10 May 1886 the English Football Association decided: "That all players taking part for England in future international matches be presented with a white silk cap with red rose embroidered on the front. These to be termed International Caps."

This tradition has spread throughout world football. The number of caps show how many times players have represented their countries. The following footballers are the most-capped players in their countries, as at 1 January 2010.

World's most-capped footballers

Player	Country	Years	Caps
Mohamed Al-Deayea	Saudi Arabia	1990–2006	181
Claudio Suárez	Mexico	1992–2006	178
Hossam Hassan	Egypt	1985–2006	169
Iván Hurtado	Ecuador	1992–2009	165

Most-capped footballers (selected countries)

Country	Player	Years	Caps
England	Peter Shilton	1970–90	125
Scotland	Kenny Dalglish	1972–87	102
Wales	Neville Southall	1982–98	92
Northern Ireland	Pat Jennings	1964–86	119
France	Lilian Thuram	1998–2008	142
Spain	Andoni Zubizarreta	1985–98	126
Germany	Lothas Matthäus	1980–2000	150
Netherlands	Edwin Van Der Sar	1995–2008	130
USA	Cobi Jones	1992–2004	164
Brazil	Cafu	1990–2006	142

Soccer timeline

500 BC Football (tsu chu, meaning to kick a ball) played in China
1314 First reference to football in England when Edward II prohibited the game because "too many people were bustling over footballs on London streets"

1800s

1848 The first rules of football drawn up at Cambridge University
1852 First inter-school football match, Westminster v Harrow
1855 Sheffield football club, the oldest still in existence, formed
1862 Notts County, the oldest current League club, formed
1863 Football Association (FA) formed
1870 First international match, England v Scotland, played at Kennington Oval
1871 FA Cup launched
1872 Corner kick introduced
1873 Scottish FA formed; Scottish Cup started
1874 Shin pads first worn
1875 The crossbar replaced a tape across the top of the goals
1876 Welsh FA formed
1878 Irish (now Northern Ireland) FA formed
1878 Referee's whistle first used
1885 Professional football legalized
1888 Football League formed
1889 The term "soccer" first used; May be an abbreviation of association football – the FA was formed to standardize the rules of the game
1890 Scottish League formed
1891 Goal nets first used
1891 Linesmen (now assistant referees) replace umpires
1891 Penalty kick adopted by the FA
1904 FIFA formed in Paris; first international match outside Britain – Belgium v France played near Brussels
1907 Professional Footballers' Association (PFA) formed (as the Football Players and Trainers Union)

The NFL abroad

The first NFL regular season game played outside the United States was at The Estadio Azteca, Mexico City, on 2 October 2005, when the Arizona Cardinals beat the San Francisco 49ers 31–14. The first regular season game played in England was at Wembley Stadium on 27 October 2007, when Miami Dolphins played the New York Giants.

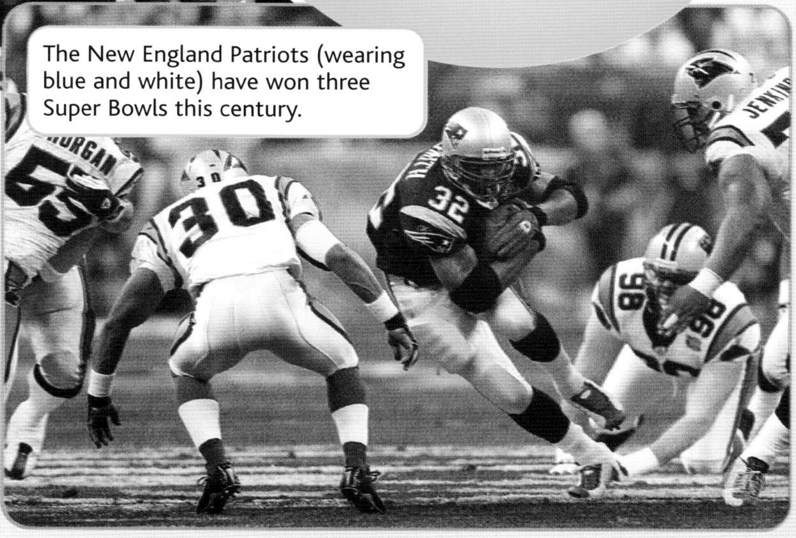

The New England Patriots (wearing blue and white) have won three Super Bowls this century.

American football

American football, or Gridiron, is the number one sport in the USA. The National Football League (NFL) is split into two conferences, the American Football Conference (AFC) and National Football Conference (NFC). Each conference is split into four divisions – North, South, East and West – and each division has four teams.

Each team plays 16 matches and the six teams with the best records in both the AFC and NFC take part in the play-offs, with the winner of each conference then meeting for the Super Bowl early in February. The Super Bowl winning team receives the Vince Lombardi Trophy.

No.	Year	Winners	No.	Year	Winners	No.	Year	Winners	No.	Year	Winners
I	1967	Green Bay Packers	XII	1978	Dallas Cowboys	XXIII	1989	San Francisco 49ers	XXXIV	2000	St Louis Rams
II	1968	Green Bay Packers	XIII	1979	Pittsburgh Steelers	XXIV	1990	San Francisco 49ers	XXXV	2001	Baltimore Ravens
III	1969	New York Jets	XIV	1980	Pittsburgh Steelers	XXV	1991	New York Giants	XXXVI	2002	New England Patriots
IV	1970	Kansas City Chiefs	XV	1981	Oakland Raiders	XXVI	1992	Washington Redskins	XXXVII	2003	Tampa Bay Buccaneers
V	1971	Baltimore Colts	XVI	1982	San Francisco 49ers	XXVII	1993	Dallas Cowboys	XXXVIII	2004	New England Patriots
VI	1972	Dallas Cowboys	XVII	1983	Washington Redskins	XXVIII	1994	Dallas Cowboys	XXXIX	2005	New England Patriots
VII	1973	Miami Dolphins	XVIII	1984	Los Angeles Raiders	XXIX	1995	San Francisco 49ers	XL	2006	Pittsburgh Steelers
VIII	1974	Miami Dolphins	XIX	1985	San Francisco 49ers	XXX	1996	Dallas Cowboys	XLI	2007	Indianapolis Colts
IX	1975	Pittsburgh Steelers	XX	1986	Chicago Bears	XXXI	1997	Green Bay Packers	XLII	2008	New York Giants
X	1976	Pittsburgh Steelers	XXI	1987	New York Giants	XXXII	1998	Denver Broncos	XLIII	2009	Pittsburgh Stealers
XI	1977	Oakland Raiders	XXII	1988	Washington Redskins	XXXIII	1999	Denver Broncos	XLIV	2010	New Orleans Saints

1900s

1921 FA of Ireland (Republic of Ireland) formed

1923 First Wembley Cup Final (Bolton v West Ham)

1928 Players' numbers introduced

1930 First World Cup in Uruguay

1932 Substitutes formally agreed by FIFA

1950 England's first World Cup (lost 1–0 to USA)

1954 Union of European Football Associations (UEFA) formed

1955 European Cup started

1960 Football League Cup started

1965 Football League agrees use of substitutes

1968 Red cards introduced (at the Mexico Olympic Games)

1975 Scottish Premier Division (now Premier League) formed

1981 Football League changed the number of points for a win from two to three

1982 Professional foul rule introduced

1992 FA Premier League formed

1993 Champions' League replaces the European Cup

2000s

2004 Greece are surprise winners of the European Championship

2007 David Beckham moves to Los Angeles Galaxy for $150 million over 5 years

2008 Spain beat Germany to win the European Championship, its first major trophy for 44 years.

2009 UEFA Europa League replaced the UEFA Cup

http://www.fifa.com search

Table tennis

Table tennis uses the lightest ball in any sport, weighing just 2.7 grams. The exact origins of the sport are uncertain, but it became very popular in England in the late 19th century when it was known as Ping-Pong, a trade name by which it is often still called today.

The first Table Tennis Association was formed in 1902 and the International Table Tennis Federation (ITTF) in 1926. The World Championship is the sport's principal tournament, and was first held in 1926. The Swaythling Cup and Corbillon Cup, presented to the respective men's and women's team champions, are the sport's most coveted trophies. China has won the men's title a record 17 times and the women's title a record 18 times. Table tennis has been an Olympic sport since 1988.

Fred Perry

The name Fred Perry became one of the first global sports clothing brands when it was given to a type of short-sleeved sport shirt, also known as a polo shirt. Fred Perry (1909–95) was a talented sportsman who was not only the last Briton to win the men's singles at Wimbledon, which he won three times, but in 1929 he also won the men's singles title at the World Table Tennis Championships.

Zhang Yining, gold medallist at the 2009 World Table Tennis Championships

Squash

Squash evolved out of the game of rackets, which in turn developed from various forms of hand and ball games played in the Middle Ages. Squash is played with a softer ball than those used in rackets, and was first played at Harrow School in 1817, but the game did not gain worldwide popularity until the 1920s.

The world governing body, the International Squash Rackets Federation, was formed in 1934 and became the World Squash Federation in 1992 after dropping the word 'rackets' from its name. It is either played by two or four players (doubles.) Currently the leading tournaments are the World Open, launched in 1976, and the British Open, first held in 1922 for women and 1930 for men. Jansher Khan of Pakistan has won the men's World Open title a record nine times and Sarah FitzGerald of Australia has won the women's title a record five times. Jahangir Khan (Pakistan) won the men's title at the British Open a record 10 times whilst the women's record is 16 (all consecutive) by Heather McKay (née Blundell) of Australia.

Lawn tennis timeline 1800s 2000s

1877 First Wimbledon Championship

1881 First US Championship

1891 First French Championship – until 1925 for French nationals

1896 Tennis played at the first Modern Olympics in Athens

1900 Davis Cup began after Dwight F. Davis donated a trophy

1905 First Australian Open

1913 International Lawn Tennis Federation founded in Paris with 12 member countries

1922 Seeding (method of ranking players) first used, at the US National Championships

1923 Women's tennis became international with the launch of the Wightman Cup (named after US team captain Hazel Wightman)

1938 Donald Budge (USA) became the first player to complete the Grand Slam

1950 Louise Brough (USA) became the first woman to complete the Grand Slam

1963 The Federation Cup, the women's equivalent of the Davis Cup, began

1968 Tennis tournaments were opened to professional players, effectively ending the amateur game

1971 The tie-break was introduced by the British LTA as an experiment

1973 Introduction of official world rankings by the ATP and LTA

1988 Tennis revived as an Olympic sport after 64 years

2004 World ranking points first allocated to competitors in the Olympic Games

2008 On 17 August Roger Federer's record run of 237 consecutive weeks at No.1 in the ATP rankings came to an end when he was deposed by Rafael Nadal

2009 Roof used on Wimbledon centre court for the first time

2009 Roger Federer won a record 15th Grand Slam Singles title

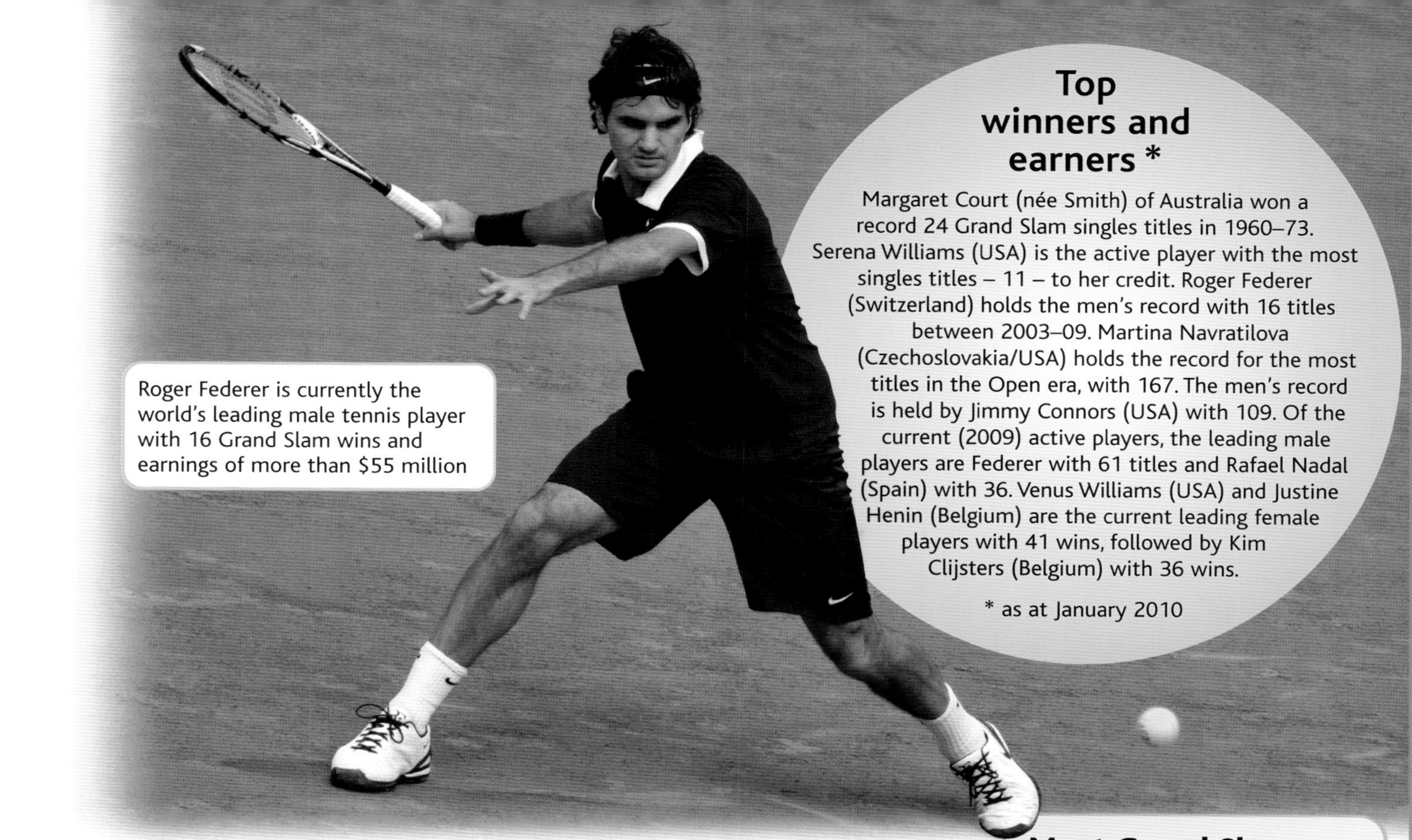

Roger Federer is currently the world's leading male tennis player with 16 Grand Slam wins and earnings of more than $55 million

Top winners and earners *

Margaret Court (née Smith) of Australia won a record 24 Grand Slam singles titles in 1960–73. Serena Williams (USA) is the active player with the most singles titles – 11 – to her credit. Roger Federer (Switzerland) holds the men's record with 16 titles between 2003–09. Martina Navratilova (Czechoslovakia/USA) holds the record for the most titles in the Open era, with 167. The men's record is held by Jimmy Connors (USA) with 109. Of the current (2009) active players, the leading male players are Federer with 61 titles and Rafael Nadal (Spain) with 36. Venus Williams (USA) and Justine Henin (Belgium) are the current leading female players with 41 wins, followed by Kim Clijsters (Belgium) with 36 wins.

* as at January 2010

Lawn tennis Grand Slam events

The Grand Slam consists of the Australian, French, Wimbledon and US Championships. A player is said to have completed the Grand Slam if he or she holds all four titles simultaneously, although not necessarily in the same year. These events were originally for amateur players but are now open to all, including professionals.

Wimbledon Championships

First held in 1877, Wimbledon is the world's most famous tennis championship. From 1877 to 1921 it was a challenge event with the defending champion qualifying for the next year's final. Women first took part in 1884. Since 1968 Wimbledon has been an open event. This means it is open to all players, including professionals.

US Open

This was first held in 1881. Until 1911, the US tournament operated as a challenge system, with the defending champion automatically going through to the following year's final. Women first competed in 1887. Two championships were held in 1968 and 1969, one for amateurs and an open championship. It became completely open in 1970.

French Open

The French Open was first held in 1891 and until 1925 it was only for French nationals. It became the French Open in 1968 and has been played at the Stade Roland Garros (named after a famous French aviator) since 1928. Women have competed since 1897.

Australian Open

This competition was first held in 1905 as the Australasian Tennis Championship. Women first competed in 1922. The competition became the Australian Championship in 1927, and since 1969 has been the Australian Open. It is played at Melbourne every January.

Junior Grand Slams

The first Junior Grand Slam event was the Boys' Singles at the 1922 Australian Open. John Newcombe (Australia) won a record 5 junior singles titles while Robyn Ebbern (Australia) and Natasha Zvereva (Soviet Union) each won a record four girls' singles titles.

Most Grand Slam Singles Titles

Men

16 Roger Federer (Switzerland)
6 x Wimbledon, 5 x USA,
3 x Australian, 1 x French

14 Pete Sampras (USA)
7 x Wimbledon, 5 x USA,
2 x Australian

Women

24 Margaret Court (neé Smith)
(Australia) 11 x Australian,
5 x USA, 5 x French,
3 x Wimbledon

22 Steffi Graf (Germany)
7 x Wimbledon, 6 x French,
5 x USA, 4 x Australian

Most Overall Grand Slam Titles

Men

28 Roy Emerson (Australia)
12 x singles, 6 x doubles

26 John Newcombe (Australia)
7 x singles, 17 x doubles,
2 x mixed doubles

Women

62 Margaret Court (neé Smith)
(Australia) 24 x singles,
19 x doubles, 19 x mixed doubles

59 Martina Navratilova
(Czechoslovakia/USA) 18 x singles,
31 x doubles, 10 x mixed doubles

Oscar de la Hoya

When Oscar de la Hoya announced his retirement in 2009, boxing lost one of its greatest fighters. A former Olympic champion, the Mexican-American won the first of his 10 world titles, the WBO Super-featherweight title, in 1994. Ten years later he won the WBO Middleweight title to become the first man ever to win world titles in six different weights. De la Hoya won 39 of his 45 professional bouts, 30 by a knockout. His last fight was an eight-round defeat by Manny Pacquiao of the Philippines.

The heaviest world champion

Nikolay Valuev of Russia is the heaviest man to hold the world heavyweight title at 148.8 kg (328 lb) when he beat Monte Barrett (USA). He is also the tallest at 2.18 m (7 ft 2 in).

Born in St Petersburg in 1973, Valuev is not surprisingly nicknamed 'The Russian Giant'. He had his first professional bout in 1993, beating John Morton in two rounds. He won the Russian heavyweight title in 1999 and in 2005 beat John Ruiz to capture the WBA heavyweight crown. He lost his title on points in 2007 before regaining it the following year, again beating Ruiz. Britain's David Haye deprived him of his title in November 2009.

Boxing's multiple world champions

The first man to win world titles at two different weights was George Dixon (Canada) who won the bantamweight title in 1890 and the featherweight title in 1891. The first to wins titles at three different weights was Bob Fitzsimmons (UK) who won the middleweight title in 1891, heavyweight title in 1897 and light-heavyweight title in 1903. Thomas Hearns (USA) became the first man to capture four different world titles when he won the WBA middleweight title in 1987. His great rival of the era, Sugar Ray Leonard, became the first man to win five different titles a year later when he added the WBC light-heavyweight title to his other titles.

These fighters all won five or more titles*
6 Oscar de la Hoya (USA)
5 Sugar Ray Leonard (USA)
5 Thomas Hearns (USA)
5 Floyd Mayweather, Jnr. (USA)
5 Manny Pacquiao (Philippines)

* As recognized by the four main bodies, WBC, WBA, IBF and WBO

www.wwe.com search

Snooker's world champions

The first snooker world professional championship was held in 1927 and won by Joe Davis, who won the first 15 titles up to 1946. The sport fell into decline in the 1950s and 1960s and there was no championship between 1953–63 and only a challenge series between 1964–68. The advent of colour television saw a surge in snooker's popularity and the world championships were revived on a knockout basis in 1969. Since 1977 and its move to its present home at Sheffield's Crucible Theatre, it has become one of Britain's most popular sporting competitions.

World Champions:

Wins	Player	Country	Year(s)
15	Joe Davis	England	1927–40, 1946
7	John Pulman	England	1964–68*
7	Stephen Hendry	Scotland	1990, 1992–96, 1999
6	Ray Reardon	Wales	1970, 1973–76, 1978
6	Steve Davis	England	1981, 1983–84, 1987–89
3	Fred Davis	England	1948–49, 1951
3	John Spencer	England	1969, 1971, 1977
3	Ronnie O'Sullivan	England	2001, 2004, 2008
3	John Higgins	Scotland	1998, 2007, 2009
2	Walter Donaldson	Scotland	1947, 1950
2	Alex Higgins	Northern Ireland	1972, 1982
2	Mark Williams	Wales	2000, 2003
1	Horace Lindrum	Australia	1952
1	Terry Griffiths	Wales	1979
1	Cliff Thorburn	Canada	1980
1	Dennis Taylor	Northern Ireland	1985
1	Joe Johnson	England	1986
1	John Parrott	England	1991
1	Ken Doherty	Ireland	1997
1	Peter Ebdon	England	2002
1	Shaun Murphy	England	2005
1	Graeme Dott	Scotland	2006

* Challenge matches only

Wrestling

The World Wrestling Federation was started in the 1960s as the WorldWide Wrestling Federation (WWWF) by Vince McMahon. In the early 1980s Vince's son, Vince McMahon Jr, renamed it WWF.

The sport changed and became widely popular. Characters such as Hulk Hogan became household names, attracting huge crowds to live matches and millions of followers via TV. The WWF is now known as WWE®, World Wrestling Entertainment, Inc. The two biggest events in the WWE calendar are Wrestle Mania, which decides the world champions, and the Royal Rumble. The first WWF Wrestle Mania was at Madison Square Garden on 31 March 1985.

Top wrestlers

- Texan Shawn Michaels is one of the most popular of all wrestlers. He weighs in at about 102 kg (225 lb). Michaels has won the WWE title, WWE World Heavyweight title, the WWE World Tag Team title and twice won the Royal Rumble, among many other top honours and titles.
- American-born Mickie James is one the leading WWE female wrestlers. She made her professional debut in 1999 under the name Alexis Laree (Laree is her middle name). At WrestleMania 22 in 2006 she beat Trish Stratus to win her first WWE women's championship. She has won the title four times and in 2009 she added the WWE Divas championship to her list of honours.
- Triple H, or "The Game", made his WWE debut in 1995 as Hunter Hearst Helmsley. He weighs around 116 kg (256 lb). He has been WWE Champion, WWE World Heavyweight Champion, WWE World Tag Team Champion, King of the Ring and Royal Rumble. He is the only man to win the Grand Slam, King of the Ring and Royal Rumble.

'The Undertaker'

Mark William Calaway, known as 'The Undertaker', started his wrestling career in 1984 under the name 'Texas Red', and is one of WWE's senior fighters. He has won seven world titles including the world heavyweight title three times. He won the 2007 Royal Rumble at the age of 42. He has also fought under other names including 'Mean' Mark Callous.

Weightlifting records

In an Olympic weightlifting competition contestants perform two types of lifts, the snatch, and the clean and jerk. They have three attempts at each. The score is the total of the best of each type of lift.

In the snatch the contestant lifts the bar from the floor directly above the head and holds it for two seconds. In the clean and jerk the contestant first takes the bar from the floor to the shoulders and then above the head.

The current men's world record is 472.5 kg (1,041.7 lb) by Hossein Rezazadeh (Iran) who set the mark at the 2000 Sydney Olympics.

The women's world record stands at 326 kg (723.1 lb), set by Jang Mi Ran of South Korea in Beijing on 16 August 2008.

Vasiliy Alekseyev

Russian weightlifter Vasiliy Alekseyev is the greatest lifter the sport has ever seen and his 80 world records make him one of the most prolific record-breakers in any sport. Between 1970 and 1978 he won two Olympic gold medals and eight world championship golds.

Olympic water sports

Sailing

The first Modern Olympics in 1896 should have included sailing, but the races could not be held because of bad weather. Sailing was included for the first time four years later in Paris and has been a full Olympic sport since 1908. Boardsailing made its debut in 1988. Men and women have competed together in sailing events over the years, but in 1988 women had events of their own. Until the 2000 Olympics, sailing was known as yachting.

Top gold-medal winning nations (1900–2008)

Great Britain 28
USA 20
Norway 17

Rowing

Rowing was to have been part of the 1896 Olympics, but the events were cancelled. It was first included in Paris four years later, and has appeared at every Olympics since. Women first competed in 1976.

Top gold-medal winning nations (1900–2008)

East Germany 33
USA 31
Great Britain 24
Germany/United Germany 23

Canoeing

Canoeing was first included as a demonstration sport in 1924, and did not become a full Olympic sport until 1936. Women took part for the first time in 1948.

Top gold-medal winning nations (1936–2008)

USSR/Unified Team 31
Germany/United Germany 29
Hungary 19
Sweden 15
East Germany 14

Michael Phelps swimming in the 2004 Olympic Games

Michael Phelps

Before he went to Beijing for the 2008 Olympics, American swimmer Michael Phelps was already one of the great Olympians with six gold medals and two bronzes to his credit from the 2004 Athens Games. Phelps also had seven golds from the previous year's world championships and had his sights firmly set on equalling the great achievement of Mark Spitz in winning seven golds at one Olympics – but went one better with eight gold medals.

Michael Phelps' gold medals at the 2008 Olympics

Event	Time (min:sec)
400 m individual medley	4:03.34 (WR)
4 x 100 m freestyle relay	3:08.24 (WR)
200 m freestyle	1:42.96 (WR)
200 m butterfly	1:52.03 (WR)
4 x 200 m freestyle relay	6:58.56 (WR)
200 m individual medley	1:54.23 (WR)
100 m butterfly	50.58 (OR)
4 x 100 m medley relay	3:29.34 (WR)

(WR) = World Record, (OR) = Olympic Record

Start of the men's coxless fours rowing final at the 2004 Olympic Games. Great Britain is the 3rd boat from the top.

Royal gold

As a 20-year-old, Crown Prince Constantine of Greece, a very good all-round sportsman, represented his country at the 1960 Rome Olympics and won a gold medal in the Yachting Dragon Class competition. Traditionally, members of the winning team received a 'dunking', and the Crown Prince was pushed into the water by his mother. He became King Constantine II in 1964.

Olympic swimming

These are the top medal-winning Olympic swimmers. Totals include medals won in relays.

Swimmer	Gold	Silver	Bronze	Total
Men				
Michael Phelps (USA)	14	0	2	16
Mark Spitz (USA)	9	1	1	11
Matt Biondi (USA)	8	2	1	11
Gary Hall Jr (USA)	5	3	2	10
Women				
Jenny Thompson (USA)	8	3	1	12
Dara Torres (USA)	4	4	4	12
Natalie Coughlin USA)	3	4	4	11
Dawn Fraser (Australia)	4	4	0	8
Kornelia Ender (GDR)	4	4	0	8
Shirley Babashoff (USA)	2	6	0	8
Inge de Bruijn (Netherlands)	4	2	2	8
Petria Thomas (Australia)	3	4	1	8

www.fina.org search

Synchronized swimming

Synchronized swimming is a cross between gymnastics and dancing in water. Although men do take part in the sport, it is open only to female competitors at both the Olympic Games and World Championships. It has been an Olympic sport since 1984 and competitors compete either as a duet or in a team. There is also a solo event at the world championships.

World swimming records*

Men

Event	mins:secs	Swimmer/country	Year
50 m freestyle	0:20.91#	César Cielo, Brazil	2009
100 m freestyle	0:46.91	César Cielo, Brazil	2009
200 m freestyle	1:42.00	Paul Biedermann, Germany	2009
400 m freestyle	3:40.07	Paul Biedermann, Germany	2009
800 m freestyle	7:32.12	Zhang Lin, China	2009
1,500 m freestyle	14:34.56	Grant Hackett, Australia	2001
50 m backstroke	0:24.04	Liam Tancock, Great Britain	2009
100 m backstroke	0:51.94#	Aaron Peirsol, USA	2009
200 m backstroke	1:51.92	Aaron Peirsol, USA	2009
50 m breaststroke	0:26.67	Cameron van Der Burgh, S.Afr.	2009
100 m breaststroke	0:58.58	Brenton Rickard, Australia	2009
200 m breaststroke	2:07.31	Christian Sprenger, Australia	2009
50 m butterfly	0:22.43	Rafael Muñoz, Spain	2009
100 m butterfly	0:49.82	Michael Phelps, USA	2009
200 m butterfly	1:51.51#	Michael Phelps, USA	2009
200 m ind. medley	1:54.10	Ryan Lochte, USA	2009
400 m ind. medley	4:03.84	Michael Phelps, USA	2008

Women

Event	mins:secs	Swimmer/country	Year
50 m freestyle	0:23.73	Britta Steffen, Germany	2009
100 m freestyle	0:52.07	Britta Steffen, Germany	2009
200 m freestyle	1:52,98	Federica Pellegrini, Italy	2009
400 m freestyle	3:59.15	Federica Pellegrini, Italy	2009
800 m freestyle	8:14.10	Rebecca Adlington, GBR	2008
1,500 m freestyle	15:42.54	Kate Ziegler, USA	2007
50 m backstroke	0:27.06	Zhao Jing, China	2009
100 m backstroke	0:58.12	Gemma Spofforth, GBR	2009
200 m backstroke	2:04.81	Kirsty Coventry, Zimbabwe	2009
50 m breaststroke	0:29.80#	Jessica Hardy, USA	2009
100 m breaststroke	1:04.45#	Jessica Hardy, USA	2009
200 m breaststroke	2:20.12	Annamay Pierse, Canada	2009
50 m butterfly	0:25.07	Therese Alshammar, Sweden	2009
10 0m butterfly	0:56,06	Sarah Sjöström, Sweden	2009
200 m butterfly	2:01.81#	Liu Zige, China	2009
200 m ind. medley	2:06.15	Ariana Kukors, USA	2009
400 m ind. medley	4:29.45	Stephanie Rice, Australia	2008

* Long course records in individual events only

Awaiting FINA ratification as at 24 January 2010

The America's Cup

The America's Cup is the top sailing trophy and one of the best known trophies in the sporting world. It began in 1851 when the English Royal Yacht Squadron organized a 10-km (6-mile) regatta of 17 boats around the Isle of Wight. The 31-m American schooner *America* entered and won the trophy, then called the One Hundred Guinea Cup.

After *America*'s win, the trophy was re-named the America's Cup and given to the New York Yacht Club. There it remained unless won by a challenger. Over the next 132 years the New York Yacht Club successfully defended the trophy against 25 challengers, until in 1983 it was won by Australia. In 2003 the trophy returned to Europe when Russell Coutts in *Alinghi* won for Switzerland – a landlocked country! The latest cup was held at Valencia in Spain in 2010 and was won by the Golden Gate Yacht Club of the USA with their yacht *USA 17*.

USA 17, winner of the 2010 America's Cup

Tour de France

The oldest and best-known of the world's great cycling tours is the Tour de France. The others are the Vuelta – Tour of Spain, and Giro – Tour of Italy.

- The Tour de France was first staged in 1903 when the course was made up of six stages over 2,428 km (1,508.7 miles). Now the race is 5,000 km (3,106.9 miles) or more and the course takes in more than 20 stages, often going into neighbouring countries.
- The famous yellow jersey (*maillot jaune*) is worn by the current overall time leader in a race. It was first worn in 1919.
- The longest race was in 1926 when Lucien Buysse of Belgium won after 5,745 km (3,569.8 miles).
- Around 15 million people every year line the streets to watch the Tour de France over its three weeks.
- The first US winner of the Tour de France was Greg LeMond who won it in 1986, and again in 1989 and 1990. He was also the first English-speaking winner of the race.
- Eddie Merckx has won more of the big three tours than any other man. He has won the Tour de France five times.

Alberto Contador of Spain won the 2009 Tour de France

Olympic cycling

Cycling was included in the first Modern Olympics in 1896. Léon Flameng (France) won the first cycling gold in the 100 km race. Only two men competed – Flameng and Georgios Kolettis of Greece – and they had to race around a 333.3 m (1,093.5 ft) track 300 times! During the race, Kolettis's bicycle needed repairing, so Flameng waited for him while the repairs were carried out. Cycling has been included in every Olympics since then. Below are the current Olympic events.

Men

Track
- Sprint
- Team Sprint
- Team pursuit
- Keirin
- Omnium*

Road
- Road race (individual)
- Time trial (individual)

Mountain bike
- Cross-country

BMX
- Individual

Women

Track
- Sprint
- Team sprint*
- Keirin*
- Omnium*

Road
- Road race (individual)
- Time trial (individual)

Mountain bike
- Cross-country

BMX
- Individual

*New in 2012

Speedway world championships

Reigning world champion Jason Crump

Racing motor cycles on dirt tracks was first recorded in the USA in 1902 and two years later in Britain. Modern-day speedway evolved from the short track races held in Australia in the 1920s with the first meeting on a cinder track at High Beech, Essex in 1928.

The first world championship was held at Wembley Stadium in 1936 and won by Lionel Van Praag (Australia). A team championship was introduced in 1960 but discontinued in 1994. An unofficial pairs event was launched in 1968 and the event became official in 1970. There are also a world long track championship (launched in 1971) and an ice speedway world championship, started in 1966.

Up to 1994 the individual world championship was decided over a single night's racing, but since 1995 the world champion is the rider who gains the most points over a season, consisting of 11 events in 2009.

The most individual world titles have been won by:

6 Ivan Mauger (New Zealand) 1968–70, 1972, 1977, 1979
6 Tony Rickardsson (Sweden) 1994, 1998–99, 2001–02, 2005
5 Ove Fundin (Sweden) 1956, 1960–61, 1963, 1967
4 Hans Nielsen (Denmark) 1986–87, 1989, 1995
4 Barry Briggs (New Zealand) 1957–58, 1964, 1966

Formula One

The Formula One World Championship usually lasts from March to October/November. In 2010 the schedule consisted of 19 races.

Since 2003 points were awarded to the first eight drivers, with the winner of each race receiving 10 points. This system was replaced in 2010 with points awarded to the first 10 drivers, with 25 being awarded to each race winner. The other drivers receive: 18–15–12–10–8–6–4–2–1 points respectively.

After more than 100 races and in his seventh season in Formula One, Jenson Button eventually won his first race in 2006. Three years later, he gained his first world title.

Best ever

German Michael Schumacher came out of retirement after three years in 2010 to drive for the Mercedes team in the hope of adding to his record of 91 race wins and seven world titles.

Motor cycle racing: champions by class

World Championship motor cycle racing is competed by class (engine size – currently 125 cc, 250 cc and 500 cc/Moto GP), with titles awarded to riders and manufacturers.

500 cc/MotoGP
Most world titles – rider:
8 Giacomo Agostini (Italy)
7 Valentino Rossi (Italy)
5 Michael Doohan (Australia)

Most world titles – manufacturer:
18 Honda (Japan)
15 MV Agusta (Italy)
12 Yamaha (Japan)

250 cc
Most world titles – rider:
4 'Max' Biaggi (Italy)
4 Phil Read (Great Britain)

Most world titles – manufacturer:
19 Honda (Japan)
14 Yamaha (Japan)
9 Aprilla (Italy)

125 cc
Most world titles – rider:
7 Angel Nieto (Spain)
6 Carlo Ubbiali (Italy)

Most world titles – manufacturer:
15 Honda (Japan)
9 Aprilla (Italy)
7 MV Agusta (Italy)

50/80 cc (last contested 1989)
Most world titles – rider:
6 Angel Nieto (Spain)
4 Stefan Dörflinger (Switzerland)

Most world titles – manufacturer:
8 Kreidler (Germany)
5 Suzuki (Japan)
5 Derbi (Spain)

Isle of Man TT
The first Tourist Trophy race on the Isle of Man was on 28 May 1907 and was won by Charlie Collier riding a single cylinder Matchless at an average speed of just over 38 mph. The most prestigious race is now the Senior TT, which was first raced in 1911. The current races take place over the 37.5 mile Snaefell Mountain Course.

Most TT wins:
26 – Joey Dunlop (Northern Ireland) 1977–2000

Most senior TT wins:
7 - Mike Hailwood (England) 1961–79

Fastest lap:
131.6 mph (211.8 km/h) John McGuinness (England) Honda CBR1000RR, Senior TT 2009

Valentino Rossi

Italian-born Valentino Rossi is one of the most successful grand prix motorcycle racers of all time, his total of 9 world titles at MotoGP, 250 cc and 125 cc putting him in joint third place behind the legendary Giacomo Agostino and Spaniard Angel Nieto. His seven MotoGP titles is just one behind fellow Italian Agostini in the senior category.

Young winners

- In 2008, Britain's Lewis Hamilton became the youngest Formula One World Champion at the age of 23 years 8 months 26 days.
- Also in 2008, Sebastien Vettel of Germany became the youngest race winner when he won the Italian Grand Prix at 21 years 2 months 12 days.
- The youngest driver to start a race is Jaime Alguersuari (Spain), who was just 19 years 4 months 3 days old when he started the 2009 Hungarian Grand Prix.
- Other young Formula One World Champions are: Fernando Alonso (Spain), aged 24 years 1 month 18 days in 2005 and Emerson Fittipaldi (Brazil), aged 25 years 8 months 29 days in 1972.

Indianapolis 500 at 100

The Indianapolis Motor Speedway was opened in 1909 and two years later, on Memorial Day, 30 May 1911, the first Indy 500 took place and was won by Ray Harroun driving a Marmon Wasp at a speed of 74.6 mph (120.1 km/h). Although it is 100 years old, the 2011 event will be the 95th as it was not run during the two World Wars.

The race is still held on Memorial Day weekend each year and drivers cover 200 laps of the 4-km (2.5-ml) course. The race has been won a record four times by three drivers: A.J. Foyt (1961, 1964, 1967, 1977), Al Unser (1970–71, 1978, 1987) and Rick Mears (1979, 1984, 1988, 1991).

Five men have won the race back-to-back, the last being Brazilian Hélio Castroneves in 2001–02. The fastest winning speed was achieved by Arie Luyendyk (Netherlands) who won the 1990 race in a speed of 185.9 mph (299.3 km/h).

www.formula1.com search

Winter Olympics

The Winter Games (officially the International Winter Sports Week, but later recognized as the first Winter Olympics) was first held in 1924. It included five events: Nordic skiing, figure skating, speed skating, bobsledding and ice hockey.

Winter Olympics were held in the same years as the Summer Olympics until 1992, but since 1994 they have taken place every four years between the Summer Games. The sports being contested at the 2010 Vancouver Games are:

- Alpine skiing
- Biathlon
- Bobsleigh
- Cross-country skiing
- Curling
- Figure skating
- Freestyle skiing
- Ice hockey
- Luge
- Nordic combined
- Short-track speed skating
- Skeleton
- Ski-jumping
- Snowboarding
- Speed skating

Top medal winners at the Winter Olympics (1924–2006)

Athlete – Men	Sport	Gold	Silver	Bronze	Total
Bjorn Dählie (Norway)	Cross-country	8	4	0	12
Ole Einar Bjoerndalen (Norway)	Biathlon	6	4	1	11
Sixten Jernberg (Sweden)	Cross-country	4	3	2	9
Ricco Gross (Germany)	Biathlon	4	3	1	8
Kjetil André Aamodt (Norway)	Alpine skiing	4	2	2	8
Sven Fischer (Germany)	Biathlon	4	2	2	8

Athlete – Women	Sport	Gold	Silver	Bronze	Total
Raisa Smetanina (USSR/Unified Team)	Cross-country	4	5	1	10
Stefania Belmondo (Italy)	Cross-country	2	3	5	10
Lyubov Yegorova (Unified Team/Russia)	Cross-country	6	3	0	9
Uschi Disl (Germany)	Biathlon	2	4	3	9
Claudia Pechstein (Germany)	Speed skating	5	2	2	9

www.vancouver2010.org search

Top medal-winning nations at the Winter Olympics (1924–2006)

Country	Gold	Silver	Bronze	Total
USA	9	15	13	37
Germany	10	13	7	30
Canada	14	7	5	26
Norway	9	8	6	23
Austria	4	6	6	16
Russia	3	5	7	15
South Korea	6	6	2	14

Winter Olympic facts and figures

1900s

1924 Chamonix, France
There were 294 competitors from 16 nations. Norway won the most medals (17) and tied with Finland for gold medals (4).

1928 St Moritz, Switzerland
Twenty-five nations and 495 competitors took part. Norway won the most medals (15) and the most golds (6).

1932 Lake Placid, USA
A total of 306 competitors from 17 nations competed. USA won the most medals (12) and the most golds (6).

1936 Garmisch-Partenkirchen, Germany
There were 755 competitors from 28 nations. Norway won most medals (15) and most gold medals (7).

1948 St Moritz, Switzerland
A total of 28 nations and 713 competitors took part. Norway, Sweden and Switzerland tied for top medal position (10). Norway and Sweden tied for most golds (4).

1952 Oslo, Norway
A total of 732 competitors from 30 nations took part. Norway held both top medal (16) and top gold (7) position.

1956 Cortina D'Ampezzo, Italy
Thirty-two nations and 818 competitors took part. USSR were top medal winners (16) with the most gold wins (7).

1960 Squaw Valley, USA
Thirty nations took part with 665 athletes. USSR again won the most medals (21) and most golds (7).

1964 Innsbruck, Austria
Thirty-six nations and 1,186 athletes took part. USSR won most medals (25) and most golds (11) for the third time.

1968 Grenoble, France
A total of 1,293 athletes competed from 37 nations. Norway won most medals (14) and most gold medals (6).

1972 Sapporo, Japan
There were 1,232 competitors from 35 nations. USSR were top of the overall medal table (16) and won most gold medals (8).

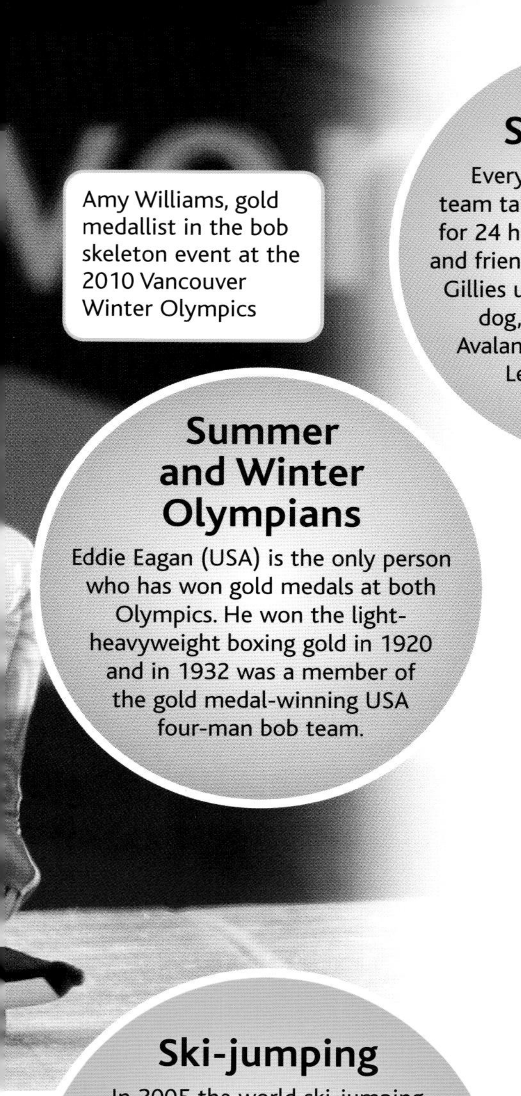

Amy Williams, gold medallist in the bob skeleton event at the 2010 Vancouver Winter Olympics

The Stanley Cup

Every player on the winning team takes the Stanley Cup home for 24 hours to show off to family and friends. New York Islander Clark Gillies used it in 1980 to feed his dog, and in 1996 Colorado Avalanche defenceman Sylvain Lefebvre baptized his daughter in it.

Ice hockey

Ice hockey probably developed from a game called bandy that was played on ice-covered pitches. The modern game is played over three 20-minute periods between two teams. Each team has six players on the ice at any one time. The object is to move the puck (a hard rubber disc) across the ice with a stick (maximum length 160 cm [63 in]) and put it into the opponent's goal.

The National Hockey League (NHL) was formed in 1917. Today the NHL is made up of 30 teams split into two conferences. The Eastern Conference has 15 teams divided into three divisions: Atlantic, North-East and South-East. The Western Conference is also divided into three divisions: Central, North-West and Pacific. At the end of season the leading teams in each conference play each other. The winner of each plays for the Stanley Cup.

Summer and Winter Olympians

Eddie Eagan (USA) is the only person who has won gold medals at both Olympics. He won the light-heavyweight boxing gold in 1920 and in 1932 was a member of the gold medal-winning USA four-man bob team.

NHL's top points-scorers

Player	Points
Wayne Gretzky	2,857
Mark Messier	1,887
Gordie Howe	1,850
Ron Francis	1,798
Marcel Dionne	1,771
Steve Yzerman	1,755

Top teams Stanley Cup wins

Montreal Canadiens	24
Toronto Maple Leafs	13
Detroit Red Wings	11
Boston Bruins	5
Edmonton Oilers	5

Ice skating

Famous skaters

- Ulrich Salchow, born in Sweden in 1877, was the greatest men's figure skater of all time. He won the first Olympic skating title at the 1908 London Olympics and between 1901 and 1911 he was the world champion on ten occasions.
- Norway's Sonja Henie won Olympic golds in 1928, 1932 and 1936. She also won ten world titles. She won nearly 1,500 cups and medals during her career. After leaving the sport in 1936 she became a film star and appeared in 11 films.

Fastest speed skaters

- Finland's Pekka Koskela set a new men's world record at Salt Lake City, USA, on 10 November 2007 when he covered 1,000 metres in 1 minute 7 seconds, which represents a speed of 53 km/h (33.39 mph).
- Cindy Klassen of Canada set a women's world record of 1 minute 13.11 seconds, a speed of 49.25 km/h (30.60 mph), at Calgary on 25 March 2006.

Canada's elusive gold

At their third attempt, Canada won its first Olympic gold medal, Summer or Winter, on home soil, at Vancouver in 2010 and went on to register a Winter Olympic record total of 14 golds.

Ski-jumping

In 2005 the world ski-jumping record was broken three times within 75 minutes! At the final meeting of the 2004–05 Ski Jumping World Cup Bjørn Einar Romøren (Norway) set a new mark at 234.5 m (769.3 ft). Then Matti Hautamaeki (Finland) put the record up to 235.5 m (772.6 ft) before Romøren re-took the record with a leap of 239 m (784.1 ft).

2000s

1976 Innsbruck, Austria
Thirty-seven nations and 1,128 athletes took part. USSR won most medals (27) and most gold medals (13).

1980 Lake Placid, USA
There were 1,067 competitors from 37 nations. USSR won most medals overall (22) and most golds (10).

1984 Sarajevo, Yugoslavia
A total of 1,278 competitors from 49 nations took part. USSR won most medals (25) but East Germany topped the gold medal table (9).

1988 Calgary, Canada
Fifty-seven nations fielded 1,423 athletes. USSR won most medals (29) and most golds (11).

1992 Albertville, France
Sixty-three nations with 1,801 competitors took part. Germany won most medals (26) and most gold medals (10).

1994 Lillehammer, Norway
1,739 athletes from 67 nations took part. Norway won most medals altogether (26) but Russia won most golds (11).

1998 Nagano, Japan
There were 72 nations taking part and 2,302 athletes. Germany won most medals (29) and most gold medals (12).

2002 Salt Lake City, USA
Seventy-eight nations fielded 2,399 athletes. Germany again won most medals (35) and most golds (12).

2006 Turin, Italy
A record 2,663 athletes from 82 nations took part. Germany were the top medal winners for the third time in a row (29) and also won most gold medals (11).

2010 Vancouver, Canada
The 21st Winter Olympics were held in Vancouver between 12 and 28 February 2010 and featured 2,628 competitors from 82 countries.

See also
The Olympics: pages 282–83

Greyhound racing

Dog racing has been popular since ancient times, when dogs were used for hunting. Modern greyhound racing takes place on an oval-shaped track over distances from 210 m (689 ft) to 1,097 m (3,599 ft). An electric "hare" goes round the track, and the dogs are released from traps to chase it.

In the UK most greyhound races are run with six dogs, but in the USA they are run with eight. There is a draw before the race to decide which trap each dog starts from. Each dog wears a coloured jacket which matches its starting trap.

Hambletonian harness race

Harness racing

In harness racing the horses pull the drivers who sit in a two-wheeled cart called a sulky. There are two forms of harness racing – pacing and trotting.

The difference between pacing and trotting is in the way the horse moves. A pacing horse moves its right front and back legs together, then its left front and back legs. A trotter moves its left front leg and right back leg at the same time, followed by its right front leg and left back leg.

Greyhound Derby

The Greyhound Derby is the most prestigious race in British greyhound racing. It was first held over 500 yards of the White City track in London in 1927. It moved to a new home at Wimbledon in 1985 and is now run over 480 metres. Only four dogs have won the race twice: the legendary Mick The Miller (1929–30), Patricia's Hope (1972–73), Rapid Ranger (2000–01) and Westmead Hawk (2005–06).

Top drivers

Herve Filion, born in Quebec, Canada, is the most famous driver in harness-racing history and set many records in his 35-year career. In 1968 he became the first driver to win 400 races in a season. He went on to achieve 400 or more wins per season in 14 other years. He was forced to retire in 1995 but made a comeback in 2002. He achieved his goal of reaching 15,000 wins before finally retiring in 2003 with 15,086 wins.

John Campbell, from Ontario, Canada, is the top money-winning jockey in the sport. He started driving in 1972 at the age of 17 and was the first man to pass the $100 million and $200 million milestones in career earnings. He won the Hambletonian six times and the 10,000th race of his career in 2008 at the age of 53.

Top horse

Moni Maker was the first horse to pass the $5 million mark. Remarkably, she achieved this during a four-year career between 1997–2000. She won 60 of her 91 trotting races and won the Horse of the Year Award in 1998 and 1999. In 2003, the Italian-bred horse Varenne surpassed Moni Maker's career winning record. He won 63 of 74 starts to amass career earnings of $5,651,061.

Rodeo

Professional rodeo developed from the early days of ranching, when bull riding and calf roping were common activities. The first known rodeo with prize money was held at Deer Trail, Colorado, in 1869. The All-Round Rodeo Cowboy World Champion is decided each year – the champion is the cowboy who wins the most money over a series of events. Top cowboys win more than $250,000 a year.

The Triple Crowns

- The Triple Crowns of the United States and England are the most prestigious of all Triple Crowns in thoroughbred racing. The US Triple Crown consists of the Kentucky Derby, Preakness Stakes and Belmont Stakes, while the English Triple Crown consist of the 2000 Guineas, Derby and St Leger.
- Only 11 horses have completed the famous treble, the last being Affirmed, ridden by Steve Cauthen in 1978.
- Fifteen horses have won the English version, the first being West Australian, ridden by Frank Butler in 1853. There were seven winners in the 20th century and none since Nijinsky, ridden by Lester Piggott, in 1970. Steve Donoghue is the only man to ride two English Triple Crown winners, Pommern (1915) and Gay Crusader (1917).

The Breeders' Cup

The Breeders' Cup Limited was started in 1982 to encourage thoroughbred racing throughout the USA. The first Breeders' Cup day was held on 10 November 1984 at Hollywood Park, Inglewood, California. Between 1984 and 2006 the championship was a single day event, but since 2007 has been spread over two days.

The Breeders' Cup attracts a crowd of around 80,000 and is televised to 120 countries around the world. The 2010 event on 5–6 November was the seventh to be staged at Churchill Downs, which is also the location of the Kentucky Derby.

Volponi, winner of the Breeders' Cup Classic 2002

Bart Cummings

Bart Cummings is the most successful trainer in Australia. His 12 Melbourne Cup wins is a remarkable achievement in itself, but his 12th win was achieved just two weeks before his 81st birthday in 2008. In addition to his Melbourne Cup triumphs, he has also won the coveted Caulfield Cup seven times.

Top horse races

England

- The Epsom Derby was first held in 1780 and is now run over one-and-a-half miles at Epsom Downs each June. The first winner was a horse named Diomed. Jockey Lester Piggott won the Derby a record nine times.
- The Grand National is the world's best-known steeplechase, a horse race over a course with obstacles to be jumped. It was first run as the Grand Liverpool Steeplechase in 1839. The race now takes place every spring over four-and-a-half miles at Aintree in England and the winning horse has to clear 30 challenging fences. The famous horse Red Rum won the race a record three times between 1972–76.

France

- The Prix de L'Arc de Triomphe was first run in 1920. It takes place on the first Sunday in October every year and covers 2,400 m over the Longchamps race course, Paris. Alleged, ridden by Lester Piggott, won the race in 1977 and 1978 and was the last horse to win two years in a row.

Australia

- The most important horse race in Australia is the Melbourne Cup which dates from 1861. It is run on the first Tuesday in November at the Flemington Park race track in Victoria. Trainer Bart Cummings won the race a record 12 times between 1965 and 2008.

United States

- The Kentucky Derby was first held in 1875. It is run over one mile two furlongs at Churchill Downs, Kentucky, on the first Saturday in May and is the most famous of all US horse races. Eddie Arcaro and Bill Hartack have been the most successful jockeys with five wins each.

Breeders' Cup records

Most wins (jockey)	15 (Jerry Bailey)
Most prize money (jockey)	$23,033,360 (Pat Day)
Most wins (trainer)	18 (D. Wayne Lukas)
Most prize money (trainer)	$19,645,520 (D. Wayne Lukas)
Most used track	Churchill Downs, Kentucky, used in 1988, 1991, 1994, 1998, 2000, 2006, 2010

Breeders' Cup record payout

When the 5-year-old Arcangues won the 1993 Breeders' Cup Classic it was the biggest upset in the history of the race. His victory paid out a record $269.20 for a $2 wager. It was the horse's first race on a dirt track.

http://www.bhs.org.uk search

BOOYAKA

Last Lists

Last *Big Brother* winner

In 2010 actor and martial arts fighter Alex Reid became the last-ever winner of *Celebrity Big Brother*. This was the seventh series of the reality show attracting an average of 3.7 million viewers. The *Celebrity* version was launched in 2001 as an extension of *Big Brother*, which was first broadcast in the UK in 2000. It had a peak audience of almost 6 million, and also screened its last series on Channel 4 in 2010, after 11 series and over 1,000 episodes.

Unusual deaths

Aeschylus
Aeschylus was a famous Greek dramatist who died in 456 BC. A prediction that he would be killed by a blow from heaven came true when an eagle carrying a tortoise dropped it on his head.

King Alexander of Greece
He died after a monkey bit him while trying to protect his dog from attack.

Francis Bacon
This Elizabethan philosopher caught a chill while trying to deep-freeze a chicken by stuffing it with snow. He died in 1626.

Hilaire Belloc
Although born in France, Hilaire Belloc was an English writer and member of parliament. He died in 1953 after a burning coal fell out of his fire and set him ablaze.

Madéleine-Sophie Blanchard
Madame Blanchard was the widow of pioneer balloonist Jean-Pierre Blanchard. She was killed in Paris in 1819, when fireworks set fire to her balloon.

Jerome Cardan
Cardan was an Italian physician, mathematician and astrologer. He starved himself to death in 1576 to make sure that his own prediction of his death would come true.

Lord Carnarvon
Carnarvon was an amateur Egyptologist who financed the excavation of Tutankhamun's tomb in 1922. Several months after opening the tomb, Carnarvon died suddenly from a mosquito bite. This began the legend of the curse of Tutankhamun.

Isadora Duncan
This American dancer was strangled in 1927 by her scarf. It became caught in the wheel of a Bugatti sports car in which she was a passenger.

Anton Dvorák
The Czech composer died in 1904 of a chill which he caught while train-spotting.

Frederick, Prince of Wales
Frederick was the son of George II and heir to the British throne. He died in 1751 after being hit by a cricket ball.

Harry Houdini (Erich Weiss)
Houdini was a famous escapologist who claimed he could withstand being punched in the stomach. He died in 1926 – after being punched in the stomach.

William Huskisson
Huskisson was a British member of parliament. He was run down by a train during the opening of the first railway in 1830.

Jean-Baptiste Lully
This Italian-French composer died in 1687 after accidentally stabbing his foot with a stick while beating time. The short conductor's baton came into use soon afterwards.

Thomas Midgley
Midgley was an American inventor who was strangled in 1944 by a machine he had invented to help him move after contracting polio. He invented three products that have since been found to be environmentally harmful: lead in petrol, CFCs in fridges and aerosols, and the insecticide DDT.

Forever young

The following are some of the most famous people who died early and so remain forever young in our minds.

Name/cause/year	Age at death
King Edward V of England, murdered, 1483	12
King Edward VI of England, natural causes, 1553	15
Anne Frank German diarist, in concentration camp, 1945	15
Lady Jane Grey Queen of England, executed, 1554	16
Thomas Chatterton English poet, took poison, 1770	22
Anastasia Grand Duchess of Russia, assassinated, 1918	17
Ritchie Valens American rock singer, plane crash, 1959	17
King Tutankhamun Egyptian pharaoh, c. 1340 BC	18
Joan of Arc French heroine, burned at the stake, 1431	19
Catherine Howard Queen of Henry VIII, beheaded, 1542	20
Billy the Kid (William H. Bonney) American outlaw, shot, 1881	21
Eddie Cochran American rock singer, car accident, 1960	21
Pocahontas Native American Indian princess, smallpox, 1617	22
Buddy Holly American rock singer, plane crash, 1959	22
Aaliyah (Aaliyah Haughton) singer, plane crash, 2001	22
River Phoenix actor, drug overdose, 1993	23
Clyde Barrow US outlaw, shot by Texas Rangers, 1934	24
James Dean American film actor, car crash, 1955	24
Lee Harvey Oswald assassin of John F. Kennedy, murdered, 1963	24
John Keats English poet, tuberculosis, 1821	25
"Red Baron" Manfred von Richthofen German flying ace, shot down, 1918	25
Jean Harlow film actress, illness, 1937	26
Brian Jones Rolling Stones guitarist, drowned, 1969	26
Jimi Hendrix rock guitarist, drugs, 1970	27
Kurt Cobain Nirvana lead singer, shooting suicide, 1994	27
Heath Ledger Australian actor, accidental drug overdose, 2008	28
Anne Brontë British writer, tuberculosis, 1849	29

Famous last words

Julius Caesar, 44 BC
Roman emperor, who was assassinated by conspirators, including Brutus, a man he thought was his friend. According to legend and Shakespeare, Caesar said: "Et tu Brute?" (You as well, Brutus?)

Caligula, AD 41
Roman emperor who was assassinated: "I am still alive!"

Catherine de Medici, 1589
Queen of France: "Ah, my God, I am dead!"

Joseph Henry Green, 1863
British doctor, after checking his own pulse: "Stopped."

General John Sedgwick, 1864
In the American Civil War, Sedgwick was shot by a sniper as he remarked: "They couldn't hit an elephant at this distance."

Viscount Palmerston, 1865
British Prime Minister: "Die, my dear doctor? That's the last thing I shall do."

Billy the Kid (aka William Bonney, Henry McCarty), 1881
American outlaw, before being shot by Sheriff Pat Garrett: "Who is it?"

Marie Antoinette, 1893
French queen, who accidentally trod on her executioner's foot as she went to the guillotine: "Pardonnez-moi, monsieur." (Pardon me, sir.)

Oscar Wilde, 1900
Opinions differ about the Irish writer's last words. Some people claim he said: "Either these curtains go/that wallpaper goes, or I do."

Prince Philippe
Prince Philippe, heir to the French throne, was killed when his horse tripped over a pig in the streets of Paris in 1131.

Pliny the Elder
Roman writer Pliny was choked by the fumes of the erupting volcano Vesuvius in AD 79.

Sir Thomas Urquhart
Urquhart was the Scottish author of books with extraordinary titles such as *Logopandecteision*. He died laughing when told of the Restoration of King Charles II in 1660.

William III
This British king died in 1701, after a fall from his horse when it stumbled over a molehill. His opponents drank a toast to the mole, calling it "The little gentleman in black velvet".

See also
Volcanic eruptions: page 46

Poster for Houdini show

Joan of Arc, 15th-century French heroine who was burned at the stake aged 19

Queen Victoria, 1901
British queen: "Oh, that peace may come." (a reference to the war at the time in South Africa). "Bertie!" (her husband, Prince Albert).

Captain Lawrence Oates, 1912
Oates was a member of Scott's expedition to the South Pole. He was terribly injured from frostbite and went to his death rather than hold up his companions. When he left the tent he said, "I am going outside and may be some time."

Anna Pavlova, 1931
Ballerina: "Get my swan costume ready!"

Lytton Strachey, 1932
English writer: "If this is dying, then I don't think much of it."

Douglas Fairbanks Sr, 1939
American film actor: "I've never felt better."

Heinrich Himmler, 1945
Nazi leader, as he committed suicide by taking poison: "I am Heinrich Himmler!"

H.G. Wells, 1946
English novelist, author of *The Time Machine*: "I'm all right."

John F. Kennedy, 1963
Moments before he was shot, Kennedy replied to "You certainly can't say that the people of Dallas haven't given you a nice welcome, Mr President" with his final words, "No, you certainly can't."

www.findagrave.com search

Entertainment lasts

Shakespeare's last play
Most people agree that *The Tempest*, 1611, is the last play Shakespeare wrote, although some think he may have written a later play that has been lost. Shakespeare died in 1616, and *The Tempest* was first published in 1623.

Charles Dickens' last story
The Mystery of Edwin Drood was Charles Dickens' last novel. It was published in monthly episodes, but ended, unfinished, when Dickens died in 1870.

The last silent film
The Four Feathers (1929) was the last silent film released by a major studio. The 1976 film *Silent Movie* does contain one word, "Non!" (French for no), which is spoken by Marcel Marceau, a mime artist.

The last Beatles concert
The Beatles last played together in public at Candlestick Park, San Francisco, on 29 August 1966. Their last publicly performed song was "Long Tall Sally".

The sixth and last Star Wars film
Star Wars: Episode III – Revenge of the Sith was released in 2005. It made almost $850 million worldwide, bringing the total for the series, which started in 1977, to $4.3 billion.

Last *Harry Potter*
The last Harry Potter novel, *Harry Potter and the Deathly Hallows*, was published on 21 July 2007, 10 years after the first. It sold 11 million copies in the first 24 hours and has gone on to sell over four times as many. The film version will be released in two parts in 2010 and 2011.

Crime and punishment lasts

Last executions for witchcraft in America
On 22 September 1692 seven women and one man were hanged for witchcraft at Salem and other places in New England.

Last beheading in the UK
On 9 April 1747, 80-year-old Simon Fraser, Lord Lovat, was beheaded for treason at Tower Hill, London.

Last person to be burned at the stake in England
Catherine Murphy belonged to a gang of coiners (coin forgers). She was strangled and then burnt at the stake at Newgate, London, on 18 March 1789.

Last public hanging in the UK
Michael Barrett was hanged outside Newgate Prison, London, on 26 May 1868 for the murder of Sarah Ann Hodgkinson. She was one of several victims who died from a bomb he had planted.

Last witness to the assassination of Abraham Lincoln
Samuel James Seymour, who died on 13 April 1956, was the last surviving witness to the assassination of the American president. Seymour was only five years old when he saw John Wilkes Booth shoot Abraham Lincoln at Ford's Theatre, Washington DC, on 14 April 1865.

Last person executed by guillotine
The last person to be executed in public was the murderer Eugene Weidmann who had his head cut off at Versailles, France, on 17 June 1939. The last official use of the guillotine in France was on 10 September 1977, when Hamida Djandoubi was executed for murder at Baumetes Prison, Marseilles.

Last prisoner of Alcatraz
Alcatraz Island, in the Bay of San Francisco, USA, was a prison for over 100 years. Surrounded by freezing water, it was considered impossible to escape. Armed rober Frank Clay Weatherman was its last prisoner. He left the island on 21 March 1963, after which Alcatraz closed.

Last men on the Moon
US *Apollo 17* astronauts Eugene A. Cernan and Harrison H. Schmitt spent three days on the Moon, blasting off to return to Earth on 14 December 1972. This was the last day on which any human walked on the surface of the Moon.

Last Aztec emperor
Montezuma II was removed from power by Spanish invaders and killed in June 1520.

Montezuma II, the last Aztec emperor

Royal lasts

The last Egyptian pharaoh
Cleopatra VII ruled from 69 BC, when she was 17 years old, until 30 BC, when Egypt became a province of the Roman empire.

The last Roman emperor
Romulus Augustus was about 14 when he was removed from power in AD 476. The Roman empire split into western and eastern divisions.

The last British king killed in battle
Richard III was killed at the battle of Bosworth on 22 August 1485.

The last British king born abroad
George II was born in Hanover, Germany, on 10 November 1683.

The last king of France
Louis-Philippe (1773–1850) reigned from 1830 until 24 February 1848, when he gave up his throne. Disguised as "Mr Smith", he travelled to England where he lived until his death.

The last emperor of China
Hsüan T'ung gave up his throne on 12 February 1912 and later took the name Henry Pu-yi. The film *The Last Emperor* (1987) is about his life.

The last tsar of Russia
Nicholas II was removed from power by the Russian Revolution of 1917, and murdered with his family at Ekaterinburg in July 1918. Their remains were reburied in St Petersburg in July 1998.

Pharos of Alexandria

Last of the Seven Wonders

The last of the Seven Wonders of the world to be built was the 124 m (406.9 ft) Pharos (lighthouse) of Alexandria, Egypt, which was completed in 279 BC. It was partly knocked down by invaders and later destroyed by an earthquake. The only one of the Seven Wonders that survives today is the Great Pyramid at Giza in Egypt.

See also

The Seven Wonders of the ancient world: pages 206–7

Transport lasts

The last stagecoach

Horse-drawn stagecoaches carried passengers and mail in Britain from the 17th century until the 19th century, when they were gradually replaced by trains. The Royal Mail between Inverness and Thurso, Scotland, last operated in October 1874.

The last horse-drawn London bus

The last horse-drawn bus ran in London on 25 October 1911.

The last Model T Ford

The Model T, first produced in 1908, was one of the most popular cars of all time. The last US-made Model T (number 15,007,033) rolled off the production line on Thursday 26 May 1927.

The last Routemaster bus

The Routemaster double-decker bus was introduced in London on 8 February 1956 and was a familiar sight in the capital for almost 50 years. The last Routemaster service ran on Friday 9 December 2005, although there are still two heritage routes in operation.

Last flight of Concorde

Concorde was the world's only supersonic airliner. It was in service for 34 years until it made its last commercial flight, from New York to London, on 24 October 2003.

Last Shuttle flights

Shuttle	Mission	Scheduled launch
Atlantis	STS-132	Landed 26 May 2010
Endeavour	STS-134	29 July 2010
Discovery	STS-133	16 September 2010

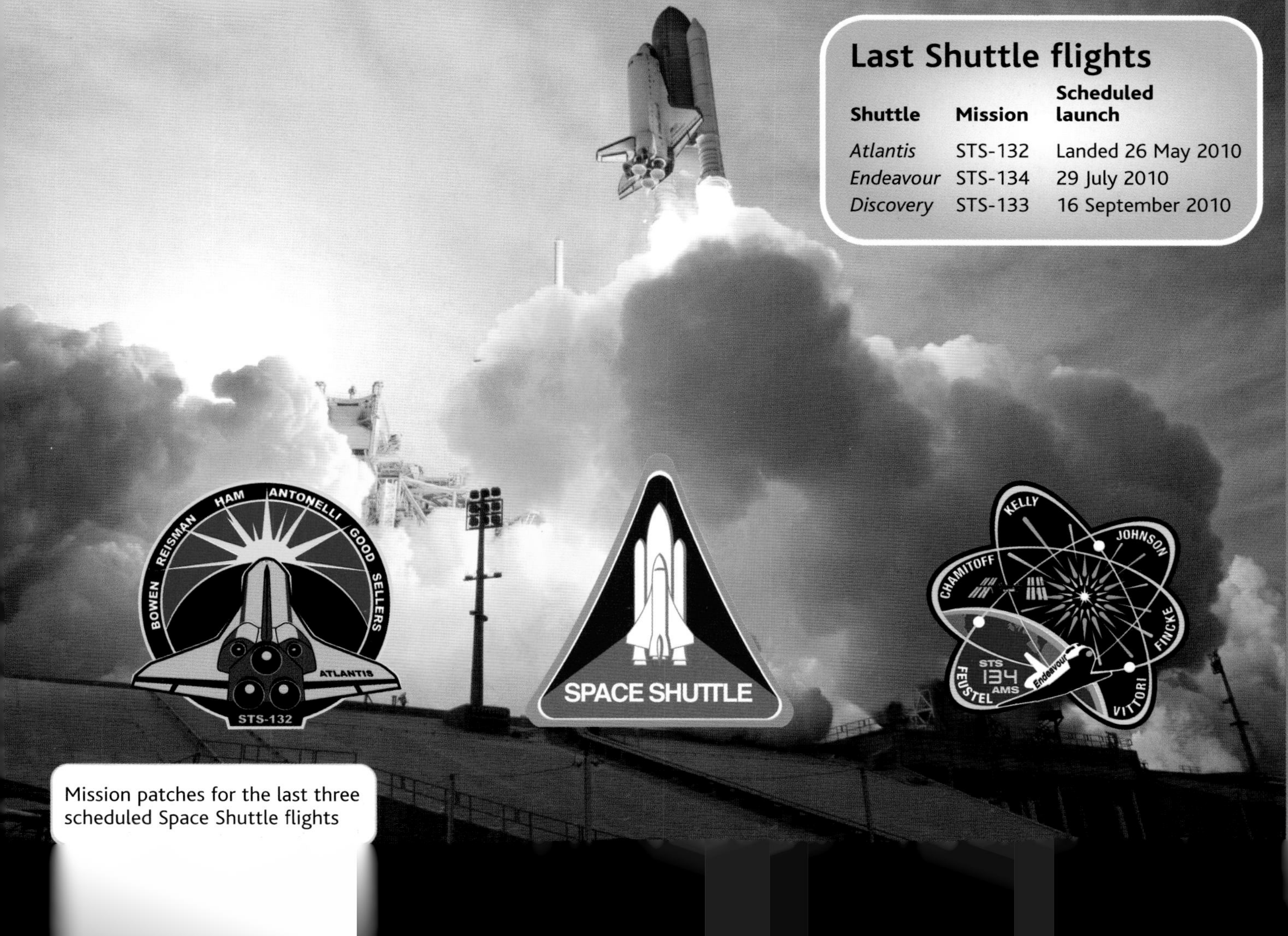

Mission patches for the last three scheduled Space Shuttle flights

Bold type indicates key entries with two or more consecutive pages of information about them.

D

E

F

Author's acknowledgements

The author would like to thank the following people, organizations and publications for kindly supplying information for this book.

Academy of Motion Picture Arts and Sciences (AMPAS)*
Alexa
American Film Institute
American Forests
Artnet
Association of Leading Visitor Attractions
Alexander Ash
Caroline Ash
Nicholas Ash
Audit Bureau of Circulations Ltd (ABC)
Box Office Mojo
BP Statistical Review of World Energy 2009
Richard Braddish
Thomas Brinkhoff
The British Council
British Film Institute
British Library
British Museum
British Phonographic Industry (BPI)
Brookfield Europe
Carbon Dioxide Information Analysis Center
Central Intelligence Agency, *The World Factbook 2010*
Christian Research
Christie's
Computer Industry Almanac
Department for Environment, Food and Rural Affairs (DEFRA)
Earth Impact Database
The Economist
Eden Project
Emporis
Energy Information Administration
Ethnologue
Euromonitor
Federal Bureau of Investigation
Food and Agriculture Organization of the United Nations (FAO)
Forbes magazine
Global Education Digest (UNESCO)
Global Forest Resources Assessment (FAO)
Golden Raspberry Award Foundation
Russell E. Gough
Monica Grady
Robert Grant
Greyhound Racing Association of America
Hollywood Reporter
Home Accident Surveillance System (HASS)
Home Office
Human Development Report (United Nations)
Imperial War Museum
Index Translationum (UNESCO)
Intellectual Property Office
International Federation of Audit Bureaux of Circulations
The International Institute for Strategic Studies, *The Military Balance 2010*
International Labour Organization
International Olympic Committee (IOC)
International Shark Attack File, Florida Museum of Natural History
International Telecommunication Union (ITU)
International Union for the Conservation of Nature (IUCN)
Internet Movie Database (IMDb)
Internet World Stats
Inter-Parliamentary Union
Claire Judd
Julien's Auctions
Dr Benjamin Lucas
Malaria Consortium
Mattel, Inc
Chris Mead
National Aeronautics and Space Administration, USA (NASA)
National Basketball Association, USA (NBA)
National Football League, USA (NFL)
National Statistics
Natural History Museum, London
AC Nielsen
The Nobel Foundation
Organisation for Economic Co-operation and Development (OECD)
Organisation Internationale des Constructeurs d'Automobiles (OICA)
Felicity Page
Parker Brothers
Tony Pattison
Periodical Publishers Association
Pet Food Manufacturers' Association
Population Reference Bureau
Quigley's Motion Picture Almanac
Recording Industry Association of America (RIAA)
Dafydd Rees
Louise Reip
Royal Astronomical Society
Royal Observatory, Greenwich
Royal Opera House, Covent Garden
Science Museum, London
Screen Digest
Robert Senior
Sotheby's
Time magazine
Tree Register of the British Isles
United Nations (UN)
United Nations Children's Fund (UNICEF)
United Nations Educational, Scientific and Cultural Organization (UNESCO)
United Nations Environment Programme
United Nations Population Division (UNPD)
Universal Postal Union
US Census Bureau International Data Base
US Geological Survey
US Mint
US Patent and Trademark Office
Variety
Lucy T. Verma
Ward's Motor Vehicle Facts & Figures 2009
WebElements
Whitaker's Almanack/Ross Fulton (country data)
World Association of Girl Guides and Girl Scouts
World Association of Newspapers
World Bank
World Christian Database
World Gazetteer
World Health Organization (WHO)
World Organization of the Scout Movement
World Tourism Organization (WTO)
World Nuclear Association

Population data
© by Stefan Helders www.world-gazetteer.com

Country names
The following abbreviations are used for country names
BUL: Bulgaria
CHN: China
CUB: Cuba
CZE: Czech Republic
DEN: Denmark
ETH: Ethiopia
FRA: France
GBR: Great Britain
GDR: German Democratic Republic (1955–90)
JAM: Jamaica
MAR: Morocco (Maroc)
POL: Poland
QAT: Qatar
ROM: Romania
RUS: Russian Federation
S.AFR: South Africa
UKR: Ukraine
USA: United States of America
USSR: Union of Soviet Socialist Republics (1922–91)

Picture acknowledgements

L = left, R = right, C = centre, T = top, B = bottom

Page **2** Jim Zuckerman/Corbis; **4** Paul Souders/Corbis; **8** Martin Puddy/Corbis; **10** Corbis; **11T** Jeremy Swinborne/iStockphoto; **12C** Jeremy Horner/Corbis; **14TL** Eileen Tweedy/The Art Archive; **15B** David Taylor/Getty Images; **16C** Mayatskyy/Dreamstime; **17TR** Regis Madec/Thaiworldview.com; **18** Courtesy of Virgin Galactic; **19B** NASA; **19T** NASA; **20TR** NASA; **20BR** NASA; **20C** NASA; **20CR** NASA; **22BL** NASA; **22CL** NASA; **22CR** NASA; **22C** NASA; **22TR** NASA; **23BL** NASA; **23BC** NASA; **23BR** NASA; **23TL** NASA; **24CR** Gianni Dagli Orti/Corbis; **24C** NASA; **24TR** NASA; **24TC** NASA; **25T** NASA; **25B** Jeff Vanuga/Corbis; **26CL** Roger Ressmeyer/Corbis; **26TR** Bettmann/Corbis; **27C** NASA; **28R** NASA; **29TL** NASA; **30C** NASA; **31CL** NASA; **31TR** NASA; **32** Jewel Samad/Getty; **34C** Charles & Josette Lenars/Corbis; **35T** Timothy Ball/iStockphoto; **36BL** Theo Allofs/ZEFA/Corbis; **36TL** iStockphoto; **37CR** Robert Paul Van Beets/Shutterstock; **38B** Andre Klaassen/iStockphoto; **38T** Frank Leung/iStockphoto; **40T** Daniel Leclair/Reuters/Corbis; **41C** Randy Miramontez/Shutterstock; **41BR** UPPA/Photoshot; **44TR** Shaun Lowe/iStockphoto; **45T** Werner H. Mueller/Corbis; **46B** Dennis M. Sabangan/epa/Corbis; **47T** Koch Valerie/iStockphoto; **48** Milse Milse/Photolibrary; **50TC** Cristi Bastian/Shutterstock; **50BL** Dr. Morley Read/Shutterstock; **51BR** Mike Norton/Dreamstime; **51C** Jon Rasmussen/iStockphoto; **52BL** Condor 36/Shutterstock; **53TR** Brad Thompson/iStockphoto; **53BR** Summer/Shutterstock; **54L** DLILLC/Corbis; **55BR** iStockphoto; **55BL** iStockphoto; **55TR** W. Wisniewski/Corbis; **56CL** Shawn Jackson/Dreamstime; **57TR** Russell Ash; **57CL** Jeffrey L. Rotman/Corbis; **58TR** Rinusbaak/Dreamstime; **58BL** Anastasiya Maksymenko/iStockphoto; **59B** Tim Davis/Corbis; **60CR** Vaeenma/Dreamstime; **60TL** Thomas Bedenk/iStockphoto; **61CL** Dave Marsden/Alamy; **61TR** Will Schmitz/iStockphoto; **62B** Dreamstime; **63BR** Blewis Photography/Shutterstock; **63TR** Steve Geer/iStockphoto; **64CR** Jack Ryan/Dreamstime; **64BL** David Scharf/Science Photo Library; **65B** Claudia Steininger/Dreamstime; **66B** Nico Smit/iStockphoto; **66TR** Sharon Morris/Dreamstime; **67TR** Stacey Bates/Shutterstock; **68T** Christoph Ermel/iStockphoto; **69BR** Rich Carey/Shutterstock; **70TR** Wayne Lawler/Ecoscene/Corbis; **70–71B** Dreamstime; **72B** Roger Milley/iStockphoto; **73BR** Doug McKinlay/Photolibrary; **73CR** Nathan Watkins/iStockphoto; **74** Walter Fogel/Festo; **75TR** Les Cunliffe/iStockphoto; **76BL** Charles O'Rear/Corbis; **78CL** Donall O Cleirigh/iStockphoto; **79BL** Bettmann/Corbis; **81T** Phil Walter/Getty Images; **84L** Hulton-Deutch Collection/Corbis; **84R** Carole Gomez/iStockphoto; **86CL** Courtesy of Apple; **86CR** One Laptop Per Child; **87T** Dean Mitchell/ Shutterstock; **89TL** Bettmann/Corbis; **89TR** Courtesy of Apple; **90** Martin Krzywinski/Science Photo Library; **91TR** Carol Munoz/iStockphoto; **92TR** Stephen Sweet/iStockphoto; **93C** Maria Boytunoa/iStockphoto; **94CL** Bettmann/Corbis; **95R** Corbis; **95BL** Corbis; **96TL** Maria Bibikova/iStockphoto; **97TR** Serghei Starus/Shutterstock; **97BL** Shutterstock; **98TL** Andresr/Shutterstock; **98CR** Hulton Archive/Getty Images; **99BL** Coca-Cola; **99BR** Jane Sweeney/JAI/Corbis; **99TL** Olivier Samson Arcand/Dinner In The Sky; **99TR** Olivier Samson Arcand/Dinner In The Sky; **100** Michael Macor/Corbis; **102–103C** Justin Sullivan/Getty Images; **102TR** Jose Marafona/iStockphoto; **103R** David Lewis/iStockphoto; **104TL** Falk Kienas/iStockphoto; **104C** Eliza Snow/iStockphoto; **105T** Bettmann/Corbis; **106B** Karim Hesham/iStockphoto; **107TR** Jivko Kazakov/iStockphoto; **107TL** Francisco Orellana/iStockphoto; **108TR** Jack Tzekov/iStockphoto; **108CL** John Woodworth/iStockphoto; **109L** Palazzo Baberini, Rome/Dagli Orti/The Art Archive; **109R** John Steele/iStockphoto; **110TR** Corbis; **110BL** Wally McNamee/Corbis; **111TR** Natalia Bratslavsky/iStockphoto; **112** Nik Wheeler/Corbis; **116BR** Prashant Vaidya/Dreamstime; **116T** Shutterstock; **117BR** Ivan Mateev/iStockphoto; **118B** James Rabinowitz/Corbis; **119T** Yann Arthus-Bertrand/Corbis; **119B** Gavin Hellier/JAI/Corbis; **120T** Randy Mayes/iStockphoto; **121B** Steven Miric/iStockphoto; **122T** Dennis Sabo/iStockphoto; **123BL** Fabian Guignard/iStockphoto; **124TC** Mike Morley/iStockphoto; **124BR** Philip Lange/Shutterstock; **125T** Rob Broek/iStockphoto; **126TL** iStockphoto; **126B** Stephen Hoerold/iStockphoto; **127TR** Ekatrina Fribus/iStockphoto; **128TL** Klemen Demsar/iStockphoto; **128BR** Marisa Allegra/iStockphoto; **129TR** Robert Lerich/Dreamstime; **130T** John Woodworth/iStockphoto; **131BR** Alan Toby/iStockphoto; **132BL** Paul Almasy/Corbis; **133TL** Andrew Cribb/iStockphoto; **133BR** Steven Tilson/iStockphoto; **134BR** Torleif Svensson/Corbis; **134TL** iStockphoto; **135TR** Birute Vijeikiene/Shutterstock; **136TL** iStockphoto; **136R** John Sigler/iStockphoto; **137TR** iStockphoto; **138B** iStockphoto; **139TR** iStockphoto; **140TL** Neale Cousland/Shutterstock; **140B** Ondrej Cech/iStockphoto; **141R** Andy Green-AGMIT/iStockphoto; **142B** Lisa Kyle Young/iStockphoto; **142TR** Felix Mockel/iStockphoto; **143C** Matthew Scholey/iStockphoto; **144** epa/Corbis; **145TR** Sandra O'Claire/iStockphoto; **146TL** Frank May/DPA/Corbis; **147CR** Bettmann/Corbis; **148TR** Gianni Dagli Orti/Corbis; **148BL** Paul Hilton/epa/Corbis; **149BL** Dave Wirtzfeld/iStockphoto; **149CL** Alan Collins/Alamy; **150CR** Historical Picture Archive/Corbis; **150CL** Peter Spiro/iStockphoto; **150TL** Russell Ash; **151B** Jeff Christensen/AFP/Getty Images; **152TL** Bettmann/Corbis; **153C** Jim Sugar/Corbis; **154TL** NASA; **154BR** The Scotsman/Corbis/Sygma; **155C** Shannon Stapleton/Corbis; **156T** Alison Wright/Corbis; **156BL** Mario Anzuoni/Reuters/Corbis; **157B** Edward Parsons/UN/EPA/Corbis; **158** Jason Hawkes/Getty Images; **160B** Sandro Vannini/Corbis; **161C** Richard A. Cooke/Corbis; **162C** Bennett Dean/Eye Ubiquitous/Corbis; **163CR** Jeremy Horner/Corbis; **164TR** Corbis; **164L** Nancy Louie/iStockphoto; **165C** Philadelphia Museum of Art/Corbis; **166C** Gianni Giansanti/Immaginazione/Corbis; **167TR** Victorian Traditions/Shutterstock; **168BL** Earl & Nazima Kowall/Corbis; **169TR** Reuters/Corbis; **169C** Nikhil Gangavane/iStockphoto; **170L** iStockphoto; **170TR** Pam Wardlaw/iStockphoto; **171TR** Cynthia Hart Designer/Corbis; **172C** Christine Balderas/iStockphoto; **172L** iStockphoto; **173B** Sharon Dominick/iStockphoto; **174B** Timo Kohlbacher/Shutterstock;

175L Joza Pojbic/iStockphoto; **176** Asmaa Waguih/Corbis; **177TR** Lise Gagne/iStockphoto; **178C** Owen Franklen/Corbis; **180C** Christie's Images/The Bridgeman Art Library; **181T** Fine Art Photography Library/Corbis; **182R** Jeff Gynane/iStockphoto; **183CL** Gianni Dagli Orti/Corbis; **183BR** Katrina Leigh/Shutterstock; **184T** Gerald French/Corbis; **184C** Dusty Cline/iStockphoto; **185B** Reuters/Corbis; **186** AFP/Getty Images; **187T** Joel Blitt/iStockphoto; **188CL** Sandro Vannini/Corbis; **188TR** Bettmann/Corbis; **190B** Kay Nietfeld/epa/Corbis; **190TR** Neema Frederic/Corbis Sygma; **191TR** David L. Moore/Alamy; **192C** Arko Datta/Reuters/Corbis; **193TL** South West News/Rex Features; **193CR** WpN/UPPA/Photoshot; **194B** Tonylady/Shutterstock; **195B** Otto Rogge/Corbis; **196** Brookfield Europe; **198C** Asier Villafranca Valasco/iStockphoto; **198B** Jim Jurica/iStockphoto; **199TC** Andrea Jemolo/Corbis; **199TR** Rizami Annuar/Dreamstime; **200BR** atref/Shutterstock; **201T** Pawel Libea/Corbis; **202L** Jose Fuste Rag/Corbis; **203T** Paul Cheyne/iStockphoto; **204T** Jean-Philippe/Corbis; **205CR** Tibor Bognar/Corbis; **206B** Liu Liqun/Corbis; **208** Nissan; **210B** Tony Arruza/Corbis; **211TR** Joe Skipper/Reuters/Getty Images; **212C** Aston Martin; **213T** Bill Nation/Corbis Sygma; **214C** Tim Wimborne/Reuters/Corbis; **214TR** Doug Pearson/JAI/Corbis; **215R** Robert Churchill/iStockphoto; **216B** Jean-Christophe Bott/epa/Corbis; **216T** Bettmann/Corbis; **217R** Bettmann/Corbis; **218TL** Eileen Tweedy/Magdalene College, Cambridge/The Art Archive; **219B** Justin Lane/epa/Corbis; **219T** Reuters/Corbis; **220B** Jaques Langevin/Corbis; **220CL** Allison Marles/iStockphoto; **221T** Galen Rowell/Corbis; **222** Uwe Anspach/epa/Corbis; **223T** Catherine dée Auvil/iStockphoto; **224BL** Alison Wright/Corbis; **225T** Andres Balcazar/iStockphoto; **226BR** Ian Poole/iStockphoto; **226TL** Robert Dawson/iStockphoto; **227T** Philip Date/Shuttertock; **227CR** Hulton-Deutsch Collection/Corbis; **228CR** Seth Joel/Corbis; **228T** iStockphoto; **229B** Qi Heng/XinHua/Xinhua Press/Corbis; **231TR** Egmont; **232C** Russell Ash; **234T** Blue Lantern Studio/Corbis; **235C** Bettmann/Corbis; **235BR** Richard Westall/Getty Images; **236R** Marvel Characters Inc./Corbis; **238** Ajay Verma/Corbis; **239TR** iStockphoto; **240** KSC Archive; **241T** Michael S Yamashita/Corbis; **242CR** Gillet Luc/iStockphoto; **242TL** The Gallery Collection/Corbis; **243CR** Justin Lane/epa/Corbis; **244C** Orjan F. Ellingvag/Corbis; **244BR** Matej Michelizza/iStockphoto; **245TR** Mitch Aunger/Shutterstock; **247TL** Gabe Palmer/Corbis; **247CR** Russell Ash; **247BR** Olga Shelego/iStockphoto; **248** Bob Krist/Corbis; **250TR** Brian Bahr/Getty Images; **251** Neville Elde/Corbis; **253T** JTB Photo/Photolibrary; **253C** Corbis; **254CL** Courtesy of Apple; **254CR** Mike Segar/Reuters/Corbis; **255C** Bettmann/Corbis; **255TR** Robert Schlesinger/epa/Corbis; **257B** Jonathan Drake/Reuters/Corbis; **256BR** Luke Daniek/iStockphoto; **258TL** Sunset Boulevard/Corbis; **258C** Josef Philipp/iStockphoto; **259R** Reuters/Corbis; **260B** Julie Lemberger/Corbis; **261TL** Joanna Hunt/Reuters/Corbis; **261BR** Robbie Jack/Corbis; **262** Walt Disney/The Kobal Collection; **264TL** Lorenzo Santini/Getty Images; **265CR** Yann Arthus-Bertrand/Corbis; **266TL** Dreamworks/The Kobal Collection; **267TR** Starstock/Photoshot; **267BL** Starstock/Photoshot; **268C** 20th Century Fox/Album/AKG-Images; **269R** Frank Trapper/Corbis; **270CR** Disney/The Kobal Collection; **271T** Album/AKG-Images; **271B** Warner Bros. Pictures/Image Move/AKG-Images; **272C** Angel Diaz/epa/Corbis; **272TL** Sunset Boulevard/Corbis; **273TR** RKO/The Kobal Collection; **275C** Dan Herrick/iStockphoto; **276** Morne de Klerk/Getty Images; **277TR** Tracy Hebden/iStockphoto; **278B** Duomo/Corbis; **279TR** Matt Campbell/epa/Corbis; **280BR** Historical Picture Archive/Corbis; **280CL** Historical Picture Archive/Corbis; **282BR** Karl Weatherly/Corbis; **283C** Everett/Photoshot; **284TL** Tim de Waele/Isosport/Corbis; **284C** Jorge Delgado/iStockphoto; **285R** Kay Nietfeld/epa/Corbis; **286TL** Tomasso DeRosa/Corbis; **286BR** Hulton-Deutsch Collection/Corbis; **287TR** Jeff Lewis/Icon SMI/Corbis; **288TR** AFP/Getty Images; **289CR** Matt A. Brown/Newsport/Corbis; **290** Kiyoshi Ota/Getty Images; **291T** Elmer Martinez/AFP/Getty Images; **292B** RIA Novosti/Alamy; **293BL** Duomo/Corbis; **294BL** Andy Clark/Reuters/Corbis; **294TR** David Gray/ Reuters/Corbis; **295BR** Manuel Queimadelos Alonso/Getty Images; **296BL** Jens Nørgaard Larsen/epa/Corbis; **296T** Tim De Waele/Corbis; **297T** Clifford White/Corbis; **298T** Jim Young/Reuters/Corbis; **300BL** Kevin R Morris/Corbis; **300TR** Kelly-Mooney Photography/Corbis; **301CR** Steve Boyle/Newsport/Corbis; **302** Rex Features; **305CL** Gianni Dagli Orti/Corbis; **305TR** Corbis; **306CR** Archivo Iconografico, SA/Corbis; **307B** NASA; **307TL** Bettmann/Corbis